ISACA®

Trust in, and value from, information systems

CISM®
REVIEW MANUAL
2015

CISM® Certified Information Security Manager®

An ISACA® Certification

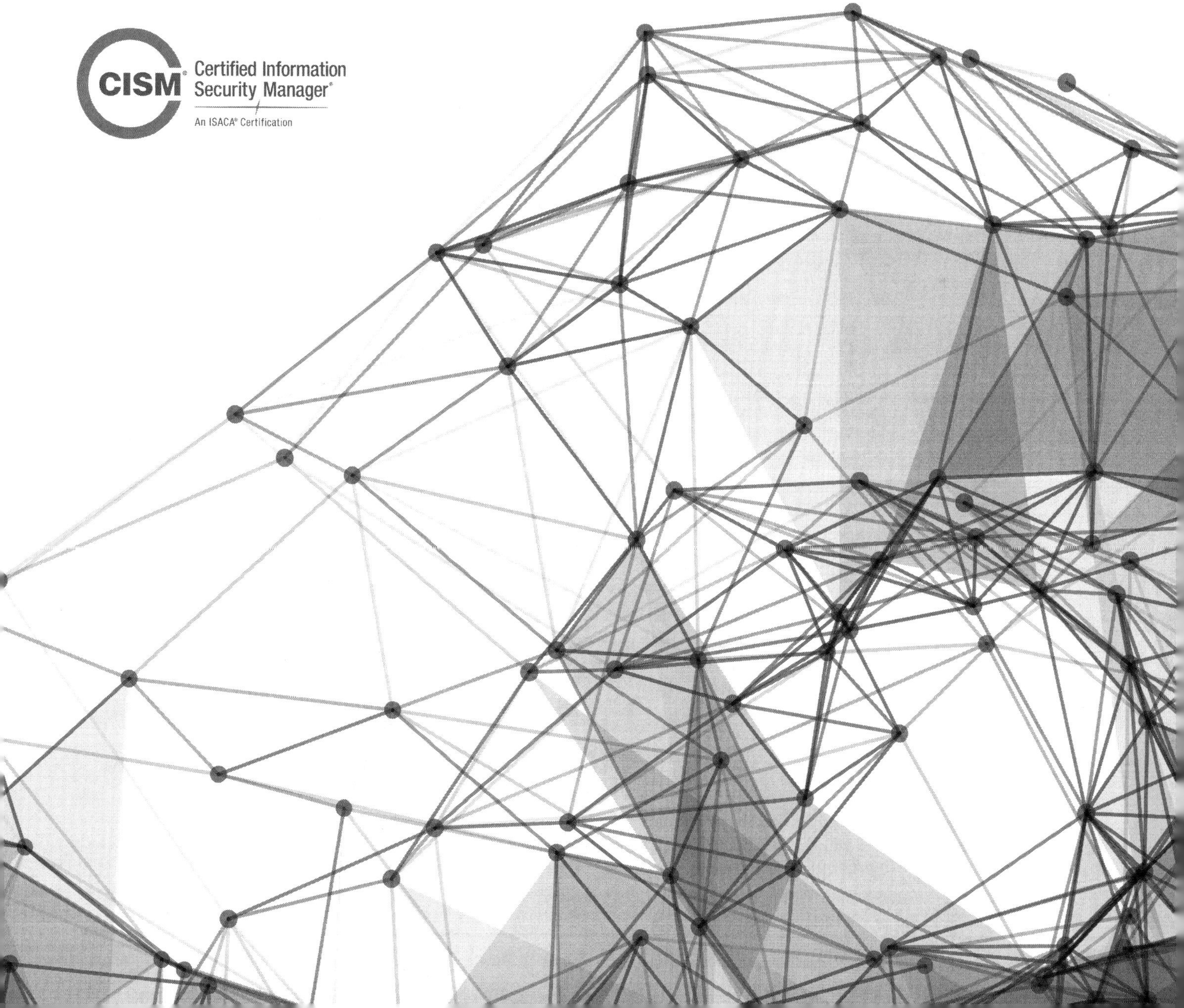

ISACA®

With more than 115,000 constituents in 180 countries, ISACA (*www.isaca.org*) helps business and IT leaders build trust in, and value from, information and information systems. Established in 1969, ISACA is the trusted source of knowledge, standards, networking, and career development for information systems audit, assurance, security, risk, privacy and governance professionals. ISACA offers the Cybersecurity Nexus™, a comprehensive set of resources for cybersecurity professionals, and COBIT®, a business framework that helps enterprises govern and manage their information and technology. ISACA also advances and validates business-critical skills and knowledge through the globally respected Certified Information Systems Auditor® (CISA®), Certified Information Security Manager® (CISM®), Certified in the Governance of Enterprise IT® (CGEIT®) and Certified in Risk and Information Systems Control™ (CRISC™) credentials. The association has more than 200 chapters worldwide.

Disclaimer

ISACA has designed and created *CISM® Review Manual 2015* primarily as an educational resource to assist individuals preparing to take the CISM certification exam. It was produced independently from the CISM exam and the CISM Certification Committee, which has had no responsibility for its content. Copies of past exams are not released to the public and were not made available to ISACA for preparation of this publication. ISACA makes no representations or warranties whatsoever with regard to these or other ISACA publications assuring candidates' passage of the CISM exam.

ISACA
3701 Algonquin Road, Suite 1010
Rolling Meadows, Illinois 60008 USA
Phone: +1.847.253.1545
Fax: +1.847.253.1443
Email: *info@isaca.org*
Web site: *www.isaca.org*

Participate in the ISACA Knowledge Center: *www.isaca.org/knowledge-center*
Follow ISACA on Twitter: *https://twitter.com/ISACANews*
Join ISACA on LinkedIn: ISACA (Official), *http://linkd.in/ISACAOfficial*
Like ISACA on Facebook: *www.facebook.com/ISACAHQ*

ISBN 978-1-60420-521-3
CISM® Review Manual 2015
Printed in the United States of America

CISM REVIEW MANUAL 2015

ISACA is pleased to offer the 2015 (13th) edition of the *CISM® Review Manual*. The purpose of this manual is to provide CISM candidates with updated technical information and references to assist in the preparation and study for the Certified Information Security Manager exam.

The *CISM® Review Manual* is updated annually to keep pace with rapid changes in the management, design, oversight and assessment of information security. As with previous manuals, the 2015 edition is the result of contributions from many qualified authorities who have generously volunteered their time and expertise. We respect and appreciate their contributions and hope their efforts provide extensive educational value to CISM manual readers.

Your comments and suggestions regarding this manual are welcome. After taking the exam, please take a moment to complete the online questionnaire (*www.isaca.org/studyaidsevaluation*). Your observations will be invaluable for the preparation of the 2016 edition of the *CISM® Review Manual*.

The sample questions contained in this manual are designed to depict the type of questions typically found on the CISM exam and to provide further clarity to the content presented in this manual. The CISM exam is a practice-based exam. Simply reading the reference material in this manual will not properly prepare candidates for the exam. The sample questions are included for guidance only. Scoring results do not indicate future individual exam success.

Certification has resulted in a positive impact on many careers. CISM is designed to provide executive management with assurance that those earning the designation have the required knowledge and ability to provide effective information security management and consulting. While the central focus of the CISM certification is information security management, all those in the IT profession with security experience will certainly find value in the CISM designation. ISACA wishes you success with the CISM exam.

ACKNOWLEDGMENTS

The 2015 edition of the *CISM® Review Manual* is the result of the collective efforts of many volunteers. ISACA members from throughout the global information security management profession participated, generously offering their talent and expertise. This international team exhibited a spirit and selflessness that has become the hallmark of contributors to this manual. Their participation and insight are truly appreciated.

All of the ISACA members who participated in the review of the *CISM® Review Manual* deserve our thanks and gratitude.

Special thanks go to W. Krag Brotby, CISM, CGEIT, a senior security consultant from the Sacramento Chapter, USA, who served as technical content project leader and editor.

Expert Reviewers
Shawna M. Flanders, CISA, CISM, CRISC, CSSGB, SSBB, Business–Technology Guidance Associates LLC, USA
Sandeep Godbole, CISA, CISM, CGEIT, AMBCI, CEH, CISSP, Syntel, India
Robert T. Hanson, CISA, CISM, CRISC, Australia
Foster J. Henderson, CISM, CRISC, CISSP, NSA-IEM, Citizant, USA
Darlene M. Tester, JD, CISM, CHSS, CISSP, Mystic Lake Hotel and Casino, USA
Edson Vittoriano P., CISM, CISSP, Ministerio Publico, Chile
Veryl White, CISA, CISM, CRISC, W. S. Badcock Corporation, USA
Larry G. Wlosinski, CISA, CISM, CRISC, CAP, CBCP, CDP, CISSP, ITIL, ActioNet Inc, USA

ISACA has begun planning the 2016 edition of the *CISM® Review Manual*. Volunteer participation drives the success of the manual. If you are interested in becoming a member of the select group of professionals involved in this global project, we want to hear from you. Please email us at *studymaterials@isaca.org*.

Table of Contents

Chapter 3:
Information Security Program Development and Management

Chapter 4:
Information Security Incident Management

About This Manual

OVERVIEW

The *CISM® Review Manual 2015* is a reference guide designed to assist candidates in preparing for the CISM examination. **The manual is one source of preparation for the exam, but should not be thought of as the only source nor viewed as a comprehensive collection of all the information and experience that are required to pass the exam.** No single publication offers such coverage and detail.

As candidates read through the manual and encounter topics that are new to them or ones in which they feel their knowledge and experience are limited, additional references should be sought. The examination will be composed of questions testing the candidate's technical and practical knowledge, and ability to apply the knowledge (based on experience) in given situations.

ORGANIZATION OF THIS MANUAL

The *CISM® Review Manual 2015* is divided into four chapters covering the CISM domains tested on the exam in the percentages listed below:

Domain 1	Information Security Governance	24 percent
Domain 2	Information Risk Management and Compliance	33 percent
Domain 3	Information Security Program Development and Management	25 percent
Domain 4	Information Security Incident Management	18 percent

Note: Each chapter defines the tasks that CISM candidates are expected to know how to do and includes a series of knowledge statements required to perform those tasks. These constitute the current practices for the information security manager. **The detailed CISM job practice can be viewed at *www.isaca.org/cismjobpractice*. The exam is based on these task and knowledge statements.**

The manual has been developed and organized to assist in the study of these areas. Exam candidates should evaluate their strengths, based on knowledge and experience, in each of these areas.

FORMAT OF THIS MANUAL

Each of the four chapters of the *CISM® Review Manual 2015* is divided into two sections for focused study. The first section contains the definitions and objectives for the four domains, with the corresponding tasks and knowledge statements that are tested on the exam.

Section one of each chapter includes:
- A definition of the domain
- Objectives for the domain as a practice area
- A listing of the task and knowledge statements for the domain
- A map of the relationship of each task to the knowledge statements for the domain
- A reference guide for the knowledge statements for the domain, including the relevant concepts and explanations
- References to specific content in section two for each knowledge statement
- Sample self-assessment questions and answers with explanations
- Suggested resources for further study of the domain

Section two of each chapter includes:
- Reference material and content that supports the knowledge statements
- Definitions of terms most commonly found on the exam

Material included is pertinent for the CISM candidate's knowledge and/or understanding when preparing for the CISM certification exam.

The structure of the content includes numbering to identify the chapter where a topic is located and headings of the subsequent levels of topics addressed in the chapter (i.e., 2.4.1 The Importance of Risk Management, is a subtopic of Risk Management Overview in chapter 2). Relevant content in a subtopic is bolded for specific attention.

Understanding the material is a barometer of the candidate's knowledge, strengths and weaknesses, and is an indication of areas in which the candidate needs to seek reference sources over and above this manual. However, written material is not a substitute for experience. **CISM exam questions will test the candidate's practical application of this knowledge.** The self-assessment questions at the end of section one of each chapter assist in understanding how a CISM question could be presented on the CISM exam and should not be used independently as a source of knowledge. Self-assessment questions should not be considered a measurement of the candidate's ability to answer questions correctly on the CISM exam for that area. The questions are intended to familiarize the candidate with question structure, and may or may not be similar to questions that will appear on the actual examination. The reference material includes other publications that could be used to further acquire and better understand detailed information on the topics addressed in the manual.

A glossary is included at the end of the manual and contains terms that apply to the material included in the chapters. Also included are terms that apply to related areas not specifically discussed. The glossary is an extension of the text in the manual and can, therefore, be another indication of areas in which the candidate may need to seek additional references.

Although every effort is made to address the majority of information that candidates are expected to know, not all examination questions are necessarily covered in the manual, and candidates will need to rely on professional experience to provide the best answer.

Throughout the manual, "association" refers to ISACA, formerly known as Information Systems Audit and Control Association, and "institute" or "ITGI®" refers to the IT Governance Institute®. Also, please note that the manual has been written using standard American English.

Note: The *CISM® Review Manual 2015* is a living document. As technology advances and information security management practices evolve, the manual will be updated to reflect such changes. Further updates to this document before the date of the exam may be viewed at *www.isaca.org/studyaidupdates*.

Suggestions to enhance the review manual or suggested reference materials should be submitted online at *www.isaca.org/studyaidsevaluation.*

EVALUATION OF THIS MANUAL

ISACA continuously monitors the swift and profound professional, technological and environmental advances affecting the information security management profession. Recognizing these rapid advances, the *CISM® Review Manual* is updated annually.

To assist ISACA in keeping abreast of these advances, please take a moment to evaluate the *CISM® Review Manual 2015*. Such feedback is valuable to fully serve the profession and future CISM exam registrants.

To complete the evaluation on the web site, please go to *www.isaca.org/studyaidsevaluation.*

Thank you for your support and assistance.

ABOUT THE CISM REVIEW QUESTIONS, ANSWERS AND EXPLANATIONS MANUAL

Candidates may also wish to enhance their study and preparation for the exam by using the *CISM® Review Questions, Answers & Explanations Manual 2014*, the *CISM® Review Questions, Answers & Explanations Manual 2014 Supplement* and the *CISM® Review Questions, Answers & Explanations Manual 2015 Supplement.*

The *CISM® Review Questions, Answers & Explanations Manual 2014* consists of 815 multiple-choice study questions, answers and explanations arranged in the domains of the current CISM job practice. The questions in this manual appeared in the *CISM® Review Questions, Answers & Explanations Manual 2012* and in the 2012 and 2013 editions of the *CISM® Review Questions, Answers & Explanations Manual Supplement.*

The 2014 and 2015 editions of the *Supplement* are the result of ISACA's dedication each year to create new sample questions, answers and explanations for candidates to use in preparation for the CISM exam. Each year, ISACA develops 100 new review questions, using a strict process of review similar to that performed for the selection of questions for the CISM exam by the CISM Certification Committee. In the 2014 and 2015 editions of the *Supplement*, the questions have been arranged in the proportions of the most recent CISM job practice.

Another study aid that is available is the CISM® Review Questions, Answers & Explanations Database - 12 Month Subscription. The database consists of the 1015 questions, answers and explanations included in the *CISM® Review Questions, Answers & Explanations Manual 2014* and the 2014 and 2015 editions of the Supplement. With this product, CISM candidates can quickly identify their strengths and weaknesses by taking random sample exams of varying length and breaking the results down by domain. Sample exams also can be chosen by domain, allowing for concentrated study, one domain at a time, and other sorting features such as the omission of previous correctly answered questions are available.

Questions in these publications are representative of the types of questions that could appear on the exam and include explanations of the correct and incorrect answers. Questions are sorted by the CISM domains and as a sample test. These publications are ideal for use in conjunction with the *CISM® Review Manual 2015*. These manuals can be used as study sources throughout the study process or as part of a final review to determine where candidates may need additional study. It should be noted that these questions and suggested answers are provided as examples; they are not actual questions from the examination and may differ in content from those that actually appear on the exam.

Note: When using the CISM review materials to prepare for the exam, it should be noted that they cover a broad spectrum of information security management issues. **Again, candidates should not assume that reading these manuals and answering review questions will fully prepare them for the examination**. Since actual exam questions often relate to practical experiences, candidates should refer to their own experiences and other reference sources, and draw upon the experiences of colleagues and others who have earned the CISM designation.

Certified Information Security Manager®
An ISACA® Certification

Chapter 1:

Information Security Governance

Section One: Overview

Section Two: Content

Section One: Overview

1.1 INTRODUCTION

This chapter reviews the body of knowledge and associated tasks necessary to develop an information security governance structure aligned with organizational objectives.

DEFINITION

COBIT 5 defines governance in terms of objectives as:

> *"Governance ensures that stakeholder needs, conditions and options are evaluated to determine balanced, agreed-on enterprise objectives to be achieved; setting direction through prioritisation and decision making; and monitoring performance and compliance against agreed-on direction and objectives."*

OBJECTIVES

The objective of this domain is to ensure that the information security manager understands the broad requirements for effective information security governance, the elements and actions required to develop an information security strategy and a plan of action to implement it.

An extension of the governance definition includes the "structure through which the objectives of the enterprise are set, and the means of attaining those objectives and monitoring performance are determined," as described by the Organisation for Economic Co-operation and Development (OECD) in its 1999 publication "OECD Principles of Corporate Governance." Structure and means include strategy, policies and their corresponding standards, procedures and guidelines, strategic and operational plans; awareness and training; risk management; controls; and audits and other assurance activities.

The *CISM® Review Manual 2015* is written from a practical perspective—that required for the implementation of effective governance—with a focus on the CISM function. Information security governance is increasingly getting the attention of organizational leaders and the information security manager is increasingly required to play a critical role in many aspects of achieving good information security governance. With this consideration, information security governance is covered extensively in this chapter.

Governance is not presented from a purely theoretical perspective, but rather from an implementation viewpoint. As a result, elements of management will be included in the governance section when it serves to illuminate the understanding of implementation requirements. Information security management functions are covered in detail in chapter 3, Information Security Program Development and Management.

This domain represents 24 percent of the CISM examination (approximately 48 questions).

1.2 TASK AND KNOWLEDGE STATEMENTS

Domain 1—Information Security Governance
Establish and maintain an information security governance framework and supporting processes to ensure that the information security strategy is aligned with organizational goals and objectives, information risk is managed appropriately and program resources are managed responsibly

TASKS

There are nine tasks within this domain that a CISM candidate must know how to perform:

T1.1 Establish and maintain an information security strategy in alignment with organizational goals and objectives to guide the establishment and ongoing management of the information security program.

T1.2 Establish and maintain an information security governance framework to guide activities that support the information security strategy.

T1.3 Integrate information security governance into corporate governance to ensure that organizational goals and objectives are supported by the information security program.

T1.4 Establish and maintain information security policies to communicate management's directives and guide the development of standards, procedures and guidelines.

T1.5 Develop business cases to support investments in information security.

T1.6 Identify internal and external influences to the organization (for example, technology, business environment, risk tolerance, geographic location, legal and regulatory requirements) to ensure that these factors are addressed by the information security strategy.

T1.7 Obtain commitment from senior management and support from other stakeholders to maximize the probability of successful implementation of the information security strategy.

T1.8 Define and communicate the roles and responsibilities of information security throughout the organization to establish clear accountabilities and lines of authority.

T1.9 Establish, monitor, evaluate and report metrics (for example, key goal indicators [KGIs], key performance indicators [KPIs], key risk indicators [KRIs]) to provide management with accurate information regarding the effectiveness of the information security strategy.

KNOWLEDGE STATEMENTS

The CISM candidate must have a good understanding of each of the areas delineated by the knowledge statements. These statements are the basis for the exam.

There are 15 knowledge statements within the information security governance domain:

KS1.1 Knowledge of methods to develop an information security strategy

KS1.2 Knowledge of the relationship among information security and business goals, objectives, functions and practices

KS1.3 Knowledge of methods to implement an information security governance framework
KS1.4 Knowledge of the fundamental concepts of governance and how they relate to information security
KS1.5 Knowledge of methods to integrate information security governance into corporate governance
KS1.6 Knowledge of internationally recognized standards, frameworks and best practices related to information security governance and strategy development
KS1.7 Knowledge of methods to develop information security policies
KS1.8 Knowledge of methods to develop business cases
KS1.9 Knowledge of strategic budgetary planning and reporting methods
KS1.10 Knowledge of the internal and external influences to the organization (for example, technology, business environment, risk tolerance, geographic location, legal and regulatory requirements) and how they impact the information security strategy
KS1.11 Knowledge of methods to obtain commitment from senior management and support from other stakeholders for information security
KS1.12 Knowledge of information security management roles and responsibilities
KS1.13 Knowledge of organizational structures and lines of authority
KS1.14 Knowledge of methods to establish new, or utilize existing, reporting and communication channels throughout an organization
KS1.15 Knowledge of methods to select, implement and interpret metrics (for example, key goal indicators [KGIs], key performance indicators [KPIs], key risk indicators [KRIs])

RELATIONSHIP OF TASK TO KNOWLEDGE STATEMENTS

The task statements are what the CISM candidate is expected to know how to perform. The knowledge statements delineate each of the areas in which the CISM candidate must have a good understanding in order to perform the tasks. The task and knowledge statements are mapped in **exhibit 1.1** insofar as it is possible to do so. Note that although there is often overlap, each task statement will generally map to several knowledge statements.

Exhibit 1.1—Task and Knowledge Statements Mapping

Task Statement	Knowledge Statements
T1.1 Establish and maintain an information security strategy in alignment with organizational goals and objectives to guide the establishment and ongoing management of the information security program.	KS1.1 Knowledge of methods to develop an information security strategy KS1.2 Knowledge of the relationship among information security and business goals, objectives, functions and practices
T1.2 Establish and maintain an information security governance framework to guide activities that support the information security strategy.	KS1.2 Knowledge of the relationship among information security and business goals, objectives, functions and practices KS1.3 Knowledge of methods to implement an information security governance framework KS1.4 Knowledge of the fundamental concepts of governance and how they relate to information security KS1.6 Knowledge of internationally recognized standards, frameworks and best practices related to information security governance and strategy development
T1.3 Integrate information security governance into corporate governance to ensure that organizational goals and objectives are supported by the information security program.	KS1.2 Knowledge of the relationship among information security and business goals, objectives, functions and practices KS1.4 Knowledge of the fundamental concepts of governance and how they relate to information security KS1.5 Knowledge of methods to integrate information security governance into corporate governance KS1.6 Knowledge of internationally recognized standards, frameworks and best practices related to information security governance and strategy development
T1.4 Establish and maintain information security policies to communicate management's directives and guide the development of standards, procedures and guidelines.	KS1.2 Knowledge of the relationship among information security and business goals, objectives, functions and practices KS1.7 Knowledge of methods to develop information security policies
T1.5 Develop business cases to support investments in information security.	KS1.8 Knowledge of methods to develop business cases KS1.9 Knowledge of strategic budgetary planning and reporting methods
T1.6 Identify internal and external influences to the organization (for example, technology, business environment, risk tolerance, geographic location, legal and regulatory requirements) to ensure that these factors are addressed by the information security strategy.	KS1.6 Knowledge of internationally recognized standards, frameworks and best practices related to information security governance and strategy development KS1.10 Knowledge of the internal and external influences to the organization (for example, technology, business environment, risk tolerance, geographic location, legal and regulatory requirements) and how they impact the information security strategy

Exhibit 1.1—Task and Knowledge Statements Mapping *(cont.)*	
Task Statement	**Knowledge Statements**
T1.7 Obtain commitment from senior management and support from other stakeholders to maximize the probability of successful implementation of the information security strategy.	KS1.11 Knowledge of methods to obtain commitment from senior management and support from other stakeholders for information security
T1.8 Define and communicate the roles and responsibilities of information security throughout the organization to establish clear accountabilities and lines of authority.	KS1.12 Knowledge of information security management roles and responsibilities KS1.13 Knowledge of organizational structures and lines of authority
T1.9 Establish, monitor, evaluate and report metrics (for example, key goal indicators [KGIs], key performance indicators [KPIs], key risk indicators [KRIs]) to provide management with accurate information regarding the effectiveness of the information security strategy.	KS1.14 Knowledge of methods to establish new, or utilize existing, reporting and communication channels throughout an organization KS1.15 Knowledge of methods to select, implement and interpret metrics (for example, key goal indicators [KGIs], key performance indicators [KPIs], key risk indicators [KRIs])

KNOWLEDGE STATEMENT REFERENCE GUIDE

The following section contains the knowledge statements and the underlying concepts and relevance for the knowledge of the information security manager. The knowledge statements are what the information security manager must know in order to accomplish the tasks. A summary explanation of each knowledge statement is provided, followed by the basic concepts that are the foundation for the written exam. Each key concept has references to section two of this chapter.

The CISM body of knowledge has been divided into four domains, and each of the four chapters covers some of the material contained in those domains. This chapter reviews the body of knowledge from the perspective of strategy and governance.

KS1.1 Knowledge of methods to develop an information security strategy

Explanation	Key Concepts	Reference in 2015 CISM Review Manual
Strategy is the plan of action to achieve the defined objectives that result in the desired outcomes, utilizing available resources within the existing constraints. A strategy for achieving defined outcomes for the information security program is necessary to develop an effective, mature security program. The strategy will guide governance requirements, policies and standards development. It will also guide the development of control objectives and the metrics necessary for effective management. Ultimately, the strategy will provide the basis for a road map for its own implementation, To be effective, the strategy must consider a variety of factors, including the available resources as well as the constraints. Resources will include people, processes, technologies and architectures. Constraints that must be considered include time, costs, resources, skills, regulatory requirements, culture and organizational structure.	The rationale for strategy development	1.4 Information Security Governance Overview 1.4.1 Importance of Information Security Governance 1.4.2 Outcomes of Information Security Governance 1.5 Effective Information Security Governance 1.5.1 Business Goals and Objectives 1.5.3 Roles and Responsibilities of Senior Management 1.10.2 Defining Objectives
	Drivers for strategy–threats, exposures, risk and impacts	1.4.2 Outcomes of Information Security Governance 1.5.4 Information Security Roles and Responsibilities
	The basis for strategy development–relationship to objectives	1.12.1 Elements of a Strategy 1.18 Information Security Program Objectives
	Relationships among strategic elements	1.13 Strategy Resources 1.13.19 Other Organizational Support and Assurance Providers 1.14.11 Risk Acceptance and Tolerance
	Strategy resources and constraints	1.12.1 Elements of a Strategy 1.14 Strategy Constraints
	How organizational objectives set requirements for security strategy	1.8 Information Security Strategy Overview 1.8.1 An Alternate View of Strategy 1.9 Developing an Information Security Strategy 1.10 Information Security Strategy Objectives 1.10.1 The Goal 1.12 Information Security Strategy Development 1.18 Information Security Program Objectives
	Developing a strategy and information security road map	1.12 Information Security Strategy Development 1.12.1 Elements of a Strategy 1.13 Strategy Resources 1.13.19 Other Organizational Support and Assurance Providers 1.14.11 Risk Acceptance and Tolerance
	Strategy as a basis for policy and the relation to control objectives	1.16 Implementing Security Governance—Example 1.16.1 Additional Policy Samples 1.18 Information Security Program Objectives Exhibit 1.2 Relationship of Governance Components

KS1.2 Knowledge of the relationship among information security and business goals, objectives, functions and practices

Explanation	Key Concepts	Reference in 2015 CISM Review Manual
In a properly governed organization, information security activities support the organizational goals and objectives while identifying and managing risk to acceptable levels. The relationship of information security to organizational functions must be understood to design and implement appropriate risk mitigation solutions. The information security manager must understand the nature and purpose of an organization's various functions in order to ensure that appropriate and effective governance structures are developed. All decisions regarding the implementation of the security program should be the result of well grounded organizational decisions. It is the role of the information security manager to identify and explain to stakeholders the risk to the organization's information, present alternatives for mitigation, and then implement an approach supported by the organization. It is also important to define and convey the opportunities available to the organization as a result of good security, such as the ability to safely conduct online organizational and financial transactions.	The relationship of information security governance to enterprise governance	1.4 Information Security Governance Overview 1.5 Effective Information Security Governance
	Defining security strategy linkages to organizational functions	1.4.2 Outcomes of Information Security Governance
	Organizational benefits of effective security	1.4.1 Importance of Information Security Governance 1.4.2 Outcomes of Information Security Governance
	Methods to determine acceptable risk	1.10.4 Risk Objectives 2.10 Risk Assessment
	Determining the effectiveness of information security governance	1.7 Information Security Governance Metrics
	Approaches to developing risk mitigation strategies	1.10.2 Defining Objectives 2.10 Risk Assessment
	How organizational objectives set requirements for security strategy	1.8 Information Security Strategy Overview 1.8.1 An Alternate View of Strategy 1.9 Developing an Information Security Strategy 1.10 Information Security Strategy Objectives 1.10.1 The Goal 1.12 Information Security Strategy Development 1.18 Information Security Program Objectives
	How security strategy relates to control objectives	1.10.2 Defining Objectives 1.10.3 The Desired State 1.10.4 Risk Objectives 1.18 Information Security Program Objectives
	How organizational objectives translate to security policies	1.13 Strategy Resources

KS1.3 Knowledge of methods to implement an information security governance framework

Explanation	Key Concepts	Reference in 2015 CISM Review Manual
All organizations operate under either a stated or implied set of goals, objectives and rules. It is essential that the information security manager be familiar with these and determine the best approach to developing a strategy that, when implemented, will achieve the objectives resulting in the desired outcomes. Properly developed, the strategy provides the road map for Implementation of the security program and governance framework. The value, effectiveness and sustainability of an information security program are functions of how well it is governed and its contribution to achieving organizational goals. A lack of an effective governance framework typically results in inefficient resource allocation and a tactical, reactive mode of operation that overprotects some assets while underprotecting others. The purpose of an information security program is to support and enhance an organization's operations. This can only be accomplished with a sound understanding of the organization, its culture and operations, and its goals and objectives.	The purpose of governance	1.4 Information Security Governance Overview 1.4.1 Importance of Information Security Governance
	Developing a governance structure	1.4.2 Outcomes of Information Security Governance 1.17 Implementing Security Governance—Example
	The criteria for effective governance	1.4.2 Outcomes of Information Security Governance 1.5 Effective Information Security Governance 1.5.1 Business Goals and Objectives
	The relationship of governance, strategy and controls	1.8 Information Security Strategy Overview 1.10.3 The Desired State Exhibit 1.2 Relationship of Governance Components
	The relationship of information security governance to enterprise governance	1.4 Information Security Governance Overview
	The relationship of governance to organizational objectives	1.4 Information Security Governance Overview 1.5.6 Business Model for Information Security
	How governance is implemented	1.15 Action Plan to Implement Strategy 1.16 Implementing Security Governance—Example

KS1.4 Knowledge of the fundamental concepts of governance and how they relate to information security

Explanation	Key Concepts	Reference in 2015 CISM Review Manual
In a properly governed organization, information security activities support the organizational goals and objectives while identifying and managing risk to acceptable levels. The relationship of information security to organizational functions must be understood to design and implement appropriate risk mitigation solutions. The information security manager must understand the nature and purpose of an organization's various functions in order to ensure that appropriate and effective governance structures are developed. All decisions regarding the implementation of the security program should be the result of well grounded organizational decisions. It is the role of the information security manager to identify and explain to stakeholders the risk to the organization's information, present alternatives for mitigation, and then to implement an approach supported by the organization.	The relationship of information security governance to enterprise governance	1.4 Information Security Governance Overview 1.5 Effective Information Security Governance
	Defining security strategy linkages to organizational functions	1.4.2 Outcomes of Information Security Governance
	Organizational benefits of effective security	1.4.1 Importance of Information Security Governance 1.4.2 Outcomes of Information Security Governance
	Methods to determine acceptable risk	1.10.4 Risk Objectives 2.10 Risk Assessment
	Determining the effectiveness of information security governance	1.7 Information Security Governance Metrics
	Approaches to developing risk mitigation strategies	1.10.2 Defining Objectives 2.10 Risk Assessment
	How security strategy relates to control objectives	1.10.2 Defining Objectives 1.10.3 The Desired State 1.10.4 Risk Objectives 1.18 Information Security Program Objectives
	The relationship between information security and the objectives of the organization	1.4 Information Security Governance Overview 1.4.1 Importance of Information Security Governance 1.4.2 Outcomes of Information Security Governance 1.5 Effective Information Security Governance 1.5.1 Business Goals and Objectives 1.5.3 Roles and Responsibilities of Senior Management 1.10.2 Defining Objectives
	Defining the outcomes of information security that support organizational objectives	1.4.2 Outcomes of Information Security Governance 1.5.4 Information Security Roles and Responsibilities
	Relating information security program objectives to organizational objectives	1.18 Information Security Program Objectives

KS1.5 Knowledge of methods to integrate information security governance into corporate governance

Explanation	Key Concepts	Reference in 2015 CISM Review Manual
Information security governance is a subset of enterprise governance. It is necessary for the information security manager to ensure that information security governance is consistent with overall governance of the enterprise. Consistency requires that the processes, methods, standards, practices and objectives are essentially the same, where applicable. It is essential to understand that information security cannot be a stand-alone activity and that it must be governed by the same rules as the rest of the organization. If there are grounded reasons why this is not prudent, either existing governance structures must be modified or acceptable variances must be devised and approved as required.	Assessing the integration of information security governance and enterprise governance	1.4 Information Security Governance Overview 1.4.1 Importance of Information Security Governance 1.8.8 Assurance Process Integration
	The possible consequences if governance activities are not integrated	1.4 Information Security Governance Overview 1.4.1 Importance of Information Security Governance 1.5 Effective Information Security Governance
	Activities that the information security manager can undertake to improve integration	1.4.2 Outcomes of Information Security Governance 1.5.1 Business Goals and Objectives

KS1.6 Knowledge of internationally recognized standards, frameworks and best practices related to information security governance and strategy development

Explanation	Key Concepts	Reference in 2015 CISM Review Manual
There are a several international standards for information security with which the information security manager should be familiar. These standards provide a consistent, time-tested set of good practices that can prove very helpful when developing or seeking to improve an information security program. ISO standards, COBIT and PCI are generally the most globally accepted standards. The CISM exam will not ask questions on any regional standards or on the specific content of international standards, but the information security manager should be generally familiar with the standards and how they can be leveraged to support strategy development and governance of the information security program.	The purpose of a standard	1.13.1 Policies and Standards
	When and how standards are used	1.7.3 Strategic Alignment Metrics 1.12.1 Elements of a Strategy 1.12.2 Strategy Resources and Constraints—Overview 1.13.1 Policies and Standards
	Common attributes of international standards	1.10.3 The Desired State
	The relationship of governance to ISO standards and COBIT	1.10.3 The Desired State 1.13.4 Technologies 1.16 Implementing Security Governance—Example Exhibit 1.9 Prevalent Standards and Frameworks
	The relationship of information security governance to enterprise governance	1.4 Information Security Governance Overview
	The relationship of governance to organizational objectives	1.4 Information Security Governance Overview 1.5.6 Business Model for Information Security
	How governance is implemented	1.15 Action Plan to Implement Strategy 1.16 Implementing Security Governance—Example

KS1.7 Knowledge of methods to develop information security policies

Explanation	Key Concepts	Reference in 2015 CISM Review Manual
The development of an information security strategy, which supports the organization's overall objectives, will drive the development of security policies. The policies will, in turn, reflect management intent, direction, and expectations and drive the development of standards and other controls that ultimately support business objectives.	The basis for policy development	1.5.4 Information Security Roles and Responsibilities 1.10.3 The Desired State 1.13.1 Policies and Standards 1.15.2 Policy Development
	Policy and strategy	1.16 Implementing Security Governance—Example 1.16.1 Additional Policy Samples 1.17 Action Plan Intermediate Goals
	Policies and control development	1.10.3 The Desired State 1.11 Determining Current State of Security 1.18 Information Security Program Objectives Exhibit 1.9 Prevalent Standards and Frameworks
	The relationship of policies and architecture	1.10.3 Architectural Approaches 1.12.1 Elements of a Strategy 1.13.2 Enterprise Information Security Architecture(s) Exhibit 1.17 SABSA Security Architecture Matrix

KS1.8 Knowledge of methods to develop business cases

Explanation	Key Concepts	Reference in 2015 CISM Review Manual
The rationale and justification for the security program and security initiatives must rest on a solid business case to optimize cost effectiveness, organizational relevance and ongoing viability. To be effective as an information security manager, it is essential to understand methods for developing an effective business case for security initiatives in order to gain the management support needed for success.	The purpose of a business case	1.5.4 Obtaining Senior Management Commitment 1.7.5 Value Delivery Metrics 1.10.3 The Desired State 3.13.6 Business Case Development
	What is included (or not) in a business case	1.10.3 The Desired State 3.13.6 Business Case Development
	The financial aspects of a business case	1.10.3 The Desired State 3.13.6 Business Case Development
	The feasibility aspects of a business case	1.10.3 The Desired State 1.16 Implementing Security Governance—Example 1.4.2 Outcomes of Information Security Governance 3.13.6 Business Case Development
	Business case recipients and presentation	1.10.3 The Desired State 3.13.6 Business Case Development

KS1.9 Knowledge of strategic budgetary planning and reporting methods

Explanation	Key Concepts	Reference in 2015 CISM Review Manual
It is important for an information security manager to understand and be able to participate in the standard organizational financial practices. Increasingly, developing, managing and implementing governance requires understanding the budgeting and reporting practices of the organization. Depending on the maturity of the organization and the state of security governance, the analysis and planning required to prepare and submit a budget can be considerable.	General management and administration concepts	1.5.3 Roles and Responsibilities of Senior Management 3.13 Security Program Management and Administrative Activities
	Budgeting	1.14.6 Costs 1.14.10 Time 3.13.7 Program Budgeting
	Financial reporting	1.5.4 Obtaining Senior Management Commitment 1.14.6 Costs 3.13.7 Program Budgeting

KS1.10 Knowledge of the internal and external influences to the organization (for example, technology, business environment, risk tolerance, geographic location, legal and regulatory requirements) and how they impact the information security strategy

Explanation	Key Concepts	Reference in 2015 CISM Review Manual
A variety of conditions will affect how an organization regards security issues and reacts to them. The information security manager must understand what those drivers are and how to address them in the security program. Internal drivers will include such things as risk tolerance and organizational objectives. External drivers can include regulatory and legal requirements, current trends in cyber attacks and factors such as economic conditions. Understanding the organizational response and reaction to these various drivers allows the information security manager to more effectively target activities to the areas of most concern and to frame security initiatives in ways more relevant to the organization.	Business sector differences in drivers	1.14.4 Culture 3.13.1 Personnel, Roles and Responsibilities, and Skills
	Regulatory drivers and their impacts	1.14.1 Legal and Regulatory Requirements
	Risk drivers and risk tolerance	1.5.5 Governance, Risk Management and Compliance 1.10.4 Risk Objectives 1.11.1 Current Risk
	Cultural aspects of organizational reactions and responses	1.9.1 Common Pitfalls 1.10.3 The Desired State 1.13.5 Personnel 1.13.6 Organizational Structure

KS1.11 Knowledge of methods to obtain commitment from senior management and support from other stakeholders for information security

Explanation	Key Concepts	Reference in 2015 CISM Review Manual
Management support and commitment is essential to an effective security program. An understanding of approaches to achieving that support is a critical skill for the information security manager. Gaining management support for a security program requires an understanding of management concerns and focus, and the ability to present a persuasive case for cost-effective solutions in organizational terms that minimize operational disruptions.	Assessing senior management commitment to information security	1.5.4 Obtaining Senior Management Commitment
	The effects of inadequate management support	1.5.4 Obtaining Senior Management Commitment 3.17 Common Information Security Program Challenges
	Options for the security manager in the absence of senior management support	1.5.4 Obtaining Senior Management Commitment 3.4 Information Security Program Management Overview
	Achieving management commitment to information security	1.5.4 Obtaining Senior Management Commitment 1.7 Information Security Governance Metrics 1.7.1 Effective Security Metrics 1.7.2 Governance Implementation Metrics
	The basis for securing management support for a security program	1.5.4 Obtaining Senior Management Commitment

KS1.12 Knowledge of information security management roles and responsibilities

Explanation	Key Concepts	Reference in 2015 CISM Review Manual
Roles and responsibilities of information security managers can vary significantly between organizations. Information security managers can have a number of titles, including chief information security officer (CISO), information security officer and chief risk officer (CRO). The role may be part of the functions of the chief security officer (CSO) or an additional responsibility of the chief information officer (CIO) or the chief technology officer (CTO). The information security function may fall under the chief financial officer (CFO), the chief executive officer (CEO), the chief operating officer (COO), the audit committee of the board of directors or under some operational department head. The responsibilities will typically be similar, but the range, scope and authority will differ dramatically. It is important for the information security manager to understand how these functions operate in various organizations and how they are impacted by different organizational structures.	Variations in roles and responsibilities of information security management	1.5.3 Roles and Responsibilities of Senior Management 1.5.3 CISO 1.5.3 Steering Committee 1.7.3 Strategic Alignment Metrics Exhibit 1.4 Relationship of Information Security Governance Outcomes to Management Responsibilities
	The impact of organizational structure on information security management	1.12.2 Strategy Resources and Constraints—Overview 1.13.6 Organizational Structure 1.16 Implementing Security Governance—Example
	The impact of other influences on the roles and responsibilities of information security management	1.12.2 Strategy Resources and Constraints—Overview 1.13.6 Organizational Structure 1.14.1 Legal and Regulatory Requirements 1.14.6 Costs

KS1.13 Knowledge of organizational structures and lines of authority

Explanation	Key Concepts	Reference in 2015 CISM Review Manual
Information security exists in an organization to support Its objectives, minimize disruptions to operations and manage risk in a cost-effective manner. To support the organization, It Is essential that the Information security manager understands the organization's structure and how responsibility and accountability Is assigned.	Organizational structure and governance	1.4 Information Security Governance Overview 1.5.2 Scope and Charter of Information Security Governance Exhibit 1.2 Relationship of Governance Components Exhibit 1.4 Relationship of Information Security Governance Outcomes to Management Responsibilities
	Responsibilities	1.5 Effective Information Security Governance Exhibit 1.2 Relationship of Governance Components Exhibit 1.4 Relationship of Information Security Governance Outcomes to Management Responsibilities

KS1.14 Knowledge of methods to establish new, or utilize existing, reporting and communication channels throughout an organization

Explanation	Key Concepts	Reference in 2015 CISM Review Manual
Effective management of a security program requires effective information flows to and from all parts of the organization. Information about events, incidents, threats and risk from all parts of the organization, as well as external sources, is essential to managing security. It is equally essential that information relevant to maintaining security is communicated to management and staff throughout the organization, on both a periodic and event-driven basis.	Types of information that should be communicated by the information security manager	1.5.4 Obtaining Senior Management Commitment 2.5.1 Risk Communication, Risk Awareness and Consulting 2.15 Risk Monitoring and Communication
	Understanding to whom and when various types of information should be reported by the information security manager	1.5.4 Obtaining Senior Management Commitment Exhibit 1.4 Relationship of Information Security Governance Outcomes to Management Responsibilities
	Information that should be communicated regularly by the information security manager	1.5.4 Obtaining Senior Management Commitment 2.15 Risk Monitoring and Communication
	Types of events that should be communicated immediately by the information security manager	1.5.4 Obtaining Senior Management Commitment 1.16.5 Action Plan Metrics
	Information that a security manager should receive, including from whom and when	1.5.4 Obtaining Senior Management Commitment Exhibit 1.7 Information Security Strategy Development Participants
	How communication channels are developed	1.4.2 Outcomes of Information Security Governance 1.5.3 Roles and Responsibilities of Senior Management 1.5.4 Obtaining Senior Management Commitment
	Integrating other assurance processes with information security	1.7.8 Assurance Process Integration (Convergence)
	Using of metrics to show trends and problem areas in the information security program	1.7 Information Security Governance Metrics 1.7.1 Effective Security Metrics 1.7.2 Governance Implementation Metrics

KS1.15 Knowledge of methods to select, implement and interpret metrics (for example, key goal indicators [KGIs], key performance indicators [KPIs], key risk indicators [KRIs])

Explanation	Key Concepts	Reference in 2015 CISM Review Manual
"Metrics" is a term used for measurements based on one or more references and involves at least two points—the measurement and the reference. Security, in its most basic meaning, is the protection from or absence of danger. Literally, security metrics should tell us about the state or degree of safety relative to a reference point. Contemporary security metrics frequently fail to do so at the operational level and in the overall management of an information security program. While there are typically numerous technical metrics available, these are of little value from a strategic management or governance standpoint. Technical metrics say nothing about strategic alignment with organizational objectives or how well risk is being managed; they provide few measures of policy compliance or whether objectives for acceptable levels of potential impact are being reached; and they provide no information on whether the information security program is headed in the right direction and achieving the desired outcomes. It is important to understand that the fundamental purpose of metrics, measures and monitoring is decision support. For metrics to be useful, the information they provide must be relevant to the roles and responsibilities of the recipient so that informed decisions can be made. For the purposes of governance metrics and monitoring, KGIs, KPIs and KRIs are typically the most useful for strategic and management purposes.	Strategic and management metrics	1.7 Information Security Governance Metrics 1.7.1 Effective Security Metrics 1.7.2 Governance Implementation Metrics
	KGIs	1.7.3 Strategic Alignment Metrics 1.7.4 Risk Management Metrics 1.7.5 Value Delivery Metrics 1.7.6 Resource Management Metrics 1.7.7 Performance Measurement 1.7.8 Assurance Process Integration (Convergence) 3.16 Security Program Metrics and Monitoring
	KPIs KRIs	1.7.1 Effective Security Metrics 1.7.2 Governance Implementation Metrics 3.16 Security Program Metrics and Monitoring

SUGGESTED RESOURCES FOR FURTHER STUDY

Allen, Julia H.; "*Governing for Enterprise Security*," Carnegie Mellon University, USA, 2005, *www.sei.cmu.edu/reports/05tn023.pdf*

Allen, Julia H.; Jody R. Westby; *Governing for Enterprise Security (GES) Implementation Guide*, Carnegie Mellon University, USA, 2007, *www.sei.cmu.edu/reports/07tn020.pdf*

Brotby, W. Krag and IT Governance Institute; *Information Security Governance: Guidance for Boards of Directors and Executive Management, 2nd Edition*, ISACA, USA, 2006

Brotby, W. Krag and IT Governance Institute; *Information Security Governance: Guidance for Information Security Managers*, ISACA, USA, 2008

Business Roundtable, "Information Security Addendum to Principles of Corporate Governance," April 2003, *www.businessroundtable.org*

Information Security Forum, The 2011 Standard of Good Practice for Information Security, UK, 2011, *www.isfsecuritystandard.com/SOGP07/index.htm*

International Organization for Standardization (ISO), Code of Practice for Information Security Management, ISO/IEC 27002:13

ISACA, *The Business Model for Information Security*, USA, 2010

ISACA, COBIT 5, USA, 2012, *www.isaca.org/cobit*

ISACA, *COBIT 5: Enabling Processes*, USA, 2012, *www.isaca.org/cobit*

ISACA, *COBIT 5 for Information Security*, USA, 2012, *www.isaca.org/cobit*

ISACA, *Unlocking Value: An Executive Primer on the Critical Role of IT Governance*, USA, 2008

Kiely, Laree; Terry Benzel; *Systemic Security Management*, Libertas Press, USA, 2006, *www.classic.marshall.usc.edu/assets/004/5347.pdf*

McKinsey and Institutional Investors Inc., "McKinsey/KIOD Survey on Corporate Governance," January 2003

National Institute of Standards and Technology (NIST), Recommended Security Controls for Federal Information Systems, NIST 800-53, USA, 2009, *www.csrc.nist.gov/publications/nistpubs/800-53-Rev3/sp800-53-rev3-final_updated-errata_05-01-2010.pdf*

Organization for Economic Co-operation and Development (OECD), *Guidelines for the Security of Information Systems and Networks: Towards a Culture of Security*, France, 2002, *www.oecd.org/dataoecd/16/22/15582260.pdf*

Sherwood, John; Andrew Clark; David Lynas; *Enterprise Security Architecture: A Business Driven Approach*, CMP Books, USA, 2005, www.sabsa.org

Tarantino, Anthony; *Manager's Guide to Compliance: Sarbanes-Oxley, COSO, ERM, COBIT, IFRS, BASEL II, OMB's A-123, ASX 10, OECD Principles, Turnbull Guidance, Best Practices, and Case Studies*, John Wiley & Sons Inc., USA, 2006

The Revolution Group, *Seventh Annual Global Information Security Survey*, USA, 2009

Note: Publications in bold are stocked in the ISACA Bookstore.

1.3 SELF-ASSESSMENT QUESTIONS

QUESTIONS

CISM exam questions are developed with the intent of measuring and testing practical knowledge in information security management. All questions are multiple choice and are designed for one best answer. Every CISM question has a stem (question) and four options (answer choices). The candidate is asked to choose the correct or best answer from the options. The stem may be in the form of a question or incomplete statement. In some instances, a scenario or a description problem may also be included. These questions normally include a description of a situation and require the candidate to answer two or more questions based on the information provided. Many times a CISM examination question will require the candidate to choose the most likely or best answer.

In every case, the candidate is required to read the question carefully, eliminate known incorrect answers and then make the best choice possible. Knowing the format in which questions are asked, and how to study to gain knowledge of what will be tested, will go a long way toward answering them correctly.

1-1 A security strategy is important for an organization **PRIMARILY** because it provides:

A. a basis for determining the best logical security architecture for the organization.
B. management intent and direction for security activities.
C. provides users guidance on how to operate securely in everyday tasks.
D. helps IT auditors ensure compliance.

1-2 Which of the following is the **MOST** important reason to provide effective communication about information security?

A. It makes information security more palatable to resistant employees.
B. It mitigates the weakest link in the information security landscape.
C. It informs business units about the information security strategy.
D. It helps the organization conform to regulatory information security requirements.

1-3 Which of the following approaches **BEST** helps the information security manager achieve compliance with various regulatory requirements?

A. Rely on corporate counsel to advise which regulations are the most relevant.
B. Stay current with all relevant regulations and request legal interpretation.
C. Involve all impacted departments and treat regulations as just another risk.
D. Ignore many of the regulations that have no penalties.

1-4 The **MOST** important consideration in developing security policies is that:

A. they are based on a threat profile.
B. they are complete and no detail is left out.
C. management signs off on them.
D. all employees read and understand them.

1-5 The **PRIMARY** security objective in creating good procedures is:

A. to make sure they work as intended.
B. that they are unambiguous and meet the standards.
C. that they be written in plain language and widely distributed.
D. that compliance can be monitored.

1-6 Which of the following **MOST** helps ensure that assignment of roles and responsibilities is effective?

A. Senior management is in support of the assignments.
B. The assignments are consistent with existing proficiencies.
C. The assignments are mapped to required skills.
D. The assignments are given on a voluntary basis.

1-7 Which of the following benefits is the **MOST** important to an organization with effective information security governance?

A. Maintaining appropriate regulatory compliance
B. Ensuring disruptions are within acceptable levels
C. Prioritizing allocation of remedial resources
D. Maximizing return on security investments

1-8 From an information security manager's perspective, the **MOST** important factors regarding data retention are:

A. business and regulatory requirements.
B. document integrity and destruction.
C. media availability and storage.
D. data confidentiality and encryption.

1-9 Which role is in the **BEST** position to review and confirm the appropriateness of a user access list?

A. Data owner
B. Information security manager
C. Domain administrator
D. Business manager

1-10 In implementing information security governance, the information security manager is **PRIMARILY** responsible for:

A. developing the security strategy.
B. reviewing the security strategy.
C. communicating the security strategy.
D. approving the security strategy.

ANSWERS TO SELF-ASSESSMENT QUESTIONS

1-1 **B** A security strategy will define management intent and direction for a security program. It should also be a statement of how security aligns with and supports business objectives, and provides the basis for good security governance.

1-2 **B** Security failures are, in the majority of instances, directly attributable to lack of awareness or failure of employees to follow procedures. Communication is important to ensure continued awareness of security policies and procedures among staff and business partners.

1-3 **C** While it can be useful to stay abreast of all current and emerging regulations, it can become a full-time job by itself. Departments such as human resources, finance and legal are most often subject to new regulations and must, therefore, be involved in determining how best to meet the existing and emerging requirements and, typically, would be most aware of these regulations. Treating regulations as another risk puts them in the proper perspective and the mechanisms to deal with them should already exist. The fact that there are so many regulations makes it unlikely that they can all be specifically addressed efficiently. Many do not currently have significant consequences and, in fact, may be addressed by compliance with other regulations. The most relevant response to regulatory requirements is to determine potential impact to the organization just as must be done with any other risk.

1-4 **A** The basis for relevant security policies must be based on viable threats to the organization, prioritized by their potential impact on the business. The strictest policies apply to the areas of greatest risk. This ensures that proportionality is maintained and great effort is not expended on unlikely threats or threats with trivial impacts.

1-5 **B** All of the answers are obviously important but the first criteria must be to ensure that there is no ambiguity in the procedures and that, from a security perspective, they meet the applicable standards and, therefore, comply with policy. While it is important to make sure that procedures work as intended, the fact that they do not may not be a security issue.

1-6 **B** The level of effectiveness of employees will be determined by their existing knowledge and capabilities, in other words, their proficiencies. Senior management support is always important, but not essential to effectiveness of employee activities. Mapping roles to the tasks that are required can be useful, but is no guarantee that people can perform the required tasks.

1-7 **B** The bottom line of security efforts is to ensure that business can continue with an acceptable level of disruption that does not unduly constrain revenue-producing activities. The other choices are useful, but subordinate outcomes as well.

1-8 **A** Integrity, availability and confidentiality are key factors for information security; however, business and regulatory requirements are the driving factors for data retention.

1-9 **A** The data owner is responsible for periodic reconfirmation of the access lists for systems he/she owns. The information security manager is in charge of the coordination of the user access list reviews but does not have any responsibility for data access. The domain administrator may technically provide the access, but he/she does not approve it. Choice D is incorrect because the business manager may not be the data owner.

1-10 **A** The information security manager is responsible for developing a security strategy based on business objectives with help of business process owners. Reviewing the security strategy is the responsibility of a steering committee. The information security manager is not necessarily responsible for communicating or approving the security strategy.

Section Two: Content

1.4 INFORMATION SECURITY GOVERNANCE OVERVIEW

Information can be defined as "data endowed with meaning and purpose." It plays a critical role in all aspects of our lives. Information has become an indispensable component of conducting business for virtually all organizations. In a growing number of companies, information is the business.

Approximately 80 percent of national critical infrastructures in the developed world are controlled by the private sector. Coupled with often ineffective bureaucracies, countless conflicting jurisdictions and aging institutions unable to adapt to dealing with burgeoning global information crime, a preponderance of the task of protecting information resources critical to survival is falling squarely on corporate shoulders.

To accomplish the task of adequate protection for information resources, the issue must be raised to a board-level activity as are other critical governance functions. The complexity, relevance and criticality of information security and its governance mandate that it be addressed and supported at the highest organizational levels.

Information security governance is the set of responsibilities and practices exercised by the board and executive management with the goal of providing strategic direction, ensuring that objectives are achieved, ascertaining that risk is managed appropriately and verifying that the organization's resources are used responsibly. Ultimately, senior management and the board of directors are accountable for information security governance and must provide the necessary leadership, organizational structures and processes to ensure that information security governance is an integral and transparent part of enterprise governance.

Increasingly, those that understand the scope and depth of risk to information take the position that, as a critical resource, information must be treated with the same care, caution and prudence that any other asset essential to the survival of the organization and, perhaps society, would receive.

Often, the focus of protection has been on the IT systems that process and store the vast majority of information rather than on the information itself. But this approach is too narrow to accomplish the level of integration, process assurance and overall security that is required. Information security takes the larger view that the content, information and the knowledge based on it, must be adequately protected, regardless of how it is handled, processed, transported or stored.

Executive management is increasingly confronted by the need to stay competitive in the global economy and heed the promise of ever greater gains from the deployment of more information resources. But even as organizations reap those gains, the increasing dependence on information and the systems that support it, and advancing risk from a host of threats, are forcing management to make difficult decisions about how to effectively address information security. In addition, scores of new and existing laws and regulations are increasingly demanding compliance and higher levels of accountability.

1.4.1 IMPORTANCE OF INFORMATION SECURITY GOVERNANCE

From an organization's perspective, information security governance is increasingly critical as dependence on information grows.

Information, defined as "data endowed with meaning and purpose," is the substance of knowledge. Knowledge is, in turn, captured, transported and stored as organized information.

More than a decade ago, Peter Drucker pointed out that, "Knowledge is fast becoming the sole factor of productivity, sidelining both capital and labor."

For most organizations, information, and the knowledge based on it, is one of their most important assets without which conducting business would not be possible. The systems and processes that handle this information have become pervasive throughout business and governmental organizations globally. This dependence of organizations on their information and the systems that handle it, coupled with the risk, benefits and opportunities that these resources present, have made information security governance a critical facet of overall governance. In addition to addressing legal and regulatory requirements, effective information security governance is simply good business. Prudent management has come to understand that it provides a series of significant benefits, including:

- Addressing the increasing potential for civil or legal liability inuring to the organization and senior management as a result of information inaccuracy or the absence of due care in its protection or inadequate regulatory compliance
- Providing assurance of policy compliance
- Increasing predictability and reducing uncertainty of business operations by lowering risk to definable and acceptable levels
- Providing the structure and framework to optimize allocations of limited security resources
- Providing a level of assurance that critical decisions are not based on faulty information
- Providing a firm foundation for efficient and effective risk management, process improvement, rapid incident response and continuity management
- Providing greater confidence in interactions with trading partners
- Improving trust in customer relationships
- Protecting the organization's reputation
- Enabling new and better ways to process electronic transactions
- Providing accountability for safeguarding information during critical business activities, such as mergers and acquisitions, business process recovery, and regulatory response
- Effective management of information security resources

In summary, because new information technology provides the potential for dramatically enhanced business performance, effective information security can add significant value to the organization by reducing losses from security-related events and providing assurance that security incidents and breaches are not catastrophic. In addition, evidence suggests that improved perception in the market has resulted in increased share value.

1.4.2 OUTCOMES OF INFORMATION SECURITY GOVERNANCE

Information security governance includes the elements required to provide senior management assurance that its direction and intent are reflected in the security posture of the organization by utilizing a structured approach to implementing a security program. Once those elements are in place, senior management can be confident that adequate and effective information security will protect the organization's vital information assets.

The objective of information security governance is to develop, implement and manage a security program that achieves the following **six basic outcomes of effective security governance**:

1. **Strategic alignment**—Aligning information security with business strategy to support organizational objectives such as:
   - Security requirements driven by enterprise requirements that are thoroughly developed to provide guidance on what must be done and a measure of when it has been achieved
   - Security solutions fit for enterprise processes that take into account the culture, governance style, technology and structure of the organization
   - Investment in information security that is aligned with the enterprise strategy, enterprise operations and well-defined threat, vulnerability and risk profile
2. **Risk management**—Executing appropriate measures to mitigate risk and reduce potential impacts on information resources to an acceptable level such as:
   - Collective understanding of the organization's threat, vulnerability and risk profile
   - Understanding of risk exposure and potential consequences of compromise
   - Awareness of risk management priorities based on potential consequences
   - Risk mitigation sufficient to achieve acceptable consequences from residual risk
   - Risk acceptance/deference based on an understanding of the potential consequences of residual risk
3. **Value delivery**—Optimizing security investments in support of business objectives such as:
   - A standard set of security practices, i.e., baseline security requirements following adequate and sufficient practices proportionate to risk and potential impact
   - Information security overheads that are maintained at a minimum level and a security program that enables the organization in achieving its objectives
   - A properly prioritized and distributed effort to areas with the greatest impact and business benefit
   - Institutionalized and commoditized standards-based solutions
   - Complete solutions, covering organization and process as well as technology based on an understanding of the end-to-end business of the organization
   - A continuous improvement culture based on the understanding that security is a process, not an event
4. **Resource optimization**—Using information security knowledge and infrastructure efficiently and effectively to:
   - Ensure that knowledge is captured and available
   - Document security processes and practices
   - Develop security architecture(s) to define and utilize infrastructure resources efficiently
5. **Performance measurement**—Monitoring and reporting on information security processes to ensure that objectives are achieved, including:
   - A defined, agreed-upon and meaningful set of metrics that are properly aligned with strategic objectives and provides the information needed for effective decisions at the strategic, management and operational levels
   - Measurement process that helps identify shortcomings and provides feedback on progress made resolving issues
   - Independent assurance provided by external assessments and audits
   - Criteria for separating the most useful metrics from the variety of things that can be measured
6. **Integration**—Integrating all relevant assurance factors to ensure that processes operate as intended from end to end:
   - Determine all organizational assurance functions.
   - Develop formal relationships with other assurance functions.
   - Coordinate all assurance functions for more cost-effective security.
   - Ensure that roles and responsibilities between assurance functions overlap.
   - Employ a systems approach to information security planning, deployment, metrics and management.

1.5 EFFECTIVE INFORMATION SECURITY GOVERNANCE

Information security governance is the responsibility of the board of directors and executive management. It must be an integral and transparent part of enterprise governance, and complement or encompass the IT governance framework. While executive management has the responsibility to consider and respond to these issues, boards of directors increasingly will be expected to make information security an intrinsic part of governance, integrated with the processes they have in place to govern other critical organizational resources.

According to the developers of the Business Model for Information Security (BMIS) (see section 1.5.6), "It is no longer enough to communicate to the world of stakeholders why we [the organization] exist and what constitutes success, we must also communicate how we are going to protect our existence."

This suggests that a clear organizational strategy for preservation is equally important to, and must accompany, a strategy for progress.

Julia Allen of Carnegie Mellon University (CMU) points out that:

> *Governing for enterprise security means viewing adequate security as a non-negotiable requirement of being in business. If an organization's management—including boards of directors, senior executives and all managers—does not establish and reinforce the business need for effective enterprise security, the organization's desired state of security will not be articulated, achieve, or sustained. To achieve a sustainable capability, organizations must make enterprise security the responsibility of leaders at a governance level, not of other organizational roles that lack the authority, accountability and resources to act and enforce compliance.*

In addition to protection of information assets, effective information security governance is required to address legal and regulatory requirements and is becoming mandatory in the exercise of due care. From any perspective, it must be considered simply good business.

1.5.1 BUSINESS GOALS AND OBJECTIVES

Corporate governance is the set of responsibilities and practices exercised by the board and executive management with the goal of providing strategic direction, ensuring that objectives are achieved, ascertaining that risk is managed appropriately and verifying that the enterprise's resources are used responsibly.

The strategic direction of the business will be defined by business goals and objectives. Information security must support business activities to be of value to the organization.

Information security governance is a subset of corporate governance; it provides strategic direction for security activities and ensures that objectives are achieved. It ensures that information security risk is appropriately managed and enterprise information resources are used responsibly.

To achieve effective information security governance, management must establish and maintain a framework to guide the development and management of a comprehensive information security program that supports business objectives.

The governance framework will generally consist of:
1. A comprehensive security strategy intrinsically linked with business objectives
2. Governing security policies that address each aspect of strategy, controls and regulation
3. A complete set of standards for each policy to ensure that procedures and guidelines comply with policy
4. An effective security organizational structure void of conflicts of interest with sufficient authority and adequate resources
5. Institutionalized metrics and monitoring processes to ensure compliance, provide feedback on effectiveness and provide the basis for appropriate management decisions

This framework, in turn, provides the basis for the development of a cost-effective information security program that supports the organization' s business goals. Implementing and managing a security program is covered in chapter 3, Information Security Program Development and Management. The objective of the program is a set of activities that provide assurance that information assets are given a level of protection commensurate with their value or with the risk their compromise poses to the organization. The relationships between enterprise governance, risk management, IT security, information security, controls, architecture and the other components of a governance framework are represented in **exhibit 1.2**. While linkage between IT and information security may occur at various higher levels, strategy is the point where information security must integrate IT in order to achieve its objectives.

1.5.2 SCOPE AND CHARTER OF INFORMATION SECURITY GOVERNANCE

Information security deals with all aspects of information, whether spoken, written, printed, electronic or relegated to any other medium, regardless of whether it is being created, viewed, transported, stored or destroyed. This is contrasted with IT security, which is concerned with security of information within the boundaries of the technology domain, usually in a custodial

Exhibit 1.2—Relationship of Governance Components

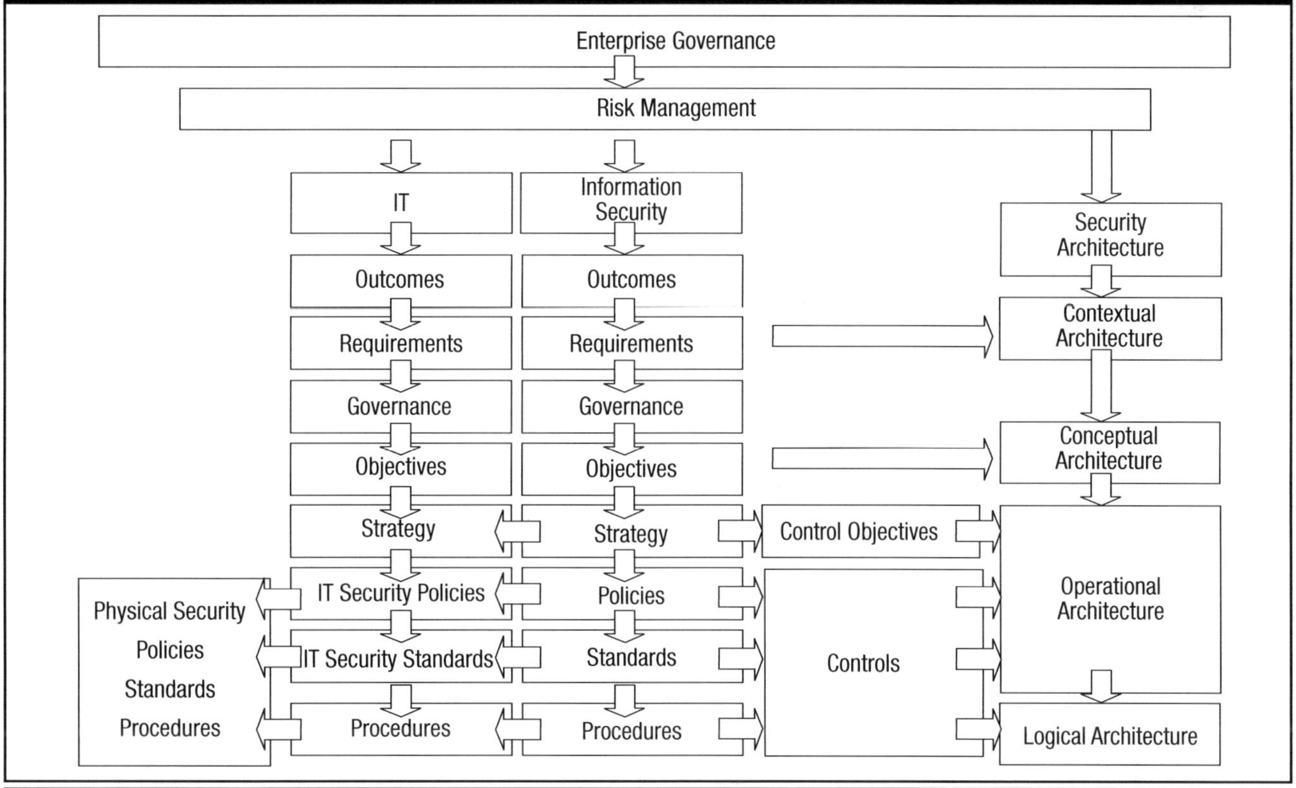

capacity. Typically, confidential information disclosed in an elevator conversation or sent via the postal mail would be outside the scope of IT security. From an information security perspective, however, the nature and type of compromise are not important; the fact that security has been breached is what is important.

In the context of information security governance, it is important that the scope and responsibilities of information security are clearly set forth in the information security strategy.

The Corporate Governance Task Force of the National Security Partnership, a task force of corporate and government leaders, has identified a core set of principles to help guide implementation of effective information security governance:
- CEOs should conduct an annual information security evaluation, review the results with staff and report on performance to the board of directors.
- Organizations should conduct periodic risk assessments of information assets as part of a risk management program.
- Organizations should implement policies and procedures based on risk assessments to secure information assets.
- Organizations should establish a security management structure to assign explicit individual roles, responsibilities, authority and accountability.
- Organizations should develop plans and initiate actions to provide adequate information security for networks, facilities, systems and information.
- Organizations should treat information security as an integral part of the system life cycle.
- Organizations should provide information security awareness, training and education to personnel.
- Organizations should conduct periodic testing and evaluation of the effectiveness of information security policies and procedures.
- Organizations should create and execute a plan for remedial action to address any information security deficiencies.
- Organizations should develop and implement incident response procedures.
- Organizations should establish plans, procedures and tests to provide continuity of operations.
- Organizations should use security good practices guidance, such as ISO/IEC 27002, to measure information security performance.

1.5.3 ROLES AND RESPONSIBILITIES OF SENIOR MANAGEMENT

Boards of Directors/Senior Management

Information security governance requires strategic direction and impetus. It requires commitment, resources and assigning responsibility for information security management as well as a means for the board to determine that its intent has been met. Effective information security governance can be accomplished only by senior management involvement in approving policy, and appropriate monitoring and metrics coupled with reporting and trend analysis.

Members of the board need to be aware of the organization's information assets and their criticality to ongoing business operations. The board should periodically be provided with the high-level results of comprehensive risk assessments and business impact analysis (BIA). A result of these activities should include board members validating/ratifying the key assets they want protected and that protection levels and priorities are appropriate to a standard of due care.

The tone at the top must be conducive to effective security governance. It is unreasonable to expect lower-level personnel to abide by security measures if they are not exercised by senior management. Executive management endorsement of intrinsic security requirements provides the basis for ensuring that security expectations are met at all levels of the enterprise. Penalties for noncompliance must be defined, communicated and enforced from the board level down.

Beyond these requirements, the board has an ongoing obligation to provide a level of oversight of the activities of information security. Given the legal and ethical responsibility of directors to exercise due care in protecting the organization's key assets, which would include its confidential and other critical information, an ongoing level of involvement and oversight of information security is required.

More specifically, there are a number of reasons why it is becoming essential for directors to be involved with, and provide oversight of, information security activities. A common concern for boards of directors is liability. Most organizations, to protect themselves from shareholder lawsuits, provide specific insurance to create a level of protection for the board in exercising its governance responsibilities. However, a typical requirement for the insurance to provide coverage requires directors to exercise a good faith effort at exercising due care in the discharge of their duties. Neglecting to address information security risk may be found to be a failure to exercise due care and may void the protection provided by insurance.

In addition, there are regulations such as the US Sarbanes-Oxley Act which mandate that every company listed on a US stock exchange maintain an audit committee with a required level of experience and demonstrable competence. This committee is often made up of members of the company's board of directors. One of the committee's key responsibilities is the ongoing monitoring of the organization's internal controls that directly affect the reliability of financial statements. Most financial controls are, in fact, technical as well as procedural, with the technical portion generally under the scope of the security manager. Therefore, it is important that the security manager maintain an open channel of communication with this committee.

Finally, institutional investors and others have come to understand that the long-term prospects for an organization are heavily impacted by the overall state of governance. A number of corporate rating organizations now provide a governance rating or metric based on a number of factors. Failure to provide an adequate level of governance and support of activities that protect the major assets of the organization is likely to be reflected in those scores. The weight and relevance of the scores will be driven by the impacts and consequences suffered by organizations that suffer the loss of significant critical and sensitive information. The bottom line is that a board of directors that does not provide a level of direction, oversight and the requirements for appropriate metrics will be subject to an increasing degree of liability and regulatory intervention.

Executive Management

Implementing effective security governance and defining the strategic security objectives of an organization can be a complex, arduous task. As with any other major initiative, it must have leadership and ongoing support from executive management to succeed. Benign neglect, indifference or outright hostility is not likely to result in satisfactory outcomes.

In addition, IT is often faced with performance pressures while security must deal with risk and regulatory issues. These imperatives all too often fall at opposite ends of the spectrum. The result can be tension between IT and security, and it is important that management promotes cooperation, arbitrates differences in perspective and is clear about priorities so that a suitable balance between performance, cost and security can be maintained.

Developing an effective information security strategy requires integration with and cooperation of business process owners. A successful outcome is the alignment of information security activities in support of business objectives. The extent to which this is achieved determines the cost effectiveness of the information security program in achieving the desired objective of providing a predictable, defined level of assurance for business processes and an acceptable level of impact from adverse events.

An organization's executive management team is responsible for ensuring that needed organizational functions, resources and supporting infrastructure are available and properly utilized to fulfill the information-security related directives of the board, regulatory compliance and other demands.

Generally, executive management looks to the information security manager to define the information security program and its subsequent management. Often, the information security manager is also expected to provide education and guidance to the executive management team. As opposed to being the decision maker, the information security manager's role in this situation is often constrained to presentation of options and key decision support information; in other words, an advisor.

Visible executive involvement is critical to the success of an information security program as well as to the effectiveness of its ongoing management. As a consequence, the information security manager should endeavor to educate the executive management team on this need. More importantly, the information security manager should coordinate their involvement in specific activities such as quarterly information risk reviews, new information systems go/no-go meetings, etc. It is important that the information security manager use the executives' time to good benefit. The information security manager must ensure that the executive has a specific role, will be provided with specific information, and has specific decisions to make when involved in information security management activities.

Executive management sets the tone for information security management within the organization. The level of visible involvement and the inclusion of information risk management in key business activities and decisions indicate to other managers the level of importance that they are also expected to apply to risk management for activities within their organizations. Often these unofficial indicators have the greatest impact on the organization's adoption of information security management as a fully recognized business function. This is the notion that auditors refer to as "tone at the top" and is reflected in the culture of the organization.

Steering Committee

To some extent, security affects all aspects of an organization. To be effective, it must be pervasive throughout the enterprise. To ensure that all stakeholders impacted by security considerations are involved, many organizations use a steering committee comprised of senior representatives of affected groups. This facilitates achieving consensus on priorities and tradeoffs. It also serves as an effective communications channel and provides an ongoing basis for ensuring the alignment of the security program with business objectives. It can also be instrumental in achieving modification of behavior toward a culture more conducive to good security.

Common topics, agendas and decisions for a security steering committee include:

- Security strategy and integration efforts, especially efforts to integrate security with business unit activities
- Specific actions and progress relative to business unit support of information security program functions, and vice versa
- Emerging risk, business unit security practices and compliance issues

The information security manager should make sure that the roles, responsibilities, scope and activities of the information security steering committee are clearly defined. This should include clear objectives and topics to prevent poor productivity or the forum becoming sidetracked with extraneous matters.

It is important that materials be distributed, reviews encouraged and solution discussions held in advance of full committee meetings so that the meeting can be focused on resolving issues and making decisions. The use of subcommittees and/or individual action assignments are appropriate to this type of management strategy.

CISO

All organizations have a chief information security officer (CISO), whether anyone holds that title or not. It may be the CIO, chief security officer (CSO), chief financial officer (CFO) or, in some cases, the chief executive officer (CEO). The scope and breadth of information security today is such that the authority required and the responsibility taken will inevitably end up with a C-level officer or executive manager. Legal responsibility will, by default, extend up the command structure and ultimately reside with senior management and the board of directors. Failure to recognize this and implement appropriate governance structures can result in senior management being unaware of this responsibility and the attendant liability. It also usually results in a lack of effective alignment of security activities with organizational objectives.

The CISO position has been gaining popularity over the past decade as more and more organizations designate a CISO or CSO role. In 2006, only 22 percent of the more than 7,000 organizations responding to PricewaterhouseCoopers' annual information security survey reported having a CISO or equivalent. By 2011, more than 80 percent of respondents reported having a CISO.

Significant changes in reporting relationships have occurred in the past few years as well as shown in **exhibit 1.3**. More organizations understand that the focus for security, a fundamentally regulatory role, is different than that of the typical CIO who is generally focused on performance. The result is that there are far fewer information security managers reporting to the CIO and increasingly reporting directly to the board of directors or to the CEO. This trend is likely to continue as security breaches increase both in severity and frequency and, at the same time, become less acceptable and subject to increasing regulatory oversight.

Exhibit 1.3—Changes in Reporting for Information Security Managers

	2007	2008	2009	2010	Three-year % change
Chief information officer (CIO)	38%	34%	32%	23%	-39%
Board of directors	21%	24%	28%	32%	+52%
Chief executive officer (CEO)	32%	34%	35%	36%	+13%
Chief financial officer (CFO)	11%	11%	13%	15%	+36%
Chief operating officer (COO)	9%	10%	12%	15%	+67%
Chief privacy officer (CPO)	8%	8%	14%	17%	+113%

Source: PricewaterhouseCooper and *CSO Magazine, Global State of Information Security Survey 2011*, figure 13, used with permission

Increasingly, prudent management is elevating the position of the information security officer to a C-level or executive position as organizations begin to understand their dependence on information and the growing threats to it. Ensuring the position exists, coupled with the responsibility, authority and required resources, demonstrates management and board of director awareness and commitment to sound information security governance.

The responsibilities and authority of information security managers vary dramatically between organizations, although they are on the rise globally. This can be attributed to the growing awareness of the importance of this function driven by increasingly spectacular failures of security and the growing losses that result. These responsibilities currently range from the CISO or vice president for security reporting to the CEO to system administrators who have part-time responsibility for security management who might report to the IT manager or CIO.

1.5.4 INFORMATION SECURITY ROLES AND RESPONSIBILITIES

Since information security spans every division and department in a company to some extent, implementing effective security governance and defining the strategic security objectives of an organization is usually a complex task. It requires leadership and ongoing support from senior management to succeed. Without senior management support and an effective information security governance structure, integrated with overall enterprise governance and defined objectives, it is difficult for the information security manager to know what goals to steer the program toward, to determine optimal governance processes or develop meaningful program metrics.

Once an information security manager has developed the security strategy with input from key business units, approval of the strategy by senior management is required. Since this is typically a complicated subject, the information security manager may need to first educate senior managers on the high-level aspects of information security and submit the overall strategy for review. A presentation to senior management describing the various aspects of the security strategy usually will take place to support and explain the documentation that the information security manager submitted. Unfortunately, in many organizations, the true value of securing information systems does not become apparent until they fail.

In some organizations, there may be an inadequate level of management commitment and information security managers may be restricted in their effectiveness. Under these circumstances, it may be useful to make an effort to educate senior management in the areas of regulatory compliance and the organization's dependence on its information assets. It may also be useful to document risk and potential impacts faced by the organization, making sure that senior management is informed of the results and finds them acceptable.

Senior management will be in a better position to support security initiatives if they are educated on how critical IT systems are to the continued operation of the enterprise as well as other aspects of information security. In addition, there is often significant confusion about which regulations apply to the organization. It will be helpful to provide an overview of pertinent regulations, compliance requirements and possible sanctions if the organization is out of compliance.

In addition, effective information security management also requires integration with and cooperation from organizational and business unit management.

An adequate level of support for information security by senior management is evident by:
- Clear approval and support for formal security strategies and policies
- Monitoring and measuring organizational performance in implementing security policies
- Supporting security awareness and training for all staff throughout the organization
- Adequate resources and sufficient authority to implement and maintain security activities
- Treating information security as a critical business issue and creating a security-positive environment
- Demonstrating to third parties that the organization deals with information security in a professional manner
- Providing high-level oversight and control
- Periodically reviewing information security effectiveness
- Setting an example by adhering to the organization's security policies and practices
- Discussing information security at board/executive management meetings

In many cases, insufficient management support of information security is not an issue of apathy, but a lack of understanding. Information security is rarely a part of general management expertise or education. As such, executive managers may not fully appreciate what is expected of them, the structure of an information security management program, or how such a program should be integrated and operated. It is often productive to coordinate workshops to assist high-level managers in gaining a clearer understanding of these issues, and establish expectations of needed support and resources.

In other cases, support for information security programs may be limited for financial or other reasons. The information security manager must recognize these constraints, prioritizing and maximizing the effects of available resources in addition to working with management to develop additional resources.

Obtaining Senior Management Commitment

A formal presentation is the most widely used technique the information security manager can use to secure senior management commitment and support of information security management policies, standards and strategy.

The formal presentation to senior management is used as a means to educate and communicate key aspects of the overall security program. Acceptance is facilitated by the information security manager applying common business case aspects throughout the acceptance process (see section 3.13.6 Business Case Development). These can include:

- Aligning security objectives with business objectives, enabling senior management to understand and apply the security policies and procedures
- Identifying potential consequences of failing to achieve certain security-related objectives and regulatory compliance
- Identifying budget items so that senior management can quantify the costs of the security program
- Utilizing commonly accepted project risk/benefit or financial models, such as total cost of ownership (TCO) or return on investment (ROI), to quantify the benefits and costs of the security program
- Defining the monitoring and auditing measures that will be included in the security program

It also should be noted that, while senior management may support the security program, it is also imperative that all employees understand and abide by the security parameters defined and put into place. Without employee acceptance, it is unlikely that the security program will be successful and it will not meet its objectives. It is very important for senior management to be seen practicing security governance. For example, if a physical access control system is implemented in the organization; senior management should comply with the same access rules and restrictions when it is implemented.

Establishing Reporting and Communication Channels

After obtaining the commitment from senior management, a proper reporting and communication channel must be established throughout the organization to ensure the effectiveness and efficiency of the entire information security governance system.

Periodic formal reporting to the board of directors/executive management is important to make senior management aware of the state of information security governance. A well organized face-to-face presentation to senior management can be conducted periodically and include business process owners as key users of the system. The presentation should be well mapped with prior presentations used to obtain support and security program commitment and can contain:

- Status of the implementation of the system based on the approved strategy
- Overall BIA result comparison (prior and post implementation)
- Statistics of detected and prevented threats as a means of demonstrating value
- Identifying the weakest security links in the organization and potential consequences of compromise
- Performance measurement data analysis supported with independent, external assessment or audit reports, if available
- Addressing ongoing alignment for critical business objectives, operation processes, or corporate environments
- Requiring the approval for renewed plans, as well as related budget items

In addition to formal presentations, routine communication channels also are crucial to the success of the information security program. There are four groups requiring different communication to consider listed below followed by suggestions of actions the information security manager should undertake to be effective:

- **Senior Management**
  - Attend business strategy meetings to become more aware and understand the updated business strategies and objectives
  - Periodic one-to-one meetings held with senior management to understand the business objectives from their perspective
- **Business Process Owners**
  - Join operation review meetings to realize the challenges and requirements of daily operations and their dependencies
  - Initiate monthly one-to-one meetings held with different process owners to gain continued support in the implementation of information security governance and address current individual security related issues
- **Other Management**
  - Line managers, supervisors and department heads charged with various security and risk management-related functions, including ensuring adequate security requirement awareness and policy compliance, must be informed of their responsibilities.
- **Employees**
  - Timely training and education programs
  - Centralized on-board training program for new hires
  - Organizational education material on updated strategies and policies
  - Personnel instructed to access the intranet or e-mail-based notifications for periodic reminders or *ad hoc* adaptations
  - Support senior management and business process owners by assigning an information security governance coordinator within each functional unit to obtain accurate feedback of daily practices in a timely manner

The relationship between the outcomes of effective security governance and management responsibilities is shown in **exhibit 1.4**. These are not meant to be comprehensive, but merely indicate some levels of management and the primary tasks for which they are responsible.

Exhibit 1.4—Relationship of Information Security Governance Outcomes to Management Responsibilities						
Management Level	**Strategic Alignment**	**Risk Management**	**Value Delivery**	**Performance Measurement**	**Resource Management**	**Process Assurance**
Board of directors	Require demonstrable alignment of security and business objectives.	• Establish acceptable risk and tolerance. • Oversee a policy on risk management. • Ensure adequate regulatory compliance.	Require reporting of security activity costs and benefits.	Require reporting of security effectiveness.	Oversee a policy of knowledge management and resource utilization.	Oversee a policy of assurance process integration.
Executive management	Institute processes to integrate security with business objectives.	• Ensure that roles and responsibilities include risk management in all activities. • Monitor regulatory compliance.	Require business case development for security initiatives.	Require monitoring and metrics for security activities.	Ensure processes for knowledge capture and efficiency metrics.	Provide oversight of all assurance functions and plans for integration.
Steering committee	Review and provide input to security strategy and requirements for effective business support.	Identify emerging risk, promote business unit security practices and identify compliance issues.	Review and advise on cost effectiveness of security activities needed to serve business functions.	Review and advise whether security initiatives meet business objectives.	Review processes for knowledge capture and dissemination and utilization of resources.	• Identify critical business processes and assurance providers. • Direct assurance integration efforts.
CISO/information security management	Develop the security strategy in alignment with business objectives, oversee the security program and liaise with business process owners for ongoing alignment.	• Ensure that risk and business impact assessments are conducted. • Develop risk mitigation strategies. • Enforce policy and regulatory compliance.	Monitor and optimize utilization, efficiency and effectiveness of security resources.	Develop, implement and report monitoring and metrics needed to support decisions at the strategic, management and operational levels.	• Develop methods for knowledge capture and dissemination. • Monitor and measure resource utilization and cost effectiveness.	• Liaise with other assurance providers. • Ensure that gaps and overlaps are identified and addressed. • Promote integration of assurance activities.
Audit executives	Evaluate and report on degree of alignment.	Evaluate and report on corporate risk management practices and results.	Evaluate and report on cost effectiveness of security program.	Evaluate and report on comprehensiveness and effectiveness of program monitoring and metrics.	Evaluate and report efficiency and utilization of resources.	Evaluate and report on integration and effectiveness of assurance processes.
Source: ISACA, *Information Security Governance: Guidance for Information Security Managers*, 2008. All rights reserved. Used by permission.						

1.5.5 GOVERNANCE, RISK MANAGEMENT AND COMPLIANCE

Governance, risk management and compliance (GRC) is an example of the growing recognition of the necessity for convergence, or assurance process integration, as discussed in section 1.8.8.

GRC is a term that reflects an approach that organizations can adopt in order to integrate these three areas. Often stated as a single business activity, GRC includes multiple overlapping and related activities within an organization, which may include internal audit, compliance programs such as the US Sarbanes-Oxley Act, enterprise risk management (ERM), operational risk, incident management and others.

Governance, as discussed previously, is the responsibility of senior executive management and focuses on creating the mechanisms an organization uses to ensure that personnel follow established processes and policies.

Risk management is the process by which an organization manages risk to acceptable levels within acceptable tolerances, identifies potential risk and its associated impacts, and prioritizes their mitigation based on the organization's business objectives.. Risk management develops and deploys internal controls to manage and mitigate risk throughout the organization.

Compliance is the process that records and monitors the policies, procedures and controls needed to ensure that policies and standards are adequately adhered to.

It is important to recognize that effective integration of GRC processes requires that governance is in place before risk can be effectively managed and compliance enforced.

According to Michael Rasmussen, an industry GRC analyst, the challenge in defining GRC is that, individually, each term has "many different meanings within organizations. There is corporate governance, IT governance, financial risk, strategic risk, operational risk, IT risk, corporate compliance, Sarbanes-Oxley (SOX) compliance, employment/labor compliance, privacy compliance, etc."

Development of GRC was initially a response to the US Sarbanes-Oxley Act, but has evolved as an approach to Enterprise Risk Management.

While a GRC program can be used in any area of an organization, it is usually focused on financial, IT and legal areas. Financial GRC is used to ensure proper operation of financial processes and compliance with regulatory requirements. In a similar fashion, IT GRC seeks to ensure proper operation and policy compliance of IT processes. Legal GRC may focus on overall regulatory compliance.

There is some disagreement on how these aspects of GRC are defined, but Gartner has stated that the broad GRC market includes the following areas:
- Finance and audit GRC
- IT GRC management
- Enterprise risk management

Gartner further divides the IT GRC management market into the following key capabilities (although the following list relates to IT GRC, a similar list of capabilities would be suitable for other areas of GRC):
- Controls and policy library
- Policy distribution and response
- IT controls self-assessment (CSA) and measurement
- IT asset repository
- Automated general computer control (GCC) collection
- Remediation and exception management
- Reporting
- Advanced IT risk evaluation and compliance dashboards

1.5.6 BUSINESS MODEL FOR INFORMATION SECURITY

The Business Model for Information Security (BMIS) originated at the Institute for Critical Information Infrastructure Protection at the Marshall School of Business at the University of Southern California in the USA. ISACA has undertaken the development of the Systemic Security Management Model. The BMIS takes a business-oriented approach to managing information security, building on the foundational concepts developed by the Institute. The model utilizes systems thinking to clarify complex relationships within the enterprise, and thus to more effectively manage security. The elements and dynamic interconnections that form the basis of the model establish the boundaries of an information security program and model how the program functions and reacts to internal and external change. The BMIS provides the context for frameworks such as COBIT.

The essence of systems theory is that a system needs to be viewed holistically—not merely as a sum of its parts—to be accurately understood. A holistic approach examines the system as a complete functioning unit. Another tenet of systems theory is that one part of the system enables understanding of other parts of the system. "Systems thinking" is a widely recognized term that refers to the examination of how systems interact, how complex systems work and why "the whole is more than the sum of its parts."

Systems theory is most accurately described as a complex network of events, relationships, reactions, consequences, technologies, processes and people that interact in often unseen and unexpected ways. Studying the behaviors and results of the interactions can assist the manager to better understand the organizational system and the way it functions. While management of any discipline within the enterprise can be enhanced by approaching it from a systems thinking perspective, its implementation will certainly help with managing risk.

The success that the systems approach has achieved in other fields bodes well for the benefits it can bring to security. The often dramatic failures of enterprises to adequately address security issues in recent years are due, to a significant extent, to their inability to define security and present it in a way that is comprehensible and relevant to all stakeholders. Utilizing a systems approach to information security management will help information security managers address complex and dynamic environments, and will generate a beneficial effect on collaboration within the enterprise, adaptation to operational change, navigation of strategic uncertainty and tolerance of the impact of external factors. The model is represented in **exhibit 1.5**.

As illustrated in **exhibit 1.5**, the model is best viewed as a flexible, three-dimensional, pyramid-shaped structure made up of four elements linked together by six dynamic interconnections. All aspects of the model interact with each other. If any one part of the model is changed, not addressed or managed inappropriately, the equilibrium of the model is potentially at risk. The dynamic interconnections act as tensions, exerting a push/pull force in reaction to changes in the enterprise, allowing the model to adapt as needed.

Exhibit 1.5—Business Model for Information Security

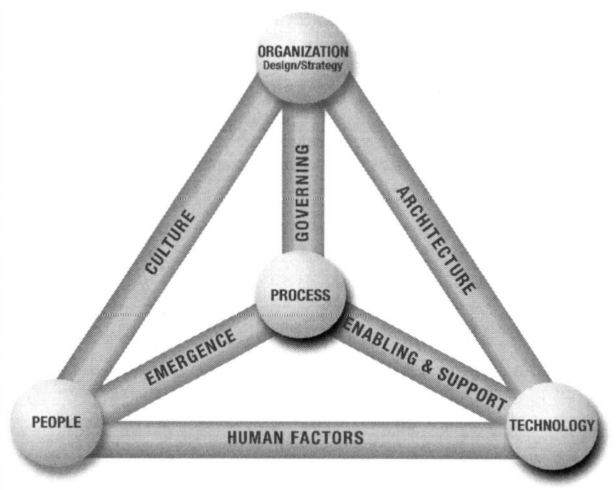

The four elements of the model are:
1. **Organization Design and Strategy**—An organization is a network of people, assets and processes interacting with each other in defined roles and working toward a common goal.

An enterprise's strategy specifies its business goals and the objectives to be achieved as well as the values and missions to be pursued. It is the enterprise's formula for success and sets its basic direction. The strategy should adapt to external and internal factors. Resources are the primary material to design the strategy and can be of different types (people, equipment, know-how).

Design defines how the organization implements its strategy. Processes, culture and architecture are important in determining the design.

2. **People**—The human resources and the security issues that surround them. It defines who implements (through design) each part of the strategy. It represents a human collective and must take into account values, behaviors and biases.

   Internally, it is critical for the information security manager to work with the human resources and legal departments to address issues such as:
   - Recruitment strategies (access, background checks, interviews, roles and responsibilities)
   - Employment issues (location of office, access to tools and data, training and awareness, movement within the enterprise)
   - Termination (reasons for leaving, timing of exit, roles and responsibilities, access to systems, access to other employees)

   Externally, customers, suppliers, media, stakeholders and others can have a strong influence on the enterprise and need to be considered within the security posture.
3. **Process**—Includes formal and informal mechanisms (large and small, simple and complex) to get things done and provides a vital link to all of the dynamic interconnections. Processes identify, measure, manage and control risk, availability, integrity and confidentiality, and they also ensure accountability. They derive from the strategy and implement the operational part of the organization element.

   To be advantageous to the enterprise, processes must:
   - Meet business requirements and align with policy
   - Consider emergence and be adaptable to changing requirements
   - Be well documented and communicated to appropriate human resources
   - Be reviewed periodically, once they are in place, to ensure efficiency and effectiveness
4. **Technology**—Composed of all of the tools, applications and infrastructure that make processes more efficient. As an evolving element that experiences frequent changes, it has its own dynamic risk. Given the typical enterprise's dependence on technology, technology constitutes a core part of the enterprise's infrastructure and a critical component in accomplishing its mission.

   Technology is often seen by the enterprise's management team as a way to resolve security threats and risk. While technical controls are helpful in mitigating some types of risk, technology should not be viewed as an information security solution.

   Technology is greatly impacted by users and by organizational culture. Some individuals still mistrust technology; some have not learned to use it; and others feel it slows them down. Regardless of the reason, information security managers must be aware that just as with physical and administrative controls, some people will try to sidestep technical controls..

Dynamic Interconnections

The dynamic interconnections link the elements together and exert a multidirectional force that pushes and pulls as things change. Actions and behaviors that occur in the dynamic interconnections can force the model out of balance or bring it back to equilibrium. The six dynamic interconnections are:

1. **Governance**—Steering the enterprise and demanding strategic leadership. Governing sets limits within which an enterprise operates and is implemented within processes to monitor performance, describe activities and achieve compliance while also providing adaptability to emergent conditions.

   Governing incorporates ensuring that objectives are determined and defined, ascertaining that risk is managed appropriately, and verifying that the enterprise's resources are used responsibly.
2. **Culture**—A pattern of behaviors, beliefs, assumptions, attitudes and ways of doing things. It is emergent and learned, and it creates a sense of comfort.

   Culture evolves as a type of shared history as a group goes through a set of common experiences. Those similar experiences cause certain responses, which become a set of expected and shared behaviors. These behaviors become unwritten rules, which become norms that are shared by all people who have that common history. It is important to understand the culture of the enterprise because it profoundly influences what information is considered, how it is interpreted and what will be done with it.

   Culture may exist on many levels, such as national (legislation/regulation, political and traditional), organizational (policies, hierarchical style and expectations) and social (family, etiquette). It is created from both external and internal factors, and is influenced by and influences organizational patterns.
3. **Enablement and Support**—Dynamic interconnection that connects the technology element to the process element. One way to help ensure that people comply with technical security measures, policies and procedures is to make processes usable and easy. Transparency can help generate acceptance for security controls by assuring users that security will not inhibit their ability to work effectively.

   Many of the actions that affect both technology and processes occur in the enablement and support dynamic interconnection. Policies, standards and guidelines must be designed to support the needs of the business by reducing or eliminating conflicts of interest, remaining flexible to support changing business objectives, and being acceptable and easy for people to follow.
4. **Emergence**—Connotes surfacing, developing, growing and evolving, and refers to patterns that arise in the life of the enterprise that appear to have no obvious cause and whose outcomes seem impossible to predict and control. The emergence dynamic interconnection (between people and processes) is a place to introduce possible solutions such as feedback loops; alignment with process improvement; and consideration of emergent issues in system design life cycle, change control, and risk management.
5. **Human Factors**—Represents the interaction and gap between technology and people and, as such, is critical to an information security program. If people do not understand how to use technology, do not embrace technology or will not follow pertinent policies, serious security problems can

evolve. Internal threats such as data leakage, data theft and misuse of data can occur within this dynamic interconnection. Human factors may arise because of experience level, cultural experiences and differing generational perspectives. Because human factors are critical components in maintaining balance within the model, it is important to train all of the enterprise's human resources on pertinent skills.

6. **Architecture**—A comprehensive and formal encapsulation of the people, processes, policies and technology that comprise an enterprise's security practices. A robust business information architecture is essential to understanding the need for security and designing the security architecture.

   It is within the architecture dynamic interconnection that the enterprise can ensure defense in depth. The design describes how the security controls are positioned and how they relate to the overall enterprise architecture. An enterprise security architecture facilitates security capabilities across lines of businesses in a consistent and a cost-effective manner and enables enterprises to be proactive with their security investment decisions.

1.5.7 ASSURANCE PROCESS INTEGRATION—CONVERGENCE

The tendency to segment security into separate but related functions has created the need to integrate the variety of assurance processes found in a typical organization. These activities are often fragmented and segmented in silos with different reporting structures. They tend to use different terminology and generally reflect different understandings of their processes and outcomes with, at times, little in common. These assurance silos can include risk management, change management, internal and external audit, privacy offices, insurance offices, human resources (HR), legal and others. Evaluating business processes from start to finish (along with their controls), regardless of which particular assurance process is involved, can mitigate the tendency for security gaps to exist among various assurance functions.

GRC, discussed earlier in section 1.5.5, is a recent effort to address integration issues between the major functions of governance, risk management and compliance.

The BMIS covered in section 1.5.6 is a current effort by ISACA to develop a totally integrated approach to information security using a systems approach.

ISO/IEC 27001:2013, covered in section 3.8.2, specifies the requirements for establishing, implementing, operating, monitoring, reviewing, maintaining and improving a documented Information Security Management System (ISMS) within the context of the organization's overall business risks.

Convergence

For several decades, it has been clear that the arbitrary division of security-related activities into physical security, IT security, risk management, privacy, compliance, information security and other disciplines has not been conducive to achieving optimal results. The increasingly dire consequences of nonintegrated security efforts has caused this separation to, increasingly, be reconsidered by professionals and management. It is becoming more common to see CISOs elevated to CSOs or the functions combined to better integrate the main security elements. Physical security for many organizations has become fairly routine and is more easily integrated into information security than the other way around. The formation of the Alliance for Enterprise Security Risk Management (AESRM) by ASIS International, ISACA and the Information Systems Security Association (ISSA) is an indication of the trend in this direction.

Because it is not possible to effectively deliver information security without a number of physical considerations, the evolution is natural. It is reasonable to expect that integration of many security activities will center around information security in the coming decade. As a result, integration of physical security and other assurance functions will, increasingly, be relevant for management to consider.

An excerpt from *Security Convergence: Current Corporate Practices and Future Trends*, commissioned by the AESRM, provides significant insight into the convergence, or assurance integration, issue. The study comprised US-based global companies with revenues from US $1 billion to more than US $100 billion.

> *The findings from the surveys and interviews point to several internal and external drivers, or "imperatives," that are forcing convergence to emerge:*
> - *Rapid expansion of the enterprise ecosystem*
> - *Value migration from physical to information-based and intangible assets*
> - *New protective technologies blurring functional boundaries*
> - *New compliance and regulatory regimes*
> - *Continuing pressure to reduce cost*
>
> *These imperatives are fundamentally altering the security landscape by forcing a change in the role security practitioners play across the value chain of the business. For example, as formal risk discussions become more integrated, cross-functional and pervasive, the expectation that physical and information security practitioners will generate joint solutions instead of independent views increases dramatically. The study identified a shift from the current state, in which security practitioners focus on their function, to a new state, in which activities are integrated to improve the value of the business.*
>
> *This new "business of security" requires security professionals to reexamine the key operating levers they have available to them. Although these operating levers (e.g., roles and responsibilities, risk management, leadership) are not new, the opportunity to use them in innovative ways may prove so. For example, the surveys and interviews presented clear evidence that, as leaders in the business, security professionals need to move from a "command and control" people model to an empowering and enabling model, and to develop an enterprisewide view of risk rather than an asset-based view*

In other words, this is a more holistic and encompassing approach that looks beyond assets and considers such factors as culture, organizational structure and processes such as the systems approach discussed in section 1.5.6, Business Model for Information Security. Analysis of the survey findings clearly shows convergence as a business trend with a great deal of momentum. Delivering on convergence is not just about organizational integration; rather, it is about integrating the security disciplines with the business's mission to deliver shareholder value through consistent, predictable operations and optimizing the allocation of security resources.

As new technologies emerge and threats become increasingly complex and unpredictable, senior security executives recognize the need to merge security functions throughout the entire enterprise. A recent incident at the Sumitomo Mitsui Bank in London, England, in which hackers attempted to steal £220 million from the bank, underlines this principle. Even though the bank had strong information technology (IT) security measures in place, a physical security lapse occurred. Adversaries posing as janitors installed devices on computer keyboards (i.e., key loggers) that allowed them to obtain valuable login information. This situation highlights and reinforces the need to bring together—in fact, converge—all components of an organization's security through an integrated and deliberate approach. To be effective, this converged approach should reach across people, processes and technology, and enable enterprises to prevent, detect, respond to and recover from any type of security incident.

In addition to the costs that companies face to deal with the immediate effects of an incident, security incidents can cause more costly, long-term harm such as damage to reputation and brand. Beyond the impact to market capitalization, if the issue threatens the public good, regulators may intervene, enacting stricter requirements to govern future business practices.

1.6 GOVERNANCE AND THIRD-PARTY RELATIONSHIPS

An important aspect of information security governance is the rules and processes employed when dealing with third-party relationships. These may include:
- Service providers
- Outsourced operations
- Trading partners
- Merged or acquired organizations

The ability to effectively manage security in these relationships often poses a significant challenge for the information security manager. This is particularly true in the case of organizations being merged. These challenges can include cultural differences that may result in approaches to security and behavior that are not acceptable to the security manager's organization. There may be technology incompatibilities between the organizations, process differences that do not integrate well or inadequate levels of baseline security. Other areas of concern can involve incident response, business continuity and disaster recovery capabilities. To ensure that the organization is adequately protected, the information security manager must assess the impacts of any of the reasonably possible security failures of any third party that may become involved with the organization. It is important to have an understanding of and a plan to manage any such potential failures sufficiently so that the potential impacts are within a range acceptable to management.

The responsibilities of the information security manager to address the potential risk and possible impacts of third-party relationships should be clear and documented. There should also be policies and standards as well as procedures establishing the involvement of information security prior to the creation of any third-party relationship so that risk can be determined and management can decide whether they are acceptable or must be mitigated. Finally, there should be a formalized engagement model between the information security organization and those groups that establish and manage third-party relationships for the organization.

1.7 INFORMATION SECURITY GOVERNANCE METRICS

"Metrics" is a term used to denote measurements based on one or more references and involves at least two points—the measurement and the reference. Security, in its most basic meaning, is the protection from or absence of danger. Literally, security metrics should tell us about the state or degree of safety relative to a reference point. Contemporary security metrics, by and large, fail to do so. It may be useful to clarify the distinction between managing the technical IT security infrastructure at the operational level and the overall management of an information security program. Technical metrics are obviously useful for the purely tactical operational management of the technical security systems—i.e., intrusion detection systems (IDSs), proxy servers, firewalls, etc. They can indicate that the infrastructure is operated in a sound fashion and that technical vulnerabilities are identified and addressed. However, these metrics are of little value from a strategic management or governance standpoint. Technical metrics say nothing about strategic alignment with organizational objectives or how well risk is being managed; they provide few measures of policy compliance or whether objectives for acceptable levels of potential impact are being reached; and, they provide no information on whether the information security program is headed in the right direction and achieving the desired outcomes.

From a management perspective, while there have been improvements in technical metrics, they are incapable of providing answers to questions such as:
- How secure is the organization?
- How much security is enough?
- How do we know when we have achieved an adequate level of security?
- What are the most cost-effective security solutions?
- How do we determine the degree of risk?
- How well can risk be predicted?
- Is the security program achieving its objectives?
- What impact is lack of security having on productivity?
- What impact would a catastrophic security breach have?
- What impact will security solutions have on productivity?

Attempts to provide meaningful answers to these questions can ultimately be addressed only by developing relevant measures—metrics that specifically address the requirements of management to make appropriate decisions about the organization's safety.

Full audits and comprehensive risk assessments are typically the only activities organizations undertake that provide this breadth of perspective. While important and necessary from a security management point of view, these provide only history or a snapshot—not what is ideally needed to guide day-to-day security management and provide the information needed to make prudent decisions.

1.7.1 EFFECTIVE SECURITY METRICS

It is generally difficult or impossible to manage any activity that cannot be measured. The fundamental purpose of metrics, measures and monitoring is decision support. For metrics to be useful, the information they provide must be relevant to the roles and responsibilities of the recipient so that informed decisions can be made. Anything that results in a change can be measured. The key to effective metrics is to utilize a set of criteria to determine which are the most suitable metrics. The criteria should include (Brotby, Krag; *Information Security Metrics,* Auerbach, USA, 2009):

- **Meaningful**—The metric must be understood by the recipients.
- **Accurate**—A reasonable degree of accuracy is essential.
- **Cost-effective**—The measurements cannot be too expensive to acquire or maintain.
- **Repeatable**—The measure must be able to be acquired reliably over time.
- **Predictive**—Measurements should be indicative of outcomes.
- **Actionable**—It should be clear to the recipient what action must be taken.
- **Genuine**—It must be clear what is actually being measured, e.g., measurements that are not random or subject to manipulation.

Standard security metrics will include things such as downtime due to viruses or Trojans, number of penetrations of systems, impacts and losses, recovery times, number of vulnerabilities uncovered with network scans, and percentage of servers patched. While these measures can be indicative of aspects of security and perhaps are useful to IT operations, none provides any actual information about how secure the organization is and probably will not meet most of the aforementioned criteria.

Operational risk and its counterpart, security is not readily measured in any absolute sense; rather, probabilities, exposures, attributes, effects and consequences are normally the gauge. Various approaches that may be useful include value at risk (VAR), return on security investment (ROSI), and annual loss expectancy (ALE). VAR is used to compute maximum probable loss in a defined period (day, week, year) with a confidence level of typically 95% or 99%. ROSI is used to calculate the return on investment based on the reduction in losses resulting from a security control. ALE provides the likely annualized loss based on probable frequency and magnitude of security compromise. These often speculative numbers can then be used as a basis for allocating or justifying resources for security activities.

Some organizations will attempt to determine the maximum impacts of potential adverse events as a measure of security. Measuring security by consequences and impacts is similar to gauging how tall a tree is by how loud a noise it makes when it falls. In other words, adverse events would have to occur to determine if security is working. An absence of adverse events provides no information on the state of security. It may mean that defenses worked, that no one attacked or that a vulnerability was not discovered. Of course, simulated attacks with penetration testing can provide some measure of the effectiveness of defenses against those specific attacks performed. However, unless a statistically relevant percentage of all possible attacks are attempted, no prediction can be made about the state of security and the organization's ability to resist attack.

It may be that all that can be stated with certainty about security is that:

1. Some organizations are attacked more frequently and/or suffer greater losses than others
2. There is a strong correlation between good security management and practices, and relatively fewer incidents and losses

Good management and good governance are inextricably linked. Measuring effective information security governance and management with any precision may be more difficult than measuring security. Metrics will, in most respects, be based on attributes, costs and subsequent outcomes of the security program. **Exhibit 1.6** presents components of an information security governance program and demonstrates that the actual course of governance, and the ability to measure and report performance, is required.

Exhibit 1.6—Components of Security Metrics

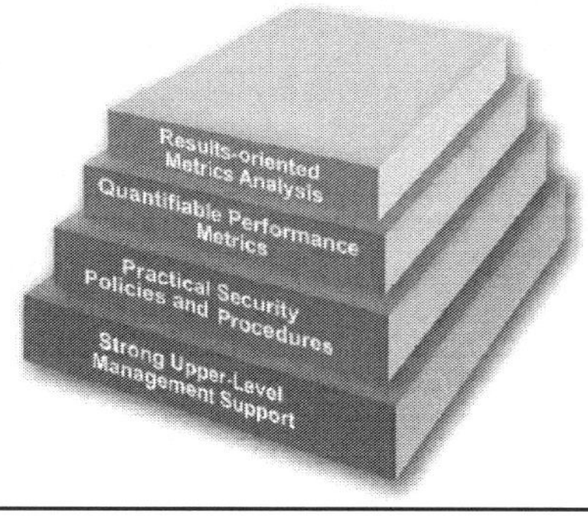

Source: NIST publication 800-55 provides an approach to security metrics.

A sensible notion suggests that a well-governed security program can be characterized by one that efficiently, effectively and consistently meets expectations and attains defined objectives. This is, however, of little help to most organizations since it often is unclear what the expectations or objectives of security are in any specific sense.

Commercial efforts to measure good governance by organizations such as Institutional Shareholder Services (ISS) and Governance Metrics International (GMI) have not stood up well to scrutiny according to a recent Yale report titled *Good Governance and the Misleading Myths of Bad Metrics* (Sonnenfeld, Jeffrey; Associate Dean for Executive Programs at Yale, Academy of Management Executive, 2004, vol. 18, no. 1). The report details studies showing that many, but not all, apparently sound governance notions are not supported by fact. The converse is also true, however; many governance notions are, indeed, supported by fact.

Because governance, in general, and security governance, in particular, is difficult to measure by a set of objective metrics, there is a tendency to use metrics that are available, regardless of demonstrated relevancy. A typical example apparent in most organizations is the use of vulnerability scans as an indication of overall security. Arguably, if it were possible to eliminate all or most vulnerabilities (which is not possible), most risk could be avoided. The fallacy is the assumption that something can be determined about risk, threat or impact by measuring just technical vulnerabilities.

While there is no universal objective scale for security or security governance, for organizations that have taken the necessary steps to develop clear objectives for information security, effective metrics can be designed to guide program development and management. Essentially, metrics can be reduced to any measure of the results of the information security program progressing toward the defined objectives. It must also be understood that different metrics are required to provide information at the strategic, tactical, and operational levels. Strategic metrics will be oriented toward high-level outcomes and objectives for the information security program.

In *Good Governance and the Misleading Myths of Bad Metrics,* the author states that:

> *The foundation of strong upper-level management support is critical, not only for the success of the security program, but also for the implementation of a security metrics program. This support establishes a focus on security within the highest levels of the organization. Without a solid foundation (i.e., proactive support of those persons in positions that control IT resources), the effectiveness of the security metrics program can fail when pressured by politics and budget limitations.*
>
> *The second component of an effective security metrics program is practical security policies and procedures backed by the authority necessary to enforce compliance. Practical security policies and procedures are defined as those that are attainable and provide meaningful security through appropriate controls. Metrics for compliance are not easily obtainable if there are no procedures in place.*
>
> *The third component is developing and establishing quantifiable performance metrics that are designed to capture and provide meaningful operational data. To provide meaningful data, quantifiable security metrics must be based on IT security performance goals and objectives, and be easily obtainable and feasible to measure. They must also be repeatable, provide relevant performance trends over time, and be useful for tracking performance and directing resources.*
>
> *Finally, the security metrics program itself must emphasize consistent periodic analysis of the metrics data. The results of this analysis are used to apply lessons learned, improve the effectiveness of existing security controls, and plan future controls to meet new security requirements as they occur. Accurate data collection must be a priority with stakeholders and users if the collected data are to be meaningful to the management and improvement of the overall security program.*
>
> *The success of an information security program implementation should be judged by the degree to which meaningful results are produced. A comprehensive security metrics analysis program should provide substantive justification for decisions that directly affect the security posture of an organization. These decisions include budget and personnel requests, and allocation of available resources. A security metrics program should provide a precise basis for preparation of required security performance-related reports.*

1.7.2 GOVERNANCE IMPLEMENTATION METRICS

Implementing an information security governance strategy and framework can require a significant effort. It is important that some form of metrics be in place during the implementation of a governance program. Performance of the overall security program will be too far downstream to provide timely information on implementation and another approach must be used. Key goal indicators (KGIs) and key performance indicators (KPIs) can be useful to provide information about the achievement of process or service goals, and can determine whether organizational milestones and objectives are being met. Because implementation of various aspects of governance will typically involve projects or initiatives, standard project measurement approaches can serve metrics requirements, e.g., achieving specific milestones or objectives, budget and time line conformance.

1.7.3 STRATEGIC ALIGNMENT METRICS

Strategic alignment of information security in support of organizational objectives is a highly desirable goal, often difficult to achieve. It should be clear that the cost effectiveness of the security program is inevitably tied to how well it supports the objectives of the organization and at what cost. Without organizational objectives as a reference point, any other gauge, including so-called best practices, may be overkill, inadequate or misdirected. From a business perspective, adequate and sufficient practices proportionate to the requirements are likely to be more cost effective than best practices. They are also likely to be received better by cost-conscious management.

The best overall indicator that security activities are in alignment with business (or organizational) objectives is the development of a security strategy that defines security objectives in business terms and ensures that the objectives are directly articulated from planning to implementation of policies, standards, procedures, processes and technology. The acid test is the reverse order evaluation of a specific control being able to be tracked to a specific business requirement. Any control that cannot be tracked directly back to a specific business requirement is suspect and should be analyzed for relevancy and possible elimination.

Indicators of alignment can include:
- The extent to which the security program demonstrably enables specific business activities
- Business activities that have not been undertaken or delayed because of inadequate capability to manage risk
- A security organization that is responsive to defined business requirements based on business owner surveys
- Organizational and security objectives that are defined and clearly understood by all involved in security and related assurance activities measured by awareness testing
- The percentage of security program activities mapped to organizational objectives and validated by executive management
- A security steering committee consisting of key executives with a charter to ensure ongoing alignment of security activities and business strategy

1.7.4 RISK MANAGEMENT METRICS

Risk management is the ultimate objective of all information security activities and, indeed, all organizational assurance efforts. While risk management effectiveness is not subject to direct measurement, there are indicators that correlate to a successful approach. A successful risk management program can be defined as one that efficiently, effectively and consistently meets expectations and attains defined objectives.

Once again, it is a requirement that expectations and objectives of risk management be defined; otherwise, there is no basis for determining whether the program is succeeding and/or heading in the right direction, and whether resource allocations are appropriate.

Indicators of appropriate risk management can include:
- A defined organizational risk appetite and tolerance in terms relevant to the organization
- The completeness of an overall security strategy and program for achieving acceptable levels of risk
- The number of defined mitigation objectives for identified significant risk
- Processes for management or reduction of adverse impacts
- The percent of systems covered by a systematic, continuous risk management processes
- Trends of periodic risk assessment indicating progress toward defined goals
- Trends in impacts
- Results from tested business continuity/disaster recovery plans
- The completeness of the asset valuation and assignment of ownership
- The percentage of business impact assessments (BIAs) of all critical or sensitive systems
- The extent of a complete and functioning asset classification process
- The ratio of security incidents from known risk compared to unidentified risk

The key goal of information security is to reduce adverse impacts on the organization to an acceptable level. Therefore, a key metric is the adverse impacts of information security incidents experienced by the organization and the extent that they do or do not exceed criteria for acceptable risk. An effective security program will show a trend in impact reduction. Quantitative measures can include trend analysis of impacts over time.

1.7.5 VALUE DELIVERY METRICS

Value delivery occurs when security investments are optimized in support of organizational objectives. Value delivery is a function of strategic alignment of security strategy and business objectives; in other words, when a business case can be convincingly made for all security activities. Optimal investment levels occur when strategic goals for security are achieved and an acceptable risk posture is attained at the lowest possible cost.

Key indicators (KGIs and KPIs) can include:
- Security activities that are designed to achieve specific strategic objectives
- The cost of security being proportional to the value of assets
- Security resources that are allocated by degree of assessed risk and potential impact
- Protection costs that are aggregated as a function of revenues or asset valuation
- Controls that are well designed based on defined control objectives and are fully utilized
- An adequate and appropriate number of controls to achieve acceptable risk and impact levels
- Control cost effectiveness that is determined by periodic testing
- Policies in place that require all controls to be periodically reevaluated for cost, compliance and effectiveness
- The utilization of controls; controls that are rarely used are not likely to be cost effective
- The number of controls to achieve acceptable risk and impact levels; fewer effective controls can be expected to be more cost effective than a greater number of less effective controls
- The effectiveness of controls as determined by testing; marginal controls are not likely to be cost effective

1.7.6 RESOURCE MANAGEMENT METRICS

Information security resource management is the term used to describe the processes to plan, allocate and control information security resources, including people, processes and technologies, for improving the efficiency and effectiveness of business solutions.

As with other organizational assets and resources, they must be managed properly. Knowledge must be captured, disseminated and available when needed. Providing multiple solutions to the same problem is, obviously, inefficient and indicates a lack of resource management. Controls and processes must be standardized, when possible, to reduce administrative and training costs. Problems and solutions must be well documented, referenced and available.

Indicators of effective resource management can include:
- Infrequent problem rediscovery
- Effective knowledge capture and dissemination

- The extent to which security-related processes are standardized
- Clearly defined roles and responsibilities for information security functions
- Information security functions incorporated into every project plan
- The percentage of information assets and related threats adequately addressed by security activities
- The proper organizational location, level of authority and number of personnel for the information security function
- Resource utilization levels
- Staff productivity
- Per seat cost of security services

1.7.7 PERFORMANCE MEASUREMENT

Measuring, monitoring and reporting on information security processes is required to ensure that organizational objectives are achieved. Methods to monitor security-related events across the organization must be developed; it is critical to design metrics that provide an indication of the performance of the security machinery and, from a management perspective, information needed to make decisions to guide the security activities of the organization.

Indicators of effective performance measurement might include:
- The time it takes to detect and report security-related incidents
- The number and frequency of subsequently discovered unreported incidents
- Benchmarking comparable organizations for costs and effectiveness
- The ability to determine the effectiveness/efficiency of controls
- Clear indications that security objectives are being met
- The absence of unexpected security events
- Knowledge of impending threats
- Effective means of determining organizational vulnerabilities
- Methods of tracking evolving risk
- Consistency of log review practices
- Results of business continuity planning (BCP)/disaster recovery (DR) tests
- The extent that key controls are monitored
- The percentage of metrics achieving defined criteria (metametrics)

1.7.8 ASSURANCE PROCESS INTEGRATION (CONVERGENCE)

Organizations should consider an approach to information security governance that includes an effort to integrate assurance functions. This will serve to increase security effectiveness and efficiency by reducing duplicated efforts and gaps in protection. It will help ensure that processes operate as intended from end to end, minimizing hidden risk. KGIs can include:
- No gaps in information asset protection
- The elimination of unnecessary security overlaps
- The seamless integration of assurance activities
- Well-defined roles and responsibilities
- Assurance providers understanding the relationship to other assurance functions
- All assurance functions are identified and considered in the strategy

In regards to management of the risk inherent in a business, Booz Allen Hamilton (in its publication titled *Convergence of Enterprise Security Organizations*) suggests that:

> *In the past, management of the risk inherent in a business was a function embedded within the individual roles of the "C Suite." The traditional approach was to treat individual risks separately and assign responsibility to an individual or small team. Managing a singular kind of risk became a distinct job, and performing that job well meant focusing exclusively on that one particular area. The problem with this stovepiped approach is that it not only ignores the interdependence of many business risks but also suboptimizes the financing of total risk for an enterprise.*
>
> *Breaking stovepipes and addressing the suboptimizing of investments requires a new way of thinking about the problem.*

This new thinking demonstrated by the BMIS discussed in section 1.5.5 brings together the various elements and stakeholders in the problem set to work closely together. A major objective of this activity is to understand how organizations can bring together diverse elements and get them to orient on a common objective.

1.8 INFORMATION SECURITY STRATEGY OVERVIEW

There are a number of definitions of strategy. While they all generally point in the same direction, they vary widely in scope, emphasis and detail. Strategy derives from the military definition which is simply "the plan to achieve an objective." As is typical, the basic concept has been expanded and grown more complex, although this does not always serve to improve understanding of the concept.

In *The Concept of Corporate Strategy, 2nd Edition*, Kenneth Andrews describes corporate strategy, which is equally applicable to the development and purpose of information security strategy:

> *Corporate strategy is the pattern of decisions in a company that determines and reveals its objectives, purposes, or goals, produces the principal policies and plans for achieving those goals, and defines the range of business the company is to pursue, the kind of economic and human organization it is or intends to be, and the nature of the economic and non-economic contribution it intends to make to its shareholders, employees, customers, and communities.*

Adding security in the appropriate places to the foregoing statement provides a workable definition of security strategy.

Exhibit 1.7—Information Security Strategy Development Participants

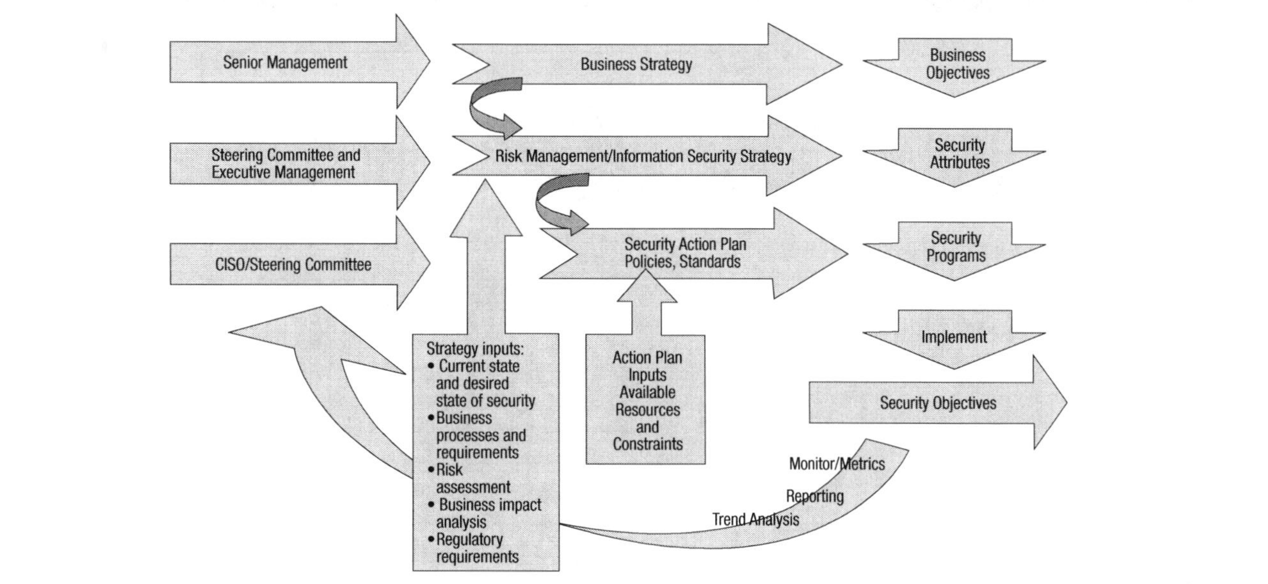

Source: ISACA, *Information Security Governance: Guidance for Information Security Managers*, 2008. All rights reserved. Used by permission.

Exhibit 1.7 shows the participants involved in developing a security strategy and their relationships and aligns them with business objectives. The arrow marked "Business Strategy" provides a road map to achieving the "Business Objectives." In addition, it should provide one of the primary inputs into "Risk Management" plans and the "Information Security Strategy." This flow serves to promote alignment of information security with business goals. The balance of inputs comes from determining the desired state of security compared to the existing, or current, state. Business processes must also be considered as well as key organizational risk, including regulatory requirements and the associated impact analysis to determine protection levels and priorities.

The objective of the security strategy is the desired state defined by business and security attributes. The strategy provides the basis for an action plan comprised of one or more security programs that, as implemented, achieve the security objectives. The action plan(s) must be formulated based on available resources and constraints, including consideration of relevant legal and regulatory requirements.

The strategy and action plans must contain provisions for monitoring as well as defined metrics to determine the level of success. This provides feedback to the CISO and steering committee to allow for midcourse correction and ensure that security initiatives are on track to meet defined objectives.

1.8.1 AN ALTERNATE VIEW OF STRATEGY

A 2004 report from McKinsey poses the caution that often the "approach to strategy involves the mistaken assumption that a predictable path to the future can be paved from the experience of the past." It goes on to suggest that strategic outcomes cannot be predetermined given today's turbulent business environment.

As a result, McKinsey proposes to define strategy as "a coherent and evolving portfolio of initiatives to drive shareholder value and long-term performance. This change in thinking requires management to develop a 'you are what you do' perspective as opposed to 'you are what you say.' In other words, companies are defined by the initiatives they prioritize and drive, not merely by mission and vision statements."

The report goes on to say that "strategy approached in this way is, by its very nature, more adaptive and less dependent upon 'big bets.' A carefully managed portfolio of initiatives is balanced across activities of adapting the core businesses to meet future challenges, shaping the portfolio in an ongoing way to respond to a changing environment, and building the next generation of businesses. By creating a portfolio of initiatives around a unifying theme, reinforced by brands, value proposition to customers, and solid operational skills, a company can successfully set the stage to drive shareholder value."

Whichever definition or approach is appropriate to a particular organization, the implementation steps remain essentially the same. The "adaptive" McKinsey model may be more appropriate to organizations experiencing a great deal of change. The more traditional model may achieve the same adaptability by increasing monitoring of KPIs and reviewing strategy suppositions more frequently.

The arguably more important criteria for good outcomes from a successful strategy is strong ongoing senior management leadership and commitment to achieving effective information security governance.

Another perspective on strategy is provided from an architectural viewpoint by Sherwood Applied Business Security Architecture (SABSA), as shown in **exhibit 1.8**.

Exhibit 1.8—SABSA Security Architecture

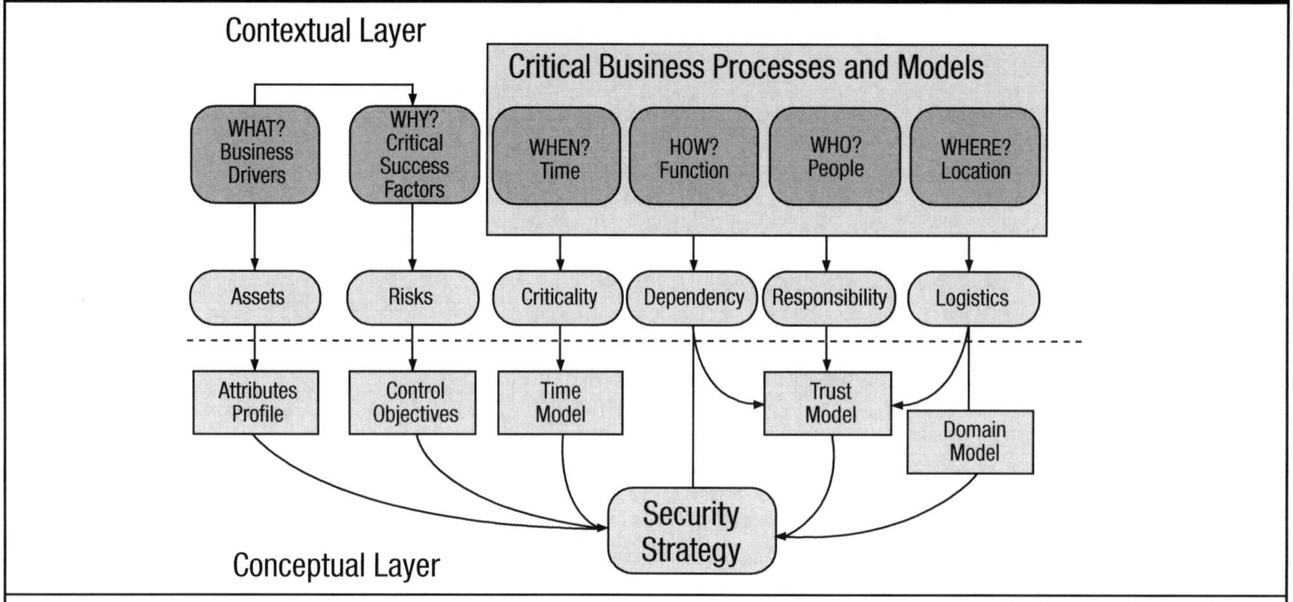

Source: Sherwood, J.; A. Clark; D. Lynas; *Enterprise Security Architecture: A Business-Driven Approach*, CMP Books, 2005, *www.sabsa.org*

1.9 DEVELOPING AN INFORMATION SECURITY STRATEGY

The process of developing an effective information security strategy requires a thorough understanding and consideration of a number of elements as shown in **exhibits 1.8** and **1.9**. In addition, it is also important for the information security manager to be aware of the common failures of strategic plans in order to avoid the pitfalls and achieve the desired outcomes.

Exhibit 1.9—Prevalent Standards and Frameworks

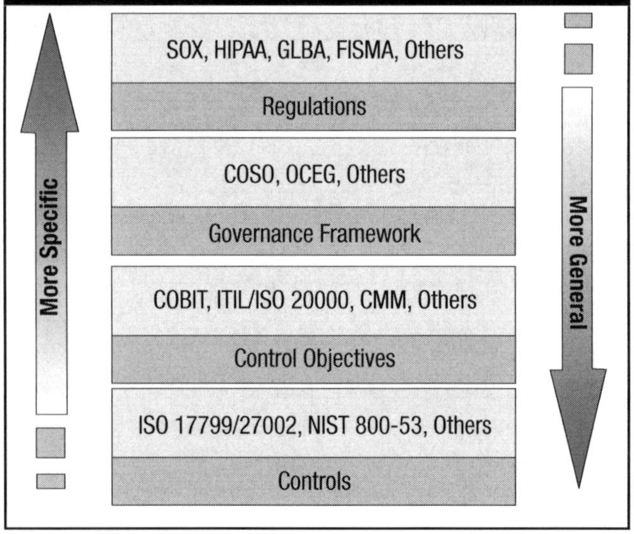

1.9.1 COMMON PITFALLS

There are a variety of reasons that security programs fail to meet expectations. It may be the lack of or an inadequate strategy. It may also result from other factors such as those in **exhibit 1.10**.

Over 9,000 respondents to the PwC survey identified underfunding and leadership as the primary obstacles to improving security. The leadership issues identified will inevitably be reflected in poor governance which in turn will result in either a poor strategy or none at all. In terms of strategy, it would be an understatement to say history is littered with examples of bad or inadequate strategies. It is surprising that, after nearly four decades of development of business strategy theory, failure of strategy continues unabated.

While some strategic plans may fail for obvious reasons such as greed, poor planning, faulty execution, unanticipated events and corporate misconduct, other causes of strategy failures are not as well understood. These failures have root causes explained by behavioral economics, a branch of psychology that studies, among other things, decision-making processes and departure from rational choice. Experiments and studies have shown a variety of underlying causes for flawed decision making. Being aware of them may allow compensation to reduce adverse effects. Some of the main reasons include:

- **Overconfidence**—Research shows a tendency for people to have excessive confidence in the ability to make accurate estimates. Most people are reluctant to estimate wide ranges of possible outcomes and prefer being precisely wrong, rather than vaguely right. Most also tend to be overconfident of their own abilities. For organizational strategies based on assessments of core capabilities, this can be particularly troublesome.
- **Optimism**—People tend to be optimistic in their forecasts. A combination of overconfidence and overoptimism can have a disastrous impact on strategies based on estimates of what may happen. Typically, these estimates will be unrealistically precise and overly optimistic.
- **Anchoring**—Research shows that once a number has been presented to someone, a subsequent estimate of even a totally unrelated subject involving numbers will "anchor" on the first number. While potentially useful for marketing purposes,

Exhibit 1.10—Obstacles to Improving Security

Question 28: "What are the greatest obstacles to improving the overall strategic effectiveness of your organization's information security function?"

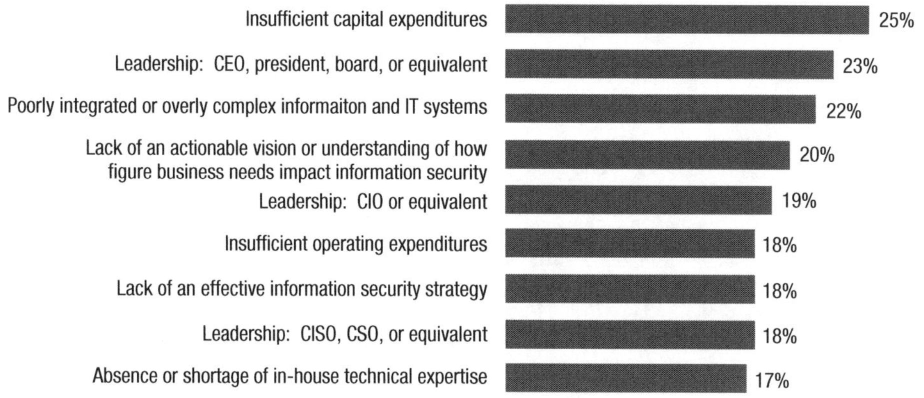

Source: PricewaterhouseCoopers and *CSO Magazine*, *Global State of Information Security 2014*, USA, figure 13, used with permission

anchoring can have serious consequences in developing strategies when future outcomes are anchored in past experiences.
- **The status quo bias**—Most people show a strong tendency toward sticking with familiar and known approaches even when they are demonstrably inadequate or ineffective. Research also indicates that concern over loss is generally stronger than excitement over possible gain. The "endowment effect" is a similar bias where people prefer to keep what they own or know, and simply owning something makes it more valuable to the owner.
- **Mental accounting**—This is defined as "the inclination to categorize and treat money differently depending on where it comes from, where it is kept, and how it is spent." Mental accounting is common even in the boardrooms of conservative, and otherwise rational, corporations. Some examples of this include:
  - Being less concerned with expenses against a restructuring charge than those against the profit and loss statement
  - Imposing cost caps on a core business while spending freely on a start-up
  - Creating new categories of spending such as "revenue investment" or "strategic investment"
- **The herding instinct**—It is a fundamental human trait to conform and seek validation of others. This can be observed by the "faddism" in security (as well as all other aspects of human activity); for example, suddenly everyone being involved in ID management or intrusion detection. Sometimes explained as "an idea whose time has come," it is more accurately described as the herding instinct behind thought leaders. The implications for strategy development should be clear. It is aptly demonstrated by the statement: "for senior managers, the only thing worse than making a huge strategic mistake is being the only person in the industry to make it."
- **False consensus**—There is a well-documented tendency for people to overestimate the extent that others share their views, beliefs and experiences. When developing strategies, false consensus can lead to ignoring or minimizing important threats or weaknesses in the plans and to persisting with doomed strategies.

A number of the more common causes have also been uncovered by research such as the study by C. F. Camerer and G. Loewenstein, including:
- **Confirmation bias**—Seeking opinions and facts that support their own beliefs
- **Selective recall**—Remembering only facts and experiences that reinforce current assumptions
- **Biased assimilation**—Only accepting facts that support an individual's current position or perspective
- **Biased evaluation**—Easy acceptance of evidence that supports their own hypotheses while contradictory evidence is challenged and, almost invariably, rejected. Critics are often charged with hostile motives or their competence is impugned.
- **Groupthink**—Pressure for agreement in team-based cultures

There have been numerous studies on the topic of departures from rational choice during the past several decades that may be worthy of study to reduce the risk of faulty decision making.

1.10 INFORMATION SECURITY STRATEGY OBJECTIVES

The objectives of developing an information security strategy must be defined and metrics developed to determine if those objectives are being achieved. Typically, the six defined outcomes of security governance will provide high-level guidance. As previously stated, the six are:
- Strategic alignment
- Effective risk management
- Value delivery
- Resource optimization
- Performance measurement
- Process assurance integration

The strategy will need to consider what each of the selected areas will mean to the organization, how they might be achieved, and what will constitute success.

1.10.1 THE GOAL

The first, and often surprisingly difficult, question that must be answered by an organization seeking to develop an information security strategy is—what is the goal?

While this seems a trivial question, most organizations fail to define the objectives of information security with any specificity. This may be because it seems obvious that the goal of information security is to protect the organization's information assets. However, that answer assumes knowledge of two things. One, that information assets are known with any degree of precision, which for most organizations is not the case. The other is that there is an assumed understanding of what it means "to protect." Everyone understands the notion in general. It is considerably more difficult to state which assets need how much protection against what.

In part, this is because organizations typically have little knowledge of what information exists within the enterprise. There is generally no process to purge useless, outdated or potentially dangerous information, data or, for that matter, unused applications. It is extremely rare to find a comprehensive catalog or index of information/processes to define what is important, what is not important or who owns it. As a result, everything typically gets saved under the assumption that storage is cheaper than data classification, ownership assignment and the identification of users. For large organizations, this can amount to terabytes of useless data and literally thousands of outdated and unused applications accumulated over decades.

This situation makes it difficult to devise a rational data protection plan since it makes little sense to expend resources protecting useless or dangerous data and information or unused applications. Dangerous data, in this context refer to information that might be used to the detriment of the organization such as damaging evidence obtained in litigation, and that could have been destroyed subject to a legal and appropriate retention policy.

Assuming current relevant information is located and identified, then it must be cataloged or classified by criticality and sensitivity. A great deal of a typical organization's data and information are neither critical nor sensitive, and it is wasteful to expend substantial resources to protect them. For many organizations, this may be a significant undertaking and they are reluctant to allocate the resources necessary. However, this is a crucial step in developing a practical and useful information security strategy and a cost-effective security program.

Just as values are assigned to an organization's physical resources, information must be assigned values to prioritize budget-constrained protection efforts and determine required levels of protection. Valuation of information is, in most cases, difficult to do with any precision. For some information, it can be the cost of creating or replacing it. In other cases, information in the form of knowledge or trade secrets is difficult or impossible to replace and may, literally, be priceless. It is obviously prudent to provide excellent protection to priceless information.

One approach commonly used is to create a few rough levels of value—for example, from zero to five—with zero being of no value and five being critical. The zero-value information, including applications, would be assigned where no owner can be determined and no use has been evidenced for a period of time. Information of zero value can then be archived for a specified period, notices sent to business owners and, if there are no objections, destroyed. Information deemed a five (critical) then becomes the priority for protection efforts.

Another approach that may be useful and substantially easier to perform is a business dependency evaluation used as an indication of value. This process starts by defining critical business processes and then determines what information is used and created. This provides a measure of the level of criticality of information resources that can be used as a guide for protection efforts.

Regardless of the methods used, the level of sensitivity must also be defined at the same time to determine a classification level needed to control access and limit disclosure. Typically, most organizations will use three or four sensitivity classifications such as confidential, internal use and public.

For most organizations, asset classification poses a daunting task, but one that must be undertaken for existing information if security governance is to be effective and relevant. This task grows exponentially more onerous over time, unless addressed. Concurrently, policies, standards and processes must be developed to mandate classification moving forward and prevent the problem from getting worse.

In summary, it will not be possible to develop a cost-effective security strategy that is aligned with business requirements prior to:
- Determining the objectives of information security
- Locating and identifying information assets and resources
- Valuation of information assets and resources
- Classifying information assets as to criticality and sensitivity
- Implementing a process to ensure that all assets have a defined owner

1.10.2 DEFINING OBJECTIVES

If an information security strategy is the basis for a plan of action to achieve security objectives, it will be necessary to define those objectives. Defining long-term objectives in terms of a "desired state" of security is necessary for a number of reasons. Without a well-articulated vision of desired outcomes for a security program, it will not be possible to develop a meaningful strategy.

It is axiomatic that, if one does not know where one is going, one cannot find a way to get there and will not know when he/she has arrived.

Without a strategy, it is not possible to develop a meaningful plan of action and the organization will continue to implement *ad hoc* tactical point solutions with nothing to provide overall integration. The resulting nonintegrated systems will be increasingly difficult to manage and become increasingly costly and difficult or impossible to secure.

Unfortunately, many organizations do not allocate adequate resources to address these issues until a major incident occurs. Experience has shown that these incidents end up far more costly than if they had been addressed properly in the beginning. A typical example is the recent breach of a major retailer resulting in the theft of 110 million customer credit card records that is estimated to ultimately cost the organization in excess of two billion dollars to resolve according to a Ponemon Institute report. The numerous security governance, management and practices flaws subsequently uncovered could have been remediated at a fraction of the expected losses.

Many objectives are stated in terms of addressing risk. Information security strategy objectives should also be stated in terms of specific goals directly aimed at supporting business activities. Some risk mitigation, such as virus and other malware protection, should apply to the organization generally. Such protection is generally not considered a specific business enabler; rather, it supports the overall health of the organization by reducing adverse impacts that hinder all activities of the organization.

A review of the organization's strategic business plans is likely to uncover opportunities for information security activities that can be directly supportive of, or enabling, a particular avenue of business by reducing risk and operational disruptions. Other sources of information to guide security efforts can include change management activities, audit reports and steering committee discussions among others. As an example, the implementation of a public key infrastructure (PKI) can enable high-value transactions between trusted trading partners or customers. Deploying virtual private networks (VPNs) may provide the sales force with secure remote connectivity, enabling improved performance. In other words, information security can enable business activities that would otherwise be too risky to undertake or, as frequently happens, are undertaken with the hope that nothing goes wrong.

According to a recent edition of *The Global State of Information Security* by PricewaterhouseCoopers:

> *Developing and maintaining an information security strategy is essential to the success of your program. This strategy serves as the roadmap for establishing your program and adapting it to future challenges. By following a consistent methodology for developing your strategy, you are more likely to achieve high-quality results during the process and complete the project in a timely manner.*

Business Linkages

Other business linkages can start from the perspective of the specific objectives of a particular line of business. A review and analysis of all the elements of a particular product line can illustrate this approach.

Consider an organization that manufactures breakfast cereal. The raw materials come into the plant on a just-in-time basis via railcar. The grains are dumped into hoppers that feed the various processing machinery. The finished cereals are packaged and moved to a warehouse in a continuous process in a matter of hours.

This relatively straightforward process relies on numerous information flows subject to a failure of availability, confidentiality or integrity. Any breakdown or significant disruption in the supply chain side—e.g., ordering, tracking or payments—is likely to cause a disruption in manufacturing. Virtually all of the activities in the plant are tied to data processing and information flows. Information security, to be effective, must understand and take into consideration all of the information streams that are critical to ensuring continuous operations. Obviously, anything that can affect the integrity or availability of the information needed in this continuous and interdependent process will be a problem. The linkage to the business, in this case, is the ability of an effective security program to prevent disruptions to the information systems essential to production.

The analysis of the foregoing example might look at the dozens of discrete pieces of information handled and processed in this manufacturing operation. Investigation into the history of the process may reveal past failures that are informative of weaknesses in the system. Most system failures are due to human error, and analysis may show that it is possible to reduce errors by either additional or better controls, or more reliable automated processes.

Typical errors include entry mistakes that might be improved by range checking or other technical processes. Procedural changes or an entry validation process may be required.

The development and analysis of business linkages can uncover information security issues at the operational level that can visibly improve the perception of the value of information security by making business processes more robust, reducing errors and improving productivity.

Improved business linkage can be one of the beneficial outcomes of an information security steering group if high-level representatives of the major departments and business units are included. Linkages may also be established by regular meetings with business owners for discussion regarding security-related issues. This may also provide an opportunity to educate business process owners on potential benefits that security may provide for their operation.

1.10.3 THE DESIRED STATE

The term "desired state" is used to denote a complete snapshot of all relevant conditions at a particular point in the future. To round out the picture, it must include principles, policies and frameworks; processes; organizational structures; culture, ethics and behavior; information; services, infrastructure and applications; and people, skills and competencies.

Defining a "state of security" in purely quantitative terms is not possible. Consequently, a "desired state of security" must, to some extent, be defined qualitatively in terms of attributes, characteristics, and outcomes. According to COBIT, it can include high-level objectives such as: "Protecting the interests of those relying on information, and the processes, systems and communications that handle, store and deliver the information, from harm resulting from failures of availability, confidentiality and integrity." This statement, while perhaps useful in stating intent and scope, provides little clarity in defining processes or objectives.

Qualitative elements such as desired outcomes should be defined as precisely as possible to provide guidance to strategy development. For example, if specific regulatory compliance is a desired outcome, a significant number of technical and process requirements become apparent.

If characteristics include a nonthreatening compliance enforcement approach consistent with the organization's culture, strategy development will have limits on the types of enforcement methods to consider.

A number of useful approaches are available to provide a framework to achieve a well-defined "desired state" for security. These, and perhaps others, should be evaluated to determine which provides the best form, fit and function for the organization. It may be useful to combine several different standards and frameworks to provide a multidimensional view into the desired state. See **exhibit 1.9**.

Several of the most accepted approaches are described in the following sections.

COBIT

COBIT 5 provides a comprehensive framework for the governance and management of enterprise IT and extensively addresses IT security, governance, risk and information security in general. Because many aspects of information security involve IT and related activities, it can serve as a framework for determining the desired state for effective information security. A new addition to this release is the *COBIT 5 for Information Security* publication, which builds on the COBIT 5 framework and focuses on information security and provides detailed and practical guidance for information security professionals and other stakeholders.

The principles espoused by COBIT 5 in **exhibit 1.11** are particularly useful and applicable to information security governance.

Exhibit 1.11—COBIT 5 Principles

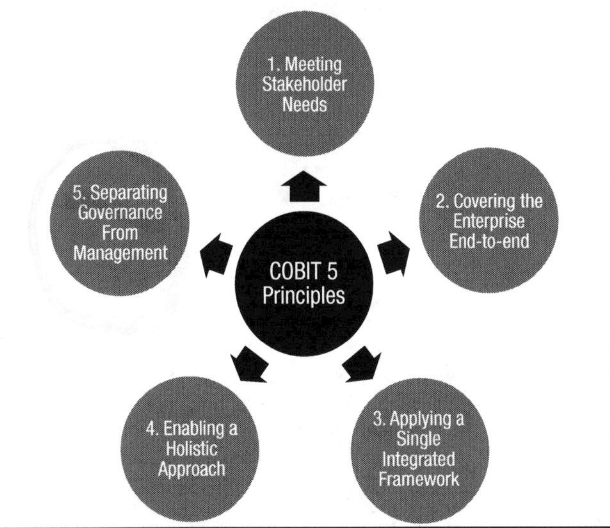

Source: ISACA, COBIT 5, USA, 2012, figure 2

COBIT 5 is based on five key principles shown in **exhibit 1.11** for governance and management of enterprise IT and information assets:

- **Principle 1: Meeting Stakeholder Needs**—Enterprises exist to create value for their stakeholders by maintaining a balance between the realization of benefits and the optimization of risk and use of resources.
- **Principle 2: Covering the Enterprise End-to-end**—COBIT 5 integrates governance of enterprise IT into enterprise governance:
  - It covers all functions and processes within the enterprise; COBIT 5 does not focus only on the "IT function," but treats information and related technologies as assets that need to be dealt with just like any other asset by everyone in the enterprise.
  - It considers all IT-related governance and management enablers to be enterprisewide and end-to-end, i.e., inclusive of everything and everyone—internal and external—that is relevant to governance and management of enterprise information and related IT.
- **Principle 3: Applying a Single, Integrated Framework**—There are many IT-related standards and good practices, each providing guidance on a subset of IT and information security activities. At a high level COBIT 5 aligns with other relevant standards and frameworks such as the ISO 27000 series.
- **Principle 4: Enabling a Holistic Approach**—Efficient and effective governance and management of enterprise IT require a holistic approach, taking into account several interacting components. COBIT 5 defines a set of enablers which are broadly defined as anything that can help to achieve the objectives of the enterprise. The COBIT 5 framework defines seven categories of enablers:
  - Principles, Policies and Frameworks
  - Processes
  - Organisational Structures
  - Culture, Ethics and Behaviour
  - Information
  - Services, Infrastructure and Applications
  - People, Skills and Competencies
- **Principle 5: Separating Governance From Management**—The COBIT 5 framework makes a clear distinction between governance and management.
  - **Governance ensures that stakeholder needs, conditions and options are evaluated to determine balanced, agreed-on enterprise objectives to be achieved; setting direction through prioritization and decision making; and monitoring performance and compliance against agreed-on direction and objectives.**

    In most enterprises, overall governance is the responsibility of the board of directors under the leadership of the chairperson. Specific governance responsibilities may be delegated to special organizational structures at an appropriate level, particularly in larger, complex enterprises.
  - **Management plans, builds, runs and monitors activities in alignment with the direction set by the governance body to achieve the enterprise objectives.**

    In most enterprises, management is the responsibility of the executive management under the leadership of the CEO.

These five principles embodied in COBIT 5 are designed to enable the enterprise to build an effective governance and management framework that optimizes information and technology investment and use for the benefit of stakeholders.

COBIT 5 Process Assessment Model

COBIT 5 has replaced the capability maturity model (CMM) with the process assessment model (PAM), providing greater granularity for assessing the current state and defining a future desired state for information security.

The PAM defined in *COBIT Process Assessment Model (PAM): Using COBIT 5* conforms to ISO/IEC 15504-2 requirements for a PAM and can be used as the basis for conducting an assessment of the capability of each COBIT 5 process, resulting in a 0 to 5 level of "maturity" similar to the CMM levels.

The process dimension uses COBIT 5 as the process reference model. COBIT 5 provides definitions of processes in a life cycle (the process reference model), together with an architecture describing the relationships among the processes.

The COBIT 5 process reference model is composed of 37 processes describing a life cycle for governance and management of enterprise IT, as shown in **exhibit 1.12**.

Exhibit 1.12—Overview of the Process Assessment Model

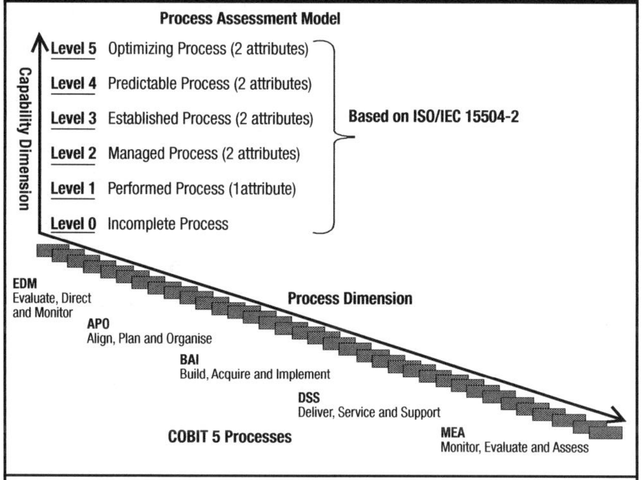

Source: ISACA, *COBIT Process Assessment Model (PAM): Using COBIT 5*, USA, 2013, figure 2

Capability Maturity Model

The desired state of security may also be defined as achieving a specific level in the Capability Maturity Model (CMM) as shown in **exhibit 1.13**. It consists of grading each defined area of security on a scale of 0 to 5, based on the maturity of processes. The maturity levels are described as:

0: Nonexistent—No recognition by organization of need for security
1: *Ad hoc*—Risk is considered on an *ad hoc* basis—no formal processes
2: Repeatable but intuitive—Emerging understanding of risk and need for security
3: Defined process—Companywide risk management policy/ security awareness
4: Managed and measurable—Risk assessment standard procedure, roles and responsibilities assigned, policies and standards in place
5: Optimized—Organizationwide processes implemented, monitored and managed

Balanced Scorecard

According to the Balanced Scorecard Institute:

> *The balanced scorecard is a management system (not only a measurement system) that enables organizations to clarify their vision and strategy, and translate them into action. It provides feedback around both the internal business processes and external outcomes in order to continuously improve strategic performance and results. When fully deployed, the balanced scorecard transforms strategic planning from an academic exercise into the nerve center of an enterprise.*

The balanced scorecard, as shown in **exhibit 1.14**, uses four perspectives, develops metrics, collects data and analyzes the data relative to each of these perspectives:

- Learning and growth
- Business process
- Customer
- Financial

Exhibit 1.13—Capability Maturity Model

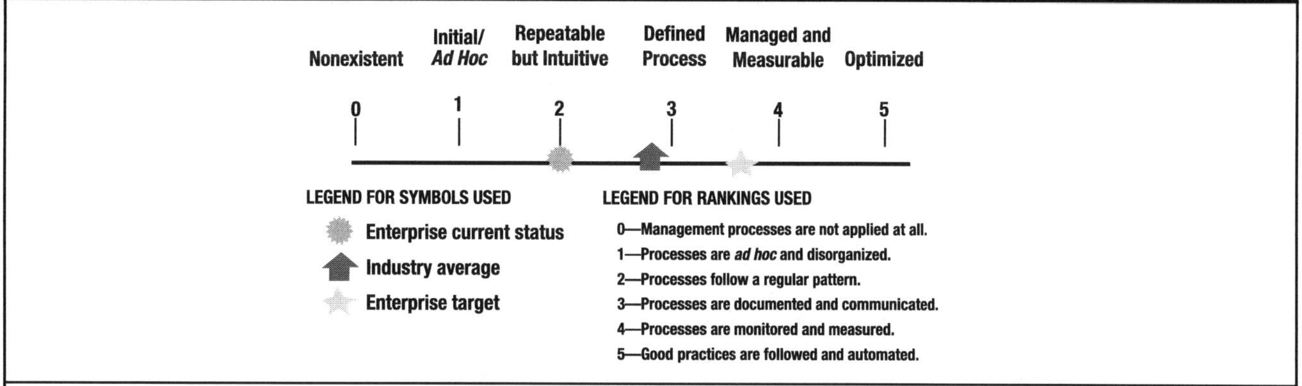

Source: ISACA, *Information Security Governance: Guidance for Information Security Managers*, 2008. All rights reserved. Used by permission.

Exhibit 1.14—Balanced Scorecard

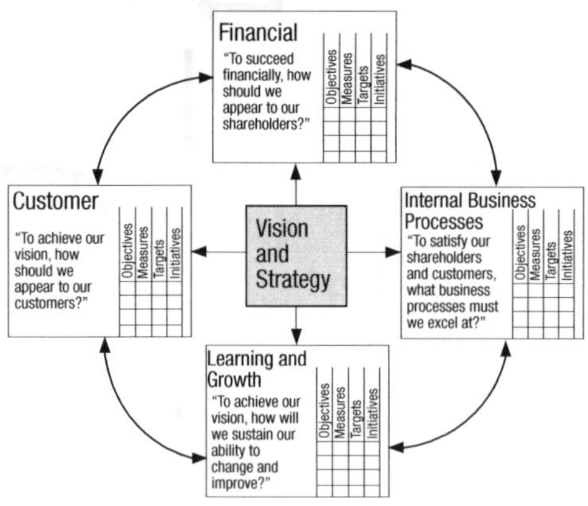

Source: Reprinted with permission from the Balanced Scorecard Institute and Pavel Arveson.

Architectural Approaches

Enterprise Information Security Architecture (EISA) is a subset of enterprise architecture. An architecture framework can be described as a foundational structure, or set of structures, which can be used for developing a broad range of different architectures, including business process architecture—sometimes referred to as the contextual architecture as well as the more traditional conceptual, logical, physical, functional and operational architectures.

There are a number of methodologies that have evolved, including process models, frameworks and *ad hoc* approaches favored by some consultancies. This evolution occurred as it became evident that an architectural perspective limited to IT was inadequate to address business design and development of security requirements. A number of architectural approaches now provide linkages and design of the business side of information protection. Architectural approaches that are inclusive of business processes that may be appropriate for defining the "desired state" of security include (but are not necessarily limited to) framework models such as: COBIT 5, the Open Group Architecture Framework (TOGAF), the Zachman Enterprise Architecture Framework, and the Extended Enterprise Architecture Framework (EA2F). These models can serve to define most or all of the "desired state" of security, provided they are properly utilized to reflect and implement the organizational security strategy. See section 1.13.2.

The architecture should describe a method for designing a target or desired state of the enterprise in terms of a set of building blocks, and for showing how the building blocks fit together. The target architecture is referred to as the reference architecture and serves to set the longer term objectives for technical, systems and process design.

ISO/IEC 27000 Series

To ensure that all relevant elements of security are addressed in an organizational security strategy, the 14 areas of the ISO/IEC 27001:2013 Standard can provide a useful framework to gauge comprehensiveness. Organizational policies and standards must be created that can track directly to each element of the standard. It is the standard on which an organization may choose to be certified and assessed (which is increasingly the case globally), while 27002:2013 is the Code of Practice for information security management that supports implementation to comply with the standard.

The 14 major headings of ISO/IEC 27001:2013 are:
- A.5: Information security policies
- A.6: Organization of information security
- A.7: Human resource security (controls that are applied before, during, or after employment)
- A.8: Asset management
- A.9: Access control
- A.10: Cryptography
- A.11: Physical and environmental security
- A.12: Operations security
- A.13: Communications security
- A.14: System acquisition, development and maintenance
- A.15: Supplier relationships
- A.16: Information security incident management
- A.17: Information security aspects of business continuity management
- A.18: Compliance (with internal requirements, such as policies, and with external requirements, such as laws)

The new and updated controls reflect changes to technology affecting many organizations, e.g., the cloud.

Whereas ISO/IEC 27001:2013 Annex A refers to 114 "controls," they are in fact just sections in ISO/IEC 27002:2013, many of which propose multiple security controls. ISO/IEC 27002:2013 suggests literally hundreds of good practice information security control measures that organizations should consider to satisfy the stated control objectives.

Like ISO/IEC 27001:2013, ISO/IEC 27002:2013 does not mandate specific controls but leaves it to the users to select and implement controls that suit them, using a risk assessment process to identify the most appropriate controls for their specific requirements. They are also free to select controls not listed in the standard, as long as their control objectives are satisfied. The ISO/IEC standard is treated as a generic controls checklist—a "menu" from which organizations select their own set.

Other Approaches

Other approaches and methods exist that may be useful such as other ISO standards on quality (ISO 9001:2000), the Six Sigma approach to quality and business management, publications from NIST and ISF, and the US Federal Information Security Management Act (FISMA). Some of these focus more on management processes and quality management than on strategic security objectives. However, the argument can be made that, if the objective of a security strategy was to fully implement relevant components of ISO/IEC 27001:2013 and 27002:2013, most or all security requirements are likely to be met. That would probably be a needlessly expensive approach, and the standards suggest that they should be carefully tailored to the specific requirements of the adopting organization. Other methodologies will undoubtedly emerge in the future that may prove to be more effective than those mentioned. The ones outlined are not meant to be exhaustive, merely some of the more widely accepted approaches to arrive at well-defined information security objectives.

It may be useful to employ a combination of methods to describe the "desired state" to assist in communications with others and as a way to crosscheck the objectives to make certain all relevant elements are considered. For example, some combination of COBIT control objectives, CMM, balanced scorecard and an appropriate architectural model would make a powerful combination. While it may seem overkill, each approach presents a different viewpoint which, in combination, is likely to make certain that no significant aspect is overlooked. Since it is unlikely that an effective security program will develop from a faulty strategy, this may be a prudent approach.

1.10.4 RISK OBJECTIVES

A major input into defining the desired state will be the organization's approach to risk and its risk appetite, that is, what management considers acceptable risk. This is another critical step since defined acceptable risk devolves into the control objectives or other risk mitigation measures employed. Control objectives are instrumental in determining the type, nature and extent of controls and countermeasures the organization employs to manage risk. **Exhibit 1.15** presents the relationship between risk, control measures and the cost of controls.

Exhibit 1.15—Optimizing Risk Costs

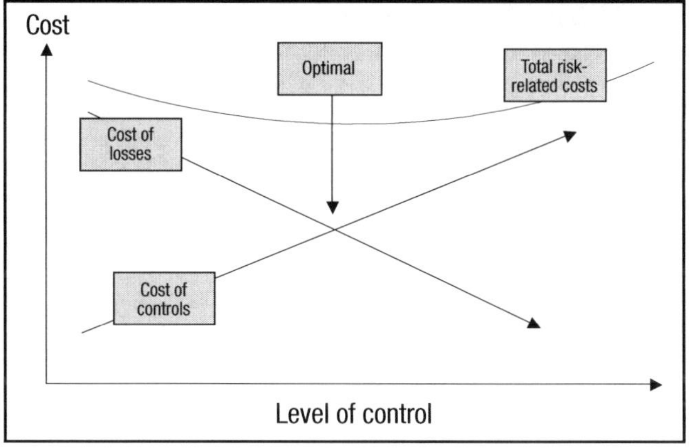

Without a reasonably clear determination of acceptable risk, it is difficult to determine whether information security is meeting its objectives and whether the appropriate level of resources has been deployed.

It must be remembered that risk is a complex subject and is often difficult to ascertain with any precision.

Operational risk management is always a trade-off—if there is a risk associated with taking a particular course of action, there is also a risk of not doing so. Furthermore, individual risk interacts in complex ways, and mitigating one risk almost certainly increases at least one other risk in response.

Risk always carries a cost whether controlled or not. Risk cost can be expressed as annual loss expectation (ALE), i.e., the amount of potential loss times the likelihood of occurrence showing the optimal level of control. Exhibit 1.15 illustrates the balance of the cost of controls against the cost of losses, showing the optimal level of control.

The acceptability of some risk can be quantified by using the business continuity approach of developing recovery time objectives (RTOs). Using a summary approach to determining RTOs may provide adequate input for strategy development. This can be an informal determination by business process owners of the amount of time critical systems can be inoperative without serious business consequences. This, in turn, provides the basis for approximating costs of achieving recovery. If this is considered too high, iteration of the process will arrive at an acceptable recovery time at an acceptable cost. This may be considered the acceptable risk.

Acceptable risk can also be approximated by examining the amount of business interruption insurance the organization carries, the amount of the deductible and its cost, i.e., annual premiums. For example, if the organization has $1 million of insurance with a $10,000 deductible at an annual cost of $50,000, the argument can be made that it is reasonable to spend up to $50,000 in control activities to reduce a $1 million risk to an acceptable risk level of $10,000, i.e., the residual risk.

Developing the right strategy objectives usually needs to be an iterative approach based upon analysis of costs to achieve the desired state and achieve acceptable risk levels. It is likely that lowering the level of acceptable risk will be more costly. However, the approach to achieving the desired state will have a significant bearing on costs as well.

For example, some risk may exist because of certain practices that are not necessary or useful to the organization, or are detrimental to its operation. This could include practices that might be considered discriminatory or contrary to law, and pose the risk of a lawsuit. Such practices, when examined, may have resulted from outmoded attitudes or approaches that can be efficiently changed at a low cost, resulting in elimination or mitigation of the risk. . In other cases, it may be possible to re-engineer certain processes or provide better architectures to reduce inherent risk. In other words, the approach to addressing or treating specific risk has a significant impact on costs.

The information security manager must understand that technical controls (e.g., firewalls, intrusion detection systems [IDSs], etc.) are merely one dimension to be considered. Physical, process and procedural controls may be more effective and less costly. In most organizations, process risk poses the greatest hazard and technical controls are unlikely to adequately compensate for poor management or faulty processes.

Once objectives have been clearly defined, there will be a number of ways to architect solutions that will vary significantly in costs and complexity. Whichever process is used, the objective is to define, in meaningful, concrete terms, the desired overall state of security at some future point.

1.11 DETERMINING CURRENT STATE OF SECURITY

A current state evaluation of information security must also be determined using the same methodologies or combination of methodologies employed to determine strategy objectives, or the desired state. In other words, whatever combination of methodologies, such as COBIT, CMM or the balanced scorecard, is used to define the desired state must also be used to determine the current state. This provides an apples-to-apples comparison between the two, providing the basis for a gap analysis that will delineate what is needed to achieve the objectives.

Using these same methodologies periodically also provides the metrics on progress toward meeting the objectives as well as a security baseline.

1.11.1 CURRENT RISK

The current state of risk must also be assessed through a comprehensive risk assessment. Just as risk objectives must be determined as a part of the desired state, so must the current state of risk be determined to provide the basis for a gap analysis of what risk exists and to what extent risk must be addressed by the strategy. A full risk assessment includes threat and vulnerability analysis, which individually will provide useful information in building a strategy as well. Since risk can be addressed in different ways, such as altering risky behavior, developing countermeasures to threats, reducing vulnerabilities or developing controls, this information will provide the basis for determining the most cost-effective strategy to address risk and developing remediation budgets. Additional periodic assessments will serve to provide the needed metrics to determine progress. Numerous approaches exist to assess risk. Some of the most commonly used methods include COBIT 5 (*COBIT 5 for Risk* publication), NIST 800-30, ISO/IEC 27005, and OCTAVE (Operationally Critical Threat, Asset, and Vulnerability Evaluation).

Business Impact Analysis/Assessment

The current state evaluation should also include a thorough business impact assessment (BIA) of critical systems and processes to help round out the current state picture. Because the ultimate objective of security is to increase stakeholder value by providing business process assurance and minimizing the impacts of adverse events, an impact analysis provides some of the information needed to develop an effective strategy. The difference between acceptable levels of impact and current level of potential impacts must be addressed by the strategy.

1.12 INFORMATION SECURITY STRATEGY DEVELOPMENT

With the information developed in the previous section, a meaningful security strategy can be developed—a strategy to move from the current state to the desired state. Knowing where one is and where one is going provides the essential starting point for strategy development; it provides the framework for creating a road map. The road map is essentially the steps that must be taken to implement the strategy.

A set of information security objectives coupled with available processes, methods, tools and techniques creates the means to construct a security strategy. A good security strategy should address and mitigate risk while complying with the legal, contractual and statutory requirements of the business as well as provide demonstrable support for the business objectives of the organization and maximize value to the stakeholders. The security strategy also needs to address how the organization will embed good security practices into every business process and area of the business.

Often, those charged with developing a security strategy think in terms of controls as the means to implement security. Controls, while important, are not the only element available to the strategist. In some cases, for example, reengineering a process can reduce or eliminate a risk without the need for controls. Or, potential impacts may be mitigated by architectural modifications rather than controls. It should also be considered that, in some cases, mitigating risk can reduce business opportunities to the extent of being counterproductive.

Ultimately, the goal of security is business process assurance, regardless of the business. This in turn serves to protect value and value creation. While the business of a government agency may not result directly in profits, it is still in the business of providing cost-effective services to its constituency and must still protect the assets for which it has custodial care. Whatever the business, its primary operational goal is to maximize the success of business processes and minimize impediments to those processes.

1.12.1 ELEMENTS OF A STRATEGY

What should go into a security strategy? The starting point and the destination have been defined. The next consideration must be what resources are available and what constraints must be considered when developing the road map. The resources are the mechanisms that will be used to achieve various parts of the strategy bound by the constraints.

Road Map

The typical road map to achieve a defined, secure desired state includes people, processes, technologies and other resources. It serves to map the routes and steps that must be taken to "navigate" to the objectives of the strategy.

The interaction and relationship between the various elements of a strategy are likely to be complex. As a consequence, it is prudent to consider the initial stages of developing a security architecture such as those discussed in section 1.14.2. Architectures can provide a structured approach to defining business drivers, resource relationships and process flows. An architecture can also help ensure that contextual and conceptual elements such as business drivers and consequences are considered in the strategy development stage.

Achieving the desired state is usually a long-term goal consisting of a series of projects and initiatives. Like most large, complex projects, it is necessary to break it down into a series of shorter-term projects that can be accomplished in a reasonable time period given the inevitable resource constraints and budget cycles. The entire road map can, and should, be charted while understanding that there is no steady state for information security, and some objectives will need to be modified over time. Some objectives, such as attaining a particular maturity level, reengineering high-risk processes, or achieving specific control objectives may not require modification.

Shorter-term projects aligned with the long-range objectives can serve to provide checkpoints and opportunities for midcourse corrections. They can also provide metrics to validate the overall strategy.

For example, one long-term objective defined in the strategy may be data classification according to sensitivity and criticality. Because of the sheer magnitude of the effort required in a large organization, it is likely to require a number of years to accomplish. The strategy may include the requirement to determine that 25 percent will be targeted for completion each fiscal year utilizing a variety of tactical approaches. A second component of the strategy might be to create policies and standards that preclude the practices that gave rise to the problem to begin with, so it does not get worse while the remediation process is underway. An example of a short-term action plan to accomplish this objective is detailed below in section 1.19.

Development of a strategy to achieve long-term objectives and the road map to get there, coupled with shorter-term intermediate goals, will provide the basis for sound policy and standards development in support of the effort.

1.12.2 STRATEGY RESOURCES AND CONSTRAINTS—OVERVIEW

The following subsections describe the typical resources for implementing an information security strategy and some of the constraints that must be considered.

Note that COBIT 5 defines enablers as factors that, individually and collectively, influence whether something will work—in this case, governance and management of information security and enterprise IT. Enablers are driven by the goals cascade, i.e., higher-level goals define what the different enablers should achieve.

The COBIT 5 framework describes seven categories of enablers (**exhibit 1.16**):
- **Principles, policies and frameworks** are the vehicle to translate the desired behavior into practical guidance for day-to-day management.
- **Processes** describe an organized set of practices and activities to achieve certain objectives and produce a set of outputs in support of achieving overall goals.
- **Organizational structures** are the key decision-making entities in an enterprise.
- **Culture, ethics and behavior** of individuals and of the enterprise are very often underestimated as a success factor in governance and management activities.
- **Information** is pervasive throughout any organization and includes all information produced and used by the enterprise. Information is required for keeping the organization running and well governed, but at the operational level, information is very often the key product of the enterprise itself.
- **Services, infrastructure and applications** include the infrastructure, technology and applications that provide the enterprise with information technology processing and services.
- **People, skills and competencies** are linked to people and are required for successful completion of all activities and for making correct decisions and taking corrective actions.

Enablers can function as resources as well as constraints and must be considered from both perspectives.

Exhibit 1.16—COBIT 5 Enterprise Enablers

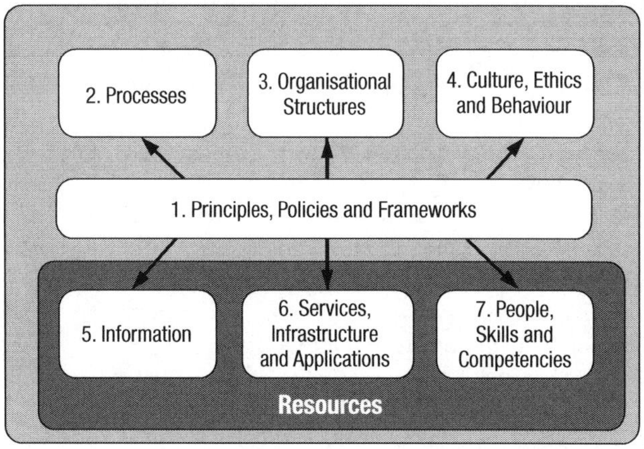

Source: ISACA, COBIT 5, USA, 2012, figure 12

Resources

The resources available to the organization need to be enumerated and considered when developing a security strategy. To the extent possible, the strategy should use existing resources to maximize utilization of existing assets and capabilities.

These resources can be considered the mechanisms, processes and systems that are available, in some optimal mix, to achieve the desired state of security over time. They will typically include:
- Policies
- Standards
- Procedures
- Guidelines
- Architecture(s)
- Controls—physical, technical, procedural
- Countermeasures
- Layered defenses
- Technologies
- Personnel security
- Organizational structure
- Roles and responsibilities
- Skills
- Training
- Awareness and education
- Audits
- Compliance enforcement
- Threat assessment
- Vulnerability analysis
- Risk assessment
- Business impact assessment
- Resource dependency analysis
- Third party service providers
- Other organizational support and assurance providers
- Facilities
- Environmental security

Constraints

There are also a number of constraints that must be considered when developing a security strategy and subsequent action plan. Constraints typically include:

- **Legal**—Laws and regulatory requirements
- **Physical**—Capacity, space, environmental constraints
- **Ethics**—Appropriate, reasonable and customary
- **Culture**—Both inside and outside the organization
- **Costs**—Time, money
- **Personnel**—Resistance to change, resentment against new constraints
- **Organizational structure**—How decisions are made and by whom, turf protection
- **Resources**—Capital, technology, people
- **Capabilities**—Knowledge, training, skills, expertise
- **Time**—Window of opportunity, mandated compliance
- **Risk appetite**—Threats, vulnerabilities, impacts

Some of the constraints, such as ethics and culture, may have been dealt with in developing the desired state. Others will undoubtedly arise as a consequence of developing the road map and action plan.

1.13 STRATEGY RESOURCES

There are typically numerous resources available to develop an information security strategy, but they will vary with the organization. The information security manager must determine what resources are available and be aware that there may be cultural, financial or other reasons that certain options may be precluded such as management reluctance to change or modify policies. This section covers some of the most essential concepts of information security and constitutes essential knowledge for the CISM candidate.

1.13.1 POLICIES AND STANDARDS

There is broad range of interpretation of policy, standards, procedures and guidelines. The definitions used in this document are in agreement with the major standards bodies and should be adopted to preclude miscommunication. Policies and standards are considered tools of governance and management, respectively, and procedures and guidelines the purview of operations. For clarity, the four are defined in the following subsections.

Policies

Policies are the high-level statements of management intent, expectations and direction. Well-developed high-level policies in a mature organization can remain fairly static for extended periods.

An example of an effective high-level policy statement on access control could be: Information resources shall be controlled in a manner that effectively precludes unauthorized access.

Policies can be considered the "constitution" of security governance and must be clearly aligned with the strategic security objectives of the organization.

Standards

Standards in this context are the metrics, allowable boundaries or the process used to determine whether procedures, processes or systems meet policy requirements. Metrics in the sense that a procedure either complies with the standard or it does not. Boundaries are set in terms of allowable limits on processes, people and technologies.

A standard for passwords used for access control could be: Passwords for medium- and low-security domains shall be composed of no less than eight characters consisting of a mixture of upper and lower case letters, and at least one number and one punctuation mark.

The standard for access control for employees on the premises can include password composition requirements, minimum and maximum password length, frequency of password changes, and rules for reuse. Generally, a standard must provide sufficient parameters or boundaries that a procedure or practice can be unambiguously determined to meet the requirements of the relevant policy. Standards must be carefully crafted to only provide necessary limits to ensure security while maximizing procedural options.

Standards must change as requirements and technologies change. Multiple standards will usually exist for each policy, depending on the security domain or classification level. For example, the password standard would be more restrictive when accessing high-security domains.

Procedures

Procedures are the responsibility of operations, including security operations, but are included here for clarity. Procedures must be unambiguous and include all necessary steps to accomplish specific tasks. They must define expected outcomes, displays and required conditions precedent to execution. Procedures must also contain the steps required when unexpected results occur.

Procedures must be clear and unambiguous, and terms must be exact. For example, the words "must," "will" and "shall" will be used for any task that is mandatory. The word "should" must be used to mean a preferred action that is not mandatory. The terms "may" or "can" must only be used to denote a purely discretionary action. Discretionary tasks should only appear in procedures, where necessary, since they dilute the message of the procedure.

Procedures for passwords would include the detailed steps required for setting up password accounts, and for changing or resetting passwords.

Guidelines

Guidelines for executing procedures are also the responsibility of operations. Guidelines should contain information that will be helpful in executing the procedures. This can include clarification of policies and standards, dependencies, suggestions and examples, narrative clarifying the procedures, background information that may be useful, tools that can be used, etc. Guidelines can be useful in many other circumstances as well, but are considered here in the context of information security governance.

1.13.2 ENTERPRISE INFORMATION SECURITY ARCHITECTURE(S)

While still not implemented by many organizations, an enterprise information security architecture (EISA) can be a powerful development, implementation and integration tool for the development and implementation of a strategy. However, to be effective it is essential that it is an integral part of enterprise architecture (EA) to help ensure that proper controls are implemented and integrated throughout the organizations infrastructure, processes and technologies. The requirement for architecture has been recognized and promoted for decades, as evidenced by the following report from the META Group in its 2002 report titled *Plan for a Security Architecture Guidelines and Relationships*, which provides a useful explanation of security architecture in the following analogy:

> *In many respects, the information security architecture is analogous to the architecture associated with buildings. It begins as a concept, a set of design objectives that must be met (e.g., the function it will serve; whether it will be a hospital, a school, etc.). It then progresses to a model, a rough approximation of the vision forged from raw materials (read: services). This is followed by the preparation of detailed blueprints, or tools that will be used to transform the vision/model into a real and finished product. Finally, there is the building itself, the realization, or output, of the prior stages.*

Given the increasing size of security staffing in most organizations, the growing cyber risk and losses coupled with increasing regulatory pressures and ever more problematic security administration, it is surprising that security architecture generally has had little impact on enterprise security efforts.

In the same report, the META Group warned:

> *Indeed, without one [security architecture], evidence suggests that enterprises will default to a haphazard, reactive, tactical approach to constructing a secure environment, regrettably wasting resources and introducing more vulnerabilities as they proceed to fix others.*

The failure of organizations to embrace the notion of security architecture appears to have several identifiable causes. One is that such projects are expensive and time-consuming, and there is little or no understanding or appreciation at most organizational levels for the necessity or the potential benefits.

It may also be that there is not an abundance of competent security architects that have sufficiently broad and deep experience to address the wide range of issues necessary to ensure a reasonable degree of success. The effect of this lack of "architecture" over time has been to have functionally less security integration and increasing vulnerability across the enterprise at the same time that technical security has seen significant improvement. This lack of integration contributes to the increasing difficulty in managing enterprise security efforts effectively.

A number of architectural frameworks and processes currently exist and some of the more prevalent ones are referenced below. Information security architecture is also covered more extensively in chapter 3, section 11.

A number of these approaches are similar and have evolved from the development of enterprise architecture. For example, the Zachman framework approach of developing a who, what, why, where, when and how matrix is shared by SABSA and EA2F. See **exhibit 1.17**.

Exhibit 1.17—SABSA Security Architecture Matrix

	Assets (What)	Motivation (Why)	Process (How)	People (Who)	Location (Where)	Time (When)
Contextual	The Business	Business Risk Model	Business Process Model	Business Organization and Relationships	Business Geography	Business Time Dependencies
Conceptual	Business Attributes Profile	Control Objectives	Security Strategies and Architectural Layering	Security Entity Model and Trust Framework	Security Domain Model	Security-related Lifetimes and Deadlines
Logical	Business Information Model	Security Policies	Security Services	Entity Schema and Privilege Profiles	Security Domain Definitions and Associations	Security Processing Cycle
Physical	Business Data Model	Security Rules, Practices and Procedures	Security Mechanisms	Users, Applications and the User Interface	Platform and Network Infrastructure	Control Structure Execution
Component	Detailed Data Structures	Security Standards	Security Products and Tools	Identities, Functions, Actions and ACLs	Processes, Nodes, Addresses and Protocols	Security Step Timing and Sequencing
Operational	Assurance of Operational Continuity	Operational Risk Management	Security Service Management and Support	Application and User Management and Support	Security of Sites, Networks and Platforms	Security Operations Schedule

Source: 1995 to 2008, Sherwood Applied Business Security Architecture. All rights reserved. Used with permission. *www.sabsa.org*

The approach for EA including security that has gained ground during the past decade is The Open Group Architectural Framework (TOGAF) which addresses the following four interrelated areas of specialization called architecture domains:

- Business architecture, which defines the business strategy, governance, organization and key business processes of the organization
- Applications architecture, which provides a blueprint for the individual application systems to be deployed, the interactions between the application systems, and their relationships to the core business processes of the organization with the frameworks for services to be exposed as business functions for integration
- Data architecture, which describes the structure of an organization's logical and physical data assets and the associated data management resources
- Technical architecture, or technology architecture, which describes the hardware, software, and network infrastructure needed to support the deployment of core, mission-critical applications

The objectives of the various approaches are essentially the same. The framework details the organization, roles, entities and relationships that exist or should exist to perform a set of business processes. The framework should provide a rigorous taxonomy that clearly identifies what processes a business performs and detailed information about how those processes are executed and secured. The end product is a set of artifacts that describe, in varying degrees of detail, exactly what and how a business operates and what security controls are required. COBIT 5 provides extensive resources and tools to achieve these objectives and has seen wide implementation globally.

The current release of COBIT 5 has changed perspective from the IT-centric approach in COBIT 4 to a holistic architectural framework. COBIT 5 was released in April 2012. COBIT 5 consolidates and integrates the COBIT 4.1, Val IT 2.0 and Risk IT frameworks, and draws from ISACA's IT Assurance Framework (ITAF) and the Business Model for Information Security (BMIS). It aligns with frameworks and standards such as Information Technology Infrastructure Library (ITIL), International Organization for Standardization (ISO), Project Management Body of Knowledge (PMBOK), PRINCE2 and The Open Group Architecture Framework (TOGAF).

The major drivers for the development of COBIT 5 for information security include:

- The need to describe information security in an enterprise context, including:
  - The full end-to-end business and IT functional responsibilities of information security
  - All aspects that lead to effective governance and management of information security, such as organizational structures, policies and culture
  - The relationship and link of information security to enterprise objectives
- An ever-increasing need for the enterprise to:
  - Maintain information risk at an acceptable level and to protect information against unauthorized disclosure, unauthorized or inadvertent modifications, and possible intrusions.
  - Ensure that services and systems are continuously available to internal and external stakeholders, leading to user satisfaction with IT engagement and services.
  - Comply with the growing number of relevant laws and regulations as well as contractual requirements and internal policies on information and systems security and protection, and provide transparency on the level of compliance.
  - Achieve all of the above while containing the cost of IT services and technology protection.

The choice of approaches may be limited by an existing organizational standard but if one does not exist, the choice should be made based on form, fit and function. In other words, a particular approach may be more consistent with existing organizational practices or may be more suitable for a particular situation. The various approaches may also entail considerably greater efforts and resources. Some are more oriented to or limited to technical architectures and will not be well suited for governance purposes.

While a specific security architecture may be of considerable benefit, it is essential that it be guided by, and tightly integrated with, the overall enterprise architecture. The development of current enterprise architecture such as TOGAF (**exhibit 1.18**) will address security as an essential component of the overall design and, in most cases, will be the preferred approach to ensure effective integration.

Alternative Enterprise Architecture Frameworks

In addition to those mentioned, a number of other approaches to enterprise and security architecture include the following (the choice of an architectural approach should be based on factors such as form, fit, function, and perhaps mandated, approaches in certain organizations):

- Integrated Architecture Framework of Capgemini
- UK Ministry of Defence (MOD) Architecture Framework (MODAF)
- NIH Enterprise Architecture Framework
- Open Security Architecture
- Service-Oriented Modeling Framework (SOMF)
- The Open Group Architecture Framework (TOGAF)
- AGATE French Délégation Générale pour l'Armement Atelier de Gestion de l'ArchiTEcture des systèmes d'information et de communication
- United States Department of Defense Architectural Framework (DoDAF)
- Interoperable Delivery (of European government services to public) Administrations, Business and Citizens (IDABC)
- United States Office of Management and Budget Federal Enterprise Architecture (FEA)
- Model-driven Architecture (MDA) of the Object Management Group
- OBASHI business and IT methodology and framework (OBASHI)
- SABSA comprehensive framework for Enterprise Security Architecture and Service Management
- Zachman framework of IBM (framework from the 1980s)
- SAP Enterprise Architecture Framework, an extension of TOGAF, to better support commercial off-the-shelf programs and Service-Oriented Architecture
- Method for an Integrated Knowledge Environment (MIKE2.0), which includes an enterprise architecture framework called the Strategic Architecture for the Federated Enterprise (SAFE)

Exhibit 1.18 depicts the TOGAF architectural process and its relationship to business operations.

Exhibit 1.18—TOGAF Enterprise Architecture Framework

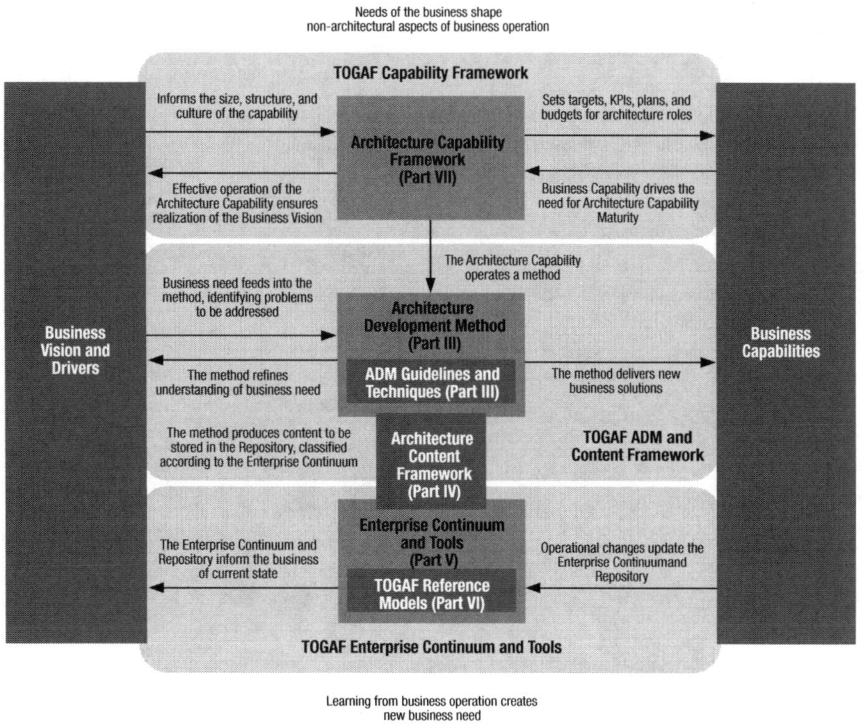

Source: ISACA, *COBIT Mapping: Mapping of TOGAF 8.1 With COBIT® 4.0*, USA, 2007

1.13.3 CONTROLS

Controls are the primary components to consider when developing an information security strategy. Controls can be physical, technical or procedural. The choice of controls must be based on a number of considerations including ensuring their effectiveness, that they are not unduly expensive or restrictive to business activities, and what the optimal form of control will be.

Extensive discussion of controls, their usage, implementation and enforcement is found in chapter 2, section 2.11.

IT Controls

COBIT focuses on IT controls, which constitute the majority of controls required in many organizations. Arguably, COBIT is one of the most developed and comprehensive approaches to determining control objectives for IT and subsequent implementation and management.

COBIT defines control objectives as "a statement of the desired result or purpose to be achieved by implementing control procedures in a particular IT activity."

Non-IT Controls

The information security manager must be aware that information security controls must be developed for non-IT-related information processes as well. This will include secure marking, handling and storage requirements for physical information. It must include considerations for handling and preventing social engineering. Environmental controls must also be taken into account so that otherwise secure systems are not subject to simply being stolen as has occurred in some well-publicized cases.

Countermeasures

Countermeasures are the protection measures that directly reduce a vulnerability or a threat. Countermeasures can simply be considered targeted controls.

Countermeasures to threats should be considered from a strategic perspective. They can be passive or active but, in many cases, may be more effective and less constricting than general controls.

A countermeasure might consist of making the most sensitive information accessible only from a separate subnet, not externally available, or it might consist of changing to an inherently more secure operating system or preventing unsecured systems from connecting to the network.

Layered Defenses

Layering defenses, or defense-in-depth, is an important and effective concept in designing an effective information security strategy or architecture. The layers must be designed so that the cause of failure of one layer does not also cause failure of the next layer.

The number of layers needed will be a function of asset sensitivity and criticality as well as the reliability of the defenses and the degree of exposure. Excessive reliance on a single control is likely to create a false sense of confidence. For example, a company that depends solely on a firewall can still be subject to numerous attack methodologies. A further defense may be the creation through education and awareness of a "human firewall," which can constitute a critical layer of defense. Segmenting the network can constitute another defensive layer.

1.13.4 TECHNOLOGIES

The past few decades have seen the development of numerous security technologies to address the ever-growing threats to information resources. Technology is one of the cornerstones of an effective security strategy. The information security manager must be familiar with how these technologies can serve as controls in achieving the desired state of security. Technology, however, cannot compensate for management, cultural or operational deficiencies, and the information security manager is cautioned to not place excessive reliance on these mechanisms. As **exhibit 1.19** demonstrates, to achieve effective defenses against security incidents, a combination of policies, standards and procedures must come together with technology.

There are a number of technologies with security mechanisms that can play a critical role in the success of an organization's security strategy. These technologies are discussed in more detail in chapter 3 and in the glossary. Given the ongoing and rapid development of technology in this area, the prudent information security manager will utilize available resources to stay current on the latest developments.

1.13.5 PERSONNEL

Personnel security is an important area the information security manager must consider as a preventative means of securing an organization. Since the most costly and damaging compromises are usually the result of insider activities, whether intentional or accidental, the first line of defense is to try to ensure the trustworthiness and integrity of new and existing personnel. Limited background checks can provide indicators of negative characteristics, but the extent of these checks may be constrained by privacy and other laws, particularly in European Union nations.

In addition, the extent and nature of background investigations should be relevant and proportional to the sensitivity and criticality of the requirements of the position held. An extensive background investigation of a receptionist might be considered an unwarranted privacy intrusion, for example. Privacy regulations of the relevant jurisdiction must be considered since they vary greatly in different countries. Nevertheless, consideration must be given to controls aimed at preventing the employment of personnel likely to harm the organization and providing ongoing intelligence indicative of emerging or potential problems with existing staff.

Methods of tracking incidents of pilfering and theft should be developed, and these events should be investigated and tracked when feasible. The appearance of what may be considered minor events may be indications of a more serious situation. It may also be an indicator of personnel who may be involved in illegal or improper activities.

If the organization's policy is that e-mail is not private and may be inspected by the company, and employees have been properly made aware of this policy, it may be appropriate to consider monitoring e-mail of personnel who have been identified as potential problems. Legal protections vary on this type of monitoring and it is the responsibility of the information security officer to understand the legal requirements of the jurisdiction involved.

It may also be prudent to develop an investigation and background checking policy and standards. These should be reviewed by the organization's legal and HR departments. These policies should also be reviewed by senior management for consistency with the organization's culture and governance approach.

Exhibit 1.19—Defense in Depth by Function

Defenses Against System Compromise	Policies, Standards, Procedures, Technology
Prevention	Authentication
	Authorization
	Encryption
	Firewalls
	Data labeling/handling/retention
	Management
	Physical security
	Intrusion prevention
	Virus scanning
	Personnel security
	Awareness and training
Containment	Authorization
	Data privacy
	Firewalls/security domains
	Network segmentation
	Physical security
Detection/notification	Monitoring
	Measurements/metrics
	Auditing/logging
	Honeypots
	Intrusion detection
	Virus detection
Reaction	Incident response
	Policy/procedure change
	Additional security mechanisms
	New/better controls
Evidence collection/ event tracking	Auditing/logging
	Management/monitoring
	Nonrepudiation
	Forensics
Recovery/restoration	Backups/restoration
	Failover/remote sites
	Business continuity/disaster recovery planning

Source: Krag Brotby

1.13.6 ORGANIZATIONAL STRUCTURE

Reporting structures for information security managers vary widely. In the *Global State of Information Security Survey 2011* conducted by PricewaterhouseCoopers and *CSO Magazine (www.pwc.com/ca/en/technology-consulting/security/security-survey.html)*, the percentage of CISOs reporting to the CIO has decreased from 38% in 2007 to 23% in 2010. During the same period, the percentage reporting directly to the board of directors has increased from 21% to 32%. and 36% now report to the CEO.

While reporting to the CIO has often been functionally adequate, it is increasingly being seen as less than optimal and should be examined by senior management as a part of governance responsibilities. There are several reasons why this is the case. One is that the increasingly broad requirements of information security transcend the purview of the typical CIO. Another reason is the inherent conflict of interest. Information security, due to efforts to ensure security, is often perceived as a constraint on IT operations. CIOs and their IT departments are usually under pressure to increase performance and cut costs. Security is often the victim of these pressures. Finally, it must be considered that for information security to be effective, it must be more aligned with the business than with technology.

Centralized and Decentralized Approaches to Coordinating Information Security

An organization's cultural makeup is a strong determinant for whether the security organization is most effective using a centralized or decentralized approach. While many benefits can be achieved through the centralization and standardization of security, often the structure of an organization makes this an ineffective approach.

Multinational companies that choose a centralized approach need to carefully consider different local legal requirements in each country where they have a presence. For example, some countries may not allow the business data to be stored or processed outside of their national boundaries; some governments may collect taxes such as a withholding tax for the software or hardware used by the entities within their jurisdiction, regardless of where the software or hardware is physically located.

One example of a distributed approach is an organization that has grown through acquisitions and operates more as independent entities rather than as a single company. In this situation, it is not unusual for separate information technology groups to exist along with different software and hardware. In this example, it would not be unusual for different security organizations to exist with separate approaches, policies and procedures. In these situations, there may still be benefits to creating a single set of overall enterprisewide security policies and then deal with local differences through local standards and procedures.

A decentralized security process has advantages in that security administrators are normally closer to the users and understand local issues better. Often, they can respond more quickly to requests for changes to access rights or security incidents.

However, there are also disadvantages. For example, the quality of service may vary by location, based on the level of training the local staff possesses and the degree to which they may be encumbered with other unrelated duties.

There may be different approaches and techniques used for security depending on whether a centralized or decentralized approach is taken, but the overall responsibilities and objectives of security will not change. They still must:
- Be closely aligned with the business objectives
- Be sponsored and approved by senior management
- Have monitoring in place
- Have reporting and crisis management in place
- Have organizational continuance procedures
- Have risk management in place
- Have appropriate security awareness and training programs

1.13.7 EMPLOYEE ROLES AND RESPONSIBILITIES

With the many tasks today's employees must complete, it is important that the strategy includes a mechanism that defines all security roles and responsibilities, and incorporates them in employee job descriptions. Ultimately, if employees are compensated based on their adherence to meeting their job responsibilities, there is a better chance of achieving security governance objectives. An employee's annual job performance and objectives can include security-related measurements.

The information security manager should work with the personnel director to define security roles and responsibilities. The related competencies required for each job position should also be defined and documented.

1.13.8 SKILLS

The skills required to implement a security strategy are an important consideration. Choosing a strategy that utilizes skills already available is likely to be a more cost-effective option, but at times, skills may need to be developed or the required activities outsourced. A skills inventory is important to determine the resources available in developing a security strategy. Proficiency testing may be useful to determine if the requisite skills are available or can be achieved through training.

1.13.9 AWARENESS AND EDUCATION

Training, education and awareness are vital in the overall strategy since security is often weakest at the end-user level. It is here, as well, that one should consider the need for the development of methods and processes that enable the policies, standards and procedures to be more easily followed, implemented and monitored. A recurring security awareness program aimed at end users reinforces the importance of information security and is now required by law, in some jurisdictions, for a number of sectors. In most organizations, evidence indicates that the majority of personnel are not aware of security policies and standards, even where they do exist. Awareness and training programs can provide for widespread acknowledgement that security is important to the organization. Since security relies heavily on individual compliance, it is important that a robust security awareness program be in place and is an element that must be considered in strategy development.

Studies have indicated that improving security awareness and training has, in many cases, resulted in the most cost-effective improvement in overall security. One study conducted by Phillip Sparks, working as a Litton Industries consultant for the US military in Europe, demonstrated the value of security awareness, as shown in **exhibit 1.20**.

According to the study conducted by Sparks:

> *Based upon direct experience with the US Military Regional Computer Emergency Response Team (RCERT) in Europe from 1994-2002, humans were the weakest link in the security chain. Security technology was purchased and implemented, but evidence indicated that the risk to information remained a human problem. Reduction of risk was achieved only after the RCERT initiated an awareness and training program that covered all 90,000 users and the 2000 IT staff personnel.*

Exhibit 1.20 depicts the relationship between risk and the awareness program. As awareness and training of personnel took place, risk was reduced as staff were taught the value of assets, the risk, and took appropriate action. Personnel became aware, then trained on security issues and procedures, which allowed the RCERT to lower the reaction time when vulnerabilities occurred in the organizations. The cost of the program increased until the program was stabilized, and then dropped as shown.

Broadening and deepening the appropriate skills of security personnel through training can do a great deal to improve an organization's overall security effectiveness. The challenge is to determine what the "appropriate" skills are and how they need to be improved to effectively protect the organization against the seemingly endless array of security risk.

Finding employees with the necessary combination of security skills to be effective in today's ever-changing, diverse environments and complex regulatory climate can be difficult and expensive. One way some organizations attempt to ensure that all needed skills are available is to hire overqualified people. The concern with this approach is that these individuals are costly to acquire and maintain and, failing to be challenged, are often dissatisfied with the position. This can lead to excessive employee turnover, unproductive attitudes or substandard performance.

Training for new or existing security personnel to equip them with the skills needed to meet specific existing and emerging security requirements can be more cost effective. This is a strong argument for an ongoing program of training targeted to the needs of the organization and, at the same time, providing a career path for employees based on continuous improvement.

For training to be an effective option, however, it must be targeted to specific systems, processes and policies and to the organization's unique and specific way of doing business, as well as its unique security context. Anything less is likely to be inadequate, and anything more wastes resources. Properly executed, this approach can seamlessly integrate into existing programs and initiatives, shore up areas of deficiency, and align security processes with business processes.

1.13.10 AUDITS

Audits—both internal and external—are one of the main processes used to determine information security deficiencies from a controls and compliance standpoint.

Internal audits in most larger organizations are performed by an internal audit department, generally reporting to either a chief risk officer (CRO) or to an audit committee of the board of directors. In most cases, a subunit of internal audit or an independent IT audit group will focus on information technology resources. In smaller organizations, internal IT audits or reviews may be performed by the information security manager or may be delegated to an information security officer. Typically, the focus is on policy compliance of people, processes and technology.

External audits are most often conducted by the finance department and often do not find their way to information security. Since these audits can provide powerful monitoring tools for the information security manager, it is important to ensure that the security department has access to this information. As with other departments, it is important for the information security manager to develop a good working relationship with the finance department in order to facilitate the flow of information that is essential to effective security management.

As regulatory oversight has increased, many organizations are required to file various audit and other reports with regulatory agencies. Many of these reports have information security implications that can provide useful intelligence and monitoring information for the information security manager. For example,

Exhibit 1.20—Impact of Awareness Training on Risk

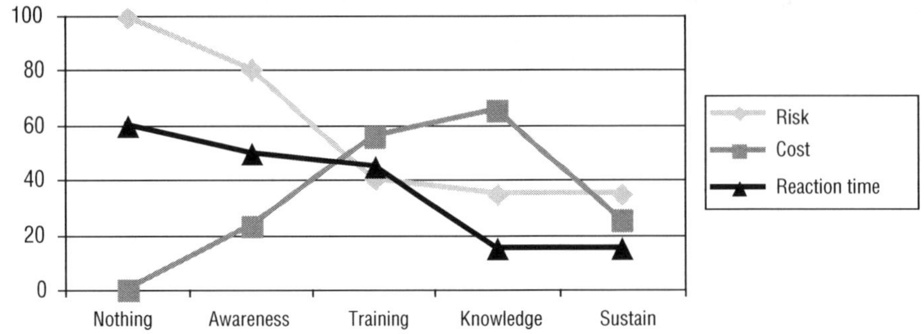

under compliance provisions of the US Sarbanes-Oxley Act, the financial controls of public companies are required to be tested annually within 90 days of reporting to the US Securities and Exchange Commission (SEC). It is important that the results of such tests are available to the information security manager and should be required as part of strategy considerations.

1.13.11 COMPLIANCE ENFORCEMENT

Security violations are an ongoing concern for information security managers, and it is important that procedures for handling them are developed. It is critical that there is senior management buy-in and backing for these procedures, especially in the area of enforcement. Security managers often find that the greatest compliance problems arise with management. If there is a lack of commitment and compliance in management ranks, it may be difficult, if not impossible, to enforce compliance across an organization.

The most effective approach to compliance in an organization where openness and trust are valued and promoted by management is likely to be a system of self-reporting and voluntary compliance based on the understanding that security is clearly in everyone's best interest. This approach usually also requires that these processes be carefully thought out, clearly communicated and cooperatively implemented. Determining how to accomplish this is an element of strategy.

1.13.12 THREAT ASSESSMENT

While threat assessment is performed as a part of overall risk assessment, it is an important element for strategic consideration by itself. One reason is that risk treatment options should consider the most cost-effective approach for addressing any particular risk. For example, mitigation measures can address threat directly, they can reduce or eliminate vulnerabilities, or they can address and compensate for impacts. The most cost-effective choice is facilitated by separately analyzing threat and vulnerability, as well as exposure and impact.

Another reason for developing a threat profile is that the strategy should consider viable threats regardless of whether a current vulnerability is known to exist. This is a proactive approach and takes into account that all vulnerabilities cannot be known and new ones are introduced continuously that may result in risk.

In addition, policy development should map to a threat profile. This is because, in a broad sense, threats are relatively constant (e.g., fire, flood, earthquake, malware, theft, fraud, attacks, mistakes), whereas vulnerabilities change frequently as a result of changes in business, processes, technology and personnel.

1.13.13 VULNERABILITY ASSESSMENT

In most organizations, technical vulnerability assessments using automated scans are common but by themselves are of limited value for security strategy development. Comprehensive vulnerability assessments are important and should include vulnerabilities in processes, technologies and facilities. Processes and facilities are frequently the most vulnerable components; yet, because of the greater difficulty in performing assessments on them, they are also the least frequently done. The process of developing a strategy will offer opportunities to address many of these vulnerabilities in a prudent, proactive approach. Even if no known or apparent threats exist for weaknesses discovered during these assessments, cost-effective opportunities to address systemic weaknesses during strategy development should be considered.

1.13.14 RISK ASSESSMENT AND MANAGEMENT

While both threat and vulnerability assessments can be useful in their own right, in considering the elements of security strategy, assessing the overall risk to the organization is also required. While threats and vulnerabilities that pose no risk to the organization may not be immediately significant, the ever-changing risk landscape makes it likely that this will not continue to be the case. In any event, to the extent that strategy development can address threats and vulnerabilities, it should do so as a matter of good practice.

Formally assessing risk is accomplished by first determining the viable threats to information resources that an organization faces. This includes physical and environmental threats (e.g., flood, fire, earthquake, pandemic) as well as technology threats (e.g., malicious software, system failure, internal and external attacks).

The next consideration is the likelihood that these threats will materialize as well as their probable magnitude. This is the risk identification phase of risk assessment. For example, it may be highly likely in some areas that an earthquake will occur, but it may be that, on average, it will not be severe enough to cause damage. In this case, the more infrequent major earthquakes that historically have caused damage should be considered. Some threats may be extreme, but too rare to warrant consideration (e.g., a comet strike) and can be ignored.

Both the frequency of occurrence as well as probable magnitude can be indicated by the extent that these threats have materialized in the past and by the experiences of peer organizations. The consideration of frequency is important, even if the magnitude is moderate. While a single event may constitute an acceptable risk, if it is a frequent occurrence, the aggregate risk may not be acceptable. For example, an organization may accept a US $10,000 loss once a year, but that level of loss every day may not be acceptable.

The next step is to determine the extent of organizational weaknesses and exposure to these threats. The combination of the frequency and magnitude and the extent of the organization's vulnerability will determine the relative level of risk. By using this information to calculate the resulting probable annual loss expectancy (ALE)—considering frequency, magnitude and exposure—management is in a position to decide on acceptability.

1.13.15 INSURANCE

Strategy resources include the option of addressing some risk with insurance. Generally, the types of risk suitable for insuring are rare, high-impact events such as floods, hurricanes or fire, embezzlement, or liability lawsuits. The most common types of insurance that can be considered include first party, third party and fidelity bonds. First-party insurance covers the organization in the event of damage from most sources and can include business interruption, direct loss and recovery costs. Third-party insurance deals with potential liability to third parties and generally includes defense against lawsuits and covers damages up to predetermined limits. Fidelity insurance or bonding involves protection against employee or agent theft or embezzlement.

1.13.16 BUSINESS IMPACT ASSESSMENT

Business impact is the "bottom line" of risk. A BIA is an exercise that determines the consequences of losing the support of any resource to an organization. The consequences are typically reduced to financial impacts. Risk that cannot result in an appreciable impact is not important. Business impact assessments are an important component of developing a strategy that addresses potential adverse impacts to the organization. A BIA must also be considered as a requirement to determine the criticality and sensitivity of systems and information. As such, it will provide the basis for developing an approach to information classification and addressing business continuity requirements.

1.13.17 RESOURCE DEPENDENCY ANALYSIS

Business dependency analysis was discussed earlier and is similar to resource dependency analysis, but is less granular and includes the elements that would be considered in a business continuity plan (BCP), including such things as staples, paper clips, etc. Resource dependency is similar to disaster recovery planning (DRP) and considers the systems, hardware and software required to perform specific organizational functions. Resource dependency can provide another perspective on the criticality of information resources. It can, to some extent, be used instead of an impact analysis to ensure that the strategy considers resources critical to business operations. The analysis is based on determining the resources (such as systems, software, connectivity, etc.) and dependencies (such as input processes and data repositories) required by operations critical to the organization.

1.13.18 OUTSOURCED SERVICES

Outsourcing is increasingly common, both onshore and offshore, as companies focus on core competencies and ways to cut costs. From an information security point of view, these arrangements can present risk that may be difficult to quantify and potentially difficult to mitigate. Typically, both the resources and skills of the outsourced functions are lost to the organization, which itself will present risk. Providers may operate on different standards and can be difficult to control. The security strategy should consider outsourced security services carefully to ensure that they either are not a critical single point of failure or that there is a viable backup plan in the event of service provider failure.

Much risk posed by outsourcing can also materialize as the result of mergers and acquisitions. Typically, significant differences in culture, systems, technology and operations between the parties present a host of security challenges that must be identified and addressed. Often, in these situations, security is an afterthought and the security manager must strive to gain a presence in these activities and assess the risk for management consideration.

1.13.19 OTHER ORGANIZATIONAL SUPPORT AND ASSURANCE PROVIDERS

When developing a security strategy, there usually are a number of support and assurance services providers within an organization that should be considered a part of information security resources. These can include a variety of departments such as legal, compliance, audit, procurement, insurance, disaster recovery, physical security, training, project office, and human resources. Other departments or groups such as change management or quality assurance also have elements of assurance as a part of their operation.

Typically, these assurance functions are not well integrated, if at all. Strategic considerations should include approaches to ensure that these functions operate seamlessly to prevent gaps that may lead to security compromises.

1.14 STRATEGY CONSTRAINTS

Numerous constraints must be considered when developing a security strategy. They will set the boundaries for the options available to the information security manager and should be thoroughly defined and understood before initiating strategy development.

1.14.1 LEGAL AND REGULATORY REQUIREMENTS

There are a number of legal and regulatory issues affecting information security that must be considered in developing a strategy. Information security is inevitably intertwined with questions of privacy, intellectual property and contractual, civil and criminal law. Any effort to design and implement an effective information security strategy must be built on a solid understanding of the pertinent legal requirements and restrictions. Different regions in a global organization may be governed by conflicting legislation. An example of this is in the area of privacy legislation, where different cultures place a different importance on privacy.

In some countries, thorough background checks may be performed on new employees but are illegal under laws in other countries. To address these situations, the global organization may need to establish different security strategies for each regional division, or it can base policy on the most restrictive requirements in order to be consistent across the enterprise.

There are also a number of legal and regulatory issues associated with Internet business, global transmissions and transborder data flows (e.g., privacy, tax laws and tariffs, data import/export restrictions, restrictions on cryptography, warranties, patents, copyrights, trade secrets, national security). These vary depending upon the organization's location, and result in constraints and boundaries on security strategies. Research into these areas must be undertaken in conjunction with legal and regulatory departments as well as any areas of the business that may be affected.

The strategy must also take into consideration that personnel safety is the subject of regulations in many jurisdictions.

Requirements for Content and Retention of Business Records

There are two main aspects an information security strategy must take into consideration regarding the content and retention of business records and compliance:
- The business requirements for business records
- The legal and regulatory requirements for records

Business requirements may exceed the legal and regulatory requirements imposed by applicable legislating bodies due to the nature of the organization's business. Some organizations have business needs requiring access to data that are 10 to 20 years old or more. This can include customer records, patient records, engineering information and many others. As a rule, the retention strategy and subsequent policy must, at a minimum, meet the legal requirements in the applicable jurisdiction and industry.

Depending upon an organization's location and industry, regulatory bodies have requirements that an organization must comply with, including legal, medical and tax.

Regulations such as Sarbanes-Oxley have imposed various mandatory retention requirements for various types and categories of information, regardless of the storage medium. The strategy will require that the information security manager stay current with these requirements and ensure compliance. Another legal requirement that should be considered is the requirements of any lawful preservation order, which would require an organization or individual to retain specific data when required by law enforcement or other authorities. It is also generally the case that archived information must be indexed sufficiently to be located and retrieved.

E-discovery

Increasingly, civil and criminal actions rely on evidence obtained from e-mail and other electronic communications in response to a production request or subpoena. If information has been archived without being classified and cataloged, retrieving the required material can be an arduous and expensive task, as has occurred in a number of high-profile cases. The increasing prevalence of this type of discovery also contributes to the need for careful consideration of a retention policy that limits the length of time that certain kinds of information such as e-mail are retained within the bounds of legal requirements.

1.14.2 PHYSICAL

There are a variety of physical and environmental factors that may influence or constrain an information security strategy. The obvious ones include such matters as capacity, space, environmental hazards and availability of infrastructure.

Others constraints that have, on occasion, been ignored include a data center that a major oil company operation placed in a basement known to periodically flood. The security strategy should make certain that provisions are made for the consideration of environmental hazards and adequate infrastructure capacity.

The strategy must include a requirement of consideration for personnel and resource safety.

1.14.3 ETHICS

The perception of ethical behavior by an organization's customers and the public at large can have a major impact on an organization and affect its value. These perceptions are often influenced by location and culture, and an effective strategy will include ethical considerations in the areas of its operations.

1.14.4 CULTURE

Internal culture of the organization must be taken into account in developing a security strategy. The culture in which the organization operates must also be considered. A strategy that is at odds with cultural norms may encounter resistance, and this may make successful implementation difficult.

1.14.5 ORGANIZATIONAL STRUCTURE

Organizational structure will have a significant impact on how a governance strategy can be devised and implemented. Often, various assurance functions exist in "silos" that have different reporting structures and authority. Cooperation between these functions is important and typically requires senior management buy-in and involvement.

1.14.6 COSTS

The development and implementation of a strategy consumes resources, including time and money. Obviously, the strategy needs to consider the most cost-effective way it can be implemented.

Organizations often justify spending based on a project's value. With security projects, however, the avoidance of specific risk or compliance with regulations are generally the primary drivers.

Generally, from a business perspective, a cost-benefit or other financial analysis is the most accepted approach to justifying expenditures and should be considered when developing a strategy.

A traditional but speculative approach is to consider the value of avoiding specific risk by estimating the potential losses incurred by a specific event and multiplying by the probability of it occurring in a given year. This results in an ALE. Thus, the cost of the controls required to preclude such an event can be compared to the ALE determine the ROI.

Many practitioners believe that ROI is not a good approach to justifying security programs. This is considered especially true for programs implemented for the purposes of regulatory compliance. For example, under Sarbanes-Oxley, enhanced penalties consisting of long sentences in federal prisons for senior executives are prescribed for some violations. The ROI on programs to prevent such penalties can be difficult to quantify.

Recently, the advances in single sign-on and user access provisioning technologies and procedures have resulted in savings in time and cost over traditional manual administration techniques, which may provide a reasonable basis for ROI calculations. There are a number of examples that compare the costs of traditional processes against the newer procedures, and these can be used in developing a business case.

1.14.7 PERSONNEL

A security strategy must consider what resistance may be encountered during implementation. Resistance to significant changes, as well as possible resentment against new constraints possibly viewed as making tasks more difficult or time consuming, should be expected.

1.14.8 RESOURCES

An effective strategy must consider available budgets, the total cost of ownership (TCO) of new or additional technologies, and the manpower requirements of design, implementation, operation, maintenance and eventual decommissioning. Typically, the TCO must be developed for the full life cycle of technologies, processes and personnel.

1.14.9 CAPABILITIES

The resources available to implement a strategy should include the known capabilities of the organization, including expertise and skills. A strategy that relies on demonstrated capabilities is more likely to succeed than one that does not.

1.14.10 TIME

Time is a major constraint in developing and implementing a strategy. There may be compliance deadlines that must be met, or support for certain strategic operations such as a merger, must be accommodated. There may be windows of opportunity for particular business activities that mandate certain timelines for implementation of certain strategies.

1.14.11 RISK ACCEPTANCE AND TOLERANCE

The level of acceptable risk and the risk tolerance of the organization play a major role in developing an information security strategy. While difficult to measure, there are a variety of methods to arrive at useful approximations. One method is to develop recovery time objectives (RTOs) for critical systems. The shorter the times decided by appropriate managers, the greater the cost and the lower the risk appetite. RTOs should be based on a business impact or dependency analysis to determine allowable downtimes for various resources. Obviously, the cost of protection should never exceed the benefit derived.

1.15 ACTION PLAN TO IMPLEMENT STRATEGY

Implementing an information strategy will typically require one or more projects or initiatives. An analysis of the gaps between the current state and the desired state for each defined metric identifies the requirements and priorities needed for an overall plan or road map to achieve the objectives and close the gaps.

1.15.1 GAP ANALYSIS—BASIS FOR AN ACTION PLAN

A gap analysis is required for various components of the strategy previously discussed, such as maturity levels, each control objective, and each risk and impact objective. The analysis will identify the steps needed to move from the current state to the desired state to achieve the defined objectives. This exercise may need to be repeated annually, or more frequently, to provide performance and goal metrics, and information on possible midcourse corrections needed in response to changing environments or other factors.
A typical approach to gap analysis is to work backward from the endpoint to the current state and determine the intermediate steps need to accomplish the objectives.

CMM or other methods can be used to assess the gap between the current and desired state. Some typical areas that should be assessed and/or ensured include:

- A security strategy with senior management acceptance and support
- A security strategy intrinsically linked with business objectives
- Security policies that are complete and consistent with strategy
- Complete standards for all relevant, consistently maintained policies
- Complete and accurate procedures for all important operations
- Clear assignment of roles and responsibilities
- An organizational structure ensuring appropriate authority for information security management without inherent conflicts of interest
- Information assets that have been identified and classified as to criticality and sensitivity
- Effective controls that have been designed, implemented and maintained
- Effective security metrics and monitoring processes, in place
- Effective compliance and enforcement processes
- Tested and functional incident and emergency response capabilities
- Tested business continuity/disaster recovery plan
- Appropriate security approvals in change management processes
- Risk that is properly identified, evaluated, communicated and managed
- Adequate security awareness and training of all users
- The development and delivery of activities that can positively influence security orientation of culture and behavior of staff
- Regulatory and legal issues are understood and addressed
- Addressing security issues with third-party service providers
- The timely resolution of noncompliance issues and other variances

1.15.2 POLICY DEVELOPMENT

One of the most important aspects of the action plan to execute the strategy is to create or modify, as needed, policies and standards. Policies are the constitution of governance, standards are the law. Policies must capture the intent, expectations and direction of management. As a strategy evolves, it is vital that supporting policies are developed to articulate the strategy. For example, if the objective is to become ISO/IEC 27001:2013 compliant over a three-year period, then the strategy must consider which elements are addressed first, what resources are allocated, how the elements of the standard can be accomplished and so forth. The road map should show the steps and the sequence, dependencies and milestones. The action plan is essentially a project plan to implement the strategy following the road map.

If the objective is ISO/IEC 27001:2013 compliance, each of the relevant 14 domains and major subsections must be the subject of a policy. In practice, this can be effectively accomplished with about two dozen specific policies for even large institutions. Each of the policies is likely to have a number of supporting standards typically divided by security domains. In other words, a set of standards for a high-security domain will be more stringent than the standards for a low-security domain. Other standards may need to be developed for different business units, depending on their activities and regulatory requirements.

The completed strategy provides the basis for creation or modification of existing policies. The policies should be directly traceable to strategy elements. If they are not, either the strategy is incomplete or the policy is incorrect. It should be apparent that a policy that contradicts the strategy is counterproductive. The strategy is the statement of intent, expectations and direction of management. The policies must, in turn, be consistent with and support the intent and direction of the strategy.

Most organizations today have some information security policies. Typically, they have evolved over time, are usually created in response to a security problem or regulations, and are often inconsistent and sometimes contradictory. These policies generally have no relationship to a security strategy (if one exists) and only a coincidental relation to business activities.

Policies are one of the primary elements of governance. They must be properly created, accepted and validated by the board and executive management, and broadly communicated throughout the organization. There may be occasions where subpolicies must be created to address unique situations separate from the bulk of the organization. An example is where a separate part of the organization is performing highly classified military work. Policies that reflect the specific security requirements for classified military work may exist as a separate set.

There are several attributes of good policies that should be considered:
- Security policies should be an articulation of a well-defined information security strategy and capture the intent, expectations and direction of management.
- Each policy should state only one general security mandate.
- Policies must be clear and easily understood by all affected parties.
- Policies should rarely be more than a few sentences long.
- There should rarely be a reason to have more than two dozen policies.

Most organizations have created security policies prior to developing a security strategy. Indeed, most organizations still have not developed a security strategy. In many cases, policy development has not followed the approach defined above and has been *ad hoc* in a variety of formats. Often, these policies have been written to include standards and procedures in lengthy, detailed documents compiled in large, dusty volumes relegated to the stock room.

In many cases, however, especially in smaller organizations, effective practices have been developed that may not be reflected in written policies. Existing practices that adequately address security requirements may usefully serve as the basis for policy and standards development. This approach minimizes organizational disruptions, communications of new policies, and resistance to new or unfamiliar constraints.

1.15.3 STANDARDS DEVELOPMENT

Standards are powerful security management tools. They set the permissible bounds for procedures and practices of technology and systems, and for people and events. Properly implemented, they are the law to the constitution of policy. They provide the measuring stick for policy compliance and a sound basis for audits. They govern the creation of procedures and guidelines.

Standards are the predominant tool of implementing effective security governance and must be owned by the information security manager. They must be carefully crafted to provide only necessary and meaningful boundaries without unnecessarily restricting procedural options. Standards serve to interpret policies and it is important that they reflect the intent of policy. Standards must be unambiguous, consistent and precise as to scope and audience. Standards must exist for the creation of standards and policies regarding format, content and required approvals.

Standards must be disseminated to those governed by them as well as those impacted. Review and modification processes must be developed as well.

Exception processes must be developed for standards not readily attainable for technological or other reasons. A process for implementing compensatory controls must be developed for out-of-compliance situations.

1.15.4 TRAINING AND AWARENESS

An effective action plan to implement a security strategy must consider an ongoing program of security awareness and training. In most organizations, evidence indicates that the majority of personnel are not aware of security policies and standards, even where they do exist. To ensure awareness of new or modified policies, all impacted personnel must be trained appropriately in order for them to see the connection between the policies and standards and their daily tasks. This information should be tailored to individual groups to ensure that it is relevant and must be presented in terms that are clear and understood by the intended audience. For example, presenting new standards on hardening servers is not likely to be meaningful to the shipping department.

In addition to providing information to those impacted by changes, it is important to ensure that staff involved in the various aspects of implementing the strategy are also appropriately trained. This includes understanding the objectives of the strategy (KGIs), the processes that will be used and performance metrics for the various activities (KPIs).

See chapter 3, section 3.13.2, Security Awareness for additional discussion on training and awareness.

1.15.5 ACTION PLAN METRICS

The plan of action to implement the strategy will require methods to monitor and measure progress, and the achievement of milestones. As with any project plan, progress and costs must be monitored on an ongoing basis to determine conformance with the plan and to allow for midcourse corrections on a timely basis. There are likely to be a variety of near-term goals—each requiring resources and a plan of action for achievement.

There are a number of approaches that can be used for ongoing monitoring and measurement of progress. One or more of the methods used to determine current state can be used on a regular basis to determine and chart how progress of current state has changed. For example, a balanced scorecard might be used effectively, by itself, as an ongoing means of tracking progress. Another commonly used approach is to utilize the CMM to define both the current state and the objectives. A straightforward approach, easily implemented and used extensively by COBIT 4, CMM provides a basis for performing ongoing gap analysis to determine progress toward achieving the goals. COBIT 5 has introduced a new, more granular approach called process assessment model (PAM) that will serve the same purpose.

In addition, however, each plan of action will benefit from developing an appropriate set of key performance indicators (KPIs), defining critical success factors (CSFs) and setting agreed-upon key goal indicators (KGIs). For example, the plan of action to achieve regulatory compliance for Sarbanes-Oxley may require, among other things:

- A detailed analysis by competent legal personnel to determine regulatory requirements for affected business units
- Knowledge of current state of compliance
- Definition of required state of compliance

Possible monitoring and metrics might include the following KGIs, CSFs and KPIs.

Key Goal Indicators

Defining clear objectives and achieving consensus on the goals are essential to developing meaningful metrics. For this particular plan, the key goals could include:

- Achieving Sarbanes-Oxley controls testing compliance mandates
- Completing independent controls testing compliance validation and attestation
- Preparation of required statement of control effectiveness

Sarbanes-Oxley requires that, for organizations publicly traded in the US, all financial controls must be tested for effectiveness within 90 days of reporting. The results of testing must be signed by the CEO and CFO, and must be attested to by the organization's auditors. The results must then be included in the organization's public filings to the Securities and Exchange Commission (US SEC).

Critical Success Factors

To achieve Sarbanes-Oxley compliance, certain steps must be accomplished to successfully meet the required objectives, including:

- Identification, categorization and definition of controls
- Defining appropriate tests to determine effectiveness
- Committing resources to accomplish required testing

Large organizations have hundreds (or more) of controls that have been developed over a period of time. In many cases, these controls are *ad hoc* and have not been subject to formal processes. It will be necessary to identify control processes, procedures, structures and technologies, so an appropriate testing regime can be developed. Determining the necessary resources and testing procedures will be critical to accomplishing the required tests.

Key Performance Indicators

Indicators of the key or critical performance factors necessary to achieve the objectives can include:

- Control effectiveness testing plans
- Progress in controls effectiveness testing
- Results of testing control effectiveness

For management to track progress in the testing effort, appropriate testing plans must be developed—consistent with the defined goals and encompassing the critical success factors. Because of the limited time (90 days) available to perform the required tests, management will need reports on the progress and results of testing.

General Metrics Considerations

Considerations for information security metrics include ensuring that what is being measured is, in fact, relevant. Because security is difficult to measure in any objective sense, relatively meaningless metrics are often used simply because they are readily available. Metrics serve only one purpose—providing the information necessary for making decisions. It is therefore critical to understand what decisions must be made, who makes them and then find ways of supplying that information in an accurate and timely fashion. Different metrics are more or less useful for different parts of the organization, and should be determined in collaboration with business process owners and management.

Metrics will generally fall into one of three categories — strategic, tactical, and operational. Senior management is typically not interested in detailed technical metrics such as the number of virus attacks thwarted or password resets but rather in information of a strategic nature. While technical metrics may be of significance to the IT security manager, senior management typically wants a summary of information important from a management perspective—information that typically excludes detailed technical data. This may include:

- Progress according to plan and budget
- Significant changes in risk and possible impacts to business objectives
- Results of disaster recovery testing
- Audit results
- Regulatory compliance status

The information security manager may want more detailed tactical information, including such things as:

- Policy compliance metrics
- Significant process, system or other changes that may affect the risk profile
- Patch management status
- Exceptions and variances to policy or standards

In organizations that have an IT security manager, it is likely that most technical security data available can be useful. This may include:

- Vulnerability scan results
- Server configuration standards compliance
- IDS monitoring results
- Firewall log analysis

Useful information security management metrics are often difficult to design and implement. Typically, the focus is on IT vulnerabilities obtained using automated scans without knowing whether a threat exists or whether there is a potential impact. From an information security management and strategic perspective, this information is of little value

This often results in the collection of vast amounts of data to try to ensure that nothing significant is overlooked. The result can be that the sheer volume of data makes it difficult to see the "big picture," and efforts should be made to develop processes to distill technical data into information needed to manage effectively.

Improvements in overall monitoring can be achieved by careful analysis of available metrics to determine their relevancy. For example, it may be interesting to know how many packets were dropped by the firewalls, but this sheds little light on risk to the organization or potential impacts. It may be information the IT department finds useful, but it is of no value to information security management. On the other hand, knowing the amount of time it takes to recover critical services after a major incident is likely to be extremely useful to all parties.

Metrics design and monitoring activities should take into consideration:

- What is important to manage information security operations
- IT security management requirements
- The needs of business process owners
- What senior management wants to know

Communications with each of the constituencies may be helpful in determining the kinds of security reports they would find useful. Reporting processes can then be devised that provide each group with the security information they require to make informed security-related decisions.

1.16 IMPLEMENTING SECURITY GOVERNANCE—EXAMPLE

The following section demonstrates an approach to implementing security governance utilizing the CMM to define objectives (KGIs), to determine a strategy, and as a metric for progress. Attaining CMM level 4 is a typical (although difficult) organizational goal and can be expressed as a desired state.

The following list, based on COBIT 4, may not delineate all attributes and characteristics of the desired state of information security and additional elements may need to be added. However, they do provide the required basics and can provide an adequate description of the desired state of security for most organizations, as follows:

- The assessment of risk is a standard procedure and exceptions to following the procedure would be noticed by IT management. It is likely that IT risk management is a defined management function with senior level responsibility. Senior management and IT management have determined the levels of risk that the organization will tolerate and have standard measures for risk/return ratios.
- Responsibilities for information security are clearly assigned, managed and enforced. Information security risk and impact analysis is consistently performed. Security policies and practices are completed with specific security baselines. Security awareness briefings have become mandatory. User identification, authentication and authorization are standardized. Security certification of staff is established. Intrusion testing is a standard and formalized process leading to improvements. Cost-benefit analysis, supporting the implementation of security measures, is increasingly being utilized. Information security processes are coordinated with the overall organization security function. Information security reporting is linked to business objectives.
- Responsibilities and standards for continuous service are enforced. System redundancy practices, including use of high-availability components, are consistently deployed.

Breaking down the individual elements of CMM 4 generates the following list:

1. The assessment of risk is a standard procedure, and exceptions to following the procedure would be noticed by security management.
2. Information security risk management is a defined management function with senior-level responsibility.
3. Senior management and information security management have determined the levels of risk that the organization will tolerate and have standard measures for risk/return ratios.
4. Responsibilities for information security are clearly assigned, managed and enforced.
5. Information security risk and impact analysis is consistently performed.
6. Security policies and practices are completed with specific security baselines.
7. Security awareness briefings are mandatory.
8. User identification, authentication and authorization are standardized.
9. Certification of security staff is established.
10. Intrusion testing is a standard and formalized process leading to improvements.
11. Cost-benefit analyses, supporting the implementation of security measures, are increasingly being utilized.
12. Information security processes are coordinated with the overall organization security function.
13. Information security reporting is linked to business objectives.
14. Responsibilities and standards for continuous service are enforced.
15. System redundancy practices, including use of high-availability components, are consistently deployed.

Depending on the structure of the organization, each significant area or process of the organization needs to be evaluated separately. For example, accounting, HR, operations, IT, business units or subsidiaries need to be evaluated to determine whether the current state meets the requirements of the 15 (or more) elements listed previously.

In most organizations, the typical results for each of the 15 defined characteristics range across the maturity levels from 1 to 4.

Policies need to be reviewed to determine whether they address each of the elements. To the extent that they do not, the following section provides suggestions for policies that address each of the requirements of CMM 4.

One objective that should be stated is: "to achieve consistent maturity levels across specific security domains"—being mindful of the notion that "security is only as good as the weakest link." For example, the maturity level of all critical processes should be the same.

Selecting a particular department, business unit or area of the organization, the maturity level of the first statement in CMM 4 can be considered.

The first statement is: "The assessment of risk is a standard procedure and exceptions to following the procedure would be noticed by security management."

If the organization is not at this maturity level, then the approach to achieving this element must be considered. Several requirements are implicit in this statement. One is that risk assessments are standard, formal procedures performed as a result of changes in systems, processes, threats or vulnerabilities and on a regular basis. It is also implicit that these assessments are based on good practices and are performed on entire processes, whether physical or electronic.

In addition, the statement implies that there is effective monitoring in place to ensure that the assessments are performed as required by policy.

First, there must be a policy that sets forth the requirement. If one exists that states it, then the requirement is addressed. Otherwise, one may need to be created or an existing policy modified.

An appropriate policy to address this requirement could state:

> *Information security risk must be assessed on a regular basis or as changes in conditions warrant utilizing standardized procedures and must include all relevant technologies and processes. Corporate security must be advised prior to commencement of such assessments, and the results of such assessments must be provided to corporate security upon completion.*

This policy should address the CMM 4 requirement for a standard procedure and a process to keep security management informed. A subsequent set of standards may need to be created to define the allowable boundaries and risk assessment requirements for various operational domains. An example of a standard is:

> High security domains comprising business-critical systems and/or confidential or protected information shall be assessed for risk annually, or more often, if there are:
> – Material changes in threats or potential impacts
> – Changes in hardware or software
> – Changes in business or objectives

Such assessments shall be the responsibility of the system or data owner, and shall be provided to corporate security for review on a timely basis. When possible, assessments shall be performed prior to implementing changes and provided to corporate security for approval of consistency with applicable policy.

The second statement in CMM 4 is: "Information security risk management is a defined management function with senior level responsibility."

To achieve this requirement, an organizational change may be necessary. Often, information security is relegated to low-level managers, which does not meet the objective. Based on the COBIT CMM model and the companion document titled "Governing for Enterprise Security," a strong business case can be made for implementing this structural change.

The third CMM criteria states: "Senior management and information security management have determined the levels of risk that the organization will tolerate and have standard measures for risk/return ratios."

A policy to address these criteria might state that risk must be managed to levels that prevent serious interruptions to critical business operations and control impacts to levels defined as acceptable.

Related standards would define limits of serious interruption and specify how the acceptable levels of impact would be determined. Standards also may set forth other definitions such as declarations criteria (who has the authority to declare an incident or disaster that requires appropriate responses) and severity criteria (a process to determine and define the severity of the event and escalation and notification requirements).

1.16.1 ADDITIONAL POLICY SAMPLES

Samples of policies that might be created to address some of the other CMM 4 statements could include:

- Clear assignment of roles and responsibilities—Roles and responsibilities of xyz Corporation shall be unambiguously defined and all required security functions formally assigned to ensure accountability. Acceptable performance shall be ensured by appropriate monitoring and metrics.
- Information assets that have been identified and classified by criticality and sensitivity—All information assets must have an identified owner and be cataloged, the value determined, and classified as to criticality and sensitivity throughout its life cycle.
- Effective controls that have been designed, implemented and maintained—Risk and potential impacts must be managed utilizing appropriate controls and countermeasures to achieve acceptable levels at acceptable costs.
- Effective monitoring processes in place—All important risk management, assurance and security activities must have processes to provide continuous monitoring necessary to ensure that control objectives are achieved.
- Effective compliance and enforcement processes—Monitoring and metrics must be implemented, managed and maintained to provide ongoing assurance that all security policies are enforced and control objectives are met.
- Tested, functional, incident and emergency response capabilities—Incident response capabilities sufficient to ensure that impacts do not materially affect the ability of the organization to continue operations must be implemented and managed.
- Tested business continuity/disaster recovery plans—Business continuity and disaster recovery plans shall be developed, maintained and tested in a manner that ensures the ability of the organization to continue operations under all conditions.

Most organizations have not achieved a consistent CMM 4 maturity level across the enterprise. This level is, however, usually sufficient to address the security needs of most organizations. It is also a difficult standard to achieve and may take a number of years to accomplish, but can serve as the objective—the desired state or reference model.

It should be noted that the foregoing sample policies may or may not be appropriate for a particular organization, but are provided as samples in terms of simple, clear construction—setting forth, at a high level, management intent and direction.

As has been previously stated, complete policies are necessary for effective information security governance. Construction, as provided in the samples, has, in practice, proven to be a preferable approach insofar as achieving management buy-in and general consensus. It must be remembered that policy construction must be consistent with, and reflect, the information security strategy and the desired state of security. The policies should also be reviewed and approved in writing by senior management.

The accompanying standards are typical examples, but must be tailored for the needs of individual organizations, and are generally not complete. Usually, multiple standards are required for each policy in each security domain.

Standards construction must be undertaken with care. Properly constructed, they provide consistent security baselines and a powerful tool for implementing information security governance.

Draft standards should be reviewed by the audit department and by affected organizational units. Audits are one of the primary policy enforcement and compliance mechanisms. Auditors' input into standards may be helpful in developing complete and effective standards, and may also assist them in performing their function. Collaboration with affected process owners is likely to achieve better cooperation with implementing proposed changes and help ensure that the standards do not needlessly interfere with the performance of their functions. While it may entail considerable give and take to achieve consensus on appropriate standards, the end result is greater alignment with business activities and better results in terms of ensuring compliance.

Implementing effective information security governance for most organizations requires a major initiative, given the often fragmented, tactical nature of typical security efforts. It requires committed support of senior management and adequate resources. It requires the elevation of security management to positions of authority equivalent to its responsibilities. This has been the trend in recent years as organizations grow totally dependent on their information assets and resources, and the threats and disruptions continue to escalate and become more costly.

1.17 ACTION PLAN INTERMEDIATE GOALS

For most organizations, a variety of specific near-term goals that align with the overall information security strategy can readily be defined once the overall strategy has been completed. Based on the BIA determination of business-critical resources and the state of security as determined by the foregoing CMM gap analysis, prioritization of remedial activities should be straightforward.

If the objectives of the security strategy are to achieve CMM 4 compliance or certification, then an example of a near-term action (or tactical) plan may state:
During the next 12 months:
- Each business unit must identify current applications in use
- Twenty-five percent of all stored information must be reviewed to determine ownership, criticality and sensitivity
- Each business unit will complete a BIA for information resources to identify critical resources
- Business units must achieve regulatory compliance
- All security roles and responsibilities must be defined
- A process will be developed to ensure business process linkages
- A comprehensive risk assessment must be performed for each business unit
- All users must be educated on an acceptable use policy
- All policies must be reviewed and revised as necessary for consistency with strategic security objectives
- Standards must exist for all policies

Near-term goals and milestones are required as part of the action plans; however, the long-term desired state needs to be clearly defined to maximize potential synergies and ensure that short- or intermediate-term action plans are ultimately aligned with the end goals. For example, a tactical solution that needs to be replaced because it will not integrate into the overall plan is likely to be more costly than one that will integrate.

It is important that the strategy and long-range plan serve to integrate near-term tactical activities. This counters the tendency to implement point solutions that are typical of the firefighting, crisis mode of operation in which many security departments find themselves. As many security managers have discovered, numerous unintegrated solutions, implemented in response to a series of crises over a period of years, become increasingly costly and difficult to manage.

1.18 INFORMATION SECURITY PROGRAM OBJECTIVES

Implementing the strategy with an action plan will result in an information security program. The program is, essentially, the project plan to implement and establish ongoing management of some part or parts of the strategy.

The objective of the information security program is to protect the interests of those relying on information and the processes, systems and communications that handle, store and deliver the information from harm, resulting from failures of availability, confidentiality and integrity.

While emerging definitions are adding concepts such as information usefulness and possession (the latter to cope with theft, deception and fraud), the networked economy certainly has added the need for trust and accountability in electronic transactions.

For most organizations, the security objective is met when:
- Information is available and usable when required, and the systems that provide it can appropriately resist attacks (availability)
- Information is observed by or disclosed to only those who have a right to know (confidentiality)
- Information is protected against unauthorized modification (integrity)
- Business transactions, as well as information exchanges between enterprise locations or with partners, can be trusted (authenticity and nonrepudiation)

The relative priority and significance of availability, confidentiality, integrity, authenticity and nonrepudiation vary according to the data within the information system and the business context in which they are used. For example, integrity is especially important relative to management information due to the impact that information has on critical strategy-related decisions. Confidentiality may be the most important based on regulatory or legal requirements regarding personal, financial or medical information or to protect trade secrets.

It is important to understand that these concepts apply equally to electronic systems as well as physical systems. Confidentiality, for example, is as much at risk from social engineering or “dumpster diving” as it is from a successful external attack. Additionally, integrity of information can be compromised at least as easily from forged physical inputs to the system as from electronic compromise.

It must also be considered that many significant losses occur from insiders as well as from external attacks. The result is that controls used to detect anomalies and ensure integrity of systems must be equally concerned with nontechnical attacks by insiders.

1.19 CASE STUDY

The following case study serves to graphically demonstrate the requirement for security governance discussed in this chapter. The case illustrates how disasters are typically caused by a sequence of failures and is a study of a dysfunctional organizational structure and culture. Failure to learn from this situation (and several other significant incidences) and take the corrective actions recommended by the seasoned external postmortem team undoubtedly contributed to the ultimate demise of this financial organization of more than 45,000 employees during the economic downturn of 2008-2009.

In a major US financial institution, low-level personnel monitoring the network operation center (NOC) noticed unusual network activity on a Sunday evening when the bank was closed. Puzzled and uncertain what they were seeing, and with no instructions to the contrary, they decided to watch the event rather than risk disturbing management on a weekend. No severity criteria, notification requirements or escalation processes had been developed by the organization. By early morning on Monday, traffic continued to increase at the main facility and then suddenly began to grow dramatically at the mirror site, hundreds of miles away. Despite having been advised of the risk by a security consultant, the IT manager (when questioned by the author of this case study), stated with a degree of pride that the totally flat network had been designed for high performance and he was confident that his experienced team could handle any adverse eventuality.

By 7 a.m. on Monday, the NOC personnel were sufficiently concerned to notify the IT managers that there was a problem and that the monitors showed the network was becoming saturated. An hour later when the external computer incident response team (CIRT) arrived, the network was totally inoperative and the team determined that the network had in fact been compromised by the Slammer worm. The CIRT team manager informed the IT manager that Slammer was memory resident and that restarting the entire network and mirror facility would resolve the issue. The manager stated that he did not have the authority to shut down the system and it would require the CIO to issue that instruction. The CIO could not be located and current emergency phone and pager numbers were only kept in a new emergency paging system that required network access. When asked about the disaster recovery plan (DRP) and what it had to say regarding declaration criteria, three different plans were produced that had been prepared by teams in different parts of the organization, unbeknownst to each other. None contained declaration criteria or specified roles, responsibilities or authority. The final resolution ultimately required the CEO, who was traveling overseas and also not immediately available, to finally issue instructions the next morning (Tuesday) to shut down the nonfunctioning network. Over thirty thousand people could not perform their work and the institution was inoperative for a full day and a half. The final direct costs were estimated by the postmortem team to exceed fifty million US dollars. The postmortem was hampered by stonewalling and lack of cooperation from most employees, fearful of being found at fault in the blame-oriented organizational culture.

The author of this case managed the postmortem team that found literally hundreds of deficient processes, a dysfunctional culture and an array of useless metrics in addition to a fatally flawed lack of adequate governance. For those monitoring the NOC, metrics indicated a problem, but they were not sufficiently meaningful to the employees for them to make any active decisions, much less the correct ones. Either better metrics or greater proficiency of the personnel could have resolved the issue quickly in the initial stages of the incident before it became a problem. Better governance would have vested adequate authority in the network manager to take the appropriate action. Better governance would have insisted that either the vulnerability patches issued a full two months prior were applied or suitable compensatory controls were implemented to address a well-known threat. Even marginally effective risk management would have insisted that a flat network with no segmentation was unacceptable and that DRP/BCP was an integrated and tested activity.

The conclusions that can be reached that are relevant to metrics and governance are that data are not information and that incomprehensible information is just data and useless. This case also illustrates that no matter how good the metrics and monitoring that provide decision support, they are useless to someone not empowered to make decisions.

As a consequence, to develop useful metrics, it must be clear what decisions must be made by whom and what information is needed to make them. It is apparent from this analysis that management metrics will typically require a variety of information from different sources that then must be synthesized to provide meaningful information needed for making decisions about what actions are required.

This case is demonstrative of the necessity for organizations to develop and implement both information security governance and the concomitant requirement to develop useful metrics.

Certified Information Security Manager®
An ISACA® Certification

Chapter 2:

Information Risk Management and Compliance

Section One: Overview

Section Two: Content

Section One: Overview

2.1 INTRODUCTION

This chapter reviews the knowledge base that the information security manager must understand in order to appropriately apply risk management principles and practices to an organization's information security program.

DEFINITION

ISO Guide 73:2009 defines risk as the "effect of uncertainty on objectives." It should be noted that this is a recent definition subject to considerable controversy. The traditional definition that many practitioners consider more useful is Threats × Vulnerabilities = Risk, or T × V = R.

Regardless of the choice of definition, information risk management is the systematic application of management policies, procedures and practices to the tasks of identifying, analyzing, evaluating, reporting, treating and monitoring information related risk.

OBJECTIVES

The objective of this domain is to ensure that the information security manager understands the importance of risk management as a tool for meeting business needs and developing a security management program to support these needs. While information security governance defines the links between business goals and objectives and the information security program, information risk management defines the extent of protection that is prudent based on business requirements, objectives and priorities.

The objective of risk management is to identify, analyze, quantify, report and manage information related risk to achieve business objectives through a number of tasks utilizing the information security manager's knowledge of key risk management techniques. Because information security is one component of enterprise risk management, the techniques, methods and metrics used to define information risk may need to be viewed within the larger context of organizational risk. As indicated in chapter 1, information risk management also needs to incorporate human resource, operational, physical, geopolitical and environmental risk.

This domain represents 33 percent of the CISM examination (approximately 66 questions).

2.2 TASK AND KNOWLEDGE STATEMENTS

Domain 2—Information Risk Management and Compliance
Manage information risk to an acceptable level to meet the business and compliance requirements of the organization

TASKS

There are nine tasks within this domain that a CISM candidate must know how to perform:

- T2.1 Establish and maintain a process for information asset classification to ensure that measures taken to protect assets are proportional to their business value.
- T2.2 Identify legal, regulatory, organizational and other applicable requirements to manage the risk of noncompliance to acceptable levels.
- T2.3 Ensure that risk assessments, vulnerability assessments and threat analyses are conducted periodically and consistently to identify risk to the organization's information.
- T2.4 Determine appropriate risk treatment options to manage risk to acceptable levels.
- T2.5 Evaluate information security controls to determine whether they are appropriate and effectively mitigate risk to an acceptable level.
- T2.6 Identify the gap between current and desired risk levels to manage risk to an acceptable level.
- T2.7 Integrate information risk management into business and IT processes (for example, development, procurement, project management, mergers and acquisitions) to promote a consistent and comprehensive information risk management process across the organization.
- T2.8 Monitor existing risk to ensure that changes are identified and managed appropriately.
- T2.9 Report noncompliance and other changes in information risk to appropriate management to assist in the risk management decision-making process.

KNOWLEDGE STATEMENTS

The CISM candidate must have a good understanding of each of the areas delineated by the knowledge statements. These statements are the basis for the exam.

There are 19 knowledge statements within the information risk management and compliance domain:

- KS2.1 Knowledge of methods to establish an information asset classification model consistent with business objectives
- KS2.2 Knowledge of methods used to assign the responsibilities for and ownership of information assets and risk
- KS2.3 Knowledge of methods to evaluate the impact of adverse events on the business
- KS2.4 Knowledge of information asset valuation methodologies
- KS2.5 Knowledge of legal, regulatory, organizational and other requirements related to information security
- KS2.6 Knowledge of reputable, reliable and timely sources of information regarding emerging information security threats and vulnerabilities
- KS2.7 Knowledge of events that may require risk reassessments and changes to information security program elements
- KS2.8 Knowledge of information threats, vulnerabilities and exposures and their evolving nature
- KS2.9 Knowledge of risk assessment and analysis methodologies
- KS2.10 Knowledge of methods used to prioritize risk
- KS2.11 Knowledge of risk reporting requirements (for example, frequency, audience, components)
- KS2.12 Knowledge of methods used to monitor risk
- KS2.13 Knowledge of risk treatment strategies and methods to apply them
- KS2.14 Knowledge of control baseline modeling and its relationship to risk-based assessments
- KS2.15 Knowledge of information security controls and countermeasures and the methods to analyze their effectiveness and efficiency
- KS2.16 Knowledge of gap analysis techniques as related to information security
- KS2.17 Knowledge of techniques for integrating risk management into business and IT processes
- KS2.18 Knowledge of compliance reporting processes and requirements
- KS2.19 Knowledge of cost/benefit analysis to assess risk treatment options

RELATIONSHIP OF TASK TO KNOWLEDGE STATEMENTS

The task statements are what the CISM candidate is expected to know how to perform. The knowledge statements delineate each of the areas in which the CISM candidate must have a good understanding in order to perform the tasks. The task and knowledge statements are mapped in **exhibit 2.1**, insofar as it is possible to do so. Note that although there is often overlap, each task statement will generally map to several knowledge statements.

Exhibit 2.1—Task and Knowledge Statements Mapping

Task Statement	Knowledge Statements
T2.1 Establish and maintain a process for information asset classification to ensure that measures taken to protect assets are proportional to their business value.	KS2.1 Knowledge of methods to establish an information asset classification model consistent with business objectives KS2.2 Knowledge of methods used to assign the responsibilities for and ownership of information assets and risk KS2.3 Knowledge of methods to evaluate the impact of adverse events on the business KS2.4 Knowledge of information asset valuation methodologies
T2.2 Identify legal, regulatory, organizational and other applicable requirements to manage the risk of noncompliance to acceptable levels.	KS2.5 Knowledge of legal, regulatory, organizational and other requirements related to information security KS2.14 Knowledge of control baseline modeling and its relationship to risk-based assessments
T2.3 Ensure that risk assessments, vulnerability assessments and threat analyses are conducted periodically and consistently to identify risk to the organization's information.	KS2.6 Knowledge of reputable, reliable and timely sources of information regarding emerging information security threats and vulnerabilities KS2.7 Knowledge of events that may require risk reassessments and changes to information security program elements KS2.8 Knowledge of information threats, vulnerabilities and exposures and their evolving nature KS2.9 Knowledge of risk assessment and analysis methodologies KS2.11 Knowledge of risk reporting requirements (for example, frequency, audience, components) KS2.14 Knowledge of control baseline modeling and its relationship to risk-based assessments
T2.4 Determine appropriate risk treatment options to manage risk to acceptable levels.	KS2.10 Knowledge of methods used to prioritize risk KS2.13 Knowledge of risk treatment strategies and methods to apply them KS2.19 Knowledge of cost/benefit analysis to assess risk treatment options
T2.5 Evaluate information security controls to determine whether they are appropriate and effectively mitigate risk to an acceptable level.	KS2.14 Knowledge of control baseline modeling and its relationship to risk-based assessments KS2.15 Knowledge of information security controls and countermeasures and the methods to analyze their effectiveness and efficiency
T2.6 Identify the gap between current and desired risk levels to manage risk to an acceptable level.	KS2.9 Knowledge of risk assessment and analysis methodologies KS2.10 Knowledge of methods used to prioritize risk KS2.16 Knowledge of gap analysis techniques as related to information security
T2.7 Integrate information risk management into business and IT processes (for example, development, procurement, project management, mergers and acquisitions) to promote a consistent and comprehensive information risk management process across the organization.	KS2.10 Knowledge of methods used to prioritize risk KS2.15 Knowledge of information security controls and countermeasures and the methods to analyze their effectiveness and efficiency KS2.17 Knowledge of techniques for integrating risk management into business and IT processes
T2.8 Monitor existing risk to ensure that changes are identified and managed appropriately.	KS2.12 Knowledge of methods used to monitor risk
T2.9 Report noncompliance and other changes in information risk to appropriate management to assist in the risk management decision-making process.	KS2.11 Knowledge of risk reporting requirements (for example, frequency, audience, components) KS2.18 Knowledge of compliance reporting processes and requirements

KNOWLEDGE STATEMENT REFERENCE GUIDE

The following section contains the knowledge statements and the underlying concepts and relevance for the knowledge of the information security manager. The knowledge statements are what the information security manager must know in order to accomplish the tasks. A summary explanation of each knowledge statement is provided, followed by the basic concepts that are the foundation for the written exam . Each key concept has references to section two of this chapter.

The CISM body of knowledge has been divided into four domains, and each of the four chapters covers some of the material contained in those domains. This chapter reviews the body of knowledge from the perspective of managing risk.

KS2.1 Knowledge of methods to establish an information asset classification model consistent with business objectives

Explanation	Key Concepts	Reference in 2015 CISM Review Manual
A classification schema is developed to define the various degrees of sensitivity and/or criticality of information that is in the care, control or custody of an organization. It serves to prioritize protection efforts and provides a basis for the degree of protection assigned to an information asset. It provides a basis to establish proportionality between the level of control and the asset value In order to avoid the cost of overprotecting or the risk of underprotecting information assets. A classification schema also facilitates effective business continuity and disaster recovery planning by identifying the most critical and sensitive information assets. Without proper criteria and a consistent process to map the sensitivity and criticality of information resources, it will not be possible to develop a cost-effective risk management program. Typically, organizations will use three or four levels of classification such as public, internal, confidential and perhaps secret. The classification schema must provide guidance on how those levels should be determined by resource owners as well as detail the level of protection that each classification requires. Criticality refers to the importance of information assets and processes to organizational activities. Sensitivity is related to the potential damage from unintended disclosure of private or confidential information such as trade secrets or protected personal data. Criticality can often be determined on a reasonably quantitative basis since the financial losses incurred as the result of the failure of a particular business function can be determined. Sensitivity is usually assessed primarily by qualitative measures.	The purpose of information asset classification	2.6.1 Ensure Asset Identification, Classification and Ownership 2.11.3 Information Asset Classification
	The requirement for asset classification in managing risk	2.11.3 Information Asset Classification 2.14 Security Control Baselines
	Determining the basis for classifications	2.11.3 Information Asset Classification
	The benefits of information asset classification	2.11.3 Information Asset Classification
	The relationship of classification to business continuity planning (BCP) and disaster recovery (DR)	2.11.3 Information Asset Classification
	The connection between classification, incident severity levels and declaration criteria	2.11.3 Information Asset Classification
	The relationship of classification to custodians, controls, monitoring, compliance, risk and impact	2.11.3 Information Asset Classification
	The purpose of determining sensitivity and criticality	2.4 Risk Management Overview 2.10.12 Impact 2.14 Security Control Baselines
	Methods for determining sensitivity and criticality	2.10.12 Impact 2.11.3 Information Asset Classification
	Approaches to determining potential impact	2.4 Risk Management Overview 2.4.1 The Importance of Risk Management 2.4.2 Outcomes of Risk Management 2.10.8 Analysis of Relevant Risk 2.10.9 Evaluation of Risk 2.10.12 Impact
	The relationships between risk, impact, sensitivity, and criticality	2.10.11 Impact

KS2.2 Knowledge of methods used to assign the responsibilities for and ownership of information assets and risk

Explanation	Key Concepts	Reference in 2015 CISM Review Manual
Accountability for ensuring compliance with policies and standards requires that a defined owner is identified for all information assets. The ownership schema consists of the policies (and standards), structure and practices that define owners, their roles and their responsibilities. It must also detail the requirements for custodians and users of information. Ensuring that systems all have identified owners also facilitates the assignment of risk. Risk is frequently tied to one or more systems, applications or processes. As such it is important to identify risk ownership based on the nature of the risk to be mitigated. Ownership should be established at the system, application, process and data levels. Risk ownership is important to ensure that there is accountability to see that the risk is mitigated or otherwise treated as required by organizational risk management guidelines.	The reason and purpose of ownership policies and structure	1.10.1 The Goal 2.6.1 Developing a Risk Management Program 2.6.2 Roles and Responsibilities 3.9.1 Operational Components
	Responsibility for ensuring that proper controls are in place	2.6.1 Developing a Risk Management Program 2.6.2 Roles and Responsibilities
	Elements of an ownership schema	1.10.1 The Goal 2.6.1 Developing a Risk Management Program 2.6.2 Roles and Responsibilities 3.14.5 Management of Security Technology 3.14.9 Outsourcing and Service Providers 1.7.4 Risk Management Metrics

KS2.3 Knowledge of methods to evaluate the impact of adverse events on the business

Explanation	Key Concepts	Reference in 2015 CISM Review Manual
Business impact assessment (BIA) and analysis is the primary process to determine the impact of the loss of an organizational function. Evaluating the impact involves a number of considerations including the effect on other operations that depend on the function that has failed. The escalation of loss over time must also be considered, i.e., loss may not be linear as a function of time but may grow exponentially. The possible cyclical nature of loss is another aspect to evaluate as this may affect the priority of remedial actions and restoration. An example of this is the urgency of recovering finance functions toward the end of a quarter based on regulatory reporting requirements. While impacts will generally be assessed in financial terms, some aspects such as the impact of reputational damage or regulatory sanctions cannot be accurately quantified in strictly monetary terms. Managing potential impacts to an acceptable level is ultimately the objective for managing risk. Knowledge of criticality and sensitivity is also needed in determining incident severity levels as well as incident management and response requirements.	Business impact assessment and evaluation	2.4 Risk Management Overview 2.10.12 Impact
	Financial aspects of impacts	2.10.12 Impact
	Nonfinancial impacts	2.10.12 Impact

KS2.4 Knowledge of information asset valuation methodologies

Explanation	Key Concepts	Reference in 2015 CISM Review Manual
The valuation process is used to determine the actual or relative value of information assets. The principal of proportionality, which determines a reasonable cost of protecting assets in relationship to their value, is not possible without implementing a valuation process. The relative value of an information asset is usually related to its criticality or sensitivity, but may not be related to its actual cost. Inexpensive equipment may process mission-critical information and therefore have a high criticality and require a high level of assurance of continued operation. High-cost systems may be used to process noncritical information, but require a high level of protection for the equipment itself against damage or theft. All three parameters (cost, criticality and sensitivity) must be known in order to define and prioritize risk and appropriate methods to mitigate risk.	The purpose and benefits of information asset valuation	2.11 Information Resource Valuation 2.11.2 Information Resource Valuation Methodologies
	The relationship of valuation and impact assessment	2.11 Information Resource Valuation 2.11.1 Information Resource Valuation Strategies
	The basis for performing information asset valuation	2.11 Information Resource Valuation 2.11.1 Information Resource Valuation Strategies 2.11.2 Information Resource Valuation Methodologies
	Asset valuation methodologies	2.10 Risk Assessment 2.11.2 Information Resource Valuation Methodologies

KS2.5 Knowledge of legal, regulatory, organizational and other requirements related to information security

Explanation	Key Concepts	Reference in 2015 CISM Review Manual
Legal and regulatory requirements must be considered in terms of risk and impact. This is necessary in order to determine the appropriate level of compliance and priority. For example, a large multinational organization is likely to be subject to Payment Card Industry (PCI) Data Security Standards (DSS) requirements as well as Sarbanes-Oxley regulations if its shares are traded on a US stock exchange. It may also need to be compliant with the US Health Insurance Portability and Accountability Act (HIPAA) and the EU Privacy Directive. In addition, there may be a number of other regulations in other jurisdictions that must be considered. These regulations must be evaluated on the basis of the risk they pose to the organization insofar as the level of enforcement and the relative position of the organization in relation to its peers; regulators will tend to concentrate enforcement on the least compliant and most visible organizations. The potential impact on the organization in both financial and reputational impacts must be evaluated as well. These evaluations provide the basis for senior management to determine the nature and extent of compliance activities appropriate for the organization. The information security manager must be aware that management may decide that risking sanctions is less costly than achieving compliance; that compliance is not binary and the decision may be to initiate these activities on a very limited basis; or that enforcement is so limited or nonexistent that compliance is not warranted.	Legal and regulatory considerations in a risk management strategy	2.5 Risk Management Strategy 2.10.14 Legal and Regulatory Requirements 2.11.3 Information Asset Classification
	Operational compliance risk	2.10.7 Risk
	Legal and regulatory considerations for asset classification	2.10.14 Legal and Regulatory Requirements 2.11.3 Information Asset Classification

KS2.6 Knowledge of reputable, reliable and timely sources of information regarding emerging information security threats and vulnerabilities

Explanation	Key Concepts	Reference in 2015 CISM Review Manual
Many sources of information regarding potential threats and vulnerabilities are available to the information security manager. These resources should be regularly monitored to provide timely warnings of new vulnerabilities in systems and software and new outbreaks of malware as well as other criminal activity such as phishing and pharming. Some of these organizations include CERT and Australian Computer Emergency Response Team (AusCERT), Network Storm Center, SANS, Computerworld, TechRepublic and others, including security vendors and software and hardware manufacturers.	External risk reporting sources	2.8.8 Other Organizational Support

KS2.7 Knowledge of events that may require risk reassessments and changes to information security program elements

Explanation	Key Concepts	Reference in 2015 CISM Review Manual
Many circumstances can create the need to reassess risk, such as new threats or newly discovered vulnerabilities; changes in architectures or business requirements; new legal or regulatory requirements; or security incidents demonstrating that prior risk assessments were inaccurate. Security baselines set by appropriate standards are the minimum security requirements for different trust domains across the enterprise. These baselines may need to change for a variety of reasons, such as the impacts from incidents growing unacceptably high or the threat landscape changing and posing new or greater risk. Baselines also may need to change as a result of new vulnerabilities introduced into systems because of changes to the organization such as mergers or acquisitions. Changes may also be required as the result of new contractual or regulatory requirements mandating improved levels of security, such as what occurred with the imposition of the Payment Card Industry (PCI) standards. These and other events that change the threat, vulnerability, exposure or impact equation will require the reassessment of risk to determine the appropriate treatment and mitigation requirements.	Purposes for creating security baselines	2.10.16 Events Affecting Security Baselines 2.14 Security Control Baselines 3.15.11 Baseline Controls
	Methods for establishing security baselines	3.15.11 Baseline Controls
	Assessing adequacy of security baselines	2.10.16 Events Affecting Security Baselines 2.14 Security Control Baselines 3.15.11 Baseline Controls

KS2.8 Knowledge of information threats, vulnerabilities and exposures and their evolving nature

Explanation	Key Concepts	Reference in 2015 CISM Review Manual
It is essential for the information security manager to understand the components of risk and the differences between threats, vulnerabilities and exposures. Threats are usually defined as any process, entity or event that can cause harm. Vulnerabilities are any weakness that can be exploited by a threat. Exposure refers to the extent to which an organization may be affected by a risk. It is critical that sound processes are developed to determine viable threats that the organization faces on a timely basis and both the logical and physical vulnerabilities that might be exploited by those threats. Threats, vulnerabilities and exposures are not static, but change based on the dynamic nature of the environment, technology and business. Regular reviews must be conducted to ensure that appropriate changes are made to address evolving risk.	The nature and kind of threats to information	2.8.1 Risk Management Process 2.8.3 Defining the External Environment 2.10.5 Threats
	Internal and external threats	2.8.3 Defining the External Environment 2.8.4 Defining the Internal Environment
	Assessing threats and risk	2.9 Risk Assessment and Analysis Methodologies 2.10 Risk Assessment
	Vulnerabilities	2.10.6 Vulnerabilities
	The components of risk assessment and risk analysis	2.10.7 Risk 2.10.8 Analysis of Relevant Risk 2.10.9 Evaluation of Risk

KS2.9 Knowledge of risk assessment and analysis methodologies

Explanation	Key Concepts	Reference in 2015 CISM Review Manual
Risk assessment and analysis is a fundamental requirement upon which all risk management activities are based. Assessing and analyzing risk to information assets is a central activity of the information security manager; risk management is the primary driver for all information security activities. Although there are many approaches to assessing and quantifying risk, all are based on understanding that both a threat and a corresponding vulnerability must exist for there to be a potential risk. When a threat is capable of exploiting a vulnerability, a risk exists. While there are qualitative, semiquantitative and quantitative approaches to assessing risk, all assessments of risk are similar, and to an extent, both subjective and speculative. When analyzing risk, this uncertainty has to be factored into the equation in respect to both frequency and magnitude of possible occurrence. Presentation of risk is often more effective if provided in terms of both maximum potential impact and probable impact. The information security manager also has to consider the aggregation of risk, which can result in some acceptable risk being exploited at the same time, collectively resulting in a potentially unacceptable impact. Another consideration is cascading risk, which is based on system and process interdependencies that can cause one exploitation to result in a domino effect of failing systems and processes.	The purpose of risk assessment and analysis	2.4 Risk Management Overview 2.6.2 Roles and Responsibilities
	Approaches to assessing and analyzing risk	2.8.1 Risk Management Process 2.8.2 Defining a Risk Management Framework 2.9 Risk Assessment and Analysis Methodologies 2.10 Risk Assessment 2.10.1 NIST Risk Assessment Methodology 2.10.2 Aggregated and Cascading Risk 2.10.3 Other Risk Assessment Approaches
	The components of risk assessment	2.8.2 Defining a Risk Management Framework 2.10.2 Aggregated and Cascading Risk
	Qualitative and quantitative assessments and analysis	2.10.8 Analysis of Relevant Risk

KS2.10 Knowledge of methods used to prioritize risk

Explanation	Key Concepts	Reference in 2015 CISM Review Manual
Possible risk is virtually unlimited. As a consequence, it is essential for the information security manager to develop processes to rank and prioritize risk based on several factors. These will include: • proximity and nature of the threat • extent that vulnerability exists • exposure of the organization to the risk • avenues of potential exploit • potential impact if the threat materializes • frequency a vulnerability can be exploited • extent of aggregated risk • potential for cascading risk The choice of approaches to prioritization should be based on sources, extent and reliability of information. All possible threats can never be known with any certainty while the degree of vulnerability can be ascertained with possibly greater reliability. Impact of the loss of certain organizational functions can usually be determined with some accuracy. Consequently, it is important to utilize the best mix of information coupled with the availability of cost-effective remediation options to prioritize risk.	Prioritizing based on frequency and magnitude	2.4 Risk Management Overview
	Evaluation based on potential impact	2.10.12 Impact 2.10.15 Costs and Benefits
	Determining likelihood	2.10.8 Analysis of Relevant Risk
	Prioritizing by cost-effectiveness of treatment options	2.10.10 Risk Treatment Options

KS2.11 Knowledge of risk reporting requirements (for example, frequency, audience, components)

Explanation	Key Concepts	Reference in 2015 CISM Review Manual
It is important for the information security manager to ensure that there is an established process and standard for reporting the state of information risk and its management on both a regular and event-driven basis. There are number of factors that will determine what is reported, to whom it is reported and when it is reported. These factors will be based on the type of organization, its culture, acceptable risk and risk tolerance, the regulatory and legal environment, and the severity, likelihood and potential consequences of risk. The various aspects and criteria of risk reporting should be defined and approved by management. The reporting process and structure should include which reports are provided to various parts of the organization on a regular basis, and the type and nature of changes in risk that must be reported. Regular reporting can serve both to communicate risk status and also as a reminder of collective responsibilities for managing risk across the organization.	The requirement for regular reporting of risk	2.5.1 Risk Communication, Risk Awareness and Consulting 2.15 Risk Monitoring and Communication 2.15.3 Reporting Significant Changes in Risk
	The kinds of events that should be reported or escalated	2.15 Risk Monitoring and Communication 2.15.3 Reporting Significant Changes in Risk
	Reporting contents to various organizational levels and recipients	2.15 Risk Monitoring and Communication 2.15.3 Reporting Significant Changes in Risk
	Key risk indicators (KRIs) and monitoring	2.15 Risk Monitoring and Communication 2.15.3 Reporting Significant Changes in Risk

KS2.12 Knowledge of methods used to monitor risk

Explanation	Key Concepts	Reference in 2015 CISM Review Manual
Since a change in either threat, vulnerability or exposure will change risk, monitoring or measuring any one or a combination can serve as a risk indicator. The concept of key risk indicators (KRI) is that certain changes internally or externally should be monitored based on their ability to provide an early warning of changes in risk. An example could be a sudden rise in emergency change requests or a significant increase in employee turnover in a particular department. Either event could signal a changing situation that should be investigated by the information security manager to determine the cause and implications for risk. Effective monitoring of security processes and related metrics provides the essential information required for successful management of an information security program. People, processes and technologies must all be monitored on a basis consistent with their degree of sensitivity and criticality. Key controls require continuous monitoring to ensure that they are functioning properly. Monitoring methods vary considerably and can range from CCTV monitors to host-based intrusion detection systems (HIDS) and network intrusion detection systems (NIDS) for detecting intrusion attempts. Many monitoring approaches can entail significant overhead from both IT resource and labor perspectives. To address this concern, automated methods such as Security Information and Event Management (SIEM) tools can reduce monitoring overhead. Important monitoring activities can also include geopolitical risk and personnel turnover, both of which may signal increasing risk levels. Prioritization of monitoring activities must be based on degree of assessed risk and level of potential impact.	Risk assessment and security posture	2.8.1 Risk Management Process 2.9 Risk Assessment and Analysis Methodologies 2.10 Risk Assessment 2.10.8 Analysis of Relevant Risk 2.15.1 Risk Monitoring
	Determining current risk posture	2.6.1 Developing a Risk Management Program 2.6.2 Roles and Responsibilities 2.15.3 Reporting Significant Changes in Risk
	What should be monitored	2.15.1 Risk Monitoring 3.16.2 Monitoring Approaches
	Monitoring key controls	3.16 Security Program Metrics and Monitoring
	Physical and technical monitoring	3.16 Security Program Metrics and Monitoring

KS2.13 Knowledge of risk treatment strategies and methods to apply them

Explanation	Key Concepts	Reference in 2015 CISM Review Manual
The selection of a risk treatment strategy should be based on a variety of factors. These include the magnitude and frequency of the potential manifestation of the risk and the potential impact. The potential impact is a function of the criticality or sensitivity of the resource. The treatment options include accepting the risk, mitigating the risk, transferring the risk or ceasing the activity that creates the risk. Mitigation, or reducing, the risk is based on three primary considerations: the availability of required resources, constraints such as regulatory requirements, time and financial resources, and an assessment of the cost-effectiveness of the approach under consideration. It is important for the security manager to ensure that the strategy selected maximizes resource utilization while still achieving the desired reduction of risk. Risk mitigation usually incurs costs in design, implementation and maintenance. In some cases, certain activities such as process reengineering may serve to reduce the risk associated with certain activities and ultimately result in cost savings as well. However, with any activity, there are expenses that must be considered, including such things as special training related to the new control as well as possible costs associated with reduced productivity. To develop and implement a risk management strategy, it is necessary to understand the current security posture of the organization as well as the "desired state" or objectives of the program. The desired state is typically defined in terms of standards of good practice, such as ISO/IEC 27002:2013. Gap analysis between the current state and the desired state will show what must be accomplished in order to move toward the objectives. Some aspects of the desired state can be quantified, but a qualitative approach to define both the current and future states will be needed as well. This can be accomplished using tools such as the capability maturity model (CMM). There are also many organizations that use a balanced scorecard (BSC) approach, which combines both quantitative and qualitative approaches.	Treatment options	2.10.10 Risk Treatment Options
	Risk mitigation	2.10.10 Risk Treatment Options
	Impact mitigation	2.10.10 Risk Treatment Options 2.10.12 Impact
	Threat countermeasures	2.10.5 Threats 2.10.10 Risk Treatment Options
	Vulnerability management	2.10.6 Vulnerabilities 2.10.10 Risk Treatment Options

KS2.14 Knowledge of control baseline modeling and its relationship to risk-based assessments

Explanation	Key Concepts	Reference in 2015 CISM Review Manual
Control baselines set the minimum security for systems, processes and people. Baselines should be based on security classifications with higher or more secure baselines set for resources of greater criticality or sensitivity because they pose the risk of greater adverse impact on the organization.	Risk management issues related to life cycles	2.10.3 Other Risk Assessment Approaches 2.13 Integration With Life Cycle Processes 2.13.1 Risk Management for IT System Development Life Cycle 2.13.2 Life Cycle-based Risk Management Principles and Practices 2.14 Security Control Baselines 3.15.11 Baseline Controls
	Information life cycles	2.11.3 Information Asset Classification
	Change management and life cycles	2.13 Integration With Life Cycle Processes 2.13.1 Risk Management for IT System Development Life Cycle 2.13.2 Life Cycle-based Risk Management Principles and Practices

KS2.15 Knowledge of information security controls and countermeasures and the methods to analyze their effectiveness and efficiency

Explanation	Key Concepts	Reference in 2015 CISM Review Manual
Controls are any regulatory process, device or technology. Controls are the primary process by which risk is mitigated. It is essential that the information security manager has a thorough understanding of control design, testing and implementation. Since controls, no matter how well devised, tend to degrade over time, it is also essential that the information security manager understands how to monitor and measure their effectiveness and efficiency on an ongoing basis.	Controls design considerations	2.4 Risk Management Overview 3.15.2 Control Design Considerations
	Testing and evaluating controls	2.10.15 Costs and Benefits 3.15.2 Control Design Considerations 3.15.3 Control Strength
	Layering controls	2.10.6 Vulnerabilities
Both technical and procedural information security controls must be assessed periodically to determine whether they still effectively meet the original control objectives. Since it is normal for control effectiveness to degrade over time, it is important to reassess them periodically. Another consideration is that controls often evolve over time in response to particular events that may no longer be relevant or related to current control objectives. Controls that are no longer needed or ineffective should be removed or modified to improve efficiency. Evaluating control effectiveness should include consideration for adverse impacts on usability and other human factors. Controls that are needlessly complex or difficult will often be circumvented, seriously affecting their effectiveness. In many organizations, controls are developed over extended periods of time, often in a reactive response to a security-related event or incident. The rationale for these controls is typically not documented and the controls simply become the accepted practice, whether the need for them still exists or other redundant controls have been implemented. An ongoing requirement for effective information security management is to ensure that all controls—whether technical, physical or procedural—are documented, meet defined control objectives, and are periodically tested both for cost and for effectiveness. Methods utilized to test controls should be objective, consistent and cost effective.	Determining control strength	3.15.3 Control Strength

KS2.16 Knowledge of gap analysis techniques as related to information security

Explanation	Key Concepts	Reference in 2015 CISM Review Manual
Gap analysis in the risk management context generally involves the analysis of difference between existing controls and control objectives or the gap between the existing risk management program and the desired program. The objectives of risk management activities should have been determined in the course of developing an information security strategy as discussed in chapter 1. These objectives can be stated in terms of capabilities and effectiveness in achieving acceptable levels of risk within acceptable tolerances at acceptable costs	Controls and control objectives	2.8.7 Gap Analysis 3.15 Controls and Countermeasures
	Assessing the gap between current and desired state	2.8.7 Gap Analysis
	Risk assessment and security posture	2.8.1 Risk Management Process 2.9 Risk Assessment and Analysis Methodologies 2.10 Risk Assessment 2.10.8 Analysis of Relevant Risk
To develop and implement a risk management strategy, it is necessary to understand the current security posture of the organization as well as the "desired state" or objectives of the program. The desired state is typically defined in terms of standards of good practice, such as ISO/IEC 27002:2013. Gap analysis between the current state and the desired state will show what must be accomplished in order to move toward the objectives. Some aspects of the desired state can be quantified, but a qualitative approach to define both the current and future states will be needed as well. This can be accomplished using tools such as the capability maturity model (CMM). There are also many organizations that use a balanced scorecard (BSC) approach, which combines both quantitative and qualitative approaches.	Determining current risk posture	2.6.1 Developing a Risk Management Program 2.6.2 Roles and Responsibilities 2.15.3 Reporting Significant Changes in Risk

KS2.17 Knowledge of techniques for integrating risk management into business and IT processes

Explanation	Key Concepts	Reference in 2015 CISM Review Manual
Risk management is a fundamental requirement in all business and IT processes. Risk changes significantly during the life cycle of resources and as business processes and procedures change. For example, risk associated with the feasibility and design phases of a project is very different from the risk that occurs during the implementation and deployment phases. Some of the primary processes to expose and manage risk include change and release management, quality assurance (QA) and user acceptance testing (UAT). The information security manager must ensure that such processes exist so that risk is identified and managed during the various life cycle stages of technologies, physical assets and processes. In addition, it is necessary to ensure that processes, procedures and practices throughout the organization are assessed for risk. Based on this assessment, the information security manager has a basis for determining the appropriate means to manage risk through implementing the various options for treating risk.	Risk management issues related to life cycles	2.10.3 Other Risk Assessment Approaches 2.13 Integration With Life Cycle Processes 2.13.1 Risk Management for IT System Development Life Cycle 2.13.2 Life Cycle-based Risk Management Principles and Practices
	Information life cycles	2.13.2 Life Cycle-based Risk Management Principles and Practices
	Change management and life cycles	2.13 Integration With Life Cycle Processes 2.13.1 Risk Management for IT System Development Life Cycle 2.13.2 Life Cycle-based Risk Management Principles and Practices

KS2.18 Knowledge of compliance reporting processes and requirements

Explanation	Key Concepts	Reference in 2015 CISM Review Manual
The necessity for compliance with legal and regulatory requirements is becoming increasingly common for many organizations. While the extent of compliance and the processes and resources allocated are decisions that must be made by senior management, it is typically a part of the information security manager's responsibilities to execute the elements that involve the various aspects of information security. Reporting on the achievement of compliance milestones will typically be required and should be established in consultation with senior management.	Risk management issues related to life cycles	2.10.3 Other Risk Assessment Approaches 2.13 Integration With Life Cycle Processes 2.13.1 Risk Management for IT System Development Life Cycle 2.13.2 Life Cycle-based Risk Management Principles and Practices
	Information life cycles	2.11.3 Information Asset Classification
	Change management and life cycles	2.13 Integration With Life Cycle Processes 2.13.1 Risk Management for IT System Development Life Cycle 2.13.2 Life Cycle-based Risk Management Principles and Practices

KS2.19 Knowledge of cost/benefit analysis to assess risk treatment options

Explanation	Key Concepts	Reference in 2015 CISM Review Manual
The choice of the best approach to treating risk should ultimately be based on cost benefit analysis. The specific approach that is most likely to be effective is one that is typically used in the organization. The benefits are typically the achievement of a defined control objective resulting in a level of risk acceptable to the organization. Costs can be analyzed using a variety of different financial approaches. These can include the most common approaches such as: • Value at risk (VAR) • Return on investment (ROI) • Return on security investment (ROSI) • Net present value (NPV) • Internal rate of return (IRR) Of course, the cost should never exceed the benefit. There are many situations where mitigation may not be an option based on the cost of the potential impact weighed against the cost of mitigation or the costs of transferring the risk. Analysis may also show that the benefits are not sufficient to justify the risk associated with the activity. Cost-benefit analysis helps provide a monetary impact view of risk and helps determine the cost of protecting what is important. However, cost-benefit analysis is also about making smart choices based on potential risk mitigation costs versus potential losses (risk exposure). Both of these concepts tie directly back to good governance practices.	Risk management benefits weighed against cost	2.10.8 Analysis of Relevant Risk 2.10.10 Risk Treatment Options 2.10.15 Costs and Benefits 3.15 Controls and Countermeasures
	Cost factors in controls	2.10.15 Costs and Benefits 2.11.1 Information Resource Valuation Strategies 2.11.3 Information Asset Classification
	Cost-benefit analysis approaches	2.10.12 Impact 2.10.15 Costs and Benefits 2.14 Security Control Baselines 3.15.11 Baseline Controls

SUGGESTED RESOURCES FOR FURTHER STUDY

Brotby, W. Krag; *Information Security Management Metrics: A Definitive Guide to Effective Security Monitoring and Measurement*, Auerbach Publications, USA, 2009

Centre for Protection of National Infrastructure, *www.cpni.gov.uk*

ISACA, *COBIT 5 for Risk*, USA, 2013, *www.isaca.org/cobit*

Daily Open Source Infrastructure Report for U.S. Department of Homeland Security, *www.dhs.gov/dhs-daily-open-source-infrastructure-report*

Information Technology Information Sharing and Analysis Centre, *www.it-isac.org*

International Organization for Standardization (ISO), ISO 27005:2011, *Information Technology—Security Technique—Information security risk management, 2nd Edition*, 2011, *www.iso.org*

ISO, ISO 31000:2009, *Risk Management—Principles and Guidelines (formerly AS/NZS 4360)*, 2009, *www.iso.org*

ISACA; *Implementing and Continually Improving IT Governance*, USA, 2010

Jaquith, Andrew; Security Metrics: Replacing Fear, Uncertainty and Doubt, Addison Wesley, USA, 2007

Kaplan, Robert S.; Anette Mikes; *Managing Risks: A New Framework*, Harvard Business Review, USA, 2012

Killmeyer, Jan; *Information Security Architecture: An Integrated Approach to Security in the Organization, 2nd Edition*, Auerbach Publications, USA, 2006

Multi-State Information Sharing & Analysis Center, *msisac.cisecurity.org*

National Institute of Standards and Technology (NIST); Guide for Applying the Risk Management Framework to Federal Information Systems: A Security Life Cycle Approach, SP 800-37 Rev. 1, USA 2010, *csrc.nist.gov/publications/nistpubs/800-37-rev1/sp800-37-rev1-final.pdf*

NIST; Managing Information Security Risk: Organization, Mission, and Information System View, SP 800-39, USA, 2011, *csrc.nist.gov/publications/nistpubs/800-39/SP800-39-final.pdf*

Peltier, Thomas R.; *Information Security Risk Analysis, 3rd Edition*, Auerbach Publications, USA, 2010

Van Grembergen, Wim; Steven De Haes; *IT Governance Domain Practices and Competencies: Measuring and Demonstrating the Value of IT*, IT Governance Institute, USA, 2005, *www.isaca.org/Knowledge-Center/Research/Documents/MeasurandDemoValueofIT.pdf*

Note: Publications in bold are stocked in the ISACA Bookstore.

2.3 SELF-ASSESSMENT QUESTIONS

QUESTIONS

CISM exam questions are developed with the intent of measuring and testing practical knowledge in information security management. All questions are multiple choice and are designed for one best answer. Every CISM question has a stem (question) and four options (answer choices). The candidate is asked to choose the correct or best answer from the options. The stem may be in the form of a question or incomplete statement. In some instances, a scenario or a description problem may also be included. These questions normally include a description of a situation and require the candidate to answer two or more questions based on the information provided. Many times a CISM examination question will require the candidate to choose the most likely or best answer.

In every case, the candidate is required to read the question carefully, eliminate known incorrect answers and then make the best choice possible. Knowing the format in which questions are asked, and how to study to gain knowledge of what will be tested, will go a long way toward answering them correctly.

2-1 The overall objective of risk management is to:

A. eliminate all vulnerabilities, if possible.
B. determine the best way to transfer risk.
C manage risk to an acceptable level.
D. implement effective countermeasures.

2-2 The information security manager should treat regulatory compliance as:

A. an organizational mandate.
B. a risk management priority.
C. a purely operational issue.
D. just another risk to be treated.

2-3 To address changes in risk, an effective risk management program should:

A. ensure that continuous monitoring processes are in place.
B. establish proper security baselines for all information resources.
C. implement a complete data classification process.
D. change security policies on a timely basis to address changing risk.

2-4 Information classification is important to properly manage risk **PRIMARILY** because:

A. it ensures accountability for information resources as required by roles and responsibilities.
B. it is a legal requirement under various regulations.
C. there is no other way to meet the requirements for availability, integrity and auditability.
D. it is used to identify the sensitivity and criticality of information to the organization.

2-5 Vulnerabilities discovered during an assessment should be:

A. handled as a risk, even though there is no threat.
B. prioritized for remediation solely based on impact.
C. a basis for analyzing the effectiveness of controls.
D. evaluated for threat, impact and cost of mitigation.

2-6 Indemnity agreements can be used to:

A. ensure an agreed-upon level of service.
B. reduce impacts on organizational resources.
C. transfer responsibility to a third party.
D. provide an effective countermeasure to threats.

2-7 Residual risk can be determined by:

A. assessing remaining vulnerabilities.
B. performing a threat analysis.
C. conducting a risk assessment.
D. implementing risk transfer.

2-8 Data owners are **PRIMARILY** responsible for creating risk mitigation strategies to address which of the following areas?

A. Platform security
B. Entitlement changes
C. Intrusion detection
D. Antivirus controls

2-9 A risk analysis should:

A. limit the scope to a benchmark of similar companies.
B. assume an equal degree of protection for all assets.
C. address the potential size and likelihood of loss.
D. give more weight to the likelihood vs. the size of the loss.

2-10 Which of the following is the **FIRST** step in selecting the appropriate controls to be implemented in a new business application?

A. Business impact analysis (BIA)
B. Cost-benefit analysis
C. Return on investment (ROI) analysis
D. Risk assessment

ANSWERS TO SELF-ASSESSMENT QUESTIONS

2-1 **C** Risk management is the process of reducing risk to an acceptable level. It is not possible to eliminate all vulnerabilities, and risk transfer and countermeasures are just some of the methods available to address risk.

2-2 **D** There are numerous regulations that may affect an organization. Priority will be a management decision based on those regulations with the greatest level of enforcement (risk) and the most severe sanctions (consequences or impact) in addition to the cost of compliance (mitigation), just as with any other risk. In some cases, management may decide that the cost of potential sanctions will be less than the cost of compliance. While it is generally preferable to be as compliant as reasonably possible, the extent of regulatory compliance is a management decision, not a security decision. All risk must be prioritized and compliance may not pose the greatest risk. Regulatory compliance is not just an operational issue, but primarily a management issue.

2-3 **A** Risk changes as threats, vulnerabilities or potential impacts change over time. The risk management program must have processes in place to monitor those changes and modify countermeasures, as appropriate, to maintain acceptable levels of residual risk.

2-4 **D** Information classification is an essential step in determining how confidential and critical information is to the business. The classification is then used to determine what information must be protected and how well during creation, handling, marking, transporting, storing and destruction. Protection could include strong encryption, robust access controls, and controls on marking, distribution and retention.

2-5 **D** Vulnerabilities uncovered should be evaluated and prioritized based on whether there is a credible threat, the impact if the vulnerability is exploited and the cost of mitigation. If there is a potential threat but little or no impact if the vulnerability is exploited, there is little risk and it may not be cost effective to address it.

2-6 **B** Indemnity agreements serve to reduce financial impacts by providing compensation for adverse events in the scope of the agreement. Indemnity agreements are not used to define service levels; these are provided by service level agreements. Legal responsibility cannot be transferred by indemnity agreements or any other instrument. Indemnity agreements are not a countermeasure to threats, but can be considered a compensatory control.

2-7 **C** Regardless of whether risk is residual or not, it is determined by a risk assessment. Determining remaining vulnerabilities after countermeasures are in place says nothing about threats, therefore risk cannot be determined. Risk cannot be determined by threat analysis alone. Transferring all risk is not relevant to determining residual risk.

2-8 **B** Data owners are concerned with and responsible for who has access to their resources and therefore need to be concerned with the strategy of how to mitigate risk of data resource usage. Platform security, intrusion detection and antivirus controls are typically IT security concerns.

2-9 **C** A risk analysis deals with the potential size and likelihood of loss. A risk analysis would not normally consider the benchmark of similar companies as providing relevant information other than for comparison purposes. Assuming equal degree of protection would only be rational in the rare event that all assets are similar in sensitivity and criticality. Since the likelihood determines (on an annualized basis) the size of the loss, both elements must be considered in the calculation.

2-10 **D** It is necessary to first consider the risk and determine whether it is acceptable to the organization. Risk assessment can identify threats and vulnerabilities and calculate the risk. Controls are evaluated by comparing the cost of the control against the potential impact if the risk were exploited. If the risk is determined to be unacceptable, a business impact analysis (BIA) can be used to determine the level of mitigation necessary. Then a cost-benefit analysis could be used to determine if mitigation cost was appropriate, considering the potential impact. Return on investment (ROI) analysis focuses on the business value of the control.

Page intentionally left blank

89-94 review

Section Two: Content

2.4 RISK MANAGEMENT OVERVIEW

Risk management is, in general terms, a process aimed at achieving an optimal balance between realizing opportunities for gain and minimizing vulnerabilities and loss. This is usually accomplished by ensuring that the impact of threats exploiting vulnerabilities is within acceptable limits at an acceptable cost. Risk management is different than "managing risk," which is often used synonymously with "risk mitigation" or "risk response."

In practical business terms, risk management means that risk is managed so that it does not materially impact the business process in an adverse way, and that an acceptable level of assurance and predictability to the desired outcomes of any important organizational activity are provided for. Risk is inherent in all activities; typically, a higher level of strategic risk will be taken to attempt to achieve higher returns. However, each organization needs to decide individually what level of risk is appropriate in order to achieve the financial and organizational results it wants.

The foundation for effective risk management is a comprehensive risk assessment, based on a solid understanding of the organization's risk universe. It is not possible to devise a relevant risk management program if there is no understanding of the nature and extent of risk to information resources and the potential impact on the organization's activities. The structure of an organization's risk function can be either centralized or decentralized. Mature organizations generally manage risk through an enterprise risk management (ERM) group or department to ensure consistency. In some organizations there is a separate IT risk department, whereas others have IT risk as a team under the ERM group. In some cases, the information security management, business resiliency and/or incident management programs may be integrated into an existing technology risk management framework. In others, risk is managed in a decentralized manner in a number of different departments and operational units, necessitating efforts to ensure continuity and integration of risk management activities.

Risk management, the development of business impact assessments, the creation of an IT asset inventory and risk analysis are fundamental prerequisites to developing a meaningful security strategy. Organizations that develop an information security governance program as detailed in chapter 1 will, by necessity, include risk management as an integral part of their overall program. However, risk management is a necessity that must be addressed regardless of the state of governance. At a high level, risk management is accomplished by balancing risk exposure against mitigation costs and implementing appropriate controls and countermeasures.

Controls are designed as part of the information risk management framework. The information risk management framework incorporates policies, procedures, practices and organizational structures and is, in essence, an architecture. This framework is designed to provide reasonable assurance that business objectives are achieved and that undesired events are prevented or detected and addressed. The framework must address people, process and technology and encompasses the physical, technical, contractual and procedural aspects of the organization. It must take into consideration the strategic, tactical, administrative and operational components of the organization to be effective.

Countermeasures include any process that serves to reduce specific threats or vulnerabilities and can be considered a targeted control. Countermeasures can range from modifying architecture or reengineering processes, to reducing or eliminating inherent technical vulnerabilities, to creating an awareness program for all employees to target social engineering and promote early recognition and reporting of security incidents.

Since risk management decisions typically have major financial implications, and can require changes across the entire organization, it is imperative that executive management is supportive of the process and fully understands and agrees with the results of the program.

Risk management can mean different things to different people in the organization. For example, a business manager might assume threats seldom occur and is not convinced of the return on investment (ROI) for security measures. An auditor's view may be that risk management means the prevention of loss, whereas an insurance manager could define it as cost-effective risk financing.

The information security manager should also understand that risk management must operate at multiple levels, including the strategic, management and operational levels. The significance of business experience and business decision making in any risk assessment process should be recognized as important to achieving realistic and successful outcomes from the process. The likelihood and relevance of a particular threat or risk will usually be a matter of judgment, and experience will be beneficial in arriving at realistic results.

Risk assessment can be quantitative or qualitative or, as is usually the case, a combination of both or semiquantitative. Whether an assessment is quantitative or qualitative is based on a variety of factors including the types of risk and impact and whether they can be readily reduced to a meaningful number. The main difference in approach is whether risk is determined by computational methods such as annual loss expectancy (ALE) or value at risk (VAR) to attempt to arrive at specific values or whether judgment and experience is used to place risk in some category such as low, medium or high. It must be understood that all risk assessments will be influenced by subjectivity because they rely on estimates, weighing of input factors, assignments of relevance and prioritization of outcomes from individuals with inherent biases.

Quantitative—One advantage of a quantitative risk assessment analysis is that it may provide an approximate measure of the magnitude of impact, usually in financial terms. This measure, in turn, can be used in the cost-benefit analysis of the recommended controls. Although a computational approach may be used to arrive at various risk aspects, the approach is nevertheless qualitative and subjective to some extent. The values used are also subject to considerable speculation and results must allow for wide margins of error. It must be understood that most risk assessments will, to a considerable extent, be semiquanitative, relying on a combination of subjective estimates and data in order to determine the relevance and outcomes. Management can tap various industry, regulatory and insurance-related resources to obtain a realistic estimate of what the cost would be at a per unit level should an event occur.

Qualitative—A qualitative risk assessment may be easier to perform and can enable prioritization of risk as well as be helpful in identifying areas of vulnerabilities requiring immediate attention. The approach involves ranking relative risk on a basis reflecting low risk to high risk. This assessment approach uses different risk scenarios and ranks the seriousness of the threats and the criticality and sensitivity of the assets. It is based on judgment, intuition and experience rather than on numbers and financial values.

Semiquantitative—A typical risk assessment will often use a combination of both quantitative and qualitative methods. This is becoming a popular first-step approach to risk assessment due to the speed and low complexity of the method and a sample of this and various other approaches is provided in section 2.10.

Whichever approach or combination of approaches is used, estimates should build in variance to account for assumption errors in the process. In other words, since risk assessment relies on predictions of future events and their frequency and magnitude, it is prudent to consider the range of probable outcomes to ensure that the worst case scenario will not result in a catastrophic outcome. With this caveat, the most likely outcomes should be the primary consideration so as to avoid an overreaction to highly improbable events. For example, when considering environmental risk, being struck by a comet while possible is highly improbable and it is unlikely that it will merit any significant mitigation efforts at least for a terrestrial facility. In addition, it would be difficult to mitigate the risk and so it is usually just accepted.

It may be useful to consider that the success of any risk management process is to some extent dependent on the feasibility of the process itself. One of the important factors is the cost and complexity of the execution of the process. As with other aspects of security, it is important to find the optimal cost-benefit balance between accuracy, complexity, effectiveness and cost.

Depending on the type of organization and the maturity with respect to risk management, a simple risk management process may have a greater chance of success then a complex one. A simple process will usually have the advantage of demonstrating the benefits at a lower cost.

2.4.1 THE IMPORTANCE OF RISK MANAGEMENT

The management of risk to information resources is a fundamental function of information security. It provides the rationale and justification for virtually all information security activities. Information security as a discipline exists to manage the risk to confidentiality, integrity and availability of information. Effective risk management is one of the main objectives of governance as discussed in chapter 1, section 1.4.2, as well as the key to managing regulatory requirements. Information security provides a level of assurance for business activities by managing risk to levels acceptable and appropriate to the mission of the business or organization. Without identifying and subsequently analyzing the spectrum of risk for a given business activity, it is not possible to determine the potential cost or impact of a particular event and, consequently, how to determine appropriate mitigation measures.

The current PricewaterhouseCoopers and *CSO Magazine Global State of Information Security Survey 2014* (*www.pwc.com*) includes the following among its significant findings:

> *"But while organizations have raised the bar on security, their adversaries have done even more. This year's survey shows that detected security incidents have increased 25% over the previous year, while the average financial costs of incidents are up 18%. The survey also reveals that many organizations have not deployed technologies that can provide insight into ecosystem vulnerabilities and threats, identify and protect key assets, and evaluate threats within the context of business objectives. And for many companies, security is not yet a foundational component of the business strategy, one that is championed by the CEO and board, and adequately funded. Put simply, few organizations have kept pace with today's escalating risks—and fewer still are prepared to manage future threats."*

The effectiveness of risk management will depend on the degree to which it is a part of an organization's culture and the extent to which it becomes everyone's responsibility.

The design and implementation of the risk management process in the organization will be influenced by:
- the organization's culture;
- the organization's mission and objectives;
- the organizational structure
- its products and services;
- its management and operation processes;
- specific organizational practices;
- the physical, environmental and regulatory conditions.

2.4.2 OUTCOMES OF RISK MANAGEMENT

Effective risk management serves to reduce the incidence of significant adverse impacts on an organization either by addressing threats, mitigating exposure and/or by reducing vulnerability or impact. To the extent this is accomplished, risk management provides a level of predictability that supports the organization's ability to operate effectively and profitably.

As stated in chapter 1, one of the outcomes of good governance is effective risk management, i.e., executing appropriate measures to mitigate risk and reduce potential impacts on information resources to an acceptable level and providing an:
- Understanding of the organization's threat, vulnerability and risk profile
- Understanding of risk exposure and potential consequences of compromise
- Awareness of risk management priorities based on potential consequences
- Organizational risk mitigation strategy sufficient to achieve acceptable consequences from residual risk

- Organizational acceptance/deference based on an understanding of the potential consequences of residual risk
- Measurable evidence that risk management resources are used in an appropriate and cost-effective manner.

2.5 RISK MANAGEMENT STRATEGY

A risk management strategy, to be effective, must be an integrated business process with defined objectives that incorporates all of the organization's risk management processes, activities, methodologies and policies. The risk management strategy sets the parameters and charts the course for the organization's risk management program. It must be consistent with and integrated into the overall security governance strategy. The information security strategy in turn must be based on the organization's overall objectives and business strategy (discussed extensively in chapter 1).

Risk management strategies are determined by a number of internal and external factors. Internal factors will include organizational maturity, history, culture, structure and acceptable risk. Various external factors such as industry sector and legal and regulatory requirements will collectively have a significant effect on the development of an effective strategy as well.

A risk management strategy must include determining the optimal approach to align processes, technology and behavior. It must take into account all credible risk and the full range of options for its appropriate management. This will include effective processes for risk identification and risk monitoring and metrics. It will also include promoting adequate robustness in defenses to withstand a wide range of viable attacks and resilience sufficient to reasonably prevent control failure.

2.5.1 RISK COMMUNICATION, RISK AWARENESS AND CONSULTING

For risk management to become part of the organization's culture, it will be necessary to communicate and create awareness of the issues across the organization at each step of the risk management process.

Communication should involve all stakeholders with efforts focused on consultation and development of a common understanding of the objectives and requirements of the program. This will allow variations in needs and perceptions to be identified and addressed more effectively. A template for risk communication is shown in **exhibit 2.2**.

2.6 EFFECTIVE INFORMATION RISK MANAGEMENT

Effective information risk management activities must be supported on an ongoing basis by all members of the organization. Executive or C-suite support lends credibility and impetus to risk management efforts. Even the best designed and implemented controls will not function as intended if operations are conducted by careless, indifferent or untrained personnel. An organizational culture that includes sound information security practices coupled with senior management commitment to effective risk management is required to achieve the objectives of the program.

Exhibit 2.2—Risk Communication Plan

A risk communication plan defines frequency, types and recipients of information about risk. The main purpose of the plan is to reduce the overload of non-relevant information (avoiding the likelihood of 'risk noise').

Life Cycle and Stakeholders	Life Cycle Stage	Internal Stakeholder	External Stakeholder	Description/Stake
	Information planning	ERM committee, audit committee		• Ensure that a risk communication plan exists and approve it. • Ensure that risk is communicated efficiently and timely.
	Information design	Risk function		• Outline the different aspects to be included in the risk communication plan (e.g., frequencies/types/recipient). • Ensure that risk is communicated efficiently and in a timely manner.
	Information build/acquire	Risk function, business process owners/CIO		• Detail the outlined aspects of the risk communication plan. • Ensure the risk communication plan includes key requirements for risk communication.
	Information use/operate: store, share, use	Board, executive management, CIO, risk function, business process owners, compliance, internal audit	External audit, regulator	Effective utilisation of the risk communication plan by the risk function ensures availability of correct and concise information about risk to the other stakeholders.
	Information monitor	Board, risk committee, audit committee, risk function	External audit	• Timely action is taken on the status of risk and risk capabilities. • The adequacy of the risk communication plan is validated regularly.
	Information dispose	Risk function		Ensure that information is disposed of in a timely, secure and appropriate manner.

Source: ISACA, *COBIT® 5 for Risk*, USA, 2013, figure 63, page 152

In addition, personnel must be aware of the risk the organization faces, understand their responsibilities and be trained in applicable control procedures. Compliance with information security controls must be monitored, tested and enforced on a continuing basis. The information security manager must also consider developing approaches to achieve a level of integration with the typically numerous risk management activities of other parts of the organization. These can include, but are not limited to, legal, facilities, physical security, HR, audit, and privacy and compliance activities. The objective is stated as one of the six outcomes identified in chapter 1 as Assurance Process Integration. Other efforts at promoting integration of risk management (as well as governance and compliance) across the enterprise are promoted by the Open Compliance and Ethics Group (OCEG) and supported by numerous vendors and consultancies.

2.6.1 DEVELOPING A RISK MANAGEMENT PROGRAM

Initial steps in developing a risk management program will include establishing:
- Context and purpose of the program
- Scope and charter
- Authority, structure and reporting relationships
- Asset identification, classification and ownership
- Objectives
- The methodology to be used
- The implementation team

Establish Context and Purpose

All organizations face a variety of risk on an ongoing basis and must deal with it either formally or on an *ad hoc* basis. Managing the risk to information is to a greater or lesser extent usually the responsibility of the information security manager. A primary requirement is to determine the organization's purpose for creating an information risk management program, determine the desired outcomes and define objectives. It might be a limited effort to reduce the impacts of Internet-based attacks and accidents or to ensure compliance with legal or regulatory requirements. If the context and scope of risk management activities are not established, the program may be far broader and encompass all aspects of organizational activity with responsibilities distributed among several departments. If the organization has one or more existing risk management function(s), it is necessary to determine how information risk management functions will be integrated with these other functions and responsibilities divided.

Setting the risk management context primarily involves defining the organization, process, project or activity, scope, and establishing goals and objectives.

As discussed in chapter 1, to establish an effective program, an essential element will be to determine the organization's risk appetite and tolerance—that is, what is considered by management to be an acceptable level of risk and the acceptable level of deviation from the acceptable risk level. Each organization has a different risk appetite for the amount and type of risk it considers acceptable and this is likely to vary by department or organizational unit as well. This is inevitably a business decision based on a number of criteria, including industry sector, regulatory considerations, ability to absorb loss, reputational concerns, mission and culture rather than any specific quantitative measures. Typically, the board of directors and executive management set the tone for the risk management program. This will manifest in the extent that the organization's security posture is risk adverse or risk aggressive. The "tone at the top" will have a pervasive influence on all aspects of the program and how well it ultimately functions. As with other aspects of security, a top-down approach is essential for an effective risk management program.

Define Scope and Charter

Since all departments and operational units in the organization have some level of responsibility for managing risk, it is important to clearly define the scope of responsibility and authority that specifically falls to the information security manager and to other stakeholders. This helps prevent gaps in the process, improves overall consistency of risk management efforts and reduces unnecessary duplication of efforts.

It should be noted that since virtually all information security activities are in some manner related to managing risk, this exercise should map closely to the security manager's job responsibilities. Regardless of the scope of responsibility of the information security manager, the total scope for risk management needs to be defined and the overall objectives determined.

While many parts of the organization will be responsible for some aspects of risk management, the main areas of information security typically interface with physical security, operational risk, IT and business management. The interface with these areas can, at times, be contentious due to lack of common or conflicting goals and poorly defined scope of responsibilities. An example of an area that needs to be defined is determining who is responsible for ensuring that sensitive information is not left at print stations, resulting in unintended disclosure or confidential documents not being shredded before being discarded (to prevent dumpster diving). While this example may seem trivial, it is important from the perspective of information security. In addition, in any organization, there are numerous points of intersection of information security, IT security, facilities and physical security as well as other assurance providers and it is important that the areas of respective authority and responsibility are clearly defined.

Define Authority, Structure and Reporting

It is essential that authority to take certain actions and make decisions is clearly defined. There are many examples (such as the case study at the end of chapter 1, section 1.19) of incidents that have resulted in unnecessarily severe consequences as a result of a lack of clarity as to who has the authority to make decisions and take certain actions.

The organizational structure in terms of lines of reporting and authority will inevitably have an impact on the ability to effectively manage risk. This may occur as a result of various parts of the organization having different parts of risk management under their control coupled with conflicting perspectives. This fractured risk management structure will be further dis-integrated if reporting goes to different decision makers in various parts of the organization. A lack of clear governance and integration of risk management activities often results in dire consequences, and the information security manager should endeavor to address such issues by assessing and presenting the risk along with recommendations to senior management.

Ensure Asset Identification, Classification and Ownership

In order to appropriately scope and prioritize risk management efforts, it is necessary to ensure that a complete and accurate information asset register exists. As part of the asset identification process, it is both typically daunting, but nevertheless imperative, that all instances of information assets be located.

In addition, information assets need to be classified in terms of business value or sensitivity and criticality to the organization. (See 2.11.3, Information Asset Classification.)

It is also essential to ensure that all information assets have an identified owner with specific responsibilities for managing risk to those assets. This will help promote accountability for policy compliance and risk management requirements throughout the organization. Policies requiring asset ownership should be in place, as well as processes established to assign ownership as assets are acquired, transferred or created.

Determine Objectives

Clear objectives and priorities for the information risk management program are essential. While the ultimate objectives, or desired state, may be to mitigate all risk to acceptable levels, even if that were possible, resource limitations will make that unlikely. As a result, it will be necessary to set priorities for the program and prioritize risk accordingly. In other words, some types of risk cannot be addressed and must be accepted, some can wait, and some should be addressed immediately. Of course, before risk can be prioritized it must be identified, and its likelihood and impact must be determined through risk analysis. Priorities can then be set, starting with types of risk that are determined to have a high likelihood of materializing as well as a high impact and working down from there.

Determine Methodologies

There are many approaches to assessing, analyzing, and mitigating risk. The following sections will discuss some of the more common approaches to these activities. In many organizations, standard approaches are already in place and should be used if they are adequate for the purpose. If these practices have not been established or are inadequate, the information security manager should evaluate the available choices and seek to implement those that are the best for the organization.

Designate Program Development Team

Once the scope of information risk management activities is defined and the objectives are clarified, the next step is to designate an individual or team responsible for developing and implementing the information risk management program. While the team is primarily responsible for the risk management plan, a successful program requires the integration of risk management at all levels of the organization. Operations staff and board members (through an oversight or steering committee) should assist the risk management committee in: identifying risk, determining acceptable risk levels, developing suitable loss-control and intervention strategies, and determining where the authority and responsibility for various aspects of risk management will reside. Of overriding importance is the need for the risk management program to be properly aligned with the strategy and direction of the business. For this reason, it is vital that participation include representatives from all key business units.

2.6.2 ROLES AND RESPONSIBILITIES

Information risk management is an integral part of security governance and it is the responsibility of the board of directors or the equivalent to ensure that these efforts are effective. Periodic reports on the efforts and effectiveness of risk management activities should be required to provide the feedback needed to ensure that management intent, direction and expectations are realized.

Executive management must ensure the availability of adequate resources and support for risk management activities and should receive status reports on a periodic and event-driven basis. Event-driven reporting will require management involvement to determine the nature and severity that triggers a report. Management must also be involved in and sign off on acceptable risk levels as well as risk management objectives. A steering committee composed of major stakeholders, as defined in chapter 1, section 1.5.3, must set risk management priorities and define risk management objectives in terms of supporting business strategy. The committee should also be charged with developing levels of acceptable risk mitigation for various business processes to be presented to senior management for agreement. Defining levels of acceptable risk and obtaining senior management support is an essential condition for effective risk management.

The information security manager is responsible for developing, collaborating and managing the information risk management program to meet the defined objectives. The information security manager must also take responsibility for maintaining liaisons with other risk management teams and assurance activities in the organization to promote the integration of activities and to provide an effective and coordinated level of business process assurance.

Key Roles

Risk management is a management responsibility. The US National Institute of Science and Technology (NIST) Publication 800-30 describes the key roles of the personnel who must support and participate in the risk management process. While the specifics in different organizations and different countries may vary, this high-level view will generally map to most organizations. It should be noted that in many organizations (such as financial institutions), the information security manager will now be the chief information security officer (CISO) with executive-level status, reporting directly to senior management.

- **Governing Boards and Senior Management**—Senior management, under the standard of due care and ultimate responsibility for mission accomplishment, must ensure that the necessary resources are effectively applied to develop the capabilities needed to accomplish the mission. They must also assess and incorporate results of the risk assessment activity into the decision-making process. An effective risk management program that assesses and mitigates IT-related mission risk requires the support and involvement of senior management.

- **Chief Risk Officer**—The chief risk officer (CRO) is generally charged with overall enterprise risk management (ERM), which may include information security in some cases. Generally, this position includes all non-information risk such as operational risk, environmental risk and sometimes credit risk.
- **Chief Information Officer**—The chief information officer (CIO) is responsible for IT planning, budgeting, and performance, including its information security components consistent with the policies and standards under the purview of the CISO or information security manager.
- **Chief Information Security Officer**—The chief information security officer (CISO) generally performs most of the same functions as an information security manager, but holds officer status in an organization usually accompanied with greater authority and typically reports to the CEO or the board of directors. The position usually includes more strategic and management elements than is typical of an information security manager.
- **Information Security Manager**—Information security managers are responsible for their organizations' security programs, usually including information risk management. Therefore, they play a leading role in introducing an appropriate, structured methodology to help identify, evaluate, and minimize risk to information resources, including the IT systems that support their organizations' missions. Information security managers also act as major consultants in support of senior management to ensure that this activity takes place on an ongoing basis.
- **System and Information Owners**—The system and information owners are responsible for ensuring that proper controls are in place to address integrity, confidentiality and availability of the IT systems and data they own. Typically, the system and information owners are responsible for changes to their IT systems. Thus, they usually have to approve and sign off on changes to their IT systems (e.g., system enhancement and major changes to the software and hardware). The system and information owners must therefore understand their role in the risk management process and fully support this process.
- **Business and Functional Managers**—The managers responsible for business operations and the IT procurement process must take an active role in the risk management process. These managers are the individuals with the authority and responsibility for making the trade-off decisions essential to mission accomplishment. Their involvement in the risk management process enables the achievement of proper security for the IT systems, which, if managed properly, will provide mission effectiveness with a minimal expenditure of resources.
- **IT Security Practitioners**—IT security practitioners (e.g., network, system, application and database administrators; computer specialists; security analysts; security consultants) are responsible for proper implementation of security requirements in their IT systems. As changes occur in the existing IT system environment (e.g., expansion in network connectivity, changes to the existing infrastructure and organizational policies, introduction of new technologies), the IT security practitioners must support or use the risk management process to identify and assess new potential risk and implement new security controls as needed to safeguard their IT systems.
- **Security Awareness Trainers (Security/Subject Matter Professionals)**—The organization's personnel are the users of the IT systems. Use of the IT systems and data according to an organization's policies, guidelines and rules of behavior is critical to mitigating risk and protecting the organization's IT resources. To minimize risk to the IT systems, it is essential that system and application users be provided with security awareness training. Therefore, the IT security trainers or security/subject matter professionals must understand the risk management process so that they can develop appropriate training materials and incorporate risk assessment into training programs to educate the end users.

2.7 INFORMATION RISK MANAGEMENT CONCEPTS

Overall risk management in most large organizations is provided by one or more separate departments. Knowledge of the subject matter is, however, required to be effective and, as a consequence, the management of information risk usually falls to the information security manager. To be effective, the information security manager requires a broad understanding of a number of concepts fundamental to security and risk management. This includes technical, strategic, tactical, administrative and operational elements. Some of the main concepts are discussed in the following section.

2.7.1 CONCEPTS

There are a number of key concepts that a security manager should be familiar with that are needed to understand this chapter and their use in the context of risk management. Most information security managers will be familiar with these concepts but it will be useful to review the definitions in the glossary to ensure a clear understanding of the definitions needed for best results in the certification exam. These concepts include:

- Threats
- Vulnerabilities
- Exposures
- Risk
- Impacts
- Controls
- Countermeasures
- Resource valuation
- Information asset classification
- Criticality
- Sensitivity
- Recovery Time Objectives (RTOs)
- Recovery Point Objectives (RPOs)
- Service Delivery Objectives (SDOs)
- Acceptable Interruption Window (AIW)
- Redundancy

Other risk management aspects related to information security that should be understood can include:

- Service level agreements (SLAs)
- System robustness and resilience
- Business continuity/disaster recovery
- Business process reengineering
- Project management timelines and complexity
- Enterprise and security architectures
- IT and information security governance
- Systems life cycle management
- Policies, standards and procedures

2.7.2 TECHNOLOGIES

There are also a variety of information security technologies and technical concepts that are important for the information security manager to have a thorough conceptual understanding of as they relate to risk management. Some of these include:
- Application security measures
- Physical security measures
- Environmental controls
- Logical access controls
- Network access controls
- Routers, firewalls and other network components (bridges, gateways)
- Intrusion detection/prevention
- Wireless security
- Platform security
- Encryption and public key infrastructure (PKI)
- Antivirus/malware, including spyware/adware
- Antispam devices
- Telecommunications and voice-over IP (VoIP)

In addition, while personnel and facilities security may not be part of a risk management program, these are areas of risk that need to be considered as a part of risk management. The information security manager must be aware of and factor in personnel issues and personnel security controls as well as environmental and facilities controls as a part of risk assessment and management activities.

2.8 IMPLEMENTING RISK MANAGEMENT

As a part of planning a risk management program, the information security manager must identify all other organizational risk management activities and seek to integrate these functions or leverage the activities within the context of the information security program. Larger organizations usually have a risk management function that deals with activities typically related to physical risk. In the case of financial institutions, there is also typically a department dealing with credit risk. Other departments or roles, such as human resources and privacy officers, and compliance functions such as audit typically are involved in managing risk within the organization. To be effective, it is critical that mechanisms be put in place to ensure good communication with other risk management and assurance functions. This is to ensure that otherwise effective information risk management is not bypassed or subverted by the lack of effective processes in other domains. It also prevents duplication of efforts and minimizes gaps in assurance functions that can adversely affect information protection activities as well as other areas of operational and business risk.

2.8.1 RISK MANAGEMENT PROCESS

Risk management consists of a series of processes, distinct from risk assessment, of weighing policy alternatives in consultation with interested parties, considering risk assessment and other factors and selecting appropriate prevention and control options that have acceptable costs.

Risk management usually consists of the following processes:
- Establish scope and boundaries
- Risk assessment
- Risk treatment
- Acceptance of residual risk
- Risk communication and monitoring

These processes are defined as follows:
- **Establish scope and boundaries**—Process for the establishment of global parameters for the performance of risk management within an organization. Both internal and external factors have to be taken into account. This will provide the context.
- **Risk assessment**—A methodic process consisting of three steps: risk identification, risk analysis and risk evaluation.
- **Risk treatment**—Process of selecting strategies to deal with identified risk, according to business' risk appetite. Risk treatment strategies are: avoiding, by cessation of risky activities, mitigating, by developing and implementing controls, transferring risk to a third party, which could be inside or outside the organization, and accepting risk. Risk will usually be accepted if there is no cost-effective way to mitigate it, if there is little exposure or potential impact, or if it is simply not feasible to address it effectively.
- **Acceptance of residual risk**—Risk acceptance can be defined as the decision and approval by management to accept the remaining risk after the treatment process is concluded.
- **Risk communication and monitoring**—A process to exchange and share information related to risk, as well as reviewing the effectiveness of the whole risk management process. Communication of risk is usually performed between decision-makers and other stakeholders inside and outside the organization. Through communication and monitoring it is assured that the scope, boundaries, evaluated risk and action plans remain relevant and updated.

The risk management process is shown in **exhibit 2.3**

Developing a systematic, analytical and continuous risk management process as shown in **exhibit 2.4** is critical to any successful security program and must be implemented as a formal process. Determining the correct or appropriate level of security is dependent on the potential risk that an organization faces, the potential impact, and the organization's ability to accept or otherwise mitigate risk. Risk can be unique to each organization.

The information security manager should set up a regular, formal process in which risk assessments are performed at the organizational, system and application levels. Ensuring that there are measurements (metrics) in place to assess the risk and the effectiveness of security measures is part of the information security manager's ongoing responsibility. The information security manager should also explore and recommend to asset owners continuous manual and automated techniques to monitor the organization's risk. This risk assessment process is important since it is necessary to focus the organization's security activities on issues that have the greatest impact and significance.

Overgeneralization by applying risk factors across industries or regions should be avoided. Furthermore, the effectiveness of an information security program is frequently challenged by organizational, technological and business/operational change. Risk management should be a continuous and dynamic process to ensure that changing threats and vulnerabilities are addressed in a timely manner.

In addition, processes must be developed to monitor the status of security controls and countermeasures to determine their ongoing effectiveness. Controls usually degrade over time and are subject to failure, mandating ongoing control monitoring and periodic testing.

Exhibit 2.3—Risk Management Process

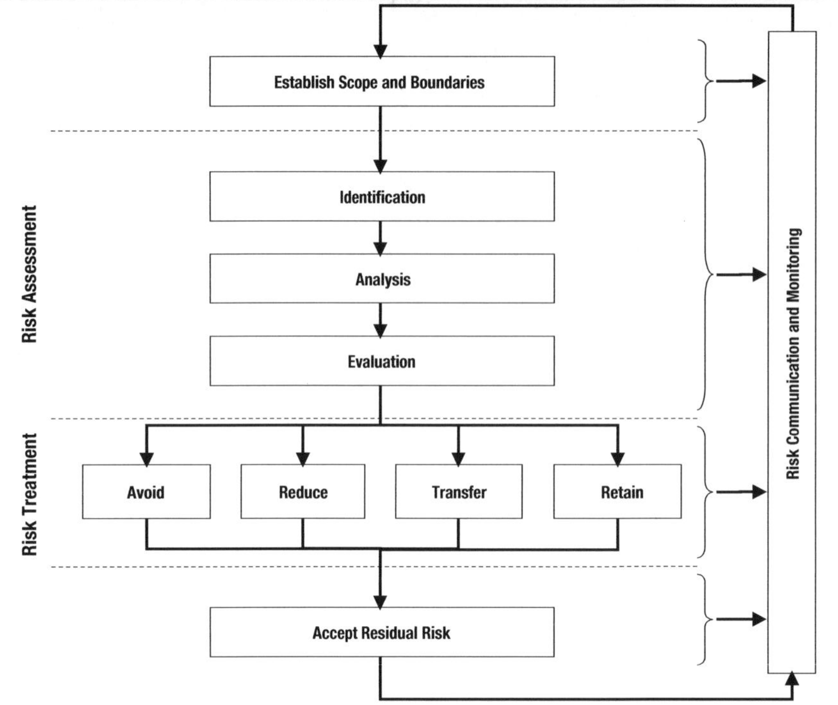

Exhibit 2.4—Continuous Risk Management Steps

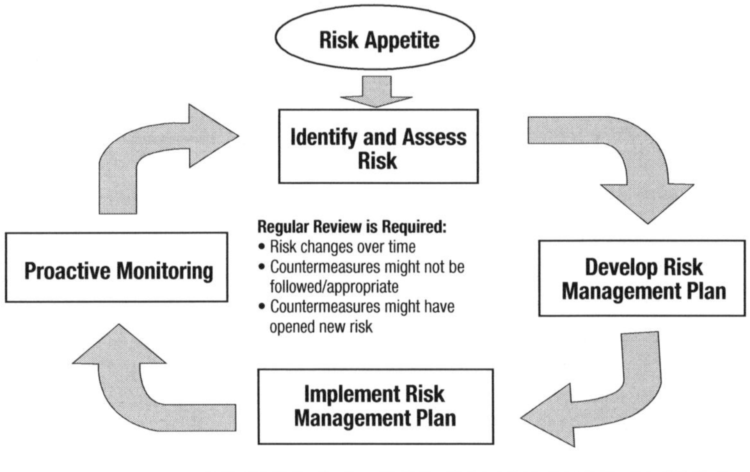

2.8.2 DEFINING A RISK MANAGEMENT FRAMEWORK

To develop an organization's systematic risk management program, a reference model should be used and adapted to the circumstances of the organization. The reference model will reflect the "desired state" discussed in chapter 1, i.e., a snapshot of a future state that meets all risk management objectives. Several excellent publication/standards are available to provide guidance on information technology and security risk management approaches. Examples include:

- COBIT 5
- ISO 31000:2009 Risk Management–Guidelines on principles and implementation of risk management
- NIST's Managing Information Security Risk: Organization, Mission, and Information System View, SP 800-39
- AS/NZS 4360:2004 Risk Management Standard, now superseded by ISO 31000:2009
- HB 158-2010: Delivering assurance based on ISO 31000:2009—Risk management—Principles and guidelines
- ISO/IEC Standard 27005:2008 Information Security Risk Management

The standards referenced above have similar risk management requirements, including:

- **Policy**—The need for an organization's senior management/ executive leadership to define and document its policy for risk

management, including objectives for, and its commitment to, risk management. The policy must be relevant to the organization's strategic context, goals, objectives and the nature of its business. Management should ensure that this policy is understood and that standards are developed, implemented and maintained at all levels in the organization.
- **Planning and resourcing**—Responsibility, authority and interrelationships of personnel who perform and verify work affecting risk management must be defined and documented. The organization must identify resource requirements and facilitate the implementation of risk management programs, through the assignment of trained personnel for ongoing management of work activities and the verification activities for internal review.
- **Implementation program**—The organization must define the steps required to implement an effective risk management system.
- **Management review**—Executive management must ensure periodic review of the risk management system in order to ensure its continuing stability and effectiveness in satisfying requirements of the program. Records of such reviews must be maintained.
- **Risk management process**—Risk management can be applied at both strategic and tactical levels in the organization—products/services, business/IT processes, projects, decisions, applications and platforms. The organization must prioritize individual risk treatment according to the organization's business objectives, risk appetite and regulatory environment for the given industry.
- **Risk management documentation**—For each stage of the process, adequate records must be kept that are sufficient to satisfy an independent audit.

By establishing the framework for the management of risk, the basic parameters within which risk must be managed are defined. Consequently, the scope for the rest of the risk management process is also set. It includes the definition of basic assumptions for the organization's external and internal environment, and the overall objectives of the risk management process and activities. Although the definition of scope and framework are fundamental for the establishment of risk management, they are independent from the particular structure of the management process, methods and tools to be used for the implementation.

In order to define an efficient framework it is important to:
- Understand the background of the organization and its risk (e.g., its core processes, valuable assets, competitive areas etc.);
- Evaluate existing risk management activities
- Develop a structure and process for the development of risk management initiatives and controls

This approach is useful for:
- Clarifying and gaining common understanding of the organizational objectives;
- Identifying the environment in which these objectives are set;
- Specifying the main scope and objectives for risk management, applicable restrictions or specific conditions and the outcomes required;
- Developing a set of criteria against which the risk will be measured;
- Defining a set of key elements for structuring the risk identification and assessment process.

The risk management program must be integrated with the organization's overall management system and, whenever possible, must adapt various elements—such as policies, organizational processes, accountability, resources and communication methods—to its specific needs.

Many organizations' existing management practices and processes include elements of risk management and many organizations have already adopted a formal risk management process for particular types of risk or circumstances. These should be critically reviewed and assessed to determine whether they meet current objectives and requirements.

2.8.3 DEFINING THE EXTERNAL ENVIRONMENT

Defining the external environment includes specifying the environment in which the organization operates. The external environment typically includes:
- The local market, the business and the competitive, financial and political environment;
- The law and regulatory environment;
- Social and cultural conditions;
- External stakeholders.

It is also important that both the perceptions and values of the various stakeholders and any externally generated threats and/or opportunities are properly evaluated and taken into consideration.

2.8.4 DEFINING THE INTERNAL ENVIRONMENT

Key areas that must be evaluated in order to provide a comprehensive view of the organization's internal environment include:
- Key business drivers (e.g., market indicators, competitive advances, product attractiveness, etc.);
- The organization's strengths, weaknesses, opportunities and threats;
- Internal stakeholders;
- Organization structure and culture;
- Assets in terms of resources (i.e., people, systems, processes, capital, etc.);
- Goals and objectives, and the strategies already in place to achieve them.

2.8.5 DEVELOPING A RISK PROFILE

A risk profile is an essential element for effective information risk management. It will serve to provide a comprehensive overview of the overall (known) risk to which the organization is exposed.

There are a variety of approaches to accomplishing this requirement, but the recent COBIT 5 approach is presented below in **exhibit 2.5** as a detailed and effective process to achieve this objective.

One important component of the risk profile is the risk register. **Exhibit 2.6** contains a sample template for a risk register entry.

Exhibit 2.5—Risk Profile

A risk profile is a description of the overall (identified) risk to which the enterprise is exposed. A risk profile consists of:

- **Risk register**
  - **Risk scenarios**
  - **Risk analysis**
- **Risk action plan**
- **Loss events (historical and current)**
- **Risk factors**
- **Independent assessment findings**

	Life Cycle Stage	Internal Stakeholder	External Stakeholder	Description/Stake
Life Cycle and Stakeholders	**Information planning**	ERM committee, board	External audit, regulator	• Internal stakeholders: Initiate and drive the implementation and appoint a CRO. Have adequate information on the exposure. • External stakeholders: To have comfort on the risk management capabilities
	Information design	Risk function, compliance, CIO, CISO, business process owners, internal audit		• CRO: To obtain information from the other roles in order to provide the overview for the governance bodies • CIO: To be able to develop an adequate information system • Other roles: To be able to provide relevant information and to ensure completeness/adequacy
	Information build/acquire	Risk function, internal audit		• CRO: Provides functional requirements and consults others. • Internal audit: Provides quality assurance services on the implementation.
	Information use/operate: store, share, use	Board, ERM committee, business executive, CIO, risk function, CISO, business process owners, compliance, internal audit	External audit, regulator	• Business process owners, business executives and CIO: To efficiently provide relevant information • Board and ERM committee: To receive relevant information and to enable decision making • Internal audit, external audit and regulator: Receive relevant information • CRO: Oversees the caption, processing and interpretation of information
	Information monitor	Board, ERM committee, risk function, internal audit	External audit	• CRO: Ongoing monitoring on adequacy, completeness and accuracy of information; semi-annual assessment of performance (MEA01) and controls (MEA02) to maintain the information • Internal audit: Annual validation of format and level of contents
	Information dispose	Risk function		• CRO: According to data retention policy, to ensure confidentiality of information and to reduce the amount of information

Source: ISACA, *COBIT® 5 For Risk*, USA, 2013, Figure 61, Page 147

Exhibit 2.6—Risk Register

Part I—Summary Data						
Risk statement						
Risk owner						
Date of last risk assessment						
Due date for update of risk assessment						
Risk category	☐STRATEGIC (IT Benefit/Value Enablement)	☐PROJECT DELIVERY (IT Programme and Project Delivery)	☐OPERATIONAL (IT Operations and Service Delivery)			
Risk classification (copied from risk analysis results)	☐LOW	☐MEDIUM	☐HIGH	☐VERY HIGH		
Risk response	☐ACCEPT	☐TRANSFER	☐MITIGATE	☐AVOID		
Part II—Risk Description						
Title						
High-level scenario (from list of sample high-level scenarios)						
Detailed scenario description—Scenario components	**Actor**					
	Threat Type					
	Event					
	Asset/Resource					
	Timing					
Other scenario information						
Part III—Risk Analysis Results						
Frequency of scenario (number of times per year)	0	1	2	3	4	5
	N ≤ 0,01 ☐	0,01 < N ≤ 0,1 ☐	0,1 < N ≤ 1 ☐	1 < N ≤ 10 ☐	10 < N ≤ 100 ☐	100 < N ☐
Comments on frequency						
Impact of scenario on business	0	1	2	3	4	5
1. Productivity	**Revenue Loss Over One Year**					
Impact rating	I ≤ 0,1% ☐	0,1% < I ≤ 1% ☐	1% < I ≤ 3% ☐	3% < I ≤ 5% ☐	5% < I ≤ 10% ☐	10% < I ☐
Detailed description of impact						
2. Cost of response	**Expenses Associated With Managing the Loss Event**					
Impact rating	I ≤ 10k$ ☐	10K$ < I ≤ 100K$ ☐	100K$ < I ≤ 1M$ ☐	1M$% < I ≤ 10M$ ☐	10M$ < I ≤ 100M$ ☐	100M$ < I ☐
Detailed description of impact						
3. Competitive advantage	**Drop-in Customer Satisfaction Ratings**					
Impact rating	I ≤ 0,5 ☐	0,5 < I ≤ 1 ☐	1 < I ≤ 1,5 ☐	1,5 < I ≤ 2 ☐	2 < I ≤2,5 ☐	2,5 < I ☐
Detailed description of impact						
4. Legal	**Regulatory Compliance—Fines**					
Impact rating	None ☐	< 1M$ ☐	< 10M$ ☐	< 100M$ ☐	< 1B$ ☐	> 1B$ ☐
Detailed description of impact						
Overall impact rating (average of four impact ratings)						
Overall rating of risk (obtained by combining frequency and impact ratings on risk map)	☐LOW	☐MEDIUM	☐HIGH	☐VERY HIGH		

Exhibit 2.6—Risk Register (cont.)

Part III—Risk Response				
Risk response for this risk	☐ACCEPT	☐TRANSFER	☐MITIGATE	☐AVOID
Justification				
Detailed description of response (NOT in case of ACCEPT)	Response Action		Completed	Action Plan
	1.		☐	☐
	2.		☐	☐
	3.		☐	☐
	4.		☐	☐
	5.		☐	☐
	6.		☐	☐
Overall status of risk action plan				
Major issues with risk action plan				
Overall status of completed responses				
Major issues with completed responses				
Part IV—Risk Indicators				
Key risk indicators for this risk	1. 2. 3. 4.			
Source: ISACA, *COBIT® 5 for Risk*, USA, 2013, figure 62, page 151				

2.8.6 DETERMINING THE RISK MANAGEMENT CONTEXT

In business terms, the process of managing risk must provide a balance between costs and benefits. The context is the scope of risk management activities and the environment in which risk management operates, including the organizational structure and culture.

Determining the risk management context involves defining the:
- range of the organization and the processes or activities to be assessed;
- duration;
- full scope of the risk management activities;
- roles and responsibilities of various parts of the organization participating in the risk management process.

The criteria by which risk will be evaluated have to be decided and agreed upon. Deciding whether risk treatment is required is usually based on operational, technical, financial, regulatory, legal, social, or environmental criteria or combinations of them. The criteria should be in line with the scope and qualitative analysis of the organization's internal policies and procedures, and must support its goals and objectives.

Important criteria to be considered are:
- impact—the kinds of consequences that will be considered;
- likelihood
- the rules that will determine whether the risk level is such that further treatment activities are required.

These criteria may need to change during later phases of the risk management process as a result of changing circumstances or as a consequence of the risk assessment and evaluation process itself.

2.8.7 GAP ANALYSIS

Gap analysis in the context of risk management generally refers to determining the gap between controls and control objectives. Control objectives should have been developed as a consequence of developing information security governance and strategy as discussed in chapter 1. Control objectives should lead to controls that achieve acceptable risk, which in turn serves to set the information security baseline.

Control objectives may change as a part of risk management activities as exposures, business objectives, or regulations change, which could create a gap between the existing control and its revised objectives. Periodically analyzing the gap between controls and their objectives should be a standard practice. This is normally accomplished as a part of the process of controls testing for effectiveness. To the extent that effectiveness of controls fails to meet the control objective and achieve acceptable risk, the controls may need to be modified, redesigned, or supplemented with additional control activities. For more information on the relationship between controls and control objectives, see chapter 3, section 3.15.

2.8.8 OTHER ORGANIZATIONAL SUPPORT

The information security industry provides many subscription services that an information security manager can integrate into an information security program. These services help to leverage expertise of external service providers without actually assigning them responsibility for executing any part of the security program. There are:

- **Good practices organizations**—Organizations such as ISACA, SANS, ISC2 can be valuable sources of comparison data with which to evaluate an information security program.
- **Security networking roundtables**—These organizations attempt to gather information security professionals from similar industries and organize discussions around topics of common interest. Some are sponsored by security technology vendors so there is no fee, but instead there might be pressure to purchase the vendor's product or service. An information security manager may consider restricting attendance to vendor-sponsored forums if they are already a client of the sponsoring vendor. Others are membership fee-based.
- **Security training organizations**—These institutions provide classes on technical topics in information security such as vulnerability analysis and platform security configuration strategies.
- **Vulnerability alerting services**—These services allow information security managers to maintain a list of technology that is in use at their organization and receive news with respect to vulnerabilities found in any technology on the list.

The field of information security changes as technology advances, and the threat landscape changes as cybercrime evolves and new laws and regulations are enacted. The information security manager should have frequent interaction with sources of new information about security products, services, threats, vulnerabilities, regulations, laws and management techniques.

2.9 RISK ASSESSMENT AND ANALYSIS METHODOLOGIES

There is no right or wrong approach to the selection of a methodology for conducting a risk assessment. However, the results must meet the goals and objectives of the organization in identifying the relative risk rating of assets and processes critical to the business. It is also essential to identify as much significant risk as possible. An approach to achieving this is to develop risk scenarios as shown in **exhibit 2.7**.

Risk assessment is the process of analyzing the threat landscape and the vulnerabilities of the organization's information assets to determine whether the organization has exposure and the risk of compromise. Coupled with either BIA or information asset classification to determine criticality, the resulting analysis is used as a basis for identifying appropriate and cost-effective controls or countermeasures to mitigate the identified risk.

Exhibit 2.7—Developing Risk Scenarios

Focus/Issue	Summary Guidance
Maintain currency of risk scenarios and risk factors.	Risk factors and the enterprise change over time; hence, scenarios will change over time, over the course of a project or over the evolution of technology. For example, it is essential that the risk function develop a review schedule and the CIO works with the business lines to review and update scenarios for relevance and importance. Frequency of this exercise depends on the overall risk profile of the enterprise and should be done at least on an annual basis, or when important changes occur.
Use generic risk scenarios as a starting point and build more detail where and when required.	One technique of keeping the number of scenarios manageable is to propagate a standard set of generic scenarios through the enterprise and develop more detailed and relevant scenarios when required and warranted by the risk profile only at lower (entity) levels. The assumptions made when grouping or generalising should be well understood by all and adequately documented because they may hide certain scenarios or be confusing when looking at risk response. For example, if 'insider threat' is not well defined within a scenario, it may not be clear whether this threat includes privileged and non-privileged insiders. The differences between these aspects of a scenario can be critical when one is trying to understand the frequency and impact of events, as well as mitigation opportunities.
Number of scenarios should be representative and reflect business reality and complexity.	Risk management helps to deal with the enormous complexity of today's IT environments by prioritising potential action according to its value in reducing risk. Risk management is about reducing complexity, not generating it; hence, another plea for working with a manageable number of risk scenarios. However, the retained number of scenarios still needs to accurately reflect business reality and complexity.
Risk taxonomy should reflect business reality and complexity.	There should be a sufficient number of risk scenario scales reflecting the complexity of the enterprise and the extent of exposures to which the enterprise is subject. Potential scales might be a 'low, medium, high' ranking or a numeric scale that scores risk importance from 0 to 5. Scales should be aligned throughout the enterprise to ensure consistent scoring.

Exhibit 2.7—Developing Risk Scenarios *(cont.)*	
Focus/Issue	**Summary Guidance**
Use generic risk scenario structure to simplify risk reporting	Similarly, for risk reporting purposes, entities should not report on all specific and detailed scenarios, but could do so by using the generic risk structure. For example, an entity may have taken generic scenario 15 (project quality), translated it into five scenarios for its major projects, subsequently conducted a risk analysis for each of the scenarios, then aggregated or summarised the results and reported back using the generic scenario header 'project quality'.
Ensure adequate people and skills requirements for developing relevant risk scenarios.	Developing a manageable and relevant set of risk scenarios requires: • Expertise and experience, to not overlook relevant scenarios and not be drawn into highly unrealistic[6] or irrelevant scenarios. While the avoidance of scenarios that are unrealistic or irrelevant is important in properly utilising limited resources, some attention should be paid to situations that are highly infrequent and unpredictable, but which could have a cataclysmic impact on the enterprise. • A thorough understanding of the environment. This includes the IT environment (e.g., infrastructure, applications, dependencies between applications, infrastructure components), the overall business environment, and an understanding of how and which IT environments support the business environment to understand the business impact. • The intervention and common views of all parties involved—senior management, which has the decision power; business management, which has the best view on business impact; IT, which has the understanding of what can go wrong with IT; and risk management, which can moderate and structure the debate amongst the other parties. • The process of developing scenarios usually benefits from a brainstorming/workshop approach, where a high-level assessment is usually required to reduce the number of scenarios to a manageable, but relevant and representative, number.
Use the risk scenario building process to obtain buy-in.	Scenario analysis is not just an analytical exercise involving 'risk analysts'. A significant additional benefit of scenario analysis is achieving organisational buy-in from enterprise entities and business lines, risk management, IT, finance, compliance and other parties. Gaining this buy-in is the reason why scenario analysis should be a carefully facilitated process.
Involve first line of defence in the scenario building process.	In addition to co-ordinating with management, it is recommended that selected members of the staff who are familiar with the detailed operations be included in discussions, where appropriate. Staff whose daily work is in the detailed operations are often more familiar with vulnerabilities in technology and processes that can be exploited.
Do not focus only on rare and extreme scenarios.	When developing scenarios, one should not focus only on worst-case events because they rarely materialise, whereas less-severe incidents happen more often.
Source: ISACA, *COBIT® 5 for Risk*, USA, 2013, figure 37, page 64	

Risk analysis is the process of combining the vulnerability information gathered during an assessment and the threat information gathered from other sources to determine risk of compromise both in terms of frequency and potential magnitude. Analysis may include statistical computations such as VAR, ALE or return on security investment (ROSI) in order to gain greater insight into risk distribution, i.e., the maximum risk and probable risk and/or impact.

See **exhibit 2.8** to identify the relationships between risk analysis, risk assessment and risk management.

Risk evaluation is the process of comparing the results of the risk analysis against established criteria for acceptability, impact, likelihood and whether further treatment is required. Deciding whether risk treatment is required is usually based on operational, technical, financial, regulatory, legal, social or environmental criteria or combinations of criteria. The criteria should be in line with the scope and qualitative analysis of the organization's internal policies and procedures, and must support its goals and objectives.

2.10 RISK ASSESSMENT

Illustrated in **exhibit 2.9**, the first step in performing the assessment is to determine asset valuation. This approach is based on the notion that if the value is low, any risk to it may not be significant and no controls or countermeasures are warranted. Assuming an asset is of significant value, the next element to be considered is to determine what vulnerabilities to loss or damage exist. If vulnerabilities exist, an assessment of viable threats must be performed. If the asset has value as well as vulnerabilities susceptible to viable threats, then there is a risk. To clarify, it is obvious that vulnerabilities for which no threats exist pose no risk. Another way to look at it is that the greater the value, and the greater the number and degree of vulnerabilities coupled with a greater number of viable threats, the greater the risk of loss.

There are numerous risk management models and assessment approaches available to the information security manager. The approach selected will be determined by the best form, fit and function. Some of these include: COBIT, OCTAVE, NIST 800-39,

Exhibit 2.8—Relationship Between Risk Analysis, Risk Assessment and Risk Management

Risk Analysis	Risk Assessment	Risk Management
Risk analysis is the identification and estimation of risk.	Risk assessment is defined as the process to identify and prioritize risk to the business. It refers mainly to the "assessing risk phase" within the larger risk management cycle. Risk analysis forms part of the risk assessment—which is the evaluation of the risk.	Risk management is the overall effort to manage risk to an acceptable level across the business. It is comprised of four primary phases: Assessing risk, conducting decision support, implementing controls and measuring program effectiveness. ISO/IEC Guide 73:2009 defines risk management as: "coordinated activities to direct and control an organization with regard to risk." Risk management is defined in AS/NZS 4360:2004 as "the culture, processes and structures that are directed towards the effective management of potential opportunities and adverse effects" and "the systematic application of management policies, procedures and practices to the tasks of establishing the context, identifying, analyzing, evaluating, treating, monitoring and communicating risk." Note: Risk management typically includes risk assessment, risk treatment, risk acceptance and risk communication.
Typical questions for risk analysis (to understand the root cause of the problem): • What caused the problem? • What does it affect? • How much does the problem cost? • Who is responsible for fixing it? • What will fix the problem? • Is the "fix" worth the investment? • Are the underlying issues ones of ineffective business processes, poor business management or insufficient employee capability?	Typical questions for risk assessment: • What is the problem? • How important is it? • What happens if we ignore the problem?	

Exhibit 2.9—Risk Analysis Framework

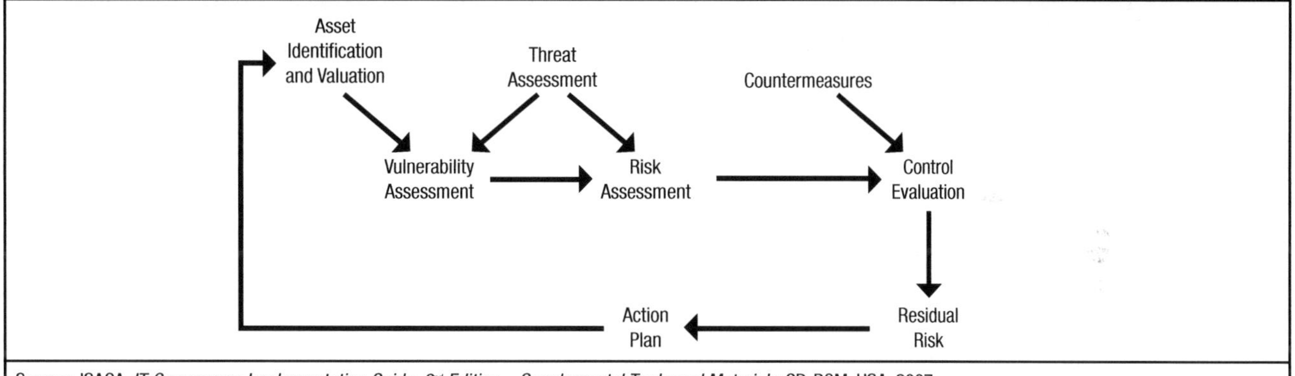

Source: ISACA, *IT Governance Implementation Guide, 2nd Edition—Supplemental Tools and Materials*, CD-ROM, USA, 2007

HB 158-2010, ISO/IEC 31000, ITIL, AND CRAMM. There are other approaches as well such as factor analysis of information risk (FAIR), risk factor analysis, value at risk (VAR), etc. that may be more suitable, depending on the organization and the specific requirements.

Whichever approach is used to identify, assess, evaluate and rank risk, the next step in risk management is the risk treatment process (how the evaluated risk is treated in the organization), discussed in section 2.10.10. The logic flow of the risk treatment process of the AS/NZS Standard 4360 (now superseded by ISO/IEC 31000) is shown in **exhibit 2.10**.

> **Note:** Information security managers should have broad knowledge of the existence of various methodologies to determine the most suitable approach or combination of approaches for their organization. Specific approaches will not be tested in the CISM examination.

The risk assessment approach developed by NIST is demonstrated in the following section as an example of a well-developed, comprehensive methodology. While primarily oriented toward IT, it can be broadened in scope to include other types of information risk.

2.10.1 NIST RISK ASSESSMENT METHODOLOGY

The risk assessment methodology encompasses nine primary steps:

- Step 1—System (or general domain) characterization
- Step 2—Threat identification
- Step 3—Vulnerability identification
- Step 4—Control analysis
- Step 5—Likelihood determination
- Step 6—Impact analysis
- Step 7—Risk determination
- Step 8—Control recommendations
- Step 9—Results documentation

Steps 2, 3, 4, and 6 can be conducted in parallel after Step 1 has been completed.

Exhibit 2.10—The Risk Treatment Process

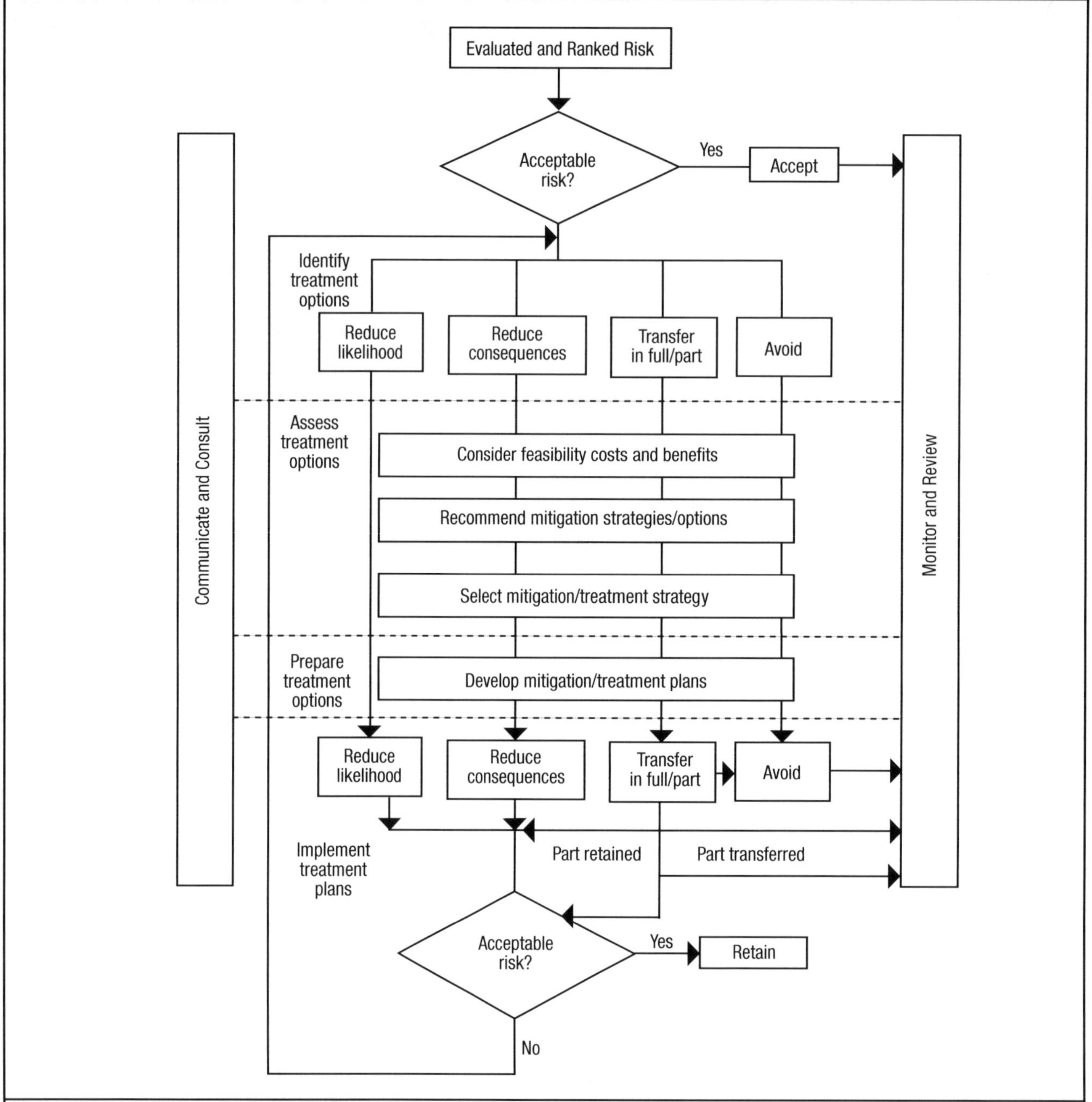

Adapted from the Australian Standard, AS/NZS: 4360:1999, Risk Management, *www.riskmanagement.com/au*

Exhibit 2.11 depicts these steps and the inputs to and outputs from each step.

2.10.2 AGGREGATED AND CASCADING RISK

Another element that must be considered is aggregated risk. This can exist where a particular threat affects a large number of minor vulnerabilities that, in the aggregate, can have a significant impact. Another possibility is that a large number of threats can simultaneously affect a number of minor vulnerabilities, resulting in a large aggregate risk. In this situation, it is possible for risk that is individually acceptable to have a catastrophic impact collectively.

Cascading risk can also manifest unacceptable impacts as a result of one failure leading to a chain reaction of failures. An example of this occurred on the east coast of the United States when a failure at a small power utility in the Midwest caused a cascade of failures across the power grid, ultimately encompassing most of the northeastern quarter of the United States. Similarly, to the extent that portions of the enterprise's IT and other operations have closely coupled dependencies, the information security manager must consider how any particular failure or combinations of failures will affect dependent systems.

Exhibit 2.11—NIST Risk Assessment Methodology

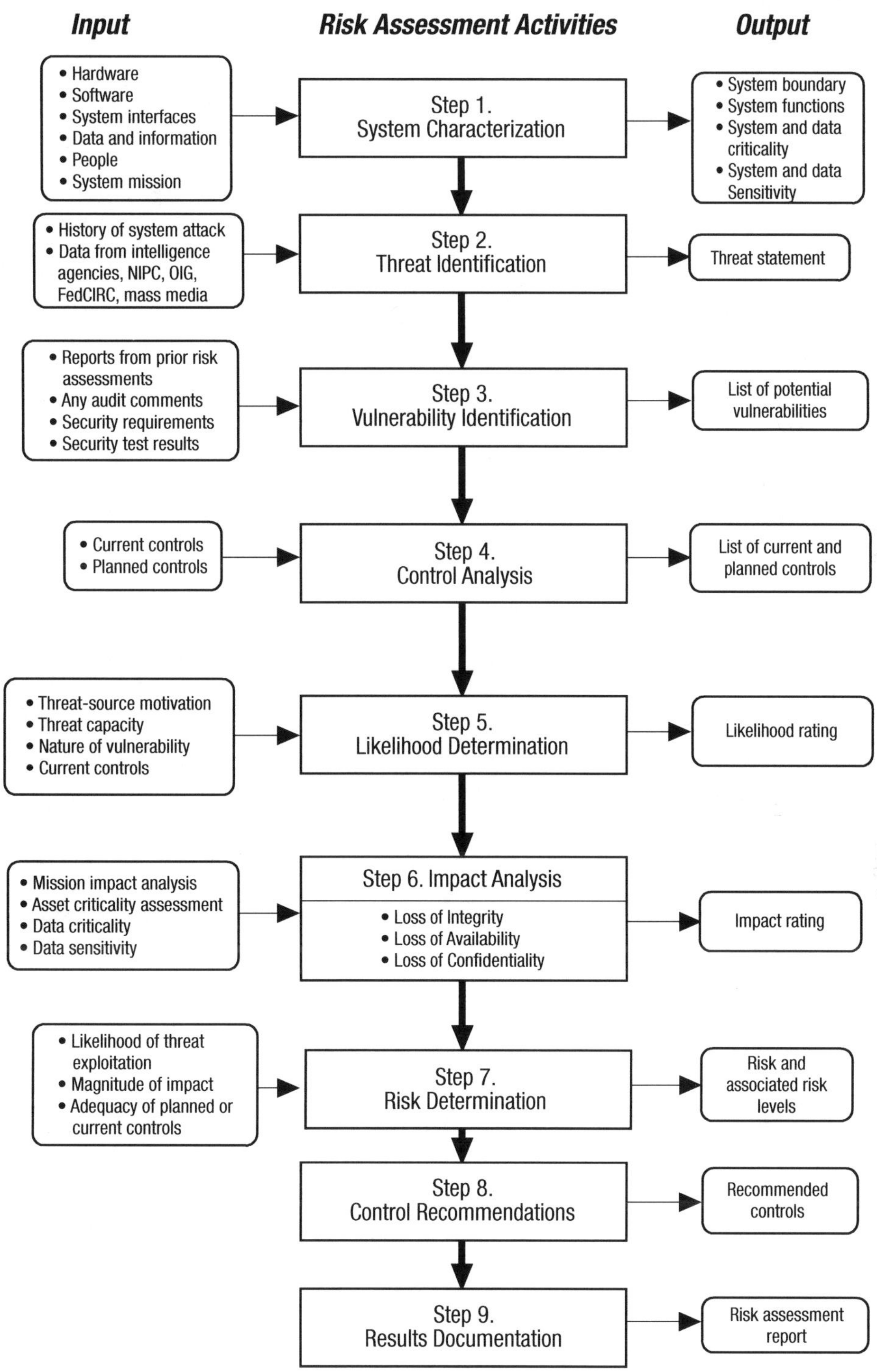

2.10.3 OTHER RISK ASSESSMENT APPROACHES

Developments over the past few decades have resulted in notable improvements in some sectors at defining the bounds of probable risk. However, few of these directly address information risk effectively. Some of these developments are starting to see adoption in the information security field and it is likely that the use of more sophisticated techniques and methods will occur in the coming years. Some of these methods are described in the following section.

Factor Analysis of Information Risk

A promising approach for decomposing risk and understanding its components is Factor Analysis of Information Risk (FAIR). The approach offers a reasoned, detailed analysis process. See **exhibit 2.12**. A white paper is available for understanding and implementing this process *(www.riskmanagementinsight.com/media/docs/FAIR_introduction.pdf)*.

FAIR provides a reasoned and logical framework for answering the following:

- **A taxonomy** of the factors that make up information risk. This taxonomy provides a foundational understanding of information risk, without which one couldn't reasonably do the rest. It also provides a set of standard definitions for our terms.
- **A method for measuring** the factors that drive information risk, including threat event frequency, vulnerability and loss.
- **A computational engine** that derives risk by mathematically simulating the relationships between the measured factors.
- **A simulation model** that allows one to apply the taxonomy, measurement method and computational engine to build and analyze risk scenarios of virtually any size or complexity.

There are four primary components of risk taxonomy for which one wants to identify threat agent characteristics—those characteristics that affect:

- The frequency with which threat agents come into contact with an organization or assets
- The probability that threat agents will act against an organization or assets
- The probability of threat agent actions being successful in overcoming protective controls
- The probable nature (type and severity) of impact to assets

Risk Factor Analysis

Other approaches to decomposing and analyzing risk include work being undertaken at Los Alamos National Laboratory. (*Risk Factor Analysis—A New Qualitative Risk Management Tool*, USA, 2000). See **exhibit 2.13.**

Probabilistic Risk Assessment

Probabilistic risk assessment (PRA) has emerged as an increasingly popular analysis tool, especially during the last decade. PRA is a systematic and comprehensive methodology to evaluate risk associated with every life-cycle aspect of a complex engineered technological entity from concept definition through design, construction and operation, and up to removal from service. Developed for use by the US National Aeronautics and Space Administration (NASA) and the nuclear power industry, the approach is complex and time consuming, but may see application in cases where high network security is required.

According to Dr. Michael Stamatelatos (NASA, *Probabilistic Risk Assessment Procedures Guide for NASA Managers and Practitioners*, USA, NASA Office of Safety and Mission Assurance, August, 2002):

> *PRA usually answers three basic questions:*
> 1. *What can go wrong with the studied technological entity, or what are the initiators or initiating events (undesirable starting events) that lead to adverse consequence(s)?*
> 2. *What and how severe are the potential detriments or the adverse consequences that the technological entity may be eventually subjected to as a result of the occurrence of the initiator?*
> 3. *How likely is occurrence of these undesirable consequences, or what are their probabilities or frequencies?*
>
> *The answer to the first question requires technical knowledge of the possible causes leading to detrimental outcomes of a given activity or action. In order to focus on the most important initiators while screening out the unimportant ones, logic tools such as master logic diagrams (MLD) or failure modes and effects analyses (FMEA) have been used successfully. The answers to the second and third questions are obtained by developing and quantifying accident (or mishap) scenarios, which are chains of events that link the initiator to the end-point detrimental consequences.*

Exhibit 2.12—Factor Analysis of Information Risk (FAIR)

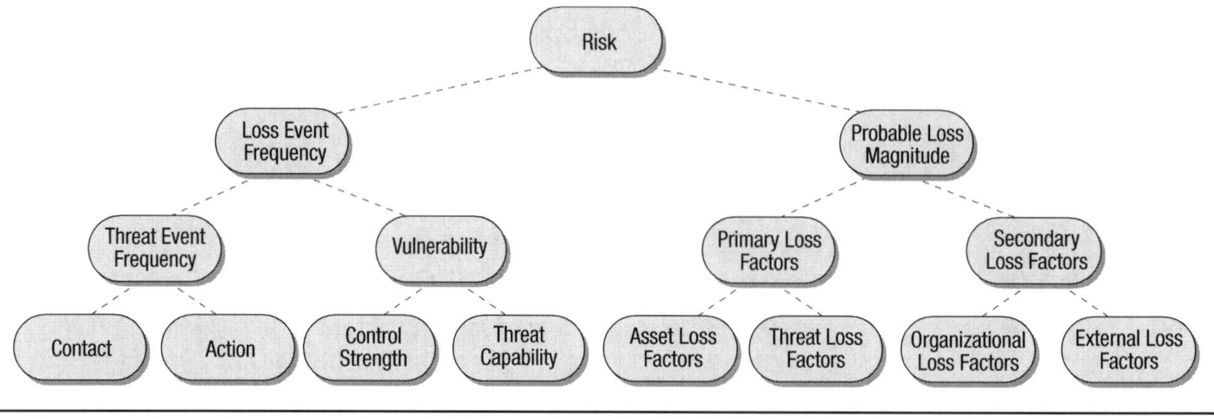

Developed by Jack Jones, Risk Management Insight LLC, 2006, *www.riskmanagementinsight.com/media/docs/FAIR_introduction.pdf*

Exhibit 2.13—Risk Factor Analysis

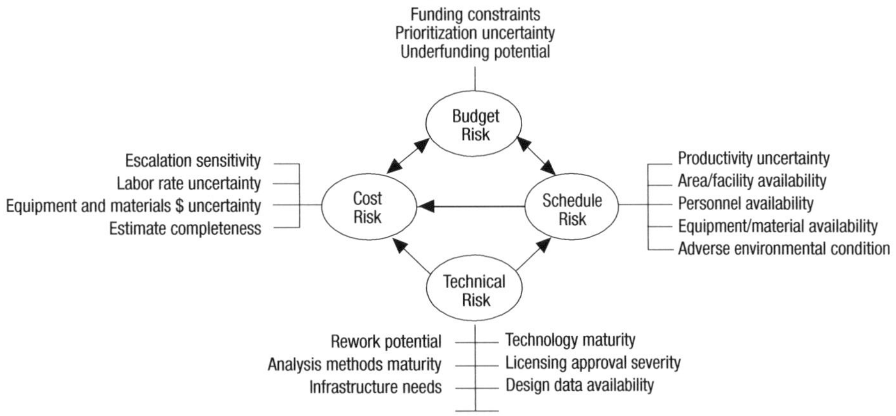

	Risk Category		
	Non/Low (0/1)	**Medium (2)**	**High (3)**
Technology Maturity	Facilities and equipment involve only proven technology or new technology for a noncritical activity.	Facilities and equipment require the adaptation of new technology from other applications critical construction or operating functions for this project.	Facilities and equipment require the development of new technology fpr critical construction or operating functions for this project.
Productivity Uncertainty	The planned rate of progress needed to reach completion as planned is conservative and well within benchmarks observed for similar tasks.	The planned rate of progress needed to reach completion as planned is aggressive but still within benchmarks observed for similar tasks.	The planned rate of progress needed to reach completion as planned is extremely aggressive or no benchmark experience is available to judge the reasonableness of the planned progress rate.
Equipment/ Material Cost Uncertainty	Equipment/material costs are well established and regulated by contracts or competitive market forces.	Equipment/material costs are well established but should be regulated by competitive market forces.	Equipment/material costs are not well established and not subject to competitve market forces.

The answer to the second question is obtained from deterministic analyses (e.g., thermal, fluid, structural or other engineering analyses) that describe the phenomena that could occur along the path of the accident scenario when the initiator and the other subsequent events (through the detrimental consequences) take place. The methods used for these deterministic evaluations depend on the specifics of the technology involved.

The answer to the third question is obtained by using Boolean logic methods for model development and probabilistic or statistical methods for the quantification portion of the model analysis. Boolean logic tools include inductive logic methods such as event tree analysis (ETA) or event sequence diagrams (ESD) analysis and deductive methods such as fault tree analysis (FTA). In cases when the probability of an event is well known from past experience, statistical actuarial data can be used if the uncertainty in these data is acceptably low. For rare events (e.g., system failures) for which there is no past failure experience or the data are very sparse, probabilistic failure models are developed with deductive logic tools such as fault trees, or inductive logic tools such as reliability block diagrams (RBD) and FMEAs.

The final result of a PRA is given in the form of a risk curve and the associated uncertainties. The risk curve is generally the plot of the frequency of exceeding a consequence value (the ordinate) as a function of the consequence values (the abscissa). If the risk assessment is qualitative, the result can be represented as a two-dimensional matrix showing probability categories versus consequence categories.

In addition to the above model of development and quantification, PRA studies require special, but often very important, analysis tools such as human reliability analysis (HRA) and dependent-failure or common-cause analysis (CCF). HRA deals with methods for modeling human error while CCF deals with methods for evaluating the effect of intersystem and intercomponent dependencies that tend to cause significant increases in overall system or facility risk.

2.10.4 IDENTIFICATION OF RISK

Technical methods, including the use of software, can be used in identifying and tracking risk as well as for providing reporting tools to record the analysis of risk. As with any process, the best tool to use is the one that is best suited to meet the unique needs of the organization. In applying risk analysis and identification methods, the information security manager should define resource requirements and establish a budget and timetable for these important tasks. Budgeting and project planning are covered in chapter 3, Information Security Program Development.

One of the initial planning steps in a risk management program is to generate a comprehensive list of sources of threats, vulnerabilities and risk, and events that might have an impact on the ability of the organization to achieve its objectives as identified in the definition of scope and the framework. These events might prevent, degrade, delay or enhance the achievement of those objectives. In general, a risk can be related to or characterized by:

- **Its origin**—e.g., threat agents such as hostile employees, employees not properly trained, competitors, governments, etc.
- **A certain activity, event or incident (i.e., threat)**—e.g., unauthorized dissemination of confidential data, competitor deployment of a new marketing policy, new or revised data protection regulations, an extensive power failure
- **Its consequences, results or impact**—e.g., service unavailability, loss or increase of market share/profits, increase in regulation, increase or decrease in competitiveness, penalties, etc.
- **A specific reason for its occurrence**—e.g., system design error, human intervention, prediction or failure to predict competitor activity
- **Protective mechanisms, exposure and controls (together with an estimate of effectiveness)**—e.g., access control and detection systems, policies, security training, market research and surveillance of market
- **Time and place of occurrence**—e.g., a flood in the computer room during extreme environmental conditions

High-quality information and thorough knowledge of the organization and its internal and external environments are very important in identifying risk. Historical information about this or similar organizations may also prove very useful since the information can lead to reasonable predictions about current and evolving issues that have not yet been faced by the organization.

Identifying what may happen is rarely sufficient. The fact that there are many ways an event can occur makes it important to study all reasonably possible and significant causes and scenarios. Methods and tools used to identify risks and its occurrence include checklists, judgments based on experience and records, flow charts, brainstorming, systems analysis, scenario analysis and systems engineering techniques.

In selecting a risk identification methodology, the following techniques should be considered:

- team-based brainstorming where workshops can prove effective in building commitment and making use of different experiences
- structured techniques such as flow charting, system design review, systems analysis, hazard and operability studies, and operational modeling
- "what-if" and scenario analysis for less clearly defined situations, such as the identification of strategic risk and processes with a more general structure as shown in **exhibit 2.14**
- threats identified internally and externally mapped to identified and suspected vulnerabilities

Exhibit 2.14—Risk Scenario Approaches

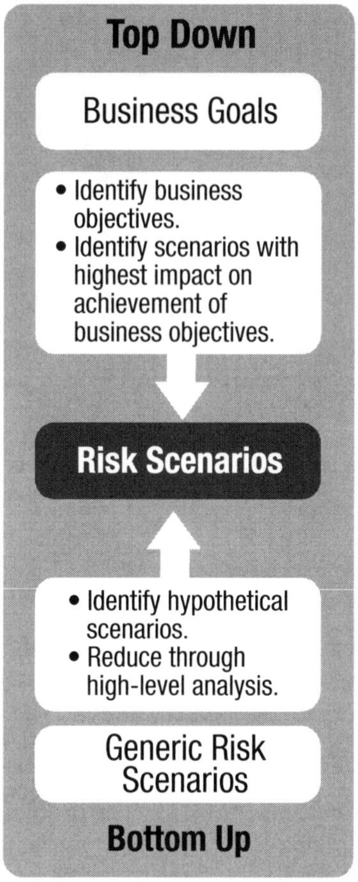

Source: Taken from ISACA, *COBIT 5 for Risk*, USA, 2013, figure 34, page 59

2.10.5 THREATS

Threats to information resources and the likelihood of their occurrence must be assessed. In this context, threats are any circumstances or events with the potential to cause harm to an information resource by exploiting vulnerabilities in the system. Threats are usually categorized as:

- **Natural**—Flood, fire, cyclones, rain/hail, plagues and earthquakes
- **Unintentional**—Fire, water, building damage/collapse, loss of utility services and equipment failure
- **Intentional physical**—Bombs, fire, water and theft
- **Intentional nonphysical**—Fraud, espionage, hacking, identity theft, malicious code, social engineering, phishing attacks and denial-of-service attacks

Advanced Persistent Threat (APT)

It is important for the information security manager to be aware that APT poses a significant risk to organizations of virtually all types globally and to ensure that appropriate steps are in place to detect and identify this threat.

APT is defined in NIST publication 800-61 as:

> *An APT is an adversary that possesses sophisticated levels of expertise and significant resources which allow it to create opportunities to achieve its objectives using multiple attack vectors (e.g., cyber, physical and deception). These objectives typically include establishing and extending footholds within the IT infrastructure of the targeted organizations for purposes of exfiltrating information, undermining or impeding critical aspects of a mission, program or organization; or positioning itself to carry out these objectives in the future. The advanced persistent threat: (i) pursues its objectives repeatedly over an extended period of time; (ii) adapts to defenders' efforts to resist it; and (iii) is determined to maintain the level of interaction needed to execute its objectives.*

In 2013, in a report titled "APT1 Exposing One of China's Cyber Espionage Units," Mandiant presented results of their research on alleged Chinese attacks using APT methodology between 2004 and 2013 that exhibited the following typical life cycle:

- **Initial compromise**—Use social engineering and spear phishing, over email, using zero-day viruses. Plant malware on a web site that the victim employees will be likely to visit.
- **Establish foothold**—Plant remote administration software in the victim's network, create network back doors and tunnels allowing stealth access to its infrastructure.
- **Escalate privileges**—Use exploits and password cracking to acquire administrator privileges over the victim's computer and possibly expand it to Windows domain administrator accounts.
- **Internal reconnaissance**—Collect information on surrounding infrastructure, trust relationships, Windows domain structure.
- **Move laterally**—Expand control to other work stations, servers and infrastructure elements and perform data harvesting on them.
- **Maintain presence**—Ensure continued control over access channels and credentials acquired in previous steps.
- **Complete mission**—Exfiltrate stolen data from the victim's network.

Exhibit 2.15 shows the typical sources of APT. Due to the required sophistication, expertise, time and costs involved, these efforts are normally only mounted against high-value targets.

The 2013 survey in **exhibit 2.16** shows the percentage of respondents that utilize various countermeasures and controls to address APT. The study indicates that nearly half of the organizations surveyed do not make an effort to address this issue at all and remain highly vulnerable to this form of exploit while a quarter of respondents are apparently not aware that the threat exists.

Exhibit 2.15—Typical Sources of APT

Threat	What They Seek	Business Impact
Intelligence agencies	Political, defense or commercial trade secrets	Loss of trade secrets or commercial, competitive advantage
Criminal groups	Money transfers, extortion opportunities, personal identity information or any secrets for potential onward sale	Financial loss, large-scale customer data breach or loss of trade secrets
Terrorist groups	Production of widespread terror through death, destruction and disruption	Loss of production and services, stock market irregularities, and potential risk to human life
Activist groups	Confidential information or disruption of services	Major data breach or loss of service
Armed forces	Intelligence or positioning to support future attacks on critical national infrastructure	Serious damage to facilities in the event of a military conflict

Source: ISACA, *Advanced Persistent Threats: How to Manage the Risk to Your Business*, USA, 2013, figure 2, page 29

Exhibit 2.16—Activities and Techniques Used to Counter Advanced Persistent Threats

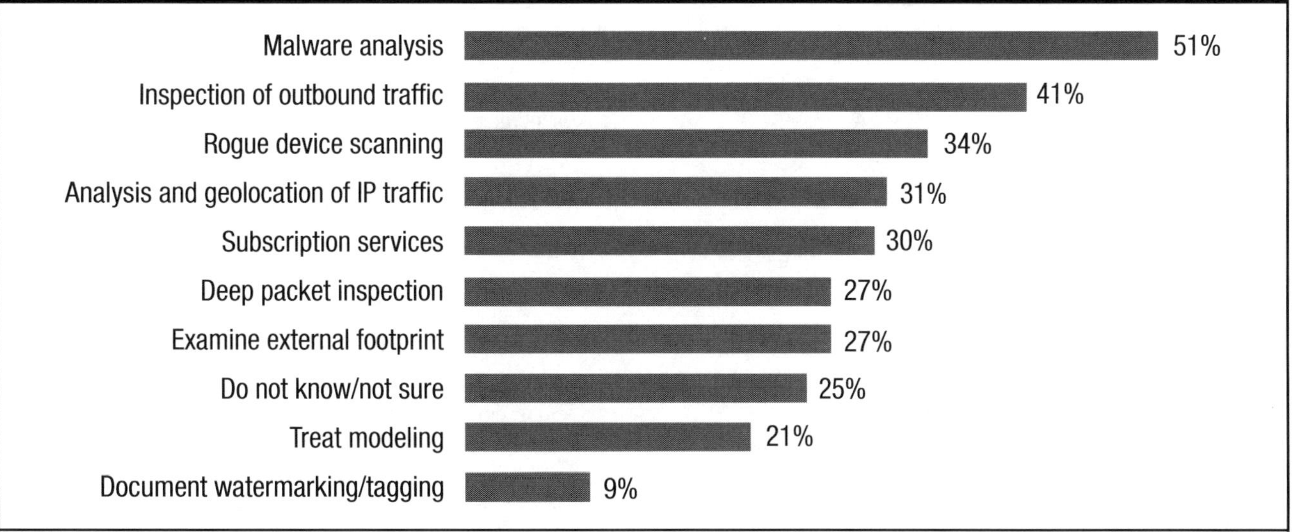

Source: *CSO Magazine*; CERT Coordination Center at Carnegie Mellon University, USA; US Federal Bureau of Investigation (FBI); PricewaterhouseCoopers; US Secret Service; *2013 US State of Cybercrime Survey*, USA, March-April 2013

2.10.6 VULNERABILITIES

The term "vulnerability" is often used as if it is a binary condition. Something "is vulnerable" or it "is not vulnerable." More accurately, assets are vulnerable to varying degrees—i.e., a particular control condition might represent a high degree of vulnerability, while another control condition represents a lower degree of vulnerability. The extent of exposure must also be considered as it affects the probability that a vulnerability is compromised. These distinctions become critical in the process of prioritizing risk management efforts, when determining the level of risk within a scenario and also when explaining conclusions and recommendations to management.

Estimating the degree of vulnerability can be accomplished through various forms of testing (when time permits and when the stakes are high) or through subject matter expert estimates. As with other valuations, estimates can be quantitative or qualitative. Whatever the approach, it is important to communicate the imprecise nature of these estimates so that management is not misled. Effective approaches for reflecting uncertainty in values include using ranges or distributions to indicate both unlikely maximums and those values that are more probable.

Determining the ultimate relevancy of a weak control also requires an understanding of the other controls in play that may mitigate the overall exposure. It would be inaccurate and a disservice to portray a control as a severe problem when, in fact, the combination of controls is relatively robust.

Many IT system weaknesses are identified using automated scanning equipment, and these can serve as leading indicators of potential compromise. Process and performance vulnerabilities are more difficult to ascertain and may require careful review and analysis to uncover. To be effective, it is essential that the assessment consider process, procedural and physical vulnerabilities in addition to technology weaknesses.

Consider the organization that does not have a formal information security training and awareness program. The vulnerability in this instance would stem from a lack of user awareness of security policies, standards and guidelines. Absent such awareness training, it has been shown that an organization is considerably more likely to suffer compromise from social engineering attacks such as phishing. Vulnerabilities can occur from numerous causes, ranging from a lack of processes for configuration control to poor personnel morale, from a vast variety of technical issues to countless human factors.

Audits, security reviews, vulnerability scans, penetration tests and key risk indicators (KRIs), among others, are usually helpful in identifying vulnerabilities. Some typical examples of vulnerabilities include:

- Defective software
- Improperly configured equipment
- Inadequate compliance enforcement
- Poor network design
- Uncontrolled or defective processes
- Inadequate governance or management
- Insufficient staff
- Lack of knowledge to support users or operations
- Lack of security functionality
- Lack of proper maintenance
- Poor choice of passwords
- Untested technology
- Transmission of unprotected communications
- Lack of redundancy
- Poor management communications

2.10.7 RISK

The traditional assessment of risk is expressed in the statement "Threats × Vulnerabilities = Risk." The result is that if there are more threats against more or greater vulnerability, there is more risk. Another current, more generalized definition of risk, also subject to considerable controversy from ISO 73:2009, is "the combination of the probability of an event and its consequence." The consequence could be a compromise or, in this context, could be a positive event as well. For most, "positive risk" is generally considered an opportunity rather than a risk, and the ISO definition does not appear to clarify the matter. Currently, most practitioners consider the notion of risk in a negative sense, and the term is used in this manual from that perspective.

Whatever definition is used, the information security manager must understand the business risk profile (in the negative sense) of the organization in terms of adversely affecting the ability to achieve its objectives.

No model provides a complete picture of all possible risk, but logically categorizing the risk areas of an organization (as illustrated in **exhibit 2.17**) facilitates focusing on key risk management strategies and decisions. It also enables the organization to develop and implement risk treatment approaches that are relevant to the business and cost effective.

A high-level categorization of risk is an inherent part of business and, because it is impractical and costly to eliminate all risk, every organization has a level of risk it will accept. The level of acceptable risk is a decision that must be made by senior management, although the information security manager may need to assist management in developing a concrete set of criteria. Approaches to assist in determining the level of acceptable risk are discussed in detail in Chapter 1, section 1.10.4 Risk Objectives.

The essential concept is that an optimal point is located where the cost of losses intersects with the costs associated with mitigating or otherwise treating the risk. This goes to the idea that the cost of protection should not exceed the value of the asset being protected.

But many factors will affect what the organization ultimately considers acceptable based on considerations such as culture, the ability of the organization to absorb losses, the effects and costs of mitigation, the extent and kind of potential impacts, and possibly legal and/or contractual requirements. In terms of culture, the organization may be generally risk adverse and opt for tighter and higher control costs, or the organization may be risk aggressive and choose to take more chances.

For most organizations the failure to adequately identify, assess, analyze, evaluate and manage risk results in risk management efforts not being properly allocated and directed at those situations with the greatest probability of compromise and the greatest impact.

It is fair to say that, for most organizations, the primary risk management efforts are typically directed at controlling unauthorized system access—which, on average, represents a relatively small proportion of losses while the majority of losses from the other identified causes such as outsourced services, electronic backup, lost or stolen laptops and paper records generally receive relatively little attention.

It also makes sense to consider the sources of risk when performing risk assessments and to consider what to monitor and where to focus. The PricewaterhouseCoopers and *CSO Magazine Global State of Information Security Survey 2014* (*www.pwc.com*) included more than 9,600 respondents covering the sources of more than 48,000 breaches. The estimated sources of these breaches are shown in **exhibit 2.18**.

For the prevalent sources of compromise one needs to consider how to allocate protection resources for the greatest benefit. Because many of the most significant threats can be addressed directly—e.g., employees and former employees, service providers, consultants, suppliers—it is prudent to consider the specific controls addressing this risk. Strong access controls, limiting access to need-to-know, network segmentation, effective termination procedures, and good monitoring will contribute to reducing risk.

It is important to recognize that the major risk to organizations does not come from technology and, to a large extent, cannot be solved by technology. Rather, risk is largely a management and personnel problem.

"I see the insider threat looming larger in my windshield than in the past," says Michael A. Mason, chief security officer for Verizon Communications, adding that Verizon defines insiders as anyone who has access to Verizon's data. "And it's important to note that insider threats are not necessarily a 'bad guy' with bad intentions; it could be a good employee doing righteous work in an insecure manner. Our problems are more human than technological."

Exhibit 2.17—Operational Risk Categories

Operational Risk Area	Description	Information or IT Mapping
Facilities and operating environment risk	Loss or damage to operational capabilities caused by problems with premises, facilities, services or equipment	Business continuity management for IT facilities
Health and safety risk	Threats to the personal health and safety of staff, customers and members of the public	Confidentiality of home addresses, travel schedules, etc.
Information risk	Unauthorized disclosure or modification to information, loss of availability of information, or inappropriate use of information	All aspects of information and IT security
Control frameworks risk	Inadequate design or performance of the existing risk management infrastructure	Business process analysis to identify critical information flows and control points
Legal and regulatory compliance risk	Failure to comply with the laws of the countries in which business operations are carried out; failure to comply with any regulatory, reporting and taxation standards; failure to comply with contracts; or failure of contracts to protect business interests	Compliance with data protection legislation, cryptographic control regulations, etc.; accuracy, timeliness and quality of information reported to regulators; and content management of all information sent to other parties
Corporate governance risk	Failure of directors to fulfill their personal statutory obligations in managing and controlling the company	Information security policy making, performance measurement and reporting
Reputation risk	The negative effects of public opinion, customer opinion and market reputation, and the damage caused to the brand by failure to manage public relations	Controlling the disclosure of confidential information; presenting a public image of a well-managed enterprise
Strategic risk	Failure to meet the long-term strategic goals of the business, including dependence on any estimated or planned outcomes that may be in the control of third parties	Managing the quality and granularity of information on which strategic business decisions are based (e.g., mergers, acquisitions, disposals)
Processing and behavioral risk	Problems with service or product delivery caused by failure of internal controls, information systems, employee integrity, errors and mistakes, or through weaknesses in operating procedures	All aspects of information systems security and the security-related behavior of employees in carrying out their tasks

Exhibit 2.17—Operational Risk Categories *(cont.)*

Operational Risk Area	Description	Information or IT Mapping
Technology risk	Failure to plan, manage and monitor the performance of technology-related projects, products, services, processes, staff and delivery channels	Failure of information and communications technology systems and the need for business continuity management
Project management risk	Failure to plan and manage the resources required for achieving tactical project goals, leading to budget overruns, time overruns or both, or leading to failure to complete the project; the technical failure of a project or the failure to manage the integration aspects with existing parts of the business and the impact that changes can have on business operations	Management of all information security-related projects
Criminal and illicit acts risk	Loss or damage caused by fraud, theft, willful neglect, gross negligence, vandalism, sabotage, extortion, etc.	Provision of security services and mechanisms to prevent all types of cybercrime
Human resources risk	Failure to recruit, develop or retain employees with the appropriate skills and knowledge or to manage employee relations	Need for policies protecting employees from sexual harassment, racial abuse, etc., through corporate e-mail systems, etc.
Supplier risk	Failure to evaluate adequately the capabilities of suppliers leading to breakdowns in the supply process or substandard delivery of supplied goods and services; failure to understand and manage the supply chain issues	Outsourced service delivery of IT or other business information processing activities
Management information risk	Inadequate, inaccurate, incomplete or untimely provision of information to support the management decision-making process	Managing the accuracy, integrity, currency, timeliness and quality of information used for management decision support
Ethics risk	Damage caused by unethical business practices, including those of associated business partners. Issues include racial and religious discrimination, exploitation of child labor, pollution, environmental issues, behavior to disadvantaged groups, etc.	Ethical collection, storage and use of information; management of information content on web sites, intranets, and in corporate e-mails and instant messaging systems
Geopolitical risk	Loss or damage in some countries, caused by political instability, poor quality of infrastructure in developing regions, or cultural differences and misunderstandings	Managing all aspects of information security and IT systems' security in regions where the enterprise has business operations but where there is special geopolitical risk
Cultural risk	Failure to deal with cultural issues affecting employees, customers or other stakeholders. These include language, religion, morality, dress codes, and other community customs and practices.	Management of information content on web sites, intranets, and in corporate e-mails and instant messaging systems
Climate and weather risk	Loss or damage caused by unusual climate conditions, including drought, heat, flood, cold, storm, winds, etc.	Business continuity management for IT facilities

Source: Sherwood, J.; A. Clark; D. Lynas; Enterprise Security Architecture: *A Business-Driven Approach*, CMP Books, 2005, *www.sabsa.org*

Exhibit 2.18—Estimated Likely Source of Incidents

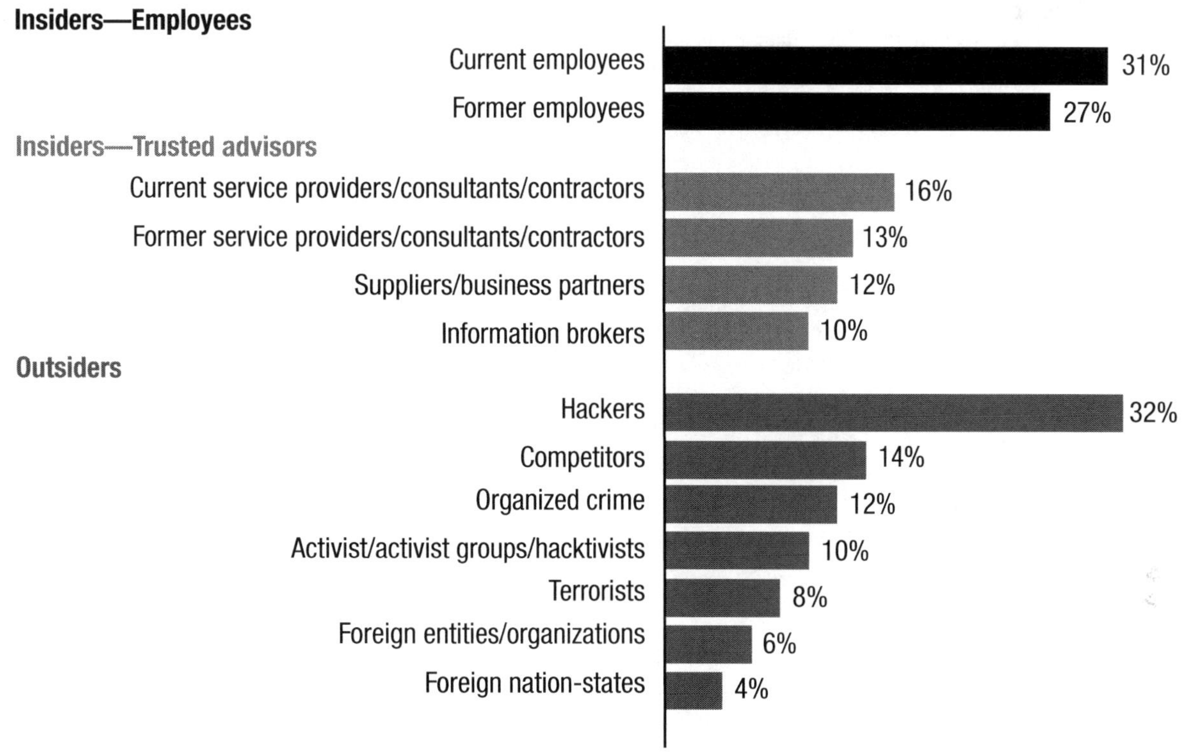

Note: Not all factors shown. Totals do not add up to 100%. Respondents were allowed to indicate multiple factors.

Source: PricewaterhouseCoopers and *CSO Magazine, Global State of Information Security Survey 2014*, used with permission, *www.pwc.com*

2.10.8 ANALYSIS OF RELEVANT RISK

Risk analysis is the phase where the level of the risk and its nature are assessed and understood. This information is the first input to decision makers on whether risk needs to be treated as well as the most appropriate and cost-effective risk treatment methodology. Risk analysis involves:
- thorough examination of the risk sources (threats and vulnerabilities);
- their positive and negative consequences;
- the likelihood that those consequences may occur and the factors that affect them;
- assessment of any existing controls or processes that tend to minimize negative risk or enhance positive outcomes (these controls may derive from a wider set of standards, controls or good practices selected according to a an applicability statement and may also come from previous risk treatment activities).

The level of risk can be estimated in various ways, including using statistical analysis and calculations combining impact and likelihood. Impact may not be clear unless business impact assessments have been performed to provide an understanding of the cost to the organization as the result of the loss of a particular function or asset.

Any formulas and methods for combining impact and likelihood must be consistent with the criteria defined when establishing the risk management context. This is because an event may have multiple consequences and affect different objectives; therefore, consequences and likelihood need to be combined to calculate the level of risk. If no reliable or statistically reliable and relevant past data are available (e.g., kept for an incident database), other estimates may be made as long as they are appropriately communicated and approved by the decision makers.

Information used to estimate impact and likelihood usually comes from:
- past experience or data and records (e.g., incident reporting);
- reliable practices, international standards or guidelines;
- market research and analysis;
- experiments and prototypes;
- economic, engineering or other models;
- specialist and expert advice.

Risk analysis techniques include:
- interviews with experts in the area of interest and questionnaires,
- use of existing models and simulations.

Risk analysis may vary in detail according to the risk, the purpose of the analysis, and the required protection level of the relevant information, data and resources. Analysis may be qualitative, semiquantitative or quantitative or a combination of these. In any case the type of analysis performed should, as stated above, be consistent with the criteria developed as part of the definition of the risk management context.

A description of the three types of analysis includes:

Qualitative Analysis

In qualitative analysis, the magnitude and likelihood of potential consequences are presented and described in detail. The scales used can be formed or adjusted to suit the circumstances, and different descriptions may be used for different risk. Qualitative analysis may be used:
- as an initial assessment to identify risk which will be the subject of further, detailed analysis;
- where nontangible aspects of risk are to be considered (e.g., reputation, culture, image, etc.)
- where there is a lack of adequate information and numerical data or resources necessary for a statistically acceptable quantitative approach.

A qualitative analysis can be accomplished by using a 5 by 5 matrix as shown in **exhibit 2.19** in the semiquantitative impact matrix.

Semiquantitative Analysis

In semiquantitative analysis, the objective is to assign values to the scales used in the qualitative assessment. These values are usually indicative and not real, which is the prerequisite of the quantitative approach. Therefore, as the value allocated to each scale is not an accurate representation of the actual magnitude of impact or likelihood, the numbers used must only be combined using a formula that recognizes the limitations or assumptions made in the description of the scales used. It also should be mentioned that the use of semiquantitative analysis may lead to various inconsistencies due to the fact that the numbers chosen may not properly reflect analogies between risks, particularly when either consequences or likelihood are extreme.

The values selected should be generally indicative and sufficient for the prioritization of one risk above another risk. For any process to operate successfully there should be a common understanding of these values and of the terms employed. The definitions shown below can be substituted with ones already in use within the organization, and it may be possible to use a subset from the enterprise risk management (ERM) framework where one exists.

Typical values for impact are:
- Insignificant (value = 1) = No meaningful impact, or of limited consequence
- Minor (value = 2) = Impact on small part of business only, or less than US $1 million impact
- Major (value = 3) = Impact on the organization's brand, or more than US $1 million impact
- Material (value = 4) = Impact more than US $200 million and requiring external reporting
- Catastrophic (value = 5) = Failure or significant downsizing of the organization

Typical values for likelihood are:
- Rare (value = 1)
- Unlikely (value = 2) = Not seen within last 5 years
- Moderate (value = 3) = Seen within last 5 years but not within last year
- Likely (value = 4) = Seen within last year
- Frequent (value = 5) = Happens on a regular basis

These values should be sufficient to allow risk prioritization according to a semiquantitative approach.

Typically, you would then calculate the risk probability and consequences as:
- Risk = impact × likelihood
- Risk = 4 (material) × 3 (moderate) = 12

Exhibit 2.19—Semiquantitative Impact Matrix

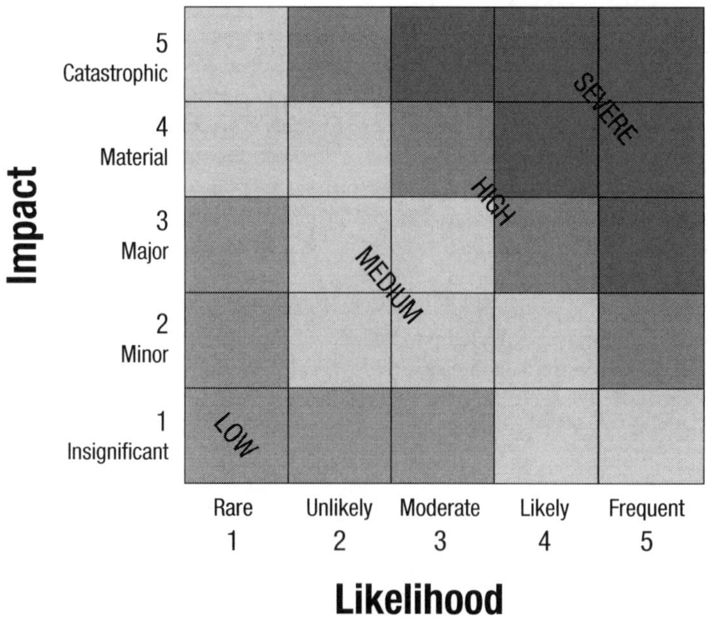

Example of a Semiquantitative Analysis

The value of the approach shown here is derived from the diversity of participants (although appropriate to the task at hand), the quality of the facilitated discussion and the consensus decision arrived at within a facilitated workshop. If this analysis is attempted in isolation, it is likely that the outcome will be flawed and incomplete:

Step 1—What are the business assets? Establish an asset register that identifies and values these assets. Identify critical assets in the register. This should be accomplished in partnership with the business owners and other relevant parties.
Step 2—What possible threats put the organization's assets at risk? Identify the possible threats.
Step 3—For each threat, what would the business impact be if the threat materialized? Identify and quantify these impacts by relating back to the asset register. For each asset, identify the business impact if the asset were no longer available, and the likelihood of that impact. This should typically be conducted in a facilitated workshop attended by the business owners, system owners, infrastructure subject matter experts (e.g., architects) and security subject matter experts.

In this model, impact is described as the cost to the business (e.g., downtime = lost revenue) if an asset is not available for a period of time.

To further enable the workshop participants to visualize the risk to the asset, a large printed (sometimes hand-drawn) grid can be used. The asset is written onto a sticky note and placed on a risk matrix or grid. The facilitator can then encourage the workshop participants to decide on impact and likelihood for the asset. From experience, it is important to strongly challenge the placement of the asset on the chart. An example grid is shown in **exhibit 2.19**.

At this point in the process, a template can be used to capture the risk that has been placed in the high and severe regions of the matrix. The template is used to record the outcomes from the following steps:
Step 1—If the impact is significant enough to be of concern, what vulnerabilities or weaknesses might there be to allow this threat to exploit the organization's assets, causing an impact? The vulnerability or weakness combined with a known threat will alter the likelihood of the event taking place. Identify and quantify these vulnerabilities or weaknesses.
Step 2—Can these vulnerabilities or weaknesses be mitigated by introducing additional controls? Identify the possible control strategies and quantify cost (total cost of ownership) for these controls.
Step 3—What is the cost-benefit analysis derived from the level of reduction of potential business impact (benefit) weighed against the cost of the additional control? Quantify the benefits and costs.

Quantitative Analysis

In quantitative analysis numerical values are assigned to both impact and likelihood. These values are derived from a variety of sources. The quality of the entire analysis depends on the accuracy of the assigned values and the validity of the statistical models used. Impact can be determined by evaluating and processing the various results of an event or by extrapolation from experimental studies or past data. Consequences may be expressed in various terms of:
- Monetary
- Technical
- Operational
- Human impact criteria

As it is made clear from the above analysis, the specification of the risk level is not unique. Impact and likelihood may be expressed or combined differently, according to the type of risk and the scope and objective of the risk management process.

Annual Loss Expectancy

Quantitative risk assessments will attempt to arrive at a numerical value, usually expressed in financial terms. The most common form will be either single loss expectancy (SLE) or annual loss expectancy (ALE). SLE is the product of the asset value (AV) multiplied by the exposure factor (EF): SLE = AV × EF.

EF is the probability that an event will occur and its likely magnitude, and equals the percentage of asset loss caused by the identified threat. The result is that the greater the value, coupled with a greater probability and greater magnitude, the greater the potential risk of loss.

ALE adds the annualized rate of occurrence (ARO) to the equation with the result that multiple occurrences will result in greater potential losses. ALE is usually expressed as:
ALE = SLE × ARO.

ALE is the annual expected financial loss to an asset, resulting from one specific threat.

ARO is the number of times a threat on a single asset is estimated to occur. The higher the risk associated with the threat, the higher the ARO. For example, if insurance data suggest that a serious fire is likely to occur once in 25 years, then the annualized rate of occurrence is 1/25 = 0.04.

EF represents the percentage of loss that a realized threat could have on a specific asset when the specific threat matches up with a specific vulnerability. Said another way, EF is the proportion of an asset's value that is likely to be destroyed by a particular risk, expressed as a percentage.

Value at Risk

Another approach required in certain financial sectors is value at risk (VAR), which can also have general risk management utility and benefit. This approach has been studied by various researchers, suggesting the suitability of the approach for information security management.

VAR is a computation based on historical data of the probability distribution of loss for a given period of time at a certainty factor typically of 95% or 99%. The probability distribution is arrived at using Monte Carlo simulations typically run through thousands of iterations with random variables based on historical information.

An approach using VAR in quantifying risk was proposed in a white paper published in 2001 at a conference in Florida. The paper summarized how VAR can be successfully used in information risk management.

> *Value at risk (VAR) summarizes the worst loss due to a security breach over a specific period of time, with a given level of confidence. More formally, VAR describes the quartile of the projected distribution of losses over a given time period. Most of the tools that are used for information risk assessment are qualitative in nature and are not grounded in theory.*
>
> *VAR is a useful tool in the hands of an expert as it provides a theoretically based, quantitative measure of information risk. Using this measure of risk, the best possible balance between risk and the cost of providing security can be achieved. Most organizations, especially those heavily invested in eBusiness, already have determined the acceptable level of risk. The dollar amount of this risk is then computed. When the total VAR of an organization exceeds this amount, the organization is alerted to the fact that an increased security investment is required.*
>
> (Value at Risk: A Methodology for Information Security Risk Assessment, Jeevan Jaisingh and Jackie Rees, *Proceedings From the INFORMS Conference on Information Systems and Technology 2001,* November 2001, Miami, FL, USA)

2.10.9 EVALUATION OF RISK

During the risk evaluation phase, decisions have to be made concerning which risk needs treatment and the treatment priorities based on the foregoing analysis. Analysts need to compare the level of risk determined during the analysis process with risk criteria established in the risk management context (i.e., in the risk criteria identification stage).

It is important to note that, in some cases, the risk evaluation may lead to a decision to undertake further analysis.

The criteria used by the risk management team must also take into account the organization objectives, the stakeholder views and, of course, the scope and objective of the risk management process itself as well as its probable margins of error. The decisions made are usually based on the level of risk, but may also be related to thresholds specified in terms of:
- consequences (e.g., impacts)
- the likelihood of events
- the cumulative (aggregated) impact of a series of events that could occur simultaneously
- the cost of treatment
- the ability of the organization to absorb losses

2.10.10 RISK TREATMENT OPTIONS

Faced with risk, organizations have four strategic choices:
- Terminate the activity giving rise to risk.
- Transfer risk to another party.
- Mitigate risk with appropriate control measures or mechanisms.
- Accept the risk.

Another alternative is that an organization may choose to accept risk by ignoring it, which can be dangerous. Ignoring a risk over time may lead to a serious underestimation of the magnitude of the risk. Accordingly, this is generally an inadvisable course of action. The only time it may be prudent to ignore a risk is when the likelihood, exposure or impact is so small that the risk is not considered material to the organization or the impact is so great and rare that there is no possibility of addressing it—e.g., a comet strike or nuclear war.

The measures (i.e., security measurements) can be selected out of sets of security measurements that are used within the information security management system (ISMS) of the organization as defined by ISO/IEC 27001:2003. At this level, security measurements are verbal descriptions of various security functions that are implemented technically (e.g., software or hardware components) or organizationally (e.g., established procedures).

Terminate the Activity

There are often ways activities might be modified or processes reengineered that can serve to mitigate or manage risk to acceptable levels. Analysis of the activity could also lead to the conclusion that it is not worth the risk. In this circumstance it should be noted that even though the organization has determined to terminate the continuation of the good or service, the liability remains as long as the product or service is being used.

Transfer the Risk

An example of risk transference is the decision by an organization to purchase insurance to address areas of risk. When an organization buys insurance, the risk is transferred to the insurance company in exchange for premium payments that reflect the insurance company's assessment of the degree of risk that it is assuming. It should be recognized that the risk is actually not transferred, rather, impact to the organization is reduced to the extent that insurance covers the costs associated with a compromise.

Risk can also be transferred by outsourcing IT functionality to a third party, provided there are indemnification clauses in the contracts; however, in transferring operational risk, third-party agreements and contracts must specifically address the liability and responsibilities of both parties in specific indemnification clauses.

Indemnity agreements that can be part of an outsourced service agreement provide a level of protection against harmful incidents. **While the possible financial impacts associated with the risk can be transferred, the legal responsibility for the consequences of compromise generally cannot be transferred.**

Risk is typically transferred to insurance companies when the probability of an incident is low, but the impact is high. An example would be earthquake or flood insurance. For the information security manager, this means that a well-managed risk program must interface with other organizational assurance providers such as the insurance department to understand what risk is covered by other assurance providers such as insurance and to what extent. Obviously, if some identified risk is adequately managed by other entities, duplication of efforts is generally not warranted.

Mitigate the Risk

Risk can be mitigated in a variety of ways. Risk can be mitigated by implementing or improving security controls or by instituting countermeasures. These controls may directly address the risk or they may be compensating controls that mitigate the effects of an occurrence. The potential impact may be reduced through procedural or technical processes. Threats and vulnerabilities may be addressed directly, reducing the likelihood of exploitation. The extent of exposure may be reduced, thus lessening the likelihood that a vulnerability is exploited.

Tolerate/Accept the Risk

There are a variety of circumstances where a defined risk may be accepted. One condition is if the cost of mitigating it is too high in proportion to the value of the asset. In other cases, it may simply not be feasible to effectively mitigate a risk or the potential impact may be low. Generally, there is an optimal point where the cost of mitigating a risk is equal to the financial impact of compromise. It must be considered that not all impacts can be readily reduced to strictly financial terms and, in many cases, will not be the only consideration.

Elements such as customer trust and confidence, legal liability, or breach of regulatory requirements may need to be considered as well. In any case, the information risk management procedure should enable accurate and appropriate documentation of the risk in order for the business manager to make the decision to accept the risk based on sufficient knowledge and understanding. Acceptance of risk should be regularly reviewed to ensure that the rationale for the initial acceptance is still valid within the current business context.

Risk Acceptance Framework

The risk acceptance framework is an important tool—with this in place, the organization can ensure that acceptance of risk is executed at the right level management.

A typical risk acceptance framework is shown below in **exhibit 2.20**.

Exhibit 2.20—Risk Acceptance Framework

Risk Level	Level Required for Acceptance
Low	Risk acceptance possible by local management
Medium	Risk acceptance possible by chief information officer (CIO)
High	Risk acceptance possible by CIO, director or chief information security officer (CISO), depending on potential impact
Severe	Risk acceptance only at board level, depending on potential impact. Risk reduction is mandatory through rigorous controls or monitoring. Management notification process is required.

2.10.11 RESIDUAL RISK

The risk that still remains after countermeasures and controls have been implemented is called residual risk. Using the example of requiring dual control to access sensitive information, one residual risk is that two individuals collude to provide unauthorized access.

Residual risk reported through a subsequent risk assessment can be used by management to identify those areas in which more control is required to further mitigate risk. Acceptable levels of risk are established as a part of developing an information security strategy as described in chapter 1. If a strategy is not developed, management must determine the acceptable risk levels, usually in terms of allowable potential impacts. Residual risk in excess of this level should be further treated with the option of additional mitigation through implementing more stringent controls. Risk below this level should be evaluated to determine whether an excessive level of countermeasures or control is being applied, and whether cost savings can be achieved by removing or modifying them. Final acceptance of residual risk takes into account:

- Regulatory compliance
- Organizational policy
- Sensitivity and criticality of relevant assets
- Acceptable levels of potential impacts
- Uncertainty inherent in the risk assessment approach
- Cost and effectiveness of implementation

In judging the appropriateness of controls or countermeasures, the full life cycle cost must be considered, including the cost of implementing and operating specific measures or mechanisms balanced against the risk and potential impacts being addressed.

2.10.12 IMPACT

Impact is the bottom line for risk management. Ultimately, all risk management activities are designed to reduce impacts to acceptable levels in order to create or preserve value to the organization. The result of any vulnerability exploited by a threat that causes a loss is an impact. Threats and vulnerabilities that do not cause an impact are usually irrelevant.

In commercial organizations, the impact is generally quantified as a direct financial loss in the short term or an ultimate (indirect) financial loss in the long term. Examples of such losses can include:

- Direct loss of money (cash or credit)
- Criminal or civil liability
- Loss of reputation/goodwill/image
- Reduction of share value
- Conflict of interests to staff or customers or shareholders
- Breach of confidence/privacy
- Loss of business opportunity/competition
- Loss of market share
- Reduction in operational efficiency/performance
- Interruption of business activity
- Noncompliance with laws and regulations resulting in penalties

As with risk calculations, impact calculations can be done either qualitatively or quantitatively. Some impacts lend themselves to quantitative representation such as the range of possible financial impact. Others, such as loss of reputation or market share, may be more difficult and may be adequately presented by qualitative statements. Impacts are determined by performing a business impact assessment and subsequent analysis, which generally includes gathering industry statistics providing a semiquantative analysis approach. This analysis will determine the criticality and sensitivity of information assets. It will provide the basis for setting access control authorizations and for business continuity planning (BCP), and will include recovery time objectives (RTOs), recovery point objectives (RPOs), maximum tolerable outages (MTOs) and service delivery objectives (SDOs). A BIA serves to prioritize risk management and, coupled with asset valuations, it provides the basis for the levels and types of protection required as well as a basis for the development of a business case for controls.

2.10.13 CONTROLS

Controls are any technology, process, practice, policy, standard or procedure that serves to regulate an activity to manage risk. It can be of an administrative, technical, management or legal nature. Controls are discussed in detail in chapter 3, section 3.15.

Because it is normal in an organization to find a number of controls of various kinds in different parts of a typical process—including logical, physical and procedural—it is important to understand the entire risk mitigation process from end to end. While layering of controls is a prudent approach, an excessive number of controls addressing the same risk are wasteful. It is also important to ensure that the various controls are not subject to the same risk, which defeats the purpose of layering them. For risk assessments to be effective and reasonably accurate, it is necessary to ensure that they are conducted from the beginning of processes through to the end. This will facilitate understanding if upstream controls minimize or eliminate some risk that may preclude the need for subsequent controls. It will also help determine whether there is unnecessary control redundancy or duplication.

2.10.14 LEGAL AND REGULATORY REQUIREMENTS

Legal and regulatory requirements must be considered in terms of risk and impact. This is necessary in order for senior management to determine the appropriate level of compliance and priority. Regulations must be first evaluated to determine to what extent the organization is already compliant. If it is found that the organization is noncompliant, then the regulations must be evaluated to determine the level of risk they pose to the organization. The organization must take into consideration the level of enforcement and its relative position in relation to its peers because enforcement actions are usually initiated against those that are least compliant. The potential impact of full compliance, partial compliance and noncompliance, in both direct financial and reputational impacts, must be evaluated as well. These evaluations provide the basis for senior management to determine the nature and extent of compliance activities appropriate for the organization. The information security manager must be aware that senior management may decide that risking sanctions is less costly than achieving compliance, or that because enforcement is limited, or even nonexistent, that compliance is not warranted. This is a management decision that should be based on risk and impact.

2.10.15 COSTS AND BENEFITS

When controls or countermeasures are planned, an organization should consider the costs and benefits. If the costs of specific controls or countermeasures (control overhead) exceed the benefits of mitigating a given risk, the organization may choose to accept the risk rather than incur the cost of mitigation. This follows the general principle that the cost of a control should never exceed the expected benefit. This is the principle of proportionality described in generally accepted security systems principles (GASSP) or its successor, generally accepted information security principles (GAISP).

> **Note:** GAISP is the successor project to GASSP. Originally carried by the International Information Security Foundation (IISF), GASSP was adopted by the Information Systems Security Association (ISSA) and renamed by substituting the word "information" for the word "system" to reflect the fact that the objective is to secure information's availability, confidentiality and integrity.

Cost-benefit analysis helps provide a monetary impact view of risk and helps determine the cost of protecting what is important. However, cost-benefit analysis is also about making smart choices based on potential risk mitigation costs versus potential losses (risk exposure). Both of these concepts tie directly back to good governance practices.

Unfortunately, most information security crime and loss metrics are not as established as traditional robbery and theft statistics. The annual CSI (Computer Security Institute) Computer Crime and Security Survey has been one measurement involving losses in the information security realm, but some practitioners suggest that its loss figures are understated, while others believe they are overstated.

Rather than debate the validity of these measures, it may be more useful to look at a few metrics that most organizations can quantify with some accuracy. Three common measurements of potential losses are employee productivity impacts, revenue losses and direct cost loss events. Virus and worm incidents are the ones most frequently cited when discussing impact on productivity. Another is the result of personally identifiable information.

Data breach losses in 2011 and 2012 as a result of a security-related incident are shown in **exhibit 2.21**. Per capita cost is shown as the average per capita cost of a data breach in US dollars for a nine country study for a two-year period.

An example of the approach suggested could be the result of a malware application which infects 10,000 employees in a 40,000-person organization. Each infected system cost each impacted employee one hour of productivity. If each employee has a fully burdened hourly wage of $30, then this is a $300,000 impact. Now that a potential loss figure has been established, it is easier to make risk remediation decisions.

Revenue losses can also be determined in a similar manner. If a business has an e-commerce web site that is producing US $1 million of revenue each day, then a denial of service (DoS) attack that lasts half a day creates a US $500,000 loss. It is debatable whether this type of attack would merely force customers to delay their purchases or whether they would simply go to a competitor. However, any public perception of an organization being the victim of a hacking attack, whether sensitive information was compromised or not, will often result in the loss of customer trust.

Exhibit 2.21—The Average Per Capita Cost of Data Breach Over Two Years

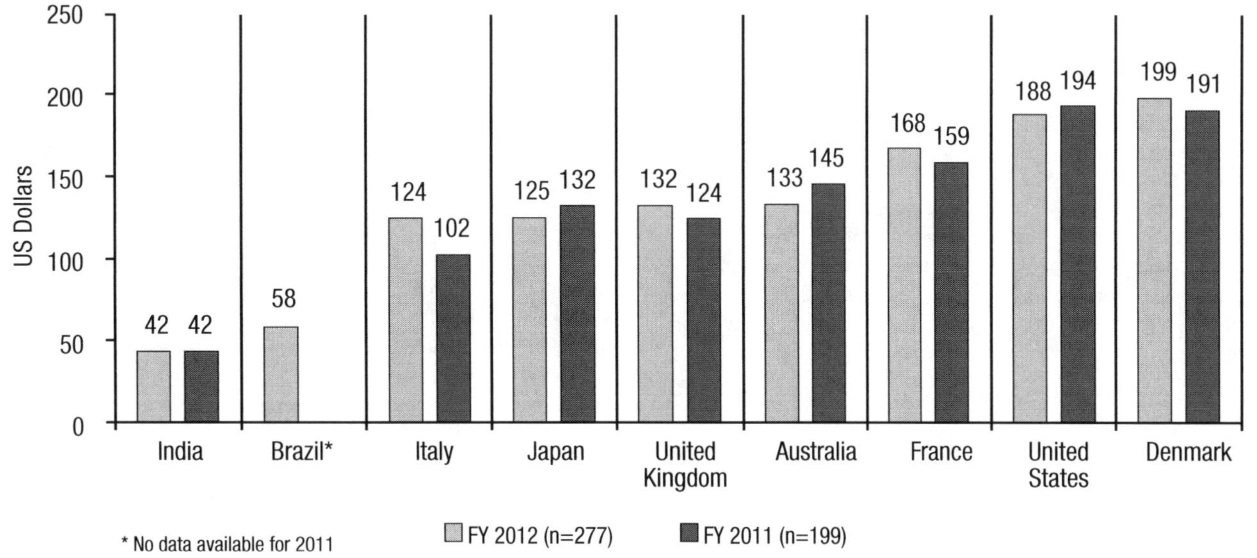

Source: 2013 Cost of Data Breach Study: Global Analysis. Benchmark research sponsored by Symantec, independently conducted by Ponemon Institute LLC, May 2013.

While productivity and revenue losses are considered direct losses, indirect losses may include the number of additional hours employees have to work to respond and recover from an incident. Another direct cost may be additional protection efforts resulting from a compromise.

When considering costs, the total cost of ownership (TCO) must be considered for the full life cycle of the control or countermeasure. This can include such elements as:
- Acquisition costs
- Deployment and implementation costs
- Recurring maintenance costs
- Testing and assessment costs
- Compliance monitoring and enforcement
- Inconvenience to users
- Reduced throughput of controlled processes
- Training in new procedures or technologies as applicable
- End of life decommissioning

2.10.16 EVENTS AFFECTING SECURITY BASELINES

A number of factors may change the risk or impact equation, necessitating that baseline security be changed. Baseline security is determined by the collective ability of controls to protect the organization's information assets. Baseline security is essentially controlled by the least restrictive aspect of collective standards and is the minimum level of security across the organization.

Any security incident can be attributed to either a control failure or the lack of a control. Any significant incident will require a risk reassessment and analysis of the root cause of the failure, which may in turn require increasing or modifying baseline security by changing the relevant standards.

Information security managers need to monitor and assess events that affect security baselines and, thus, might affect the organization's security program. Based on this assessment, the information security manager must determine if the organization's security plans and test plans require modification to address changing risk.

Security baselines may be modified for various reasons; for example, a vendor identifies that a parameter in its software or hardware that must be changed to achieve or maintain the desired protection levels. Another reason could be an outside event that requires increased baselines. For example, if there is a protest or other civil unrest near the organization's facility, the baseline for physical security may need to be increased for a period of time until that threat passes. Other drivers could include new or changing laws or regulations, identifying unacceptable risk levels as a result of new or changing threats, degradation of controls over time, and changes to systems creating new vulnerabilities.

2.11 INFORMATION RESOURCE VALUATION

The process of valuation, which consists of relating all values in a common financial form, may be straightforward for some assets. Hardware can be easily valued based on replacement costs. The value of information, in some cases, is the cost of recreating or restoring it. In other cases, the value is related to the consequential costs and possible regulatory sanctions stemming from the exposure of confidential information or trade secrets.

The impact or consequences of a breach of personally identifiable information can be regulatory sanctions and may also include the individuals suffering identity theft losses filing lawsuits for damages, as well as possible class-action lawsuits on behalf of thousands of victims. Another consequence is the reputational damage, often resulting in loss of share value. Clearly, in this case, the valuation cannot be based on the intrinsic value of the information, which may be low or zero. Rather, valuation must be based on the total range of potential losses and impacts.

Marketing materials are another type of information with no intrinsic value but which can, nevertheless, create unintended liabilities and, therefore, risk that must be considered. Inaccurate representations of products or services, or information leading to wrong investor decisions can result in significant losses as a consequence of various legal actions. Therefore, a prudent organization must consider ensuring systematic review and control of information to manage the risk of potential liability created by publicly released information.

Categories of typical information assets that must be protected include:
- Proprietary information of all types
- Current financial records
- Acquisition or merger plans
- Strategic marketing plans
- Trade secrets
- Patent-related information
- Personally identifiable information (PII)

2.11.1 INFORMATION RESOURCE VALUATION STRATEGIES

Companies typically find resource valuation problematic and often don't undertake the effort. Often companies do not have an accurate list of their information assets, and the effort to inventory and categorize these assets can appear an insurmountable task. Another reason is that even when assets are known, it is often difficult to place an exact value on assets such as PII or trade secrets, although a high degree of accuracy is not necessary.

In most cases, effective resource valuation is best based on loss scenarios. Information can be classified and put into a matrix with each loss scenario to make a complex problem more manageable and understandable. See **exhibit 2.22**.

The accuracy of the valuation is not as critical as having an approach to prioritize efforts. Values within the same order of magnitude as the actual loss (should it occur) are sufficient for planning purposes. There are many well-documented loss scenarios and loss amounts with which to base a valuation in media reports. One good source of information is *www.attrition.org,* which maintains a database of data breaches and loss amounts for a number of years.

2.11.2 INFORMATION RESOURCE VALUATION METHODOLOGIES

Asset or resource valuation can be complex and time consuming, but it is an essential undertaking required for an effective information risk management program. The various information resource valuation methodologies utilize many different variables. These variables can include the level of technical complexity and the level of potential direct and consequential financial loss. Quantitative valuation methodologies will generally be the most precise, but can be quite complex once actual and downstream impacts have been analyzed. Another valuation methodology that is sometimes used is judgmental or qualitative in nature, where an independent decision is made based upon business knowledge, executive management directives, historical perspectives, business goals and environmental factors. There are situations in which quantitative data are not available and this alternative method is the only option. Many information systems managers use a combination of techniques. In some cases, simply assigning value based on a subjective scale of low, medium and high may be satisfactory.

The most straightforward approach is the monetary value that represents the purchase price, replacement cost or book value if that is representative of the importance to the organization. If it is not, other approaches must be considered. If it is an asset that directly or indirectly generates revenue, a computed value such as net present value (NPV) may be a reasonable approach.

Another approach is to consider value-add or other more intangible but arguably more important values. For example, an e-commerce application and server may only have hardware and software costs of US $50,000, but are an essential component in generating millions in revenue every month. In this situation,

Exhibit 2.22—Matrix of Loss Scenarios

Scenario	Type of Data	Size of Loss	Reputation Loss	Lawsuit Loss	Fines/ Reg Loss	Market Loss	Expected Loss per year	Notes
Hacker steals data; publicly blackmails company	Customer data	1K records 10K records	US $1M US $20M	US $1M US $10M	US $1 US $35M	US $1M US $5M	US $10M	Regulatory loss of ability to make acquisitions for 1 year
Employee steals data; sells data to competitors	Strategic plan	3-year plan	Minimal	Minimal	Minimal	US $20M	US $2M	Competitor duplicates new products; brings to market faster
Contractor steals data; sells data to hackers	Employee data	10K records	US $5M	US $10M	Minimal	Minimal	US $200,000	
Backup tapes and data found in garbage; makes front-page news	Customer data	10M records	US $20M	US $20M	US $10M	US $5M	US $200,000	

value may be computed in terms of revenue generation or the financial impact for any unanticipated down time.

Intangible assets that may prove difficult to quantify are the organization's reputation and consumer trust. Although a hacking incident itself may not create any direct losses, customers may leave due to lack of confidence in the organization, especially if there are strong competitors.

One PGP-Vontu study of 31 compromised organizations found that 19% of customers ceased doing business with those organizations and another 40% were considering doing so. Such a dramatic defection is likely to have serious economic impact on any organization.

Another example could result from someone stealing customers' personal credit data. This could cause the organization to incur the costs of notifying a large number of people about the incident (under laws such as the US State of California Senate Bill [SB] 1386). Additionally, this type of incident could result in potential costs related to legal defense; for example, if a lawsuit is filed by those impacted. In the case where credit cards are compromised, the affected banks typically insist on recovering the costs of reissuing new cards in addition to any fraud costs they had to cover. This typically is in the range of $10 or more for each card. In the recent case in which a well-known retailer had a reported 110 million card records stolen, the total costs will be considerable.

In a publicly traded company, intangible assets represent the difference between the tangible assets as recorded in the financials and the company's market capitalization value. For example, a company with a US $5 billion market capitalization has US $1 billion in tangible assets and US $4 billion in intangible assets. Therefore, 80% of the company's value (US $4 billion) is made up of intangible assets. Intangible assets are usually comprised of intellectual property such as trade secrets, patents and copyrights, knowledge management, brand reputation, corporate culture, customer loyalty and trust, and innovation. It is obvious that most of these intangible assets fall under the purview of information security for the purposes of protecting them and preserving their value.

In addition, the information security manager needs to be aware of ongoing changes in the organization and should alter the use of valuation methodologies to best meet the needs as a result of these changes. If quantitative data are outdated and cannot be updated in a reasonable time frame, it may be desirable to use qualitative data either in place of or to augment the quantitative data.

While a detailed discussion on methods for establishing intangible asset values is beyond the scope of this manual, it is important for the information security manager to understand valuation approaches and the necessity for this activity.

2.11.3 INFORMATION ASSET CLASSIFICATION

Information asset classification is required to determine the relative sensitivity and criticality or business value of information assets. Criticality is determined by the impact on the organization as a result of the loss of an asset, i.e., how important the asset is to the business. Sensitivity is based on the potential damage to the organization as a result of unauthorized disclosure. This will provide the basis for protection efforts, business continuity planning, and user access control. For larger organizations, this can be a daunting task because there are likely to be peta- or terabytes of electronic data, warehouses of documents, and thousands of individuals and devices. Yet, without determining the business value, sensitivity and criticality (and increasingly, legal and regulatory requirements) of information resources, it is not possible to develop an effective risk management program that provides appropriate protection proportional to business value or sensitivity and criticality.

In cases where comprehensive classification is not possible due to resource constraints or other reasons, a less effective option is a business dependency assessment that can be used to provide a basis for allocating proportional protective activities. This approach is based on the information resources that critical business functions utilize.

The first step in the classification process is locating and identifying information resources. In many organizations, this may prove difficult since there is often no comprehensive inventory of information-related assets. This may be especially true in larger organizations with multiple independent business units lacking a strong centralized security function. The identification process must include determining the location of the data, and the data owners, users and custodians. The security manager must also determine what data are housed by external service providers. These service providers can include media vaulting and archival firms, mailing list processors, firms that process mail containing company information, firms that act as couriers or transporters of information, and third-party service providers. Service providers may also include data centers providing hosting functions, payroll services or health insurance administration.

The information security manager working with the business units should ascertain the appropriate information classification based on business value or levels of sensitivity and criticality of information resources, and ensure that all business and IT stakeholders have the opportunity to review and approve the established guidelines for access control levels. The number of levels should be kept to a minimum. Classifications should be simple such as designations by differing degrees for sensitivity and criticality. End-user managers in coordination with the security administrator can then use these classifications in their risk and impact assessment process and to assist with determining access levels of users. The information security manager must also be aware that in a risk-adverse organization or one with a blame culture there will be an incentive to overclassify, and it will be necessary to consider controls to limit this tendency.

A major benefit of information asset classification is the reduced risk of underprotection and the cost of overprotection of information resources by tying security to business objectives. Although it is a complicated undertaking to implement data classification, the long-term benefits to the organization are substantial. The alternative is to provide all information assets with the same level of protection, which is unlikely to be cost effective. And if the organization is risk adverse and requires a high level of security, providing the same high level of protection to all assets can be very costly.

There are a number of questions that should be asked in any information asset classification model, including but not limited to:

- How many classification levels are suitable for the organization?
- How will information be located?
- What process is used to determine classification?
- How will classified information be identified?
- How will it be marked?
- How will it be handled?
- How will it be transported?
- How will confidential information be stored and archived?
- What is the life cycle of the information (create, update, retrieve, archive, dispose)?
- What are the processes associated with the various stages in the information asset life cycle?
- How will it be retained according to policy or law?
- How will it be safely destroyed at the end of the retention period?
- Who has ownership of information?
- Who has access rights?
- Who has authority for determining access to the data?
- What approvals are needed for access?

An important part of information classification is not just applying a classification label to each piece of information, but identifying security measures that can consistently be applied to each level. As the level of sensitivity or criticality increases, security measures should increase in rigor so that, at the highest level, security mechanisms are the most restrictive or provide the greatest level of protection. It must also be remembered that sensitivity and criticality require different security mechanisms and processes. For any piece of information, an owner may have to make both a sensitivity and a criticality decision.

Methods to Determine Criticality of Resources and Impact of Adverse Events

A number of methods exist to determine the sensitivity and criticality of information resources, and the impact of adverse events. A BIA is often performed to identify the impact of adverse events. Methods outlined within COBIT, NIST and the Software Engineering Institute's Octave framework are representative of the resources the information security manager may utilize in this effort.

It is a generally accepted practice to focus on the impact that a loss of information resources has on the organization rather than on a specific adverse event. Since there are numerous adverse events that could occur, it is a daunting task to completely list all of them. Such an effort, obviously, is not practical or cost effective.

The first step to determine information resource importance is to break the corporate or organizational structure into business units or departments. See **exhibit 2.23**. Under the corporate or top-level organizational structure, each of the business units should be rated by its importance or value to the business.

In **exhibit 2.23**, Business Unit B is given a number one rating since it is the most important. The importance usually equates to revenue, but the value may equate to critical functions being performed. There can be as many units or departments as exist, but it may be more manageable to stay at a higher level.

Exhibit 2.23—Top Layer of Business Risk Structure

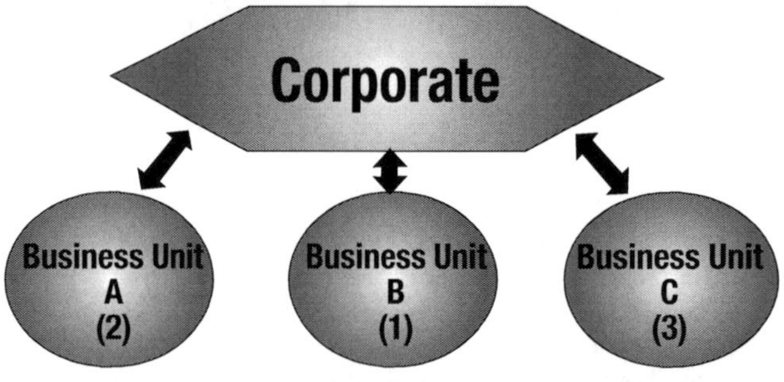

Courtesy of Kenneth D. Biery, 2008

Exhibit 2.24—Critical Function Layer of Business Risk Structure

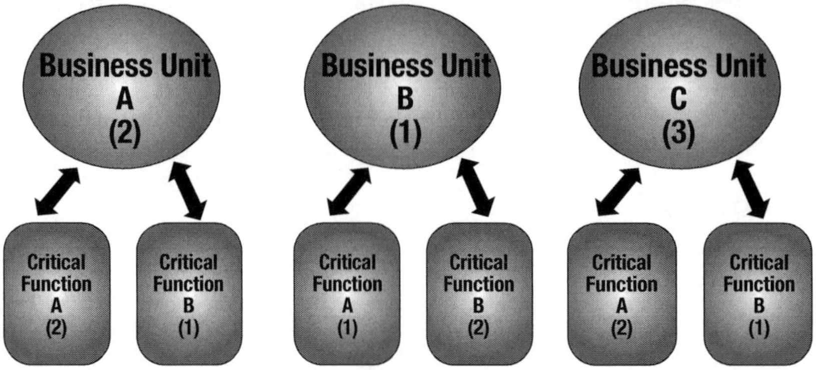

Courtesy of Kenneth D. Biery, 2008

The rating should be done by the senior management team, based on their understanding of the organization. This is the foundation for establishing the risk management structure. The relative importance or value of the business units or departments is going to flow down into critical functions, assets and resources.

The next step is identifying the critical organizational functions. The focus for each business unit or department is to define what tasks are important to the unit in achieving its goals. There can be a two-level structure within the critical function layer to represent complex operations. The critical business functions are also numerically rated against each other to help with prioritization of subsequent risk remediation efforts.

Once critical functions have been identified, as shown in **exhibit 2.24**, the basic structure of the organization has been mapped. It is important to recognize that the structure has been focused only on operational elements, not technologies, applications or data. This progressive drill-down structure looks similar to a BIA that is performed when conducting business continuity planning. The structure will provide a management-level view of risk and where it resides in the organization.

In the structure shown in **exhibit 2.25**, assets and resources are the containers of risk. Because there are vulnerabilities identified with the assets that can be exploited by threats, there is risk. Assets, like business units and critical functions, are numerically rated as well. Because assets are associated with the critical business function they support, they will be rated against each other from the most important to the least important in their group.

The risk represented in **exhibit 2.26** is the composite of vulnerabilities that a threat can exploit to cause a negative impact to an asset. With the approach represented in the preceding diagrams, an organization can see where risk originates and how it can potentially impact business operations. The roll-up and drill-down nature of this approach is useful for management throughout the organization. For example, business owners may want to see at what level of risk their critical functions are in order to be able to set a prioritization schedule for fixing vulnerabilities or prioritizing protection efforts.

The ability to determine how identified risk can impact business operations is demonstrated in **exhibit 2.27** which is the combined elements discussed above. It shows how risk exposure can potentially impact some of the company's most valuable assets. The structure shown in the diagram helps both management and the security team align and prioritize their efforts accordingly.

2.11.4 IMPACT ASSESSMENT AND ANALYSIS

A BIA is an exercise that determines the impact of losing the availability of any resource to an organization, establishes the escalation of that loss over time, identifies the minimum resources needed to recover, and prioritizes the recovery of processes and supporting systems. While a BIA is often thought of in the

Exhibit 2.25—Aligning Assets to the Critical Function Layer

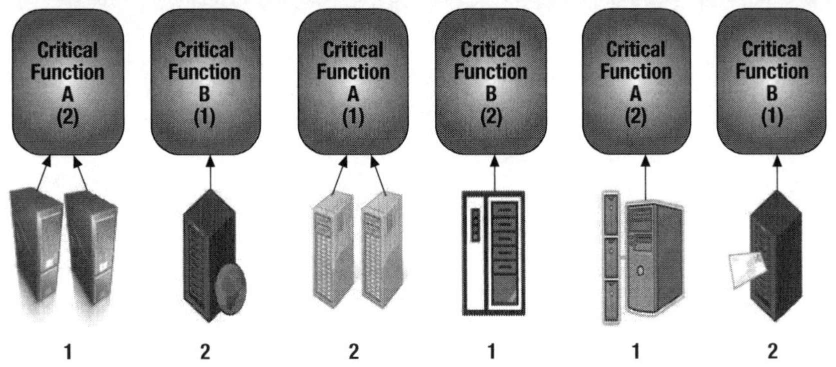

Courtesy of Kenneth D. Biery, 2008

Exhibit 2.26—Asset Vulnerabilities

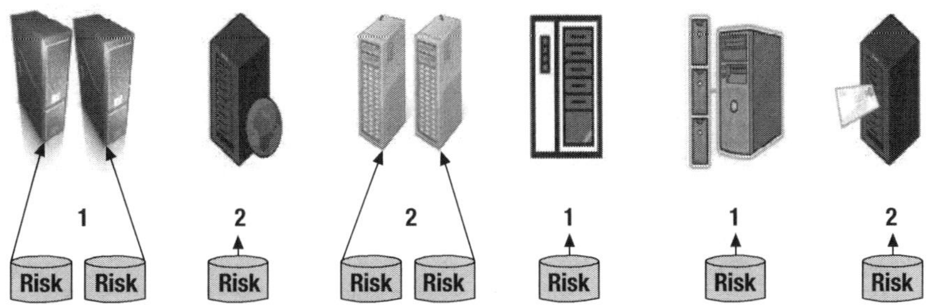

Courtesy of Kenneth D. Biery, 2008

Exhibit 2.27—Combined Risk Impact Structure

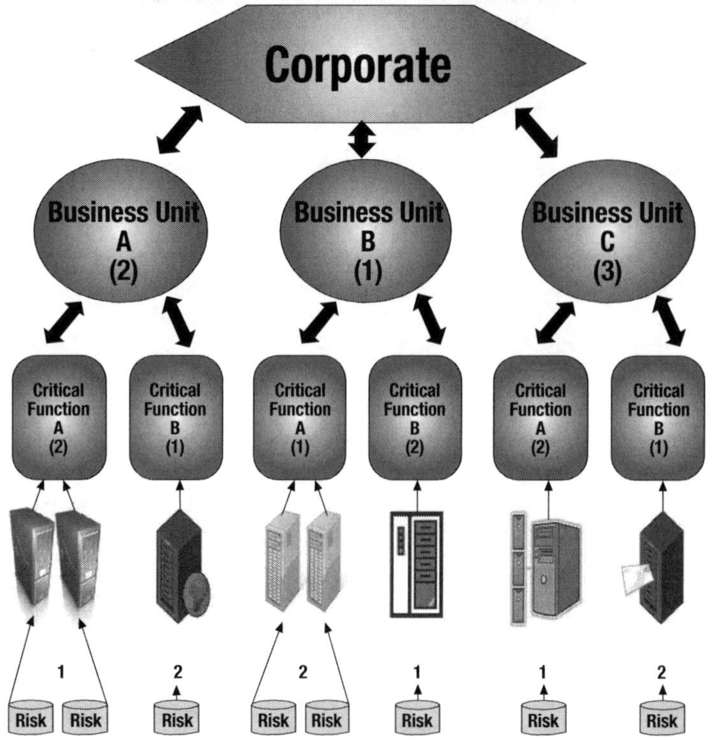

Courtesy of Kenneth D. Biery, 2008

context of business continuity and disaster recovery, whether potential impact is determined by this process or another process is not important. Impact is the bottom line of risk, and the range of severity in terms of the organization must be determined to provide the information needed and to guide risk management activities. Obviously, even high risk with little or no impact is not of concern.

It is common for these assessments to determine only a worst-case outcome, which experience shows occurs in a minority of events. As a result of this "impact inflation," management often discounts these assessments as unrealistic and excessively pessimistic.

A more effective approach involves performing a reasonably small set of scenario analyses with key organization stakeholders, where a range of potential outcomes is determined. This range of outcomes is then used to define a quantitative distribution of impact magnitudes, including minimum, maximum, and most likely including values as well as a confidence level. These values can then be used as inputs to quantitative analysis methods (e.g., Monte Carlo simulations to determine probability distribution) that more accurately describe for management the real impact potential.

The other advantage this approach provides is that it more closely resembles the type of impact data that management receives from other business risk domains (e.g., investment, marketing, credit, etc.). This alignment improves management's ability to make an apples-to-apples comparison and well-informed risk decisions.

Before beginning the impact analysis of a specific set of resources, it is necessary to obtain the following information:

- System mission (e.g., objectives of the processes performed by the IT system or personnel)
- System (manual or technical) and data criticality (e.g., the system's value or importance to an organization)
- System, personnel and data criticality (the impacts associated with unintended disclosure)

This information can be obtained from performing a BIA or from existing organizational documentation such as a mission impact analysis report or asset criticality assessment report, if they exist. A mission impact assessment and analysis or BIA prioritizes the impact levels associated with the compromise of an organization's information assets based on a qualitative or quantitative assessment of the criticality of those assets. An asset criticality or resource dependency assessment identifies and prioritizes the critical organization information assets (e.g., hardware, software, systems, services, and related technology assets) that support the organization's critical missions.

If this documentation does not exist or such assessments for the organization's information assets have not been performed, the system and data sensitivity can be determined based on the level of protection required to maintain the availability, integrity, and confidentiality of the system and data.

The adverse impact of a security event can be described in terms of loss or degradation or any combination of integrity, availability, and confidentiality.

- **Loss of Integrity**—System and data integrity refers to the requirement that information be protected from improper modification. Integrity is lost if unauthorized or erroneous

changes are made to the data or IT system by either intentional or accidental acts. If the loss of system or data integrity is not corrected, continued use of the contaminated system or corrupted data could result in broader corruption, fraud, or misinformed decisions. Also, violation of integrity may be the first step in a successful attack against system availability or confidentiality.
- **Loss of Availability**—If a mission-critical IT system or process is unavailable to its end users, the organization's mission may be affected. Loss of system functionality and operational effectiveness, for example, may result in loss of productive time, thus impeding the end users' performance of their functions in supporting the organization's mission.
- **Loss of Confidentiality**—In this context, confidentiality refers to the protection of information from unauthorized disclosure. The impact of unauthorized disclosure of confidential information can range from the jeopardizing of national security to the disclosure of private consumer data. Unauthorized, unanticipated, or unintentional disclosure of private consumer or other regulated data can result in loss of public confidence, loss of customer base, and legal action against the organization.

Some tangible impacts can be measured quantitatively in lost revenue, the cost of repairing the system or the level of effort required to correct problems caused by a compromise. Other impacts (e.g., loss of public confidence, loss of credibility, damage to an organization's interest) cannot be measured in specific units but can be described qualitatively in terms of high, medium, and low impacts.

In conducting an impact analysis, consideration should be given to the advantages and disadvantages of quantitative versus qualitative assessments. The main advantage of the qualitative impact analysis is that it prioritizes the risk and identifies areas for immediate improvement in addressing the vulnerabilities. The disadvantage of the qualitative analysis is that it does not provide specific quantifiable measurements of the magnitude of the impacts, therefore making a cost-benefit analysis of any recommended controls difficult.

The major advantage of a quantitative impact analysis is that it provides a measurement of the impacts' magnitude, which can be used in the cost-benefit analysis of recommended controls.

The disadvantage is that, depending on the numerical ranges used to express the measurement, the meaning of the quantitative impact analysis may be unclear, requiring the result to be interpreted in a qualitative manner. Additional factors must also be considered to determine the magnitude of impact, such as the range of possible errors in estimation or computations.

2.12 RECOVERY TIME OBJECTIVES

The information security manager must understand recovery time objectives (RTOs) and how they apply to the organization's information resources as part of the overall evaluation of risk. The organization's business needs will dictate the RTO, which is usually defined as the amount of time to recover an acceptable level of normal operations. The information resource's functional criticality, recovery priorities, and interdependencies offset by costs are variables that will determine the RTO.

Determining RTO can depend upon a number of factors including the cyclical need (time of day, week, month or year) of the information and organization, interdependencies among the information and the organization's requirements as well as the cost of available options. The organization's requirements can be based upon customer needs, contractual obligations or SLAs, and possibly regulatory requirements. The information security manager should consider that the RTO may vary with the timing of the month or year. Financial information may not be as critical at the beginning of the month when the new fiscal month is being opened. This same information is likely to be highly critical at the end of the month when the monthly financial reports are being prepared and the accounting period is being closed. The timing of business cycles and their dependence on information needs to be considered as part of information classification.

RTOs are determined by performing a BIA in coordination with developing a business continuity plan (BCP). The BIA is generally conducted by interviewing information owners to obtain their perspective on the cost associated with an extended interruption in service for a business system or process. Often there are two perspectives for RTO. One is the perspective of the individuals whose job it is to utilize the information, and the other is the view of senior management who must consider costs and may need to arbitrate between business units competing for resources. An information resource that a divisional supervisor may believe is critical may not be critical in the eyes of the vice president of operations, who is able to include the overall organizational risk in the evaluation of the RTO.

The information security manager should understand that both perspectives are important and work toward an RTO that considers them. The result will factor into the BCP, the scope of the services to be restored and priority order for the recovery of systems. In the end, the final decision is that of senior management. Senior management is in the best position to arbitrate the needs and requirements of the different components of the business, such as the regulatory requirements to which the organization is subject, and determine which processes are the most critical to the continued survival of the business as well as determine acceptable costs.

2.12.1 RTO AND ITS RELATION TO BUSINESS CONTINUITY PLANNING AND CONTINGENCY PLANNING OBJECTIVES AND PROCESSES

Knowledge of the RTO for information systems and their associated data is needed for an organization to develop and implement an effective BCP program. Once the RTOs are known, the organization can identify and develop contingency strategies that will meet the RTOs of the information resources. The RTOs will drive the order of priority for restoration of services and, in certain cases, the selection of specific recovery technologies in situations where the RTO is short.

One critical factor when developing contingency processes is cost. System owners invariably prefer shorter RTOs, but the tradeoffs in cost may not be warranted. Near instantaneous recovery can be achieved, where needed, using technologies such as mirroring of information resources, so that, in the event of a disruption, the information resources are always available quickly. In general, the cost of recovery is less if the RTO for a given resource is longer.

There is a breakeven point of the time period to determine the RTO, where the impact of the disruption begins to be greater than the cost of recovery. The length of this time period depends on the nature of the business disruption and the resources involved. Qualitative as well as quantitative issues must be taken into consideration since loss of customer confidence, even if it cannot be estimated, can have a long-term negative impact on the organization. Most organizations can reduce their RTOs, but there is an associated cost.

2.12.2 RECOVERY POINT OBJECTIVES

The recovery point objective (RPO) is determined based on the acceptable data loss in case of disruption of operations. It indicates the most recent point in time to which it is acceptable to recover the data. RPO effectively quantifies the permissible amount of data loss in case of interruption. While this is typically the scope of business continuity and disaster recovery planning, it is an important consideration when developing a risk management strategy.

In particular, the RPO will have an effect on the achievability of short RTOs, which must be considered from a risk management perspective. If the RPO is too distant and the restoration of data is time consuming, it may not be possible to achieve a short recovery time.

2.12.3 SERVICE DELIVERY OBJECTIVES

Service delivery objectives (SDOs) are defined as the minimal level of service that must be restored after an event to meet business requirements until normal operations can be resumed. SDOs will be affected by both RTOs and RPOs and must also be considered in any risk management strategy and implementation. Higher levels of service will generally require greater resources as well as more current RPOs.

2.12.4 THIRD-PARTY SERVICE PROVIDERS

A typical organization uses many information resources in support of its business processes. These resources can originate within the organization or be provided by entities external to the organization. Most organizations will use a combination of the two. The information security manager needs to be aware of the location and access permissions for all information resources since they all require protection regardless of who is processing them.

For the information security manager, there are a number of considerations to address when outsourcing, which include:

- Ensuring that the organization has appropriate controls and processes in place to facilitate outsourcing
- Ensuring that there are appropriate information risk management clauses in the outsourcing contract
- Ensuring that a risk assessment is performed for the process to be outsourced
- Ensuring that an appropriate level of due diligence is performed prior to contract signature
- Managing the information risk for outsourced services on a day-to-day basis
- Ensuring that material changes to the relationship are flagged and new risk assessments are performed as required
- Ensuring that proper processes are followed when relationships are ended

Considerations when outsourcing services:

- Outsourcing or planning to outsource business critical functions generally increases information risk.
- The complexity of managing information risk is increased in outsourcing arrangements by the separation of responsibility for control specification and control implementation.
- The separation of responsibility for control specification and control implementation is bridged by the outsourcing contract. This underlines the contract's importance as the primary method through which the organization can manage its information risk.
- Where the outsourced business function operates within a regulated industry, the outsourcing contract needs to explicitly address regulatory requirements.
- The complexity of information risk assessment is increased in outsourcing arrangements since there are three types of information risk to assess: the business function, the outsourcing provider and outsourcing itself.
- The style of the overall contract and the amount of innovation contributed by the provider has a major impact on the way in which information risk management requirements are specified.
- The relationship between the organization and the outsourcing provider often contributes more to effective information risk management in an outsourcing arrangement than the contract.
- Because few businesses remain static, information risk management within the outsourcing arrangement must evolve so that it continues to be relevant to the organization's needs.
- The exit strategy for the outsourcing arrangement is at least as important as the initial transition. It should be developed at the planning stage and included in the contract to facilitate the continued availability of the outsourced business function. The exit strategy is far too important to leave until the outsourcing arrangement comes to its conclusion.

The information risk management requirements for outsourced business functions are different from those for in-house functions and, in many instances, are greater. After the information risk has been analyzed and the controls have been identified, these controls need to be defined within the contract for the provider to implement. Outsourcing results in a disconnection between setting the controls and their implementation. **Exhibit 2.28** provides a simplistic view of this separation of the responsibilities of the organization versus those of the provider.

The information security manager should be aware that, although the organization can outsource information risk management to a third party, it generally cannot outsource responsibility.

The disconnection between control definition and control implementation makes managing the risk associated with outsourcing business functions complex and makes the outsourcing contract essential in managing information risk. The challenge for the information security manager is in how to define and implement information risk management controls in different outsourced business functions throughout the organization.

The business problem is the need to define and implement information risk management measures to protect the information within business functions that have been handed to a third party to operate on a day-to-day basis.

Exhibit 2.28—Disconnect of Responsibilities With Outsourced Providers

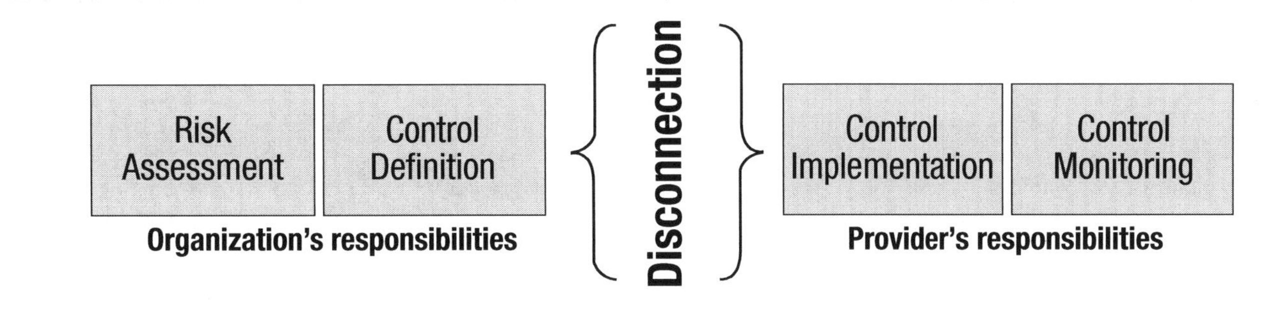

The disconnection between control definition and control implementation in an outsourcing arrangement

Information risk recommendations for outsourcing initiatives:
- Timely involvement of information risk management professionals to ensure the risk assessment and controls definition
- Ensure that key information risk management controls are negotiated within the contract
- Ensure mechanisms to negotiate small changes to information risk management controls since they may be costly
- Ensure that changes to information risk management controls are not difficult and complicated
- Ensure mechanisms to get information on whether information risk are being managed effectively
- Ensure mechanisms to compensate for the lack of trust in the provider's staff

Outsourced information resources may present an information security manager with other challenges, including external organizations that may be reluctant to share technical details on the nature and extent of their information protection mechanisms. This makes it critical to ensure that adequate specified levels of protection are included in SLAs and other outsourcing contracts. One common approach is to specify requirements for specific audits such as SOC 2 (*Report on Controls at a Service Organization Relevant to Security, Availability, Processing Integrity, Confidentiality or Privacy,* developed by the AICPA) or ISO 27001:2013 certification. It is also important to analyze SOC 2 or other audit reports upon receipt for third-party auditor comments and, if present, comments about customer control effectiveness and policy compliance. Note that SOC 2 reports are often not sufficient on their own because the criteria have been defined by the organization in question. For high-risk relationships, it is generally preferable to rely on periodic compliance assessments conducted directly by the sourcing organization or a contracted third party.

From a risk management perspective, it is also important that incident management and response, BCP/DRP, and testing include all important outsourced services and functions. This includes implementing a well-defined and tested incident detection, escalation and response plan in concert with the outsourcing entities.

For regulated organizations such as financial institutions there is often a time requirement for notification of regulatory agencies regarding suspicious events involving regulated information. Contracts with third parties must ensure that processes are established to support such notifications.

Another often-neglected area concerns third-party vendor financial viability. Since outsourcing contracts are often awarded to low-cost bidders, the risk of the outsourcing organization to continue to operate according to the contract and to honor any indemnity agreements may be a function of their financial capabilities. Financial information can be obtained from a variety of sources, including credit reports, US Securities and Exchange Commission filings of publicly traded firms, annual reports, etc. If such certifications are not available, information must be obtained from providers—information sufficient to determine how external entities are securing information assets.

Some portion of risk associated with outsourced information services can be transferred by incorporating indemnity clauses in SLAs. Key clauses that should be part of a third-party contract must include, but are not restricted to:
- Right to source code in event of default of provider (e.g., source code escrow)
- Requirement to remain timely with compliance to industry and regulatory requirements
- Right to audit vendor's books of accounts and premises
- Right to review their processes
- Insistence on standard operating procedures (SOPs)
- Right to assess the skill sets of the vendor resources
- Advance information if the resources deployed are to be changed

An SLA should also be developed and formally agreed that explains timeliness of response (system and human), scanning expectations, etc.

2.13 INTEGRATION WITH LIFE CYCLE PROCESSES

Ensuring that risk identification, analysis and mitigation activities are integrated into life cycle processes is an important task of information security management. Most organizations have change management procedures that can provide the information security manager with an approach to implementing risk management processes on an ongoing basis. Since changes to any information resource are likely to introduce new vulnerabilities and change the overall risk equation, it is important that the information security manager is aware of proposed modifications.

Change management is a tenet of well-managed organizations. But, as distributed computing became the norm and changes were made more easily in a dispersed environment by people with limited knowledge, organizations often experienced a lack of standardization in their hardware and software environments. Realizing this, management in most organizations have instituted more robust change management procedures and, as a consequence, have begun to achieve better control over the enterprise information resources. This is, of course, a moving target, and organizations with remote operations are, in some cases, still finding effective change management an elusive goal.

Organizations have also typically instituted change management for other areas of the business and for a variety of business activities as well as environmental factors and facilities. The benefit of these activities is that many organizations now have change management procedures that span the entire organization. The information security manager must be aware of these change management activities and ensure that security is well entrenched so changes are not made without considering the implications to the overall security of the organization's information resources. One method of helping to ensure this is for information security management to participate as a member of the change management committee and ensure that all significant changes are subject to review and approval by security and meet policy and standards requirements.

While the normal focus in change management addresses hardware and software changes (testing, sign-offs, etc.) and possibly security impact, the change management process should extend well beyond the system owners and IT population. The change management process must include facilities management with respect to data center infrastructure and any other area that may impact overall information security (e.g., physical access control of sensitive or critical areas).

The impact of change management must address system and facilities maintenance windows with facilities personnel (often outsourced) and business continuity management. Quite often changes are not documented on a timely basis within these areas. Facilities may not have current single-line drawings and blue prints. Correspondingly, computer infrastructure/configuration management may not have the changes properly documented or updated on a timely basis. Business continuity may also fall behind on relevant updates when those updates occur in cycles. Emergency response and business continuity may also suffer communications lapses when current and changing processes are not reviewed within facility infrastructure areas.

Facilities personnel often have access to environmental monitoring and control systems (building management system [BMS]/ supervisory control and data acquisition [SCADA] systems) for heating, ventilating and air conditioning (HVAC), water and electricity, or even physical access control systems. These are often programmed for remote computer access, an area that often escapes information security oversight. Physical security and control systems have been designed within the context of their being deployed within a closed/controlled environment.

Closed-circuit camera systems once configured to transmit data over the backbone network are often integrated with the IT infrastructure, posing the risk of compromise to these systems from IT facilities and the network.

IT systems can also be compromised due to vulnerabilities in the physical security system. Physical security and control systems, because of their importance in the protection of facilities and people, may be part of the organization's critical infrastructure. The protection of these systems, their system code and data may need to be integrated into security classification schemes. Facilities service contracts in support of physical and control systems often have emergency-response clauses. However, those contracts should be reviewed because they may lack adequate SLAs or fail to provide sufficient details and accountability for an adequate emergency response. A high-availability application may suffer unforeseen business impacts as a result of facilities failures.

Internal or external parties managing the facilities are sometimes overlooked from a risk management perspective. These are also the vulnerable areas because human beings pose the greatest threat to information security. Human beings are subject to negligence in compliance with established processes, ignorance of known threats, collusion or emotional behavior. It is important to include this factor in assessing the risk for critical information resources. Examples of internal parties are the operators who are granted, by job roles, direct physical access to the systems and facilities. External parties that may pose a risk include the servicing agents, e.g., cleaning or maintenance crew, etc. Possible controls are background screening, employment terms, annual signing of compliance to code of conducts, or contractual terms in the case of external parties.

By integrating risk identification, analysis and mitigation activities into change management (life cycle processes), the information security manager can ensure that critical information resources are adequately protected. This is a proactive approach, enabling the information security manager to better plan and implement security policies and procedures in alignment with the business goals and objectives of the organization. It also permits information security controls to be interjected into an activity that holds the greatest potential for degrading existing controls.

2.13.1 RISK MANAGEMENT FOR IT SYSTEM DEVELOPMENT LIFE CYCLE

According to NIST publication 800-30, minimizing negative impact on an organization and need for a sound basis in decision making are the fundamental reasons organizations implement a risk management process for their IT systems. Effective risk management must be totally integrated into the system development life cycle (SDLC). An IT system's SDLC has five phases: initiation, development or acquisition, implementation, operation or maintenance, and disposal. In some cases, an IT system may occupy several of these phases at the same time. However, the risk management methodology is the same, regardless of the SDLC phase for which the assessment is being conducted. Risk management is an iterative process that can be performed during each major phase of the SDLC. **Exhibit 2.29** describes the characteristics of each SDLC phase and indicates how risk management can be performed in support of each phase.

2.13.2 LIFE CYCLE-BASED RISK MANAGEMENT PRINCIPLES AND PRACTICES

Since risk management is a continuous process, the information security manager should view risk management itself as having a life cycle. This life cycle can comprise assessment, treatment and monitoring phases. Employing a life cycle-based risk management approach and integration with change management improves costs in that a full risk assessment does not have to be performed periodically. Instead, updates may be made to the risk assessment and risk management processes on an incremental basis.

2.14 SECURITY CONTROL BASELINES

Implementing baselines for security processes sets the minimum security requirements throughout the organization so they are consistent with acceptable risk levels. Different baselines must be set for different security classifications, with more stringent security controls required for more critical or sensitive resources. If the organization has not implemented a classification scheme, it will be difficult for the information security manager to develop a rational basis for setting baselines without the risk of overprotecting some resources or underprotecting others. Acceptable levels of risk for each security classification must also be determined and standards developed or modified to set the lower boundaries of protection for each security domain. Standards provide the basis for measurement and testing approaches for evaluating whether security baselines are being met by existing controls.

Regular evaluation of baselines is necessary due to the dynamic nature of IT hardware and software as well as external factors such as changing geopolitical risk, emerging regulatory requirements or volatility in financial markets. These combine to create constantly changing vulnerabilities and attack vectors.

A baseline is defined as "a line serving as a basis"; "a line of known measure or position used to calculate or locate something"; or "an initial set of critical observations or data used for comparison or a control." In order to formulate a baseline of security controls, some measurement of the effectiveness and efficiency of controls is necessary. A baseline is usually not based on a single test of controls, but based upon the overall capacity of controls to collectively mitigate risk to acceptable levels.

To establish control baselines, security managers can refer to many of the published standards that may be implemented within the organization. Based on these standards, a test of the control is performed multiple times to establish an evaluation of the effectiveness and efficiency of the control required by the standard.

In order to establish a baseline for antivirus processes the information security manager will require periodic (weekly, monthly) reports of infected systems, virus alerts, virus incidents reported to the help desk, definition file updates and other pertinent information. Based upon this information, it is possible to evaluate the effectiveness of the control, and based on additional information—such as man hours required, software costs and latent risk—to evaluate the efficiency of the antivirus process as an IT control.

Exhibit 2.29—Characteristics of the SDLC Phases

SDLC Phase	Phase Characteristics	Support from Risk Management Activities
Phase 1—Initiation	The need for an IT system is expressed and the purpose and scope of the IT system is documented.	Identified risk is used to support the development of the system requirements, including security requirements and a security concept of operations (strategy).
Phase 2—Development or Acquisition	The IT system is designed, purchased, programmed, developed, or otherwise constructed.	Risk identified during this phase can be used to support the security analyses of the IT system that may lead to architecture and design trade-offs during system development.
Phase 3—Implementation	The system security features should be configured, enabled, tested and verified.	The risk management process supports implementation against its requirements and within its modeled operational environment. Decisions regarding risk identified must be made prior to system operation.
Phase 4—Operation or Maintenance	The system performs its functions. Typically the system will undergo periodic updates or changes to hardware and software; the system may also be altered in less obvious ways due to changes to organizational processes, policies and procedures.	Risk management activities are performed for periodic system reauthorization (or reaccreditation or whenever major changes are made to an IT system in its operational, production environment (e.g., new systems interfaces).
Phase 5—Disposal	This phase may involve the disposition of information, hardware and software. Activities may include moving, archiving, discarding or destroying information and sanitizing the hardware and software.	Risk management activities are performed for system components that will be disposed of or replaced to ensure that the hardware and software are properly disposed of, that residual data are appropriately handled, and that system migration is conducted in a secure and systematic manner.

The antivirus process example presented above is an example of a security metric insofar as it is a measure from a point of reference. Based upon regular evaluation of metrics, security managers can develop effective control baselines. Good metrics for information security management, including evaluating controls, have the following characteristics:

- Manageable
- Meaningful
- Actionable
- Unambiguous
- Reliable/consistent
- Accurate
- Timely
- Predictive

Ideally, the metrics should be quantifiable measurements based upon ordinal numbers or percentages of a given requirement. Ideally, it should be inexpensive to gather the necessary information to perform the measurements

As the cost to gather measurements increases and the ability to quantify results decreases, the organizational value of the metric decreases. If the measurement is not quantifiable in such a way that the results are supportable, then users of the data will tend to discount the value of the data. If the cost to gather data increases too much, security managers should look to other measurement methods such as indirect analysis or extrapolation based upon other related measurements obtained.

Setting security baselines for an organization's operational enterprise has a number of benefits. It standardizes the minimum amount of security measures that must be employed throughout the organization; this results in positive benefits for risk management. Secondly, it provides a convenient point of reference to measure changes to security and identify corresponding effects on risk.

Working in conjunction with the organization's enterprise architecture group, an information security technology baseline of controls can be developed that is appropriate for the organization's operating environment.

There is a wealth of information available from NIST, COBIT, ISO/IEC 27001:2013 and security vendors regarding standards for information security controls. However, the information security manager has to keep in mind that every organization has its own needs and its own priorities. While NIST, ISO, COBIT and vendor information resources can provide starting points of support for developing controls, specific analysis should always be performed.

Controls suitable for the organization must be developed based on a variety of factors such as culture, structure, risk appetite and tolerance, etc. It is also important to keep in mind that, in addition to technology in the definition of a risk analysis program, people and processes must be considered as well. The information security manager will also need to develop procedural and physical security baselines. This will often present more of a challenge since these are areas typically outside the areas of security department control. Appropriate standards as described in chapter 1, with approval of the steering committee, can be the most effective approach to address this issue. Internal audit and regular security reviews can help provide assurance of compliance.

There is a general consensus among many vendors, security organizations, information security professionals and systems auditors about security configuration specifications that represent a prudent level of due care. These cooperative efforts continue to define consensus-based, good-practice security configurations for various systems and platforms. The information security manager should examine these specifications and, where appropriate, they should be tailored and incorporated into organizational security baselines.

While industry standard baselines are important for the information security manager to be aware of, the information security manager must assess the level of security that should be employed in the organization in various security domains. The commingling of different technologies can often introduce new risk and change a secure system or platform into one that has new vulnerabilities. A tailored risk assessment that recognizes these interactions and dependencies will enable the information security manager to determine whether security processes and procedures above the accepted baselines are necessary to provide adequate security commensurate with the organizations defined levels of acceptable risk. Some organizations and industries may require higher baselines. Regulatory requirement for certain industries and regions may set a higher standard. Another issue may be that some of the organization's information is classified as highly critical or sensitive, and it must have control mechanisms that provide a higher level of security commensurate with its classification.

2.15 RISK MONITORING AND COMMUNICATION

Implementing an effective risk management program requires monitoring and communication. Monitoring the effectiveness of controls will be an ongoing effort required to manage risk. Communication channels must be established both for reporting and disseminating information relevant to managing risk as well as providing the information security manager with information about risk-related activities throughout the enterprise, which includes reporting significant changes in risk and training and awareness.

2.15.1 RISK MONITORING

An important component of the risk management life cycle is continuously monitoring, evaluating, assessing and reporting risk. The results and status of this ongoing analysis needs to be documented and reported to senior management on a regular basis. To facilitate such reporting, visual aids such as graphs or charts and summarized overviews can be useful. **Exhibit 2.30** shows a risk report format from COBIT 5 that can serve as a standard approach for communicating risk status.

Senior management will typically have little interest in technical details and is likely to want an overview of the current status and indicators of any immediate or impending threat that requires attention.

Red-amber-green reports, often referred to as security dashboards, heat charts, or stoplight charts are often used to show an overall assessment of the security posture. Depending on the recipients, other forms of representing security status such as bar graphs or spider charts are often more effective at conveying trends. Whatever the form of reporting, the information security manager is responsible for the management of this reporting process to ensure that it takes place that the results are analyzed adequately and acted on appropriately in a timely manner. This responsibility includes identifying the types of events that will trigger reporting required by regulatory agencies and/or law enforcement and advising management of this requirement.

2.15.2 KEY RISK INDICATORS (KRIs)

One approach seeing increasing use is to report and monitor risk through the use of key risk indicators (KRIs). KRIs can be defined as measures that, in some manner, indicate when an enterprise is subject to risk that exceeds a defined risk level. Typically, these indicators are trends in factors known to increase risk and are generally developed based on experience. They can be as diverse as increasing absenteeism or increased turnover in key employees to rising levels of security events or incidents. KRIs can provide early warnings on possible issues or areas that pose particular risk.

A variety of risk indicators can be developed for various parts of an organization as a means of ongoing monitoring. A KRI is differentiated by being highly relevant and possessing a high probability of predicting or indicating major risk. Selection of KRIs, in addition to experience, can be based on sources such as industry benchmarks, external threat reporting services, or any other factor that can be monitored which indicates changes in risk to the organization.

Exhibit 2.30—Risk Report

A risk report includes information on current risk management capabilities and actual status and trends with regard to risk. This report will be based on the risk profile and will be tailored to the requirements of recipients.

	Life Cycle Stage	Internal Stakeholder	External Stakeholder	Description/Stake
Life Cycle and Stakeholders	**Information planning**	Risk function		Risk management capabilities, actual status and trends are communicated timely and accurately to the right people, based on their needs and requirements.
	Information design	Risk function		Risk management capabilities, actual status and trends are communicated timely and accurately to the right people, based on their needs and requirements.
	Information build/acquire	Risk function, business process owners/CIO		Ensure that the risk report includes the latest information on risk management capabilities, latest status and trends with regard to risk of the entire organisation.
	Information use/operate: store, share, use	Board, executive management, CIO, risk function, business process owners/CIO, compliance, internal audit	External audit, regulator	Effective utilisation and availability of information item by all involved stakeholders.
	Information monitor	Board, risk committee, audit committee, risk function, business process owners/CIO	External audit	Verifies that information remains actual and alerts on changes.
	Information dispose	Risk function		Ensures information is disposed of in a timely, secure and appropriate manner.
Goals	Quality Subdimension and Goals	Description—The extent to which information is...	Relevance	Goal—The risk report...
Intrinsic	**Accuracy**	correct and reliable	High	should accurately define the risk management capabilities and actual status and trends with regard to risk, in such a way that it does not arouse confusion
	Objectivity	unbiased, unprejudiced and impartial	High	information is based on the enterprise's risk culture and confirmed by observations.
	Believability	regarded as true and credible	Medium	should be realistic and accurate
	Reputation	regarded as coming from a true and credible source	High	source information is collected from competent and recognised sources.

Source: ISACA, *COBIT® 5 for Risk*, USA, 2013, figure 64, page 155

KRIs are specific to each enterprise, and their selection depends on a number of parameters in the internal and external environment—such as the size and complexity of the organization, whether it operates in a highly regulated market, and its business strategy. Identifying useful risk indicators includes the following considerations:

- Including the different stakeholders in the enterprise. Risk indicators should not focus solely on the operational or the strategic side of risk. Rather, they should be identified for all stakeholders. Involving the right stakeholders in the selection of risk indicators will also ensure greater buy-in and ownership.
- Balancing the selection of risk indicators covering performance indicators that indicate risk after an event has occurred, lead indicators that indicate what capabilities are in place to prevent events from occurring, and trends based on analyzing indicators over time or correlating indicators to gain insight
- Ensuring that the selected indicators drill down to the root cause of events rather than just focusing on symptoms

Additionally, it is important to determine which measures are likely to serve as effective KRIs. These are differentiated by being highly relevant and possessing a high probability of predicting or indicating important risk. The criteria for selecting effective KRIs include:

- **Impact**—Indicators for risk with high potential impact are more likely to be KRIs.
- **Effort to implement, measure and report**—For different indicators of equivalent sensitivity to changing risk, the ones that are easier to measure are preferred.
- **Reliability**—The indicator must possess a high correlation with the risk and be a good predictor or outcome measure.
- **Sensitivity**—The indicator must be representative of the risk and capable of accurately indicating variances in the risk level.

Since the enterprise's internal and external environments are constantly changing, the risk environment is also highly dynamic and the set of KRIs will more than likely change over time. Each KRI is related to the risk appetite and tolerance so that trigger levels can be defined that will enable stakeholders to take appropriate action in a timely manner.

2.15.3 REPORTING SIGNIFICANT CHANGES IN RISK

As changes occur in an organization, the risk assessment must be updated to ensure its continued accuracy. Reporting these changes to the appropriate levels of management at the proper time is a primary responsibility of the information security manager. The information security manager should have periodic meetings with upper management to present a status on the organization's overall risk profile, including changes in risk level as well as the status of any open (untreated) risk.

In addition, the security program should include a process in which a significant security breach or security event will trigger a report to upper management and a reassessment of risk and applicable controls because all security events or incidents are the result of the failure of, or lack of, controls. The information security manager should have defined processes by which security events are evaluated based on impact to the organization. This evaluation may warrant a special report to upper management to inform them of the event, the impact and the steps being taken to mitigate the risk. Refer to chapter 4, Information Security and Incident Management, for more detailed information on establishing and managing an incident response program.

2.16 TRAINING AND AWARENESS

People typically constitute the greatest risk to any organization generally through accident, mistake, a lack of knowledge/ information and, occasionally, through malicious intent. Appropriate training and awareness campaigns can have significant positive contribution on managing risk. Many controls are procedural and require some operational knowledge and compliance. Technical controls must be configured and operated correctly to provide the expected level of assurance. Ensuring users are educated in procedures and understand risk management processes is the responsibility of the information security manager, and appropriate training and awareness activities should be included in any risk management program.

The training and awareness program should be targeted to different staffing and security levels (e.g., senior management, middle management/IT staff and end users).

End-user information security training should include, among other things, sessions on:

- The importance of adhering to the security policies and procedures of the enterprise
- Responding to emergency situations
- Significance of logical access in an IT environment
- Privacy and confidentiality requirements
- Recognizing and reporting security incidents
- Recognizing and dealing with social engineering

2.17 DOCUMENTATION

Appropriate documentation that is readily available regarding risk management policies and standards, as well as other relevant risk-related matters, is required to effectively manage risk. Decisions concerning the nature and extent of documentation involve costs and related benefits. The risk management strategy, policy and program define the documentation needed. Specifically, at each stage of the risk management process, documentation should include:

- Objectives
- Audience
- Information resources
- Assumptions
- Decisions

A risk management policy document may include information such as:

- Objectives of the policy and rationale for managing risk
- Scope and charter of information risk management
- Links between the risk management policy and the organization's strategic and corporate business plans
- Extent and range of issues to which the policy applies
- Guidance on what is considered acceptable risk levels
- Risk management responsibilities

- Support expertise available to assist those responsible for managing risk
- Level of documentation required for various risk-management-related activities, e.g., change management
- A plan for reviewing compliance with the risk management policy
- Incident and event severity levels
- Risk reporting and escalation procedures, format and frequency

In some circumstances, a compliance and due diligence statement may be required to ensure that managers formally acknowledge their responsibility to comply with risk management policies and procedures.

Typical documentation for risk management should include:

- A risk register—For each risk identified, record the:
  - Source of risk
  - Nature of risk
  - Selected treatment option
  - Existing controls
  - Recommended controls not implemented and the reasons why they should be implemented
- Consequences and likelihood of compromise, including:
  - Income loss
  - Unexpected expense
  - Legal risk (compliance and contractual)
  - Interdependent processes
  - Loss of public reputation or public confidence
- Initial risk rating
- Vulnerability to external/internal factors
- An inventory of information assets, including IT and telecommunication assets, that lists:
  - Description of the asset
  - Technical specifications
  - Number/quantity
  - Location
  - Special licensing requirements, if any
- A risk mitigation and action plan, providing:
  - Who has responsibility for implementing the plan
  - Resources to be utilized
  - Budget allocation
  - Timetable for implementation
  - Details of mechanism/control measures
  - Policy compliance requirements
- Monitoring and audit documents, which include:
  - Outcomes of audits/reviews and other monitoring procedures
  - Follow-up of review recommendations and implementation status

Finally, it is essential that all documentation be subject to an effective version control process as well as a standard approach to marking and handling. Documentation should be conspicuously labeled with classification level, revision date and number, effective dates, and document owner.

Page intentionally left blank

Certified Information Security Manager® An ISACA® Certification

Chapter 3:

Information Security Program Development and Management

Section One: Overview

Section Two: Content

Section One: Overview

3.1 INTRODUCTION

This chapter reviews the diverse areas of knowledge needed to develop and manage an information security program.

DEFINITION

An information security program includes the coordinated set of activities, projects and/or initiatives to implement the information security strategy and manage the program. The strategy, as discussed in chapter 1, is the plan to achieve the objectives of information security that support the goals of the organization. Information security program management includes directing, overseeing and monitoring activities related to information security in support of organizational objectives. Management is the process of achieving the objectives of the business organization by bringing together human, physical and financial resources in an optimum combination with process and technology, and making the best decision for the organization while taking into consideration its operating environment.

OBJECTIVES

The objective of this domain is to ensure that the information security manager understands the broad requirements and activities needed to create, manage and maintain a program to implement an information security strategy. The information security program may consist of a series of projects and initiatives to achieve the objectives the strategy is designed to address as well as ongoing management and administration. The strategy can be used to chart a comprehensive road map to achieve a "desired state" as discussed in chapter 1. In some cases, however, the objectives may be more simply defined as a maturity level on the Capability Maturity Model (CMM) scale, addressing the most serious risk determined by a risk assessment, or achieving compliance with a particular set of regulations or standards. Regardless, objectives of the program must be clearly defined and a plan and methodology devised to achieve those goals.

The information security manager must know how to define and utilize the resources required to achieve the goals, consistent with organizational objectives, through a number of tasks utilizing the security manager's knowledge of people, process and technology.

Chapters 1 and 2 in this manual cover governance of information security and risk management. The concepts and information from these chapters is applied in the development and management of an information security program.

This domain represents 25 percent of the CISM examination (approximately 50 questions).

3.2 TASK AND KNOWLEDGE STATEMENTS

Domain 3—Information Security Program Development and Management
Establish and manage the information security program in alignment with the information security strategy

TASKS

There are nine tasks within this domain that a CISM must know how to perform:

- T3.1 Establish and maintain the information security program in alignment with the information security strategy.
- T3.2 Ensure alignment between the information security program and other business functions (for example, human resources [HR], accounting, procurement and IT) to support integration with business processes.
- T3.3 Identify, acquire, manage and define requirements for internal and external resources to execute the information security program.
- T3.4 Establish and maintain information security architectures (people, process, technology) to execute the information security program.
- T3.5 Establish, communicate and maintain organizational information security standards, procedures, guidelines and other documentation to support and guide compliance with information security policies.
- T3.6 Establish and maintain a program for information security awareness and training to promote a secure environment and an effective security culture.
- T3.7 Integrate information security requirements into organizational processes (for example, change control, mergers and acquisitions, development, business continuity, disaster recovery) to maintain the organization's security baseline.
- T3.8 Integrate information security requirements into contracts and activities of third parties (for example, joint ventures, outsourced providers, business partners, customers) to maintain the organization's security baseline.
- T3.9 Establish, monitor and periodically report program management and operational metrics to evaluate the effectiveness and efficiency of the information security program.

KNOWLEDGE STATEMENTS

The CISM candidate must have a good understanding of each of the domains delineated by the knowledge statements. These statements are the basis for the exam.

There are 12 knowledge statements within the information security program development domain:

- KS3.1 Knowledge of methods to align information security program requirements with those of other business functions
- KS3.2 Knowledge of methods to identify, acquire, manage and define requirements for internal and external resources
- KS3.3 Knowledge of information security technologies, emerging trends, (for example, cloud computing, mobile computing) and underlying concepts
- KS3.4 Knowledge of methods to design information security controls

KS3.5 Knowledge of information security architectures (for example, people, process, technology) and methods to apply them
KS3.6 Knowledge of methods to develop information security standards, procedures and guidelines
KS3.7 Knowledge of methods to implement and communicate information security policies, standards, procedures and guidelines
KS3.8 Knowledge of methods to establish and maintain effective information security awareness and training programs
KS3.9 Knowledge of methods to integrate information security requirements into organizational processes
KS3.10 Knowledge of methods to incorporate information security requirements into contracts and third-party management processes
KS3.11 Knowledge of methods to design, implement and report operational information security metrics
KS3.12 Knowledge of methods for testing the effectiveness and applicability of information security controls

RELATIONSHIP OF TASK TO KNOWLEDGE STATEMENTS

The task statements are what the CISM candidate is expected to know how to perform. The knowledge statements delineate each of the areas in which the CISM candidate must have a good understanding in order to perform the tasks. The task and knowledge statements are mapped in **exhibit 3.1**, insofar as it is possible to do so. Note that although there is often overlap, each task statement will generally map to several knowledge statements.

Exhibit 3.1—Task and Knowledge Statements Mapping

Task Statement	Knowledge Statements
T3.1 Establish and maintain the information security program in alignment with the information security strategy.	KS 3.1 Knowledge of methods to align information security program requirements with those of other business functions KS3.2 Knowledge of methods to identify, acquire, manage and define requirements for internal and external resources KS3.3 Knowledge of information security technologies, emerging trends, (for example, cloud computing, mobile computing) and underlying concepts KS3.4 Knowledge of methods to design information security controls KS3.5 Knowledge of information security architectures (for example, people, processes, technology) and methods to apply them
T3.2 Ensure alignment between the information security program and other business functions (for example, human resources [HR], accounting, procurement and IT) to support integration with business processes.	KS3.1 Knowledge of methods to align information security program requirements with those of other business functions
T3.3 Identify, acquire, manage and define requirements for internal and external resources to execute the information security program.	KS3.2 Knowledge of methods to identify, acquire, manage and define requirements for internal and external resources KS3.3 Knowledge of information security technologies, emerging trends, (for example, cloud computing, mobile computing) and underlying concepts
T3.4 Establish and maintain information security architectures (people, process, technology) to execute the information security program.	KS3.2 Knowledge of methods to identify, acquire, manage and define requirements for internal and external resources KS3.3 Knowledge of information security technologies, emerging trends, (for example, cloud computing, mobile computing) and underlying concepts KS3.4 Knowledge of methods to design information security controls KS3.5 Knowledge of information security architectures (for example, people, process, technology) and methods to apply them KS3.9 Knowledge of methods to integrate information security requirements into organizational processes KS3.12 Knowledge of methods for testing the effectiveness and applicability of information security controls
T3.5 Establish, communicate and maintain organizational information security standards, procedures, guidelines and other documentation to support and guide compliance with information security policies.	KS3.4 Knowledge of methods to design information security controls KS3.6 Knowledge of methods to develop information security standards, procedures and guidelines KS3.7 Knowledge of methods to implement and communicate information security policies, standards, procedures and guidelines
T3.6 Establish and maintain a program for information security awareness and training to promote a secure environment and an effective security culture.	KS3.7 Knowledge of methods to implement and communicate information security policies, standards, procedures and guidelines KS3.8 Knowledge of methods to establish and maintain effective information security awareness and training programs

Exhibit 3.1—Task and Knowledge Statements Mapping *(cont.)*	
Task Statement	**Knowledge Statements**
T3.7 Integrate information security requirements into organizational processes (for example, change control, mergers and acquisitions, development, business continuity, disaster recovery) to maintain the organization's security baseline.	KS3.4 Knowledge of methods to design information security controls KS3.9 Knowledge of methods to integrate information security requirements into organizational processes
T3.8 Integrate information security requirements into contracts and activities of third parties (for example, joint ventures, outsourced providers, business partners, customers) to maintain the organization's security baseline.	KS3.4 Knowledge of methods to design information security controls KS3.10 Knowledge of methods to incorporate information security requirements into contracts and third-party management processes
T3.9 Establish, monitor and periodically report program management and operational metrics to evaluate the effectiveness and efficiency of the information security program.	KS3.3 Knowledge of information security technologies, emerging trends, (for example, cloud computing, mobile computing) and underlying concepts KS3.11 Knowledge of methods to design, implement and report operational information security metrics KS3.12 Knowledge of methods for testing the effectiveness and applicability of information security controls

KNOWLEDGE STATEMENT REFERENCE GUIDE

The following section contains the knowledge statements and the underlying concepts and relevance for the knowledge of the information security manager. The knowledge statements are what the information security manager must know in order to accomplish the tasks. A summary explanation of each knowledge statement is provided, followed by the basic concepts that are the foundation for the written exam. Each key concept has references to section two of this chapter.

The CISM body of knowledge has been divided into four domains, and each of the four chapters covers some of the material contained in those domains. This chapter reviews the body of knowledge from the perspective of management of the security program.

KS3.1 Knowledge of methods to align information security program requirements with those of other business functions

Explanation	Key Concepts	Reference in 2015 CISM Review Manual
The requirement for strategic alignment discussed in chapter 1 must be made operational by the information security manager as a part of program development. This requires an understanding of the various business functions of the organization. These in turn will drive many of the requirements for information security. Meeting these requirements will maximize the effectiveness and benefits provided by information security activities to the organization.	The functions of other organizational units related to information security	3.4.2 Outcomes of Information Security Program Management 3.14.1 Information Security Liaison Responsibilities 3.14.2 Cross-organizational Responsibilities
	Factors affecting interdepartmental collaboration	3.14.1 Information Security Liaison Responsibilities 3.14.2 Cross-organizational Responsibilities
	Policy, governance and assurance process integration	3.6 Information Security Program Concepts 3.7 Scope and Charter of Information Security Program 3.14.1 Information Security Liaison Responsibilities 3.14.2 Cross-organizational Responsibilities
	Structural and cultural considerations for alignment	3.7 Scope and Charter of an Information Security Program 3.10.1 Elements of a Road Map 3.13.1 Personnel, Roles and Responsibilities, and Skills 3.14.1 Information Security Liaison Responsibilities 3.14.2 Cross-organizational Responsibilities

KS3.2 Knowledge of methods to identify, acquire, manage and define requirements for internal and external resources

Explanation	Key Concepts	Reference in 2015 CISM Review Manual
The security manager must have knowledge of implementation and management of information security processes and technologies. Depending on the scope of a security program development effort, it can be a major undertaking requiring managing a number of activities in diverse areas. This will typically include managing people, processes and technology. The personnel involved can include management, direct reports, consultants, contractors, and service providers as well as individuals in other departments and organizational units. Security program implementation will inevitably affect business processes, and will include many aspects of information technology as well. An information security manager should have broad exposure to and be competent in all of these areas in order to effectively manage the overall security program implementation. Developing an information security program of any significant size requires a number of different resources, including people, finances, processes and technologies. Organizations have established processes, policies and practices that must be followed for acquiring these resources. The information security manager must be familiar with these practices to be effective and minimize potential obstacles. This typically includes knowledge of areas such as finance, procurement (including contracting procedures and policies), and HR. Most organizations have departments that are responsible for these activities and the information security manager should understand how they function and then develop working relationships with key contacts within each group. The information security manager must be able to identify required skills for each role related to information security and to encourage employees to acquire those skills necessary to competently perform their assigned duties. Prior to training, actual skill and proficiency should be measured against the required levels through testing and observation. This will provide an understanding of the skills gap and what is required to close the gap, and it will help define the level and depth of the training required. The required skills can be developed through any number of methods, including self-study, on-the-job training and instructor-led training. This activity may also determine proficiency levels beyond what is required in particular job functions, providing an opportunity to assign greater responsibilities and career advancement for individuals.	Effective project planning and management	3.4.2 Outcomes of Information Security Program Management 3.9.3 Administrative Components 3.10.1 Elements of a Road Map 3.10.2 Developing an Information Security Program Road Map 3.11.2 Objectives of Information Security Architectures 3.13.1 Personnel, Roles and Responsibilities, and Skills 3.14.9 Outsourcing and Service Providers 3.14.11 Integration With IT Processes
	Resources required for information security program implementation	3.4.2 Outcomes of Information Security Program Management 3.6.2 Technology Resources 3.9.3 Administrative Components 3.10.1 Elements of a Road Map 3.10.2 Developing an Information Security Program Roadmap 3.11.2 Objectives of Information Security Architectures 3.13.1 Personnel, Roles and Responsibilities, and Skills 3.13.7 Program Budgeting 3.14.9 Outsourcing and Service Providers 3.14.11 Integration With IT Processes
	Personnel required for program implementation	3.13.1 Personnel, Roles and Responsibilities, and Skills 3.13.10 Vendor Management 3.14.9 Outsourcing and Service Providers
	Security requirements for outsourced functions and services	3.14.9 Outsourcing and Service Providers 3.14.10 Cloud Computing
	SLAs and service contracts	3.14.9 Outsourcing and Service Providers 3.14.10 Cloud Computing
	Addressing risk and liabilities posed by third parties	3.13.2 Security Awareness, Training and Education 3.14.9 Outsourcing and Service Providers 3.14.10 Cloud Computing 3.15 Controls and Countermeasures 3.15.10 Control Testing and Modification

KS3.3 Knowledge of information security technologies, emerging trends, (for example, cloud computing, mobile computing) and underlying concepts

Explanation	Key Concepts	Reference in 2015 CISM Review Manual
Developing an information security program requires a solid understanding of available technologies, their capabilities and their use. A majority of information security controls will be technical, and it is necessary to understand the capabilities, costs and benefits of specific technologies as well as their limitations. As an example, the information security manager does not need to know how to configure a firewall or harden a server, but must know what these technologies are, how these activities are performed and how they affect the implementation and management of information security.	The types of security technologies	3.14.5 Management of Security Technology 3.15 Controls and Countermeasures
	The use and purpose of security technologies	3.6 Information Security Program Concepts 3.15 Controls and Countermeasures 3.17 Common Information Security Program Challenges
	Control technologies	3.6.2 Technology Resources 3.15 Controls and Countermeasures 3.15.2 Controls as Strategy Implementation Resources 3.15.7 Physical and Environmental Controls 3.15.8 Control Technology Categories
	Security of information technology	3.11 Information Security Infrastructure and Architecture

KS3.4 Knowledge of methods to design information security controls

Explanation	Key Concepts	Reference in 2015 CISM Review Manual
Any policy, practice, procedure, process or technology that serves to regulate activities is a control. Effective development of controls requires a controls policy and architecture that collectively meet the control objectives defined in the strategy. The controls policy will include considerations such as whether controls fail open or closed or whether activities are denied unless explicitly allowed or allowed unless denied. Controls design must consider control strength, reliability, effectiveness, user and productivity impact, cost, and how to utilize appropriate layering to achieve acceptable risk levels. To a large extent, the core function of information security program development is the ongoing process of designing, developing, implementing, testing and modifying controls—whether technical, physical or procedural. Translating an information security strategy into a control architecture is an essential competence for the information security manager. Controls in this context are often thought of as primarily technology implementations, but for information security, physical and procedural considerations are equally important. Servers that are well-secured from a technical point of view are at risk if they are subject to weak facilities security such as poor access controls for personnel. Inadequate or inconsistent compliance with critical procedures is often the cause of systems failures and must be considered as well in a controls implementation approach.	The kinds of controls and their use	3.6 Information Security Program Concepts 3.6.2 Technology Resources 3.10.1 Elements of a Road Map 3.15 Controls and Countermeasures
	Controls design criteria	3.14.7 Compliance Monitoring and Enforcement 3.15.2 Control Design Considerations 3.16 Security Program Metrics and Monitoring
	Controls design policy	3.8 The Information Security Management Framework 3.15.2 Control Design Considerations Exhibit 3.5 Information Security Management System Controls Process
	Controls testing and maintenance	3.13.3 Documentation 3.14.4 Security Reviews and Audits 3.15.10 Control Testing and Modification 3.16.13 Monitoring and Communication
	Basis and requirement for control objectives	3.4 Information Security Program Management Overview 3.4.2 Outcomes of the Information Security Program 3.15 Controls and Countermeasures 3.15.10 Control Testing and Modification 3.16.10 Measuring Effectiveness of Technical Security Architecture 3.16.12 Measuring Operational Performance
	Types and uses of controls	3.8 The Information Security Management Framework 3.11 Information Security Infrastructure and Architecture 3.14.8 Assessment of Risk and Impact 3.15 Controls and Countermeasures
	Control development, performance and deployment criteria	3.9 Information Security Framework Components 3.13.2 Security Awareness, Training and Education 3.13.3 Documentation 3.13.8 General Rules of Use/Acceptable Use Policy 3.14.4 Security Reviews and Audits 3.14.7 Compliance Monitoring and Enforcement 3.14.8 Assessment of Risk and Impact 3.14.11 Integration With IT Processes 3.15 Controls and Countermeasures 3.16.8 Measuring Security Cost-Effectiveness 3.16.10 Measuring Effectiveness of Technical Security Architecture
	Testing controls for effectiveness	3.14.9 Outsourcing and Service Providers 3.15.10 Control Testing and Modification

KS3.5 Knowledge of information security architectures (for example, people, process, technology) and methods to apply them

Explanation	Key Concepts	Reference in 2015 CISM Review Manual
Depending on scope, development and implementation, an information security program can consist of a variety of projects and involve a large number of elements. In addition, these activities may extend over several years and will invariably benefit from the implementation of several levels of security architecture. This may include contextual and conceptual architectures based on the business requirements that define the relationship between organizational functions and, at a high level, how process and technology will support them. It will usually include logical and physical architectures as well and may include component, functional and operational architectures. One of the key functions of architecture is to provide a framework within which complexity can be managed successfully. As the size and complexity of a project grows, many designers and design influences must work as a team to create something that has the appearance of being created by a single design authority. As the complexity of the business environment grows, many business processes and support functions must integrate seamlessly to provide effective services and management to the business, its customers and its partners. Architecture provides a means to manage that complexity. Architecture also acts as a road map for a collection of smaller projects and services that must be integrated into a single program or initiative. It provides a framework within which many members of large design, delivery and support teams can work together and serves to integrate tactical security elements.	The purposes of security architecture	1.13.2 Enterprise Information Security Architecture(s) 3.11 Information Security Infrastructure and Architecture 3.11.1 Enterprise Information Security Architecture 3.11.2 Objectives of Information Security Architectures Exhibit 1.17 TOGAF Enterprise Architecture Framework
	The elements of an architecture	Exhibit 3.8 The SABSA Matrix for Security Architecture Development
	The types of security architectures	1.13.2 Enterprise Information Security Architecture(s) Exhibit 1.17 TOGAF Enterprise Architecture Framework Exhibit 3.6 The SABSA Model for Security Architecture Development Exhibit 3.7 The SABSA Model for Security Architecture Development From the Operational Security Architecture Perspective

KS3.6 Knowledge of methods to develop information security standards, procedures and guidelines

Explanation	Key Concepts	Reference in 2015 CISM Review Manual
Many organizations have created governance documents over a period of time and with different authors and approaches. The result is generally an unwieldy collection of unclear, confusing and often contradictory mandates that are seldom read and nearly impossible to follow. It is essential, as a part of developing an information security program, to create or modify policies to be clear, well-organized and consistent high-level statements of management intent, expectations and direction. This must be followed by ensuring development of clear, concise and minimally restrictive standards as well as a requirement for reviewing and modifying procedures as needed. A detailed approach is provided in chapter 1, section 1.12.1. While there are many approaches to developing security governance documentation, in order to support the organization's objectives, the approaches must all begin with understanding the structure, culture, practices and goals of the business. The security policies must define a strategy that supports those objectives. Metrics to assess progress should also be developed. The strategy must include the processes for developing, implementing, communicating and maintaining governance documentation such as policies, standards and procedures. Chapter 1, section 16, contains an example of an approach to developing security governance documentation. The various governance documents (policies, standards, procedures) may be created or modified during the development of a strategy or during program development. This is also the phase where implementation of new or modified policies and standards is likely to occur, as well as the processes necessary for their periodic review, modification and communication.	Policy support for information security program development	1.13.1 Policies and Standards 1.15.2 Policy Development 3.10.2 Developing an Information Security Program Road Map 3.13.3 Documentation
	Standards requirements and compliance for program development	1.13.1 Policies and Standards 1.15.2 Policy Development 3.10.2 Developing an Information Security Program Road Map 3.13.3 Documentation
	Procedure development during program development and implementation	1.13.1 Policies and Standards 3.8 The Information Security Management Framework 3.13.3 Documentation 3.15.4 Control Methods 3.15.8 Control Technology Categories 3.15.10 Control Testing and Modification 3.16.6 Measuring Compliance 3.16.13 Monitoring and Communication
	Policy support for information security program development	1.13.1 Policies and Standards 1.15.2 Policy Development 3.10.2 Developing an Information Security Program Road Map 3.13.3 Documentation

KS3.7 Knowledge of methods to implement and communicate information security policies, standards, procedures and guidelines

Explanation	Key Concepts	Reference in 2015 CISM Review Manual
Security policies, standards, procedures and guidelines are the primary tools for guiding the implementation and management of an information security program. Policies are high-level statements of management intent, direction and expectations. The topic is covered extensively in chapter 1, sections 1.13.1 and 1.15.2. From the perspective of managing an information security program, policies will already have been developed, although they may require additions, review or modification. Typically, the task of managing the security program will be concerned with interpreting these policies by developing or modifying a collection of appropriate standards. The specific nature and content of the standards is governed by the requirements of managing risk. Policies are implemented by designing, developing or modifying and deploying controls consistent with these standards. Compliance with the standards on a consistent ongoing basis will also be a major focus for the information security manager. It is essential to develop policies that ensure that program development is aligned with and supports organizational objectives. Policies may exist, or have been developed, as a part of strategy, but they may require modification during security program development as conditions or constraints change. It may be determined that policies do not adequately address unanticipated circumstances, that the legal or regulatory requirements have changed or different business objectives have emerged. The information security manager must ensure that processes exist for security policy review, modification, management approval and dissemination to all stakeholders. When policies are modified or created, standards must also be reviewed to ensure that they continue to reflect the intent of the policy. All parties subject to the policies must be made aware of the changes in policy and standards, and they should be instructed to review their procedures to ensure that they make any modifications necessary due to the changes in standards. Policy development or modification must be linked to the organization's overall objectives. An appropriate balance must be struck supporting business activities while providing protection against unacceptable risk at an acceptable cost. The linkage to business objectives is the result of clearly defining the objectives of the security program, what constitutes acceptable risk, and the types of controls that are minimally disruptive while achieving the required degree of mitigation.	Requirement for control (governance) documentation	1.4 Information Security Governance Overview 1.4.1 Importance of Information Security Governance 3.13.3 Documentation
	Implementation of policies and standards	1.13.1 Policies and Standards 1.15.2 Policy Development 3.10 Defining an Information Security Program Road Map 3.14.2 Cross-organizational Responsibilities 3.17 Common Information Security Program Challenges Exhibit 3.14 Security Review Alternatives
	Circumstances requiring control documentation changes	3.13.1 Personnel, Roles and Responsibilities, and Skills 3.13.3 Documentation 3.14.7 Compliance Monitoring and Enforcement
	Requirements for evaluating control documentation	3.14.7 Compliance Monitoring and Enforcement Exhibit 3.14 Security Review Alternatives

KS3.8 Knowledge of methods to establish and maintain effective information security awareness and training programs

Explanation	Key Concepts	Reference in 2015 CISM Review Manual
Awareness education and training can serve to mitigate some of the biggest organizational risk and achieve the most cost-effective improvement in security. This can generally be achieved by educating an organization's staff in required procedures and policy compliance, as well as ensuring that staff can identify and understand the information risk that threatens the organization. It is critical that the training effectively communicate the risk and its potential impact in order for staff to understand the justification for what many see as inconvenient extra steps that security controls often require. The information security manager must also understand the organization's structure and culture, as well as the types of communication that are most effective, in order to develop awareness and training programs that will be effective in the environment. Periodically changing security awareness messages and the means of delivery will help maintain a higher level of security awareness. Procedural controls can be complex and it is essential to provide training as needed to ensure that staff understand the procedures and can correctly perform the steps. Awareness of information security policies, standards and procedures by all personnel is essential to achieving effective risk management. However, employees cannot be expected to comply with policies or standards that they are not aware of, or follow procedures they do not understand. The information security manager must devise a standardized approach, such as short computer- or paper-based quizzes to gauge awareness levels. Periodic use of a standardized testing approach provides metrics for awareness trends and training effectiveness. Training needs can be determined by a skills assessment or employing a testing approach. Indicators for additional training requirements can come from various sources such as tracking help desk activity, operational errors, security events and audits.	Determining adequate levels of security awareness	3.13.2 Security Awareness, Training and Education

KS3.9 Knowledge of methods to integrate information security requirements into organizational processes

Explanation	Key Concepts	Reference in 2015 CISM Review Manual
Development of a security program must take into consideration the existing organizational structure, culture and practices. Implementation of the security program components will be most efficiently accomplished by integrating the program into the existing organizational processes and thereby minimize disruption and organizational resistance to change. If there are existing standards for risk management practices such as change management, user acceptance testing or release management, they should be utilized to the extent possible. Numerous other functions important to information security exist in most organizations. Among the most important are audit, procurement, human resources, contracting, procurement, legal, and the project management office (PMO). To the extent possible, the security program should be integrated with these functions during information security program development. There are many specific approaches to life cycle methodologies, including the common system development life cycle (SDLC) version typically used in information systems. The approaches are similar, but differ somewhat in the terms used and the number of steps in the model. The typical steps will include some variation of: feasibility, design, development, deployment, maintenance and end-of-life decommissioning. The relevance for the development of an information security program is primarily that risk changes with the life cycle stage and must be addressed appropriately. The risk at the design stage for a technical control, such as a firewall, is that the design is inadequate or faulty, while at the maintenance stage, the risk to be managed is that maintenance activities are insufficient to ensure an aspect of security such as availability. One of the most common causes of information security breaches is inadequate assessment and management of risk as a result of system or process changes. Managing an information security program effectively requires that the security manager ensure that change management policies and processes exist and are documented, that they are followed and that security is considered an integral part of the process. This generally requires the direct, ongoing participation of the information security manager in the change management process.	Application of security standards in organizational processes	3.4.2 Outcomes of Information Security Program Management 3.14.11 Integration With IT Processes 3.14.9 Outsourcing and Service Providers

KS3.10 Knowledge of methods to incorporate information security requirements into contracts and third-party management processes

<table>
<tr><th>Explanation</th><th>Key Concepts</th><th>Reference in 2015 CISM Review Manual</th></tr>
<tr><td rowspan="3">Contracts that have implications for information security will usually be reviewed by the legal department. However, they must also be reviewed by the information security manager to ensure that risk is assessed and management is either prepared to accept the risk or make appropriate changes.

Risk related to third parties is often the most difficult to manage to acceptable levels, and it is essential that the security manager understand the processes and options available to address these issues. Each relationship with a third party must undergo a risk assessment, and appropriate mitigation measures must be agreed to and budgeted prior to contract execution

An information security program must take into consideration all third-party relationships, including trading partners, outsourced functions and service providers. Security vulnerabilities are often introduced by these relationships, and it is essential that the information security program consider these vulnerabilities as part of the overall organizational risk profile. Contractual relationships must be governed by appropriate contract language and service level agreements (SLAs) must include adequate provisions regarding security.

It is essential that appropriate security provisions are a part of any service contract. The information security manager must assess the risk of outsourcing any activity or service and ensure that appropriate provisions exist in the contract. These provisions should be introduced as early as possible in the contract negotiation process. Provisions can include right to audit, specific security requirements, security SLAs or other reporting and monitoring requirements, and indemnification clauses in the event of security breaches caused by the service provider.

Effectively monitoring the risk created by third-party providers can present a significant challenge that must be addressed by the information security manager. Monitoring and metrics requirements for outsourced services must be carefully conceived and defined in SLAs, based on the organization's control objectives and the assessed risk. The nature of the risk presented by third parties will depend on a number of factors, but primarily on the services that are provided and the impact of interruptions to those services. Every requirement in the SLA must be supported by a specific control and monitoring process.</td><td>The types and degree of information security risk posed by contractual relationships</td><td>3.14.9 Outsourcing and Service Providers
3.14.10 Cloud Computing</td></tr>
<tr><td>Contract and relationship monitoring and metrics</td><td>3.14.9 Outsourcing and Service Providers</td></tr>
<tr><td>Liabilities posed by third parties</td><td>3.14.9 Outsourcing and Service Providers</td></tr>
</table>

KS3.11 Knowledge of methods to design, implement and report operational information security metrics

Explanation	Key Concepts	Reference in 2015 CISM Review Manual
Metrics serve to provide the information needed to make decisions. Information security management metrics must be carefully devised to provide information that is meaningful to the recipient, accurate, reliable and timely. As a consequence, metrics must be developed based on understanding the responsibilities of the various managers that are the recipients of the information. For example, the chief financial officer (CFO) is unlikely to care about the number of packets dropped by a firewall whereas that may be useful information for the IT security officer. The tendency to provide data simply because they are available must be avoided and the focus shifted to provide the information needed as a basis for prudent decisions.	Types of strategic, management and operational metrics	1.7 Information Security Governance Metrics 3.4 Information Security Program Management Overview 3.4.2 Outcomes of Information Security Program Management 3.16 Security Program Metrics and Monitoring
	The purpose and use of metrics and monitoring	3.4 Information Security Program Management Overview 3.5.1 Defining Objectives 3.11.2 Objectives of Information Security Architectures 3.13.3 Documentation 3.13.12 Plan-Do-Check-Act 3.14.7 Compliance Monitoring and Enforcement 3.16 Security Program Metrics and Monitoring 3.16.3 Measuring Information Security Management Performance 3.16.12 Measuring Operational Performance 3.17 Common Information Security Program Challenges
	Essential criteria for relevant metrics	3.16 Security Program Metrics and Monitoring
	What should be monitored?	3.4.2 Outcomes of Information Security Program Management 3.16 Security Program Metrics and Monitoring
	Types of metrics: strategic, management, operational	1.7 Information Security Governance Metrics 3.16 Security Program Metrics and Monitoring

KS3.12 Knowledge of methods for testing the effectiveness and applicability of information security controls

Explanation	Key Concepts	Reference in 2015 CISM Review Manual
Controls generally evolve over time in response to a particular event or circumstance, usually without the benefit of an overall controls strategy and architecture. An important aspect of information security program development is to establish a process to periodically assess and evaluate controls to ensure that they continue to be relevant and effective. Assessing effectiveness and applicability must include a cost-benefit analysis encompassing inconvenience to users and impacts on productivity, as well as the total cost of ownership (TCO) of the control, including acquisition, deployment, training, testing, maintenance and eventual decommissioning. In many organizations, controls are developed over extended periods of time, often in a reactive response to a security-related event or incident. The rationale for these controls is typically not documented and the controls simply become the accepted practice, whether the need for them still exists or other redundant controls have been implemented. An ongoing requirement for effective information security management is to ensure that all controls—whether technical, physical or procedural—are documented, meet defined control objectives, and are periodically tested both for cost and for effectiveness. Methods utilized to test controls should be objective, consistent and cost-effective.	Purpose of testing controls	3.14.4 Security Reviews and Audits 3.15 Controls and Countermeasures
	Methods of testing controls	3.14.4 Security Reviews and Audits 3.15.10 Control Testing and Modification
	Control testing criteria	3.14.4 Security Reviews and Audits
	Legal and regulatory control testing requirements	3.13.13 Legal and Regulatory Requirements

SUGGESTED RESOURCES FOR FURTHER STUDY

Bonham, Stephen S.; *IT Project Portfolio Management*, Artech House Inc., USA, 2005

Brancik, Kenneth C.; *Insider Computer Fraud: An In-depth Framework for Detecting and Defending Against Insider IT Attacks*, Auerbach Publications, USA, 2007

Brotby, W. Krag; *Information Security Management Metrics: A Definitive Guide to Effective Security Monitoring and Measurement*, Auerbach Publications, USA, 2009

Cendrowski, Harry; James P. Martin; Louis W. Petro; *The Handbook of Fraud Deterrence*, John Wiley & Sons Inc., USA, 2006

Cloud Security Alliance (CSA), *cloudsecurityalliance.org*

International Federation of Accountants (IFAC), "Managing Security of Information Guidelines," 2006, *www.ifac.org*

International Information Systems Security Certification Consortium, Inc. (ISC)², *www.isc2.org*

International Organization for Standardization (ISO), "Guidelines for the Management of IT Security, ISO/IEC 13335," 2006, *www.iso.org*

ISACA, *Cloud Computing: Business Benefits With Security, Governance and Assurance Perspectives*, 2009, *www.isaca.org/Knowledge-Center/Research/Documents/Cloud-Computing-28Oct09-Research.pdf*

ISACA, COBIT 5, USA, 2012, *www.isaca.org/cobit*

ISACA, *COBIT 5 for Information Security*, USA, 2012

ISACA, *COBIT 5: Enabling Processes*, USA, 2012, *www.isaca.org/cobit*

Krause Nozaki, Micki; Harold F. Tipon; *Handbook of Information Security Management, 6th Edition*, Volume 6, CRC Press, USA, 2012

Longstaff, Dr. Thomas; David S. Brown; Eugene Schultz; *Responding to Computer Security Incidents: Guidelines for Incident Handling*, UCRL-ID-104689, USA, 23 July 1990

Marcella Jr., Albert J.; Doug Menendez; *Cyber Forensics: A Field Manual for Collecting, Examining and Preserving Evidence of Computer Crime, 2nd Edition*, Auerbach Publications, USA, 2008

Natan, Ron Ben; *Implementing Database Security and Auditing*, Elsevier Digital Press, USA, 2005

National Institute of Standards and Technology (NIST) Special Publications, *csrc.nist.gov/publications/PubsSPs.html*

SANS Institute, *www.sans.org*

Senft, Sandra; Frederick Gallegos; Aleksandra Davis; *Information Technology Control and Audit, 4th Edition*, Auerbach Publications, USA, 2012

Stamp, Mark; *Information Security: Principles and Practice, 2nd Edition*, John Wiley & Sons Inc., USA, 2011

Vacca, John; *Biometric Technologies and Verification Systems*, Elsevier Inc., USA, 2007

Van Grembergen, Wim; Steven De Haes; *IT Governance Domain Practices and Competencies: Measuring and Demonstrating the Value of IT*, IT Governance Institute, USA, 2005, *www.isaca.org/Knowledge-Center/Research/Documents/MeasurandDemoValueofIT.pdf*

Wells, Joseph T.; *Fraud Casebook, Lessons From the Bad Side of Business*, John Wiley & Sons Inc., USA, 2007

Wulgaert, Tim and ISACA; *Security Awareness: Best Practices to Secure Your Enterprise*, ISACA, USA, 2005

Wysocki, Robert K.; *Effective Project Management: Traditional, Agile, Extreme, 6th Edition*, Wiley Publishing Inc., USA, 2011

Note: Publications in bold are stocked in the ISACA Bookstore.

3.3 SELF-ASSESSMENT QUESTIONS

QUESTIONS

CISM exam questions are developed with the intent of measuring and testing practical knowledge in information security management. All questions are multiple choice and are designed for one best answer. Every CISM question has a stem (question) and four options (answer choices). The candidate is asked to choose the correct or best answer from the options. The stem may be in the form of a question or incomplete statement. In some instances, a scenario or a description problem may also be included. These questions normally include a description of a situation and require the candidate to answer two or more questions based on the information provided. Many times a CISM examination question will require the candidate to choose the most likely or best answer.

In every case, the candidate is required to read the question carefully, eliminate known incorrect answers and then make the best choice possible. Knowing the format in which questions are asked, and how to study to gain knowledge of what will be tested, will go a long way toward answering them correctly.

3-1 When designing an intrusion detection system, the information security manager should recommend that it be placed:

A. outside the firewall.
B. on the firewall server.
C. on a screened subnet.
D. on the external router.

3-2 Which of the following is the **BEST** metric for evaluating the effectiveness of security awareness training? The number of:

A. password resets.
B. reported incidents.
C. incidents resolved.
D. access rule violations.

3-3 Security monitoring mechanisms should **PRIMARILY**:

A. focus on business-critical information.
B. assist owners to manage control risks.
C. focus on detecting network intrusions.
D. record all security violations.

3-4 When contracting with an outsourcer to provide security administration, the **MOST** important contractual element is the:

A. right-to-terminate clause.
B. limitations of liability.
C. service level agreement (SLA).
D. financial penalties clause.

3-5 Which of the following is **MOST** effective in preventing security weaknesses in operating systems?

A. Patch management
B. Change management
C. Security baselines
D. Configuration management

3-6 Which of the following is the **MOST** effective solution for preventing internal users from modifying sensitive and classified information?

A. Baseline security standards
B. System access violation logs
C. Role-based access controls
D. Exit routines

3-7 Which of the following is the **MOST** important consideration when implementing an intrusion detection system (IDS)?

A. Tuning
B. Patching
C. Encryption
D. Packet filtering

3-8 Which of the following practices is **BEST** used to remove system access for contractors and other temporary users when it is no longer required?

A. Log all account usage and send it to their manager.
B. Establish predetermined automatic expiration dates.
C. Require managers to email security when the user leaves.
D. Ensure that each individual has signed a security acknowledgement.

3-9 Which of the following is **MOST** important for a successful information security program?

A. Adequate training on emerging security technologies
B. Open communication with key process owners
C. Adequate policies, standards and procedures
D. Executive management commitment

3-10 An enterprise is implementing an information security program. During which phase of the implementation should metrics be established to assess the effectiveness of the program over time?

A. Testing
B. Initiation
C. Design
D. Development

ANSWERS TO SELF-ASSESSMENT QUESTIONS

3-1 **C** An intrusion detection system (IDS) should be placed on a screened subnet, which is a demilitarized zone (DMZ). Placing it on the Internet side of the firewall is not advised because the system will generate alerts on all malicious traffic—even though 99 percent will be stopped by the firewall and never reach the internal network. The same would be true of placing it on the external router, if such a thing were feasible. Since firewalls should be installed on hardened servers with minimal services enabled, it would be inappropriate to install the IDS on the same physical device.

3-2 **B** Reported incidents will provide an indicator of the awareness level of staff. An increase in reported incidents could indicate that the staff is paying more attention to security. Password resets and access rule violations may or may not have anything to do with awareness levels. The number of incidents resolved may not correlate to staff awareness.

3-3 **A** Security monitoring must focus on business-critical information to remain effectively usable by and credible to business users. Control risk is the possibility that controls would not detect an incident or error condition, and therefore is not a correct answer because monitoring would not directly assist in managing this risk. Network intrusions are not the only focus of monitoring mechanisms; although they should record all security violations, this is not the **primary** objective.

3-4 **C** Service level agreements (SLAs) provide metrics to which outsourcing firms can be held accountable. This is more important than a limitation on the outsourcing firm's liability, a right-to-terminate clause or a hold-harmless agreement which involves liabilities to third parties.

3-5 **A** Patch management corrects discovered weaknesses by applying a correction (a patch) to the original program code. Change management controls the process of introducing changes to systems. Security baselines provide minimum recommended settings. Configuration management controls the updates to the production environment.

3-6 **C** Role-based access controls help ensure that users only have access to files and systems appropriate for their job role. Violation logs are detective and do not prevent unauthorized access. Baseline security standards do not prevent unauthorized access. Exit routines are dependent upon appropriate role-based access.

3-7 **A** If an intrusion detection system (IDS) is not properly tuned it will generate an unacceptable number of false positives and/or fail to sound an alarm when an actual attack is underway. Patching is more related to operating system hardening, while encryption and packet filtering would not be as relevant.

3-8 **B** Predetermined expiration dates are the most effective means of removing systems access for temporary users. Reliance on managers to promptly send in termination notices cannot always be counted on, while requiring each individual to sign a security acknowledgement would have little effect in this case.

3-9 **D** Sufficient executive management support is the most important factor for the success of an information security program. Open communication, adequate training, and good policies and procedures, while important, are not as important as support from top management; they will not ensure success if senior management support is not present.

3-10 **C** In the design phase, security checkpoints are defined and a test plan is developed. The testing phase is too late since the system has already been developed and is in production testing. In the initiation phase, the basic security objective of the project is acknowledged. Development is the coding phase and is too late to consider test plans.

Section Two: Content

3.4 INFORMATION SECURITY PROGRAM MANAGEMENT OVERVIEW

An information security program encompasses all the activities and resources that collectively provide information security services to an organization. Primary program activities entail design, development and integration of enterprisewide controls related to information security, as well as the ongoing administration and management of these controls. The controls can range from simple policies and processes to highly complex technology solutions. Depending on the size and nature of the organization, these activities can be executed by a chief information security officer (CISO) managing a large staff with diverse skills, or, at the other end of the spectrum, a single individual that carries all the responsibilities for the information security program.

In some instances, the information security manager may be required to initiate an information security program from its inception. More often, the job of the information security manager will involve managing, modifying and improving an existing program. In either case, it is important for the information security manager to have a solid understanding of the many aspects and requirements of effective program design, implementation and management.

Successful security program management is not significantly different from managing any other organizational activity. The primary difference is that, despite great strides gained over the last decade, information security remains a somewhat ill-defined and frequently misunderstood discipline.

Many individuals working in the capacity of information security manager come from a technical background. Most did not embark on a management career; rather, they were technologists that found themselves increasingly faced with management functions and responsibilities. Additionally, this move toward a broader management role has been driven by the increased desire of the business to understand why specific security controls are required and how the business benefits specifically from them. In short, senior management wants to understand the specific risk that the information security program is addressing, and why the controls it mandates are a sound investment and actually benefit the business. This trend has compelled security professionals to step out of their comfort zone in the technology realm and develop a greater understanding and appreciation for the business activities they are seeking to protect.

These trends of growing security organizations and increased pressure from the business to ensure that the security program is aligned with and supports the business objectives have broadened the body of knowledge security managers must master. A broad set of business knowledge and understanding must now be added to the base of information security knowledge all security professionals should possess. However, until the last decade, information security management was not a recognized field of study. The result was that, unlike virtually all other organizational functions, there was not a large pool of well-seasoned information security managers with decades of experience. There was also not a well-codified standard body of knowledge backed by years of practice and educational underpinnings. This situation was the basis for the development of the ISACA CISM program in 2003, and continues today to drive the efforts of ISACA, ISO, and similar organizations that are seeking to assist enterprises around the globe to develop effective information security programs.

Information Security Management Trends

In an increasing number of medium and larger organizations, the information security manager is at the executive level, designated as vice president of security, CISO, or simply chief security officer (CSO). In the latter case, a number of security functions may report to an independent corporate-level security organization. These functions may include, but are not limited to, physical and information security, some or all of IT security, compliance, privacy, business continuity planning/disaster recovery (BCP/DR) and security architecture. In some large multinational organizations, many or all these functions are currently included under a senior corporate risk manager, or chief risk officer (CRO).

The benefits of this trend are apparent. All of these functions serve the basic need of ensuring the safety and preservation of the organization and are, to a large extent, interdependent. Aggregating these assurance activities under a single corporate function is likely to gain favor as it becomes increasingly apparent that a disintegrated, stovepipe approach to security is inefficient, costly and, all too often, ineffective.

While the trend will be toward greater integration and the increasing elevation of information security, for many organizations it is not likely to occur in the near term, and information security management will continue to be a fragmented, low-level IT effort. In many sectors it will continue to be seen as primarily a technical activity largely dealing with compliance issues as opposed to a vital strategic business activity.

Regardless of trends and optimal considerations for security, the reality in the majority of organizations is something less than optimal, but security must still be managed on a continuous, ongoing basis.

In addition to understanding security concepts and technologies, information security managers will increasingly need to gain expertise in a range of management functions such as budgeting, planning, business case development, recruiting and other personnel related functions.

Essential Elements of an Information Security Program

There are three elements essential to ensure successful security program design, implementation and ongoing management:

1. The program must be the execution of a well-developed information security strategy closely aligned with and supporting organizational objectives.
2. The program must be well-designed with cooperation and support from management and stakeholders.
3. Effective metrics must be developed for program design and implementation phases as well as the subsequent ongoing

security program management phases to provide the feedback necessary to guide program execution to achieve the defined outcomes.

Most standard frameworks for information security show the development of an information security program as starting with risk assessment and leading to the definition of a strategy to manage risk. While, in some cases, this may be adequate, it is not likely to be optimal and does not address the balance of important outcomes for information security including strategic alignment, resource management, value delivery, assurance process integration and performance measurement.

The comprehensive approach to security strategy development presented in chapter 1 goes beyond just addressing risk by also defining overall objectives for information security. These objectives in turn should be explicitly linked to organizational objectives. The outlined approach also describes methodologies for defining the desired state of security and provides the basis for developing a comprehensive and effective strategy to achieve those objectives. Beyond just focusing on managing risk, this preferred approach considers how information security should be linked to and actively support the organization's strategic objectives, ensure its preservation, and optimize security resources and activities.

The reality is that many organizations are not yet ready to undertake the costs and efforts to implement information security governance. In these cases, the information security manager may need to "shortcut" objectives development. This can be accomplished by utilizing a standard framework such as COBIT or ISO/IEC 27001:2013 in conjunction with a capability maturity model (CMM) scale or the more recent ISO/IEC 15504 process assessment reference model used in COBIT 5. This approach will allow the information security manager to determine the current state of the information security program, set specific goals and determine a strategy to achieve them.

In any event, it is essential for the information security manager to develop defined objectives for the information security program and to gain management and stakeholder consensus. Without defined objectives for information security, it will be impossible to devise effective information security management metrics because there will be no point of reference to show progress and development is likely to be *ad hoc* and haphazard.

Regardless of how the objectives of information security are devised and a strategy for achieving them developed, the goal of an information security program is to implement the strategy and achieve the defined objectives. Once developed, the information security program should clearly represent the elements of the strategy.

Information security program development is likely to entail a variety of activities, projects and initiatives involving people, processes and technology over a protracted period of time. The information security manager should keep in mind that the objectives and expected benefits of the information security program will be the most useful if defined in business terms to help nontechnical stakeholders understand and endorse the program goals. This is also more likely to promote feedback and participation from business owners which, in turn, will make it more likely that the security program will be aligned with overall organizational objectives. The information security manager should also consider that programs and initiatives that do not have specific identifiable business or organizational benefits must be carefully examined to determine whether they are justified or resources can produce greater benefits elsewhere.

3.4.1 IMPORTANCE OF THE INFORMATION SECURITY PROGRAM

Achieving adequate levels of information security at a reasonable cost requires good planning, an effective strategy and capable management. Information security program management is an ongoing requirement that serves to protect information assets, satisfy regulatory obligations, and minimize potential legal and liability exposures. Properly designed, implemented and managed, it provides critical support for many business functions that simply would not be feasible without it.

To be of any use, a strategy as discussed in chapter 1 must be implemented and made operational. One or more processes must be devised to achieve the objectives of the strategy. The security program is the process by which the organization's security systems are designed, engineered, built, deployed, modified, managed and maintained as well as removed from service. This critical aspect of the information security manager's responsibilities covers a broad area, and it requires substantial expertise and broad technical and managerial skills.

A well-executed security program will serve to effectively design, implement, manage and monitor the security program, transforming strategy into actuality. While providing the capabilities to meet security objectives, it will also accommodate the inevitable changes in security requirements, taking advantage of security expertise, tools and techniques already available in the infrastructure. It also increases the likelihood that the efforts are well-integrated, decreasing costs of maintenance and administration and providing a consistent level of security across the enterprise.

It should be clear that an effective security program requires a great deal of planning as well as expertise and resources. Effective planning can be significantly aided by developing an enterprise security architecture at the conceptual, logical, functional and physical levels. Well-defined models and frameworks exist that can assist in this process as detailed in section 3.12.

3.4.2 OUTCOMES OF INFORMATION SECURITY PROGRAM MANAGEMENT

Effective information security program management should achieve the objectives defined in the security strategy discussed in chapter 1. As with other management activities, the goals must be defined in specific, objective and measurable terms. Appropriate metrics must then be established to determine whether the goals have been achieved and, if not, by how much they were missed and how performance might be improved.

Whether formal information security governance has been implemented or not, an acceptable level of the following six outcomes should be considered the basis for developing the objectives of an effective information security program:
- Strategic alignment
- Risk management
- Value delivery
- Resource management
- Assurance process integration
- Performance measurement

Developing a strategy and defining the attributes of the information security program are primarily conceptual and logical exercises. Development of the security program will require transforming these concepts and logical relationships into technologies and processes. From an architectural perspective, this will require developing the physical, functional and operational components that are necessary to achieve the defined objectives.

If this is a major initiative or series of initiatives, the information security manager should consider the development of a full security architecture to ensure that the goals and desired outcomes are realized. If enterprise architecture(s) already exist, then a security architecture that is consistent with it should be incorporated into the existing enterprise architecture(s). As with any complex structure with numerous moving parts, architecture can serve to define logical, physical and operational component and process relationships. It can also clarify potential issues and provide traceability from concept to implementation and operation.

Strategic Alignment

Effective alignment of information security with business or mission objectives requires regular interaction with business owners and an understanding of their plans and objectives. It often depends on garnering input from and building consensus between the major operating units within the organization. In the realm of the information security manager, this consensus involves topics such as understanding:
- Organizational information risk
- Selection of appropriate control objectives and standards
- Agreement on acceptable risk and risk tolerance
- Definitions of financial, operational and other constraints

This can be accomplished through a security steering committee, if business owners or their delegates are members and active participants. The security program can support the alignment of business objectives and information security by implementing processes that ensure that defined business objectives provide the ongoing input to guide security activities.

Both old and new issues requiring attention should be tracked and communicated regularly. Action items related to issue investigation, resolution and disposition should be monitored and reported as organizational security performance metrics. A regular information security strategy report should be delivered to executive management to provide visibility into successes and setbacks around strategic alignment. This information can range from progress on projects of interest to new risk or capabilities that may affect a particular line of business.

These day-to-day operational interactions are also powerful in their ability to build rapport and cooperation throughout the organization. In addition to facilitating timely action on information security issues, active relationships fostered by the information security manager can also increase awareness and a sense of responsibility around information security.

If the organization has a strategic business planning unit, active participation in its activities may also provide insight into future business directions and ensure that security considerations are included in the planning process. This may provide opportunities to orient security activities to support those objectives and identify potential risk.

Efforts to align security with business objectives must include consideration of security solutions that are a good fit for current and planned business initiatives. Alignment must also take into account enterprise processes as well as cost, culture, governance, existing technology and structure of the organization.

Risk Management

Managing the risk to information assets is a primary responsibility of the information security manager and provides the foundation and rationale for virtually all information security activities. Risk analysis must be based on business requirements as well as on an understanding of the organization's processes, culture and technology. To effectively manage risk, the information security manager must develop a comprehensive understanding of threats the organization faces, its vulnerabilities, its risk profile and the level of risk that management determines is acceptable. The potential impacts of threats that can materialize must be evaluated and used to establish treatment priorities. Risk must be managed to a level that is acceptable to the organization. However, the risk landscape is always changing, and new risk will inevitably arise during program development and administration. It is important that a continuous process of risk management be maintained during program development, implementation and evolution.

Value Delivery

Value delivery as an objective requires that information security delivers the required level of security effectively and efficiently. The execution of the security program can have a considerable effect on achieving this goal. Good planning and project management skills are needed to implement the strategy efficiently.

Security investments should be managed to optimize support of business objectives and deliver clear value to the organization. The information security manager should direct efforts toward achievement of a standard set of security practices and establishment of security baselines proportionate to risk. Protection efforts must be prioritized to allocate limited resources to areas of greatest need and benefit.

Continued delivery of value requires that security solutions be institutionalized as normal and expected practices based on standards. Solutions must comprehensively address logical, technical, operational and physical concerns based on an understanding of the end-to-end operating processes of the organization. Security management cannot remain static and must strive to develop a culture of continuous improvement.

Resource Management

A number of resources are utilized in developing and managing a security program. These resources include people, technology and processes. The information security manager must endeavor to utilize human, financial, technical and knowledge resources efficiently and effectively. An important aspect of resource management is accomplished by ensuring that knowledge is captured and made available to those who need it. Human resources are utilized efficiently by ensuring adequate knowledge and skills, proper management, and performance tracking. Security processes and practices must be documented, and they must be consistent with standards and policies. Project planning, technology selection and skill acquisition or development will significantly factor into the effectiveness of resource management. Security architectures should be developed to define and utilize infrastructures to achieve security objectives efficiently. These efforts help promote recognition of the resource needs and shortfalls and provide the basis for good resource management.

Assurance Process Integration

It is important for the information security manager to be aware of and understand all organizational assurance functions because they invariably have significance for information security. The information security manager should develop formal relationships with other assurance providers and endeavor to integrate those activities with information security activities. In the typical organization, this might include physical security, risk management, privacy office, quality assurance, audit, change management, insurance, HR, business continuity, disaster recovery and perhaps others.

As dictated by the governance objectives discussed in chapter 1, an information security manager should seek to increase information assurance and the predictability of business operations through mitigation measures that reduce information-related risk to defined and agreed upon levels of acceptability. As discussed in chapter 2, acceptable risk at an acceptable cost can be determined by developing recovery time objectives (RTOs), which will serve to balance the cost of restoration against acceptable outages. In other cases, acceptable risk may be determined in terms of reliability, integrity, performance levels, confidentiality, acceptable downtimes and financial impacts.

Performance Measurement

If an information security strategy has been developed, it should have identified a variety of important monitoring and metrics requirements. It is likely that during the evolution and management of a security program, additional opportunities to develop meaningful metrics or points of useful monitoring will become apparent. There may be opportunities to "roll up" groups of metrics to provide a more holistic picture for managing security. Considerable new work has been done by ISACA with the goal of developing processes to provide better security management metrics. This topic is covered in greater detail in section 3.16.

The development and implementation of the security program itself will require a means of measuring progress and monitoring activities. An effective information security program results in processes designed to achieve governance objectives as well as measurable artifacts that demonstrate whether the objectives are met. Security processes should be designed with measurable control points that allow independent auditors to attest that the program is in place and effectively managed.

The information security manager must develop monitoring processes and associated metrics to provide continuous reporting on the effectiveness of information security processes and controls. Good metrics design and implementation requires an understanding of the information needed by various constituencies to manage effectively. Metrics must be developed at multiple levels, including strategic, management and operational levels. The metrics utilized should be defined, agreed on by management and aligned with strategic objectives. Care must be taken to ensure that metrics provide useful information relevant to managing security activities to achieve defined objectives. These measurement processes help identify shortcomings and failures of security activities, and provide feedback on progress made in resolving issues.

3.5 INFORMATION SECURITY PROGRAM OBJECTIVES

The objective of the information security program is to implement the strategy in the most cost-effective manner possible, while maximizing support of business functions and minimizing operational disruptions. Chapters 1 and 2 explain how governance and risk management objectives for a security program are defined and incorporated into an overall strategy. The success of these initial steps will determine the degree of clarity in understanding the information security program development objectives. If the security strategy has been well developed, the primary task will be turning high-level strategy into logical and physical reality through a series of projects and initiatives. But even with a well-developed security strategy, it is inevitable that there will be elements that must be modified or reconsidered during program design, development and ongoing administration. This can occur for a variety of reasons, such as changes in business requirements, underlying infrastructure, topology, technologies or risk level. It can also be the case that better solutions become available during the course of the program development or subsequently. Even unanticipated resistance by those affected by the changes introduced by the new or modified program can drive significant changes to design, implementation or operation of a security program.

Whether the strategy has been developed in significant detail or only to the conceptual level, program development will include a great deal of planning and design to achieve working project plans. It is likely that standard SDLC approaches will be useful, including feasibility, requirements and design phases. Developing these plans in a collaborative fashion is important to gain consensus and cooperation from various stakeholders and to minimize subsequent implementation and operational problems.

3.5.1 DEFINING OBJECTIVES

Rarely is an information security manager faced with a situation where there is no information security activity present in an organization. Therefore, building an information security program is often a process of comparing existing organizational activity to what is required to achieve a desired state by performing a gap analysis. If the processes outlined in chapter 1 have been utilized to develop information security objectives, this will already have been accomplished at a high level, but it may be necessary to further define these objectives down to a more concrete and practical level. This may require a substantial amount of effort, but it is a critical component for developing the security program.

It is essential to determine the forces that drive the business need for the information security program. Primary drivers for an information security program may include:
- The ever increasing requirements for regulatory compliance
- Higher frequency and cost related to security incidents
- Concerns over reputational damage
- Growing commercial demands of Payment Card Industry (PCI) Data Security Standard (DSS)
- Business processes or objectives that may increase organizational risk

Determining the drivers will help clarify objectives for the program and provide the basis for the development of relevant metrics.

Once the objectives have been clearly defined, the purpose of the security program development activities is to develop the processes and projects that close the gap between the current state and those objectives. Typically, much of the basic work will be to identify necessary controls, implement them, develop suitable metrics and then monitor control points in support of control objectives.

Whether or not there is an existing information security program, there are some basic building blocks that need to be in place to support control activity and know that it is effective. As has been previously stated, the first step is always to determine management objectives for information security, develop key goal indicators (KGIs) that reflect those objectives, and then develop ways to measure whether the program is heading in the right direction to meet those objectives.

3.6 INFORMATION SECURITY PROGRAM CONCEPTS

As an information security program is developed, it is important that the developers keep in mind the fundamental purpose of the security program, i.e., to implement the security strategy and achieve the defined outcomes as detailed in chapter 1.

In situations where security governance has not been implemented and/or a strategy has not been developed, it will still be necessary to define overall objectives for security activities. Off-the-shelf, ready-made objectives can include conformance to a particular set of standards or achieving a defined maturity level based on the CMM model.

Whether set forth in a strategy or not, a security program implementation effort should also include a series of specific control objectives as defined in COBIT or ISO 27001. It is likely that a great deal of any security program will consist of designing, developing and implementing controls, whether technical, procedural or physical. As these controls are developed, monitoring and metrics must also be considered. Processes to measure control effectiveness will be essential as will approaches to determining control failure. Some metrics development approaches and processes are detailed in section 3.16.

Implementation will typically consist of a series of projects and initiatives. It generally involves project management skills, including resource utilization, budgeting, setting and meeting time lines and milestones, quality assurance and user acceptance testing.

Many projects involve unusual or complex technical elements and may require detailed specification, design and engineering efforts. This often requires skills outside of the information security managers' capabilities and it is generally prudent to consider engaging the services of consultants or contractors with subject matter expertise.

3.6.1 CONCEPTS

Both implementing and managing a security program will require the information security manager to understand and have a working knowledge of a number of management and process concepts including:
- SDLCs
- Requirements development
- Specification development
- Control objectives
- Control design and development
- Control implementation and testing
- Control monitoring and metrics
- Architectures
- Documentation
- Quality assurance
- Project management
- Business case development
- Business process reengineering
- Budgeting, costing and financial issues
- Deployment and integration strategies
- Training needs assessments and approaches
- Communications
- Problem resolution
- Contingency planning
- Variance and noncompliance resolution
- Risk management
- Compliance monitoring and enforcement
- Personnel issues

Note: This is not an all inclusive list, but merely representative of many of the major concepts with which that the information security manager must be familiar.

3.6.2 TECHNOLOGY RESOURCES

An information security program will, in most cases, involve a variety of technologies in addition to processes, policies and people. The information security manager must be qualified to make decisions with respect to technology, including the viability and applicability of available solutions in terms of the program goals and objectives. It is also essential that the information security manager understand where a given technology fits into the basic prevention, detection, containment, reaction and recovery framework, and how it will serve to implement strategic elements.

Below is a sampling of the technologies related directly to information security that the information security manager should be familiar with:

- Firewalls
- Backup and archiving approaches such as redundant array of inexpensive disks (RAID)
- Antivirus systems
- Security features inherent in networking devices (e.g., routers, switches)
- Intrusion detection systems (IDSs), including host-based intrusion detection systems (HIDSs), network intrusion detection systems (NIDSs)
- Intrusion-prevention systems (IPSs)
- Cryptographic techniques (e.g., public key infrastructure [PKI], Advanced Encryption Standard [AES], etc.)
- Digital signatures
- Smart cards
- Authentication and authorization mechanisms (one-time passwords [OTPs], challenge-response, PKI certificates multifactor authentication, biometrics)
- Wireless security methodologies
- Mobile computing
- Application security methodologies
- Remote access methodologies (virtual private network [VPNs], etc.)
- Web security techniques
- Log collection, analysis and correlation tools (i.e., Security Information and Event Management [SIEM])
- Vulnerability scanning and penetration testing tools
- Data leak prevention methodologies (removable media security, content filtering, etc.) and associated technologies
- Data integrity controls, e.g., backups, data snapshots, data replication, RAID, SAN real-time replication, etc.
- Identity and access management systems

While many of these technologies are specifically related to security and most function as controls, the information security manager must recognize that virtually all deployed technologies will have security implications.

In addition to technologies that are security related, the information security manager must be familiar with the broader aspects of information technology including, but not limited to:

- Local area networks (LANs)
- Wide area networks (WANs)
- Storage area networks (SANs)
- Internet and network protocols (TCP/IP, UDP, etc.)
- Operating Systems
- Network Routing concepts and protocols
- Databases
- Servers
- Enterprise architectures (two- and three-tier client servers, messaging, etc.)
- Virtualization
- Cloud computing
- Web-related technologies and architectures

To reiterate, these lists are not meant to be comprehensive, but representative of the areas and types of technologies the information security manager should be familiar with to successfully manage an information security program. If unfamiliar with any of the terms listed above, the CISM candidate should first review the glossary at the end of this manual. Additionally, the Knowledge Center on the ISACA web site (*www.isaca.org*) contains a fully searchable store of information in the form of white papers, journal articles and other ISACA publications that address many technologies, trends and concepts important to information security managers.

3.7 SCOPE AND CHARTER OF AN INFORMATION SECURITY PROGRAM

Whether an information security manager is forming a new security department or coming into one already established, there are several important considerations to be aware of. It will be important to determine the scope, responsibilities and charter of the department. It is rare to find these elements clearly identified and documented, unlike general technical responsibilities for items such as firewalls, IDSs, virus detection, etc., which are usually documented. The lack of defined responsibilities will make it difficult to determine what to manage or how well the security function is meeting objectives.

The information security manager coming into a new situation is advised to invest considerable effort in gaining an understanding from those he or she reports to regarding expectations, responsibilities, scope, authority, budgets, reporting requirements, etc. It will be useful to specifically document these elements and obtain agreement with management.

In terms of the chain of command, it is vital to understand the organizational structure and where the security function falls within that structure. In many situations, there will be inherent structural conflicts that the manager should be aware of and give careful consideration to. It may also be prudent to discuss any potential conflicts of interest with management and understand how it will be handled. The information security department largely serves as an internal regulatory function, and its ability to function effectively precludes reporting to those it is supposed to regulate. While there may be exceptions, it is generally true that information security managers who report in the technology chain of command or to other operational managers are likely to be very limited in their ability to provide effective information security across the enterprise.

If the department is established and has been functioning well, it is likely that many security department functions will already be accepted practice. Nevertheless, it will be useful to determine whether responsibilities are clearly defined and well documented.

In many instances, a prior manager will have assumed a variety of functions and taken on responsibilities that were not formally defined and documented. Such managers may have been effective through being particularly persuasive and influential rather than through defined and documented processes and structure. If the prior manager is available for orientation, it would be prudent to utilize whatever time is available to gain insight into the existing situation. If the prior manager is not available, it may take a thorough investigation to determine what the manager's responsibilities were and how tasks were accomplished.

The ability to be effective in a particular organization will be heavily impacted by culture and the information security manager's understanding of it. Security is often politically charged, and success may hinge more on developing the right relationships than on any particular expertise. To a varying extent, organizations do not operate in the manner defined by organizational charts, but by undocumented relationships and influence. Much as the Google™ search engine determines relative importance by the number of links to a particular site, so can the influence of particular individuals in an organization be charted by their number of links to others.

It is also essential to gain a thorough understanding of the current state of security functions in the organization. This may include all or many of the assessment elements discussed in prior chapters such as risk and business impact assessments. The state of governance and strategy will need to be ascertained, as will the condition of policies and standards, compliance, etc. Reviews of recent audits and other pertinent reports will be useful as well. Once completed, the balance of the elements identified in chapter 1 on governance can be considered, and the information security manager will have a basis to move forward with implementing an information security management framework.

Exhibit 3.2 shows a summary of the steps in developing an information security program.

The scope of an information security program is established by the development of a strategy as discussed in chapter 1, in combination with risk management responsibilities covered in chapter 2. The extent to which management supports the implementation of the strategy and risk management activities determines the charter.

Implementation of a security program invariably impacts an organization's established way of doing things. Within an existing structure of people, processes and technology, the information security manager must strive to integrate changes to these established processes and policies. Inevitably, this will result in some degree of resistance to change that must be anticipated and planned for.

In the absence of an adopted information security strategy and where no formal charter is documented, an information security manager can fall back to industry standards such as a customized version of ISACA's description of a mature information security program that might read:

> *"Information security is a joint responsibility of business, information security and IT management, and is integrated with corporate business objectives. Information security requirements are clearly defined, optimized and included in a verified security plan. Security functions are integrated with applications at the design stage and end users are increasingly accountable for managing security. Information security reporting provides early warning of changing and emerging risk, using automated active monitoring approaches for*

Exhibit 3.2—Steps in Information Security Program Development

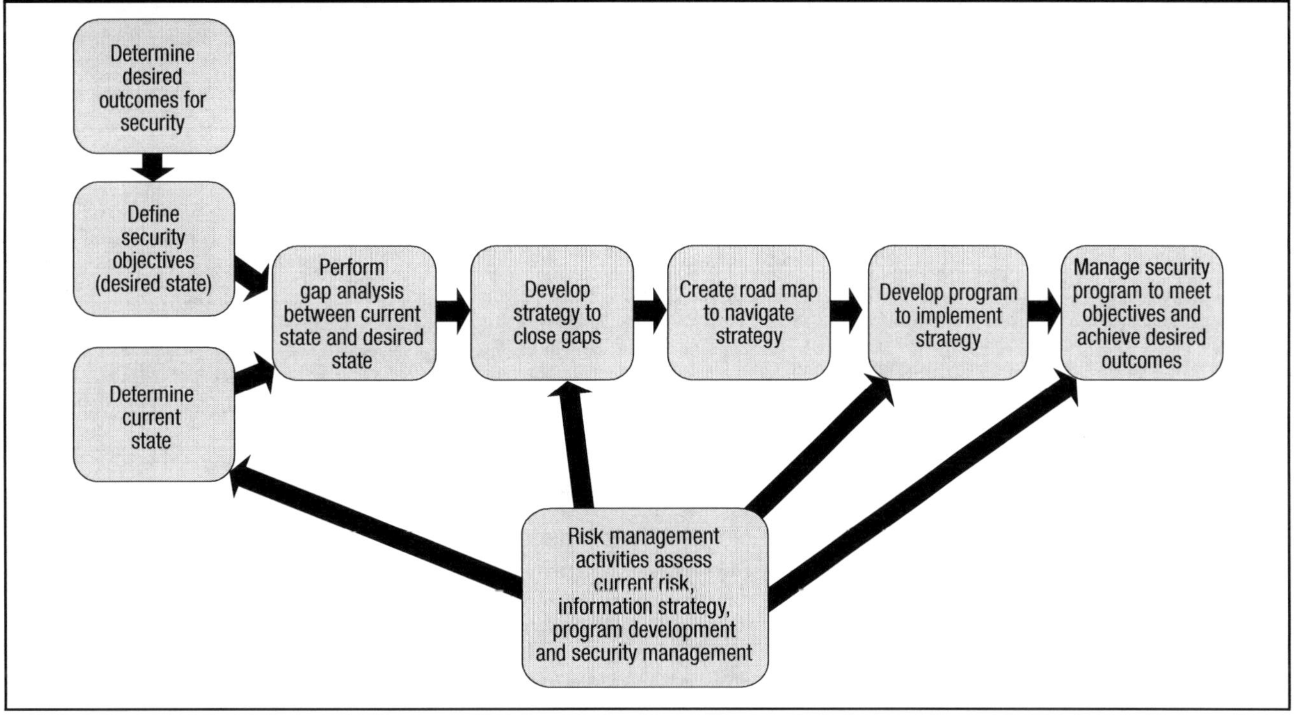

critical systems. Incidents are promptly addressed with formalized incident response procedures supported by automated tools. Periodic security assessments evaluate the effectiveness of implementation of the security plan. Information on new threats and vulnerabilities is systematically collected and analyzed, and adequate mitigating controls are promptly communicated and implemented. Intrusion testing, root cause analysis of security incidents and proactive identification of risk is the basis for continuous improvements. Security processes and technologies are integrated organizationwide."

This approach, coupled with COBIT 5 or ISO/IEC 27001 Information Security Management System (ISMS), can serve as the basis for a strategy and help define the scope and charter of the information security program.

3.8 THE INFORMATION SECURITY MANAGEMENT FRAMEWORK

The information security management framework is a conceptual representation of an information security management structure. It should define the technical, operational, administrative and managerial components of the program; the organizational units and leadership responsible for each component; the control or management objective that each component should deliver; the interfaces and information flow between the components; and each component's tangible outputs. Although formats and detail levels vary, the framework should fundamentally describe the information security management components (e.g., roles, policies, standard operating procedures [SOPs], management procedures, security architectures) and their interactions in broad strokes. This is, in essence, an operational architecture as described in section 3.12.

Other outcomes of an effective security management framework focus on shorter-term needs. For example, organizational decision makers require awareness of risk and mitigation options in support of corporate initiatives such as external hosting of information systems. Implementers of solutions often require the services of technical security subject matter expertise, which the information security manager should facilitate either through internal or external resources. Ensuring that initiatives and existing operations adhere to policies and standards is also an area that the information security manager and the security department are expected to manage.

The information security manager is typically expected to craft information security management options that deliver outcomes that are less direct, but no less important, to achieving security goals. These objectives include demonstrating, both directly and indirectly, that:
- The program adds tactical and strategic value to the organization.
- The program is being operated efficiently and with concern to cost issues.
- Management has a clear understanding of information security drivers, activities, benefits and needs.
- Information security knowledge and capabilities are growing as a result of the program.
- The program fosters cooperation and goodwill between organizational units.
- There is facilitation of information security stakeholders understanding their roles, responsibilities and expectations.
- The program includes provisions for the organization's continuity of business.

These soft goals revolve around directly and indirectly demonstrating to security steering committees, senior management and boards of directors that the information security program is delivering results and the information security manager is managing the program effectively.

There are a number of different frameworks that can be utilized by the information security manager for developing the information security program. Two of the most common internationally recognized approaches, COBIT and ISO/IEC 27001, are described in the following sections.

3.8.1 COBIT 5

COBIT 5 provides a comprehensive framework with a focus on helping enterprises create optimal value from IT by maintaining a balance between realizing benefits and optimizing risk levels and resource use. COBIT 5 enables IT and information to be governed and managed in a holistic manner for the enterprise, addressing the business and IT functional areas of responsibility, considering the information-related interests of internal and external stakeholders.

Exhibit 3.3—COBIT 5 Principles

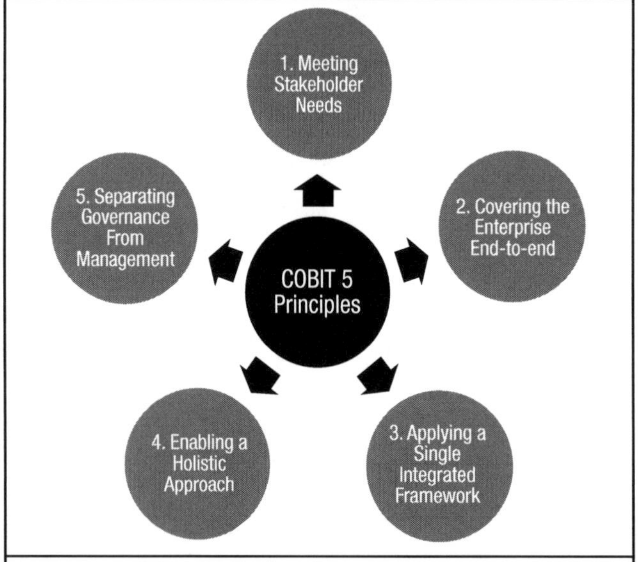

Source: ISACA, COBIT 5, USA, 2012, figure 2

COBIT 5 is based on five key principles (shown in **exhibit 3.3**) for governance and management of enterprise IT:

- **Principle 1: Meeting Stakeholder Needs**—Enterprises exist to create value for their stakeholders, by maintaining a balance between the realization of benefits and the optimization of risk and use of resources. COBIT 5 provides all of the required processes and other enablers to support business value creation through the use of IT. Because every enterprise has different objectives, an enterprise can customize COBIT 5 to suit its own context through the goals cascade, translating high-level enterprise goals into manageable, specific, IT-related goals and mapping these to specific processes and practices.
- **Principle 2: Covering the Enterprise End-to-End**—COBIT 5 integrates governance of enterprise IT into enterprise governance:
  - It covers all functions and processes within the enterprise; COBIT 5 does not focus only on the "IT function," but treats information and related technologies as assets that need to be dealt with just like any other asset by everyone in the enterprise.
  - It considers all IT-related governance and management enablers to be enterprisewide and end-to-end, i.e., inclusive of everything and everyone—internal and external—that is relevant to governance and management of enterprise information and related IT.
- **Principle 3: Applying a Single, Integrated Framework**—There are many IT-related standards and best practices, each providing guidance on a subset of IT activities. COBIT 5 aligns with other relevant standards and frameworks at a high level, and thus can serve as the overarching framework for governance and management of enterprise IT.
- **Principle 4: Enabling a Holistic Approach**—Efficient and effective governance and management of enterprise IT requires a holistic approach, taking into account several interacting components. COBIT 5 defines a set of enablers to support the implementation of a comprehensive governance and management system for enterprise IT. Enablers are broadly defined as anything that can help to achieve the objectives of the enterprise. The COBIT 5 framework defines seven categories of enablers:
  - Principles, Policies and Frameworks
  - Processes
  - Organizational Structures
  - Culture, Ethics and Behavior
  - Information
  - Services, Infrastructure and Applications
  - People, Skills and Competencies
- **Principle 5: Separating Governance from Management**—The COBIT 5 framework makes a clear distinction between governance and management. These two disciplines encompass different types of activities, require different organizational structures and serve different purposes. COBIT 5's view on this key distinction between governance and management is:
  - **Governance ensures that stakeholder needs, conditions and options are evaluated to determine balanced, agreed-on enterprise objectives to be achieved; setting direction through prioritization and decision making; and monitoring performance and compliance against agreed-on direction and objectives.**

    In most enterprises, overall governance is the responsibility of the board of directors under the leadership of the chairperson. Specific governance responsibilities may be delegated to special organizational structures at an appropriate level, particularly in larger, complex enterprises.
  - **Management plans, builds, runs and monitors activities in alignment with the direction set by the governance body to achieve the enterprise objectives.**

    In most enterprises, management is the responsibility of the executive management under the leadership of the chief executive officer (CEO). Together, these five principles enable the enterprise to build an effective governance and management framework that optimizes information and technology investment and use for the benefit of stakeholders.

COBIT 5 FOR INFORMATION SECURITY

COBIT® 5 for Information Security leverages the comprehensive view of COBIT 5 while focusing on providing guidance for professionals involved in maintaining the confidentiality, availability and integrity of enterprise information. The framework provides tools to help understand, utilize, implement and direct core information security related activities and make more informed decisions. It enables information security professionals to effectively communicate with business and IT leaders and manage risk associated with information, including those related to compliance, continuity, security and privacy.

3.8.2 ISO/IEC 27001:2013

The security standard ISO/IEC 27001:2013 Information Security Management System (ISMS) and the accompanying code of practice 27002:2013 provide a widely accepted framework and approach to information security management. The 114 control objectives in the 14 domains of 27001:2013 can be generally mapped to COBIT, but are less business oriented, less comprehensive and do not provide complete tool sets. These standards do provide high-level comprehensive requirements for information security programs. Based on the British Standard (BS), this standard has been slightly expanded to include 14 broad control areas:

- A.5: Information security policies
- A.6: Organization of information security
- A.7: Human resource security (controls that are applied before, during, or after employment)
- A.8: Asset management
- A.9: Access control
- A.10: Cryptography
- A.11: Physical and environmental security
- A.12: Operations security
- A.13: Communications security
- A.14: System acquisition, development and maintenance
- A.15: Supplier relationships
- A.16: Information security incident management
- A.17: Information security aspects of business continuity management
- A.18: Compliance (with internal requirements, such as policies, and with external requirements, such as laws)

The ISO 27xxx set of published standards and practices now cover virtually all aspects of security. They include:
- ISO/IEC 27000 overview and vocabulary
- ISO/IEC 27001 formal ISMS specification
- ISO/IEC 27002 infosec controls
- ISO/IEC 27003 ISMS implementation guide
- ISO/IEC 27004 infosec metrics
- ISO/IEC 27005 infosec risk management
- ISO/IEC 27006 ISMS certification guide
- ISO/IEC 27007 management system auditing
- ISO/IEC TR 27008 technical auditing
- ISO/IEC 27010 for interorganizational communications
- ISO/IEC 27011 for telecommunications industry
- ISO/IEC 27013 for ISMS + service management
- ISO/IEC 27014 infosec governance
- ISO/IEC TR 27015 for financial services
- ISO/IEC TR 27016 infosec economics
- ISO/IEC TR 27019 process control
- ISO/IEC 27031 ICT business continuity
- ISO/IEC 27032 cybersecurity
- ISO/IEC 27033-1 to -5 network security
- ISO/IEC 27034 application security
- ISO/IEC 27035 incident management
- ISO/IEC 27036-3 ICT supply chain
- ISO/IEC 27037 digital evidence
- ISO 27799 ISO27k for healthcare industry

3.9 INFORMATION SECURITY FRAMEWORK COMPONENTS

Most standard frameworks for information security show the development of an information security program as starting with risk assessment and the identification of control objectives and key controls defined by standards such as COBIT and ISO/IEC 27002. But it should be understood that control objectives must be based on individual organizational objectives and tailored to achieve the desired outcomes as discussed in chapter 1. As the program develops and matures, additional controls may be required to comply with changing conditions, new regulations and contractual obligations as depicted in **exhibit 3.4**.

Exhibit 3.4—Security Program Implementation Strategy

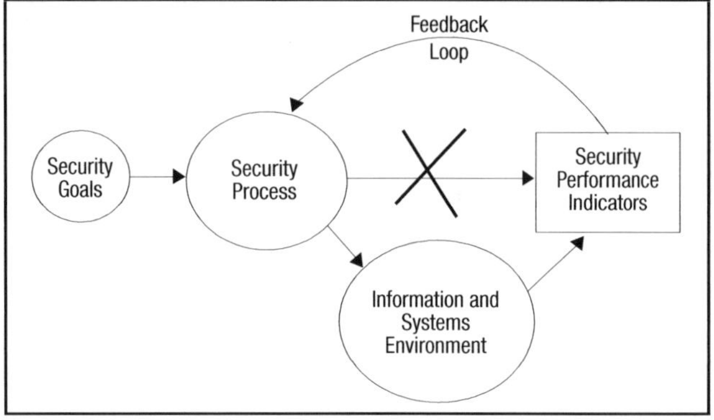

The various components that make up the management framework can be broken down into their functional elements. This can be helpful in ensuring that each aspect is adequately represented in the framework.

3.9.1 OPERATIONAL COMPONENTS

Operational components of a security program are the ongoing management and administrative activities that must be performed to provide the required level of security assurance. These operational components include items such as standard operating procedures, business operations security practices, and maintenance and administration of security technologies. They are generally conducted on a daily to weekly time line.

The information security manager must provide ongoing management of operational components. Because it is common for many of these components to fall outside of the information security domain (e.g., operating system patching procedures), the information security manager must work with IT, business units and other organizational units to ensure that operational needs are covered. Examples of common operational components include:
- Identity management and access control administration
- Security event monitoring and analysis
- System patching procedures and configuration management
- Change control and/or release management processes
- Security metrics collection and reporting
- Maintenance of supplemental control technologies and program support technologies
- Incident response, investigation and resolution
- Retirement and sanitization of data processing equipment and media storage

For each operational component, the information security manager will need to identify the owner and collaborate to document key information needed for management of the necessary functions. This information includes the component ownership and execution roles, activity schedule or triggers, needed information or data inputs, actual procedural steps, success criteria, failure escalation procedures and approval/review processes. It also includes processes for providing suitable management metrics for the feedback necessary for effective ongoing management.

In addition, the information security manager should ensure that procedures for work log maintenance, issue escalation, management oversight and periodic quality assurance reviews are developed and implemented. It is important for the information security manager to update the roles and responsibilities documentation as new tasks arise in operational component development. For example, a new operational procedure that requires a monthly chief operating officer (COO) review of security issues related to business activities needs to be added to the appropriate task lists and schedules.

3.9.2 MANAGEMENT COMPONENTS

In addition to a variety of ongoing technical and operational security tasks, the information security manager will have a number of management components to consider. These will typically include strategic implementation activities such as standards development or modification, policy reviews and oversight of initiatives or program execution. These are activities that generally take place less frequently than operational components, perhaps on a time line measured in months, quarters or years.

Management objectives, requirements and policies are key in shaping the rest of the information security program which, in turn, defines what must be managed. The information security manager must ensure that this process is executed with appropriate consideration to legal, regulatory, risk and resource issues as well as a suite of metrics needed for decision support.

Ongoing or periodic analysis of assets, threats, risk and organizational impacts must continue to be the basis for modifying security policies and developing or modifying standards. It should be considered that early versions are often too permissive, too restrictive or misaligned with operational realities. As a result, the information security manager is well advised to exercise flexibility in making adjustments to standards and policy interpretation during the initial stages of a security program.

Ongoing communication with business and operational units is critical to providing the feedback that can provide guidance to information security management, ensure its effectiveness, and maintain alignment with, and support of, the objectives of the organization.

During development of operational and technical management components, it is important that there is management oversight ensuring fulfillment of requirements and consistency with strategic direction. This oversight often occurs in the form of management reviews of program components, for example, the chief information officer (CIO), chief executive officer (CEO), steering committee or executive committee performing a quarterly review of security operations. Topics for review might include modifications to operational or technical components, general effectiveness of program components, review of metrics and key performance indicators (KPIs), root-cause analysis of detrimental events such as outages or compromises, issues hampering component effectiveness that require management attention, and/or review of action items and commitments from previous review sessions.

3.9.3 ADMINISTRATIVE COMPONENTS

As the scope and responsibilities of the information security management function grows, so do the resources, personnel and financial aspects involved. This means that information security management must address the same business administration activities as other business units. The information security manager in charge of such an organization must ensure that financial, HR and other management functions are effective.

Financial administration functions generally consist of budgeting, time line planning, total cost of ownership (TCO) analysis/management, return on investment (ROI) analysis/management, acquisition/purchasing and inventory management. These functions, particularly budgeting and time line planning, often require updates throughout the fiscal year as financial realities and organizational goals change. The information security manager should establish a working rapport with the organization's finance department to ensure a strong working relationship, support, and compliance with financial policies and procedures.

HR management functions generally include job description management, organizational planning, recruitment and hiring, performance management, payroll and time tracking administration, employee education and development, and termination management. The information security program should account for the time and resources needed for these activities, particularly as program staffing grows over time. Those charged with management of larger information security programs must also address the need to develop an efficient organizational structure with appropriate layers of management and supervisory personnel. In all issues related to HR management, it is important that the information security manager work closely with HR leadership and adhere to established procedures to prevent legal liabilities and other types of risk.

Effective management functions require the information security manager to balance project efforts and ongoing operational overhead with staff head count, utilization levels and external resources. Rarely does any information security program have an optimal number of resources, and it is always necessary to prioritize efforts. The information security manager should work with the steering committee and executive management to determine priorities and to establish consensus on what project items may be delayed because of resource constraints. Spikes in activity or unexpected project efforts can often be addressed with third-party resources such as contractors. The information security manager should maintain relationships with the vendors most likely to be called on in such cases.

It is not unusual for the information security manager to be under pressure to shortcut security management, quality assurance (QA) and development processes, or to divert resources from daily operations to accelerate project efforts. It is the role of the information security manager to document and ensure that executive management understands the risk implications of moving an initiative ahead without full security diligence; it is up to executive management to decide if the initiative is important enough to warrant the risk. If this situation occurs, the information security manager should make every effort to utilize the first available opportunity to revisit systems or initiatives that are not certified or accredited.

To ensure that the existing security environment operates as needed, security operational resources should only be diverted to project efforts if they are not fully utilized. Even in this situation, it needs to be clearly communicated that operational security resources are provided *ad hoc*, and a spike in operational activities (e.g., an intrusion) requires the immediate attention of the operational staff.

3.9.4 EDUCATIONAL AND INFORMATIONAL COMPONENTS

Information security management activities must include employee education and awareness regarding security risk. Information security awareness training is often integrated with employee orientation and initial training. General organizational policies and procedures, such as acceptable use policies and employee monitoring policies, should be communicated and administered at the organization's HR level. Issues and responsibilities that are specific to an employee's role or organization, e.g., call center authentication of customers, should be communicated and administered at the business unit level. Interactive education techniques such as online testing and role-playing are often more effective than a purely informational approach. Examples include incident response and contingency plan training and exercises. In all cases, the information security manager should collaborate with HR and business units to identify information security education needs. Pertinent metrics (e.g., average employee quiz scores, average time elapsed since last employee training) should be tracked and communicated to the steering committee and executive management.

3.10 DEFINING AN INFORMATION SECURITY PROGRAM ROAD MAP

The key goals of strategic alignment, risk management, value delivery, resource management, assurance process integration and performance measurement are universal and are defined to some extent in the development of a security strategy. The process of program development requires that each of the six key goals is considered in detail and clarified in light of the evolving road map. As specific project plans for various parts of the road map develop, approaches to best achieve each key goal should become apparent.

These may be concepts that are not well understood by management and other stakeholders, which could lead to unrealistic expectations and poor outcomes. To maximize the chances for success, it may be most effective to develop a road map for the information security program in stages starting with relatively simple objectives designed to demonstrate the value of the program and provide feedback on achievement of the key goals.

> As an example: The first stage might be to create that subcomponent of the program necessary to demonstrate strategic alignment. To get started, an information security manager can interview stakeholders such as department heads in HR, legal, finance and major business units to determine important organizational issues and concerns. Information taken from such interviews will point to candidates for information security steering committee members. In stage 2, that forum can be used to draft basic security policies for the implementation of an information security program for approval by upper management. Because members of the information security steering committee, by definition, represent business interests, the forum can be used to list specific business goals for security with reference to business processes (and thus also to systems as depicted in **exhibit 3.5**). In stage 3, members of the information security steering committee hold functional roles that can promote awareness of the policy and conduct internal security reviews to see if they are in compliance. In stage 4, the compliance gaps identified in the security reviews can be used to effect change, and an approach to monitor the organizational policy compliance strategy could be simultaneously developed. From that foundation, the information security manager can begin the work of building consensus around roles and responsibilities, processes, and procedures in support of the policy.

3.10.1 ELEMENTS OF A ROAD MAP

A road map to implement the information security strategy must consider a number of factors. If a well-developed strategy exists, then a high-level road map should also exist. Objectives, resources and constraints will have been defined. The work that remains is to transform the conceptual or logical architecture or design into a physical one. Construction of specific projects and initiatives must be planned along with budgets, timetables, personnel and other tactical project management aspects that will result collectively in achieving the strategy objectives. It is similar to the differences between the architecture of a house and the tasks required to build the house.

If, however, a strategy is not developed and risk management objectives are not defined, there is a risk that the diverse elements that must be developed for the information security program will not be integrated or prioritized. In addition, there will be a lack of useful metrics and, over time, the results are likely to be less than optimal.

Much of an information security program development effort will involve designing controls that meet control objectives, then developing projects to implement, deploy and test the controls. One factor to consider is the ability of the organization to absorb new security activities. These activities would be initiated to address control weaknesses and meet new objectives. Consideration must be given to the extent that these activities are disruptive to other organizational activities. See section 3.15 Controls and Countermeasures.

3.10.2 DEVELOPING AN INFORMATION SECURITY PROGRAM ROAD MAP

An important skill to have in developing an information security program road map is the ability to thoroughly review the security level of existing data, applications, systems, facilities and processes. This will provide insight into the specific projects required to meet strategic objectives. Approaches to performing security reviews and evaluating the security program is discussed in section 3.14.4.

An implementation road map can essentially be a high-level project plan or an architectural design which can serve the same purpose. Either can serve to define the steps necessary to achieve a particular objective of the program. The purpose is to have an overall view of the steps required as well as the sequence. In more complex projects, it can be a benefit to have both. A road map should include various milestones that will provide KGIs, indicate KPIs and define critical success factors (CSFs).

3.10.3 GAP ANALYSIS—BASIS FOR AN ACTION PLAN

Once the organizational roles and responsibilities seem appropriately established and inventory is taken of the required versus existing technology and processes, an information security manager can identify where control objectives are not adequately supported by controls. The information security manager should get those people accountable to identify control points and assist in developing processes to monitor them. Those executing new processes and procedures should concentrate on KGIs and KPIs, frequently validating that control objectives are being met and that progress toward control objectives achieves information security program goals. It is more important that the procedure for monitoring achievement of control objectives is established than it is that all processes are right on the first pass. It is this monitoring that, if effective, will provide a basis for the security program to evolve and mature.

Exhibit 3.5—Information Security Management System Controls Process

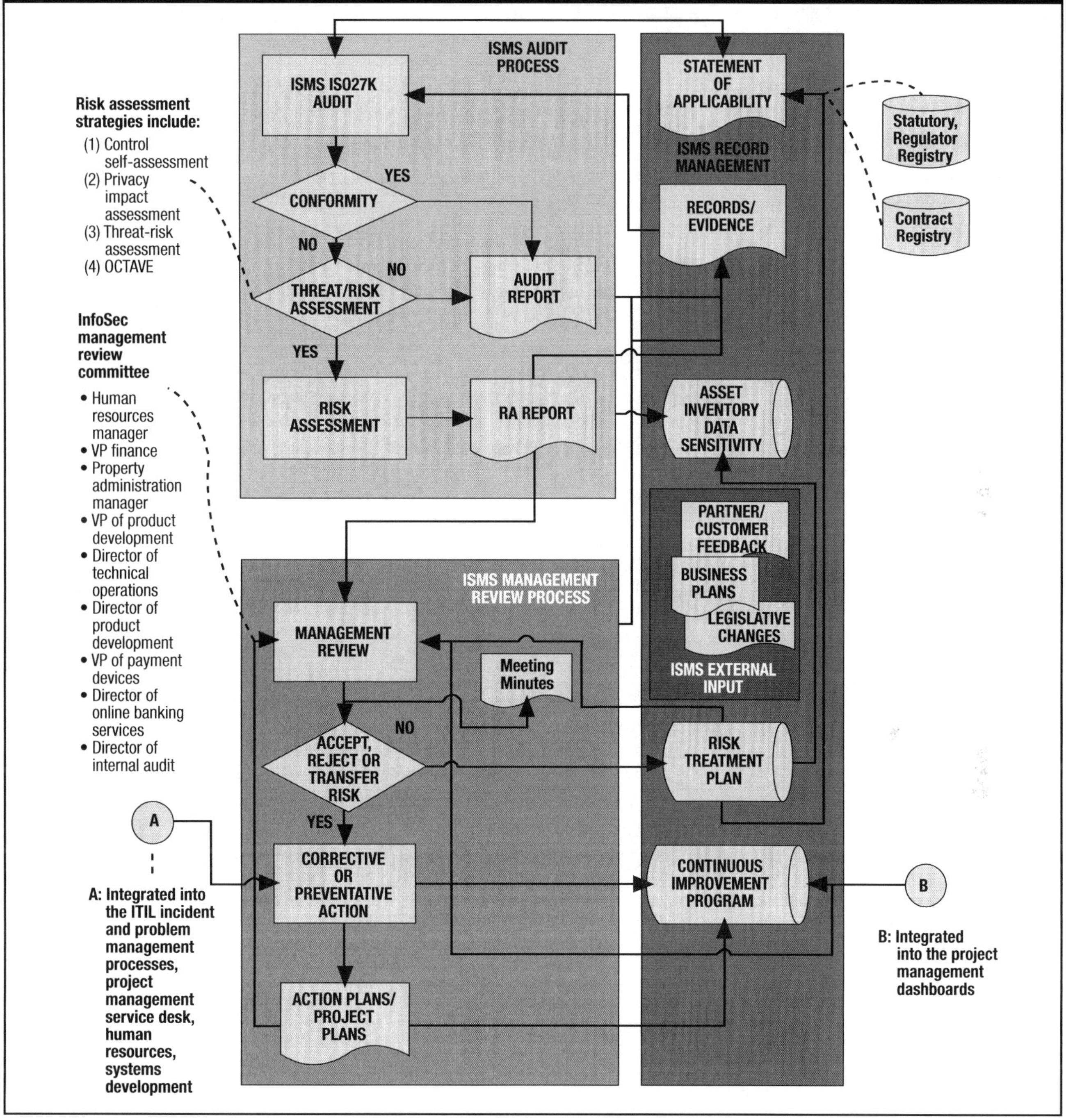

3.11 INFORMATION SECURITY INFRASTRUCTURE AND ARCHITECTURE

Infrastructure refers to the underlying base or foundation on which information systems are deployed. Generally, infrastructure comprises the computing platforms, networks and middleware layers, and it supports a wide range of applications. In previous sections, the information security program has been presented as the foundation that enables security resources to be deployed. Infrastructure and security infrastructure refer to the same thing. When infrastructure is designed and implemented and is consistent with appropriate policies and standards, the infrastructure should essentially be secure.

3.11.1 ENTERPRISE INFORMATION SECURITY ARCHITECTURE

Considerable development of architectural approaches for security, as a part or subset of enterprise information architecture, has occurred during the past decade. There are few things as complex as the information systems in a large organization. These systems are often constructed without a comprehensive architecture or extensive design efforts. Information systems have traditionally evolved organically with bits and pieces added as needed. The result has been a lack of integration, haphazard security standardization and a host of other weaknesses and vulnerabilities evident in most systems.

The objective of enterprise information security architecture (EISA) is to apply comprehensive and rigorous methods to describe current and/or future structure and behavior for an organization's security processes, information security systems, personnel and organizational subunits, so that they align with the organization's goals and strategic direction.

EISA development is not exclusively about information security technology, but rather includes security as it relates to business structure, performance management and security processes.

Financial and other organizations requiring a more robust security posture are increasingly utilizing information security enterprise architecture integrated with enterprise information architecture. One of the primary purposes is to achieve strategic alignment, i.e., to ensure that business strategy and IT security are aligned. Properly developed, EISA provides the ability to trace business strategy down through process elements to the underlying technology. This promotes effective value delivery by ensuring that the processes and technologies deployed are relevant to the business objectives and not simply a solution in search of a problem. It supports the goal of proportionality and prioritization by providing visibility of the processes and technologies that support the most important business functions.

EISA was introduced by Gartner in their white paper titled "Incorporating Security into the Enterprise Architecture Process" and published in 2006. Since then, security architecture has gone from being a largely standalone, silo-based, security-focused activity to a much more appropriate and effective enterprise-focused solution incorporating business, information and technology.

In the past, business architecture, information architecture and technology architecture was referred to as BIT, but with the addition of security the acronym has changed to BITS.

The objectives of EISA include:
- Provide overarching structure, coherence and cohesiveness.
- Serve as a program development road map.
- Ensure strategic alignment between business and security.
- Support and enable achievement of business strategy.
- Implement security policies and strategy.
- Ensure traceability back to the business strategy, specific business requirements and key principles.
- Provide a level of abstraction independent of specific technologies and preferences.
- Establish a common "language" for information security within the organization.
- Allow many individual contributors to work together to achieve objectives.

A number of architectural approaches have been developed for the enterprise, some of which include security and some of which deal exclusively with security as discussed in chapter 1, section 1.13.2. Some of the approaches include:
- Integrated Architecture Framework of Capgemini
- UK Ministry of Defence (MOD) Architecture Framework (MODAF)
- National Institutes of Health (NIH) Enterprise Architecture Framework
- Open Security Architecture
- Service-Oriented Modeling Framework (SOMF)
- The Open Group Architecture Framework (TOGAF)
- AGATE French Délégation Générale pour l'Armement Atelier de Gestion de l'ArchiTEcture des systèmes d'information et de communication
- United States Department of Defense Architectural Framework (DoDAF)
- Interoperable Delivery (of European government services to public) Administrations, Business and Citizens (IDABC)
- United States Office of Management and Budget Federal Enterprise Architecture (FEA)
- Model-driven Architecture (MDA) of the Object Management Group
- Ownership, Business Processes, Applications, Systems, Hardware, and Infrastructure business and IT methodology and framework (OBASHI)
- SABSA comprehensive framework for Enterprise Security Architecture and Service Management
- Zachman framework of IBM (framework from the 1980s)
- SAP Enterprise Architecture Framework, an extension of TOGAF, to better support commercial off-the-shelf programs and Service-Oriented Architecture
- Method for an Integrated Knowledge Environment (MIKE2.0), which includes an enterprise architecture framework called the Strategic Architecture for the Federated Enterprise (SAFE)

While a detailed discussion of each of these approaches is beyond the scope of this manual, it should be noted that these approaches fall into two basic categories: process approaches and frameworks. Frameworks such as COBIT, Zachman, SABSA and TOGAF allow a great deal of flexibility in how each element of the architecture is developed. The essence of the frameworks is to describe the elements of architecture and how they must relate to each other. Process models are more directive in the processes used for the various elements. While the objectives of all the models are essentially the same, the approach varies widely.

In some cases, an organization has already adopted a standardized architectural approach which must be utilized to the extent possible. If no standard approach has been devised, the various methods mentioned in this manual should be evaluated for the most appropriate form, fit and function.

Although many options exist for enterprise architecture, the current approaches that seem to be gaining favor include COBIT and TOGAF.

Exhibit 3.6 is a brief overview of the Architecture Development Method (ADM) and is iterative over the entire process, between phases and within phases. The phases include:
- **Preliminary phase**—Deals mainly with the definition of the architecture framework, as discussed above, as well as the architecture principles. In addition, the overall scope, constraints, objectives and assumptions are identified.
- **Architecture vision**—Deals with defining the vision and scope of the architecture and specific segments of work to be performed

- **Business architecture**—Addresses the description of the as-is business architecture domain, the development of the to-be business architecture and the gap analysis between the two
- **Information systems architecture**—Provides the description of the as-is and to-be data, applications domains and conducting the gap analyses
- **Technology architecture**—Deals with the description of the as-is and to-be technology domains, and conducting a gap analysis
- **Opportunities and solutions**—Deals with the formulation of a high-level implementation and migration strategy to transform the as-is architectures into the to-be architecture
- **Migration planning**—Deals with formulation of a detailed implementation and migration road map, including the analysis of costs, benefits and risk
- **Implementation governance**—Ensures that the implementation projects conform to the defined architecture
- **Architecture change management**—Deals with keeping the architecture up-to-date and ensures that the architecture responds to the needs of the enterprise, as changes arise
- **Requirements management**—Ensures that the architecture projects are based on business requirements and that the business requirements are validated against the architecture

Exhibit 3.6—TOGAF Architecture Development Model (ADM)

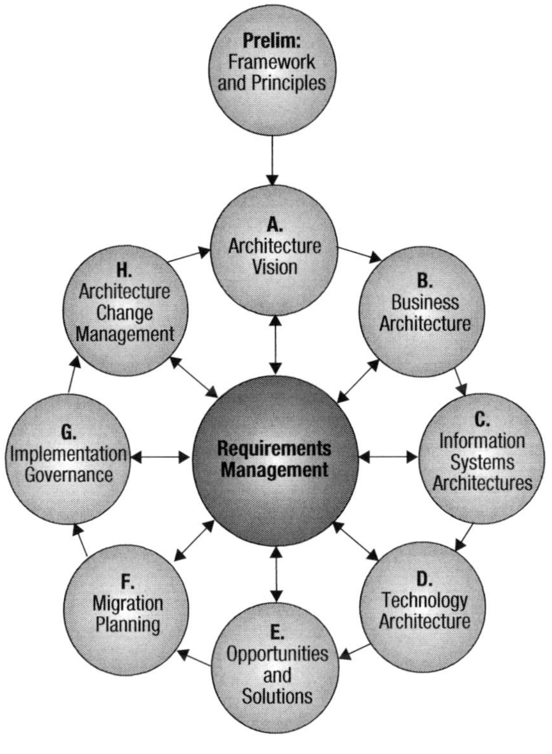

Source: ISACA, *COBIT MAPPING: MAPPING OF TOGAF 8.1 WITH COBIT® 4.0*, USA, 2007, figure 6, page 23

Enterprise Architecture Domains

There are four types of architecture that are commonly accepted as subsets of an overall enterprise architecture, as shown in **exhibit 3.7**, all of which TOGAF and COBIT are designed to support:

- A business (or business process) architecture defines the business strategy, governance, organization and key business processes.
- A data architecture describes the structure of an organization's logical and physical data assets, and data management resources.
- An applications architecture provides a blueprint for the individual application systems to be deployed, their interactions and their relationships to the core business processes of the organization.
- A technology architecture describes the architectural principles, component relationships, and hardware and software infrastructure intended to support the deployment of core, mission-critical applications.

There are many other approaches to both enterprise and security architecture. However, an effective approach must start with the enterprise business architecture. The subsequent designs, such as application, security, data architectures, etc., function as subsets to ensure alignment with and support of business strategy and objectives.

Complexity of developing and implementing some approaches has proven to be a hindrance to adoption. For example, some notions of information security architecture frameworks include six layers, from contextual to physical. Like a building architecture, the highest or contextual level defined in the Sherwood Applied Business Security Architecture (SABSA) and the Zachman frameworks is the "business" or utility layer. That is, what is the structure to be used for? A theater is designed very differently than an office building because the buildings are used for different purposes. The design, or architecture, is tightly aligned with the purpose, i.e., linked to the business objective. The contextual architecture serves to define the relationships between various required business attributes. These include who, what, when, where and how, which drive the next layer, the conceptual layer, which integrates the architectural design concepts with the business requirements.

The next layer, the logical architecture, describes the same elements in terms of the relationships of logical elements. This is followed by a physical layer, which identifies the relationships between various security "mechanisms" that will execute the logical relationships and the component architecture consisting of the actual devices and their interconnections. Finally, there is the operational architecture, describing how security service delivery is organized. The steps required to define these levels are shown in **exhibit 3.8**.

While arguably comprehensive, organizations that have attempted to implement SABSA or Zachman frameworks have often found this framework complex and costly to develop and difficult to maintain as organizations experience rapid change and new business objectives are defined.

The important consideration, regardless of the approach, is that at the point of the development and implementation of an information security program, some form of high-level architecture or design should have been prepared. This is particularly the case for major implementations comprised of many parts and projects that must integrate well to achieve the program objectives. Although many organizations have not developed enterprise or security architectures, the adoption of an appropriate one can be essential to developing and implementing an effective information security program.

Exhibit 3.7—Architecture Concerns of the Stakeholders

Architecture Views May address user, planner and business management business concerns	Data Architecture Views May address database designer administrator and system engineer concerns	Applications Architecture Views May address system and software engineer concerns	Technology Architecture Views May address acquires, operator, administrator and manager concerns
Business function view	Data entity view	Software engineering view	Networked computing/hardware view
Business services view			
Business process view			
Business information view			Communications engineering view
Business locations view	Data flow view (organisation data use)	Applications interoperability view	
People view (organisation chart)			Processing view
Workflow view			
Useability view			
Business strategy and goals view			
Business objectives view	Logical data view	Software distribution view	Cost view
Business rules view			
Business events view			Standards view
Business performance view			
	System engineering view		
Enterprise security view			
Enterprise manageability view			
Enterprise quality of service view			
Enterprise mobility view			
Source: ISACA, *COBIT MAPPING: MAPPING OF TOGAF 8.1 WITH COBIT® 4.0*, USA, 2007, figure 7, page 24			

3.11.2 OBJECTIVES OF INFORMATION SECURITY ARCHITECTURES

One of the key functions of "architecture" as a tool of the modern business is to provide a framework within which complexity can be managed successfully. As the size and complexity of a project grows, many designers and design influences must all work as a team to create something that has the appearance of being created by a single "design authority."

As the complexity of the business environment grows, many business processes and support functions must integrate seamlessly to provide effective services and management to the business, its customers and its partners. Architecture provides a means to manage that complexity.

Providing a Framework and Road Map

Architecture also acts as a road map for a collection of smaller projects and services that must be integrated into a single homogenous whole. It provides a framework within which many members of large design, delivery and support teams can work harmoniously, and toward which tactical projects can be migrated.

Simplicity and Clarity Through Layering and Modularization

In the same way that conventional architecture defines the rules and standards for the design and construction of buildings, information systems architecture addresses these same issues for the design and construction of computers, communications networks and the distributed business systems that are required for the delivery of business services. Information systems architecture must, therefore, take account of:

- The goals that are to be achieved through the systems
- The environment in which the systems will be built and used
- The technical capabilities of the people to construct and operate the systems and their component subsystems

Business Focus Beyond the Technical Domain

Information systems architecture is concerned with much more than technical factors. It is concerned with what the enterprise wants to achieve and with the environmental factors that will influence those achievements. The word "enterprise" implies not just a large organization, but one in which all the parts of that organization exhibit a "joined up" quality and in which the organization is seen at the highest level as a single entity with an integrated mission and purpose.

In some organizations, this broad view of information systems architecture is not well understood. Technical factors are often

Exhibit 3.8 SABSA Master Matrix

	ASSETS (What)	MOTIVATION (Why)	PROCESS (How)	PEOPLE (Who)	LOCATION (Where)	TIME (When)
CONTEXTUAL ARCHITECTURE	Business Decisions	Business Risk	Business Processes	Business Governance	Business Geography	Business Time Dependence
	Taxonomy of Business Assets, including Goals & Objectives	Opportunities & Threats Inventory	Inventory of Operational Processes	Organisational Structure & the Extended Enterprise	Inventory of Buildings Sites, Territories, Jurisdictions, etc.	Time dependencies of business objectives
CONCEPTUAL ARCHITECTURE	Business Knowledge & Risk strategy	Risk Management Objectives	Strategies for Process Assurance	Roles & Responsibilities	Domain Framework	Time Management Framework
	Business Attributes Profile	Enablement & Control Objectives; Policy Architecture	Process Mapping Framework; Architectural strategies for ICT	Owners, Custodians and Users; Service Providers & Customers	Security Domain Concepts & Framework	Through-Life Risk Management Framework
LOGICAL ARCHITECTURE	Information Assets	Risk Management Policies	Process Maps & Services	Entity & Trust Framework	Domain Maps	Calendar and Timetable
	Inventory of Information Assets	Domain Policies	Information Flows; Functional Transformations; Service Oriented Architecture	Entity Schema; Trust Models; Privilege Profiles	Domain Definitions; Inter-domain associations & interactions	Start Times, Lifetimes & Deadlines
PHYSICAL ARCHITECTURE	Data Assets	Risk Management Practices	Process Mechanisms	Human Interface	ICT Infrastructure	Processing Schedule
	Data Dictionary & Data Inventory	Risk Management Rules & Procedures	Applications; Middleware; Systems; Security Mechanisms	User Interface to ICT Systems; Access Control Systems	Host Platforms, Layout & Network	Timing & Sequencing of Processes and Sessions
COMPONENT ARCHITECTURE	ICT Components	Risk Management Tools & Standards	Process Tools & Standards	Personnel Management Tools & Standards	Locator Tools & Standards	Step Timing & Sequencing Tools
	ICT Products, including Data Repositories and Processors	Risk Analysis Tools; Risk Registers; Risk Monitoring and Reporting Tools	Tools and Protocols for Process Delivery	Identities; Job Descriptions; Roles; Functions; Actions & Access Control	Nodes, Addresses and other Locators	Time Schedules; Clocks, Timers & Interrupts
SERVICE MANAGEMENT ARCHITECTURE	Service Delivery Management	Operational Risk Management	Process Delivery Management	Personnel Management	Management of Environment	Time and Performance Management
	Assurance of Operational Continuity & Excellence	Risk Assessment; Risk Monitoring & Reporting; Risk Treatment	Management & Support of Systems, Applications & Services	Account Provisioning; User Support Management	Management of Buildings, Sites, Platforms & Networks	Management of Calendar and Timetable

Source: SABSA matrix, SABSA Enterprise Security Architecture, used with permission

the main influences on the architecture and, under these conditions, the architecture can fail to deliver what the business expects and needs.

Architecture and Control Objectives

Where security control objectives are considered, a systems architect can use combinations of technologies to provide control points in a system's infrastructure. Combined with control activities and associated procedures, these control points may be used to ensure that policy compliance is preserved as new systems are deployed that use the infrastructure. For example, if a network is structured such that there is only one connection to the Internet, then all network traffic that is destined for the Internet must travel through that connection. This would allow technology to be deployed in one place that could inspect all documents destined for the Internet to ensure that the information contained in the document is authorized to be sent to an external entity. Often, no technology will be specified by the architecture; this leaves a wide range of design choices for control points that would inspect documents being sent to the Internet.

3.12 ARCHITECTURE IMPLEMENTATION

Some organizations have enough experience with combinations of technologies used for a specific purpose that they elevate architectural decisions to the policy level. That is, choices of combinations of technology used for a given purpose are mandated by policy, because certain combinations allow easy implementation of security features that accomplish specific control objectives. Often, architectural policies are warranted where potential damage from data exposure warrants redundant controls. Some examples of architecture policy domains are:

- Database management systems (to restrict application access)
- Telecommunications (to mitigate threats of phone fraud)
- Web application access

For example, web application access is often protected from unauthorized access via user IDs and passwords. Yet inherent vulnerabilities in communicating on publicly available networks prompted security architects to require the use of transport layer security (TLS) on web servers that hosted applications that exchanged sensitive information with clients.

This configuration is often mandated by policy to ensure that traffic between client and server is encrypted to prevent the user ID and password, and the subsequent data flow, from being observed on the public network. However, such a policy does not provide any assurance that the client has not been compromised or that the user password has not been stolen. Mitigation of this impersonation threat requires a technology control in addition to passwords and basic TLS encryption.

There are multiple alternatives that an application may employ to achieve the level of client identification necessary to mitigate the risk of impersonation. In financial applications such as online banking, regulators now require that banks utilize some form of multifactor authentication to provide additional assurance of the identity of the individual initiating the client request. Applying this requirement uniformly on all applications (making it part of the organization's security architecture) will allow the organization to mitigate the impersonation threat in a uniform and efficient, thus supportable, manner.

A number of approaches to architecture for components of information systems exist (e.g., architectures for data and databases, servers, technical infrastructures, identity management, etc.). However, few organizations have developed an overall comprehensive enterprise security architecture, its management and its relationship to business objectives. This is somewhat analogous to a situation in which there exists separate, unintegrated designs for aircraft wings, engines, navigational equipment, passenger seats, etc., but no designs for the complete aircraft and how the various components fit together. The result would be unlikely to function well, if at all, and few would be inclined to trust it with their lives. Admittedly, information systems are designed to operate in a far more loosely-coupled fashion but the point is, nevertheless, relevant.

A number of architectural frameworks have been developed during the past decade to address this issue and they offer useful insights and approaches to dealing with many current design, management, implementation and monitoring issues. Some specific approaches are listed in section 3.11.1.

The framework approaches offer a great deal of flexibility in utilizing a variety of standards and methods such as COBIT, ITIL and ISO/IEC 27001:2013. It is true that many of the approaches may be more sophisticated and complex than many organizations are prepared to deal with. However, with the growing reliance on increasingly complex systems coupled with the escalating problems of manageability and security, organizations will eventually have little choice but to "get organized." The ISO27001:2013 approach to implementation of the Information Security Management System (ISMS) is shown in **exhibit 3.9**.

Exhibit 3.9—The SABSA Framework for Security Management

	Assets (What)	Motivation (Why)	Process (How)	People (Who)	Location (Where)	Time (When)
Contextual	Business Requirements Collection; Information Classification	Business Risk Assessment; Corporate Policy Making	Business Risk Assessment; Corporate Policy Making	Business Security Organisation Management	Business Field Operations Program	Business Calendar and Timetable Management
Conceptual	Business Continuity Management	Security Audit; Corporate Compliance; Metrics, Measures and Benchmarks; SLAs	Change Control Incident Management; Disaster Recovery	Security Training; Awareness; Cultural Development	Security Domain Management	Security Operations Schedule Management
Logical	Information Security; System Integrity	Detailed Security Policy Making; Policy Compliance Monitoring; Intelligence Gathering	Intrusion Detection; Event Monitoring Security Process Development Security Service Management; System Development Controls; Configuration Management	Access Control; Privilege and Profile Administration	Applications Security Administration and Management	Applications Deadline & Cut-off Management
Physical	Database Security; System Integrity	Vulnerability Assessment; Penetration testing; Threat Assessment	Rule Definition; Key Management ACL Maintenance Backup Admin; Computer Forensics; Event Log Administator Anti-Virus Administrator	User Support; Security Help desk	Network Security Management; Site Security Management	User A/C Aging; Password Aging; Crypto Key Aging; Admin. of Access Control Time Windows
Component	Product and Tool Security and Integrity	Threat Research; Vulnerability Research; CERT Notifications	Product Procurement; Project Management; Operations Management	Personnel Vetting; Supplier Vetting; User Admin.	Platform Workstation and Equipment Security Management	Time-out Configuration; Detailed Security Operations Sequencing

For the information security manager, the approach may be helpful in developing long-term objectives or suggesting approaches to address current issues. Some organizations have adopted elements of the architectural approach, piecemeal, with the long-term objective of full implementation over time.

3.13 SECURITY PROGRAM MANAGEMENT AND ADMINISTRATIVE ACTIVITIES

Information security program management includes directing, overseeing and monitoring activities related to information security in support of organizational objectives. Management is the process of achieving the objectives of the business organization by bringing together human, physical and financial resources in an optimum combination with process and technology and making the best decision for the organization while taking into consideration its operating environment.

In the typical organization, information security program management will include short- and long-range planning and day-to-day administration in addition to directing various projects and initiatives. It generally also includes a variety of risk management activities and incident management and response functions; it will usually include a variety of oversight and monitoring functions as well. Program management typically includes aspects of governance whether in terms of policy and standards development or in terms of procedural controls and general rules of use for end users. As with other aspects of information security, governance cannot remain static in a changing risk environment and must evolve to be effective.

The information security manager has the responsibility for managing information security program activities to achieve the outcomes listed in section 3.4.2. It is the responsibility of senior management to support those objectives and provide adequate resources and authority to ensure that objectives are achieved. In addition, the roles and responsibilities of other assurance providers must be clearly defined to prevent gaps in protection between them.

As the scope of the information security manager's responsibilities continues to expand, there is the risk is that important security elements may be overlooked or neglected. It may be useful for the information security manager to consider the following checklist for a comprehensive, well-managed security program:

- A security strategy intrinsically linked with business objectives that has senior management acceptance and support
- Security policy and supporting standards that are complete and consistent with strategy
- Complete and accurate security procedures for all important operations
- Clear assignment of roles and responsibilities
- Established method to ensure continued alignment with business goals and objectives such as a security steering committee
- Information assets that have been identified and classified by criticality and sensitivity
- Security architecture that is complete and consistent with strategy, and in line with business objectives
- Effective controls that have been well-designed, implemented and maintained
- Effective monitoring processes in place
- Tested and functional incident and emergency response capabilities
- Tested business continuity/disaster recovery plans
- Appropriate information security involvement in change management, SDLC and project management processes
- Established processes to ensure that risk is properly identified, evaluated, communicated and managed
- Established security awareness training for all users
- Established activities that create and sustain a corporate culture that values information security
- Established processes to maintain awareness of current and emerging regulatory and legal issues
- Effective integration with procurement and third-party management processes
- Resolution of noncompliance issues and other variances in a timely manner
- Processes to ensure ongoing interaction with business process owners
- Business supported processes for risk and business impact assessments, development of risk mitigation strategies, and enforcement of policy and regulatory compliance
- Established operational, tactical and strategic metrics that monitor utilization and effectiveness of security resources
- Established methods for knowledge capture and dissemination
- Effective communication and integration with other organizational assurance providers

Note that this list is not comprehensive, nor will it fit all organizations. It is simply meant to demonstrate the range of activities and established practices that would constitute a mature security program. This list must be tailored for the size and nature of each organization.

Program Administration

Administration of a security program will typically involve a series of repetitive functions similar to that required in other organizational units. There will be differences in administration of program development projects and the ongoing administration of the operations aspects of the program which need to be considered.

Ongoing administration might include such tasks as:
- Personnel performance, time tracking and other record keeping
- Resource utilization
- Purchasing and/or acquisition
- Inventory management
- Project monitoring and tracking
- Awareness program development
- Budgeting, financial management and asset control
- Business case development and financial analysis
- HR administration and personnel management
- Project and program management
- Operations and service delivery management
- Implementation and administration of metrics and reporting
- Information technology development life cycle management

There may be a number of technical administrative and operational requirements as well. These may include:
- Cryptographic key management
- Log reviews and monitoring
- Change request review and oversight
- Configuration, patch and other life cycle management review and oversight

- Vulnerability scanning
- Threat monitoring
- Compliance monitoring
- Penetration testing

An effective information security manager should be familiar with existing frameworks and major international standards for IT and security management (e.g., COBIT, ISO/IEC 27001 and 27002) and be able to extract relevant elements to utilize for the management approach best suited to the organization. Some may prove to be a better fit than others, depending on organizational structure, culture, available resources, business sector, etc.

The information security manager has many responsibilities, and one may be as a facilitator to help resolve competing objectives between security and performance. As an active facilitator, the information security manager gains senior management support and organizational acceptance and compliance for the information security program's policies, standards and procedures. Through a facilitative approach, the information security manager can work with the different departments to discuss information security risk and suggest solutions that address both security requirements and minimizing the impact on business activities. Through this consultative role, the information security manager also needs to ensure that the organization's life cycle processes incorporate information security. By working in a consultative role, the information security manager can facilitate the enterprise's information security program while staying informed about the organization's activities that may impact information security.

3.13.1 PERSONNEL, ROLES AND RESPONSIBILITIES, AND SKILLS

The information security manager must plan personnel resources around the technical and administrative skills required to effectively operate the program. Staff members can include security engineers, QA and testing specialists, access administrators, project managers, compliance liaisons, security architects, awareness coordinators, and policy specialists. The information security manager should develop positions in accordance with specific program needs, even merging responsibilities of multiple roles into one personnel position for small organizations.

The information security manager must ensure that personnel within the security organization as well as other responsible organizations maintain the appropriate skills needed to carry out program functions. Each organization's skill requirements vary, generally revolving around the existing information systems and security technologies implemented.

Personnel requirements for information security program development differ after the program is implemented. In other words, architects, designers, builders, developers, testers and others involved in the construction of a security program are likely to be different from the personnel that will administer systems once they are functioning normally. Skills that are only rarely needed are best acquired through engagement of service providers such as integrators or consulting firms. When faced with the need for a specialized skill, the information security manager should analyze the cost, timing and intellectual capital implications of hiring staff versus using an external service provider. Additionally, in some organizations there may be a need for background checks, especially if classified, confidential or highly sensitive information is involved with the job.

Project management will be a normal activity in managing the development of a security program. Larger organizations usually have a project management office (PMO), which may be available to the information security manager to assist in development and implementation projects. Existing functions within the organization should be used whenever possible both to maximize organizational involvement in the program and leverage existing capabilities.

Roles

RACI (Responsible, Accountable, Consulted, Informed) charts can be used effectively in defining the various roles associated with aspects of developing an information security program. Clear designation of roles and responsibilities is necessary to ensure effective implementation.

A role is a designation assigned to an individual by virtue of a job function or other label. A responsibility is a description of some procedure or function related to the role that someone is accountable to perform. Roles are important to information security because they allow responsibilities and/or access rights to be assigned based on the fact that an individual performs a function rather than having to assign them to individual people. There are typically many job functions in the organization that support security functions and the ability to assign access authorizations based on roles simplifies administration.

Skills

Skills are the training, expertise and experience held by the personnel in a given job function. It is important to understand the proficiencies of available personnel to ensure that they map to competencies required for program implementation. Specific skills needed for program implementation can be acquired through training or utilizing external resources. External resources such as consultants are often a more cost-effective choice for skills required for only a short time for specific projects.

Once it has been agreed that certain personnel will have specific information security responsibilities, formal employment agreements should be established that reference those responsibilities, and these must be considered when screening applicants for employment.

Culture

Culture represents the organizational behavior, methods for navigating and influencing the organization's formal and informal structures to get the work done, attitudes, norms, level of teamwork, existence or lack of turf issues, and geographic dispersion. Culture is impacted by the individual backgrounds, work ethics, values, past experiences, individual filters/blind spots and perceptions of life that individuals bring to the workplace. Every organization has a culture, whether it has been purposely designed or simply emerged over time as a reflection of the leadership.

While information security primarily involves logical and analytical activities, building relationships, teamwork, and influencing the organizational attitudes toward a positive security culture relies more on good interpersonal skills. The astute information security program manager will recognize the importance of developing both types of skills as essential to being an effective manager.

Building a security-aware culture depends on individuals in their respective roles performing their jobs in a way that protects information assets. Each person, no matter what level or role within the organization, should be able to articulate how information security relates to their role. For this to happen, the security manager must plan communications, participate in committees and projects, and provide individual attention to the end users' or managers' needs. The security department should be able to answer "What is in it for me?" or "Why should I care?" for every person in the organization. Once these questions have been answered, effective communications can be tailored to these messages.

Some indicators of a successful security culture are: the information security department is brought into projects at the appropriate times, end users know how to identify and report incidents, the organization can identify the security manager, and people know their role in protecting the information assets of the organization and integrating information security into their daily practices.

3.13.2 SECURITY AWARENESS, TRAINING AND EDUCATION

Risk that is inherent in using computing systems cannot be addressed through technical security mechanisms. An active security awareness program can greatly reduce risk by addressing the behavioral element of security through education and consistent application of awareness techniques. Security awareness programs should focus on common user security concerns such as password selection, appropriate use of computing resources, e-mail and web browsing safety, and social engineering, and the programs should be tailored to specific groups. In addition, users are the front line for the detection of threats that may not be detectable by automated means, e.g., fraudulent activity and social engineering. Employees should be educated on recognizing and escalating such events to enhance loss prevention.

An important aspect of ensuring compliance with the information security program is the education and awareness of the organization regarding the importance of the program. In addition to the need for information security, all personnel must be trained in their specific responsibilities that are related to information security. Particular attention must be paid to those job functions that require virtually unlimited data access. People whose job is to transfer data may have access to data in most systems, and those doing performance tuning can change most operating system configurations. People whose job is to schedule batch jobs have the authority to run most system jobs applications. Programmers have access to change application code. These functions are not typically managed by an information security manager. Although it is possible to set up elaborate monitoring controls, it is not technically feasible or financially prudent for an information security manager to provide oversight adequate to ensure that all data transfer jobs that transmit reports send them only to appropriately authorized recipients. Though the information security manager can ensure that there is clear policy, develop applicable standards and assist in process coordination, management in all areas must assist in providing oversight.

Employee awareness should start from the point of joining the organization (e.g., through induction training) and continue regularly. Techniques for delivery need to vary to prevent them from becoming stale or boring, and may also need to be incorporated into other organizational training programs.

Security awareness programs should consist of training, often administered online; simple quizzes to gauge retention of training concepts; security awareness reminders such as posters, newsletters, or screen savers; and a regular schedule of refresher training. In larger organizations, there may be a large enough population of middle and senior management to warrant special management-level training on information security awareness and operations issues.

All employees of an organization and, where relevant, third-party users must receive appropriate training and regular updates on the importance of security policies, standards and procedures in the organization. This includes security requirements, legal responsibilities and business controls, as well as training in the correct use of information processing facilities, e.g., login procedures, use of software packages. For new employees, this should occur before access to information or services is granted and be a part of new employee orientation.

The information security manager should take a methodical approach to developing and implementing the education and awareness program, and consider various aspects including:
- Who is the intended audience (senior management, business managers, IT staff, end users)?
- What is the intended message (policies, procedures, recent events)?
- What is the intended result (improved policy compliance, behavioral change, better practices)?
- What communication method will be used (computer-based training [CBT], all-hands meeting, intranet, newsletters, etc.)?
- What is the organizational structure and culture?

A number of different mechanisms available for raising information security awareness include:
- Computer-based security awareness and training programs
- E-mail reminders and security tips
- Written security policies and procedures (and updates)
- Nondisclosure statements signed by the employee
- Use of different media in promulgating security (e.g., company newsletter, web page, videos, posters, login reminders)
- Visible enforcement of security rules
- Simulated security incidents for improving security
- Rewarding employees who report suspicious events
- Periodic reviews
- Job descriptions
- Performance reviews

3.13.3 DOCUMENTATION

Oversight of the creation and maintenance of security-related documentation is an important administrative component of an effective information security program. Documents that commonly pertain to the program include:
- Policies, standards, procedures and guidelines
- Technical diagrams of infrastructure and architectures, applications and data flows
- Training and awareness documentation

- Risk analyses, recommendations and related documentation
- Security system designs, configuration policies and maintenance documentation
- Operational records such as shift reports and incident tracking reports
- Operational procedures and process flows
- Organizational documentation such as organization charts, staff performance objectives and RACI models

Each document should be assigned an owner who is responsible for updating documentation (or templates in the case of operational records). Changes should be made under the recommendations of management or the security steering committee; the person or group should also approve changes prior to their distribution. The owner is also responsible for ensuring that access to documentation is appropriate, controlled and auditable.

Exhibit 3.10—COBIT 5 Enterprise Enablers

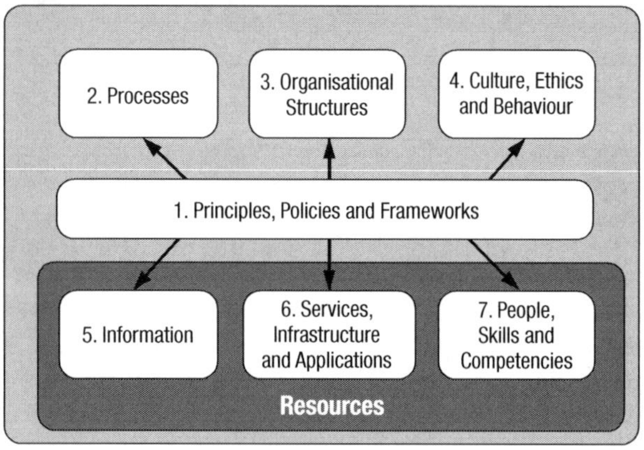

Source: ISACA, COBIT 5, USA, 2012, figure 12

The information security manager should ensure that enablers (principles, policies and frameworks; processes; organizational structures; culture, ethics and behavior; information; services, infrastructure, and applications; people, skills and competencies; as shown in **exhibit 3.10**) are available that address creation, approval, change, maintenance, controlled distribution and retirement of documentation. In many cases, these services are provided as part of a larger enterprise document management system, an ideal situation considering that the information security manager does not necessarily maintain custodianship of all security-related documentation. The information security manager should also ensure that sensitive technical and operational documents are protected by controls and practices equal to or stronger than those implemented for other sensitive corporate information assets. Security documentation must also follow the organizational standards for appropriate classification and labeling.

A number of documents will be required to design, initiate and implement an information security program. Documentation requirements will change at various stages and it is important to make sure they are current. Standards and procedures must change as required to address changes in risk, technology, business activities or baselines, but must remain consistent with published policies, which typically change with far less frequency.

Version control is essential to ensure that all parties are operating from the same document revisions, and a reliable notification and publication process will be required.

Some of the documentation required will typically include:
- Program objectives
- Road maps
- Business cases
- Resources required
- Controls
- Budgets
- Systems designs/architectures
- Policies, standards, procedures, guidelines
- Project plan milestones, time lines
- KGIs, KPIs, CSFs, other metrics
- Training and awareness requirements
- Business impact and risk analysis
- Service level agreements (SLAs)
- Severity criteria
- Declaration criteria

Document Maintenance

Documentation will typically need to be updated as the information security program is implemented and as the organization evolves. The information security manager must implement procedures for adding; modifying; and, in some cases, retiring information security policies, standards, procedures and other documentation.

An important consideration for all documentation activities is to ensure that an appropriate version control process is in place so that all recipients are using current documentation. Processes must also be developed to retire documentation that has been superseded by later releases. Automated systems utilizing a single source for all documentation will help ensure that only current policies, standards and procedures are being used. Also, all documentation must have standardized markings, including effective release date, owner and classification.

A process for change proposals can be based on policy reviews or as stakeholders recognize the need for a policy change. The information security manager should track proposed changes to policies for review in the appropriate forums.

Modification of standards will probably occur more frequently than modification of policies. These changes are often driven by changes in technology such as availability of new security capabilities, changes in risk, evolution of the technical infrastructure and requirements of new business initiatives. Proposed standards should be reviewed by the steering committee and/or by departments impacted by them. The opportunity to provide input and suggested modification should be afforded as well to optimize cooperation and compliance. Standards should be reviewed periodically or as warranted by environmental changes, changing risk, request of stakeholders or audit determination of insufficiency. Changes to standards should be managed in a similar manner to policy changes and should also include technical or operational risk analysis relative to the proposed change in standards.

Modifications to either policies or standards should trigger procedures to modify compliance monitoring tools and processes. It is suggested that changes be periodically shared with auditors and compliance personnel who are not already involved in the change management process to ensure awareness and acceptance of changes prior to auditing activities.
Changes in standards will necessitate a review of procedures that may require modification to be in compliance. Other documentation such as acceptable use policies, guidelines, QA and procurement processes, and others may also require modification.

3.13.4 PROGRAM DEVELOPMENT AND PROJECT MANAGEMENT

Information security programs are rarely static and must undergo ongoing development to meet changing conditions and risk. The basis for development will be the strategy to achieve defined objectives. These objectives include achieving the desired maturity levels and managing risk to acceptable levels while effectively supporting business operations.

The information security gap analysis described in section 3.10.3 typically identifies the need for projects that result in improvements to the information security program. The processes described in section 3.14.11 should also be reviewed to identify projects that can fill gaps between the existing organization and the program as envisioned. Many of these projects will be technology implementations or reconfigurations that will make existing technology more secure. Each project should have time, budget and measurable result. Each must make the environment more secure without causing control weaknesses in other areas.

As would any professional project manager, an information security manager should prioritize the portfolio of projects in such a way that those that overlap are not delayed by each other, resources are appropriately allocated, and the results are smoothly integrated into or transitioned from existing operations. The information security manager should employ generally accepted project management techniques such as setting goals, measuring progress, tracking deadlines, and assigning responsibilities in a controlled and repeatable manner. This helps ensure that the security program's design and implementation will be successful.

3.13.5 RISK MANAGEMENT

Virtually all aspects of program management serve to manage risk to acceptable levels. Since the risk landscape changes continuously, it is essential that information security changes and adapts as required to ensure the business is capable of dealing effectively with current conditions.

Regardless of the effectiveness of information security, few organizations will escape the effect of security incidents. An essential aspect of program management is to ensure that the organization can respond effectively to security incidents that disrupt business operations.

Risk Management Responsibilities

Managing information risk is an integral part of the information security manager's ongoing responsibilities and a primary requirement in both program development and management. The information security manager must have a good understanding and develop the requisite skills regarding evaluation and management of risk. This should include:
- Knowledge of program development life cycle risk
- Knowledge of program management risk
- Knowledge of methods for assessing the vulnerabilities in technical and operational environments
- Ability to analyze exposures, the general threat environment and threats specific to the information security manager's organization
- Knowledge of risk analysis approaches including quantitative and qualitative methods
- Knowledge of risk management processes including mitigation, elimination, transfer, and informed acceptance
- Ability to understand and assess potential impacts if risk are exploited
- Knowledge of methods for tracking, documenting and communicating risk and impact issues

3.13.6 BUSINESS CASE DEVELOPMENT

The purpose of a business case is to capture the reasoning for initiating a project or task, and the business case should include all the factors that can materially affect the project's success or failure. The method of presentation should be consistent with the organization's usual approach and can be electronic, a well-structured written document or a slide presentation. It must persuasively encompass benefits, costs and risk. The benefits must be tangible, supportable and relevant to the organization. Particular attention must be given to the financial aspects of the proposal. The TCO and risk must be realistically represented for the full life cycle of the project. It is important to avoid overconfidence, overly optimistic projections and excessive precision for what are likely to be somewhat speculative results. (See section 1.9.1 Common Pitfalls.)

The principal purposes of the formal business case process are:
- Introduce a way of thinking that causes people with the authority to recommend projects to consider their value, risk and relative priority as a fundamental element of submitting the project proposal.
- Require those proposing a project to justify its value to the enterprise and to eliminate any proposal that is not of demonstrable value.
- Enable management to determine whether the project proposed is of value to the business and achievable compared to the relative merits of alternative proposals.
- Enable management to objectively measure the subsequent achievement of the benefits of the business case.

While there are many possible formats for developing a business case, utilizing formal project management methodologies is likely to be the most persuasive. The case should include the options considered and the reasons for rejecting them. The options presented should include the case for not initiating a particular project. The business case should include some or all of the following:
- **Reference**—Project name/reference, origins/background/ current state
- **Context**—Business objectives/opportunities, business strategic alignment (priority)

- **Value Proposition**—Desired business outcomes, outcomes road map, business benefits (by outcome), quantified benefits value, costs/ROI financial scenarios, risk/costs of not proceeding, project risk (to project, benefits and business)
- **Focus**—Problem/solution scope, assumptions/constraints, options identified/evaluated, size, scale and complexity assessment
- **Deliverables**—Outcomes, deliverables and benefits planned; organizational areas impacted (internally and externally); key stakeholders
- **Dependencies**—CSFs
- **Project metrics**—KGIs, KPIs
- **Workload**—Approach, phase/stage definitions (project [change] activities, technical delivery activities, workload estimate/breakdown, project plan and schedule, critical path analysis)
- **Required resources**—Project leadership team, project governance team, team resources, funding
- **Commitments (required)**—Project controls, review schedule, reporting processes, deliverables schedule, financial budget/schedule

Business Case Evaluation

Evaluation and review of a business case should include determining that:
- The investment has value and importance.
- The project will be properly managed.
- The enterprise has the capability to deliver the benefits.
- The enterprise's dedicated resources are working on the highest value opportunities.
- Projects with interdependencies are undertaken in the optimal sequence.

Business Case Objectives

The business case process should be designed to be:
- **Adaptable**—It is tailored to the size and risk of the proposal.
- **Consistent**—The same basic business issues are addressed by every project.
- **Business oriented**—It is concerned with the business capabilities and impact, rather than having a technical focus.
- **Comprehensive**—All factors relevant to a complete evaluation are included.
- **Understandable**—The contents are clearly relevant, logical and, although demanding, are simple to complete and evaluate.
- **Measurable**—All key aspects can be quantified so their achievement can be tracked and measured.
- **Transparent**—Key elements can be justified directly.
- **Accountable**—Accountabilities and commitments for the delivery of benefits and management of costs are clear.

3.13.7 PROGRAM BUDGETING

Budgeting is an essential part of information security program management and can have a significant impact on the program's success. Effective preparation and defense of a budget can mean the difference between having or not having sufficient staff and other resources to accomplish the objectives of the information security program.

As with many business activities, self-education and advance preparation are key factors in successfully navigating this frequently challenging process. Well before the budget cycle begins, the information security manager should ensure familiarity with the budgeting process and methods used by the organization. It will also be important to consider the timing of the various stages of the organization's budget cycle.

Another key consideration before beginning the budgeting process is the information security strategy. All budget expenditures for information security should be derived from and supported by the information security strategy. Ideally, elements of the security strategy are laid out in a security road map, as discussed in section 3.10. Having the strategy communicated and approved before entering into the budgeting process is a key element in a successful budget proposal.

Elements of an Information Security Program Budget

Many costs associated with an information security program are fairly straightforward. Expenses such as personnel (salaries, training, etc.), basic hardware and software, and subscription services fall into this category. In addition to the typical program start-up and yearly operational costs, there will likely be short- and long-term projects that represent various objectives on the security road map. These projects will consume resources over the course of months (or years) and must be accounted for in the budget as accurately as possible. The information security manager should collaborate with the organization's PMO and the appropriate subject matter experts (SMEs) to help estimate costs for projects that will start within the fiscal year. Elements of each project that should be considered include:
- Employee time
- Contractor and consultant fees
- Equipment (hardware, software) costs
- Space requirements (data center rack space, etc.)
- Testing resources (personnel, system time, etc.)
- Training costs (staff, users, etc.)
- Travel
- Creation of supporting documentation
- Ongoing maintenance
- Contingencies for unexpected costs

While it will be impossible to be 100 percent accurate, engaging the appropriate SMEs and skilled project managers can be invaluable in arriving at a fairly accurate estimate.

Finally, it is important to keep in mind that some aspects of an information security program are not entirely predictable and can incur unanticipated costs—particularly in the area of incident response. These costs are often the result of the need for external resources to assist with a security event that exceeds the skills or bandwidth of the organization's staff. One approach to budget for these situations is to use historical data of incidents and remediation costs of previous security events that required unbudgeted external resources.

Even if the organization has recently initiated its security program, there may have been prior events that necessitated external resources. If the planned program does not anticipate having these skills on staff, it is likely external resources will be needed again in the future. For example, if during the past three years the organization has engaged external forensic consultants to assist with security events because the required skill sets were not on staff, the security manager should consider adding a line item in the budget to account for this situation. Costs can be estimated based on the average costs over the previous years as a starting point. If this information is not available, industry statistics from peer organizations may be useful as an indicator of risk and remediation costs.

3.13.8 GENERAL RULES OF USE/ACCEPTABLE USE POLICY

While specific procedures provide the detailed steps required for many functions at the operational level, there is still a large group of users that may benefit from a user-friendly summary of what they should and should not do to comply with policy. An effective way of assisting these general users in understanding security-related responsibilities is the development of an acceptable use policy. This policy can detail, in everyday terms, the obligations and responsibilities of all users in a straightforward and concise manner. It is then necessary to effectively communicate the use policy to all users and ensure it is read and understood. The use policy should be provided to all new personnel that will have access to information assets regardless of employment status.

Typically, these rules of use for all personnel include the policy and standards for access control, classification, marking and handling of documents and information, reporting requirements and disclosure constraints. They may also include rules on e-mail and Internet usage as well as other information resources and assets. The rules of use provide a general security baseline for the entire organization. It is often necessary to provide supplemental or additional information to specific groups in the organization, consistent with their responsibilities.

3.13.9 INFORMATION SECURITY PROBLEM MANAGEMENT PRACTICES

In addition to crisis or event management practices, the information security manager needs to understand the various aspects of an effective problem management approach. Problem management typically requires a systematic approach to understanding the various aspects of the issue, defining the problem and designing an action program along with assigning responsibility and assigning due dates for resolution. A reporting process should also be implemented for tracking the results and ensuring that the problem is resolved.

As the information systems environment is continually going through changes via updates and additions, it is not unusual for the security controls in place to occasionally develop a problem and not work as intended. It is at this point that the information security manager must identify the problem and assign a priority to it.

The information security manager should also be familiar with mitigating controls that may have to be employed if the primary security control fails. Rather than allowing the security vulnerability to put the organization at risk, it may be necessary for the information security manager to take alternative actions to protect the information resources until the problem is resolved. For example, if a firewall fails, the information security manager may elect to disconnect the system from the outside until the firewall problem is corrected. While this would protect the information resources from outside risk, it would likely affect the organization's ability to perform business. Therefore, it is important that specific authority and limits are established by management.

3.13.10 VENDOR MANAGEMENT

An ongoing management and administrative responsibility for the typical information security manager is the oversight and monitoring of external providers of hardware and software, general supplies, and various services.

This is to provide assurance that risk introduced in acquisition processes, implementation and service delivery is managed appropriately. Other organizational units will typically be involved in aspects of managing vendors including legal, finance, procurement, and possibly some business units.

Security service providers are a common feature of many information security programs and often the most cost-effective approach to various monitoring and administrative functions. They can provide the information security manager with specialist skills as needed, longer-term staff augmentation while recruiting for open positions and even offloading of routine daily tasks. Outsourced security service providers can deliver a range of services such as assessment and audit, engineering, operational support, security architecture and design, advisory services, and forensics support.

Security service providers can free up internal resources to focus on projects or operations where preservation of intellectual capital is at a premium. The use of external security resources can also provide an objective, fresh perspective on the information security program. If the information security manager is to utilize an outsourced security provider, the capabilities and approaches that the vendor takes should align with the organization's information security program.

The use of external parties to provide security-related functions usually creates risk that must be managed by the information security manager. Issues such as financial viability, quality of service, adequate staffing, adherence to the organization's security policies and right to audit must be addressed.

3.13.11 PROGRAM MANAGEMENT EVALUATION

Certain situations call for the information security manager to assess the current state of an existing information security program, e.g., if promoted or hired into an existing CSO role. It is also important for the information security manager to periodically reevaluate the effectiveness of the program relative to the changes in organizational demands, environment and constraints. The results of such analysis should be shared with the information security steering committee or other stakeholders for review and development of strategies for needed program modifications.

While the information security manager must determine the most appropriate scope for assessing current state, the following section outlines several critical areas for evaluation.

Program Objectives

The information security manager must evaluate the documented security objectives established for the program. Key considerations include:
- Were program goals aligned with governance objectives (if they exist)?

- Are objectives measurable, realistic and associated with specific time lines?
- Do program objectives align with organizational goals, initiatives, compliance needs and operational environment?
- Is there consensus on program objectives? Were objectives developed collaboratively?
- Have metrics been implemented to measure program objective success and shortfalls?
- Are there regular management reviews of objectives and accomplishments?

Compliance Requirements

Alignment with and fulfillment of compliance requirements are among the most visible indications of security management status. Because many standards establish program management requirements, the information security manager must evaluate the management program itself—framework and components—against compulsory and/or voluntary compliance standards. Key considerations include:

- Is there facilitation of close communication between compliance and information security groups? Are information security compliance requirements clearly defined?
- Does the information security program specifically integrate compliance requirements into policies, standards, procedures, operations and success metrics?
- Do the program's technical, operational and managerial components align with the components required by regulatory standards?
- What have been the results of recent audit and compliance reviews of the information security program?
- Are program compliance deficiencies tracked, reported and addressed timely?
- Are compliance management technologies used to increase the efficiency of fulfilling security compliance demands?

Program Management

Evaluation of program management components will reveal the extent of management support and the overall depth of the existing program. Very technical, tactically-driven security programs will tend to implement fewer management components, where strategic programs driven by standards, compliance and governance will implement a more comprehensive set of management activities that ensures that requirements are established and fulfilled. Considerations of program management components include:

- Is there thorough documentation of the program itself? Have key policies, standards and procedures been reduced to accessible operating guidelines and distributed to responsible parties?
- Do responsible individuals understand their roles and responsibilities?
- Are roles and responsibilities defined for members of senior management, boards, etc.? Do these organizations understand and engage their responsibilities?
- Are responsibilities for information security represented in business managers' individual objectives and part of their individual performance rating?
- Are policies and standards defined, formally approved and distributed?
- Are business unit managers involved in guiding and supporting information security program activities? Is there a formal steering committee?
- How is the program positioned within the organization? To whom is the program accountable? Does this positioning impart an appropriate level of authority and visibility for the objectives that the program must fulfill?
- Does the program implement effective administration functions, e.g., budgeting, financial management, HR management, knowledge management?
- Are meaningful metrics used to evaluate program performance? Are these metrics regularly collected and reported?
- Are there forums and mechanisms for regular management oversight of program activities? Does management regularly reassess program effectiveness?

Security Operations Management

The information security manager must evaluate the effectiveness with which the information security program implements security operational activities, both within the security organization and in other organizational units. Some key considerations include:

- Are security requirements and processes included in security, technology and business unit standard operating procedures?
- Do security-related standard operating procedures (SOPs) provide for accountability, process visibility and management oversight?
- Are there documented SOPs for security-related activities such as access management, security systems maintenance, event analysis and incident response?
- Is there a schedule of regularly performed procedures, e.g., technical configuration review? Does the program provide for records of scheduled activities?
- Is there separation of duties between system implementers, security administrators and compliance personnel?
- Does the program provide for effective operational metrics reporting that provide management with needed information for oversight? Are there other oversight mechanisms in place?
- Does management regularly review security operations? Is there a forum for operational issues to be escalated to management for resolution?

Technical Security Management

Management of the technical security environment is critical to ensuring that information processing systems and security mechanisms are implemented effectively. In addition to evaluating the current technical environment itself, the information security manager should consider the following issues regarding management of technical security concerns:

- Are there technical standards for the security configuration of individual network, system, application and other technology components?
- Do standards exist that address architectural security issues such as topology, communication protocols and compartmentalization of critical systems?
- Do standards support and enforce high-level policies and requirements? Are standards a collaborative effort between technology, operations and security staff?
- Are technical standards uniformly implemented? Do procedures exist to regularly evaluate and report on compliance with technical standards? Is there a formal process to manage exceptions?
- Is separation of development, test and production environments enforced?

- Do systems enforce separation of duty, especially where high levels of administrative access are concerned?
- Is there reliable and comprehensive visibility (logging) into system activities, configurations, accessibility and security-related events? Is this visibility continual or intermittent?
- Are proper decommissioning processes in place to prevent data leakage?

Resource Levels

The information security manager must assess the level of financial, human and technical resources allocated to the program. Areas of deficiency must be identified and escalated to senior management and/or the steering committee. Considerations include the following areas:

- Financial resource allocations
  - What is the current funding level for the program?
  - Is a comprehensive capital and operating budget maintained?
  - Do financial allocations align with program budget expectations?
  - Are there linkages between resource allocation and business objectives?
  - Are functions within the program prioritized in terms of financial allocation?
  - Which functions are likely to suffer from underfunding?
- HR
  - Does the program implement a workload management methodology?
  - What is the current staffing level for the program?
  - Are existing resources fully utilized in terms of time and skills?
  - Are existing resources adequately skilled for the roles they are in?
  - Are there low-value tasks that other resources could be leveraged to complete?
  - What other human resources (e.g., information technology staff) is the program dependent on to operate effectively? Is information security a formal part of these resources' job descriptions and activity plans?
- Technical resources
  - What technologies currently support information security program objectives?
  - Is the capacity of supporting technologies sufficient to support current demands? Will these technologies scale to meet future needs?
  - Does the program account for maintenance, administration and eventual replacement of supporting technologies?
  - Are there other technologies that could make the program more efficient or effective?

3.13.12 PLAN-DO-CHECK-ACT

The information security program is based on the effective, efficient management of controls designed and implemented to treat or mitigate threats, risk and vulnerabilities. The unique dependency on the effective, efficient management of a business process such as information security lends itself to the concepts and methodologies encompassed within the total quality management (TQM) system. TQM is based on four primary processes, Plan-Do-Check-Act (PDCA), as depicted in **exhibit 3.11**.

The TQM approach, combined with a governance methodology that focuses on strategic program alignment with organizational goals, will provide the information security manager with tools that he or she can use to implement and maintain a highly effective, efficient program. As described in chapter 1, the basic elements of a governance methodology includes a strategic vision, objectives, KGIs, CSFs, KPIs, and key actions or tactical and annual action plans. These elements are defined as follows and depicted in **exhibit 3.12**.

- **Vision** is a broadly defined, clear and compelling statement about the organization's purpose. This should include the desired outcomes of the information security program.
- **Strategic objectives** are a set of goals that are necessary and sufficient to move the organization toward its vision. These goals should be reflected in KGIs.
- **CSFs** are a set of circumstances or events that are necessary to achieve the strategic objectives.
- **KPIs** are concrete metrics tracked to ensure that the CSFs are being achieved.
- **Key actions, including tactical and annual action plans** are the initiatives to be delivered in order to achieve the strategic objectives and KGIs.

3.13.13 LEGAL AND REGULATORY REQUIREMENTS

Corporate legal departments are often primarily focused on contracts and securities, or company stock-related matters. The result is that they are, in many cases, not aware of regulatory requirements, and the information security manager should not rely on the legal department to identify them. Typically, the impacted department will be the most knowledgeable about legal and regulatory issues. It is, however, prudent for the information security manager to request legal review and interpretation of legal requirements that have security implications to ensure clarity on the organization's official position on the matter.

In addition, the information security manager may be required to support legal standards related to privacy of information and transactions, the collection and handling of audit records, e-mail retention policies, incident investigation procedures, and cooperation with legal authorities. Legal issues also must be taken into careful consideration whenever an employee of the organization is investigated or monitored, or when disciplinary action is to be taken for inappropriate behavior.

3.13.14 PHYSICAL AND ENVIRONMENTAL FACTORS

The confidentiality, integrity and availability of information can be compromised through unauthorized physical access and damage or destruction to physical components. The level of security surrounding any IT hardware and software, or any physical information assets such as documents or other media, should depend on the criticality of the systems, sensitivity of the information that can be accessed, the significance of applications processed, the cost of the equipment and the availability of backup equipment. A wide range of physical security controls, such as electronic locks, motion detectors, cameras, steel wire caging and radio-frequency tracking devices, are available to the information security manager to implement physical security.

Exhibit 3.11—PDCA Methodology

The PDCA Methodology is an iterative process model

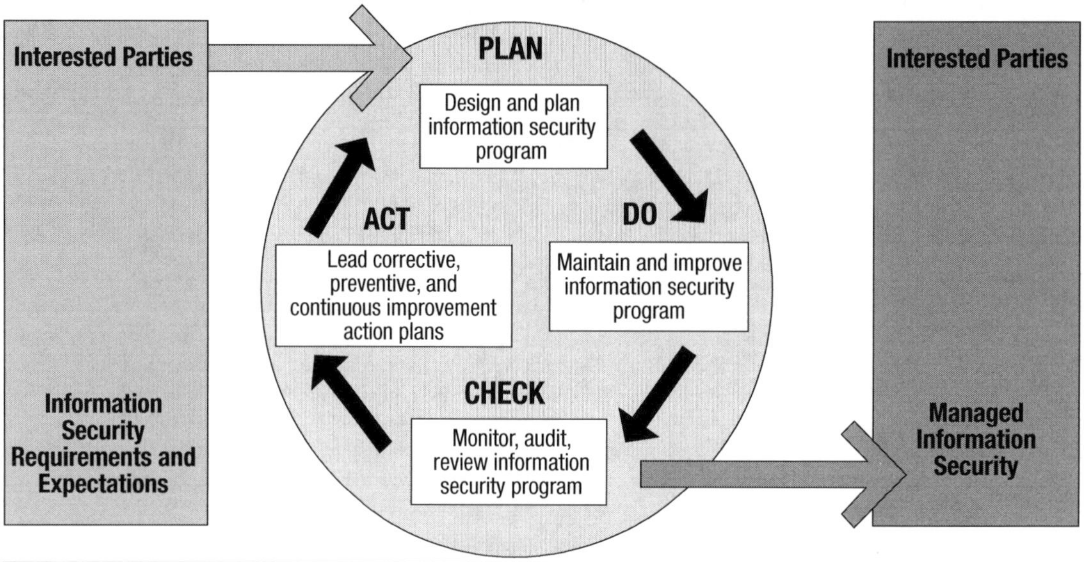

PLAN	Design, plan and initiate the information security program. These activities include creating a strategy, socialization concepts, creating policies, goals, objectives and practices as necessary to manage risk.
DO	Execute and control the information security strategy including the integration into organizational practices.
CHECK	Facilitate semiannual audits to determine conformance to the statement of applicability and identify opportunities for improvement. Wherever appropriate, develop and integrate performance matrices which support information security program goals and objectives.
ACT	Upon the discovery of nonconformities and/or opportunities, create and track corrective, preventive and continuous improvement action plans. Present findings from internal/external audit and risk assessments to the Management Review Committee for decisions regarding the acceptance, rejection, or transfer of risk and the commitment of resources and capital to facilitate subsequent efforts.

Exhibit 3.12—Strategic Objectives, CSFs, KPIs, Key Actions

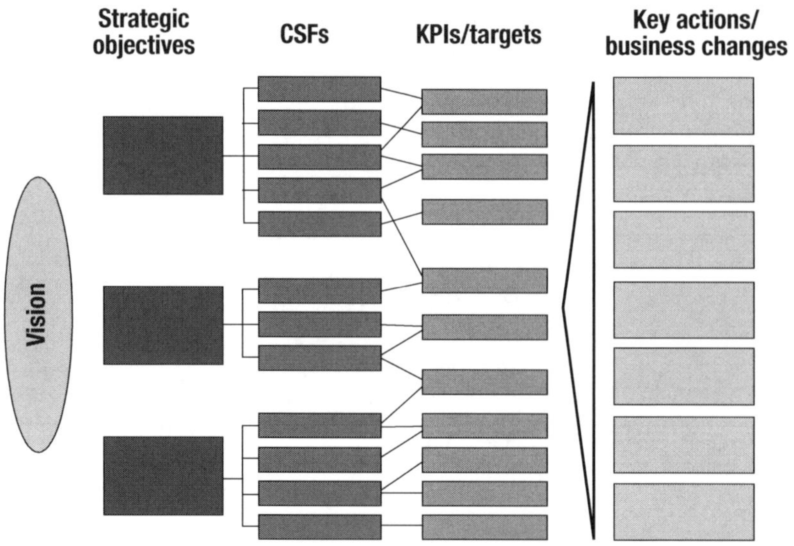

Physical security policies and standards must be established in addition to control processes. Physical control of access to computing resources should be applied based on the sensitivity of information accessed, processed and stored there. Access should be provided on an as-needed basis.

Location within facilities and environmental factors are also concerns. Locating critical systems in areas with unstable environments or in proximity to water pipes or other potential hazards should be avoided. Computing environments should incorporate systems to monitor and control environmental factors such as temperature, humidity and electrical power quality.

Personal computers are often used in less-secure user areas and may require special consideration to ensure adequate levels of security. If a workstation has a particularly sensitive function or is required to store sensitive information, isolating it may be desirable. Other physical workstation controls can include physically securing the device to prevent theft, locking the chassis to prevent tampering, removal or disabling external device interfaces (e.g., universal serial bus [USB], serial ports), and enforcement of local area network (LAN) based storage to minimize sensitive data on workstation disks.

Laptops and portable devices also require special consideration, particularly given the significant risk of theft or loss. The information security manager should consider the use of whole disk encryption to protect sensitive information in the event of loss.

Security of electronic and print media should also be protected. Disclosure of sensitive information on paper, microfilm, tape, CD-ROM or other physical media is as great a risk to the organization as an online compromise and must be stored in secure locations. The transport and storage of backup tapes, if not encrypted, can also present significant risk, particularly when stored offsite. The information security manager should also consider a clean desk policy to prevent unauthorized access to sensitive information in less-secure office areas.

Geographic concerns also need to be considered, particularly where organizational facilities and disaster recovery sites are involved. Regions with a risk of earthquakes, hurricanes, flooding or other natural disasters should be avoided when selecting facility sites. Proximity to facilities that present special risk (e.g., nuclear power plants, chemical production facilities, airports) should be considered. Finally, primary processing facilities, disaster recovery sites and offsite data storage facilities should be located far enough from one another to ensure that a disaster event does not impact more than one site.

3.13.15 ETHICS

Many organizations have implemented ethics training to provide guidance on what the organization considers legal and appropriate behavior. This approach is most common when individuals are required to engage in activities of a particularly sensitive nature such as monitoring user activities, penetration testing, and access to sensitive personal data. Information security personnel must be sensitive to potential conflicts of interest or activities that may be perceived in a manner detrimental to the organization.

The code of ethics should be reviewed and acknowledged by each employee involved in information security management and other applicable duties. The signed acceptance of the code should be kept as a part of employee records.

3.13.16 CULTURE AND REGIONAL VARIANCES

The information security manager should be aware of differences in perceptions, customs and appropriate behavior across different regions and cultures and that what is viewed as reasonable in one culture may not be acceptable in another. The information security manager needs to identify the audience and those who will be affected by the information security activities.

In addition, laws in different countries restrict certain sharing of personal information. The information security manager needs to be aware of these complications and work to develop an information security program that meets the individual needs of the organization.

Policies, controls and procedures should be developed and implemented with respect to these differences. Elements that might be culturally offensive to others must be avoided, particularly if alternate elements are available that meet control requirements. If in doubt, the information security manager should work with the legal and HR department to develop appropriate strategies for addressing differences across the regions and cultures represented within the organization to identify potential conflicts and work toward solutions.

3.13.17 LOGISTICS

The information security manager must address logistical issues effectively, particularly given the significant amount of interaction with other business units and individuals that is required by an effective information security program. Some of the logistic issues that the information security manager needs to be able to manage include:

- Cross-organizational strategic planning and execution
- Project and task management
- Coordination of committee meetings and activities
- Developing schedules of regularly performed procedures
- Resource prioritization and workload management
- Coordination of security resources and activities with larger projects and operations

Existing corporate resources, such as online scheduling and resource management systems, can assist with these concerns. In addition, the information security manager should develop logistics management skills either through training, self-study or mentoring.

3.14 SECURITY PROGRAM SERVICES AND OPERATIONAL ACTIVITIES

The typical information security program has a number of operational responsibilities in addition to providing various security related services. While the nature of these operations and services vary considerably between different organizations, the following section describes those most typically found in larger organizations.

3.14.1 INFORMATION SECURITY LIAISON RESPONSIBILITIES

In addition to the roles discussed in the forgoing section, it is essential for an effective information security manager to maintain ongoing relationships with a number of other groups and departments in the organization. These other organizational functions will have a great deal of impact on the ability of the information security manager to be effective in implementing and managing the security program. While the names of these departments may vary, most organizations will have the majority of these functions.

While the information security program will achieve greater success by integrating assurance activities with the following departments to the extent possible, effective integration with IT is essential. Integration with IT is covered in greater detail in section 3.14.11.

Physical/Corporate Security

Most organizations will have a corporate security department charged with physical security responsibilities. These departments are typically managed by individuals from law enforcement and often will have limited exposure to information security. Nevertheless, physical security issues invariably impact information security and it is essential that a close working relationship exists with this department.

IT Audit

IT or internal audit is generally charged with providing assurance of policy compliance and identifying risk. Often, especially in the absence of complete policies and standards, these auditors will have findings on information security based on what they consider good or acceptable practices. Depending on the expertise of the auditors, these findings may or may not agree with the information security manager's perspective, and this underscores the necessity for complete governance documentation. Since internal audit activities invariably impact the information security program, it is essential for the information security manager to develop and maintain a good working relationship with internal audit. A good relationship with internal audit can also provide considerable support for achieving information security objectives.

Information Technology Unit

As the hands-on implementers and operators of information processing systems, an organization's information technology unit has a critical role in information security program development and management. It is important for the information security manager to develop a strong working relationship with the information technology unit and strive to foster an environment of rapport, trust and communication. This can be a challenge since IT often perceives security as an impediment to their efforts.

IT often has conflicting requirements to ensure that policies and standards are met at the same time that performance and efficiency requirements are being addressed. This conflict between safety and performance can result in sacrificing security to meet operational objectives.

Typically, security requirements encompass implementation of control mechanisms in the network, systems and application environments as well as ensuring that technology operations address security requirements. This can be a challenging task for the information technology unit since they must fulfill security needs while also addressing issues such as functionality, accessibility, performance, capacity and scalability. The information security manager should work with the information technology unit to determine solutions that both fulfill security requirements and still meet performance requirements.

In addition to configuring security within the actual technical environment, many organizations utilize the information technology unit to design, deploy, and operate security systems such as firewalls, identity management systems and encryption technologies (e.g., VPNs, secure sockets layer [SSL] accelerators).

The separation of operational responsibilities between the information security department and the information technology unit is often based on the impact that a particular security system has on the production technology environment. While failure of a passive control such as an NIDS is unlikely to create a systemwide outage, the failure of an in-line system such as a firewall could cause the Internet or critical business partner connections to go down.

Business Unit Managers

It is important for the information security manager to engage business unit management when developing the information security program, and to continue to develop those relationships in ongoing security management activities. The business unit manager's responsibility for front-line business operations is ensuring that business operations meet security requirements as well as identifying and escalating security incidents and other risk concerns. It is essential that the information security manager ensures that business unit managers recognize and engage their responsibilities in ensuring secure day-to-day operational security. Business unit managers should be members of the information security steering committee, and the information security manager should establish close ties with managers of business units predisposed to information-related risk (e.g., call centers, support desks).

In addition to daily operational business units, most organizations have business units responsible for the development of new products or services targeted at internal users, an external marketplace or both. It is important that the information security manager engages in the development process for any products or services related to the organization's information resources, which includes virtually any such initiative. The product development business unit should utilize an established baseline of standing security requirements (e.g., authentication controls, activity logging) for any new development project and work with the information security manager to develop additional controls to safeguard against application-specific risk. Early involvement in the product development cycle and standard baseline information security requirements helps the information security manager ensure that resources and time are allocated for effective controls implementation. If the information security group has a security architecture team, this is an appropriate area for their involvement.

Human Resources

The HR department within most organizations has significant information security responsibilities with regards to employee policy distribution, education and enforcement. The information security manager should work with HR leadership to establish the best means to administer employee education on, and in agreement with, computer resource usage policies and procedures.

The information security manager must ensure that the HR and legal departments are intimately involved in any action involving monitoring of an employee's actions or suspected abuse of computing resources. Because of the legal implications involved with personnel actions in most localities, this cooperation is crucial. The information security manager should establish procedures and escalation as part of the incident management procedures so that all involved parties understand their roles and responsibilities and are prepared for immediate action when an event does occur. A senior representative of the HR department should be assigned to the information security steering committee.

Legal Department

Information security issues are frequently related to compliance, liability, corporate responsibility and due diligence. In most organizations, all of these areas are the domain of the legal department. The information security manager should liaise with a representative of the legal department, who should also be on the security steering committee. By ensuring that the legal department has ongoing awareness of information security issues and acting with their consensus, the information security manager can help protect the organization from legal liability.

Employees

Employees serve as the first line of defense in the security of information. It is essential that appropriate security training on relevant policies, standards and applicable procedures is provided periodically or as needed. Testing should be used to confirm understanding and signed acknowledgement of the training should be kept with personnel records.

Once trained, it is the responsibility of all employees to follow policies, standards and procedures. Employees should be trained to report potential threats and incidents as well as offer suggestions for improvement to the information security program, based on their day-to-day involvement with the program.

Procurement

Most organizations will employ a formal procurement process that can have consequences for information security in terms of product acquisitions. It is important that the information security manager has visibility into the process and input into acquisition practices. Mature organizations will have an approved equipment list that has been evaluated for policy and standards compliance to manage and minimize vulnerabilities introduced as a result of new equipment acquisitions. In the absence of such a process, it is important for the information security manager to be advised of proposed acquisitions and provided the opportunity to determine what risk may be introduced as a result.

Compliance

As a consequence of the increasingly complex legal and regulatory landscape that organizations must navigate, many organizations have implemented a compliance office which may be an independent department or a part of the legal department. Since there may need to be policy, standards and procedural recognition of applicable legal and regulatory requirements, it is necessary for the information security manager to establish a working relationship with the compliance office.

Privacy

Privacy regulations have become increasingly common and more restrictive in many parts of the world. In response, many organizations have instituted a privacy office or a privacy officer. In some cases, this is a part of the compliance office or it may be a separate function. In any event, privacy requirements in some jurisdictions are vigorously enforced and compliance must be a major focus of information security. To ensure requirements are met, the information security manager must maintain coordination with the privacy office to avoid sanctions that have grown increasingly severe.

Training

Many larger organizations have a separate training and education department. The information security manager should have contact with this function for assistance in providing security awareness training and education in needed security skills.

Quality Assurance

Quality assurance must include acceptable levels of security-related controls. Understanding the QA process and ensuring that it includes testing of security-related aspects is an important consideration for information security. The information security manager should maintain a relationship with the QA department in order to ensure that risk is addressed as a standard part of the process.

Insurance

Most organizations maintain various insurance policies such as business interruption coverage that has relevance for information security activities insofar as incident response, business continuity and disaster recovery. It is incumbent on the information security manager to understand the kinds and extent of insurance the organization has in order to include it in risk management and recovery planning.

Third Party Management

Third party management includes outsourced functions and services. Some services may be under the direct control of information security such as outsourced IDS monitoring but most are likely managed by other departments. It is incumbent on the information security manager to understand what functions or services are provided by external parties and to understand the associated risk. Managing risk to acceptable levels can pose a challenge and may require a variety of preventive, detective and compensatory controls.

Project Management Office

The information security organization should maintain a strong relationship with any PMOs within the enterprise. It is important that the information security manager or representatives have an awareness of all projects, particularly IT projects, across the organization. Maintaining a relationship with not only business and IT groups, but also with any organizational PMOs, provides another layer of protection that no projects will be completed without at least being reviewed by the information security team for potential risk or required security measures.

3.14.2 CROSS-ORGANIZATIONAL RESPONSIBILITIES

The information security manager is directly responsible for many critical aspects of the information security program. It is important to be aware that there can be separation of duty issues if the same manager is responsible for overlapping aspects of policy, implementation and monitoring. While in smaller organizations it may be difficult to achieve an optimal level of separation, the information security manager must be aware of the risk presented and endeavor to provide compensating controls to the extent feasible. It also generally falls to the information security manager to provide assurance that these areas of responsibility are appropriately assigned across senior managers within the organization to avoid possible conflicts of interest (see **exhibit 3.13**).

Exhibit 3.13—Information Security Roles and Responsibilities

Role	Associated Information Security Process Responsibility	Sample Key Performance Indicator
Executive management	Security strategy oversight and alignment	Organizational responsibility for executing all security program elements is assigned.
Business risk management	IT risk assessment	Prioritized list of IT risks to be addressed is maintained and periodically updated.
Department management	Security requirements sign-off and acceptance testing	Security features to be incorporated into application are formally approved.
	Access authorization	Individuals or groups to have access to data are formally approved.
Legal advisor to executive management	Information protection counsel	Information protection policies are consistent with applicable laws and regulations, formally approved, and those affected are aware of them.
IT operations management	Security monitoring	Security incidents are identified before they cause damage.
	Incident response	Appropriate responses to security incidents are embedded in operational procedures.
	Crisis management	Recovery procedures are periodically and successfully tested.
	Site inventory	All purchased computing devices are accounted for and correlate with a business purpose.
Quality manager	Security review participation	Security-policy-compliant systems are configured.
	Security requirements capture	Business requirements for confidentiality, integrity, and availability are documented.
	Application security design	Technical implementation plans for meeting business process security requirements are established.
	Change control	Secure archival, retrieval and compilation plans of organization-maintained source code and product customizations are established.
	Security upgrade management	Ensure testing and application of security software fixes
Purchasing	Security requirements capture	Formal requirements for security in all requests for product information and proposals are established.
	Contract requirements	Business requirements for confidentiality, integrity and availability in information service provider and technology maintenance contracts are established.

As each phase of a security program is developed, executive management, managers with risk management responsibilities and department management should be made aware of the content of the information security program so that activities can be coordinated and specific areas of responsibility confirmed. Information security programs typically cross numerous department boundaries; therefore, fostering awareness and getting consensus early in the process is important. The role of the information security manager itself often becomes that of "ambassador" for the information security program.

The information security manager must work closely with management to ensure that those in various departments and business units understand, accept and have the resources necessary to implement their part of the information security program.

A strategy for incorporating the ideas and support of the organization's management can include the formation of an information security steering committee or an executive security council as discussed in chapter 1. These committees can also serve to coordinate activities among groups involved in other aspects of risk management and assurance functions, thereby helping to achieve assurance process integration. The members of these committees are selected for their ability to support the information security program and to represent the organization's interests. They will help ensure that information security requirements are identified and organizationwide support is achieved. The steering committee will typically own the information security strategy and is commonly designated as the group empowered to approve changes to policy or standards.

An important part of program development is the review, modification and/or creation of policies required to establish a framework for the development of organizational standards with respect to security. Documents that reflect the decisions set by security strategy should be clearly set forth in the form of policy mandates. Policy documents identify management intent and direction and form the basis for the organizational standards that comply with management and regulatory objectives for data confidentiality, integrity and availability.

Next, awareness is required to educate those affected by security policy on their roles and responsibilities. Awareness activities should be conducted by all business areas that are responsible for maintaining processes in conformance with security policy. These need not always be formal training classes, but should fit in with the culture of the organization and management's preferred method of communication. Depending on the organization, executives may fulfill their awareness responsibilities with a variety of alternatives, including videos, memos, e-mail reminders, posters, seminars and formal security training classes. A variety of parallel approaches are most likely to be effective.

Considerations for implementation of security measures are rarely limited to a few central security architecture projects or major initiatives that the information security manager personally manages. Security implementation responsibilities might range from protecting a personal laptop from theft to configuring telecommunications equipment. For this reason, most managers and executives will have some aspect of security implementation within their scope of responsibilities.

Those with monitoring responsibility should establish processes that create and maintain alerts, logs and metrics on system security configuration and activity. The information security manager is often the point of escalation for security issues identified by monitoring processes as well as the primary contact for incidents that may require investigation. Security monitoring must be implemented in a manner that ensures separation of duties. This is important because in order to be effective, regulatory functions such as security, audit and quality control cannot be under the control of those being monitored. This is also true for compliance and enforcement.

Finally, compliance will include any activity that tracks security issues and helps ensure that resources facilitate the resolution of security issues. Executives with responsibility for security compliance should establish programs that track trends in metrics, and investigate anomalies as well as known security violations. A strong compliance program will further ensure that conclusions of these investigations are reported to others in executive management in such a way that risk is well understood. These reports should, if possible, be accompanied by recommendations for changes necessary to achieve satisfactory compliance levels. The information security manager will often be an SME within this process or may lead the program.

3.14.3 INCIDENT RESPONSE

Incident response is typically an operational requirement for the information security department. The incident response capability discussed in chapter 4 provides first responders to the inevitable security incidents experienced in virtually all organizations. The objective is to quickly identify and contain incidents to prevent significant interruptions to business activities; restore affected services and determine root causes so that improvements can be implemented to prevent recurrence.

3.14.4 SECURITY REVIEWS AND AUDITS

During the development and management of an information security program, it is essential for the manager to have a consistent standardized approach to assessing and evaluating the state of various aspects of the program. Using a consistent approach will provide trend information over time and can serve as a metric for improvements to various aspects of the information security program. This can be accomplished using a security review process similar to an audit.

As with standard approaches to auditing, security reviews will have:
- An objective
- A scope
- Constraints
- An approach
- A result

A review objective is a statement of what is to be determined in the course of a review. For example, the objective of a review may be to determine whether an Internet banking application can be exploited to gain access to internal systems.

Objective defines what the information security manager wants to get out of the review. Usually, it is to determine whether or not a given systems environment meets some security standard. In the above example, the review objective is that of a typical external penetration study, i.e., to make sure that users of web services cannot exploit system vulnerabilities to gain access to the systems that host those services.

Scope refers to the mapping of the objective to the aspect that is to be reviewed. Thus, the review objective dictates scope. For example, the review objective in the previous example dictates that the scope includes the Internet access points of the application and all of the underlying technology that enables that access. If the scope is hard to describe, the review objective should be clarified to ensure that the result of the review will be well defined and thus actionable.

Constraint is the situation within which a reviewer operates that may impact aspects of conducting the review. It may or may not hinder his/her ability to review the entire scope and complete the review objective. In the example, a constraint may be a prohibition on accessing the application during business hours.

An information security manager must evaluate his/her ability to fulfill the objective of the review in the context of constraints.

Approach is a set of activities that cover the scope in a way that meets the objective of the review, given the constraints. There are usually alternative sets of activities that can cover the scope and objective. The idea is to identify the set that is hampered by the fewest constraints. In the previous example, a constraint could be that the information security manager would not be given the credentials necessary to create a web session as an authorized user of the application under review. Recall that the objective requires the reviewer to provide a determination on whether application Internet access can be exploited to gain access to internal systems. To meet this objective, the review must have "application Internet access" as part of the scope. An information security manager, in this situation, should identify the lack of authorization for application access as a constraint and find some other way to achieve the same objective. One approach could be to set up the system in a test environment where access authorization is not an issue.

Result is an assessment of whether the review objective was met. It is an answer to the question, "Is this secure?" If it is not possible to answer the question with any level of assurance, the review should be declared incomplete. This would occur in the case above if the application access required for covering the scope was not achieved.

Exhibit 3.14 depicts some common types of reviews and the objective, scope, constraint and approach results of each.

In the course of performing security reviews, an information security manager can gather data not only about policy and process at various levels of the organization, but also data about specific control weaknesses that may put information at risk. This data can be used to help prioritize program development efforts.

Audits

Like security reviews, audits have objectives, scope, constraints, approach and results. The professional practice of information systems audit is based on an approach in which auditors identify, evaluate, test and assess the effectiveness of controls. Effectiveness is judged on the basis of whether controls meet a given set of control objectives such as compliance with policies and standards. In performing an audit, an audit team assembles documentation 1) that maps controls to control objectives, 2) states what they did to test those controls and 3) links those test results to their final assessment. This documentation, called "work papers," may or may not be delivered with the final report.

Exhibit 3.14—Security Review Alternatives

Review Type	Control Self-assessment	Security Architecture or Design Review	Security Spot Check
Objective	To establish that the controls implemented to maintain security are sufficient to do so in the systems environment required to effect security	To establish that a system is capable of securing data, and identify configuration parameters	To decide whether a given security process is working
Scope	The systems environment housing the data that an organization is charged to secure documents on system security mechanisms	Network and operating system placement diagrams, as well as detailed technical design	Process description, system security parameters of system directly supporting the process
Constraint	• Unknowns or lack of expertise in security mechanisms in third-party products • Time • The possible bias of participants who are also responsible for system maintenance	• Unknowns or lack of expertise in security mechanisms in third-party products • Time	Reliance on assumptions with respect to systems interfaces and supporting systems (e.g., data feeds, network, OS)
Approach	• Identify risks, exposures and potential perpetrators. • Evaluate ability of controls to protect, detect or recover from exploits.	Compare settable parameters of all system components to known secure configurations and/or security policy.	• Review all system security procedures and settings. • Identify expected user community. • Evaluate whether expected controls are in place.
Result	List of control weaknesses	List of issues to address, iterative process	Yes or no

When an information security program has established policies and standards, an audit is extremely useful in identifying whether those policies and standards have been fully implemented. However, when an information security program is under development, those policies and standards may not yet be set. In this situation, an information security manager may select an externally published standard and engage an audit team to determine the extent to which the organization is in compliance. An external standard or framework, such as COBIT or ISO/IEC 27001, 27002, provides a structure for control objectives that enables an audit team to organize their examination of existing controls. The work papers from such an audit can often be more useful than the final report. The value in the analysis of existing controls and their mapping to a set of external standards is most useful if the set of external standards closely resembles those that the information security manager intends to put in place as part of the information security program.

Different standards focus on different aspects of controls. The following examples start at the most comprehensive in scope, followed by those whose scope narrows into specific technology domains:
- COBIT lists control objectives, and for each control objective, a list of control practices.
- The Standard of Good Practice for Information Security catalogs information security management practices and lists corresponding requirements for resources and responsibilities.
- ISO/IEC 27001 and 27002 lists control practices in the domain of IT security, followed by an appendix listing security-related control objectives and, for each control objective, a list of control practices.

Auditors

Audits are an essential part of any security program and it is essential for the information security manager to develop a good working relationship with the auditors. While it is not unusual for auditors to be viewed in a negative light by IT and information security staff and others in the organization, effective information security managers understand that audits are both an essential assurance process and a critical and influential ally in achieving good security governance and compliance. They can be instrumental in implementing security standards by providing feedback to senior management through audit findings that can serve to influence the "tone at the top" and create high-level support for security activities. Involving auditors in overall security management can be a powerful tool for improving an organization's security culture.

The information security program must integrate with internal and/or external auditing activities. Some audits are compulsory, as those required to establish compliance with some regulatory standard. Others are voluntary, as when an independent auditor makes an attestation to compliance with an industry standard.

The information security manager should coordinate with organizational audit coordinators to ensure that time and resources are allocated to address audit activities. Procedures should be established in advance for scheduling, observation of employee activities, and provision of configuration data from technical systems.

In some cases, a deficiency identified by an auditor may not be applicable to the information security manager's specific organization. If concerns are identified during an audit, the information security manager should work with the auditors to agree on associated risk, mitigating factors and satisfactory control objectives. With this information in hand, the information security manager may craft one or more potential solutions that fit the organization's operational, financial and technical environment. Any combination of mitigating or compensating controls that enforce the agreed-on control objectives should satisfy the issue.

Audit findings provide strong, independent feedback for the steering committee and/or management to utilize in assessing the effectiveness of the information security program.

3.14.5 MANAGEMENT OF SECURITY TECHNOLOGY

The typical security program employs a number of technologies that require effective management and operation if optimal value delivery and resource management is to be achieved. While a newer organization may utilize contemporary technologies, more mature organizations are often constrained by the legacy architecture of the organization. However, these constraints can be minimized because there is usually a wide range of technology alternatives available to address a given control objective. Features that are available within a given set of legacy devices will differ depending on the technical footprint of the organization. Yet, through decades of development of alternative preventive, detective and recovery controls, solid tools and techniques to achieve information security goals are usually available.

Technology Competencies

Although information security spans technical, operational and managerial domains, a significant portion of the actual implementation of information security program is likely to be technical. The information security manager and security department personnel are often considered the primary source for technical security subject matter expertise within an organization. It is important that the information security manager works with the security steering committee, senior management and other security stakeholders to establish the scope and approach of technical skills delivery in which the information security manager and security organization are expected to engage.

Organizations differ with regard to the technical scope of the information security department. At one end of the spectrum is the approach in which the information security program operates at the corporate level and primarily sets security standards at a high level. Another common approach is to utilize the information security personnel as technical SMEs, providing consultative services to system administrators and other information technologists who, in turn, implement technical controls and security systems. At the other end of the spectrum are organizations in which the information security group takes ownership of specific pieces of infrastructure, such as access control systems, intrusion detection and monitoring systems, and compliance and vulnerability assessment automation tools.

For the individual information security manager, the technology skills that are needed vary based on his/her operational role, the organizational structure and technical scope. More technically-focused information security managers, e.g., those in system administration roles, will obviously need more in-depth technical knowledge and should make training and educational arrangements accordingly. Information security managers operating at a higher level, e.g., as a CISO, may not require hands-on technical skills, but should be knowledgeable about the information technologies implemented by their organization from architectural and data flow perspectives. Regardless of operating level, all information systems managers should have a thorough understanding of security architecture, control implementation principles, and commonly implemented security processes and mechanisms. This understanding should include the strengths, limitations, opportunities and risk of common security controls in addition to the financial and operational implications of deployment.

It is important for information security managers to take into consideration all levels of technology as they plan for skills development, both personally and for the overall information security program. While traditional perimeter, network and systems security are still crucial to a strong technical security environment, information security managers are increasingly expected to address issues of application security (e.g., coding practices, functional application security mechanisms, data access control mechanisms), database security (e.g., data access control methods, application integration, content protection) and, increasingly, elements of physical, operational and environmental security issues. Highly integrated and tightly coupled systems, such as enterprise resource planning (ERP) implementations, can create an additional challenge; the entire system has to be considered from a security perspective because compromise of one element can disrupt the operations of the entire enterprise. It is important that the information security manager understand and plan for the potential "domino effect" of cascading risk.

3.14.6 DUE DILIGENCE

Due diligence is essentially a term related to the notion of the "standard of due care." It is the idea that there are steps that should be taken by a reasonable person of similar competency in similar circumstances. In the case of an information security manager, this means ensuring that the basic components of a reasonable security program are in place. Some of these components might include:

- Senior management support
- Comprehensive policies, standards and procedures
- Appropriate security education, training and awareness throughout the organization
- Periodic risk assessments
- Effective backup and recovery processes
- Implementation of adequate security controls
- Effective monitoring and metrics of the security program
- Effective compliance efforts
- Tested business continuity and disaster recovery plans
- Protection data (in transit and at rest)

It is also important to take into consideration that the third parties the organization uses and relies on can present risk to information resources. Due diligence regarding placement of appropriate security language into contracts and agreements with third parties, as well as subsequent third party performance against security requirements, must also take place. Because contracts are usually prepared by the legal department, it is important to collaborate to ensure language needed to provide adequate levels of protection is included. An organization's information must be protected as specified by its policies, regardless of its location.

Periodic reviews of the infrastructure, preferably by an independent knowledgeable third party, may be a reasonable requirement as well. The infrastructure is a critical component that the organization relies on to meet its business objectives. Risk must be identified and reasonably addressed.

Managing and Controlling Access to Information Resources

The information security manager must be aware of the various standards for managing and controlling access to information resources. It should also be considered that, depending on the organization's industry sector, specific regulatory bodies may have defined standards that must be addressed.

Increasingly, information security management is defined by the need to satisfy regulatory requirements. While these regulatory requirements establish specific protection measures that need to be in place, they are not comprehensive in their approach. More broadly defined guidance for information security program development and administration is provided by various standards bodies and by not-for-profit organizations whose members are involved with governance, assurance or information protection. The following list, while not meant to be complete, identifies some of the more widely recognized organizations that provide reference materials of interest to information security managers:

- American Institute of Certified Public Accountants (AICPA)
- Canadian Institute of Chartered Accountants (CICA)
- The Committee of Sponsoring Organisations of the Treadway Commission (COSO)
- German Federal Office for Information Security (BSI)
- International Organization for Standardization (ISO)
- ISACA
- International Information Systems Security Certification Consortium, Inc. $(ISC)^2$
- IT Governance Institute
- National Fire Protection Association (NFPA)
- Organisation for Economic Co-operation and Development (OECD)
- US Federal Energy Regulatory Commission (FERC)
- US Federal Financial Institution Examination Council (FFIEC)
- US National Institute of Standards and Technology (NIST)
- US Office of the Comptroller of the Currency (OCC)

Vulnerability Reporting Sources

Today, threats to information systems are global. Requirements for rapid time to market and other issues have resulted in a variety of vulnerabilities in both hardware and software. These vulnerabilities are constantly being discovered and reported by a variety of organizations. It is an important part of any effective security program to maintain daily monitoring of relevant entities that publish this information, which includes CERT, MITRE's Common Vulnerabilities and Exposures database, Security Focus'

BUGTRAQ mailing list, SANS Institute, OEMS and numerous software vendors. Having the most current possible vulnerability information makes it possible for the information security manager to respond promptly with appropriate mitigation, compensation or elimination action to address newly discovered software and system flaws.

3.14.7 COMPLIANCE MONITORING AND ENFORCEMENT

Compliance enforcement processes must be considered during program development to ensure subsequent effectiveness and manageability once the program is implemented. Compliance enforcement refers to any activity within the information security program that is designed to ensure compliance with the organization's security policies, standards and procedures.

Compliance, especially with procedural controls, may pose one of the major challenges for managing a security program, and must be given careful attention when designing controls during program development. Ease of monitoring and enforcement will often be the most important factors in control selection. Complex control processes that are not readily enforceable, or that are difficult to monitor for compliance are generally of little value and may pose a considerable risk themselves.

Enforcement procedures should be designed to assume that control activities are in place in support of control objectives. These procedures are an added layer of control that checks that the procedures established by management are actually followed. For example, in a password reset procedure, an enforcement procedure may consist of a supervisor listening to randomly selected help desk calls and listing any help desk staff who neglect to ask a user for a security identification code prior to resetting the passwords. The enforcement procedure would be to use the list to first, warn and, then, discipline help desk staff who did not follow the password reset procedure.

Policy Compliance

Policies form the basis for all accountability with respect to security responsibilities throughout the organization. Policies must be comprehensive enough to cover all situations in which information is handled, yet flexible enough to allow different processes and procedures to evolve for different technologies and still be in compliance. Except in very small organizations, an information security manager will not have direct control over SDLC activities of all information systems in the organization. Consequently, it is necessary to designate formal security roles that establish which department head is responsible for putting processes in place that maintain security policy compliance and meet the appropriate standards for a given set of information systems.

It is the responsibility of the information security manager to ensure that, in the assignment process, there are no "orphan" systems or systems without policy-compliance owners. It is also the responsibility of the information security manager to provide oversight and ensure that policy compliance processes are properly designed. An information security manager can accomplish this oversight via a combination of security review, metrics gathering and reporting processes.

Information security management literature often refers to a policy exception process. This is a method by which business units or departments can review policy and decide not to follow it based on a various factors. Several justifications can exist for policy exceptions. It may be based on a risk/reward decision where the benefit of not following the policy justifies the risk. It may be financially or technically infeasible to comply with specific policies or standards. Such trade-offs should be considered in the policy development process when possible to minimize the need for subsequent exceptions. As part of the program development, a formal waiver process should be implemented to manage the life cycle of these exceptions to ensure that they are periodically reviewed and when possible closed.

Standards Compliance

Standards provide the boundaries of options for systems, processes, and actions that will still comply with policy. The standards must be designed to ensure that all systems of the same type within the same security domain are configured and operated in the same way based on criticality and sensitivity of the resources. These will allow platform administration procedures to be developed using standards documents as reference to ensure that policy compliance is maintained. Standards also provide economy of scale; the configuration mapping to policy needs to be done only once for each security domain, and technology and process engineering efforts are reused for systems of the same type.

As much as possible, compliance with standards should be automated to ensure that system configurations do not, through intentional or unintentional activity, deviate from policy compliance. However, as policy should state only management intent, direction and expectations to allow flexibility for different standards to develop and provide many options to comply with policy, exceptions to standards should always be reviewed to see if they deviate from the intent of policy. It may also be that a business situation justifies a deviation from existing standards but, nevertheless, may be determined to fall within the intent of policy.

Resolution of Noncompliance Issues

Noncompliance issues usually result in risk to the organization, so it is important to develop specific processes to deal with these issues in an effective and timely manner. Depending on how significant the risk is, various approaches can be taken to address it. If a particular noncompliance event is a serious risk, then resolution needs to occur quickly. The security manager benefits from a method of determining criticality and then having a risk-based response process.

Typically, a timetable is developed to document each noncompliance item and responsibility for addressing it is assigned and recorded. Regular follow-up is important to ensure that the noncompliance issue and other variances are satisfactorily addressed in a timely manner. Noncompliance issues and other variances can be identified through a number of different mechanisms including:

- Normal monitoring
- Audit reports
- Security reviews
- Vulnerability scans
- Due diligence work

Compliance Enforcement

Compliance enforcement is an ongoing set of activities that endeavor to ensure fulfillment of information security and other standards. Audits are a snapshot of compliance in time; compliance enforcement is an ongoing process that helps reduce risk as well as ensure positive audit opinions.
Compliance enforcement responsibilities are usually shared across organizational units, and the results are commonly shared with executive management and the board's audit or compliance committees. The legal and internal audit departments often have responsibility for assessment of business strategies and operations, respectively. The information security unit is often responsible for implementing independent evaluation of technical standards, preferably utilizing automated tools. In larger organizations and heavily regulated industries, an independent compliance organization may be established to handle and coordinate these activities.

The information security program itself is also a target of compliance evaluation and performance. The information security manager should be prepared to work closely with compliance and/or internal audit personnel to demonstrate compliance of the information security program with pertinent standards and regulations. As with a formal audit, issues identified should be defined in terms of risk, mitigating factors and acceptable control objectives. Depending on the magnitude of the issue, the information security manager may address the concern independently or may collaborate with executive management and/or the security steering committee to affect a solution.

3.14.8 ASSESSMENT OF RISK AND IMPACT

A primary operational responsibility for the information security manager and the fundamental purpose of the program is to manage risk to acceptable levels. The objective is to minimize disruptions to organizational activities balanced against an acceptable cost. A number of ongoing tasks are required to achieve this objective. While the topic is covered in depth in chapter 2, the following section summarizes the ongoing activities required in a typical information security program.

Vulnerability Assessment

The organization's information systems environment should be constantly monitored for development of vulnerabilities that could threaten confidentiality, integrity or availability. In addition to searching for known vulnerabilities, this process should also detect unexpected changes to technical systems. This process is best implemented using automated, network- or host-based tools that deliver concise reports to information security management, including immediate alerts if severe vulnerabilities are noted.

In addition to regularly scheduled scanning, the information security manager should ensure that scheduled changes to existing technical environments (e.g., installation of a new service, hosts being relocated, firewall upgrades) do not inadvertently create architectural vulnerabilities. Human error and unexpected system behaviors can cause the enforcement policies of technical security control mechanisms to change, creating opportunities for exploit and organizational information systems impact.

Threat Assessment

Technical and behavioral threats to an organization evolve as a result of several internal and external factors. Implementation of new technologies, granting broader network and application access to partners and customers, and the ever-growing capabilities of attackers warrant periodic reassessment of the threat landscape that an organization faces. This activity is particularly important for organizations too small or resource-constrained to adopt a continuous assessment approach to threat management.

The information security manager should perform this analysis at least annually by evaluating changes in the technical and operating environments of the organization, particularly where external entities are granted access to organizational resources. Internal factors such as new business units, new or upgraded technologies, changes to products and services, and changes in roles and responsibilities all represent areas where new threats may emerge.

As new threats are identified and prioritized in terms of impact, the information security manager must evaluate the ability of existing controls to mitigate risk associated with new threats. In some cases, the technical security architecture may need to be modified, a threat-specific countermeasure may be deployed, or a compensating mechanism or process may be implemented until mitigating controls are developed. Threat sources can include technical/cyber, human, facility-based, natural and environmental, and pandemic events.

Numerous threats exist that may impact security program development efforts and objectives. The range of possible threats must be evaluated to determine if they are viable, the likelihood they will materialize, their potential magnitude and the potential impact to systems or operations, to personnel or facilities.

Risk and Business Impact Assessment

Risk assessment is a process used to identify, analyze and evaluate risk, the probability of compromise and its potential impact on an organization in quantitative or qualitative terms. A business impact analysis (BIA) is an exercise that determines the impact of losing the availability of any resource to an organization, establishes the escalation of that loss over time, identifies the minimum resources needed to recover, and prioritizes the recovery of processes and supporting systems. While a BIA is often thought of in the context of business continuity and disaster recovery, whether potential impact is determined by this process or another process is not important. Impact is the bottom line of risk and the range of severity in terms of the organization must be determined to provide the information needed and to guide risk management activities. Obviously, even high risk with little or no impact is not of concern.

In developing KGIs necessary for achieving control objectives, an information security manager must make choices about the impact that achieving control objectives will have on the confidentiality, integrity and availability of information resources. However, even if a risk management process has been developed as described in chapter 2, mapping control benefits and impact onto key business goals for security is not necessarily a straightforward process. The relationship of developing and implementing security controls to achieving organizational objectives will usually require a well-developed business case (see section 3.13.6) to achieve the level of buy-in needed to achieve success.

The business case must address the fact that regardless of the level of control, residual risk will always remain, and it must address the fact that risk may aggregate into levels that are unacceptable. In other words, even with effective controls apparently managing risk to acceptable levels, the aggregate effect of a number of types of acceptable risk may not be acceptable and may pose a serious threat to the organization.

Numerous studies show that disasters are typically not a single calamitous occurrence but rather the result of a number of small incidents and mistakes that collectively contribute to a major event. The lesson is that while, individually, types of residual risks might be low, collectively, they can be disastrous.

As threats and vulnerabilities emerge, the information security manager must take steps to analyze and communicate the impact on the organization's risk posture. This process is critical to ensuring that security stakeholders are aware of potential business impact and may take actions to mitigate risk accordingly. This entire process should be completed annually, or the information security manager may choose to take an incremental approach, analyzing portions of the enterprise monthly or quarterly.

The information security manager should also recognize that asset values and risk characteristics can also change, requiring reanalysis of risk posture. For example, a company can grow increasingly revenue-dependent on an application that was initially not considered to be critical to the enterprise. Asset value can increase or decrease over time in terms of real monetary value or strategic value to the organization. In addition, the risk associated with an asset can grow. A small database may initially only contain a few dozen personal information records; the same database five years later might contain 10,000, representing a much higher impact if compromised.

Periodic risk assessment results should be provided to the steering committee and/or senior management for use in guiding information security priorities and activities. The information security manager should manage this process and guide the committee through making appropriate decisions based on risk analysis results. More details on risk assessment are in chapter 2, section 2.10 Risk Assessment.

Resource Dependency Assessment

If resource or other constraints do not allow for comprehensive business impact assessments, a business dependency assessment may be a less costly alternative to provide the basis for allocating available resources based on the criticality of the function. A business dependency assessment reviews the resources that are used to conduct business, i.e., servers, databases etc. Depending on the criticality of the business function, the assets and resources needed for that function are identified, providing a basis for prioritizing protection efforts. In other words, a business dependency assessment is based on determining the various applications, and infrastructure used by a business for day-to-day operations. While it should also identify interdependencies and other resources needed to perform the required functions, it does not capture the financial and operational impact of potential disruptions and does not replace a BIA.

3.14.9 OUTSOURCING AND SERVICE PROVIDERS

The two types of outsourcing that an information security manager may be required to deal with include third-party providers of security services and outsourced IT or business processes that must be integrated into the overall information security program. Most of the security requirements are similar, depending on criticality and sensitivity of assets and extent of services involved, but the ownership will be different, i.e., the information security manager will normally be the process owner for outsourced security services whereas other outsourced services are typically the responsibility of the process owner. The risk posed by third parties connected to the organization's internal network can be substantial and must be carefully considered.

Economics are the primary driver of outsourcing. As a result, early engagement by the information security manager is essential to ensure that those making the decisions do not unduly compromise security for the sake of cost. A variety of risk as a result of outsourcing must be considered. A few of the common issues experienced include:
- Loss of essential skills
- Lack of visibility into security processes
- New access and other control risk
- Viability of the third-party vendor
- Complexity of incident management
- Cultural and ethical differences
- Unanticipated costs and service inadequacies

The adequacy of the vendor's controls needs to be audited and monitored through the life of the contract to ensure that security measures are not marginalized over time as a result of cost pressures. This can be accomplished by independent audit or onsite visits at the third-party facility to ensure that the proper controls are in place.

The existence and enforcement of privacy laws to protect a company's data also needs to be considered. This is particularly true as individuals in different cultures may treat information differently (i.e., what your firm considers sensitive information may not be considered sensitive in another country).

While technical controls for the IT component of outsourced processes may seem obvious, arrangements that deal with business processes require that training, awareness, manual controls and monitoring be put in place to ensure that employees in third-party facilities are treating the processes and physical and electronic data to acceptable standards.

Third-party security providers are a viable strategy that the information security manager can use to assist in the design and operation of the organization's information security program or to provide other IT services. One of the main concerns for security is the extent that the third-party provider can and will meet the organization's security policies and standards on an ongoing, verifiable basis. Since a 2006 study by PGP-Vontu shows that about one-fifth of all security breaches are caused by external service providers, this is a critical issue to consider.

The maturity of a vendor's security program and their assurance of compliance with the contracting organization's security policies, should be high on the list of decision factors when selecting a vendor. This proposal and evaluation process is often used when evaluating whether to use an organization's autonomous division or subsidiary for certain security services.

The issues requiring attention are broad and must be enumerated based on the scope, type and risk associated with the initiative. Some common issues to be considered include:
- Isolation of external party access to resources
- Integrity and authenticity of data and transactions
- Protection against malicious code or content
- Privacy/confidentiality agreements and procedures
- Security standards for transacting systems
- Data transmission confidentiality
- Identity and access management of the third party
- Incident contact and escalation procedures

Outsourcing Contracts

The fundamental purpose of contracts is to ensure that the parties to the contract are aware of their responsibilities and rights within the relationship and to provide the means to address disagreements once the contract is in force. Within that framework, there are certain provisions for security and information protection with which the information security manager should be familiar. While the information security manager may or may not be included in contract reviews, the following issues should be addressed with the legal department to ensure an understanding of security requirements that should be covered.

The most common security provision addresses confidentiality or nondisclosure. Each party will typically agree that any confidential or sensitive information it receives as part of the agreement, or about the other party, will be kept confidential through appropriate measures. This may also include the requirement to return or destroy any proprietary or confidential information upon termination of the contract or after a specified period of time. The information security manager will need to determine the specific level of destruction that will be required (e.g., document shredding, disk and tape degaussing, etc.).

The contract may also stipulate that either or both parties must maintain appropriate security controls to ensure that the systems and information used under the agreement are protected by appropriate means. The contract should explicitly define what is meant by "appropriate" and the requirements for demonstrating the effectiveness of those protections. Whether it is through the production of a current third-party audit report (e.g., SSAE16) or compliance with an industry-standard security framework (such as ISO/IEC 27001:2013, 27002:2013 or COBIT 5), the standards by which the program will be judged should be defined in the contract. Additionally, if the contracted product or service includes network connectivity between the buyer and the seller, the contract should address responsibility for the security of that connection. Specifications as to the level of security expected (e.g., firewalls, intrusion detection/prevention, monitoring, etc.) or specific technical requirements should be addressed as well.

A contract with a service provider that has been determined (through a risk assessment) to be beyond a predetermined risk threshold should always contain a right-to-audit provision. This would typically be for any third party that accesses, stores or processes any sensitive or otherwise business-critical information, that provides mission-critical services, or that connects to the network infrastructure of the contracting organization. The right-to-audit clause should allow the customer, upon proper notice, the right to conduct an in-depth audit of the third party's security program and processes to verify the effectiveness of all associated controls. If this provision is included in the contract, the parameters for an audit, such as compliance criteria, notification, scope limitations, frequency, and responsibility for incurred costs, should be explicit.

In the event that a security breach happens at either party, the contract should specify the roles each party will play in the investigation and remediation process. Issues such as which party will lead the investigation, notification procedures and responsibilities (including law enforcement or regulatory notifications), and timing must all be addressed. During an active incident, pressure is high, tempers can flair, and fairness and equity are much harder to come by, so addressing these issues in the contract is easier and can be done much more equitably. Finally, the contract should contain indemnity clauses that ensure compensation for impacts caused by the service provider.

The contract between the parties is a key element of establishing an appropriate level of control of the organization information processing facilities (IPFs). Depending on the business processes and operational needs of the organization requiring the services of a third-party vendor outsourcing, contracts may need to deal with a number of complex security questions. Points that should be covered in the contract (from the perspective of the information security manager) can include, but are not limited to:
- Detailed specification of outsourced service
- Specific security requirements
- Restrictions on copying information and securing assets
- Prohibiting access without explicit authorization and maintaining a list of individuals who have access
- Right to audit and/or inspect
- Indemnity clauses to mitigate impacts caused by the service provider
- Requirements for incident response and BCPs
- Level of service quality
- Integrity and confidentiality of business assets
- Nondisclosure agreements to be signed by the employees/agents of third parties
- Protection of intellectual property
- Ownership of information
- Requirement that applicable legal and regulatory requirements are met
- Ensure return and/or destruction of information/assets at the end of the contract
- Duration up to which the confidentiality shall be maintained
- Employees or agents of the third party required to comply with security policies of the organization
- Escalation processes

Third-party Access

Third-party access to the information security manager's organization's processing facilities under any circumstances should be controlled based on risk assessment and must be clearly defined in a service level agreement (SLA). Access should be granted based on the principles of "least privilege," "need-to-know" and "need-to-do." It is important to bear in mind that third parties may have a different set of ethics and business culture that must be considered in terms of risk.

Providing access to third parties must be based on clearly defined methods of access, access rights and level of functionality, and access must require the approval of the asset owner.

Access usage should be fully logged and reviewed by the security manager on a regular basis. The review frequency should be decided based on factors such as:
- Criticality of information to which access rights are given
- Criticality of privileges given
- Period of contract

Anomalies noticed should be immediately reported to the asset owner and escalations done wherever required. The access rights given to third parties should be removed immediately after the contract expires.

Network and information access should not be granted to a third party until the contract has been signed. The contract should define the terms for access, control requirements and make allowances for assurance that appropriate safeguards are in place and remain for the duration of the contract.

3.14.10 CLOUD COMPUTING

Cloud computing is the evolution of a concept that dates back to the 1960s when the notion of "utility computing" was first suggested. The idea was based on the notion of an electric utility or telephone service provider. The intervening decades have provided the technological basis to make the concept practical through increased bandwidth and near universal Internet availability.

While current offerings vary considerably in scope and capabilities, there is growing consensus on the definition. The US National Institute of Science and Technology (NIST) defines cloud computing as "a model for enabling convenient, on-demand network access to a shared pool of configurable computing resources (e.g., networks, servers, storage, applications, and services) that can be rapidly provisioned and released with minimal management effort or service provider interaction."

The defining characteristic of cloud computing is that processing and data are somewhere in "the cloud" as opposed to being in a specific known location. Cloud computing can be provided as either public hosting for a number of unrelated entities or private hosting, in the case of large organizations wanting greater control over the environment. The topic is covered extensively in the ISACA white paper "Cloud Computing: Business Benefits With Security, Governance and Assurance Perspectives" dated 28 October 2009 (*www.isaca.org/Knowledge-Center/Research/ResearchDeliverables/Pages/Cloud-Computing-Business-Benefits-With-Security-Governance-and-Assurance-Perspective.aspx*).

As with any emerging technology, cloud computing offers the possibility of high reward in terms of containment of costs and features such as agility and provisioning speed. However, as a "new" initiative, it can also bring the potential for high risk. Cloud computing introduces a level of abstraction between the physical infrastructure and the owner of the information being stored and processed. Traditionally, the data owner has had direct or indirect control of the physical environment affecting his/her data. In the cloud, this is no longer the case. Due to this abstraction, there is already a widespread demand for greater transparency and a robust assurance approach of the cloud computing supplier's security and control environment.

Once it has been determined that cloud services are a plausible solution for an enterprise, it is important to identify the business objectives and risk that accompany the cloud. This will assist enterprises in determining what types of data should be trusted to the cloud, as well as which applications and services might deliver the greatest benefit.

Advantages

Proponents of cloud computing cite a number of benefits including:
- **Cost**—Computing becomes an operational cost rather than a capital expenditure since the cloud provider typically supplies the infrastructure as needed. In addition, far less in-house expertise is needed reducing technical staffing requirements. Centralization of computing resources by the provider results in economies of scale that reduce costs as well.
- **Scalability**—Provides on-demand provisioning of resources reducing or eliminating requirements for capacity planning.
- **Reliability**—Large cloud computing providers have redundant sites which may address most business continuity and disaster recovery issues.
- **Performance**—Improved performance as result of provider continuous and consistent monitoring.
- **Agility**—Improved agility as a result of rapid re-provisioning of infrastructure resources as needed.

The cloud model can be thought of as being composed of three service models (**exhibit 3.15**) and four deployment models (**exhibit 3.16**). Overall risk and benefits will differ per model, and it is important to note that when considering different types of service and deployment models, enterprises should consider the risk that accompanies them.

Security Considerations

For organizations where security is not considered a high priority, security provided by a reputable cloud provider may be a significant improvement. However, for the information security manager, security considerations are an issue that must be carefully assessed. The loss of control over sensitive data must be considered. The location of data may be an issue as well. In organizations that store and transmit data across state or national boundaries, the information security manager may need to consider myriad laws, regulations and compliance requirements of various jurisdictions. Requirements for handling incidents may vary from one jurisdiction to another, e.g., breach notification laws. Availability of audit logs may also be limited or nonexistent from the cloud provider, and the actual level of security may be difficult to ascertain.

Exhibit 3.15—Cloud Computing Service Models

Service Model	Definition	To Be Considered
Infrastructure as a Service (IaaS)	Capability to provision processing, storage, networks and other fundamental computing resources, offering the customer the ability to deploy and run arbitrary software, which can include operating systems and applications. IaaS puts these IT operations into the hands of a third party.	Options to minimize the impact if the cloud provider has a service interruption
Platform as a Service (PaaS)	Capability to deploy onto the cloud infrastructure customer-created or acquired applications created using programming languages and tools supported by the provider	• Availability • Confidentiality • Privacy and legal liability in the event of a security breach (as databases housing sensitive information will now be hosted offsite) • Data ownership • Concerns around e-discovery
Software as a Service (SaaS)	Capability to use the provider's applications running on cloud infrastructure. The applications are accessible from various client devices through a thin client interface such as a web browser (e.g., web-based e-mail).	• Who owns the applications? • Where do the applications reside?

ISACA, *Cloud Computing: Business Benefits With Security, Governance and Assurance Perspectives*, USA, 2009, fig. 1, p. 5, *www.isaca.org/Knowledge-Center/Research/ResearchDeliverables/Pages/Cloud-Computing-Business-Benefits-With-Security-Governance-and-Assurance-Perspective.aspx*

Exhibit 3.16—Cloud Computing Deployment Models

Deployment Model	Description of Cloud Infrastructure	To Be Considered
Private cloud	• Operated solely for an organization • May be managed by the organization or a third party • May exist on-premise or off-premise	• Cloud services with minimum risk • May not provide the scalability and agility of public cloud services
Community cloud	• Shared by several organizations • Supports a specific community that has shared mission or interest. • May be managed by the organizations or a third party • May reside on-premise or off-premise	• Same as private cloud, plus: • Data may be stored with the data of competitors.
Public cloud	• Made available to the general public or a large industry group • Owned by an organization selling cloud services	• Same as community cloud, plus: • Data may be stored in unknown locations and may not be easily retrievable.
Hybrid cloud	A composition of two or more clouds (private, community or public) that remain unique entities but are bound together by standardized or proprietary technology that enables data and application portability (e.g., cloud bursting for load balancing between clouds)	• Aggregate risk of merging different deployment models • Classification and labeling of data will be beneficial to the security manager to ensure that data are assigned to the correct cloud type.

ISACA, *Cloud Computing: Business Benefits With Security, Governance and Assurance Perspectives*, USA, 2009, fig. 2, p. 5, *www.isaca.org/Knowledge-Center/Research/ResearchDeliverables/Pages/Cloud-Computing-Business-Benefits-With-Security-Governance-and-Assurance-Perspective.aspx*

As with IT outsourcing, failure of the provider or the interconnections can leave the organization without computing resources and although the occurrence is unlikely, it should be considered as well.

3.14.11 INTEGRATION WITH IT PROCESSES

It is important to provide defined interfaces between the organization's security-related functions and ensure that there are clear channels of communication. For example, information security risk management activities should integrate well with the activities of an organizational risk manager to ensure continuity and efficiency of efforts. Business continuity planning is often a separate function that must integrate with incident response activities of the information security department.

Integration

The information security manager must ensure that the information security program interfaces effectively with other organizational assurance functions. These interfaces are often bidirectional; that is, security-related information is received from these departments and, in turn, information security should provide relevant information to these units. The assurance functions provide input, requirements and feedback to the information security program which, in turn, provides metrics and evaluation data for assurance evaluation. It is important that the organization's assurance units are part of the steering committee to ensure broader awareness of security issues. Broad ongoing involvement also helps prevent the unintegrated silo effect created when assurance functions operate in isolation.

To be effective, information security must be pervasive, affecting every aspect of the enterprise. As a consequence, the range of responsibilities for effective security management is broad and, in most cases, exceeds the direct authority of the information security manager. As a result, the information security manager is most likely to be successful by operating in a collaborative fashion, being a good communicator and developing a persuasive business case for security initiatives.

System Life Cycle Processes

Achieving effective information systems security is easiest when risk and protection considerations are included in the SDLC. Since these activities are usually the responsibility of other departments but have significant impact on security, it is essential that the information security manager develops approaches to integrating these functions with information security activities.

The various SDLC processes generally consist of:
- Establishing requirements
- Feasibility
- Architecture and design
- Proof of concept
- Full development
- Integration testing
- Quality and acceptance testing
- Deployment
- Maintenance
- System end-of-life

Change Management

Virtually all organizations employ some form of change management process. In some cases, it may not be formal. Security needs to be an integral part of the change management process because new vulnerabilities may be introduced as a result of system or process changes. The information security manager should identify all change management processes used by the organization for notification that changes are taking place that may impact security. The information security manager needs to implement processes to ensure that security implications are considered as a standard practice. As changes are made to systems and processes over time, there is often a tendency for existing security controls to become less effective. Therefore, it is critical for the security manager to ensure that security controls and countermeasures are updated regularly and are adapted to organizational changes.

Decentralized organizations can pose a special challenge to the security manager. Often, many of these divisions are highly autonomous, and it may be difficult to monitor and ensure compliance with corporate policies and procedures. It is important to understand the organizational structure during development and implementation of a security program to develop an effective approach.

To maintain accountability for policy compliance through frequent change, an information security program must identify where in the organization IT changes are initiated, funded and deployed. The information security manager must negotiate hooks into these processes so that those in job functions that specify, purchase and deploy new systems have policy compliance as part of their job functions. This gives the information security manager time to identify vulnerabilities in new systems, identify new threats presented by the systems and assist the implementation team in developing policy-compliant standards that can be handed to a release manager as preapproved for production deployment. This is a key element of integrating the security program into the day-to-day work of the organization, thereby ensuring its long-term adoption.

Configuration Management

Studies have shown that improper configuration is the major cause of security breaches to information systems. As a consequence, it is essential that strong procedural and/or technical controls are implemented to effectively manage this risk.

The typical underlying causes for failure to properly configure systems are either a lack of clear standards or procedures for configuration or shorthanded staff failing to properly follow procedures or taking improper shortcuts. The information security manager must ensure that proper documentation exists on correct configuration and that IT staff has sufficient training in performing these activities. If proper documentation does exist, the workload of those responsible should be examined to see if time is the issue or if some form of compliance enforcement is required to ensure correct configuration.

Release Management

When properly implemented, release management reduces the chances of operational failure by ensuring adequate testing has been performed and required conditions exist for the correct operation of new software or systems. It is incumbent on the information security manager to ensure that proper standards and procedures exist so that products are not deployed to production prematurely. In addition, it is important to provide adequate monitoring and oversight to ensure that procedures are followed to avoid unexpected production system failure.

3.15 CONTROLS AND COUNTERMEASURES

In designing the information security program, an information security manager's focus will need to shift between general and application-level controls. In the course of performing security reviews, step-by-step breakdown of interrelated activity is segmented into control activities that cover the infrastructure and operating environment (general controls), and security measures over and above those it takes to run business software securely (application controls).

General controls are control activities that support the entire organization in a centralized fashion. Because infrastructure is often shared among different departments in the same organization, the term "general controls" is often used to describe all controls over infrastructure. These are typically control activities in support of an operating system, network and facility security. They may include centralized user administration procedures as well. In determining how to protect data critical to a business process, it is important that an information security manager be able to rely on the existence of adequate general controls. These are the foundation on which specific control activities supporting business information resource protection rest. Where specific, noncentralized business information processing is supported by technology, the control activities over that technology are often referred to as application-level controls.

In most organizations, general controls and application controls are managed by different groups. With the help of management, the information security manager must identify and define the roles and responsibilities with respect to security for these and all other groups. Thus, a vital element of any information security program is a roles and responsibilities matrix such as the one in **exhibit 1.3** in chapter 1. The information security manager must design the information security program to facilitate both enterprisewide and department-level control activities that build on organizational responsibility for general and application controls. In addition, the information security manager must take into account organizational interfaces with third-party service providers, regulators and other entities with which the organization must cooperate to meet its data protection, privacy, confidentiality, and compliance requirements.

Within the constraints of the roles and responsibilities assignments, an information security manager may be able to identify key technology elements that facilitate the achievement of control objectives. The information security manager must enlist key stakeholders with roles and responsibilities that correspond to the control objectives in the design of corresponding technology controls. The information security manager must ensure that these technology goals are seen to contribute to stakeholders' objectives to ensure that they are adopted and supported. Ideally, the technology must be easy to use, reusable and promote operational efficiency. These technology elements, when supported centrally and used by various parts of the organization, become part of the information security architecture, and the processes and procedures that support them become general controls. They essentially become the building blocks on which the entire program rests. Because technology itself is inadequate to implement general controls, adoption of security architecture and the ability to formally delegate responsibility for operating within it according to policy are key criteria in selecting technical elements of an information security road map.

However, it is rare that enterprisewide or general controls are sufficient to guard against all situations where data could be at risk due to unauthorized access and use. As information must be distributed through the organization to be used by business processes, the information security manager should be aware of those situations in which general controls are inadequate to protect against information misuse. Therefore, a critical element of the information security road map is the SDLC process that provides for security reviews at early stages of projects to determine whether application-level controls are necessary. This allows an information security manager to identify and recommend methods to implement access or other controls at the application level. The choice of security "touchpoints" to be established to ensure access controls are effective as illustrated in **exhibit 3.17**. These touchpoints are where controls as well as monitoring or metrics may be needed.

A major part of security management is the design, implementation, monitoring, testing and maintenance of controls. Controls are defined as the policies, procedures, practices, technologies and organizational structures designed to provide reasonable assurance that business objectives are achieved and that undesirable events are prevented or detected and corrected.

Controls are essentially any regulatory process, whether physical, technical or procedural. The choice of controls can be based on a number of considerations, including their effectiveness, cost or restrictions to business activities, and what the optimal form of control is.

Controls are one of the primary methods of managing information security risk and a major responsibility of information security management. It is important to understand that controls for physical elements, such as administrative processes and procedures, are just as critical as controls applied to technology. **Most security failures can ultimately be attributed to failures of management, and it must be remembered that management problems typically do not have technical solutions.** Inevitably, people and physical processes exist at each end of technical processes and constitute the greatest risk to information security. As a consequence, the information security manager must be careful not to place excessive focus and reliance on technology.

The information security manager must be aware that standards or procedures which are too restrictive or prevent the organization from meeting its business objectives are likely to circumvented. The objective is to balance the need for controls with the requirements of the business. Therefore, the information security manager must have a good business perspective, understand the risk to the organization's

Exhibit 3.17—Touchpoints for Security Tollgates

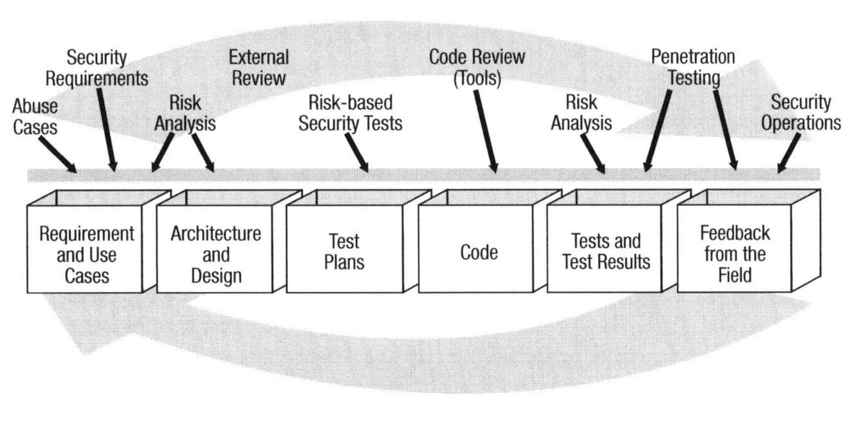

Source: Adapted by permission from the book "*Software Security: Building Security In*" by Gary McGraw (Addison-Wesley, USA, 2006) *www.swsec.com*

information resources, interpret the information security policies and implement security controls that consider all of these aspects. An important perspective is to use the approach that is least restrictive and disruptive to the business that nevertheless meets the criteria for acceptable risk. The trade-offs between the greatest security and least impact on business activities is the fine line that the effective information security manager must strive to achieve.

Information security controls must be developed for both IT- and non-IT-related information processes. This includes secure marking, handling, transport and storage requirements for physical information as well as considerations for handling and preventing social engineering. Environmental controls must also be taken into account, so that otherwise secure systems are not subject to simply being stolen, as has occurred in some well-publicized cases.
There are a number of standards and guides available for information security management that should be familiar to the information security manager. Two of the most accepted references for information security are COBIT and ISO/IEC ISO 27001 and 27002. Numerous other sources of guidance are available such as the US Federal Information Processing Standards (FIPS) Publication 200, NIST 800-53 and the Standard of Good Practice for Information Security published by the Information Security Forum.

3.15.1 CONTROL CATEGORIES

- **Preventive**—Preventive controls inhibit attempts to violate security policy and include such controls as access control enforcement, encryption and authentication.
- **Detective**—Detective controls warn of violations or attempted violations of security policy and include such controls as audit trails, intrusion detection methods and checksums.
- **Corrective**—Corrective controls remediate vulnerabilities. Backup restore procedures are a corrective measure as they enable a system to be recovered if harm is so extensive that processing cannot continue without recourse to corrective measures.
- **Compensatory**—Compensatory controls compensate for increased risk by adding control steps that mitigate a risk; for example, adding a challenge response component to weak access controls can compensate for the deficiency.
- **Deterrent**—Deterrent controls provide warnings that can deter potential compromise; for example, warning banners on login screens or offering rewards for the arrest of hackers. Controls and their effect are shown in **exhibit 3.18**.

Note that compensatory and corrective controls are often combined.

3.15.2 CONTROL DESIGN CONSIDERATIONS

Based on today's regulatory environment, controls and countermeasures are most efficiently approached based on a top-down, risk-based approach. After applying industry-recognized frameworks such as COBIT or ISO 27001, design of the controls implemented must include measurability. Effectiveness of controls cannot be evaluated unless they can be tested and measured. Further, confidence levels and sampling sizes for testing the effectiveness of these controls closely mirror audit and regulatory compliance objectives. For example, when designing a control for daily IDS log reviews in an organization subject to the US Sarbanes-Oxley Act, it is logical to create a process that shows daily affirmative reviews (review notes, sign-offs, approvals, etc.) and that sampling sizes follow US Sarbanes-Oxley testing requirements based on the frequency of the control, i.e., 25 samples for daily, 10 for weekly, and three for monthly.

Controls as Strategy Implementation Resources

Controls are any regulatory device, system, procedure or process that regulates or controls some operational activity. Security controls need to address people, technology and processes. Controls should necessarily result in corrective or preventive action, paving the way for improvement of information security measures.

> For example, access control is a preventive control that prevents unauthorized access that may result in harm to systems. Intrusion detection is a detective control because it enables unauthorized access to be detected. Backup and restoration procedures are a corrective control that enables a system to be recovered if harm is so extensive that data are lost or irreparably damaged. Sometimes compensatory controls are mentioned, which are similar to corrective controls but compensate for some security weakness.

Exhibit 3.18—Control Types and Effect

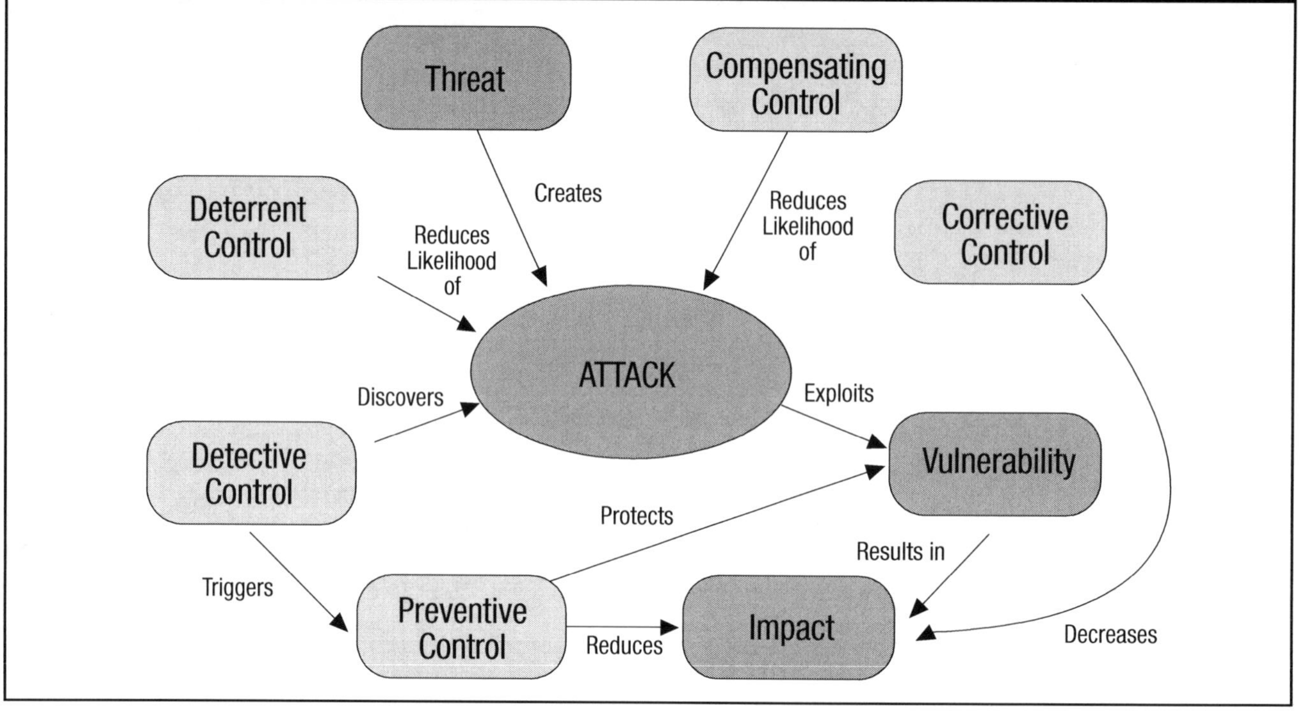

Security products often provide various combinations of these different types of controls. A typical control is a firewall, which is a product that filters network traffic to limit what protocols (or ports) can be used to enter or exit an internal network, as well as what address or address range is allowed as a source and destination. This is a preventive control because it prevents access to specific network ports, protocols or destinations not specifically allowed. The same firewall may have more advanced features that allow it to examine inbound network traffic for malware and sends alerts to an operations center if they pass through the device. This is a detective control. The firewall may also have a feature that allows operations to divert incoming traffic to a backup site (although this would typically be accomplished by changes at the Internet router) if, upon responding to the virus alert, they find that a virus has reduced the capacity at the primary site. That is a recovery, or corrective, control because it allows the systems to resume normal operations. The proxy service that runs on the firewall may be capable of displaying a warning banner as a deterrent control against unauthorized access.

Note that the deterrent, preventive, detective or corrective (or compensatory) control features of the firewall are fully describable, technically, without using the word "firewall." The point is that the information security manager must recognize the security value of technology product features independently of the label given to a product by the product vendor. It is the features and how they are used that enable control points to be established, not the choice of product or its name.

As far as possible, controls should be automated so that it is technically infeasible to bypass them. (See section 3.15.6, Countermeasures.) Some common control practices that make it hard for users to bypass controls are mechanisms that embody these principles:

- **(Logical) Access control**—Users of information should be identified, authenticated and authorized prior to accessing information. There are a variety of ways to implement access control. Most access control models fall into one of two types: mandatory access control (MAC) or discretionary access control (DAC). MAC refers to a means of restricting access to data based on security requirements for information contained in the data and the corresponding security clearance of users. MAC is typically used for military applications where, for example, a secret clearance is required to access data classified as "secret." There is generally also a second requirement of "need to know" for access authorization. DAC refers to means of restricting access to objects based on the identity of subjects and/or groups to which they belong. The controls are discretionary in the sense that rules may allow a subject with certain access permission to pass that permission on to another subject. The choice of appropriate access control mechanisms in a given situation depends on organizational requirements for data protection.
- **Secure failure**—This refers to a device designed to shut down and stop processing information whenever it detects a malfunction that may affect its access control mechanisms. Secure failure as a control policy must be carefully considered since it obviously affects availability. It may also pose an obvious hazard when electrically controlled physical access fails in a locked condition, preventing egress in the case of fire or other disaster.
- **Principle of least privilege**—This refers to a resource access design strategy that provides administrative capability to partition resource access so that those requiring fewer resources than others have the minimum system privileges that they require to accomplish their responsibilities.
- **Compartmentalize to minimize damage**—This refers to the capacity of system architecture to contain access to subsets of system resources by requiring a separate set of authorization controls per subset. For example, a system in

which administrative privileges are not granted when they are requested on certain network interfaces can be combined with network port restrictions to lock Internet users out of administrative functions.
- **Segregation of duties**—This refers to the ability of software to restrict a user from having two functions that are meant to provide supervisory or oversight features. For example, software should prevent a person who has the ability to print checks from being able to change the name of the check recipient before and after it is printed.
- **Transparency**—This refers to the ability of the average layperson to understand how system security is supposed to work so that all stakeholders can easily see what effect their activities have on systems security. Users, administrators, engineers and architects should be able to converse about system controls in a way that all can verify that they are working as expected. Transparency is often achieved by keeping the technology design as simple as possible to avoid confusion as to system functionality.
- **Trust**—This refers to a design strategy that includes the existence of a security mechanism whereby the identity of a user can be determined by its relationship to an "identity provider" which is "trusted" by a "relying party." The relying party has some mechanism for determining the authenticity of a connection from the identity provider and relies on that information to allow the identity provider to pass to it the identity of the user. A typical application is the use of a trusted third party in PKI architecture known as the certificate authority (CA), which attests to the identity of an entity by issuing a certificate.
- **Trust no one**—This refers to a design strategy that includes oversight controls as part of the information system design rather than designating trusted individuals to administer the system and expecting them to follow procedure or relying on subsequent audit to verify if they had. A typical application is the use of closed-circuit television (CCTV) to monitor activities.

3.15.3 CONTROL STRENGTH

Strength of controls can be measured by the type of control being evaluated (preventive, detective, manual, automated, etc.) and its quantitative and qualitative compliance testing results. As such, although an automated control is typically preferable to manual control, detailed analysis may reveal that a manual control is better. An automated control design may create alerts and generate automatic reports. However, careful evaluation of the process may determine that no evidence of review can be produced and subsequent response actions up to and including resolution cannot be measured. In this scenario, the control fails. On the other hand, if handwritten notes were recorded within IDS log reports on a daily basis with initials and dates, and the same notes contained analysis, action plans, ticket numbers and resolution, then the manual control is far more effective than the automated one. Of course, no conclusion can be reached as to the strength of the control until it has been adequately tested.

The strength of a control can be measured in terms of its inherent or design strength, and the likelihood of its effectiveness. An example of an inherently strong control is balancing the books to account for all cash and/or segregating accounting responsibilities among multiple employees. An example of an inherently strong control by design is requiring dual control to access sensitive areas or materials.

In order to demonstrate value and alignment with business objectives, risk mitigation must be tied to supported business functions. This ensures that information security and IT governance initiatives are inherently followed, and cost justification for the treatment process is readily available and self-explanatory.

3.15.4 CONTROL METHODS

Security controls encompass the use of technical and nontechnical methods. Technical controls are safeguards that are incorporated into computer hardware, software, or firmware (e.g., access control mechanisms, identification and authentication mechanisms, encryption methods, intrusion detection software). Nontechnical controls are management and operational controls such as security policies; operational procedures; and personnel, physical, and environmental security.

Controls, such as two-factor authentication required for high-security situations, can include both technical and manual processes, e.g., smart cards requiring a PIN.

3.15.5 CONTROL RECOMMENDATIONS

Elements of controls that should be considered when evaluating control strength include whether the controls are preventive or detective, manual or automated, and formal (documented in procedure manuals and evidence of their operation is maintained) or ad hoc. During this step of the process, controls that could mitigate or eliminate the identified risk (as appropriate to the organization's operations) are provided. The goal of the recommended controls is to reduce the level of risk to information resources to an acceptable level. The following factors should be considered in recommending controls and alternative solutions to minimize or eliminate identified risk:
- Effectiveness of recommended options
- Compatibility with other impacted systems, processes and controls
- Relevant legislation and regulation
- Organizational policy and standards
- Organizational structure and culture
- Operational impact
- Safety and reliability

The control recommendations are the results of the risk assessment and analysis process and provide input to the risk mitigation process. During the risk mitigation process the recommended procedural and technical security controls are evaluated, prioritized and implemented. To determine which ones are required and appropriate for a specific organization, a cost-benefit analysis should be conducted for the proposed controls to demonstrate that the costs of implementing the controls can be justified by the reduction in the level of risk. In addition, the operational impact (e.g., effect on system or personnel performance) and feasibility (e.g., technical requirements, user acceptance) of introducing the recommended options should be evaluated carefully during the risk mitigation process.

3.15.6 COUNTERMEASURES

In addition to the general safeguarding that standard controls provide, the information security manager may occasionally require a control against a specific threat. Such a control is termed a "countermeasure." A countermeasure can be considered a targeted control. Countermeasures often provide specific protection, making them less efficient than broader, more general safeguards—although not necessarily less cost-effective depending on the original and residual annual loss expectancy (ALE) associated with the threat countered.

Countermeasures are controls that are put into place in response to a specific threat and/or vulnerability that is known to exist. They may be preventive, detective or corrective, or any combination of the three. Countermeasures are not recognized in ISO/IEC 27001:2013 and can simply be considered a form of targeted control.

Countermeasures deployed to narrowly address specific threats or vulnerabilities are often expensive, both operationally and financially, and can become a distraction from core security operations. Their deployment should commence only with clear justification, with due caution, and only when an existing or more general control cannot adequately mitigate the threat.

Countermeasures can be used just like any other control. But because they are in response to a specific threat or vulnerability, they are often applied as incremental enhancements to existing controls. For example, an organization that scans all e-mail to block incoming viruses may encounter a threat to its e-mail infrastructure due to an influx of spam. The organization may implement a countermeasure to the spam attacks by enhancing the virus scanner to block incoming mail from a list of known spammers. Countermeasures can be nontechnical as well, such as offering a reward for information leading to the arrest of hackers.

An information security program must be flexible enough to be able to implement a countermeasure with very little warning. Emergency changes may need to bypass standard change control processes, but they must be employed with caution and be thoroughly documented, and they must pass through the change management process, even if it is after the fact.

Countermeasures are frequently not technical in nature. A very common countermeasure is deployed in response to threats of impersonation. Where it has been reported that a social engineer has called an end user, posing as an administrator and asking the user for his/her passwords, a countermeasure may be in the form of awareness activity such as a broadcast to all end users directing them not to divulge their passwords to anyone, under any circumstances, and to immediately report such suspicious activity to security.

3.15.7 PHYSICAL AND ENVIRONMENTAL CONTROLS

When implementing an information security program, it is critical to understand that all efforts to protect information have as their foundation a strong physical barrier protecting the physical media on which the information resides. In many organizations, physical security is a service provided as part of facilities management. The physical security organization may set requirements on a building-by-building basis, and enforce these requirements using a combination of physical security technology measures and manual procedures. An information security manager should validate technology choices in support of physical security processes and must ensure that policies and standards are developed to ensure adequate physical security.

Physical and environmental controls are a specialized set of general controls on which all computing facilities as well as personnel depend. In addition, some technologies have features that allow physical mechanisms to override logical controls. For example, unauthorized physical access to technology devices may allow unauthorized access to information. Though the information security manager is often not responsible for physical access controls, it is important that roles and responsibilities with respect to these controls are assigned and that the information security manager has an escalation path to ensure that requirements are met. It is important to ensure that it is not possible for an unauthorized person to physically connect equipment to the network and that equipment and removable media (including documents and discarded items such as removable media) are protected from theft.

Methods to keep unauthorized individuals from gaining access to tangible information resources include identification badges and authentication devices such as smart cards or access controls based on biometrics, security cameras, security guards, fences, lighting, locks and sensors. A variety of intrusion sensors are available, including vibration sensors, motion detectors and many others.

Physical controls are also intended to prevent or mitigate damage to facilities and other tangible resources that might be caused by natural or technological events (e.g., backup power sources can sustain operations if a hurricane damages the power lines serving the facility or if the power grid fails). Environmental controls include air conditioning, water drainage, fire suppression and other measures designed to ensure that the facilities in which systems are stored is designed with the physical limitations of computer system operation as requirements. Without adequate environmental controls to prevent, detect and recover from physical damage to information systems, other general and application control activities could be rendered ineffective or useless.

In a large and geographically dispersed organization, an IT site operations manager may be assigned at each site to ensure that all equipment is inventoried and configured to policy-compliant standards. An information security manager may establish this role and responsibility as a resource to interface with local physical security organizations on behalf of the information security program.

3.15.8 CONTROL TECHNOLOGY CATEGORIES

When determining the types of control technologies that must be considered by the information security manager, it may be useful to consider operational authority and the types of controls available. Since the majority of technical controls will be the direct responsibility of the IT department, consideration must be given to how security will be maintained. Technologies will typically fall under one of three different categories in terms of the type of controls that are available: native, supplemental, and support control technologies. In some cases, operational authority may be split between IT and the security department.

Native Control Technologies

Native control technologies are out-of-the-box security features that are integrated with business information systems. For example, most web servers include functions providing authentication capabilities, access logging and SSL transport encryption. All of these controls would be considered native to the web server technology.

Although the policies and standards governing their use are established by the information security function, most native control technologies are generally configured and operated by IT. This is because native controls often directly impact production operations, and providing information security staff with configuration rights to core production systems often violates the separation of duty principal and can create risk by complicating change control processes and system ownership issues.

Native technology controls exist on all information technology devices including:
- Servers
- Databases
- Routers
- Switches

Supplemental Control Technologies

Supplemental control technologies are usually components that are added on to an information systems environment. Supplemental security technologies often provide some function that is not available from native components (e.g., network intrusion detection) or that is more appropriate to implement outside of primary business application systems for architectural or performance reasons (e.g., a single network firewall versus individual host-based network filtering).

Supplemental control technologies tend to be more specialized than native control technologies, and therefore they are often operated by security specialists. Even when these technical security specialists are resources of the information security group, security technical operations can benefit by leveraging the support of information technology units. In some cases, it may be appropriate to share responsibility for a particular supplemental control technology, particularly if it is deeply embedded in both the security and business application domains. Federated identity and access management technologies are a common example of a supplemental technology for which responsibilities are shared across the security and technology organization. Typical supplemental control technologies include:
- Federated identity management systems
- Single sign on (SSO)
- Intrusion prevention systems (IPS)
- Firewalls

Management Support Technologies

Management support technologies serve to automate a security-related procedure, provide management information processing, or otherwise increase management efficiency or capabilities. A few examples include security information management (SIM) tools, security event analysis systems and compliance monitoring scanners. These technologies are primarily used by the security organization, and they do not directly impact the production environment. For these reasons and to help enforce separation of duties, technologies that support security operations are commonly implemented and operated by the information security group in relative independence from the information technology department.

Security-related procedures can frequently be automated to increase the information security program's efficiency or capabilities. The use of these supporting technologies to increase resource productivity is an important strategy in developing an efficient and effective program. Some of the most common supporting technologies include:
- SIM tools
- Security information and event management (SIEM) systems
- Compliance monitoring and management tools
- Access management workflow systems
- Vulnerability scanning tools
- Security configuration monitoring tools
- Policy management and distribution systems

3.15.9 TECHNICAL CONTROL COMPONENTS AND ARCHITECTURE

Information security management includes dealing with a wide range of technical components. Generally, these technical mechanisms have been previously categorized as native control technologies, supplementary control technologies and management support technologies.

Analysis of Controls

Control and support technologies collectively form the technical security architecture. This construct can be applied to individual business applications, or the enterprise as a whole, with the objective of revealing how the interaction of individual technical components provide for overall enterprise or application security. This holistic view of technical component capabilities prevents a point-solution perspective that leads to poor overall security. Technical security architecture analysis should be coordinated closely with reviews and analysis of threat and risk factors. The information security manager must ensure that the components of the technical security architecture are aligned with the organization's risk and threat postures as well as business requirements. Provided that the technical architecture is in alignment with the higher levels of architecture, this alignment with business objectives should occur naturally.

When analyzing technical security architecture, the information security manager should use a clearly defined set of measurable criteria to enable tracking of performance metrics. A common approach to the development of metrics is to pose questions that need to be answered and then develop methods to provide answers. A few possible criteria for analyzing technical security architecture and components and developing suitable metrics and monitoring include:
- **Control placement**
  - Where are the controls located in the enterprise?
  - Are controls layered?
  - Is control redundancy needed?
  - Are controls on or near the perimeter efficient providers of broad access protection?

- Are there uncontrolled access channels to processing services or data? (Consider physical, network, system-level, application and message access vectors.)
- **Control effectiveness**
  - Are controls reliable?
  - Are they the minimum required?
  - Do they inhibit productivity?
  - Are they automated or manual?
  - Are key controls monitored? In real-time?
  - Are they easily circumvented?
- **Control efficiency**
  - How broadly do the controls protect the environment?
  - Are they specific to one resource or asset?
  - Can they and should they be more fully utilized?
  - Is any one control a single point of application failure?
  - Is any one control a single point of security failure?
  - Is there unnecessary redundancy in controls?
- **Control policy**
  - Do controls fail secure or fail open?
  - Do controls implement a restrictive policy (denial unless explicitly permitted) or a permissive policy (permission unless explicitly denied)?
  - Is the principal of least-needed functionality and access enforced?
  - Does the rationale for the control configuration align with policy, corporate expectations and other drivers?
- **Control implementation**
  - Is each control implemented in accordance with policies and standards?
  - Are controls self-protecting?
  - Will controls alert security personnel if they fail or detect an error condition?
  - Have controls been tested to verify that they implement the intended policy?
  - Are control activities logged, monitored and reviewed?
  - Do controls meet defined control objectives?
  - Are control objectives mapped to organizational goals?

Details of specific security technologies, technical control architecture and analysis of technical control requirements are an important component of information security program development, as well as ongoing management and administration. The information security manager should be well-versed in the technologies that are part of the technical security architecture and have access to technical specialists who will be responsible for installing, configuring and maintaining these technologies.

3.15.10 CONTROL TESTING AND MODIFICATION

Changes to the technical or operational environment can often modify the protective effect of controls or create new weaknesses that existing controls are not designed to mitigate. Periodic testing of controls should be implemented to ensure that mechanisms continually enforce policies and that procedural controls are being carried out consistently and effectively.

Changes to technical or operational controls must be made with caution. Changes to technical controls should be made under change control procedures and stakeholder approval. The information security manager should analyze the proposed control environment to determine if new or recurring vulnerabilities exist in the design and to ensure that the control is properly designed (i.e., self-protecting, contains a failure policy, can be monitored). Upon implementation, acceptance testing must be conducted to ensure that prescribed policies are enforced by the mechanisms.

Changes to operational procedures should also undergo review and approval by appropriate stakeholders. Requisite changes to process inputs, activity steps, approvals or reviews, and process results should be considered and modifications to related processes and technologies should be coordinated. Workload considerations should also be taken into consideration to ensure that changes to operational controls do not overload resources and impact operational quality. If additional staff training is required to implement changes, it should be coordinated and completed prior to implementation of the change. The operational control should be reviewed in the form of a walk-through shortly after implementation to ensure that all elements are understood and appropriately implemented.

Extensive information is available on developing control objectives and implementing specific controls from COBIT and other sources such as ISO/IEC 27001 and 27002.

3.15.11 BASELINE CONTROLS

Defined baseline security controls should be a standing requirement for all new systems development. Security requirements should be defined and documented as an essential part of the system documentation. Adequate traceability of the security requirements should be ensured and supported across the different phases of the life cycle. A few examples include authentication functions, logging, role-based access control and data transmission confidentiality mechanisms. The information security manager should refer to industry and regional sources to determine a baseline set of security functions appropriate to their organizational policies and other needs. Supplemental controls may be warranted based on vulnerability, threat and risk analysis, and these controls should be included in the requirements-gathering process.

The information security team may be consulted during the design and development phases to evaluate the ability of solution options to fulfill requirements. Rarely is a perfect solution found, and there will always be trade-offs between security requirements, performance, costs and other demands. It is important that the information security manager exercise diligence in identifying and communicating solution deficiencies and developing mitigating or compensating controls as required. The information security manager should also employ internal or external resources to review coding practices and security logic during development to ensure that adequate practices are being employed.

During the quality and acceptance phases, the information security manager should coordinate testing of originally established functional security requirements in addition to testing system interfaces for vulnerabilities. This testing should verify that the system's security mechanisms meet control objectives and provide the information security team with needed administrative and feedback functions. If functional security shortcomings, coding vulnerabilities or exploitable logic flaws are identified, the information security manager should work with the project team to prioritize and resolve issues. If issues cannot be repaired or mitigated prior to planned rollout, the senior management team should review security issues and associated risk to decide if the system should be deployed prior to resolution of identified vulnerabilities. If the system is to be deployed with unresolved security issues, the security manager should ensure that the issues are documented and that there is an agreed-on timetable to resolve issues or, if there is no viable resolution available at the time, track and periodically reassess the issue and to determine whether a viable resolution has become available.

The information security manager should ensure that appropriate segregation of duties is considered throughout the SDLC. Personnel promoting code to production (deployment) should not be the same personnel that developed, tested or approved the code. Testing and QA plans must also be subject to review by the information security manager to ensure that the security elements are properly tested and certified. In some cases, for software developed for critical operations, it may be necessary to perform a code review in addition to the QA testing process. Code reviews are often outsourced for an independent review.

3.16 SECURITY PROGRAM METRICS AND MONITORING

In the process of information security program management, several aspects of metrics must be considered. First, are the metrics necessary to track and guide program development itself at the project, management and strategic levels? Second, will the development of metrics be needed for ongoing management of the results of the program? Since one of the essential elements of controls selection is whether they can be effectively monitored and measured, it is critical to consider this aspect during program design and development. Key controls that cannot be monitored pose a risk that should be avoided.

To understand the concepts of security measurement, the two words—security and measurement—must be defined. The security of an organization involves much more than specific technical controls like policy, firewalls, passwords, intrusion detection and disaster recovery plans. Security is certainly comprised of technical controls, but it also includes processes that surround technical controls and people issues. These three characteristics of security make it a complex system, and when they are combined it can be called a security program.

For any complex system, applying basic system engineering concepts will improve the performance of the system. The concepts of design, planned implementation, scheduled maintenance and management can significantly increase the effectiveness and performance of a security program. One of the fundamental principles of systems engineering is the ability to measure and quantify. Measurement enables proper design, accurate implementation to specifications, and effective management activities including goal setting, tracking progress, benchmarking and prioritizing. In essence, measurement is a fundamental requirement for security program success.

An effective security program involves design and planning, implementation, and ongoing management of the people, processes and technology that impact all aspects of security across an organization.

It may be useful to clarify the distinction between managing the technical IT security systems at the operational level and the overall management of an information security program. Technical metrics are obviously useful for the purely tactical operational management of the technical security infrastructure (e.g., antivirus servers, intrusion detection devices, firewalls, etc.) They can indicate that the infrastructure is operated in a sound fashion and that technical vulnerabilities are identified and addressed. However, these metrics are of less value from a strategic management standpoint. That is, they say nothing about strategic alignment with organizational objectives or how well risk is being managed; they provide few measures of policy compliance or whether objectives for acceptable levels of potential impact are being reached. They also provide no information on information security program direction, velocity or objective proximity.

From a management perspective, while there have been improvements in technical metrics, they are generally incapable of providing answers to such questions as:

- How secure is the organization?
- How much security is enough?
- How do we know when we have achieved security?
- What are the most cost-effective solutions?
- How do we determine the degree of risk?
- How well can risk be predicted?
- Are we moving in the right direction?
- What impact is lack of security having on productivity?
- What impact would a catastrophic security breach have?
- What impact will the solutions have on productivity?

3.16.1 METRICS DEVELOPMENT

The information security governance process described in chapter 1, section 1.4, Information Security Governance Overview, should produce a set of goals for the information security program—goals that are tailored to the organization. As discussed in section 3.6.1 Concepts, these goals will generate control objectives and corresponding planning activity designed to achieve the objectives that result in the desired outcomes. Information security program metrics that directly correspond to these control objectives are essential for managing the program.

It should be evident that it will not be possible to develop meaningful security management metrics without the foundation of governance to set goals and create points of reference. That is to say, measurements without a reference in the form of objectives or goals are not metrics and not likely to be useful in program guidance.

Ultimately, metrics serve only one purpose—decision support. We measure to manage. We measure to provide the information upon which to base informed decisions relative to what we are trying to accomplish, i.e., the goals.

There are a number of considerations when developing useful and relevant metrics in the course of program development. Since the purpose of metrics is decision support, it is essential to know what decisions are made at various levels of the organization and subsequently, what metrics information is needed to make those decisions correctly. That means that roles and responsibilities have to be defined in order to know what information is required by whom. The primary parameter of metrics design can be summed up as:

- Who needs to know?
- What do they need to know?
- When do they need to know it?

Metrics need to provide information at one or more of the following three levels:

- Strategic
- Management
- Operational

Strategic

Strategic metrics are often a compilation of other management metrics designed to indicate that the security program is on track, on target and on budget to achieve the desired outcomes. At the strategic level, the information needed is essentially "navigational," i.e., determining whether the security program is headed in the right direction to achieve the defined objectives leading to the desired outcomes. This information is needed by both the information security manager as well as senior management to provide appropriate oversight.

Management

Management (or tactical) metrics are those needed to manage the security program such as the level of policy and standards compliance, incident management and response effectiveness, manpower and resource utilization. At the security management level, information on compliance, emerging risk, resource utilization, alignment with business goals, etc., will be needed to make the decisions required for effective management. The information security manager also requires a summary of technical metrics to ensure that the machinery is operating properly in acceptable ranges, much as the driver of an automobile wants to know that there is fuel in the tank and that oil pressure and water temperature are in an acceptable range.

Operational

Operational metrics are the more common technical and procedural metrics such as open vulnerabilities, patch management status, etc. Purely technical metrics will primarily be useful for IT security managers and system administrators. These include the usual malware mitigation measures, firewall configuration data, syslog reviews and other operational matters.

There are a number of other considerations for developing metrics. The essential attributes that must be considered include:

- **Manageable**—This attribute suggests that the data should be readily collected, condensed, sorted, stored, correlated, reviewed and understood.
- **Meaningful**—This attribute suggests that the data should be understandable to the recipient, relevant to the objectives and provide a basis for the decisions needed to manage.
- **Actionable**—Just as a compass makes it clear to a pilot in which direction to head to stay on course, so should management metrics make it clear whether to turn left or right. Information that merely invites further investigation may just be clutter.
- **Unambiguous**—Information that is not clear may be not be useful.
- **Reliable**—It is essential to be able to rely on the various feedback mechanisms and that they provide the same result for the same conditions each time they are measured. For example, when the gas tank is actually empty, the gauge should indicate it every time it is measured. In addition, to be reliable, the metric must measure what you think it is measuring, not an unrelated event or spurious artifact.
- **Accurate**—Showing a heading of north when going south is worse than having no information at all. The degree of accuracy depends on how critical the measure is and varies considerably. Qualitative metrics may be approximations, but nevertheless are adequate. Quantitative metrics need to be accurate to be of any use, e.g., if the gauge shows 10 gallons of fuel, but the actual amount is only five, the metric can be dangerous.
- **Timely**—To be useful, feedback must occur when needed. It is better to know that the barn door is open before the horse escapes.
- **Predictive**—To the extent possible, leading indicators are very valuable.
- **Genuine**—Metrics subject to manipulation are less reliable and may suffer accuracy as well.

These attributes can be utilized as meta-metrics (i.e., a measure of metrics themselves) serving to rank the metrics and determine which are most useful. Any metric that substantially fails to meet these criteria is suspect. In many cases, the metrics in use by most organizations will not rate well on these criteria, but nevertheless may be the best available. It must also be understood that even well-rated metrics can fail. A prudent approach is to strive to create a system of metrics that cross-reference each other for the purpose of validation. This can be accomplished by measuring two separate aspects of the same thing and ensuring agreement between them. For example, if an engine consumes five gallons of fuel each hour, a 10-gallon tank should last two hours. After one hour, the fuel gauge should indicate that half of the tank remains, assuming it was full at the start. In a similar manner, discrepancies between internal measures of compliance and the results of an audit must be investigated to determine which measure is faulty. If they both indicate approximately a similar level of compliance, it serves to validate the measures.

A number of other descriptive attributes can be developed, but the ones listed above are the most significant. The question then becomes whether these attributes can be prioritized or whether any metrics or combinations of metrics that do not include most or all of the characteristics above should be discarded.

Security management metrics must be implemented to determine the ongoing effectiveness of security to meet the defined objectives at the strategic, management and operational levels. The information required to make decisions about security will be different for each of these levels, as will be the metrics to capture it.

Monitoring processes are required to ensure compliance with applicable laws and regulations to which the organization is subject. Monitoring of all relevant metrics is required to ensure that they are operating and that the information they provide is properly distributed and handled.

In recent years, a number of industries have become subject to specific regulations to ensure the security and privacy of sensitive information, especially in financial and healthcare organizations, and to reduce operational risk in national critical infrastructure organizations. Compliance failure in these cases can have adverse legal implications, so adequate monitoring is a requirement.

To assess the effectiveness of an organization's security program(s), the information security manager must have a thorough understanding of how to monitor security programs and controls on an ongoing basis. Some monitoring is technical and quantitative in nature while other aspects are, by necessity, imprecise and qualitative.Technical metrics can be used to provide quantitative metrics for monitoring and can include elements such as:

- Number of unremediated vulnerabilities
- Number of open or closed audit items
- Number or percentage of user accounts in compliance with standards
- Perimeter penetrations
- Unresolved security variances

Qualitative metrics that should be monitored can be used to determine trends and can include such things as:

- CMM levels at periodic intervals
- KGIs
- KPIs
- Business balanced scorecard (BSC)
- Six Sigma quality indicators
- ISO 9001 quality indicators
- COBIT 5 Process Assessment Model

Other relevant measures of significance can include the cost-effectiveness of controls and the extent of control failures.

Other monitoring activities relate to organizational compliance, with security policies and procedures established by the organization as a security baseline. As information resources change over time, it is important to be aware that the security baseline and the resources must adapt to changing threats and new vulnerabilities. It is important that all stakeholders are aware of these changes and an appropriate consensus is reached.

3.16.2 MONITORING APPROACHES

It is important for the security manager to develop a consistent, reliable method to determine the overall ongoing effectiveness of the program. One way is to regularly conduct risk assessments and track improvements over time. Another standard tool is the use of external and internal scanning and penetration testing to determine system vulnerabilities, although this will only indicate the effectiveness of one facet of the overall program. Doing so on a regular basis and tracking the results can be a useful indicator of trends in technical security. Most organizations conduct regular vulnerability scans to determine if open vulnerabilities are addressed and to see if new ones appear. Steady improvement is the hallmark of an effective program—although of limited value from a management perspective unless accompanied by information about viable threats and potential impacts to provide enough information to inform appropriate security decisions.

In addition to monitoring automated security activities, the organization's change management activities should also feed the information security's monitoring program. Metrics are important, but of little use if adverse trends are not dealt with in a timely manner. The information security manager should have a process in place whereby metrics are reviewed on a regular basis and any unusual activity is reported. An action plan to react to the unusual activity should be developed as well as a proactive plan to address trends in activity that may lead to a security breach or failure.

Monitoring Security Activities in Infrastructure and Business Applications

Since the organization's vulnerability to security breaches likely exists 24/7, continuous monitoring of security activities is a prudent business practice that the information security manager should implement. A great deal of this monitoring will be technical and may be performed by IT personnel. In this case, the monitoring requirements must be defined in suitable operating standards along with severity criteria and escalation processes.

Continuous monitoring of IDSs and firewalls can provide real-time information of attempts to breach perimeter defenses. Training help desk personnel to escalate suspicious reports that may signal a breach or an attack can serve as an effective monitoring and early warning system. This information can be critical to taking corrective action in a timely manner.

Determining Success of Information Security Investments

It is important for the information security manager to have processes in place to determine the overall effectiveness of security investments and the extent to which objectives have been met. There is always competition for resources in organizations, and senior management will seek to obtain the best returns on investment and justify costs.

During the design and implementation of the security program, the information security manager should ensure that KPIs are defined and agreed to, and that a mechanism to measure progress against those indicators is implemented. This way, the information security manager can assess the success or failure of various components of the security program and whether they are cost-justifiable. This will be helpful when developing a business case for other elements of a security program.

Actual costs for various components of a security program need to be accurately calculated to determine cost-effectiveness. It is useful to use the concept of TCO for evaluating the various components of a security program. In addition to initial procurement and implementation costs, it is important to include:

- Costs to administer controls
- Training costs
- Maintenance costs
- Monitoring costs
- Update fees
- Consultant or help desk fees
- Fees associated with other interrelated systems that may have been modified to accommodate security objectives

3.16.3 MEASURING INFORMATION SECURITY MANAGEMENT PERFORMANCE

The information security manager should understand how to implement processes and mechanisms that provide for the ability to assess the success and shortcomings of the information security program. Measuring success consists of defining measurable objectives, tracking the most appropriate metrics and periodically analyzing results to determine areas of success and improvement opportunities. The specific objectives of the information security program will vary according to the scope and operating level of the security department, but must be conceptually and chronologically aligned with business goals.

An information security program generally includes a core set of common objectives:
- Minimize risk and loss related to information security issues.
- Support achievement of overall organizational objectives.
- Support organizational achievement of compliance.
- Maximize the program's operational productivity.
- Maximize security cost-effectiveness.
- Establish and maintain organizational security awareness.
- Facilitate effective logical, technical and operational security architecture.
- Maximize effectiveness of program framework and resources.
- Measure and manage operational performance.

While each organization must develop their organization's specific goals, the following sections cover the most common objectives and suggest methodologies for measuring their successful delivery.

3.16.4 MEASURING INFORMATION SECURITY RISK AND LOSS

The primary objective of an information security program is to ensure that risk is managed appropriately and that impacts from adverse events fall within acceptable limits. Attaining perfect security while retaining system usability is virtually impossible. Determining whether the security program is functioning at a suitable level—balancing operational efficiency against adequate safety—can be approached in a number of ways from different perspectives.

The following are possible approaches to periodically measuring the program's success against risk management and loss prevention objectives:
- The technical vulnerability management approach poses the following questions:
  - How many technical or operational vulnerabilities exist?
  - How many have been resolved?
  - What is the average time to resolve them?
  - How many recurred?
  - How many systems (critical or otherwise) are impacted by them?
  - How many have the potential for external exploit?
  - How many have the potential for gross compromise (e.g., remote privileged code execution, unauthorized administrative access, bulk exposure of sensitive printed information)?
- The risk management approach is concerned with the following questions:
  - How many high-, medium- and low-risk issues are unresolved? What is the aggregate ALE?
  - How many were resolved during the reporting period? If available, what is the aggregate ALE that has been eliminated?
  - How many were completely eliminated versus partially mitigated versus transferred?
  - How many were accepted because no mitigation nor compensation method was tenable?
  - How many remain open because of inaction or lack of cooperation?
- The loss prevention approach is concerned with the following questions:
  - Were there loss events during the reporting period? What is the aggregate loss including investigation, recovery, data reconstruction and customer relationship management?
  - How many events were preventable (i.e., risk or vulnerability identified prior to the loss event)?
  - What was the average amount of time taken to identify loss incidents? To initiate incident response procedures? To isolate incidents from other systems? To contain event losses?

In addition to these quantitative metrics, a number of qualitative measures can be applied to risk management success monitoring. Some of these include:
- Do risk management activities occur as scheduled?
- Have incident response and BCPs been tested?
- Are asset inventories, custodianships, valuations and risk analyses up-to-date?
- Is there consensus among information security stakeholders as to acceptable levels of risk to the organization?
- Do executive management oversight and review activities occur as planned?

3.16.5 MEASURING SUPPORT OF ORGANIZATIONAL OBJECTIVES

As discussed in other portions of this book, the information security program must support core organizational objectives. Measuring this set of objectives is largely subjective, and organizational objectives can change rapidly in the face of evolving operational pressures and market conditions. The following qualitative measures can be reviewed by the information security steering committee and/or executive management:
- Is there documented correlation between key organizational milestones and the objectives of the information security program?
- How many information security objectives were successfully completed in support of organizational goals?
- Were there organizational goals that were not fulfilled because information security objectives were not met?
- How strong is consensus among business units, executive management and other information security stakeholders that program objectives are complete and appropriate?

The information security manager should recognize that much of a successful measure's value is in analysis of why an objective was or was not met. Qualitative measures such as those represented by support of organizational objectives should be handled as such. For missed objectives, the reasons why they were not accomplished should be analyzed and the feedback used to guide ongoing optimization of the information security program.

3.16.6 MEASURING COMPLIANCE

An essential, ongoing and primary concern for information security program management is policy and standards compliance. Given that most security failures are the result of personnel failing to follow procedures in compliance with standards, compliance is an essential element of security management. Criticality and sensitivity must be known as they mandate the level of compliance that must be achieved to manage risk to acceptable levels. Anything less than 100% compliance is unacceptable when piloting passenger jets or operating nuclear power plants since impacts are likely to be catastrophic and unacceptable. For any activity that is not life- or organization-threatening, the cost of compliance efforts must be weighed against the benefits and potential impacts.

Measuring compliance with technical standards is often straightforward and can frequently be automated. Compliance with procedural or process standards is generally more difficult and may pose a challenge. Since this is frequently the area of failure leading to security compromise, it requires careful consideration. Some compliance requirements are sufficiently critical to warrant direct continuous monitoring such as access controlled by guards and sign-in procedures. In other cases, detective controls such as logging and checklists may suffice.

Compliance requirements may either be statutory, contractual or internal. If the organization must comply with compulsory or voluntary standards involving information security, the information security manager must ensure that program goals are aligned with these requirements. Likewise, the policies, procedures and technologies implemented by the program must fulfill requirements of adopted standards. Measurements of compliance achievement are often tied to the results of internal or external audits. The information security manager may also wish to implement automated or manual compliance monitoring with higher frequency and/or broader scope than achievable with incremental audits. In addition to actual point-in-time compliance, the program should be measured on the effectiveness of resolving identified compliance issues.

3.16.7 MEASURING OPERATIONAL PRODUCTIVITY

No information security program has unlimited resources. Couple this reality with the rapid growth of information technology enterprises, and the need for the information security manager to maximize operational productivity is apparent.

Ways in which productivity can be improved include the use of automation technologies, outsourcing of low-value operational tasks and leveraging the activities of other organizational units. Security management automation technologies can act as workforce multipliers, increasing the accomplishment of operational tasks many times over. Vulnerability scanning tools are an outstanding example of this effect; manual vulnerability assessment that took several individuals a number of weeks can now be accomplished in hours or days. The personnel cost savings can often justify the expense of such tools.

Productivity measures are most useful when employed in a time-based comparison analysis. This approach provides a powerful demonstration of security automation value by showing productivity before and after a productivity-boosting technology was applied. Using this approach, the information security manager can demonstrate returns on security investments.

Productivity is a measure of work product generated per resource. For example, if "event log entries analyzed" is the work product and "security analyst" is the resource, the measure of productivity is "events analyzed per analyst." Productivity measures can be applied to technology resources in addition to personnel, e.g., "network packets processed per IDS node."

The information security manager should set periodic goals for increasing the productivity of the information security program through specific initiatives. These goals should be reviewed to determine the productivity gains achieved. Where possible, the information security manager should analyze data such as hourly employee cost and effort expended per task to demonstrate the financial value of productivity improvement initiatives to senior management.

3.16.8 MEASURING SECURITY COST-EFFECTIVENESS

It is important that the information security program is financially sustainable, lest security controls degrade due to poor maintenance and support. Financial constraints are a common reason for security lapses, including failure to plan for ongoing maintenance requirements. The information security manager must work to maximize the value of each security investment in order to control information security expenses and ensure sustainable achievement of objectives.

This process begins with accurate cost forecasting and budgeting. The success of this activity is generally established by monitoring budget utilization versus original projections and can help identify issues with security cost planning. In addition to measuring budgeting effectiveness, the information security manager should implement procedures to measure the ongoing cost-effectiveness of security components, most often accomplished by tracking cost/result ratios. This approach establishes cost-efficiency goals for new technologies and improvement goals for existing technologies by measuring the total cost of generating a specific result.

To be accurate, costs must include maintenance, operations and administration costs for the period analyzed (e.g., month, quarter, year). Including all pertinent costs provides the information security manager with the TCO for the security investment being analyzed. Ratios of result-units per currency-unit (e.g., 7,400 network packets analyzed per US dollar annually) or vice versa (0.04 euros per thousand e-mails scanned annually) can be used to demonstrate cost efficiency and cost of results. Other examples include:

- Costs of vulnerability assessment per application
- Costs for workstation security controls per user
- Costs for e-mail spam and virus protection per mailbox

Technology purchase and deployment efforts represent only a fraction of full life cycle costs. The information security manager must regularly consider the total costs of maintaining, operating and administering technical security components. In addition, the personnel costs associated with ongoing operational and management activities should also be considered. These analyses should be shared with the security steering committee to help identify areas of opportunity for improving cost-effectiveness and to assist with forecasting future resource needs.

3.16.9 MEASURING ORGANIZATIONAL AWARENESS

Even in a tightly controlled technical environment, personnel actions can present threats that can only be mitigated through education and awareness. It is important for the information security program to implement processes for tracking the ongoing effectiveness of awareness programs.

Tracking organizational awareness is most commonly achieved at the employee level. As such, the information security manager should work with his/her organization's HR department to implement metrics for tracking organizational awareness success. Records of initial training, acceptance of policies and usage agreements, and ongoing awareness updates are useful metrics relative to the actual training program. In addition to identifying individuals in need of training, this helps identify organizational units that may not be fully engaged in the security awareness program.

Another measure of awareness program effectiveness is employee testing. The information security manager should develop tools such as short online or paper examinations that are administered immediately following training to determine the effectiveness of the training. In addition, conducting additional quizzing on a random sampling of employees several months after training will help determine the long-term effectiveness of awareness training and other efforts (e.g., information security newsletters).

3.16.10 MEASURING EFFECTIVENESS OF TECHNICAL SECURITY ARCHITECTURE

The technical security architecture is often one of the most tangible manifestations of an information security program. It is important for the information security manager to establish quantitative measures of the effectiveness of the technical control environment. The range of possible technical metrics is quite broad, and the information security manager should identify those metrics most meaningful to the identified recipients. Technical security metrics can be categorized for reporting and analysis purposes by protected resource and geographic location. Some examples of technical security effectiveness metrics include:

- Probe and attack attempts repelled by network access control devices; qualify by asset or resource targeted, source geography and attack type
- Probe and attack attempts detected by IDSs on internal networks; qualify by internal versus external source, resource targeted and attack type
- Number and type of actual compromises; qualify by attack severity, attack type, impact severity and source of attack
- Statistics on viruses, worms and other malware identified and neutralized; qualify by impact potential, severity of larger Internet outbreaks and malware vector
- Amount of downtime attributable to security flaws and unpatched systems
- Number of messages processed, sessions examined, and kilobytes (KB) of data examined by IDSs

In addition to the quantitative success metrics above, there are a number of important qualitative measures that apply to the technical control environment. Some examples include:

- Individual technical mechanisms have been tested to verify control objectives and policy enforcement.
- The security architecture is constructed of appropriate controls in a layered fashion.
- Control mechanisms are properly configured and monitored in real-time, self-protection implemented, and information security personnel alerted to faults.
- All critical systems stream events to information security personnel or to event analysis automation tools for real-time threat detection.

The information security manager should bear in mind that, although these measures and metrics are useful for IT and information security management and others, most will have little meaning to senior management and most are probably of little interest. A composite summary indicating the security department is performing according to expectations will probably be much more useful to senior and executive management.

3.16.11 MEASURING EFFECTIVENESS OF MANAGEMENT FRAMEWORK AND RESOURCES

Efficient information security management maximizes the results produced by the components and processes it implements. Mechanisms for capturing process feedback, identifying issues and opportunities, tracking consistency of implementation, and effectively communicating changes and knowledge help maximize program effectiveness. Methods of tracking the program's success in this area include:

- Tracking the frequency of issue recurrence
- Monitoring the level of operational knowledge capture and dissemination
- The degree to which process implementations are standardized
- Clarity and completeness of documented information security roles and responsibilities
- Information security requirements incorporated into every project plan
- Efforts and results in making the program more productive and cost-effective
- Overall security resource utilization and trends
- Ongoing alignment with, and support of, organizational objectives

The information security manager should implement such mechanisms with the goal of extracting additional "latent" value from the framework, procedures and resources that make up the program.

3.16.12 MEASURING OPERATIONAL PERFORMANCE

Measuring, monitoring and reporting on information security processes helps the information security manager ensure that operational components of the program effectively support control objectives. Measures of security operational performance include:

- Time to detect, escalate, isolate and contain incidents
- Time between vulnerability detection and resolution
- Quantity, frequency and severity of incidents discovered after their occurrence
- Average time between vendor release of vulnerability patches and their application

- Percentage of systems that have been audited within a certain period
- Number of changes that are released without full change control approval

The information security manager should determine the most appropriate metrics for tracking security operations within all organizational units. These metrics should be compiled, analyzed and distributed to stakeholders and responsible management on a regular basis. Performance issues should be analyzed for root cause by the security steering committee and improvement solutions implemented.

3.16.13 MONITORING AND COMMUNICATION

There are a number of monitoring considerations in implementing or managing a security program, regardless of its scope. New or modified controls in addition to numerous other design considerations will require methods to determine if they are operating as intended. Monitoring technical controls will often consist of reviewing logs and various alerts such as an IDS or firewalls for potential security vulnerabilities or emerging threats.

Other monitoring activities that are just as important and, typically, more difficult will include procedural and process controls. Technical monitoring of physical processes is likely to be the most efficient and effective. Personnel usually interface with information systems at various points in typical processes and these will be the most promising control points to monitor. Monitoring earlier in processes, in addition to watching for suitable outcomes, will provide earlier warning of impending problems.

Monitoring of information systems security is a critical operational component of any information security program. The information security manager should consider the development of a central monitoring environment that provides analysts visibility into all enterprise information resources. There is a broad range of security events that are logged and that could be monitored, and each organization needs to determine which events are the most pertinent in terms of affected resource and event type. Some commonly monitored event types include:
- Failed access attempts to resources
- Processing faults that may indicate system tampering
- Outages, race conditions and faults related to design or other issues
- Changes to system configurations, particularly security controls
- Privileged system access and activities
- Technical security component fault detection

Procedures for analyzing events and taking appropriate responsive action must be developed. Security monitoring analysts should be trained on these procedures, and monitoring supervisors should have response procedures to address anomalies. Usually response procedures involve analyzing related events and system states, capturing additional event-related information, investigating suspicious activity, or escalating the issue to senior analysts or management. The escalation path for security events and incident initiation should be tested regularly.

In addition to real-time monitoring, the information security manager should periodically conduct analysis of trends in security-related events such as attempted attack types or most frequently targeted resources. The longer view associated with this type of analysis can often reveal threat and risk patterns that would otherwise go unrecognized.

All key controls should be monitored in real time, if possible. Log reviews and IDS alerts are after the fact, detective controls and not ideal to ensure rapid reaction.

Results of ongoing monitoring may be rolled up to provide assurance to management that security is providing the appropriate levels of operational assurances and control objectives are being met.

3.17 COMMON INFORMATION SECURITY PROGRAM CHALLENGES

Initiating or expanding a security program will often result in a surprising array of unexpected impediments for the information security manager. These can include:
- Organizational resistance due to changes in areas of responsibility introduced by the program
- A perception that increased security will reduce access required for job functions
- Overreliance on subjective metrics
- Failure of strategy
- Assumptions of procedural compliance without confirming oversight
- Ineffective project management, delaying security initiatives
- Previously undetected, broken or buggy security software

There are always cultural and organizational challenges in any job function and the path is not cleared for the information security manager simply by virtue of gaining senior management support. In order to implement a truly successful program, the cooperation of many others in the organization will be important as well.

Exhibit 3.19 identifies some constraints inherent in road map development for three different organizations. An information security manager must be aware of the type of constraints inherent in the organization when designing control activities and must strive to minimize their impact on the information security program objectives.

The last line in **exhibit 3.19** shows the information security program capabilities that result from the set of constraints associated with the corresponding organization. Organization 1is the organization that introduces the most constraints on the implementation of a successful information security program. Organization 3 is the most controlled and, therefore, most conducive to developing an effective information security program. These examples are contrasted to demonstrate that the capability of an information security manager to produce an effective information security program is almost totally dependent on the environment in which they operate.

Many organizations still view information security as a low-level, technology-based cost center, forgoing security governance and strategic information security management. While universally recognized as necessary, information security is often viewed as

Exhibit 3.19—Constraints on Developing an Information Security Road Map

	Organization 1	Organization 2	Organization 3
Legal and regulatory requirements	Compliance requires major changes in application data flow.	Frequent spot checks interrupt progress on longer-term projects.	Restrictions exist on the sharing of data with service providers.
Physical and environmental factors	Computer room is located on easily accessible floor and subject to flooding.	Data center operation is outsourced.	Data center on fourth floor is a suitable environment control.
Ethics	Attitude is "if I see it on my screen, it is mine."	Attitude is "if I can use it to make money, it should be mine."	Attitude is "if I need it, my request should be approved."
Culture/regional variances	Culture promotes freedom of information sharing.	Turf wars forestall policy approval processes.	The tone at the top promotes information security goals.
Costs	Company is in bankruptcy and cannot spend money on IT.	All information security projects must be cost-justified.	Information security budget is approved and adequate.
Personnel	Former hackers are hired by departments seeking competitive information.	Background checks are done sporadically based on human resources risk assessments.	Personnel screening processes are uniformly implemented.
Logistics	The information security manager is located in a branch with limited network access.	The information security manager is located at headquarters and has no data center access.	The information security manager is well situated between headquarters and the data center.
Resources	No staff or equipment is dedicated to security.	The information security manager staff lacks technical skills.	The information security manager staff has IT experience and daily access to technology.
Capabilities	Documentation only	Process coordination	Control implementation

obstructionist and an impediment to getting the job done. This situation can create a challenging environment for an information security manager. A few common manifestations of such an environment may include a lack of management support, poor resource levels for information security, a shortsighted approach to strategy, and poor cooperation from other business units. Typically, the information security manager in this situation reports far down in the hierarchy and has the daunting task of trying to drive security up the organizational structure.

The situation is gradually changing for the better for a number of reasons, including legal and regulatory mandates that require improved security as a matter of national security and commercial necessity. Expectations of customers and business partners are an important consideration that has provided a positive push toward enhanced security. Another is the credit card industry's rigorous security requirements from the Payment Card Industry (PCI) data security standards (DSS) council for organizations that process credit card information. Since this impacts a very wide range of organizations, it is likely to significantly improve many aspects of information security globally. Whether the rate of adoption and improved security will match the pace of increasingly sophisticated and profitable criminal elements remains a challenge.

In the near future, other drivers will include increased litigation that is likely to result in substantial damage awards. Finally, the emergence of the necessity for cyber-insurance, with the attendant requirements of insurers for adequate risk management, will be a driver for better, more effective security. This is likely to come about in the same manner in which insurance has been instrumental in gradually improving automobile, product and fire safety.

Although the overall situation in terms of security is improving, the information security manager must deal with the situation as it exists. Regardless of organizational circumstances, a persuasive information security manager with a clear vision of the role of information security in the organization can often improve the overall security posture with an ongoing campaign to educate stakeholders in the role and relevance of information security. This can include defining and seeking agreement on information risk control objectives, determining the organization's risk appetite and identifying mission-critical information assets.

It is also beneficial for information security activities to align with and support defined business objectives. This will be most effective if it is an ongoing effort and suitably communicated to stakeholders. Developing meaningful KPIs and metrics will also be useful in supporting information security objectives. Each information security manager must determine the appropriate breadth and depth of metrics for their own organization to provide the information needed for management, but should also implement some form of consistent reporting to promote awareness of the importance that information security management has in the achievement of organizational objectives.

Other issues the information security manager may need to deal with occur in situations where information security is a relatively new function within an organization. Even for mature information security programs, the requirements and demands are rapidly changing, driven by technical and regulatory pressures. The challenges below do not represent an exhaustive list, but illustrate methods for assessing and addressing several of the most common concerns. The information security manager should be cognizant of common challenges to effective information security management, the reasons behind those challenges and strategies for addressing them.

Management Support

Lack of management support is most common in smaller organizations and those that are not in security-intensive industries. Such organizations often have no compulsory requirement to address information security and, therefore, often view it as a marginally important issue that adds cost with little value. These views often reflect misunderstanding of the organization's dependence on information systems, the threat and risk environment, or the impact that the organization faces or may be unknowingly experiencing.

In such circumstances, the information security manager must utilize resources, such as industry statistics, organizational impact and dependency analyses, and reviews of common threats to the organization's specific information processing systems. In addition, management may require guidance in what is expected of them and approaches that industry peers are taking to address information security. Even if initial education does not result in immediate strengthening of support, ongoing education should still be conducted to develop awareness of security needs.

Funding

Inadequate funding for information security initiatives is perhaps one of the most frustrating and challenging issues that the information security manager must address. While this issue might be a symptom of an underlying lack of management support, there are often other factors that the information security manager is able to influence. Some funding-related issues that may need to be addressed by the information security manager include:
- Management not recognizing the value of security investments
- Security being viewed as a low-value cost center
- Management not understanding where existing money is going
- The organizational need for a security investment not being understood
- The need for more awareness of industry trends in security investment

If additional funding to close financial gaps is not available, the information security manager must exercise strategies that minimize the impact of the financial shortfall on the organization's information risk posture. Some common strategies that can be applied include:
- Leveraging the budgets of other organizational units (e.g., product development, internal audit, information systems) to implement needed security program components
- Improving the efficiency of existing information security program components
- Working with the information security steering committee to reprioritize security resource assignments and providing senior management with analysis of what security components will become underresourced and the associated risk implications.

It is important for the information security manager to pay close attention to funding issues and work on them on an ongoing basis. It is often too late for analyzing needs and educating management once the actual budgeting process begins, delaying needed investments by months or years.

It is also important for the information security manager to understand that financing an information security program is often difficult. If the program is working successfully, management may not see where the money is going and may wonder why they are spending so much. If the program is not successful, management may not understand why they are budgeting significant amounts of money for systems that are still being compromised. It is essential for the information security manager to find ways to show that security is important, functional and business related.

Staffing

The root causes of funding issues extend to the challenge of inadequate staff levels to meet security program requirements. Obstacles toward obtaining effective staffing levels might include:
- Poor understanding of what activities new resources will do
- Questioning the need or benefit of new resource activities
- Lack of awareness of existing staff utilization levels or activities
- Belief that existing staff are underutilized
- Desire to examine outsourcing alternatives

When presented with these issues, the information security manager should utilize workload management procedures to generate personnel workload analyses, utilization reports and other metrics that demonstrate the level of effort currently expended. In addition, charts that associate specific information security roles or teams with the protection that they provide to enterprise information systems are helpful. Demonstrating high or growing levels of productivity also help demonstrate that the information security program is utilizing resources effectively and efficiently.

If the organization is unable to allocate additional human resources to the program, the information security manager may wish to consider implementing the following strategies to minimize the impact of understaffing on information security program effectiveness:
- Collaborate with other business units to determine if they can assume more information security responsibilities; delegate appropriate tasks with oversight
- Analyze outsourcing possibilities, especially for high-volume operational activities; be prepared to demonstrate how freed resources would be immediately redeployed to higher-value activities
- Work with the information security steering committee to reprioritize security personnel assignments; provide senior management with analysis of what security activities will not be addressed with current staff and communicate risk implications

Page intentionally left blank

Certified Information Security Manager®
An ISACA® Certification

Chapter 4:

Information Security Incident Management

Section One: Overview

Section Two: Content

Section One: Overview

4.1 INTRODUCTION

This chapter reviews the essential knowledge necessary to establish an effective program to respond to and subsequently manage incidents that threaten an organization's information systems and infrastructure.

DEFINITION

Incident management is defined as the capability to effectively manage unexpected disruptive events with the objective of minimizing impacts and maintaining or restoring normal operations within defined time limits. Incident response is the operational capability of incident management that identifies, prepares for and responds to incidents to control and limit damage; provide forensic and investigative capabilities; and maintain, recover and restore normal operations as defined in service level agreements (SLAs).

OBJECTIVES

The objective of this domain is to ensure that the information security manager has the knowledge and understanding necessary to identify, analyze, manage and respond effectively to unexpected events that may adversely affect the organization's information assets and/or its ability to operate. This will usually include disruptions to, or failures or misuse of, information processing functions, but will also include events that may adversely impact other information assets of the organization. Typically, incidents will come about as a result of accidents, mistakes, intentional acts of malice, theft, embezzlement, extortion, fraud, espionage or environmental occurrences such as storms, earthquakes, fires, etc.

This domain represents 18 percent of the CISM examination (approximately 36 questions).

4.2 TASK AND KNOWLEDGE STATEMENTS

Domain 4—Information Security Incident Management
Plan, establish and manage the capability to detect, investigate, respond to and recover from information security incidents to minimize business impact

TASKS

There are 10 tasks within this domain that a CISM candidate must know how to perform:

T4.1 Establish and maintain an organizational definition of, and severity hierarchy for, information security incidents to allow accurate identification of and response to incidents.

T4.2 Establish and maintain an incident response plan to ensure an effective and timely response to information security incidents.

T4.3 Develop and implement processes to ensure the timely identification of information security incidents.

T4.4 Establish and maintain processes to investigate and document information security incidents to be able to respond appropriately and determine their causes while adhering to legal, regulatory and organizational requirements.

T4.5 Establish and maintain incident escalation and notification processes to ensure that the appropriate stakeholders are involved in incident response management.

T4.6 Organize, train and equip teams to effectively respond to information security incidents in a timely manner.

T4.7 Test and review the incident response plan periodically to ensure an effective response to information security incidents and to improve response capabilities.

T4.8 Establish and maintain communication plans and processes to manage communication with internal and external entities.

T4.9 Conduct postincident reviews to determine the root cause of information security incidents, develop corrective actions, reassess risk, evaluate response effectiveness and take appropriate remedial actions.

T4.10 Establish and maintain integration among the incident response plan, disaster recovery plan and business continuity plan.

KNOWLEDGE STATEMENTS

The CISM candidate must have a good understanding of each of the areas delineated by the knowledge statements. These statements are the basis for the exam.

There are 14 knowledge statements within the information security incident management area:

KS4.1 Knowledge of the components of an incident response plan

KS4.2 Knowledge of incident management concepts and practices

KS4.3 Knowledge of business continuity planning (BCP) and disaster recovery planning (DRP) and their relationship to the incident response plan

KS4.4 Knowledge of incident classification methods

KS4.5 Knowledge of damage containment methods

KS4.6 Knowledge of notification and escalation processes

KS4.7 Knowledge of the roles and responsibilities in identifying and managing information security incidents

KS4.8 Knowledge of the types and sources of tools and equipment required to adequately equip incident response teams

KS4.9 Knowledge of forensic requirements and capabilities for collecting, preserving and presenting evidence (for example, admissibility, quality and completeness of evidence, chain of custody)

KS4.10 Knowledge of internal and external incident reporting requirements and procedures

KS4.11 Knowledge of postincident review practices and investigative methods to identify root causes and determine corrective actions

KS4.12 Knowledge of techniques to quantify damages, costs and other business impacts arising from information security incidents

KS4.13 Knowledge of technologies and processes that detect, log and analyze information security events
KS4.14 Knowledge of internal and external resources available to investigate information security incidents

RELATIONSHIP OF TASK TO KNOWLEDGE STATEMENTS

The task statements are what the CISM candidate is expected to know how to perform. The knowledge statements delineate each of the areas in which the CISM candidate must have a good understanding in order to perform the tasks. The task and knowledge statements are mapped in **exhibit 4.1** insofar as it is possible to do so. Note that although there is often an overlap, each task statement will generally map to several knowledge statements.

Exhibit 4.1—Task and Knowledge Statements Mapping

Task Statement	Knowledge Statements
T4.1 Establish and maintain an organizational definition of, and severity hierarchy for, information security incidents to allow accurate identification of and response to incidents.	KS4.1 Knowledge of the components of an incident response plan KS4.4 Knowledge of incident classification methods
T4.2 Establish and maintain an incident response plan to ensure an effective and timely response to information security incidents.	KS4.1 Knowledge of the components of an incident response plan KS4.3 Knowledge of business continuity planning (BCP) and disaster recovery planning (DRP) and their relationship to the incident response plan
T4.3 Develop and implement processes to ensure the timely identification of information security incidents.	KS4.2 Knowledge of incident management concepts and practices KS4.4 Knowledge of incident classification methods KS4.7 Knowledge of the roles and responsibilities in identifying and managing information security incidents KS4.13 Knowledge of technologies and processes that detect, log and analyze information security events
T4.4 Establish and maintain processes to investigate and document information security incidents to be able to respond appropriately and determine their causes while adhering to legal, regulatory and organizational requirements.	KS4.1 Knowledge of the components of an incident response plan KS4.3 Knowledge of business continuity planning (BCP) and disaster recovery planning (DRP) and their relationship to the incident response plan KS4.4 Knowledge of incident classification methods KS4.8 Knowledge of the types and sources of tools and equipment required to adequately equip incident response teams KS4.9 Knowledge of forensic requirements and capabilities for collecting, preserving and presenting evidence (for example, admissibility, quality and completeness of evidence, chain of custody) KS4.11 Knowledge of postincident review practices and investigative methods to identify root causes and determine corrective actions KS4.13 Knowledge of technologies and processes that detect, log and analyze information security events KS4.14 Knowledge of internal and external resources available to investigate information security incidents
T4.5 Establish and maintain incident escalation and notification processes to ensure that the appropriate stakeholders are involved in incident response management.	KS4.2 Knowledge of incident management concepts and practices KS4.5 Knowledge of damage containment methods KS4.6 Knowledge of notification and escalation processes KS4.7 Knowledge of the roles and responsibilities in identifying and managing information security incidents KS4.10 Knowledge of internal and external incident reporting requirements and procedures
T4.6 Organize, train and equip teams to effectively respond to information security incidents in a timely manner.	KS4.7 Knowledge of the roles and responsibilities in identifying and managing information security incidents KS4.8 Knowledge of the types and sources of tools and equipment required to adequately equip incident response teams KS4.9 Knowledge of forensic requirements and capabilities for collecting, preserving and presenting evidence (for example, admissibility, quality and completeness of evidence, chain of custody) KS4.10 Knowledge of internal and external incident reporting requirements and procedures KS4.12 Knowledge of techniques to quantify damages, costs and other business impacts arising from information security incidents KS4.14 Knowledge of internal and external resources available to investigate information security incidents

Exhibit 4.1—Task and Knowledge Statements Mapping *(cont.)*	
Task Statement	**Knowledge Statements**
T4.7 Test and review the incident response plan periodically to ensure an effective response to information security incidents and to improve response capabilities.	KS4.3 Knowledge of business continuity planning (BCP) and disaster recovery planning (DRP) and their relationship to the incident response plan
T4.8 Establish and maintain communication plans and processes to manage communication with internal and external entities.	KS4.6 Knowledge of notification and escalation processes KS4.10 Knowledge of internal and external incident reporting requirements and procedures
T4.9 Conduct postincident reviews to determine the root cause of information security incidents, develop corrective actions, reassess risk, evaluate response effectiveness and take appropriate remedial actions.	KS4.5 Knowledge of damage containment methods KS4.11 Knowledge of postincident review practices and investigative methods to identify root causes and determine corrective actions KS4.12 Knowledge of techniques to quantify damages, costs and other business impacts arising from information security incidents
T4.10 Establish and maintain integration among the incident response plan, disaster recovery plan and business continuity plan.	KS4.3 Knowledge of business continuity planning (BCP) and disaster recovery planning (DRP) and their relationship to the incident response plan

KNOWLEDGE STATEMENT REFERENCE GUIDE

The following section contains the knowledge statements and the underlying concepts and relevance for the knowledge of the information security manager. The knowledge statements are what the information security manager must know in order to accomplish the tasks. A summary explanation of each knowledge statement is provided, followed by the basic concepts that are the foundation for the written exam. Each key concept has references to section two of this chapter.

The CISM body of knowledge has been divided into four domains, and each of the four chapters covers some of the material contained in those domains. This chapter reviews the body of knowledge from the perspective of incident management and response.

KS4.1 Knowledge of the components of an incident response plan

Explanation	Key Concepts	Reference in 2015 CISM Review Manual
Incident response is the operational capability to respond appropriately to security-related events and incidents to effectively minimize disruptions to the organization. There are several capabilities essential to effective response. The first is the capability to determine that, in fact, an incident has occurred. The second is the ability to quickly assess the type and nature of the incident. Third, is the ability to mobilize needed resources to triage the effects and provide the appropriate remedies in order to limit damage and maintain or restore affected services.	Identifying an incident	4.4 Incident Management Overview 4.5 Incident Response Procedures 4.5.4 Concepts
	Incident response team responsibilities	4.4 Incident Management Overview 4.5 Incident Response Procedures 4.5.2 Outcomes of Incident Management 4.7.3 Personnel 4.7.4 Roles and Responsibilities
	Incident management team responsibilities	4.4 Incident Management Overview 4.7.3 Personnel 4.7.4 Roles and Responsibilities
	Incident triage	4.4 Incident Management Overview 4.5 Incident Response Procedures 4.5.4 Concepts 4.10.1 Detailed Plan of Action for Incident Management

KS4.2 Knowledge of incident management concepts and practices

Explanation	Key Concepts	Reference in 2015 CISM Review Manual
The goal of incident management is to detect and respond to information security-related incidents in such a way that service operations as are restored to normal as quickly as possible and that overall adverse effects to the enterprise are minimized. While many specific aspects of incident management will depend on the individual organization, the overall objectives will be the same. These include: • Detect incidents quickly • Diagnose incidents accurately • Manage incidents properly • Contain and minimize damage • Restore affected services • Determine root causes • Implement improvements to prevent recurrence or minimize the impact of future, similar events	Incident management life cycle	4.10.1 Detailed Plan of Action for Incident Management
	Incident management and response purpose	4.4 Incident Management Overview 4.5 Incident Response Procedures 4.5.3 Incident Management 4.8 Incident Management Objectives 4.8.3 Strategic Alignment
	Incident management processes	4.4 Incident Management Overview 4.5 Incident Response Procedures 4.10.1 Detailed Plan of Action for Incident Management
	Incident response capabilities	4.5 Incident Response Procedures 4.10 Defining Incident Management Procedures 4.11.1 History of Incidents

KS4.3 Knowledge of business continuity planning (BCP) and disaster recovery planning (DRP) and their relationship to the incident response plan

Explanation	Key Concepts	Reference in 2015 CISM Review Manual
Disaster recovery planning (DRP) and business continuity planning (BCP) are handled in different ways by different organizations. Some organizations have a separate department that handles both functions. Others have each function reporting into a different part of the organization. Some companies outsource both activities. Regardless of where these functions are located in the organization, it is essential that the information security manager understands the process and how it relates to incident management and response. If an incident has significant impacts that disable portions or all of an organization's information systems, then typically, a disaster must be declared and the disaster recovery and business continuity plans would be activated. The handoff from the incident response team to those in charge of disaster recovery must be integrated, well planned and smoothly executed. The involved personnel must have appropriate training and understanding of their own and each others' processes. It is critical that a disaster declaration be handled appropriately since the consequences of declaring a disaster that could have been avoided can be as costly as failing to declare an actual one in a timely manner. Acceptable service levels must be agreed on in advance and documented in operating and service level agreements (OLAs and SLAs). The information security manager must also review all disaster recovery and business continuity plans to ensure that any risk to information security resulting from execution of the plans are highlighted and treated appropriately. While often not responsible for declaring a disaster, the information security manager will typically coordinate the collected information from the damage assessment phase of the incident response process to provide needed information to senior management so they will be able to make an informed decision regarding whether to declare a disaster.	Disaster recovery planning (DRP)	4.4 Incident Management Overview 4.13 Business Continuity and Disaster Recovery Procedures 4.15 Executing Response and Recovery Plans
	Business continuity planning (BCP)	4.13 Business Continuity and Disaster Recovery Procedures 4.15 Executing Response and Recovery Plans
	Severity criteria	4.4 Incident Management Overview 4.5.2 Outcomes of Incident Management
	Declaration criteria	4.4 Incident Management Overview 4.5.2 Outcomes of Incident Management 4.13.1 Recovery Planning and Business Recovery Processes
	Acceptable service levels	4.4 Incident Management Overview 4.13.10 Integrating Recovery Objectives and Impact Analysis With Incident Response

KS4.4 Knowledge of incident classification methods

Explanation	Key Concepts	Reference in 2015 CISM Review Manual
The classification of an incident needs to be accurate and must be completed as quickly as possible. Both of these factors help to ensure an appropriate response and that the impact is minimized. The classification will be in terms of the type of incident; e.g., whether it is accidental, or a malicious code or an actual penetration of the network. The nearly endless possibilities can make this task challenging and the information security manager should develop a network of experts that can be called on to classify the type of incident as well as advise on remedial options. Once the nature and extent of the incident is identified, the appropriate severity levels can be determined and the incident response plan activated.	Incident classification	4.10.1 Detailed Plan of Action for Incident Management
	Incident triage	4.5.4 Concepts 4.10.1 Detailed Plan of Action for Incident Management
	Severity levels	4.10.1 Detailed Plan of Action for Incident Management

KS4.5 Knowledge of damage containment methods

Explanation	Key Concepts	Reference in 2015 CISM Review Manual
The objective of incident management and response is to minimize impact stemming from information security incidents. To achieve this objective, it is necessary for the incident manager to understand all aspects of the incident and the most effective way to contain and minimize operational disruption and other negative factors such as data loss. This will require a thorough understanding of the systems architecture and organizational processes in order to isolate and contain problems to only the affected areas. As an example, a virus infection is commonly addressed most effectively by determining the systems infected, isolating them and removing the infection. It must be understood, however, that this may result in conflict with problem management efforts, which would focus on determining the source or root cause of the infection. The conflict comes about because removing the virus and restoring the systems to production quickly may destroy evidence needed by the problem management team to determine the source of the infection and operational requirements may not permit the isolation or disabling of mission-critical systems. The security manager will need to decide whether to forgo the potential to determine the source of the problem or to incur the cost of keeping systems down long enough to complete the investigation. As with most decisions regarding security, there is risk inherent in each course of action.	Incident triage	4.4 Incident Management Overview 4.5.4 Concepts 4.10.1 Detailed Plan of Action for Incident Management
	Containment	4.12.2 Elements of a Business Impact Analysis
	Problem management	4.5.4 Concepts
	Response capability	4.10.1 Detailed Plan of Action for Incident Management 4.11 Current State of Incident Response Capability 4.13.3 Recovery Strategies 4.13.17 Updating Recovery Plans

KS4.6 Knowledge of notification and escalation processes

Explanation	Key Concepts	Reference in 2015 CISM Review Manual
It is critical for the information security manager to determine who must be notified and under what circumstances in order to both receive and provide critical information about incidents. Operational personnel must understand which situations and events would require notification of the information security manager. The information security manager must develop clear requirements and processes to provide notification and escalation criteria for events, risk or other circumstances to various parts of the organization. The development of severity criteria and educating personnel in their use is a key component of developing notification and escalation requirements.	Severity criteria	4.4 Incident Management Overview 4.5 Incident Response Procedures 4.5.2 Outcomes of Incident Management 4.10.1 Detailed Plan of Action for Incident Management
	Communication and reporting channels	4.5.2 Outcomes of Incident Management 4.5.4 Concepts 4.7.5 Skills 4.10.1 Detailed Plan of Action for Incident Management 4.12.7 Incident Notification Process 4.12.8 Challenges in Developing an Incident Management Plan
	Escalation procedures	4.12.3 Escalation Process for Effective Incident Management

KS4.7 Knowledge of the roles and responsibilities in identifying and managing information security incidents

Explanation	Key Concepts	Reference in 2015 CISM Review Manual
All personnel in an organization must have basic guidance for and awareness of events that may be considered a security incident. This is to ensure early notification of possible incidents so that actual security incidents may be quickly identified, assessed and mitigated to minimize damage and operational interruptions. Members of both the incident management team (IMT) and the incident response team (IRT) must understand their specific responsibilities and must be proficient in carrying them out. This may require specialized training and testing to ensure that all team members possess the level of skills required.	Event, incident and problem definitions	4.4 Incident Management Overview 4.5.4 Concepts
	Incident recognition training and education	4.7.6 Awareness and Education
	Incident management and response roles and responsibilities	4.7.4 Roles and Responsibilities 4.12.6 Organizing, Training and Equipping the Response Staff 4.13.2 Recovery Operations
	Skills and personnel requirements	4.7.5 Skills
	Evidence collection and handling	4.16.3 Establishing Procedures 4.16.4 Requirements for Evidence 4.16.5 Legal Aspects of Forensic Evidence

KS4.8 Knowledge of the types and sources of tools and equipment required to adequately equip incident response teams

Explanation	Key Concepts	Reference in 2015 CISM Review Manual
Incidents are, by nature, unexpected and vary widely ranging from physical or logical intrusions to procedural errors and accidents. Incidents can be accidental or due to intentionally malicious activates. As a consequence, effective incident response teams must be equipped and prepared for a wide variety of possible events and response strategies. The types of tools, equipment and methodologies required will depend on the systems and processes utilized by the enterprise as well as the scope and charter of the incident response capability. It is essential that the information security manager clearly identify the type and nature of incidents and events that the team will be expected to handle, and then ensure, that they are properly trained and equipped to do so. Often, skill sets or tool sets that are too expensive and/or too rarely needed to justifiably maintain in house can be handled by a service agreement with a firm that specializes in incident response activities. An example is digital forensics services.	Incident response team capability requirements	4.4 Incident Management Overview 4.6 Incident Management Organization 4.10.1 Detailed Plan of Action for Incident Management 4.11 Current State of Incident Response Capability
	Investigative tools	4.16.5 Legal Aspects of Forensic Evidence

KS4.9 Knowledge of forensic requirements and capabilities for collecting, preserving and presenting evidence (for example, admissibility, quality and completeness of evidence, chain of custody)

Explanation	Key Concepts	Reference in 2015 CISM Review Manual
Forensics is a systematic, detailed set of procedures and associated tools that are utilized to locate, collect and handle information stored on computing systems in order to assist in determining the root cause and impact of an information security incident. Frequently, this involves the collection, handling and preservation of evidence in a manner that meets criminal or civil legal requirements for admittance as evidence in a court of law. Until the full scope of an incident is understood, the best assumption is to treat investigative activities and evidence collection as if there is a criminal investigation. The essential elements of this approach include the steps needed to meet local legal requirements for evidence collection, preservation and transport (chain of custody). It is also important to avoid contamination of a possible crime scene. Improper handling of evidence can result in limiting options for prosecution and/or determining the causes of an event. The information security manager should understand that objectives of forensics and incident management are typically in conflict. Incident management seeks to resolve problems and restore normal operations as quickly as possible while forensics seeks to determine causes and responsibility and thereby typically delays restoration of services. The information security manager should use a risk-based approach to manage the situation appropriately.	Collection and preservation of evidence	4.16.2 Documenting Events
	Chain of custody	4.16.2 Documenting Events 4.16.4 Requirements for Evidence 4.16.5 Legal Aspects of Forensic Evidence
	Investigative techniques	4.16.1 Identifying Causes and Corrective Actions 4.16.2 Documenting Events

KS4.10 Knowledge of internal and external incident reporting requirements and procedures

Explanation	Key Concepts	Reference in 2015 CISM Review Manual
Depending on the industry sector and legal jurisdiction, certain types of events may require reports to regulatory agencies, law enforcement or authorities. The information security manager must understand the legal requirements for reporting to external authorities as well as the types of events that require reporting to internal management and other stakeholders. Reporting requirements must be properly documented in the appropriate policies, standards and procedures. Documentation should detail: • The types of events that must be reported • To whom (and by what manner) they must be reported • What information must be conveyed • The required reporting time frame • Other associated actions that must be taken in conjunction with the reporting In most organizations, reports required by authorities are not submitted directly by the information security manager, but rather by the organization's legal department, which has the responsibility for ensuring proper format and content.	Legal and regulatory reporting requirements	4.4 Incident Management Overview 4.5.2 Outcomes of Incident Management 4.5.4 Concepts 4.6.1 Responsibilities 4.8.3 Strategic Alignment

KS4.11 Knowledge of postincident review practices and investigative methods to identify root causes and determine corrective actions

Explanation	Key Concepts	Reference in 2015 CISM Review Manual
Incidents must be reviewed in a systematic and standardized manner in order to facilitate understanding the root causes, the underlying vulnerabilities and, possibly, the parties responsible for the incident. The specific approach used by the information security manager can vary significantly and depends on the organization, capabilities and other factors. The primary purpose of the postmortem analysis is to document "lessons learned," enabling better detection of new incidents and more effective response to an incident in the future. Even if formal forensics techniques are not employed, incidents should be investigated in a systematic manner to determine whether the causes are technical or procedural and to expose process failures that gave rise to the incident. This information will provide the basis and rationale for activities that improve the organization's overall security posture.	Postmortem assessments, analysis and reporting	4.16 Postincident Activities and Investigation
	Problem management and root cause analysis	4.4 Incident Management Overview 4.5.2 Outcomes of Incident Management 4.16.1 Identifying Causes and Corrective Actions
	Investigative techniques and practices	4.16.2 Documenting Events
	Forensics	4.16.5 Legal Aspects of Forensic Evidence

KS4.12 Knowledge of techniques to quantify damages, costs and other business impacts arising from information security incidents

Explanation	Key Concepts	Reference in 2015 CISM Review Manual
The information security manager must have access to the appropriate resources to perform financial analysis for the purposes of determining impacts associated with information security incidents. Financial impacts will include not only the direct costs of an incident, but must include all related and consequential costs. These can include disruptions to productivity, the costs of subsequent mitigation measures, possible reputational damage, and regulatory sanctions. This analysis is necessary both for accurate financial reporting as well as to provide a basis for immediate and longer term risk mitigation strategies.	Financial impact assessments and analysis	4.4 Incident Management Overview 4.5.4 Concepts 4.12.2 Business Impact Assessment
	Techniques for quantifying financial impacts	4.12.2 Business Impact Assessment 4.13.10 Integrating Recovery Objectives and Impact Analysis With Incident Response
	Liability and exposure posed by third parties	4.5.3 Incident Management 4.13.16 Insurance

KS4.13 Knowledge of technologies and processes that detect, log and analyze information security events

Explanation	Key Concepts	Reference in 2015 CISM Review Manual
Effective risk management includes capabilities for quickly detecting events that have security implications. Responding appropriately requires the ability to accurately analyze the nature and extent of these events. Effective analysis is, in turn, dependent on complete and accurate logs. A variety of technologies are available to detect, log and analyze security events. These include Incident detection and prevention systems (IDS, IPS), host-based IDS (HIDS) and network-based IDS (NIDS), firewalls, security information management (SIM) and security information and event management (SIEM) tools. Contemporary SIEM tools have the capability to correlate information from a variety of devices and systems to detect security events, provide notification capabilities, and then track events during remediation. Another significant feature of incident management systems is their ability to track an incident during its life cycle. Tracking is a powerful feature that ensures that incidents are not overlooked and that they receive the necessary attention based on criticality. It enables users to provide more information and receive status updates along the event life cycle until the event is closed. The system is most likely offered in a web-based format for easy accessibility. An effective incident management system should: • Consolidate and correlate inputs from multiple systems • Identify incidents or potential incidents • Prioritize incidents based on business impact • Track incidents until they are closed • Provide status tracking and notifications • Integrate with major IT management systems	Security Information and Event Management	4.5.5 Incident Management Systems 4.13.4 Addressing Threats
	Intrusion Detection Systems (IDS, IPS, HIDS, NIDS)	4.5.5 Incident Management Systems 4.13.4 Addressing Threats

KS4.14 Knowledge of internal and external resources available to investigate information security incidents

Explanation	Key Concepts	Reference in 2015 CISM Review Manual
The effective information security manager should have general expertise in investigative techniques, postmortems and legal requirements in the event of a security breach. A primary reason is to gain an understanding of the vulnerabilities that were exploited in order to improve security and prevent recurrence. In many cases, there are also legal requirements for notification if personal information or critical infrastructure is compromised It is also essential that staff understand the requirements for the preservation of evidence and maintaining the chain of custody. Determining the causes of an incident generally requires expertise in applicable technologies and may require competency in forensics. Sophisticated attackers may erase most or all of their tracks and can present a significant challenge in determining the source and nature of a compromise. In many cases, the target is not aware of an intrusion until considerable time has passed. The Association of Certified Fraud examiners found that the average time taken to discover a fraud was 14 months. Adequate specialized investigative skills may not be available internally, in which case it is prudent to have arrangements with external providers of these skills. Many consulting firms can provide this expertise as needed. In addition, it may not be cost effective for the organization to acquire specialized forensics software such as EnCase® and the associated training needed for only occasional use.	Postmortem assessments, analysis and reporting	4.16 Postincident Activities and Investigation 4.16.3 Establishing Procedures 4.16.4 Requirements for Evidence Exhibit 4.2 Roles and Responsibilities
	Problem management and root cause analysis	4.5.2 Outcomes of Incident Management 4.16 Postincident Activities and Investigation 4.16.1 Identifying Causes and Corrective Actions 4.16.3 Establishing Procedures 4.16.4 Requirements for Evidence Exhibit 4.2 Roles and Responsibilities
	Investigative techniques and practices	4.16 Postincident Activities and Investigation 4.16.2 Documenting Events 4.16.3 Establishing Procedures 4.16.4 Requirements for Evidence Exhibit 4.2 Roles and Responsibilities
	Forensics	4.16.4 Requirements for Evidence 4.16.5 Legal Aspects of Forensic Evidence

SUGGESTED RESOURCES FOR FURTHER STUDY

Albert, Cecilia; Audrey J. Dorofee; Georgia Killcrece; Robin Ruefle; Mark Zajicek; Defining Incident Management Processes for CSIRTs: A Work in Progress, Software Engineering Institute, Carnegie Mellon University, USA, 2004, *www.sei.cmu.edu/library/abstracts/reports/04tr015.cfm*

Burtles, Jim; *Principles and Practice of Business Continuity: Tools and Techniques*, Rothstein Associates Inc., USA, 2007

Carnegie Mellon University, Software Engineering Institute, CERT® Coordination Center; Creating a Computer Security Incident Response Team: A Process for Getting Started, February 2006, *www.cert.org/csirts/Creating-A-CSIRT.html*

Endorf, Carl; Eugene Schultz; Jim Mellander; *Intrusion Detection and Prevention*, McGraw-Hill, USA, 2004

Federal Emergency Management Agency, USA, *www.fema.org*

Graham, Julia; David Kaye; *A Risk Management Approach to Business Continuity*, Rothstein Associates Inc., USA, 2006

Grance, Tim.; Karen Scarfone; Kelly Masone; *Computer Security Incident Handling Guide: Recommendations of the National Institute of Standards and Technology*, NIST Publication 800-61 rev. 2, 2012, *www.csrc.nist.gov/publications/nistpubs/800-61-rev2/sp800-61rev2.pdf*

Hiles, Andrew; *The Definitive Handbook of Business Continuity Management, 2nd Edition*; John Wiley & Sons Inc., USA, 2008

Kabay, M.E.; CSIRT Management, USA, 2009, p 15, *www.mekabay.com/infosecmgmt/csirtm.pdf*

Snedaker, Susan; *Business Continuity & Disaster Recovery Planning for IT Professionals*, Syngress Publishing Inc., USA, 2007

Symantec; Managing Security Incidents in the Enterprise, *www.symantec.com/avcenter/reference/incident.manager.pdf*

Note: Publications in bold are stocked in the ISACA Bookstore.

4.3 SELF-ASSESSMENT QUESTIONS

QUESTIONS

CISM exam questions are developed with the intent of measuring and testing practical knowledge in information security management. All questions are multiple choice and are designed for one best answer. Every CISM question has a stem (question) and four options (answer choices). The candidate is asked to choose the correct or best answer from the options. The stem may be in the form of a question or incomplete statement. In some instances, a scenario or a description problem may also be included. These questions normally include a description of a situation and require the candidate to answer two or more questions based on the information provided. Many times a CISM examination question will require the candidate to choose the most likely or best answer.

In every case, the candidate is required to read the question carefully, eliminate known incorrect answers and then make the best choice possible. Knowing the format in which questions are asked, and how to study to gain knowledge of what can be tested, will go a long way toward answering them correctly.

4-1 The **PRIMARY** goal of a postincident review is to:

A. gather evidence for subsequent legal action.
B. identify individuals who failed to take appropriate action.
C. prepare a report on the incident for management.
D. derive ways to improve the response process.

4-2 Which of the following is the **MOST** appropriate quality that an incident handler should possess?

A. Presentation skills for management report
B. Ability to follow policy and procedures
C. Integrity
D. Ability to cope with stress

4-3 What is the **PRIMARY** reason for conducting triage?

A. Limited resources in incident handling
B. As a part of the mandatory process in incident handling
C. To mitigate an incident
D. To detect an incident

4-4 Which of the following is **MOST** important when deciding whether to build an alternate facility or subscribe to a hot site operated by a third party?

A. Cost to rebuild information processing facilities
B. Incremental daily cost of losing different systems
C. Location and cost of commercial recovery facilities
D. Estimated annualized loss expectancy (ALE) from key risk

4-5 Which of the following documents should be contained in a computer incident response team (CIRT) manual?

A. Risk assessment
B. Severity criteria
C. Employee phone directory
D. Table of all backup files

4-6 Which of the following types of insurance coverage would protect an organization against dishonest or fraudulent behavior by its own employees?

A. Fidelity
B. Business interruption
C. Valuable papers and records
D. Business continuity

4-7 Which of the following practices would **BEST** ensure the adequacy of a disaster recovery plan?

A. Regular reviews of recovery plan information
B. Table top walk-through of disaster recovery plans
C. Regular recovery exercises, using expert personnel
D. Regular audits of disaster recovery facilities

4-8 Which of the following procedures would provide the **BEST** protection if an intruder or malicious program has gained superuser (e.g., root) access to a system?

A. Prevent the system administrator(s) from accessing the system until it can be shown that they were not the attackers.
B. Inspect the system and intrusion detection output to identify all changes and then undo them.
C. Rebuild the system using original media.
D. Change all passwords, then resume normal operations.

4-9 Which of the following is likely to be the **MOST** significant challenge when developing an incident management plan?

A. Plan does not align with organizational goals
B. Implementation of log centralization, correlation and event tracking
C. Development of incident metrics
D. Lack of management support and organizational consensus

4-10 If a forensics copy of a hard drive is needed, the copied data is **MOST** defensible from a legal standpoint if which of the following is used?

A. A compressed copy of all contents of the hard drive
B. A copy that includes all files and directories
C. A bit-by-bit copy of all data
D. An encrypted copy of all contents of the hard drive

ANSWERS TO SELF-ASSESSMENT QUESTIONS

4-1 **D** The goal of a postincident review is to derive ways in which the incident response process can be improved. It should not be focused on finding and punishing those individuals who did not take appropriate action or learning the identity of the attacker. Evidence should have already been gathered earlier in the process. Although postincident review can be used to prepare a report/presentation to management, it is not the primary goal.

4-2 **D** Incident handlers work in high-stress environments when dealing with incidents. Incorrect decisions are likely made if the person is unable to cope with stress; thus, the primary quality of those listed is to cope with stress.

4-3 **A** Triage is conducted primarily because there are limited incident handling resources. With categorization, prioritization and assignment of incidents based on their criticality, resources can be allocated more efficiently. Other choices are part of incident handling processes.

4-4 **C** The decision whether to build an alternate facility or rent hot site facilities from a third party should be based entirely on business decisions of cost and whether the location is susceptible to the same environmental risk as the primary facility.

4-5 **B** Severity criteria will remain relatively static and is the only one of the choices that is appropriate for the manual. The other choices will change frequently and it would not make sense to reprint the manual every time phone numbers change or backup files change.

4-6 **A** Fidelity coverage means insurance coverage against loss from dishonesty or fraud by employees.

4-7 **A** The most common failure of disaster recovery plans is a lack of maintaining the current information. The various types of recovery exercises, including walk-throughs, are important, yet must be based on an up-to-date recovery plan to add value. Recovery exercises using expert personnel are typically not realistic since it is uncertain what personnel would be available during an actual disaster. Audits may be useful in uncovering deficiencies in the plan, but would not provide a high level of assurance of successful plan execution.

4-8 **C** If someone, or a malicious program, gains superuser privileges on a system without authorization, the organization never really knows what the perpetrator or program has done to the system. The only way to assure the integrity of the system is to wipe the system clean (usually after making a complete data backup for the purpose of further analysis and also to prevent the destruction of data that may not exist elsewhere) and start over again by reinstalling the operating system and applications. Note that choice D would be defensible if the system was rebuilt first, but the way this alternative is worded makes it wrong because it omits any mention of the need to rebuild the system. To be correct, choice D would have to be worded "rebuild the system and then change all passwords."

4-9 **D** Getting senior management buy-in is often difficult, but is the necessary first step in order to move forward with any incident management plan. The incident management plan is a subset of the security strategy, which already aligns to organizational goals and therefore does not represent a major challenge. Implementation of log centralization, correlation and event tracking, as well as the development of incident metrics, are also required, but they are not the most significant challenges.

4-10 **C** There is no alternative to making a bit-by-bit copy, if one wants forensic evidence that is "air tight." Only a bit copy will result in capturing all data on a hard drive. Copying all files and folders will, in contrast, miss certain data such as data between the end of a file and the end of the disk sector ("slack space").

Section Two: Content

4.4 INCIDENT MANAGEMENT OVERVIEW

Incident management and response can be considered the emergency operations part of risk management. Included are activities that result from unanticipated attacks, losses, theft, accidents or any other unexpected adverse events that occur as a result of the failure or lack of controls.

The purpose of incident management is to identify and respond to unexpected disruptive events with the objective of controlling impacts within acceptable levels. These events can be technical, such as attacks mounted on the network via viruses, denial of service (DoS) or system intrusion, or they can be the result of mistakes, accidents, or system or process failure. Disruptions can also be caused by a variety of physical events such as theft of proprietary information, social engineering, lost or stolen backup tapes or laptops, environmental conditions such as floods, fires, or earthquakes. Any type of incident that can significantly affect the organization's ability to operate, or that may cause damage, must be considered by the information security manager and will normally be a part of incident management and response capabilities.

Incident management can include activities that either serve to minimize the possibility of occurrences or lessen impacts, or both, although this is usually one of the functions of risk management. An example would be securing laptops physically to lessen the possibility of theft as well as encrypting hard disks to reduce the impact of theft or loss.

As with other aspects of risk management, risk and business impact assessments form the basis for determining the priority of resource protection and response activities.

Incident management, problem management and disaster recovery planning (part of business continuity planning [BCP]) are separate but complementary processes. As "first responders" to adverse events related to information security, the objective of incident management is to prevent incidents from becoming problems and to prevent problems from becoming disasters.

The extent of incident management and response capabilities must be carefully balanced with baseline security, business continuity and disaster recovery. For example, if there is little or no response capability, it may be prudent to raise baseline security levels. The level of incident management capability must also be considered in the context of BCP and disaster recovery planning (DRP). There is some point where it will be more cost effective to resort to alternate processing options than to maintain a high level of incident management and response capability.

The goal of incident management and response activities can be summarized as:
- Detect incidents quickly
- Diagnose incidents accurately
- Manage incidents properly
- Contain and minimize damage
- Restore affected services
- Determine root causes
- Implement improvements to prevent recurrence
- Document and report

By definition, incidents are unexpected and often confusing. The ability to detect and assess the situation, determine the causes, and quickly arrive at solutions can mean the difference between an inconvenience and a disaster. An important consideration is knowing the point at which an incident becomes a problem and, consequently, when the inability to adequately address a problem calls for the declaration of a disaster. The time to make those determinations is not in the middle of a crisis.

Rigorous planning and commitment of resources are necessary to adequately plan for such events. As with other aspects of security, it is critical to achieve stakeholder consensus and senior management support for an effective incident management capability. Support can be achieved as a result of the impacts of prior incidents to the organization or to other incidents, and/or from developing a persuasive business case. Incident management and response can result in lower overall security costs by setting baselines to address common events, but providing protection against relatively rare occurrences with a response, containment and recovery capability. This is similar to the common approach for protecting against fire by a combination of reasonable preventive controls, coupled with an effective fire detection system, evacuation plans and triggers for fire department response. These controls should be complemented with insurance policies in the rare event that incident management and response measures fall short. While a totally fireproof structure could be built, optimal cost effectiveness utilizes a combination of risk management approaches.

Many organizations have a separate department responsible for BCP and disaster recovery (DR) and the extent of information security involvement and authority will vary widely. However these departments are structured, it is essential that they work together closely and that the plans are complementary and well integrated. Who is in charge of what kind of events must be clearly defined and there must be clear severity and declaration criteria. Severity criteria should be consistent, concisely described and easy to understand so that severity levels of similar events will be uniformly determined. Declaration criteria must also be established so that it is clear who has the authority to determine the response level, activate the teams, and declare a disaster and mobilize the recovery process. Severity criteria and their use must be widely published. Personnel must be trained to recognize potential incidents and proper classification and must be trained in notification, reporting and escalation requirements. The information security manager should be aware that, regardless of how well incidents are planned for and handled, there is always the possibility that events will escalate to a disaster.

Considering the need for incident response, business continuity (BC) and DR to work together, this chapter will cover the following topics:
- Incident response procedures
- Business continuity and disaster recovery procedures
- Testing of plans
- Postincident and event activities and investigations

4.5 INCIDENT RESPONSE PROCEDURES

There is no guarantee that even the best possible controls will prevent disruptive, and sometimes even catastrophic, incidents from occurring. Adverse events such as security breaches, power outages, fires and natural disasters can bring IT and business operations to a halt. Response management enables a business to respond effectively when an incident occurs, to continue operations in the event of disruption, and to survive interruptions or security breaches in information systems.

The following section covers the necessity for incident response capabilities and the typical responsibilities of an information security manager. These responsibilities can vary significantly in different organizations and, in some cases, may include some DR and BC activities as well.

4.5.1 IMPORTANCE OF INCIDENT MANAGEMENT

As organizations increasingly rely on information processes and systems, and significant disruption to those activities results in unacceptably severe impacts, the criticality of effective incident management and response has grown. Some of the factors that compound the necessity include:
- The trend of both increased occurrences and escalating losses resulting from information security incidents
- The increase of vulnerabilities in software or systems affecting large parts of an organization's infrastructure and impact operations
- Failure of security controls to prevent incidents
- Legal and regulatory groups requiring the development of an incident management capability
- The growing sophistication and capabilities of profit-oriented attackers

4.5.2 OUTCOMES OF INCIDENT MANAGEMENT

Incident management is a term that includes incident detection, response and postincident review.

An outcome of good incident management and response will be an organization that can deal effectively with unanticipated events that might threaten to disrupt the business. The organization will have sufficient detection and monitoring capabilities to ensure that incidents are detected in a timely manner. There will be well-defined severity and declaration criteria as well as defined escalation and notification processes. Personnel will be trained in the recognition of incidents, the application of severity criteria, and proper reporting and escalation procedures. The organization will have response capabilities that demonstrably support the business strategy by being responsive to the criticality and sensitivity of the resources protected. The organization will serve to proactively manage the risk of incidents appropriately in a cost-effective manner and will provide integration of security-related organizational functions to maximize effectiveness. The organization will provide monitoring and metrics to gauge performance of incident management and response capabilities, and it will periodically test its capabilities and ensure that information and plans are updated regularly, are current and accessible when needed.

These activities will ensure that:
- Information assets are adequately protected and the risk level is within acceptable limits.
- Effective incident response plans are in place and understood by relevant stakeholders (e.g., management, IT departments, end users, incident handlers).
- Incidents are identified and contained, and the root cause is addressed to allow recovery within an acceptable interruption window (AIW).
- There is good control of communication flows to different stakeholders and external parties as documented in the communication plan.
- Lessons learned are documented and shared with stakeholders to increase the level of security awareness and serve as a basis for improvement.
- Assurance is provided to internal and external stakeholders (e.g., customers, suppliers, business partners) that the organization has adequate control and is prepared to ensure business survivability in the long term.

4.5.3 INCIDENT MANAGEMENT

Depending on the organization, the extent of the information security manager's involvement in BCP/DR, BCP/DRP, and incident response will vary considerably. The typical situation is that the information security manager has, at a minimum, responsibility as first responder to information security related incidents, regardless of the causes.

To effectively deal with security incidents, it is important for the information security manager to have a good conceptual and practical understanding of what is required to adequately address those responsibilities. In addition, there must be a good understanding of the BC and DR processes. This is to ensure that incident management and response plans and activities integrate well with the overall BCP and DRP in the event that an incident escalates to a disaster.

4.5.4 CONCEPTS

Carnegie Mellon University (CMU) Software Engineering Institute (SEI) provides the following definitions:
- **Incident handling** is one service that involves all the processes or tasks associated with handling events and incidents. It involves multiple functions:
  - Detection and reporting—The ability to receive and review event information, incident reports, and alerts
  - Triage—The action taken to categorize, prioritize and assign events and incidents
  - Analysis—The attempt to determine what has happened, the impact and threat, the damage that has resulted, and the recovery or mitigation steps that should be followed
  - Incident response—The action taken to resolve or mitigate an incident, coordinate and disseminate information, and implement follow-up strategies to prevent recurring incidents
- **Effective incident management** will ensure that incidents are detected, recorded and managed to limit impacts. Recording incidents is required so that no aspect of an incident is inadvertently overlooked, so that incident response activities can be tracked and so that information can be provided to aid planning activities. Recording is also required to properly document information that potentially includes forensics data that

can be used to pursue disciplinary or legal options. Incidents must be classified to ensure that they are correctly prioritized and routed to the correct resources. Incident management includes initial support processes that allow new incidents to be checked against known errors and problems so that any previously identified workarounds can be quickly identified.

In summary, incident management provides a structure by which incidents can be investigated, diagnosed, resolved and then closed. The process ensures that the incidents are owned, tracked and monitored throughout their life cycle. There may be occasions when major incidents occur that require a response above and beyond that provided by the normal incident process and may require activating BCP/DR capabilities.

Incident management often includes other functions such as vulnerability management and security awareness training. It may include proactive activities intended to help prevent incidents.

- **Incident response** is the last step in an incident handling process that encompasses the planning, coordination and execution of appropriate mitigation, containment and recovery strategies and actions.

The information security manager also must be aware of the possibility of nontechnical incidents that must be planned for and addressed. These incidents can include social engineering, lost or stolen backup tapes or laptop computers, physical theft of sensitive materials, natural disasters, etc.

4.5.5 INCIDENT MANAGEMENT SYSTEMS

The sheer amount of information and activities in increasingly complex systems has driven the development of automated incident management systems in recent years. These systems automate many manual processes that provide filtered information that can identify possible technical incidents and alert the incident management team (IMT).

An example of a distributed incident management system is one that contains multiple specific incident detection capabilities, e.g., network intrusion detection systems (NIDSs), host intrusion detection systems (HIDSs) and server/appliance logs.

An example of a centralized incident management system is a security information and event manager (SIEM). This tool essentially combines critical events and logs from many different systems and correlates them into more meaningful incident information. Further processing can be done from there, e.g., prioritizing incidents based on their business impacts or performing specific notifications/escalations based on the impact ratings.

Another significant feature of incident management systems is their ability to track an incident during its life cycle. Tracking is a powerful feature that ensures that incidents are not overlooked and that they receive necessary attention based on criticality. Tracking enables users to provide more information and receive status updates along the event life cycle until the event is closed. The system is most often offered in a web-based format for easy accessibility.

An effective security information and event management system (SIEM) should:
- Consolidate and correlate inputs from multiple systems
- Identify incidents or potential incidents
- Prioritize incidents based on business impact
- Track incidents until they are closed
- Provide status tracking and notifications
- Integrate with major IT management systems
- Implement good practices guidelines

There are potential efficiencies and cost savings that can be realized using automated incident management systems. Some considerations for the information security manager can include:
- **Operating costs**—In the absence of an automated and centralized incident management system, information security staff may be required to monitor different security devices, correlate events and process the information manually. With this approach, there are additional costs for training and maintaining the staff over the long term. There also is a higher probability of human error.
- **Recovery costs**—An automated system, when configured properly, is able to detect and escalate incidents significantly faster than when a manual process is used. The amount of damage can be controlled and further damage prevented when the recovery actions are initiated earlier rather than later. In the case of a manual management system, a longer analysis process may contribute to further damage before incidents are contained.

4.6 INCIDENT MANAGEMENT ORGANIZATION

The incident management capability in an organization is, figuratively, the fire brigade and ambulance service for a variety of incidents, including information processing and processes. It is there to respond to and manage incidents in order to contain and minimize damage. Poorly managed incidents have the capacity to become disasters if they are not handled effectively. A typical example would be a financial institution being infected with Trojan malware. The absence of a tested incident response plan and the lack of appropriate response while the Trojan captured data unhindered could result in the viability of the entire organization being at stake due to substantial financial losses as well as the reputational damage.

Just as there are requirements for addressing fire and medical emergencies utilizing trained individuals and appropriate equipment, so must the prudent information security manager plan for the inevitable range of incidents likely to disrupt the organization's business operations to an unacceptable extent.

Incident management is, nominally, a component of risk management and can be considered the operational and reactive element. That is, if managing risk was insufficient to prevent a threat from materializing and causing an impact, incident management and response capabilities should be available to react appropriately to limit the damage and restore operations.

The information security manager should understand the various activities involved in a response and recovery program. This includes meeting with emergency management officials (federal, state/provincial, municipal/local) to understand what governmental capabilities exist. These officials are likely to have information concerning the nature of the risk to which the location or area is susceptible. Most countries and governments have civil defense and/or emergency management agencies that are tasked with advising and assisting the population in dealing with a wide range of natural and human-initiated threats.

Emergency management activities typically focus around the activities immediately after an incident. This can include activities during or after a physical disaster, fire, electrical failure or security-related incident. These events may require prompt action to recover operational status. Actions may necessitate restoration of hardware, software and/or data files. Emergency management activities also typically include measures to assure the safety of personnel such as evacuation plans and creation of a command center from which emergency procedures can be executed. It also is important that information about an incident only be communicated on a need-to-know basis.

4.6.1 RESPONSIBILITIES

Typically, there are a number of incident management responsibilities that the information security manager must undertake. These will generally include:
- Developing information security incident management and response plans
- Handling and coordinating information security incident response activities effectively and efficiently
- Validating, verifying and reporting of protective or countermeasure solutions, both technical and administrative
- Planning, budgeting and program development for all matters related to information security incident management and response

The approach to incident response may vary depending on the situation, but the goals are constant and include:
- Containing and minimizing the effects of the incident so that damage and losses do not escalate out of control
- Notifying the appropriate people for the purpose of recovery or to provide needed information
- Recovering quickly and efficiently from security incidents
- Responding systematically and decreasing the likelihood of recurrence
- Balancing operational and security processes
- Dealing with legal and law enforcement-related issues

The information security manager also needs to define what constitutes a security-related incident. Typically, security incidents include:
- Malicious code attacks
- Unauthorized access to IT or information resources
- Unauthorized utilization of services
- Unauthorized changes to systems, network devices or information
- DoS
- Misuse
- Surveillance and espionage
- Hoaxes/social engineering

It should be noted that many incidents that initially appear to be malicious turn out, instead, to be the result of human error. Studies show that organizations experience nearly double the number of incidents due to human error than to externally-initiated security breaches.

4.6.2 SENIOR MANAGEMENT COMMITMENT

As is the case with other aspects of information security, senior management commitment is critical to the success of incident management and response.

A business case can be made so that effective incident management and response may be a less costly option than attempting to implement controls for all possible conditions. Incident management and response can be part of the trade-off that may reduce the cost of risk management efforts by allowing higher levels of acceptable risk.

Adequate incident response, in combination with effective information security, creates a practical risk management solution that may be more cost effective in the long run and may be the most prudent resource management decision.

4.7 INCIDENT MANAGEMENT RESOURCES

There are a number of resources available in the typical organization that must be identified and utilized in the development of an incident management and response plan. As with other aspects of information security, it is essential to develop a clear scope and objectives as well as an implementation strategy. The strategy must consider the elements needed to move from the current state of incident management to the desired state. This will clarify what resources are required and how they must be deployed.

4.7.1 POLICIES AND STANDARDS

The incident response plan must be backed by well-defined policies, standards and procedures. A documented set of policies, standards and procedures is important to:
- Ensure that incident management activities are aligned with the IMT mission
- Set correct expectations
- Provide guidance for operational needs
- Maintain consistency and reliability of services
- Clearly understand roles and responsibilities
- Set requirements for identified alternates for all important functions

The lack of suitable policies and supporting standards may hinder incident management capabilities.

4.7.2 INCIDENT RESPONSE TECHNOLOGY CONCEPTS

The following security concepts and technologies must be familiar to IRTs:
- Security principles—General understanding of basic security principles such as:
  - Confidentiality
  - Availability
  - Authentication
  - Integrity
  - Access control
  - Privacy
  - Nonrepudiation
  - Compliance

Knowledge of security principles is important in order to understand potential problems that can arise if appropriate security measures have not been implemented correctly and to understand the potential impacts to the organization's systems:

- **Security vulnerabilities/weaknesses**—Understanding how any specific attack is manifested in a given software or hardware technology. The most common types of vulnerabilities and associated attacks involve:
  - Physical security issues
  - Protocol design flaws (e.g., man-in-the-middle attacks, spoofing)
  - Malicious code (e.g., viruses, worms, Trojan horses)
  - Implementation flaws (e.g., buffer overflow, timing windows/race conditions)
  - Configuration weaknesses
  - User errors or lack of awareness
- **The Internet**—There must be security in the underlying protocols and services used on the Internet. A good understanding is important to anticipate the threats that might occur in the future. The following technologies that enable the Internet should be addressed in the incident response program:
  - Network protocols—Common (or core) network protocols such as Internet Protocol (IP), Transmission Control Protocol (TCP), User Datagram Protocol (UDP), Internet Control Message Protocol (ICMP), Address Resolution Protocol (ARP), and Reverse Address Resolution Protocol (RARP); how they are used; common types of threats or attacks against the protocol; strategies to mitigate or eliminate such attacks; and Internet technologies
  - Network applications and services—For example: domain name system (DNS), network file system (NFS) and secure shell (SSH); how they work; common usage; secure configurations; and common types of threats or attacks against the application or service and mitigation strategies
  - Network security issues—To recognize vulnerable points in network configurations. Basic perimeter security, network firewalls (design, packet filtering, proxy systems, demilitarized zone [DMZ], bastion hosts, etc.) and router security are relevant to recognize the potential for information disclosure of data traveling across the network (e.g., packet monitoring or "sniffers") or threats relating to accepting untrustworthy information.
- **Operating systems**—Knowledge of operating systems such as UNIX, Windows, MAC, Linux, Android, or any other operating systems used by the team or constituency is important, specifically how to:
  - Configure (harden) the system
  - Review configuration files for security weaknesses
  - Identify common attack methods
  - Determine whether a compromise attempt occurred
  - Determine whether an attempted system compromise was successful
  - Review log files for anomalies
  - Analyze the results of attacks
  - Manage system privileges
  - Recover from a compromise
- **Malicious code (viruses, worms, Trojan horse programs)**—Can have different types of payloads that can cause a denial-of-service attack or web defacement, or the code can contain more "dynamic" payloads that can be configured to result in multifaceted attack vectors; how malicious code is propagated through some of the obvious methods (CDs, thumb drives, email, programs, etc.) and how it can propagate through other means such as macros, multipurpose Internet mail extension (MIME), peer-to-peer file sharing or viruses that affect operating systems running on PC and Macintosh platforms
- **Programming skills**—The range of programming languages utilized by the organization's operating systems, concepts and techniques for secure programming and how vulnerabilities can be introduced into code (e.g., through poor programming and design practices).

4.7.3 PERSONNEL

An IMT usually consists of an information security manager, steering committee/advisory board, permanent/dedicated team members and virtual/temporary team members.

The information security manager usually leads the team. In larger organizations, it may be more effective to appoint a separate IRT leader/manager who focuses on responding to incidents. Above the information security manager, there is a set of senior management executives in a group, typically a security steering group (SSG), security advisory board or perhaps an executive committee. Whatever it is called, the SSG function is responsible for approving the charter and serves as an escalation point for the IMT. The SSG also approves deviations and exceptions to normal practice.

Permanent/dedicated team members have full-time work inside the IMT. They perform the primary tasks in the IMT/IRT. As information systems are broad and complex, it is inefficient and expensive to have all individuals covering all disciplines in performing IMT/IRT. Virtual/temporary team members may have specialized skills and are recruited when necessary to fill gaps within the internal skills portfolio.

Incident Response Team Organization

Incident handlers analyze incident data, determine the impact of the incident, and act appropriately to limit the damage to the organization and restore normal services. Often, the team will depend on the participation and cooperation of complementary groups and of general users. Incident response team models that have proven to work in many organizations include:

- **Central IRT**—A single IRT handles all incidents for the organization, usually either a small organization or one that is centrally located.
- **Distributed IRT**—Each of several teams is responsible for a logical or physical segment of the infrastructure, usually of a large organization or one that is geographically dispersed.
- **Coordinating IRT**—The central team may provide guidance to distributed IRTs, develop policies and standards, provide training, conduct exercises, and coordinate or support response to specific incidents. Distributed teams manage and implement incident response.
- **Outsourced IRT**—Successful IRTs may be comprised entirely of employees of the organization, or may be fully or partially outsourced.

Permanent team members may include incident handlers, investigators and forensics experts, and IT and physical security

specialists. Virtual team members normally consist of business representatives (middle management), legal staff, communications staff (public relations), human resources (HR) staff, other security groups (physical security), risk management and IT specialists. The composition of incident response staff varies from team to team and depends on a number of factors such as:
- Mission and goals of the incident response program
- Nature and range of services offered
- Available staff expertise
- Constituency size and technology base
- Anticipated incident load
- Severity or complexity of incident reports
- Funding

4.7.4 ROLES AND RESPONSIBILITIES

Exhibit 4.2 provides common roles and responsibilities of IRT personnel. Note that each position should have an alternate in case the designee is incapacitated or unavailable.

Exhibit 4.2—Roles and Responsibilities

No.	Position	Roles	Responsibilities
1.	Security steering group	Highest structure of an organization's functions related to information security	1. Take responsibility for overall incident management and response concept 2. Approve IMT charter 3. Approve exceptions/deviations 4. Make final decisions
2.	Information security manager	IMT leader and main interface to SSG	1. Develops and maintains incident management and response capability 2. Effectively manages risk and incidents 3. Performs proactive and reactive measures to control information risk level
3.	Incident response manager	IRT leader	1. Supervises incident response tasks 2. Coordinates resources to effectively perform incident response tasks 3. Takes responsibility for successful execution of incident response plan 4. Presents incident response report and lessons learned to SSG members
4.	Incident handler	IMT/IRT team member	1. Performs incident response tasks to contain exposures from an incident 2. Documents steps taken when executing incident response plan 3. Maintains chain of custody and observes incident handling procedures for court purposes 4. Writes incident response report and lessons learned
5.	Investigator	IMT/IRT team member	1. Performs investigative tasks to a specific incident 2. Finds root cause of an incident 3. Writes report of investigation findings
6.	IT security specialist	IMT/IRT team member; subject matter expert in IT security	1. Performs complex and in-depth IT security-related tasks as part of Incident response plan 2. Performs IT security assessment/audit as proactive measure and part of vulnerability management
7.	Business managers	Business function owners; information assets/system owners	1. Make decisions on matters related to information assets/systems when an incident happens, based on IMT/IRT recommendations 2. Provide clear understanding of business impact in BIA process or in incident response plan
8.	IT specialists/representatives	Subject matter experts in IT services	1. Provide support to IMT/IRT when resolving an incidents 2. Maintain information systems in a good condition per company policy and best practices
9.	Legal representative	Subject matter expert in legal	1. Ensures that incident response actions and procedures comply with legal and regulatory requirements. 2. Acts as the liaison to law enforcement and outside agencies.
10.	HR	Subject matter expert in HR area	1. Provides assistance in incident management/response when there is a need to investigate an employee suspected of causing an incident 2. Integrates HR policy to support incident management/response (sanctions to employees found to violate acceptable use of policy or involved in an incident)
11.	Public relations (PR) representative	Subject matter expert in PR area	1. Provides controlled communication to internal and external stakeholders to minimize any adverse impact to ongoing incident response activities and to protect an organization's brand and reputation 2. Provides assistance to IMT/IRT in communication issues, thus relieving the team to work on critical issues on resolving an incident
12.	Risk management specialist	Subject matter expert in risk management	1. Works closely with business managers and senior management to determine and manage risk 2. Provides input (e.g., BIA, risk management strategy) to incident management
13.	Physical security/ facilities manager	Knowledgeable about physical plant and emergency capabilities	1. Responsible for physical plant and facilities 2. Ensures physical security during incidents

4.7.5 SKILLS

To build an incident response team with capable incident handlers, organizations need people with certain skill sets and technical expertise, with abilities that enable them to respond to incidents, perform analysis tasks and communicate effectively with the constituency and external contacts. They must also be competent problem solvers, must easily adapt to change, and must be effective in their daily activities.

The set of basic skills that incident response team members need can be separated into two broad groups:

- **Personal skills**—Major parts of the incident handler's daily activity, including:
  - Communication—The ability to communicate effectively is a critical component of the skills needed by incident response teams. They need to be effective communicators to ensure that they obtain and supply the information necessary to be helpful. They need to be good listeners, understanding what is said (or not said), to enable them to gain details about an incident that is being reported. They also remain in control of these communications to most effectively determine what is happening, what facts are important and what assistance is necessary. They need to communicate with:
    - Team members
    - IT staff
    - Application owners
    - Users of the systems
    - Technical experts
    - Management and other administrative staff
    - Human resources
    - Law enforcement
    - Media/public relations staff
    - Vendors

    Communication can take many forms, including:
    - Responses in email concerning incidents
    - Documentation of event or incident reports, vulnerabilities and other technical information
    - Notifications and/or guidelines that are provided to the constituency
    - Internal development policies and procedures
    - Other external communications to staff, management, or other relevant parties
  - Leadership skills—Members of a response team are often faced with directing and getting support of other members of the organization and leadership is an important attribute.
  - Presentation skills—An incident response team's skills are needed for a technical presentation, management or sponsor briefings, a panel discussion at a conference, or some other form of public-speaking engagement. The specialist member's skills might extend to providing expert testimony in legal or other proceedings on behalf of the team or users.
  - Ability to follow policies and procedures—Team members need the ability to follow and support the established policies and procedures for incident response management.
  - Team skills—The ability to work in a team environment as productive and cordial team players, be aware of responsibilities, contribute to the goals of the team, and work together to share information, workload and experiences. Members must be flexible and willing to adapt to change. There may be a need for one or more team members to act in a leadership role to support the smaller groups or technical teams.
  - Integrity—Team members often deal with information that is sensitive and, occasionally, they may have access to information that is newsworthy. Members must be trustworthy, discrete and able to handle information in confidence.
  - Self understanding—Team members must be able to recognize their limitations and actively seek support from their team members, other experts or management.
  - Coping with stress—The incident response team is likely to face stressful situations. They need to be able to recognize when they are becoming stressed, be willing to make their fellow team members aware of the situation, and take the necessary steps to control and maintain their composure.
  - Problem solving—Without good problem-solving skills, team members could become overwhelmed with the volumes of data related to incidents and other tasks that need to be handled. Problem-solving skills also include an ability to "think outside the box" or look at issues from multiple perspectives to identify relevant information or data. This includes knowing who else to contact or approach for additional information, creative ideas or added technical insight.
  - Time management—Team members might be confronted with a multitude of tasks ranging from analyzing, coordinating and responding to incidents, to performing duties such as prioritizing their workload, attending and/or preparing for meetings, completing time sheets, collecting statistics, conducting research, giving briefings and presentations, traveling to conferences, providing onsite technical support, and prioritizing tasks. Team members must be able to balance efforts between completing the tasks and recognizing when to seek help or guidance.
- **Technical skills**—The basic technical skills required by incident management team members are of two types:
  - Technical foundation skills—Require a basic understanding of the underlying technologies used by the organization
  - Incident handling skills—Require an understanding of the techniques, decision points and supporting tools (software or applications) required in daily activities

4.7.6 AWARENESS AND EDUCATION

If an organization is unable to find internal experts or hire/train staff to provide the necessary specialist skills, the organization may be able to develop relationships with experts in the field to provide the necessary skills. When a situation arises where in-house knowledge is not enough, these technical specialists can be called on to fill the gap in expertise.

When more complex incidents are reported, the organization may need to supplement or expand the staff's basic skills to include more in-depth knowledge so that staff members can understand, analyze, and identify effective responses to reported incidents.

4.7.7 AUDITS

Internal and external audits are performed to verify compliance with policies, standards and procedures defined for an organization. Internal audits are conducted by specialists within the organization and are usually intended to support compliance requirements or to improve an existing situation. External audits involve a third party who performs the tasks. While most external audits are exercised as part of mandatory requirements, external audits are also often imposed as part of business collaboration.

Both types of audits can be useful in reviewing incident management and response plans and capabilities. Periodic audits of the processes and procedures specified in the plans can provide validation that security will not be compromised in the event of an incident and that policy compliance and legal requirements are addressed appropriately. Audits can also provide an objective view of the overall completeness and functionality of the incident management and response plans and provide assurance that major gaps in the processes do not exist.

4.7.8 OUTSOURCED SECURITY PROVIDERS

Outsourcing incident management capability may be a cost-effective option for an organization. For example, organizations that have outsourced their information technology operations may benefit from close integration if incident management is outsourced to the same vendor. Organizations would still require an incident response plan overseen by an incident response team, even if components of incident management are outsourced.

4.8 INCIDENT MANAGEMENT OBJECTIVES

Incident management exists to address the inevitable events that threaten the operation of any organization. It serves as the next-to-last safety net after controls have failed to prevent or contain a threatening event. Its purpose is to respond to and contain a threatening incident or to quickly restore normal operations in the event of damage. Failing to do so will result in the declaration of a disaster and recovery operations will move to an alternative site to restore operations according to a BCP/DR.

4.8.1 DEFINING OBJECTIVES

The objectives of incident management are:
- Handle incidents when they occur so that the exposure can be contained or eradicated to enable recovery within an AIW.
- Restore systems to normal operations.
- Prevent previous incidents from recurring by documenting and learning from past incidents.
- Deploy proactive countermeasures to prevent/minimize the probability of incidents from taking place.

4.8.2 THE DESIRED STATE

Since incident management and response serves as the fire brigade, ambulance service and emergency room for the organization's information assets, it must effectively address a wide range of possible unexpected events, both electronic and physical. It will need to have well-developed monitoring capabilities for key controls, whether procedural or technical, to provide early detection of potential problems. It will have personnel trained in assessing the situation, capable of providing triage, managing effective responses that maximize operational continuity and minimize impacts. Incident managers will have made provisions to capture all relevant information and apply previously learned lessons. They will be prepared for a disaster through well-defined criteria, experience, knowledge and authority to invoke the disaster recovery processes necessary to maintain or recover operational status.

4.8.3 STRATEGIC ALIGNMENT

Similar to many other support functions, incident management must be aligned with an organization's strategic plan. The following components may help to accomplish this alignment:
- **Constituency**—To whom does the IMT provide services? It is important to know who the stakeholders are for this function and to identify their expectations and their information needs. For example, senior management in financial institutions may be bound by BASEL II or another regulation. Thus, incident management is an important function and it is expected that the IMT should meet certain performance and reporting requirements.
- **Mission**—The mission defines the purpose of the team and the primary objectives and goals that are provided by IMT.

  An example of a possible IMT mission statement follows: "The mission of the incident management team is to develop, maintain and deliver incident management capabilities and services to safeguard the organization's information assets against computer incidents. We strive to provide assurance to our stakeholders that risk and computer incidents are dealt with in an efficient and effective manner and that we will prevent/minimize losses resulting from such incidents."
- **Services**—Services provided by IMT should be clearly defined to manage stakeholder expectations. Services offered in organizations may differ significantly, and normally have a positive correlation with the size of the organization and the extent of senior management buy-in.
- **Organizational structure**—The structure of the IMT should effectively support the organization's structure. For multinational companies, a geography-based structure may be the best. For organizations with multiple subsidiaries, one IMT may be developed for each major subsidiary. The best structure would provide business with the maximum availability of IMT services on the most cost-effective basis.
- **Resources**—Sufficient staffing is needed to be effective. Because incident management covers a wide range of services, most of the time it is not possible to have all the resources available within one IMT. One way to solve this issue is to establish virtual team members and/or complement the team with external resources.
- **Funding**—The IMT usually consists of highly specialized members. In the course of providing services, the equipment that they use may also be specialized, requiring greater capital expenditures. In view of this, sufficient funding is required to ensure the continuity of critical incident response services.
- **Management buy-in**—Senior management buy-in is essential for establishing and supporting the incident management function. The lack of buy-in normally results in suboptimal IMT performance since there may be significant limitation in budgets or the availability of suitable personnel.

4.8.4 RISK MANAGEMENT

Successful outcomes of risk management include effective incident management and response capabilities. Any risk that materializes that is not prevented by controls will constitute an incident that must be managed and responded to with the intent that it does not escalate into a disaster.

4.8.5 ASSURANCE PROCESS INTEGRATION

The type and nature of incidents that the information security manager may deal with will often require the involvement of a number of other organizational functions. This may include physical security, legal, HR and, perhaps, others. As a consequence, it is important to ensure incident management and recovery plans actively incorporate and integrate those functions where required. An effective outcome is a set of plans that defines which departments are involved in various incident management and response activities, and that those linkages have been tested under realistic conditions.

4.8.6 VALUE DELIVERY

Incident management capabilities must be closely integrated with business functions and provide the last line of defense of cost-efficient risk management. Incident management should not just be considered technology to prevent or respond to incidents, but a set of processes that, as a component of risk management, can provide the optimal balance between prevention, containment and restoration.

To deliver value, incident management should:
- Integrate with business processes and structures as seamlessly as possible
- Improve the capability of businesses to manage risk and provide assurance to stakeholders
- Integrate with BCP
- Become part of an organization's overall strategy and effort to protect and secure critical business function and assets
- Provide the backstop and optimize risk management efforts

4.8.7 RESOURCE MANAGEMENT

Resource management spans time, people, budget and other factors to achieve objectives efficiently under given resource constraints. Incident management and response activities consume resources that must be managed to achieve optimal effectiveness. When it is not possible to achieve all objectives, effective resource management ensures that the most important priorities are addressed first.

4.9 INCIDENT MANAGEMENT METRICS AND INDICATORS

Incident management metrics, measures and indicators are the criteria used to measure the effectiveness and efficiency of the incident management function. Metrics based on key performance indicators (KPIs) and program goals established for incident management should be presented to senior management as a basis of justification for continuous support and funding. It enables senior management to understand the incident management capability of their organization and areas of risk that need to be addressed.

Incident management reports and measures are useful for the IMT for self-assessment and to understand what has been done satisfactorily and where improvements need to be made. Common criteria that are used as part of incident management metrics may include:
- Total number of reported incidents
- Total number of detected incidents
- Average time to respond to an incident relative to the AIW
- Average time to resolve an incident
- Total number of incidents successfully resolved
- Proactive and preventive measures taken
- Total number of employees receiving security awareness training
- Total damage from reported and detected incidents if incident response was not performed
- Total savings from potential damages from incidents resolved
- Total labor responding to incidents
- Detection and notification times

4.9.1 PERFORMANCE MEASUREMENT

The performance measurements for incident management and response will focus on achieving the defined objectives and optimizing effectiveness. Key goal indicators (KGIs) and KPIs for the activity should be defined and agreed on by stakeholders and ratified by senior management. The typical range of KGIs encompasses the successful handling of incidents whether by live testing or under actual conditions. Key performance measures can be identified by meeting recovery time objectives or by successfully handling incidents that threaten business operations.

4.10 DEFINING INCIDENT MANAGEMENT PROCEDURES

There is no single, fixed and one-size-fits-all set of incident management procedures for every organization. However, there are a number of good practices that most organizations adopt and customize to meet their own specific needs. Commonly adopted approaches are available from CMU/SEI and the SANS Institute, among others.

4.10.1 DETAILED PLAN OF ACTION FOR INCIDENT MANAGEMENT

The incident management action plan is also known as the incident response plan (IRP). There are a number of approaches to developing the IRP.

In the CMU/SEI technical report titled *Defining Incident Management Processes*, the approach, shown in **exhibit 4.3**, is as follows:
- **Prepare/improve/sustain (prepare)**—This process defines all preparation work that has to be completed prior to having any capability to respond to incidents. It contains subprocesses to evaluate incident handling capability and postmortem review of incidents for improvements. Subprocesses in this process include:
  - Coordinate planning and design:
    - Identify incident management requirements.
    - Establish vision and mission.
    - Obtain funding and sponsorship.
    - Develop implementation plan.
  - Coordinate implementation:
    - Develop policies, processes and plans.
    - Establish incident handling criteria.
    - Implement defined resources.
    - Evaluate incident management capability.
    - Conduct postmortem review.
    - Determine incident management process changes.
    - Implement incident management process changes.

Exhibit 4.3—Incident Response Plan Process Flow

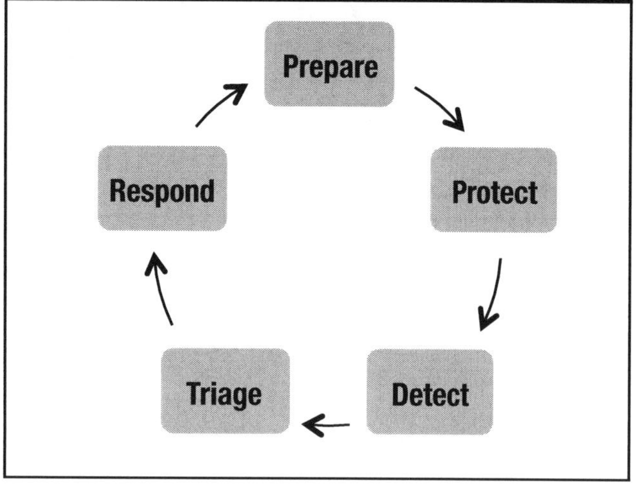

- **Protect infrastructure (protect)**—The protect process aims to protect and secure critical data and computing infrastructure and its constituency when responding to incidents. It also proposes improvement on a predetermined schedule while keeping the appropriate security context in consideration. Subprocesses in this process include:
  - Implement changes to computing infrastructure to mitigate ongoing or potential incident.
  - Implement infrastructure protection improvements from postmortem reviews or other process improvement mechanisms.
  - Evaluate computing infrastructure by performing proactive security assessment and evaluation.
  - Provide input to detect process on incidents/potential incidents.
- **Detect events (detect)**—The detect process identifies unusual/suspicious activity that might compromise critical business functions or infrastructure. Subprocesses in this process include:
  - Proactive detection—The detect process is conducted regularly prior to an incident. The IMT monitors various information from online/periodic vulnerability scanning, network monitoring, antivirus and personal firewall alerts, commercial vulnerability alert services, risk analysis and security audit/assessment.
  - Reactive detection—The detect process is conducted when there are reports from system users or other organizations. Users may notice unusual or suspicious activity and report them to the IMT. It is also possible that another organization's IMT provides advisories when their system has received malicious activity from your organization.

    For the IMT to receive the report promptly, there should be multiple communication channels from end users to the IMT. This can be in the form of phone calls, faxes, email messages, web-form reporting and automated intrusion detection systems (IDSs).
- **Triage events (triage)**—Triage is a process of sorting, categorizing, correlating, prioritizing and assigning incoming reports/events. It is an essential element of any incident management capability. When there are multiple reports coming into the IMT, triage allows events to be prioritized appropriately, thus receiving a prompt response. It also serves as a single point of entry for any IMT correspondence and information.

  Triage provides a snapshot of the current status of all incident activity reported, a central location for incident status reporting, and an initial assessment of incoming reports for further handling. Triage can be done at two levels:
  - Tactical—Based on a set of criteria
  - Strategic—Based on the impact of business.

  Subprocesses in this process include:
  - Categorization—Using predetermined criteria, classify all incoming reports/events. There are many ways to categorize, for example, the US National Institute of Science and Technology (NIST), in its *Computer Security Incident Handling Guide* (SP 800-61), uses:
    - DoS
    - Malicious code
    - Unauthorized access
    - Inappropriate usage
    - Multiple components
  - Correlation—Correlates a report/event with other relevant information. A higher correlation of a report/event provides more information that is useful for the IMT to decide the appropriate response.
  - Prioritization—In an ideal world, every undesirable event is followed-up as soon as possible. However, resources are limited and it may not always be possible. To ensure minimal impact to critical business function or information assets, incidents are prioritized based on their potential impact. Assignments start from highest priority down to lowest priority.
  - Assignment—When an incident or potential incident has been identified, it is assigned to the IMT in the next process (respond). Assignment may be based on:
    - Workload of IMT members
    - IMT members who have handled similar incidents
    - Category or priority of the event
    - Relevant functional business unit
- **Respond**—The response process includes steps taken to address, resolve or mitigate an incident. CMU/SEI defines three types of response activities:
  - Technical response—Appropriate for technical IMT members, such as incident handlers and IT representatives, to analyze and resolve an incident. Technical response forms may include the following:
    - Collecting data for further analysis
    - Analyzing incident supporting information such as log files
    - Researching corresponding technical mitigation strategies and recovery option
    - Telephone or email technical assistance
    - Onsite assistance
    - Analysis of logs
    - Development and deployment of patches and workarounds
  - Management response—The management response includes activities that require supervisory or management intervention, notification, interaction, escalation or approval as part of response to be undertaken. This response is normally executed by business managers and senior management, and spreads across business units.
  - Legal response—The legal response is associated with activity that relates to investigation, prosecution, liability, copyright and privacy issues, laws, regulations and nondisclosure agreements. Because this response may require in-depth

knowledge on legal matters, it is usually referred to the corporate legal team.

A detailed flow diagram of the incident management process is shown in **exhibit 4.4**.

4.11 CURRENT STATE OF INCIDENT RESPONSE CAPABILITY

Most organizations have some sort of incident response capability, either *ad hoc* or formal. The information security manager must identify what is already in place as a basis for understanding the current state. There are many ways to do this; several methods that can be used are:

- **Survey of senior management, business managers and IT representatives**—Using a collection of senior management, business line managers and technology representatives, surveys and focus groups provide a mechanism to help determine the past performance and perception of the incident management team and its process capabilities.
- **Self-assessment**—Self-assessment is conducted by the IMT against a set of criteria to develop an understanding of current capabilities. This is the easiest method since it does not require participation from many stakeholders. The disadvantage of this method is that it includes a limited view on current capability and may not be in line with stakeholders' perceived capability.
- **External assessment or audit**—This is the most comprehensive option and it combines interviews, surveys, simulation and other assessment techniques in the assessment. This option is normally used for an organization that already has an adequate incident management capability, but is further improving it or reengineering the processes.

4.11.1 HISTORY OF INCIDENTS

Past incidents (both internal and external) can provide valuable information on trends, types of events, and business impacts. This information is used as an input to the assessment of the types of incidents that must be planned for and considered.

4.11.2 THREATS

Threats are any event that may cause harm to an organization's assets, operations or personnel. There are a number of threats that must be considered, including:

- **Environmental**—Environmental threats cover natural disasters. While natural disasters vary between locations, some natural disasters may occur between prolonged periods of time and others may occur annually. It is hard to guard against certain natural disasters since their destructive nature is high.
- **Technical**—Technical threats include fire, electrical failure, heating, ventilating and air conditioning (HVAC) failure,

Exhibit 4.4 – Incident Handling Process Flow

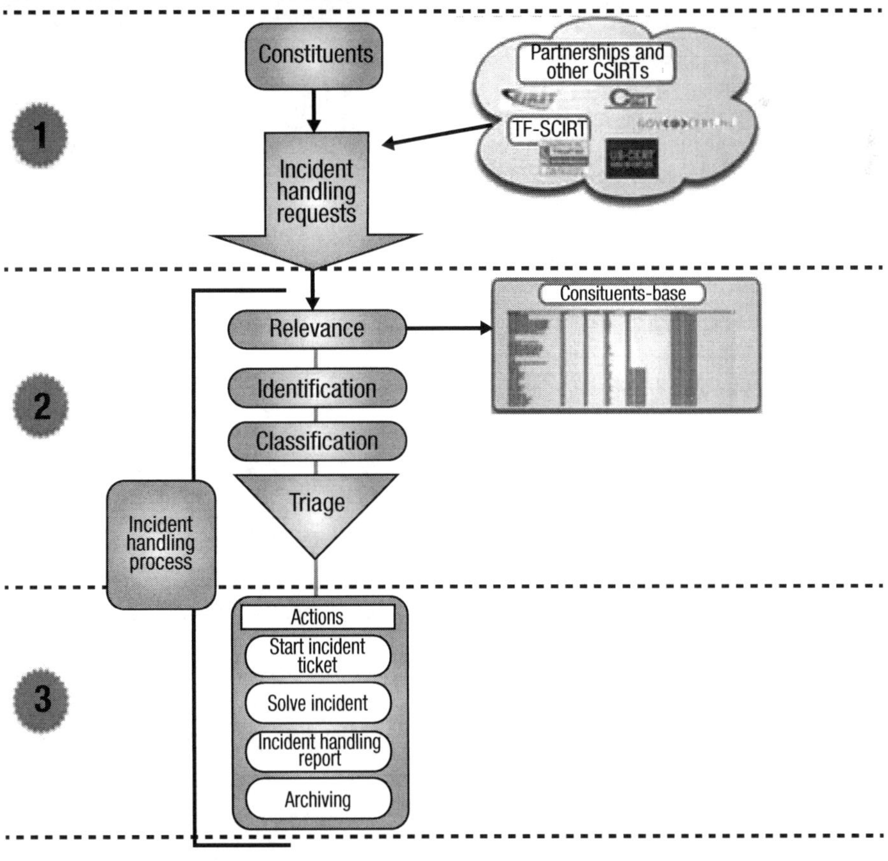

Source: European Union Agency for Network and Information Security, *http://www.enisa.europa.eu/activities/cert/support/incident-management/browsable/workflows/proposed-workflows/proposed-workflows-i*

information system and software issues, telecommunication failure and gas/water leakage. Technical threats are normally found in every organization and are quite common. With sufficient planning, technical threats can be managed adequately.
- **Man-made**—Threats that arise from man-made actions may include damage by disgruntled employees, corporate sabotage/espionage and political instability that interrupts business functions. Such threats are normally easy to identify from location/context and to guard against with proper planning.

4.11.3 VULNERABILITIES

A weakness in a system, technology, process, people or control that can be exploited and result in exposure is a vulnerability. A vulnerability that can be exploited by threats results in risk. One aspect of risk management is managing vulnerabilities to maintain risk within acceptable limits as determined by the organization's risk appetite and tolerance. Vulnerability management is part of the incident management capability; it is the proactive identification, monitoring and fixing of any weaknesses.

4.12 DEVELOPING AN INCIDENT RESPONSE PLAN

The incident response plan is the operational component of incident management. The plan details the actions, personnel and activities that take place in case adverse events result in the loss of information systems or processes.

Elements of an Incident Response Plan

The following model proposed by Schultz, Brown and Longstaff in a University of California technical report "Responding to Computer Security Incidents: Guidelines for Incident Handling" (UCRL-ID-104689, July 23, 1990), presents the six-phase model of incident response including preparation, identification, containment, eradication, restoration and follow-up:
- **Preparation**—This phase prepares an organization to develop an incident response plan prior to an incident. Sufficient preparation facilitates smooth execution. Activities in this phase include:
  - Establishing an approach to handle incidents
  - Establishing policy and warning banners in information systems to deter intruders and allow information collection
  - Establishing communication plan to stakeholders
  - Developing criteria on when to report an incident to authorities
  - Developing a process to activate the incident management team
  - Establishing a secure location to execute the incident response plan
  - Ensuring equipment needed is available
- **Identification**—This phase aims to verify if an incident has happened and find out more details about the incident. Reports on possible incidents may come from information systems, end users or other organizations. Not all reports are valid incidents, as they may be false alarms or may not qualify as an incident. Activities in this phase include:
  - Assigning ownership of an incident or potential incident to an incident handler
  - Verifying that reports or events qualify as an incident
  - Establishing chain of custody during identification when handling potential evidence
  - Determining the severity of an incident and escalating it as necessary
- **Containment**—After an incident has been identified and confirmed, the IMT is activated and information from the incident handler is shared. The team will conduct a detailed assessment and contact the system owner or business manager of the affected information systems/assets to coordinate further action. The action taken in this phase is to limit the exposure. Activities in this phase include:
  - Activating the incident management/response team to contain the incident
  - Notifying appropriate stakeholders affected by the incident
  - Obtaining agreement on actions taken that may affect availability of a service or risks of the containment process
  - Getting the IT representative and relevant virtual team members involved to implement containment procedures
  - Obtaining and preserving evidence
  - Documenting and taking backups of actions from this phase onward
  - Controlling and managing communication to the public by the public relations team
- **Eradication**—When containment measures have been deployed, it is time to determine the root cause of the incident and eradicate it. Eradication can be done in a number of ways: restoring backups to achieve a clean state of the system, removing the root cause, improving defenses and performing vulnerability analysis to find further potential damage from the same root cause. Activities in this phase include:
  - Determining the signs and cause of incidents
  - Locating the most recent version of backups or alternative solutions
  - Removing the root cause. In the event of worm or virus infection, it can be removed by deploying appropriate patches and updated antivirus software.
  - Improving defenses by implementing protection techniques
  - Performing vulnerability analysis to find new vulnerabilities introduced by the root cause
- **Recovery**—This phase ensures that affected systems or services are restored to a condition specified in the service delivery objectives (SDO) or business continuity plan (BCP). The time constraint up to this phase is documented in the RTO. Activities in this phase include:
  - Restoring operations to normal
  - Validating that actions taken on restored systems were successful
  - Getting involvement of system owners to test the system
  - Facilitating system owners to declare normal operation
- **Lessons learned**—At the end of the incident response process, a report should always be developed to share what has happened, what measures were taken and the results after the plan was executed. Part of the report should contain lessons learned that provide the IMT and other stakeholders valuable learning points of what could have been done better. These lessons should be developed into a plan to enhance the incident management capability and the documentation of the incident response plan. Activities in this phase include:
  - Writing the incident report
  - Analyzing issues encountered during incident response efforts
  - Proposing improvement based on issues encountered
  - Presenting the report to relevant stakeholders

4.12.1 GAP ANALYSIS—BASIS FOR AN INCIDENT RESPONSE PLAN

Gap analysis will provide information on the gap between current incident response capabilities compared with the desired level. By comparing the two levels, the improvements in capabilities, skills and technology can be identified, including:

- Processes that need to be improved to be more efficient and effective
- Resources needed to achieve the objectives for the incident response capability

The resulting gap analysis report can be used for planning purposes to determine the steps needed to resolve the gap between the current state and the desired state. It can also be useful in determining the most effective strategy to achieve the objectives and prioritize efforts. The priorities should be based on the areas of greatest potential impact and the best cost benefit.

4.12.2 BUSINESS IMPACT ASSESSMENT

The first step in the incident response management process is to consider the potential impact of each type of incident that may occur. The argument is that one cannot properly plan for and prioritize response to an undesirable event if there is little idea of the likely impacts of different possible incident scenarios on the business/organization. The analysis of potential incidents and related business impacts is accomplished by conducting a BIA—a systematic activity designed to assess the impact of disruption, unauthorized access and/or tampering, or total loss of availability of the support of any critical information resource (system, network device, application, personnel and/or data) to an organization.

A BIA must:

- Determine the loss to the organization resulting from a function being unavailable
- Establish the escalation of that loss over time
- Identify the minimum resources needed for recovery
- Prioritize the recovery of processes and supporting systems

The purpose of a BIA is to create a report that helps stakeholders understand what impact an incident would have on the business. The impact may be in the form of a qualitative (rating) or quantitative value (monetary value).

To perform this phase successfully, it is essential to understand the structure and culture of the organization, key business processes, acceptable risk and risk tolerance, and critical IT and physical resources. A successful BIA requires participation from business process owners, senior management, IT, physical security and end-users.

BIAs have three primary goals:

- **Criticality prioritization**—Every critical business unit process must be identified and prioritized. The impact of an incident must be evaluated—the higher the impact, the higher the priority.
- **Downtime estimation**—The assessment is also used to estimate the maximum tolerable downtime (MTD) or maximum tolerable outage (MTO) that the business can tolerate and still remain viable. This can also mean the longest period of unavailability of critical processes/services/information assets before the company may cease to operate.
- **Resource requirement**—Resource requirements for critical processes are also identified at this time, with the most time-sensitive and highest-impact processes receiving the most resource allocation.

An assessment includes the following activities:

- **Gathering assessment material**—The initial step of the BIA is to identify which business units are critical to an organization. This step can be drilled down to the critical tasks that must be performed to ensure business survival.
- **Analyzing the information compiled**—During this phase, several activities take place such as documenting required processes, identifying interdependencies and determining the acceptable period of interruption. Tasks in this phase include:
  - Identify interdependencies between these functions and departments.
  - Discover all possible disruptions that could affect the mechanism necessary to allow these departments to function together.
  - Identify and document potential threats that could disrupt interdepartmental communication.
  - Gather quantitative and qualitative information pertaining to those threats.
  - Provide alternative methods of restoring functionality and communication.
  - Provide a brief statement of rationale for each threat and corresponding information.
- **Documenting the result and presenting recommendations**—The last step of an assessment is documenting assessment results from the previous activities and creating a report for business units and senior management.

Another way of viewing a BIA is that it is an exercise designed to identify the resources that are most important to an organization and the impact resulting from disruption, unauthorized access and/or tampering, or availability loss. If conducted properly, a BIA facilitates understanding the amount of potential loss (and various other unwanted effects) that could occur from certain types of events. Potential loss includes not only direct financial loss, but other less tangible types of loss such as reputational damage, failure to achieve regulatory compliance, etc.

Despite the extremely high level of importance of understanding the business impact of incidents on the business process, many organizations fail to undertake this assessment.

Another common problem is the failure to update BIAs when systems and business functions are added or changed.

A BIA is related to risk assessment (both qualitative and quantitative risk assessment) insofar as the degree of exposure will correlate to the potential for impact. A BIA is not, however, the same as a risk assessment. A BIA is a more specialized function that involves identifying the kinds of impacts related to disruption, unauthorized access and/or tampering, and total loss of availability, and identifying the effect on business processes. Risk assessment, on the other hand, examines sources of threat, associated vulnerabilities and the probability of occurrence, which provides estimates of the level of risk.

Elements of a Business Impact Analysis

The way in which BIAs are conducted varies from organization to organization. However, BIAs have the following elements in common in that they:
- Describe the business mission of each particular business/cost center
- Identify the functions that characterize each business function
- Determine dependencies such as required inputs from other operations
- Determine other subsequent operations dependent on function
- Identify critical processing cycles (in terms of time intervals) for each function
- Estimate the impact of each type of incident on business operations
- Identify the resources and activities required to restore an acceptable level of operation
- Determine work-around possibilities such as manual or PC-based operation, or workload shifting
- Estimate the amount of time that recovering from each type of incident is likely to take

Exhibit 4.5 provides a sample BIA.

Exhibit 4.5—Key Elements of Response Management

Outage Duration (hrs)	Cost (US $)	Recovery Resources Needed	Priority of Recovery Process
8	$80,000	Electrical technicians	7
16	$160,000	Electrical technicians, applications support	8
24	$250,000	Electrical technicians, applications support	8
36	$1,000,000	Electrical technicians, applications support, computer support	9
48	$2,000,000	Electrical technicians, applications support, computer support, outside consultants	9
72	$4,000,000	Electrical technicians, applications support, computer support, outside consultants	10
96	$8,000,000	Electrical technicians, applications support, computer support, outside consultants	10

Benefits of Conducting a Business Impact Analysis

Conducting BIAs produces several important major benefits, including:
- Increasing the understanding of the amount of potential loss, and various other undesirable effects that could occur from certain types of incidents
- Facilitating all response management activities
- Raising the level of awareness for response management within an organization

4.12.3 ESCALATION PROCESS FOR EFFECTIVE INCIDENT MANAGEMENT

The information security manager should implement an escalation process to establish the events to be managed (i.e., in the event of a telecommunications shutdown). Events that appear routine can be related to a security compromise and constitute an incident (e.g., data corruption may not be due to an application problem, but rather to a virus or worm infection). As part of the emergency management and incident management policies and procedures, a detailed description of the escalation process should be documented.

For every event, a list of actions should be described in the sequence to be performed. Every action listed should identify the responsible person and an estimated time for execution.

When all the actions have been completed successfully, the process should continue in the section dedicated to "end of emergency." If any action cannot be executed or if the estimated time is reached, the process should continue in the next action. Each unsuccessful action wastes time. If the accumulated elapsed time reaches a predetermined limit, the emergency status may change to an alert condition (low, medium, high). An alert situation prompts notification of individuals and organizations with executive responsibilities. Alert notification may include senior management, response and recovery teams, HR, insurance companies, backup facilities, vendors and customers.

The process should continue until the emergency is resolved or the last alert has occurred. At this point, the emergency management team will meet to evaluate the damages and mitigation alternatives, determine whether to declare a disaster and/or launch the response and recovery plan, and to determine the appropriate strategy. The information security manager should develop a communication plan in consultation with public relations, legal counsel and appropriate senior management to ensure the appropriateness of any information disclosures.

After the escalation process, numerous tasks such as notifying personnel, activating backup facilities, containing security threats to information resources, making transportation arrangements and carrying them out, retrieving and unloading data, testing, etc., must be executed. The total elapsed time should be in accordance with the established RTO as discussed in chapter 2.

The escalation process includes prioritizing event information and the decision process for determining when to alert various groups, including senior management, the public, shareholders and stakeholders, legal counsel, HR staff, vendors and customers.

The information security manager should develop these escalation processes through consultation with public relations, legal counsel and appropriate senior management. This process should also include vendors and utility services.

Many organizations define the level of events and define the escalation procedures differently for each level. These levels can be based on the severity of the event as well as the number of organizations that may be affected by the event and their specific need to be notified. The information security manager should also have mechanisms to communicate crisis or event information. These mechanisms may include using email if computing systems and networks are operational, cellular phones, fax machines, electronic pagers, web sites or an emergency telephone number at which a message can be placed. Note, however, that some types of communication, such as email messages, are by default in cleartext, making them subject to potential interception. The information security manager should also develop methods to encrypt email personal digital assistants (PDAs) and other communications used in communicating crisis or event-related information to ensure that information is released only as prudent or according to plans.

4.12.4 HELP DESK PROCESSES FOR IDENTIFYING SECURITY INCIDENTS

The information security manager should have processes defined for help desk personnel to distinguish a typical help desk request from a possible security incident. The help desk is likely to receive the first reports indicating a security-related problem. Prompt recognition of an incident in progress and quick referral to appropriate parties is critical to minimizing the damage resulting from such incidents.

By defining appropriate criteria and by improving the awareness of help desk personnel, the information security manager develops another important method to detect a security incident. Proper training also helps to reduce the risk that the help desk could be successfully targeted in a social-engineering attack designed to obtain access to accounts, such as a perpetrator pretending to be a user who has been locked out and requiring immediate access to the system. In addition to identifying a possible security incident, help desk personnel should be aware of the proper procedures to report and escalate a potential issue.

4.12.5 INCIDENT MANAGEMENT AND RESPONSE TEAMS

The plan must identify teams and define their assigned responsibilities in the event of an incident. To implement the strategies that have been developed for business recovery, key decision-making, technical and end-user personnel to lead teams need to be designated and trained. Depending on the size of the business operation, the team may consist of a single person. The involvement of these teams depends on the level of the disruption of service and the types of assets lost, compromised, damaged or endangered. A matrix should be developed that indicates the correlation between the functions of the different teams. This will facilitate estimating the magnitude of the effort and activating the appropriate combination of teams. Examples of the kinds of teams usually needed include:

- **Emergency action team**—Designated fire wardens and "bucket crews" whose function is to deal with fires or other emergency response scenarios
- **Damage assessment team**—Qualified individuals who assess the extent of damage to physical assets and make an initial determination regarding what is a complete loss vs. what is restorable or salvageable
- **Emergency management team**—Responsible for coordinating the activities of all other recovery teams and handling key decision making
- **Relocation team**—Responsible for coordinating the process of moving from the affected location to an alternate site or to the restored original location
- **Security team**—Often called a computer security incident response team, it is responsible for monitoring the security of systems and communication links, containing any ongoing security threats, resolving any security issues that impede the expeditious recovery of the system(s), and assuring the proper installation and functioning of every security software package.

A number of key decisions must be agreed on during the planning, implementation and evaluation phases of the response and recovery plan. These include:

- Goals/requirements/products for each phase
- Key goal and performance indicators
- Critical success factors and critical path aspects of implementation
- Alternate facilities in which tasks and operations can be performed
- Critical information resources to deploy (e.g., data and systems)
- Persons responsible for completion
- Available resources, including financial, personnel and technical, to aid in deployment
- Scheduling of activities with established priorities

4.12.6 ORGANIZING, TRAINING AND EQUIPPING THE RESPONSE STAFF

Training the response teams is essential; the information security manager should develop event scenarios and test the response and recovery plans to ensure that team participants are familiar with their tasks and responsibilities. Through this process, the teams will also identify the resources they require for response and recovery, providing the basis for equipping the teams with needed resources. An added value of training is detecting and modifying ambiguous procedures to achieve clarity and determining recovery resources that may not be adequate or effective.

IMT members should undergo the following training program:

- **Induction to the IMT**—The induction should provide the essential information required to be an effective IMT member.
- **Mentoring team members regarding roles, responsibilities and procedures**—Existing IMT members can provide valuable knowledge to aid new members after induction. To facilitate effective mentoring, the buddy system can be used, pairing new members with experienced members.
- **On-the-job training**—May serve to provide an understanding of company policies, standards, procedures, available tools and applications, acceptable code of conduct, etc.
- **Formal training**—Team members may require formal training to attain an adequate level of competence necessary to support the overall incident management capability.

4.12.7 INCIDENT NOTIFICATION PROCESS

Having an effective and timely security incident notification process is a critical component of any security program. The information security manager should understand how obtaining timely and relevant information can help the organization respond quickly and efficiently and will ultimately protect the organization from potential loss and damage that may occur as the result of

an incident. Mechanisms that enable an automated detection system or monitor to send email or phone messages to designated personnel exist. The following functions are most likely to need information concerning incidents when they occur:
- Risk management
- HR (when a security compromise appears to involve insiders)
- Legal
- Public relations
- Network operations

Notification activities are effective only if knowledgeable personnel understand their responsibilities and perform them in an efficient and timely manner. The information security manager therefore needs to define the responsibilities and communicate them to key personnel. It can also be effective to work with HR to determine how these responsibilities can be documented in employee's job descriptions.

4.12.8 CHALLENGES IN DEVELOPING AN INCIDENT MANAGEMENT PLAN

When developing and maintaining an incident management plan, there may be unanticipated challenges as the result of:
- **Lack of management buy-in and organizational consensus**—Most challenges result from a lack of management buy-in and consensus among the business units. When an incident occurs, management response may not be provided as expected, thus hindering incident management efforts. This may happen when senior management and other stakeholders or constituents are not involved in incident management planning and implementation.

  Challenges can also be caused by the lack of regular meetings between the IMT and constituents. A sense of ownership among constituents in incident management helps to ensure that sufficient resources and support are available for the IMT.
- **Mismatch to organizational goals and structure**—Business operates at an accelerated rate and may change significantly over a short period of time. Incident management may not be able to cope with the speed or nature of changes happening within the organization. Consider a situation where the business expands to emerging countries. The presence in new countries may grow at a significant rate; however, it may be difficult to expand incident management capabilities. A round of discussions may be needed to identify critical business functions and local stakeholders, and to understand local regulations. Senior management is usually occupied with business matters at this stage and may not be able to invest time in incident management. It is the responsibility of the IMT to identify any critical issues and make these known to executive management.
- **IMT member turnover**—Developing an incident management plan may take a significant amount of time with frequent interaction with various stakeholders. The champion of incident management, who is normally either a member of senior management or the information security manager, may leave the company unexpectedly, causing any planning or development efforts to come to a halt. The lack of a champion is likely to reduce the focus and resources devoted to implementing the plan.
- **Lack of communication process**—Ineffective communication processes may result either in undercommunication or overcommunication. In the case of undercommunication, relevant stakeholders may not receive the information that they need. This may result in different understandings about the need for incident management planning, the benefits that can be obtained, or their role in developing, implementing and maintaining an incident management capability. Overcommunication may turn stakeholders against incident management since they may feel that the plan is too much to handle or that it competes with priorities that they have established.
- **Complex and wide plan**—The proposed plan may be good and cover many issues, but it is too complex and too wide. Constituents may not be prepared to participate and commit to plans that appear overreaching.

4.13 BUSINESS CONTINUITY AND DISASTER RECOVERY PROCEDURES

There are a number of considerations when developing response and recovery plans, including available resources, expected services, and the types, kinds and severity of threats faced by the organization. The state of monitoring and detection capabilities must also be known, and the level of risk the organization is willing to accept must be determined. An effective strategy for recovery plans will strike the most cost-effective balance between risk management efforts, incident management and response, and BC/DRP.

4.13.1 RECOVERY PLANNING AND BUSINESS RECOVERY PROCESSES

The information security manager must understand the basic processes required to recover operations from incidents such as DoS attacks, natural disasters and other potential disruption of business operations.

Disaster recovery (DR) has traditionally been defined as the recovery of IT systems after disruptive events such as hurricanes and floods. Business recovery is defined as the recovery of the critical business processes necessary to continue or resume operations. Business recovery includes not only disaster recovery, but also all other required operational aspects.

Planning must include the requirements for determining when an incident cannot be resolved by the available recovery processes and a disaster must be declared. The declaration of a disaster pursuant to defined declaration criteria will generally require moving operations to the alternate processing site.

Not all events, incidents or critical disruptions should be classified as security incidents. For example, disruption in service can be caused by system malfunctions or accident. Regardless of the cause of operational disruption, satisfactory resolution will require prompt action to maintain or recover operational status. Actions may, among other things, necessitate restoration of hardware, software and/or data files.

Each of these planning processes typically includes several main phases, including:
- Risk and business impact assessment
- Response and recovery strategy definition
- Documenting response and recovery plans
- Training that covers response and recovery procedures

- Updating response and recovery plans
- Testing response and recovery plans
- Auditing response and recovery plans

Prior to creating a detailed business continuity plan, it is important to perform BIAs to determine the incremental daily cost of losing different systems. This provides the basis for deciding on appropriate RTOs. This, in turn, affects the location and cost of offsite recovery facilities, and the composition and mission of individual response and recovery teams.

4.13.2 RECOVERY OPERATIONS

Once the organization is up and running in recovery mode (which is usually from a disaster recovery site in the case of damage or inaccessibility of the primary facility), the business continuity teams should monitor the restoration progress at the primary site. This is done to assess when it is safe to return and perform tests to evaluate whether the primary data center and facilities are accessible, operational and capable of functioning at normal capacities and processing load.

The teams that were responsible for relocating to the alternate site and making it operational perform a similar operation to return to the primary site. On complete restoration of the primary facility and data processing capabilities, the recovery teams update the business continuity leader, who will then declare normalcy in consultation with the crisis management team and migrate operations back to the primary site.

In the event that the primary site is completely destroyed or severely damaged, the organization may make a strategic decision to transform the alternate recovery site to the primary operations site or identify, acquire and set up another site where operations will eventually be restored and will function as the primary site. This is especially true in cases where the organization subscribes to a third-party disaster recovery site since the costs of operating from such a site for an extended period of time may prove to be prohibitively high.

To ensure effective and comprehensive contingency planning, organizations setting up a business continuity plan should not only address the processes, roles and responsibilities of identifying an incident, and declaring a disaster and managing operations in a disaster mode, but it should also define processes to restore operations at the primary site and announce the return to normalcy. A cold site may be identified during the strategy phase to be upgraded to a primary operating facility in the event that the incident renders the primary facility useless.

It is important to remember that information resources must still be protected, even during the potentially chaotic environment of a business interruption or disaster. The information security manager must ensure that information security is incorporated into all response and recovery plans. The security manager should carefully review these plans to ensure that their execution does not compromise information security standards and requirements. In cases where such a compromise is unavoidable, other mitigations should be explored. Minimally, a focused risk assessment should be conducted to make management aware of the extent and potential impacts of the security risk introduced by execution of the plan.

In the likely event that the crisis is not catastrophic and the organization has switched to disaster recovery mode for only a limited time, it is important that the disaster recovery site be restored to an acceptable state of readiness after operations are reinstated at the primary facility.

Lessons learned and gaps identified in the plan when either switching to the disaster recovery site or reverting to the primary facility should be recorded and recommendations should be implemented to enhance the effectiveness of the plan. A realistic plan should cover all aspects of reestablishing the operations at the primary site, including people, facilities and technology areas.

4.13.3 RECOVERY STRATEGIES

Various strategies exist for recovering critical information resources. The most appropriate strategy is likely to be one that demonstrably addresses probable events with acceptable recovery times at a reasonable cost.

The total cost of a recovery capability is the cost of preparing for possible disruptions (i.e., purchasing, maintaining and regularly testing redundant computers; maintaining alternate network routing, training and personnel costs, etc.) and the cost of putting these into effect in the event of an incident. Impacts of disruptions can, to some extent, be mitigated by various forms of business interruption insurance, which should be considered as a strategy option.

Depending on the size and complexity of the organization and the state of recovery planning, the information security manager should understand that the development of an incident management and response plan is likely to be a difficult and expensive process that may take considerable time. It may require the development of several alternative strategies, encompassing different capabilities and costs, to be presented to management for a final decision. Each alternative must be sufficiently developed to provide an understanding of the trade-offs between scope, capabilities and cost. It may be prudent to consider outsourcing some or all of the needed capabilities and determine costs for the purpose of comparisons. Once the decision is made for which strategy best meets management's objectives, it provides the basis for the development of detailed incident management and response plans.

4.13.4 ADDRESSING THREATS

In the case of threats, some possible strategies to consider may include:

- **Eliminate or neutralize a threat**—Although removing or neutralizing a threat might seem like the best alternative, doing so when the threat is external is generally an unrealistic goal. If the threat is internal and specific, it may be possible to eliminate it. For example, the threat of a particular activity creating a security incident might be addressed by ceasing the activity.
- **Minimize the likelihood of a threat's occurrence**—The best alternative is often to minimize the likelihood of a threat's occurrence by reducing or eliminating vulnerabilities or exposure. This goal can be achieved by implementing the appropriate set of physical, environmental and/or security controls. For example, deploying firewalls, IDSs and strong authentication methods might substantially reduce the risk of a successful attack. Reducing exposure may be achieved by compartmentalization, such as network segmentation.

- **Minimize the effects of a threat if an incident occurs**—There are usually a number of ways to minimize impact if an incident occurs, such as effective incident management and response, insurance or redundant systems with automatic failover, or other compensatory or corrective controls.

Each critical information processing system will require an approach to restoring operations in the event of disruption. There are many alternative strategies that can be considered both in terms of the incident management and response capability and from a disaster recovery perspective. These can range from redundant and mirrored systems to ensuring a high degree of system or process resilience and robustness.

4.13.5 RECOVERY SITES

The most appropriate alternatives must be based on probability, impacts and cost. Lengthier and more costly outages or disasters that impair the primary physical facility are likely to require offsite backup alternatives. The types of offsite backup facilities that can be considered include:

- **Hot sites**—Hot sites are configured fully and ready to operate within several hours. The equipment, network and systems software must be compatible with the primary installation being backed up. The only additional needs are staff, programs, data files and documentation.
- **Warm sites**—Warm sites are complete infrastructures, but are partially configured in terms of IT, usually with network connections and essential peripheral equipment such as disk drives, tape drives and controllers. Sometimes a warm site is equipped with a less-powerful central processing unit (CPU) than the primary site.
- **Cold sites**—Cold sites have only the basic environment (electrical wiring, air conditioning, flooring, etc.) to operate an information processing facility (IPF). The cold site is ready to receive equipment, but does not offer any components at the site in advance of the need. Activation of the site may take several weeks.
- **Mobile sites**—Mobile sites are specially designed trailers that can be quickly transported to a business location or an alternate site to provide a ready-conditioned IPF. These mobile sites can be attached to form larger work areas and can be preconfigured with servers, desktop computers, communications equipment, and even microwave and satellite data links. They are a useful alternative when there are no recovery facilities in the immediate geographic area. They are also useful in case of a widespread disaster and may be a cost-effective alternative for duplicate IPFs for a multisite organization.
- **Duplicate sites**—These facilities are dedicated recovery sites that are functionally similar or identical to the primary site that can quickly take over for the primary site. They range from a standby hot site to facilities available through a reciprocal agreement with another company. (Note that although, in the past, reciprocal agreements were common, they are now seldom used.) The assumption is that there are fewer problems in coordinating compatibility and availability in the case of duplicate sites. Large organizations with multiple data facilities can often develop failover capabilities between their own geographically dispersed data centers.

  Adhering to the following principles helps ensure the viability of this approach:
  - The site chosen should be located so it is not subject to the same disaster event as the primary site. If, for example, the primary site is in an area subject to hurricanes, the recovery site should not be subject to the same hurricanes.
  - Coordination of hardware/software strategies is necessary. A reasonable degree of hardware and software compatibility must exist to serve as a basis for backup.
  - Resource availability must be assured. The workloads of the sites must be monitored to ensure that sufficient availability for emergency backup use exists.
  - There must be agreement concerning the priority of adding applications (workloads) until all the recovery resources are fully utilized.
  - Regular testing is necessary. Whether duplicate sites are under common ownership or under the same management, testing of the backup operation on a regular basis is necessary to ensure that it will work in the event of a disaster.
- **Mirror sites**—If continuous uptime and availability is required, a mirror site may be the best option. By definition, a mirror site is very similar or identical to the primary site. The mirror site is operational in concert with the primary site on a load-sharing basis. Typically, applications are launched by an automatic scheduler that balances the loads between the sites based on available operational capacity and applications can be executed in either one. Provided that sufficient reserve capacity exists, applications are seamlessly switched between the sites without interruption. Once again, organizations with multiple data facilities can often develop this capability between their own geographically dispersed data centers.

The type of site most suitable will largely be based on operational requirements determined by the BIA, the costs and benefits, and the risk appetite of management. It may be determined that some critical operational aspects must be mirrored to meet service level requirements while others can be adequately supported by hot, warm or cold site capabilities at the same or other facilities.

4.13.6 BASIS FOR RECOVERY SITE SELECTIONS

The type of site selected for a response and recovery strategy should be based on the following considerations:

- **Interruption window**—The total time that the organization can wait from the point of failure to the restoration of critical services/applications. After this time, the cumulative losses caused by the interruption may threaten the existence of the organization.
- **RTOs**—The length of time from the interruption to the time that the process must be functioning at a service level sufficient to limit financial and operational impacts to an acceptable level. Some organizations express it as partial moments, i.e., from point of failure to technical recovery, or point of disaster declaration to full operations.
- **RPOs**—Refer to the age of the data that the organization needs to be able to restore in the event of a disaster. Sometimes this is expressed as the point of last known good data. This will be the starting point for operations at the recovery site. If full backups are infrequent, it may take too much time to recreate the amount of data that is needed and the result would be RTOs not being met.

- **Services delivery objectives (SDOs)**—Level of services to be supported during the alternate process mode until the normal situation is restored. This must be directly related to business needs.
- **MTOs**—The maximum time that the organization can support processing in the alternate mode. Various factors will determine the MTO, including increasing backlogs of deferred processing. This, in turn, is affected by the SDO if it is less than that required during normal operations.
- **Proximity factors**—The distance from potential hazards, which can include flooding risk from nearby waterways, hazardous material manufacturing or storage, or other situations that may pose a risk to the operation of a recovery site
- **Location**—Sufficient distance needed to minimize the likelihood of both the primary and recovery facilities being subject to the same occurrence of an environmental event. When planning, consideration should be given to the typical impact area of the types of events that have a higher likelihood of occurrence for a given location. For example, in the case of hurricanes vs. tornados, the impact area of a hurricane is typically much larger than the impact area of a tornado, requiring greater distance between sites for a location where hurricanes frequently occur.
- **Nature of probable disruptions**—This must be considered in terms of the MTO. For example, a major earthquake is likely to render a primary site inoperable for a number of months. Clearly, the MTO in an area subject to this disruption must be greater than the probable duration of such an event.

To prepare a suitable recovery strategy, the information security manager must balance all of these parameters with the capabilities of different types of recovery sites, their costs and locations.

The complexity and cost of the response and recovery plans, as well as the type and cost of the recovery site, are proportionally inverse to these time objectives. An interruption window of two hours, for instance, dictates a hot or mirrored solution that is generally very expensive, but the corresponding recovery process is likely to be simple and inexpensive. In contrast, an interruption window of a month may permit the use of a cold site that is inexpensive, but the associated recovery process is likely to be complex and expensive.

4.13.7 RECIPROCAL AGREEMENTS

If the recovery strategy is to use reciprocal agreements with one or more internal or external entities, it is essential that similar equipment and applications are available. Under the typical agreement, participants promise to provide computing time and network operations to each other when an emergency arises.

Although the principles concerning recovery strategies are straightforward, they seldom work as planned in real-world settings. IT resources are generally used in a manner that approaches their maximum capacity and may not be able to support the requirements for recovery operations; organizations do not generally have sufficient reserve resources to satisfy even fairly small recovery requirements related to CPU, network bandwidth or storage capacity. The availability of competent personnel at an alternate facility must also be considered. It is likely that in the event of a serious incident or disaster, the availability of staff resources will be adversely affected. Extra expenses, integrating external personnel into operations and additional threats to physical security are some of the difficult and immediate problems inherent in this type of solution.

Additionally, creating a contract that provides adequate protection can be a difficult task, and the cost of dealing with changes over time is likely to be significant. It is important that contractual provisions for the use of third-party sites should cover important issues such as configuration of third-party hardware and software, speed of availability, reliability, duration of usage, nature of intersite communications, and period of usage.

There are several alternatives available for securing backup hardware and physical facilities, including:

- **Vendor or third party**—Hardware vendors are usually the best source for replacement equipment. However, this may often involve a waiting period that is not acceptable for critical operations. It is unlikely that any vendor will guarantee a specific reaction to a crisis. Vendor arrangements are utilized best when an organization plans to move from a hot site to a warm or cold site, so advance planning is critical. Another source of equipment replacement is the used hardware market. This market can supply critical components or entire systems on relatively short notice, often at a substantially reduced cost. Establishing relationships with dealers well in advance of any actual emergency is critical.
- **Off-the-shelf**—Such components are often available from the inventory of suppliers on short notice, but may require special arrangements. To make use of this approach, several strategies must be utilized, including:
  - Avoiding the use of unusual and hard-to-get equipment
  - Regularly updating equipment to keep current
  - Maintaining software compatibility to permit the operation of newer equipment

Because data and software are required for these strategies, special arrangements need to be considered for their backup to removable media and their safe, secure storage offsite.

Additionally, part of the recovery of IT facilities involves telecommunications, for which the strategies usually considered include elements of network disaster prevention:

- Alternative routing
- Diverse routing
- Long-haul network diversity
- Protection of local resources
- Voice recovery
- Availability of appropriate circuits and adequate bandwidth
- Availability of out-of-band communications in case of failure of primary communications methods

Once a strategy for the recovery of sufficient IT facilities to support critical business processes has been developed, it is critical that the strategies work for the entire period of recovery until all facilities are restored. The strategies may include:

- Doing nothing until recovery facilities are ready
- Using manual procedures
- Focusing on the most important customers, suppliers, products, systems, etc., with the resources that are still available
- Using PC-based systems to capture data for later processing or performing simple local processing

4.13.8 STRATEGY IMPLEMENTATION

Based on the response and recovery strategy selected by management, a detailed response and recovery plan should be developed. It should address all issues involved in recovering from a disaster. Various factors should be considered while developing the plan, including:

- Preincident readiness
- Evacuation procedures
- How to declare a disaster
- Identification of the business processes and IT resources that should be recovered
- Identification of the responsibilities in the plan
- Identification of the persons responsible for each function in the plan
- Identification of contact information
- The step-by-step explanation of the recovery options
- Identification of the various resources required for recovery and continued operations
- Ensuring that other logistics such as personnel relocation and temporary housing are considered

The response and recovery plan should be documented and written in simple language that is clear and easy to read. It is also common to identify teams of personnel who are responsible for specific tasks in case of incidents or disasters.

4.13.9 RECOVERY PLAN ELEMENTS

Most business continuity plans are created as a set of procedures that accommodate system, user and network recovery strategies. Copies of the plan must be kept offsite to ensure that it is available when needed; this includes at the recovery facility, at the media storage facility and at the homes of key decision-making personnel. Components of the plan must include key decision-making personnel, a backup of required supplies, the organization, and the assignment of responsibilities, telecommunication networks and insurance provisions.

4.13.10 INTEGRATING RECOVERY OBJECTIVES AND IMPACT ANALYSIS WITH INCIDENT RESPONSE

The information security manager should be aware that incident management also includes BCP and DRP. DRP generally comprises the plan to recover an IT processing facility or the plan by business units to recover an operational facility. The recovery plan must be consistent with and support the overall IT plan of the organization. BCP, DRP and incident response does not necessarily have to be combined into a single plan. To have a viable response and recovery strategy, however, each must be consistent with the other and integrated so that transition on declaration of a disaster is effective.

Effective integration of incident response and BCP/DR requires the relationship between RTO, RPO, SDO and MTO to be carefully considered. Since the transition from incident response to disaster recovery operations for any but mirrored sites will require some time, RTO and AIW will be impacted.

Risk Acceptance and Tolerance

The general issues of risk have been addressed in chapter 2. Risk specific to incident response and recovery operations are numerous and must be considered from a magnitude and frequency basis as well as from the perspective of the potential for impact.

Risk tolerance is the acceptable degree of variance to acceptable risk which, in the final analysis, must be determined by management. The essential consideration from an information security perspective is to ensure that an incident or disaster does not result in a security compromise. Since the focus will be on recovery or restoration of services, there is a significant possibility that expediency and procedural shortcuts will pose increased risk exposure.

Business Impact Analysis

No matter how good controls may be, the risk of an incident cannot be completely eliminated. Accordingly, the information security manager should oversee the development of response and recovery plans to ensure that they are properly designed and implemented. These plans should, as described previously, be based on the BIA.

Next, response and recovery strategies should be identified and validated and then approved by senior management. Once senior management approves these strategies, the information security manager should oversee the development of the response and recovery plans. During this process, response and recovery teams should be identified and team members mobilized. The plans must provide the teams guidance concerning the steps to be taken to recover business processes.

Recovery Time Objectives

RTO is defined as the amount of time allowed for the recovery of a business function or resource to a predefined operational level after a disaster occurs. Exceeding this time would mean organization survival would be threatened or the losses would exceed acceptable levels. RTOs are determined as a result of management deciding the level of acceptable impact as a result of the unavailability of information resources. Generally, the optimal RTO is the point where the ongoing cost of loss is equal to the cost of recovery.

Recovery Point Objectives

RPO is defined as a measurement of the point prior to an outage to which data are to be restored; that is, the last point of known good data. RTO and RPO must be closely linked to facilitate effective incident management and response. This is because a short RTO may be adversely impacted by the RPO if there is a large amount of data that must be restored prior to achieving acceptable levels of operation.

An example of a procedural statement that specifies both RTO and RPO could be: "In the event of main web server hard drive failure, restoration to the latest backup version should be complete within two hours."

Service Delivery Objectives

The SDO is the level of acceptable service that must be achieved within the RTO. In many cases, an acceptable level may be substantially less than normal operations, less costly and easier to achieve. The SDO will be determined by various factors, including business requirements, costs and sustainability over the likely duration of operation in an alternate facility.

Maximum Tolerable Outage

MTO is the total time that operations can be sustained at an alternate site. A number of factors must be considered to arrive at this value. It must be related to the probable types of events that may require operations to move to an alternate site and their probable duration. If the threats such as a major earthquake are likely to result in long-term damage, the MTO may need to be measured in months whereas other types of events might typically be much shorter.

4.13.11 NOTIFICATION REQUIREMENTS

The recovery plan must cover notification responsibilities and requirements. It should also include a directory of key decision-making personnel, information systems owners, end users and others required to initiate and carry out response efforts. This directory should also include multiple communication methods (telephone, cellular phone, texting, email, etc).

The directory should include at least the following individuals:
- Representatives of equipment and software vendors
- Contacts within companies that have been designated to provide supplies and equipment or services
- Contacts at recovery facilities, including hot site representatives or predefined network communications rerouting services
- Contacts at offsite media storage facilities and the contacts within the company who are authorized to retrieve media from the offsite facility
- Insurance company agents
- Contact information for regulatory bodies
- Contacts at HR and/or contract personnel services
- Law enforcement contacts

Note that the decision to bring in law enforcement during such an incident rests solely with senior management. It is not the role of an information security manager to directly contact external organizations, except perhaps in the context of a cross-organizational response team that includes members of an organization's legal and, possibly, media relations functions. The information security manager is, instead, expected to provide information security expertise as well as evidence when called on to do so during organization-endorsed communication with external entities such as clients, law enforcement and the media. The information security manager should also help to identify and escalate law enforcement and legal issues; an appropriate escalation process is thus imperative.

There are companies that handle automated emergency response communications, which may be a good option for some organizations. However, as with any other outsourced service, careful consideration should be given to the required processes that must be in place to ensure the effectiveness of this solution.

4.13.12 SUPPLIES

The plan must include provisions for all supplies necessary for continuing normal business activities during the recovery effort. This includes detailed, up-to-date hard-copy procedures that can be followed easily by staff and contract personnel who are unfamiliar with the standard and recovery operations. This is to ensure that the plan can be implemented, even if members of the regular staff are unavailable. Also, a supply of special forms, such as check stock, invoice forms and order forms, should be secured at an offsite location.

If the data entry function is dependent on certain hardware devices and/or software programs, these programs and equipment, including specialized electronic data interchange (EDI) equipment and programs, must also be provided at the recovery site.

4.13.13 COMMUNICATION NETWORKS

The plan must contain details of the organization's telecommunication networks needed to restore business operations. Because of the criticality of these networks, the procedures to ensure continuous telecommunication capabilities should be given a high priority. Telecommunication networks are susceptible to the same natural disasters as data centers, but are also are vulnerable to disruptive events unique to telecommunications. These include central switching office disasters, cable cuts, communication software glitches and errors, security breaches from hacking (phone hackers are known as "phreakers"), and a host of other human errors. The local exchange carrier is typically not responsible for providing backup services. Although many carriers normally back up main components within their systems, the organization should make provisions for backing up its own telecommunication facilities.

Telecommunications capabilities to consider include telephone voice circuits, wide area networks (WANs) (connections to distributed data centers), local area networks (LANs) and third-party electronic data interchange providers. Options can include satellite and microwave links, and depending on criticality and location, wireless links or even single sideband radiotelephone communications. Critical capacity requirements should be identified for the various thresholds of outage, such as two hours, eight hours or 24 hours, for each telecommunications capability. Uninterruptable power supplies (UPSs) should be sufficient to provide backup for telecommunications equipment as well as for computer equipment.

4.13.14 METHODS FOR PROVIDING CONTINUITY OF NETWORK SERVICES

These methods can include:
- **Redundancy**—Achieving redundancy involves a variety of solutions, including:
  - Providing extra capacity with a plan to use the surplus capacity should the normal primary transmission capability not be available. In the case of a LAN, a second cable could be installed through an alternate route for use in the event that the primary cable is damaged.
  - Providing multiple paths between routers
  - Using special dynamic routing protocols such as the Open Shortest Path First (OSPF) and External Gateway Routing Protocol (EGRP)
  - Providing for failover devices to avoid single point of failures in routers, switches, firewalls, etc.
  - Saving configuration files for recovery of network devices, such as routers and switches, in the event that they fail
- **Alternative routing**—Alternative routing means routing information via an alternate medium such as copper cable or fiber optics. This involves use of different networks, circuits

or end points, if the normal network is unavailable. Most local carriers are deploying counter-rotating, fiber-optic rings. These rings have fiberoptic cables that transmit information in two different directions and in separate cable sheaths for increased protection. Currently, these rings connect through one central switching office. However, future expansion of the rings may incorporate a second central office in the circuit. Some carriers are offering alternate routes to different points of presence or alternate central offices. Other examples include dial-up circuits as an alternative to dedicated circuits, a cellular phone and microwave communications as alternatives to land circuits, and couriers as an alternative to electronic transmissions.

- **Diverse routing**—The method of routing traffic through split cable facilities or duplicate cable facilities. This can be accomplished with different and/or duplicate cable sheaths. If different cable sheaths are used, the cable may be in the same conduit and, therefore, subject to the same interruptions as the cable it is backing up. The communication service subscriber can duplicate the facilities by having alternate routes, although the entrance to and from the customer's premises may be in the same conduit. The subscriber can obtain diverse routing and alternate routing from the local carrier, including dual entrance facilities; however, acquiring this type of access is time consuming and costly. Most carriers provide facilities for alternate and diverse routing, although most services are transmitted over terrestrial media. These cable facilities are usually located in the ground or the basement of buildings that house computer equipment. Ground-based facilities are at great risk due to the aging infrastructures of cities. In addition, cable-based facilities usually share space with mechanical and electrical systems that can impose great risk due to human error and disastrous events.
- **Long-haul network diversity**—Many vendors of recovery facilities provide diverse long-distance network availability, utilizing high-speed data circuits among the major long-distance carriers. This ensures long-distance access if any single carrier experiences a network failure. Several of the major carriers have now installed automatic rerouting software and redundant lines that provide instantaneous recovery if a break in their lines occurs. The information security manager should confirm that the recovery facility has these vital telecommunications capabilities.
- **Last-mile circuit protection**—Many recovery facilities provide a redundant combination of local carrier high-speed data circuits, microwave and/or coaxial cable access to the local communications loop. This enables the facility to have access during a local carrier communication disaster. Alternate local carrier routing is also utilized.
- **Voice recovery**—With many service, financial and retail industries dependent on voice communication, redundant cabling and alternative routing should be provided for voice communication lines as well as data communication lines.

4.13.15 HIGH-AVAILABILITY CONSIDERATIONS

The loss or disruption of servers managing sensitive and critical business processes could have catastrophic effects on an organization. Plans should include operational failover methods to prevent servers from going offline for an extended period of time. Server recovery should also be included in the disaster recovery plan. Some of the techniques for providing failover or fault-tolerant capabilities include UPSs and the use of failover systems to prevent power failures of varying levels.

Redundant array of inexpensive disks (RAID) provides performance improvements and fault-tolerant capabilities via hardware or software solutions, breaking up data and writing them to a series of multiple disks to improve performance and/or save large files simultaneously. These systems provide the potential for cost-effective continuous data availability onsite or offsite.

A storage area network (SAN) is a high-speed, special-purpose network that provides mass storage using remote interconnected devices—such as disk arrays, tape libraries or optical jukeboxes—with associated data servers that function as if they were attached locally. SANs are typically part of the overall network of computing resources for larger enterprises, but may also serve as remote resources for backup and archival storage. SANs typically support disk mirroring, backup and restore functions, data migration between storage devices, and the sharing of data among different servers in one or more networks.

Fault-tolerant servers provide for fail-safe redundancy through mirrored images of the primary server. Using this approach may also entail distributed processing of a server load, a concept referred to as "load balancing" or "clustering," where all servers take part in processing. In this arrangement, there is an intelligent cluster unit that provides for load balancing for improved performance. This type of server architecture is transparent to users. The only thing that may be noticeable to a user is performance degradation if a server fails.

4.13.16 INSURANCE

The plan should also contain key information concerning the organization's insurance. The information systems processing insurance policy is usually a multi-peril policy designed to provide various types of IT coverage. It should be constructed modularly so it can be adapted to the insured's particular IT environment.

Specific types of coverage that are available include:

- **IT equipment and facilities**—Provides coverage of physical damage to the IPF and owned equipment. An organization should also insure leased equipment if it is obtained when the lessee is responsible for hazard coverage. The information security manager should review these policies carefully; many policies are worded such that insurers are obligated to replace damaged or destroyed equipment with "like kind and quality," not necessarily the identical brand and model.
- **Media (software) reconstruction**—Covers damage to computer-related media that are the property of the insured and for which the insured may be liable. Insurance is available for on-premises, off-premises or in-transit disasters and covers the actual reproduction cost of the property. Considerations in determining the amount of coverage needed are programming costs to reproduce the media damaged, backup expenses and physical replacement of media devices such as tapes, cartridges and disks.
- **Extra expense**—Designed to cover the extra costs of continuing operations following damage or destruction at the IPF. The amount of insurance needed is based on the availability and cost of backup facilities and operations. Extra expense can also

cover the loss of net profits caused by computer media damage. This provides reimbursement for monetary losses resulting from suspension of operations due to the physical loss of equipment or media as in the case when IPFs are on the sixth floor and the first five floors are burned out. In this case, operations would be interrupted even though the IPF remained unaffected.
- **Business interruption**—Covers the loss of profit due to the disruption of the activity of the company caused by any covered IT malfunction or security-related event in which an attacker or malicious code causes loss of availability of computing resources.
- **Valuable papers and records**—Covers the actual cash value of papers and records (not defined as media) on the insured's premises against unauthorized disclosure, direct physical loss or damage.
- **Errors and omissions**—Provides legal liability protection in the event that the professional practitioner commits an act, error or omission that results in financial loss to a client. This insurance originally was designed for service bureaus, but it is now available from several insurance companies for protecting against actions of systems analysts, software designers, programmers, consultants and other IS personnel.
- **Fidelity coverage**—Usually takes the form of banker's blanket bonds, excess fidelity insurance and commercial blanket bonds, and covers loss from dishonest or fraudulent acts by employees. This type of coverage is prevalent in financial institutions operating their own IPF.
- **Media transportation**—Provides coverage for potential loss or damage to media in transit to off-premises IPFs. Transit coverage wording in the policy usually specifies that all documents must be filmed or otherwise copied. When the policy does not specifically require that data be filmed prior to being transported and the work is not filmed, management should obtain from the insurance carrier a letter that specifically describes the carrier's position and coverage in the event data are destroyed.

4.13.17 UPDATING RECOVERY PLANS

Finally, since organizations constantly evolve and change, the response and recovery plans also need to change. The information security manager must establish a process in which recovery plans are updated as changes occur within an organization. Assessing the response and recovery plan requirements during the change management process within an organization is an essential part of effective response management.

Plans and strategies for response and recovery should be reviewed and updated according to a schedule to reflect continuing recognition of changing requirements. The following factors as well as others may impact requirements and the need for the plan to be updated:
- A strategy that is appropriate at one point in time may not be adequate as the needs of an organization change.
- New applications may be developed or acquired.
- Changes in business strategy may alter the significance of critical applications or result in additional applications being deemed as critical.
- Changes in the software or hardware environment may make current provisions obsolete or inappropriate.
- Changing physical and environmental circumstances may also need to be considered.

The responsibility for maintaining the business continuity and disaster recovery plan often falls to a business continuity plan coordinator while the information security manager may be responsible for maintaining the incident response plan. However these responsibilities are allocated, specific plan maintenance activities include:
- Developing a schedule for periodic review and maintenance of the plan, and advising all personnel of their roles and the deadline for receiving revisions and comments
- Calling for revisions out of schedule when significant changes have occurred
- Reviewing revisions and comments, and updating the plan within a reasonable period (e.g., 30 days) after the review date
- Arranging and coordinating scheduled and unscheduled tests of the plan to evaluate its adequacy
- Participating in scheduled plan tests, which should be performed at least once each year. For scheduled and unscheduled tests, the coordinator should write evaluations and integrate changes to resolve unsuccessful test results into the response plan within a reasonable period (e.g., 30 days).
- Developing a schedule for training personnel in emergency and recovery procedures, as set forth in the plan. Training dates should be scheduled within a reasonable period (e.g., 30 days) after each plan revision and scheduled plan test.
- Maintaining records of plan maintenance activities—testing, training and reviews
- Updating, at least quarterly, the notification directory to include all personnel changes, including phone numbers and responsibilities or status within the company

4.14 TESTING INCIDENT RESPONSE AND BUSINESS CONTINUITY/DISASTER RECOVERY PLANS

Testing all aspects of the incident recovery plans is the most important factor in achieving success in an emergency situation. The main objective of testing is to ensure that executing the plans will result in the successful recovery of the infrastructure and critical business processes.

Testing should focus on:
- Identifying gaps
- Verifying assumptions
- Testing time lines
- Effectiveness of strategies
- Performance of personnel
- Accuracy and currency of plan information

Testing promotes collaboration and coordination among teams and is a useful training tool. Many organizations require complete testing annually. In addition, testing should be considered on the completion or major revision of each draft plan or complementary plans and following changes in key personnel, technology or the business/regulatory environment.

Testing must be carefully planned and controlled to avoid placing the business at increased risk. To ensure that all plans are regularly tested, the information security manager should maintain a "testing schedule" of dates and tests to be conducted for all critical functions.

Prior to each test, the security manager should ensure that:
- The risk and impact of disruption from testing is minimized
- The business understands and accepts the risk inherent in testing
- Fallback arrangements exist to restore operations at any point during the test

All tests must be fully documented with pretest, test and posttest reports. Test documentation should be retained for audit review and reference. The security manager must ensure that information security is also tested and not compromised during testing.

4.14.1 PERIODIC TESTING OF THE RESPONSE AND RECOVERY PLANS

As discussed in prior sections, the scope and nature of incident response and recovery teams and their capabilities will vary with different organizations as will business continuity and disaster recovery operations. The exact relationship between these functions must be clearly defined and their scope and capabilities understood and integrated. Regardless of the specific scope at any particular organization, it is essential that the information security manager has a good understanding of the entire business continuity process, including incident management and disaster recovery.

Whatever the structure, it is necessary to ensure that the full scope of incident management responsibilities are tested up to the point of a disaster declaration, including the escalation, and involvement of or handover to the disaster management and recovery operation if this is the responsibility of another group. The discussion in this section includes full disaster recovery, which the information security manager should understand regardless of the specific scope of incident management and response responsibilities.

The information security manager, helped by the recovery team's organization, should implement periodic testing of response and recovery plans. Testing should include:
- Developing test objectives
- Executing the test
- Evaluating the test
- Developing recommendations to improve the effectiveness of testing processes as well as response and recovery plans
- Implementing a follow-up process to ensure that the recommendations are implemented

Response and recovery plans that have not been tested leave an organization with an unacceptable likelihood that plans will not work, even though care is taken in developing and documenting these plans. Because testing plans cost time and resources, an organization should carefully plan tests and develop test objectives to be methodical and help ensure that measurable benefits can be achieved.

Once test objectives have been defined, the information security manager should ensure that an independent third party is present to monitor and evaluate the test. Internal or external audit or other assurance personnel can often assume this role. A result of the evaluation step should be a list of recommendations that an organization should complete to improve its response and recovery plans. It is extremely unlikely that no recommendations will result and that everything works as planned. If it does, it is likely that a more challenging test should be planned.

The information security manager should also implement a tracking process to ensure that any recommendations resulting from testing are implemented in a timely fashion. Personnel should be tasked with making any necessary changes.

4.14.2 TESTING FOR INFRASTRUCTURE AND CRITICAL BUSINESS APPLICATIONS

The information security manager needs to understand that testing recovery and response plans need to include infrastructure and critical applications. With today's organizations relying heavily on information technology, the information security manager is not only tasked with securing these systems during normal operations, but also during disaster events.

Based on the risk assessment and business impact information, the information security manager can identify critical applications that the organization requires and the infrastructure needed to support them. To ensure that these are recovered in a timely fashion, the information security manager needs to perform appropriate recovery tests.

4.14.3 TYPES OF TESTS

- **Checklist review**—A preliminary step to a real test. Recovery checklists are distributed to all members of a recovery team to review and ensure that the checklist is current.
- **Structured walkthrough**—Team members physically implement the plans on paper and review each step to assess its effectiveness, identify enhancements, constraints and deficiencies.
- **Simulation test**—The recovery team role play a prepared disaster scenario without activating processing at the recovery site.
- **Parallel test**—The recovery site is brought to a state of operational readiness, but operations at the primary site continue normally.
- **Full interruption test**—Operations are shut down at the primary site and shifted to the recovery site in accordance with the recovery plan; this is the most rigorous form of testing, but is expensive and potentially disruptive.

Testing should start simply and increase gradually, stretching the objectives and success criteria of previous tests so as to build confidence and minimize risk to the business. At a minimum, "full-interruption" tests should be performed annually after individual plans have been tested separately with satisfactory results.

Tests that are progressively more challenging can include:
- Table-top walk-through of the plans
- Table-top walk-through with mock disaster scenarios
- Testing the infrastructure and communication components of the recovery plan
- Testing the infrastructure and recovery of the critical applications

- Testing the infrastructure, critical applications and involvement of the end users
- Full restoration and recovery tests with some personnel unfamiliar with the systems
- Surprise tests

Most response and recovery tests fall short of a full-scale test of all operational portions of the corporation. This should not preclude performing full or partial testing because one of the purposes of the business continuity test is to determine how well the plan works or the portions of the plan that need improvement. Although surprise tests are potentially advantageous from the standpoint that they are similar to real-life incident response situations, they have some severe potential downsides. They can be terribly disruptive to production and operations, and they can alienate individuals who are in some way disrupted by them. The information security manager should carefully consider the ramifications before deciding to use this approach. It is not unheard of that a serious extended outage resulted from the inability to restore systems as planned.

The test should be scheduled during a time that will minimize disruptions to normal operations. Weekends are generally a good time to conduct tests. It is important that the key recovery team members are involved in the test process and are also allotted the necessary time to devote their full effort. The test should address all critical components and simulate actual prime-time processing conditions, even if the test is conducted during off hours.

4.14.4 TEST RESULTS

The test should strive to, at a minimum, accomplish the following tasks:
- Verify the completeness and precision of the response and recovery plan.
- Evaluate the performance of the personnel involved in the exercise.
- Appraise the demonstrated level of training and awareness of individuals who are not part of the recovery/response team.
- Evaluate the coordination among the team members and external vendors and suppliers.
- Measure the ability and capacity of the backup site to perform prescribed processing.
- Assess the vital records retrieval capability.
- Evaluate the state and quantity of equipment and supplies that have been relocated to the recovery site.
- Measure the overall performance of operational and information systems processing activities related to maintaining the business entity.

To perform testing, each of the following test phases should be completed:
- **Pretest**—The pretest consists of the set of actions necessary to set the stage for the actual test. This ranges from placing tables in the proper operations recovery area to transporting and installing backup telephone equipment. These activities are outside the realm of those that would take place in the case of a real emergency, in which there is generally no forewarning of the event and thus no time to take preparatory actions.
- **Test**—This is the real action of the business continuity test. Actual operational activities are executed to test the specific objectives of the plan. Data entry, telephone calls, information systems processing, handling orders and movement of personnel, equipment and suppliers should take place. Evaluators should review staff members as they perform the designated tasks. This is the actual test of preparedness to respond to an emergency.
- **Posttest**—The posttest is the cleanup of group activities. This phase comprises assignments such as returning all resources to their proper place, disconnecting equipment, returning personnel to their normal locations and deleting all company data from third-party systems. The posttest cleanup also includes formally evaluating the plan and implementing indicated improvements.

In addition, the following types of tests may be performed:
- **Paper tests**—Paper tests are an on-paper walk-through of the plan involving the major players in the plan's execution who reason out what might happen in a particular type of service disruption. They may walk through the entire plan or just a portion. The paper test usually precedes preparedness tests.
- **Preparedness tests**—Preparedness tests are usually localized versions of a full test, wherein actual resources are expended in the simulation of a system crash. These tests are performed regularly on different aspects of the plan and can be a cost-effective way to gradually obtain evidence about how good the plan is. They also provide a means to improve the plan in increments.
- **Full operational tests**—These tests are one step away from an actual service disruption. An organization should have tested the plan well on paper and locally before endeavoring to completely shut down operations. For purposes of BCP testing, the full operational testing scenario is the disaster.

During every phase of the test, detailed documentation of observations, problems and resolutions should be maintained. Each team should have a diary with specific steps and information recorded. This documentation serves as important historical information that can facilitate actual recovery during a real disaster. The documentation also aids in performing detailed analysis of the strengths and weaknesses of the plan.

4.14.5 RECOVERY TEST METRICS

Just as with nearly everything else in information security, metrics should be developed and used in measuring the success of the plan and testing against the stated objectives. Results must thus be recorded and evaluated quantitatively, as opposed to an evaluation based only on verbal descriptions. The resulting metrics should be used not only to measure the effectiveness of the plan, but more importantly, to improve it. Although specific measurements vary depending on the test and the organization, the following general types of metrics usually apply:
- **Time**—Elapsed time for completion of prescribed tasks, delivery of equipment, assembly of personnel and arrival at a predetermined site. This is essential to refine the response time estimated for every task in the escalation process.
- **Amount**—Amount of work performed at the backup site by clerical personnel and the amount of information systems processing operations.
- **Percentage and/or number**—The number of vital records successfully carried to the backup site versus the required number, and the number of supplies and equipment requested versus actually received. The number of critical systems

successfully recovered can be measured with the number of transactions processed.

- **Accuracy**—Accuracy of the data entry at the recovery site versus normal accuracy (as a percentage). The accuracy of actual processing cycles can be determined by comparing output results with those for the same period processed under normal conditions.

This testing process enables the information security manager to achieve initial successes and modify the plan based on information gained from the initial tests. It is important to note that performing a robust test costs resources and requires coordination between various departments. A minor error or mishap (e.g., a missing set of backup media) could make completing the full test impossible.

In case normal business operations are destroyed or inaccessible, the information security manager needs to have alternative operating plans based on the response and recovery strategy. The information security manager needs to test these alternate capabilities and should also report the response and recovery capability of the organization to senior management.

4.15 EXECUTING RESPONSE AND RECOVERY PLANS

Given that a major incident usually causes considerable confusion and a host of unexpected conditions, it is essential that the incident management and response plans have been tested under realistic conditions. It is virtually guaranteed that untested plans will not work. It is also safe to assume that the more severe the incident, the greater the potential chaos, confusion and problems facing the incident management and response teams. Incidents can range from a virus attack bringing down IT systems to an earthquake bringing down the building. To provide reasonable assurance that the organization is preserved under foreseeable circumstances, all reasonably possible events must be anticipated and prepared for and the planning must be thorough, realistic and tested.

4.15.1 ENSURING EXECUTION AS REQUIRED

To ensure the response and recovery plans are executed as required, the plans need a facilitator or director to direct the tasks within the plans, oversee their execution, liaise with senior management and make decisions as necessary. The information security manager may or may not be the appropriate person to act as the recovery plan director or coordinator, but must be certain the role is assigned to someone who can perform this critical function.

Developing appropriate response and recovery strategies as well as alternatives is an essential component in the overall process of executing the response and recovery plans. It will provide reasonable assurance that the organization can recover its key business functions in the event of a disruption and that it responds appropriately to a security-related incident.

Testing the plans is essential to ensuring that plans can be executed as required. By testing the plans in a scenario designed to mimic real-life conditions, personnel can become familiar with the tasks and their responsibilities as defined in the plan. This familiarity will increase the probability that the plan is executed effectively during an actual incident.

The information security manager should also appoint an independent observer to record progress and document any exceptions that occur during both testing and during an actual event. Through a postevent review, the information security manager and key recovery personnel can then review the observations and make adjustments to the plan accordingly.

4.16 POSTINCIDENT ACTIVITIES AND INVESTIGATION

Understanding the purpose and structure of postincident reviews and follow-up procedures enables the information security manager to continuously improve the security program. A consistent methodology should be adopted within the information security organization so that, when a problem is found, an action plan is developed to reduce/mitigate it. Once the action plan is devised, steps should then be taken to implement the solution. By repeating these basic principles, the information security program is able to adapt to changes in the organization and the threats it faces. In addition, this reduces the amount of time personnel need to react to security incidents so they are able to spend more time on proactive activities.

The follow-up process in incident response is potentially the most valuable part of the effort. Lessons learned during incident handling can improve a security practice as well as the incident response process itself. Additionally, the information security manager needs to calculate the cost of the incident once all response efforts are done by adding the cost of any loss or damage plus the cost of labor and any special software or hardware needed to handle the incident. The cost provides a useful metric, especially in justifying the existence of the response team to senior management, and may be used as evidence in a court case.

The information security manager should manage postevent reviews to learn from each incident and the resulting response and recovery effort, and to use the information to improve the organization's response and recovery procedures. The information security manager may perform these reviews with the help of third-party specialists if detailed forensic skills are needed.

4.16.1 IDENTIFYING CAUSES AND CORRECTIVE ACTIONS

Security incidents may not always be the result of externally initiated attacks, or even internally initiated attacks, but also can be the result of failures in security controls that have been implemented. For a systematic review of security events, the information security manager should appoint an event review team. This team should review any evidence and develop recommendations to enhance the information security program by identifying root (most fundamental) causes of a specific event and necessary measures to prevent the same/similar events from recurring. The root cause of many break-ins to systems, for example, is often weak or nonexistent vulnerability assessment and patch management efforts.

The analysis should be done to determine answers to questions such as:

- Who is involved?
- What has happened?
- Where did the attack originate from?
- When (what time frame)?
- Why did it happen?
- How was the system vulnerable or how did the attack occur?
- What was the reason for the attack?

4.16.2 DOCUMENTING EVENTS

During and subsequent to any actual or potential security incident, it is essential for the information security manager to have processes in place to develop a clear record of events. By preserving this information, events can be investigated and provided to a forensics team or authorities if necessary. To ensure this occurs, there should be one or more individuals specifically charged with incident documentation and the preservation of evidence. Documentation of any event that has possible security implications can provide clarity as to whether an incident is merely an accident, mistake or a deliberate attack.

A serious incident is typically chaotic and good documentation will prove invaluable in postincident investigation and forensics as well as possibly helpful in incident resolution.

4.16.3 ESTABLISHING PROCEDURES

Having a good legal framework is important to provide options to the organization. The information security manager should develop data preservation procedures with the advice and assistance of legal counsel, the organization's managers and knowledgeable law enforcement officials to assure that the procedures provide sufficient guidance to IT and security staff. With the assistance of these specialized resources, the information security manager can develop procedures to handle security events in a manner that preserves evidence, ensures legally sufficient chain of custody and is appropriate to meet business objectives.

There are a few basic actions that the information systems staff must understand. This includes doing nothing that could change/modify/contaminate potential or actual evidence. Trained forensics personnel can inspect computer systems that have been attacked, but if the organization's personnel contaminate the information, the data may not be admissible in a court of law and/or the forensics staff may be unable to use the data in investigating an incident. Computer forensics, gathering and handling information and physical objects relevant to a security incident in a systematic manner so that they can be used as evidence in a court of law should usually be performed by a specially trained staff, third-party specialists, security incident response team or law enforcement officials. The initial response by the system administrator should include:

- Retrieving information needed to confirm an incident
- Identifying the scope and size of the affected environment (e.g., networks, systems, applications)
- Determining the degree of loss, modification or damage (if any)
- Identifying the possible path or means of attack

4.16.4 REQUIREMENTS FOR EVIDENCE

The information security manager should understand that any contamination of evidence following an intrusion could prevent an organization prosecuting a perpetrator and limit its options. In addition, the modification of data can inhibit computer forensic activity necessary to identify the perpetrator and all the changes and effects resulting from an attack. It may also preclude the possibility of identifying how the attack occurred, and how the security program should be changed and enhanced to reduce the risk of a similar attack in the future.

The usual recommendation for a computer that has been compromised is to disconnect the power to maximize the preservation of evidence on the hard disk. This approach is generally the recommendation of law enforcement based on the risk of the evidence being compromised. This can occur as a result of the system swap files overwriting evidence or an intruder or malware erasing evidence of compromise. There is also the risk of contaminating evidence.

This approach is not universally accepted as the best solution. One argument against disconnecting power is that data in memory is lost and sudden power loss may result in corruption of critical information on the hard disk. Since some malware is only memory resident, the cause of an incident and the avenue of attack may be difficult to establish.

Since the best approach is subject to controversy, the information security manager will need to establish the most appropriate approach for their organization and train personnel in the appropriate procedures.

Whichever procedure is used to secure a compromised system, trained personnel must use forensic tools to create a bit-by-bit copy of any evidence that may exist on hard drives and other media to ensure legal admissibility. To avoid the potential for alteration or destruction of incident-related data, any testing or data analysis should be conducted using this copy. The original should be given to a designated evidence custodian who must store it in a safe location. The original media must remain unchanged and a record of who has had custody of it—the chain of custody—must be maintained for the evidence to be admissible in court.

When taking a copy of a hard drive, the technician should take a bit level image of all the data on the drive, using a cable with a write-protect diode to prevent writing anything back onto the source drive. Hash values of both the source and destination drive should be calculated to ensure that the copied drive is an exact image of the original.

4.16.5 LEGAL ASPECTS OF FORENSIC EVIDENCE

As noted above, in order for evidence to be admissible in legal proceedings, it must have been acquired in a forensically sound manner and its chain of custody maintained. The information security manager in charge of an incident must have established and documented procedures for acquisition of evidence by properly trained personnel.

The required documentation to maintain legally admissible evidence must include:

- Chain of custody forms that include:
  - Name and contact information of custodians
  - When, why and by whom an evidence item was acquired or moved
  - Detailed identification of the evidence (serial numbers, model information, etc.)
  - Where it is stored (physically or logically)
  - When/if it was returned
- Checklists for acquiring technicians (including details of legally acceptable forensic practices)
- Detailed activity log templates for acquiring technicians
- Signed nondisclosure/confidentiality forms for all technicians involved in recovering evidence
- An up-to-date case log that outlines:
  - Dates when requests were received
  - Dates investigations were assigned to investigators
  - Name and contact information investigator and requestor
  - Identifying case number
  - Basic notes about the case and its requirements and completed procedures
  - Date when completed
- Investigation report templates that include:
  - Name and contact information of investigators
  - Date of investigation and an identifying case number
  - Details of any interviews or communications with management or staff regarding the investigation
  - Details of devices or data that was acquired (serial numbers, models, physical or logical locations)
  - Details of software or hardware tools used for acquisition or analysis (these must be recognized forensically sound tools)
  - Details of findings including samples or copies of relevant data and/or references to their storage location
  - Final signatures of investigator in charge

Procedures for initiating a forensics investigation need to be agreed to, documented, followed carefully and understood by everyone in the enterprise. The information security manager should work with management and HR (and other stakeholders) to establish a process that ensures that all investigations are fair, unbiased and well documented.

It is important to be aware that legal requirements vary in different jurisdictions. As a result, informed legal advice for appropriate processes that meet judicial standards will be required.

GENERAL INFORMATION

REQUIREMENTS FOR CERTIFICATION

To earn the CISM designation, information security professionals are required to:

1. Successfully pass the CISM exam
2. Adhere to the ISACA Code of Professional Ethics
3. Agree to comply with the CISM continuing education policy
4. Submit verified evidence of five (5) years of work experience in the field of information security. Three (3) of the five (5) years of work experience must be gained performing the role of an information security manager. In addition, this work experience must be broad and gained in three of the four job practice domains. A processing fee of US $50 must accompany CISM applications for certification.

   Substitutions for work performed in the role of an information security manager are not allowed. However, a maximum of two (2) years for general work experience in the field of information security may be substituted as follows:
   - Two years of general work experience may be substituted for currently holding one of the following broad security-related certifications or a postgraduate degree:
     - Certified Information Systems Auditor (CISA) in good standing
     - Certified Information Systems Security Professional (CISSP) in good standing
     - Postgraduate degree in information security or a related field (for example, business administration, information systems, information assurance)

   OR

   - A maximum of one (1) year of work experience may be substituted for one of the following:
     - One full year of information systems management experience
     - Currently holding a skill-based security certification (e.g., SANS Global Information Assurance Certification [GIAC], Microsoft Certified Systems Engineer [MCSE], CompTIA Security+, Disaster Recovery Institute Certified Business Continuity Professional [CBCP])
     - Completion of an information security management program at an institution aligned with the ISACA-sponsored Model Curriculum

   Experience must have been gained within the 10-year period preceding the application for certification or within five (5) years from the date of initially passing the exam. Application for certification must be submitted within five (5) years from the passing date of the CISM exam. All experience must be verified independently with employers.

It is important to note that a CISM candidate may choose to take the CISM exam prior to meeting the experience requirements.

Please note that certification application decisions are not final as there is an appeal process for certification application denials. Appeals undertaken by a certification exam taker, certification applicant or by a certified individual are undertaken at the discretion and cost of the exam taker, applicant or individual. Inquiries of denials of certification can be sent to *certification@isaca.org*.

DESCRIPTION OF THE EXAM

The CISM Certification Committee oversees the development of the exam and ensures the currency of its content. Questions for the CISM exam are developed through a multitiered process designed to enhance the ultimate quality of the exam. Once the CISM Certification Committee approves the questions, they go into the item pool from which all CISM exam questions are selected.

The purpose of the exam is to evaluate a candidate's knowledge and experience in information security management. The exam consists of 200 multiple-choice questions, administered during a four-hour session, that cover the CISM job practice domains. The exam covers four information security management domains created from the CISM job practice analysis and reflects the work performed by information security managers. The job practice was developed and validated using prominent industry leaders, subject matter experts and industry practitioners.

REGISTRATION FOR THE CISM EXAM

The CISM exam will be administered in June, September and December in 2015. Please refer to the *ISACA Exam Candidate Information Guide* at *www.isaca.org/examguide* for specific exam registration dates, deadlines and registration forms, as well as important key information for exam day. Exam registrations can be placed online at *www.isaca.org/examreg*.

CISM PROGRAM ACCREDITATION RENEWED UNDER ISO/IEC 17024:2003

The American National Standards Institute (ANSI) has voted to continue the accreditation for the CISA, CISM and CGEIT certifications, as well as accredit CRISC for the first time, under ISO/IEC 17024:2003, General Requirements for Bodies Operating Certification Systems of Persons. ANSI, a private, nonprofit organization, accredits other organizations to serve as third-party product, system and personnel certifiers.

ISO/IEC 17024 specifies the requirements to be followed by organizations certifying individual against specific requirements. ANSI describes ISO/IEC 17024 as "expected to play a prominent role in facilitating global standardization of the certification community, increasing mobility among countries, enhancing public safety, and protecting consumers."

ANSI's accreditation:
- Promotes the unique qualifications and expertise that ISACA's certifications provide
- Protects the integrity of the certifications and provides legal defensibility
- Enhances consumer and public confidence in the certifications and the people who hold them
- Facilitates mobility across borders or industries

Accreditation by ANSI signifies that ISACA's procedures meet ANSI's essential requirements for openness, balance, consensus and due process. With this accreditation, ISACA anticipates that significant opportunities for CISAs, CISMs, CGEITs and CRISCs will continue to open in the USA and around the world.

ANSI Accredited Program
PERSONNEL
CERTIFICATION

PREPARING FOR THE CISM EXAM

The CISM exam evaluates a candidate's practical knowledge of the job practice domains listed in this manual and online at www.isaca.org/cismjobpractice. That is, the exam is designed to test a candidate's knowledge, experience and judgment of the proper or preferred application of information security management principles, methods and practices. Since the exam covers a broad spectrum of information security issues, candidates are cautioned not to assume that reading CISM study guides and reference publications will fully prepare them for the exam. CISM candidates are encouraged to refer to their own experiences when studying for the exam and refer to CISM study guides and reference publications for further explanation of concepts or practices with which the candidate is not familiar.

No representation or warranties are made by ISACA in regard to CISM exam study guides, other ISACA publications, references or courses assuring candidates' passage of the exam.

TYPES OF EXAM QUESTIONS

CISM exam questions are developed with the intent of measuring and testing practical knowledge and the application of general concepts and standards. All questions are multiple choice and are designed for one best answer.

Every question has a stem (question) and four options (answer choices). The candidate is asked to choose the correct or best answer from the options. The stem may be in the form of a question or incomplete statement. In some instances, a scenario may also be included. These questions normally include a description of a situation and require the candidate to answer two or more questions based on the information provided. The candidate is cautioned to read each question carefully. An exam question may require the candidate to choose the appropriate answer based on a qualifier, such as **MOST** or **BEST**. In every case, the candidate is required to read the question carefully, eliminate known incorrect answers and then make the best choice possible. To gain a better understanding of the types of question that might appear on the exam and how these questions are developed, refer to the Item Writing Guide available at *www.isaca.org/itemwriter*. Representations of CISM exam questions are available at *www.isaca.org/cismassessment*.

ADMINISTRATION OF THE EXAM

ISACA has contracted with an internationally recognized testing agency. This not-for-profit corporation engages in the development and administration of credentialing exams for certification and licensing purposes. It assists ISACA in the construction, administration and scoring of the CISM exam.

SITTING FOR THE EXAM

Candidates are to report to the testing site at the report time indicated on their admission ticket. NO CANDIDATE WILL BE ADMITTED TO THE TEST CENTER ONCE THE CHIEF EXAMINER BEGINS READING THE ORAL INSTRUCTIONS. Candidates who arrive after the oral instructions have begun will not be allowed to sit for the exam and will forfeit their registration fee. To ensure that candidates arrive in time for the exam, it is recommended that candidates become familiar with the exact location of, and the best travel route to, the exam site prior to the date of the exam. Candidates can use their admission tickets only at the designated test center on the admission ticket.

To be admitted into the test site, candidates must bring the email printout OR a printout of the downloaded admission ticket and an acceptable form of photo identification such as a driver's license, passport or government-issued ID. This ID must be a current and original government-issued identification that is not handwritten and that contains both the candidate's name as it appears on the admission ticket and the candidate's photograph. Candidates who do not provide an acceptable form of identification will not be allowed to sit for the exam and will forfeit their registration fee.

The following conventions should be observed when completing the exam:

- Do not bring study materials (including notes, paper, books or study guides) or scratch paper or notepads into the exam site. For further details regarding what personal belongings can (and cannot) be brought into the test site, please visit *www.isaca.org/cismbelongings*.
- Candidates are not allowed to bring any type of communication device (e.g., cell phone, tablet, smart watches, mobile devices, etc.) into the test center. If candidates are viewed with any such device during the exam administration, their exams will be voided and they will be asked to immediately leave the exam
- Candidates who leave the testing area without authorization or accompaniment by a test proctor will not be allowed to return to the testing room and will be subject to disqualification.
- Candidates should bring several no. 2 pencils since pencils will not be provided at the exam site.
- Include your exam identification number as it appears on your admission ticket and any other requested information. Failure to do so may result in a delay or errors.
- Read the provided instructions carefully before attempting to answer questions. Skipping over these directions or reading them too quickly could result in missing important information and possibly losing credit points.
- Mark the appropriate area when indicating responses on the answer sheet. When correcting a previously answered question, fully erase a wrong answer before writing in the new one.
- Remember to answer all questions since there is no penalty for wrong answers. Grading is based solely on the number of questions answered correctly. Do not leave any question blank.
- Identify key words or phrases in the question (**MOST, BEST, FIRST …**) before selecting and recording the answer.

BUDGETING TIME

The following are time-management tips for the exam:

- It is recommended that candidates become familiar with the exact location of, and the best travel route to, the exam site prior to the date of the exam.
- Candidates should arrive at the exam testing site at the time indicated on their admission ticket. This will give time for candidates to be seated and get acclimated.
- The exam is administered over a four-hour period. This allows for a little over one minute per question. Therefore, it is advisable that candidates pace themselves to complete the entire exam. In order to do so, candidates must complete an average of 50 questions per hour.
- Candidates are urged to record their answers on their answer sheet. No additional time will be allowed after the exam time has elapsed to transfer or record answers should candidates mark their answers in the question booklet.

RULES AND PROCEDURES

- Candidates are asked to sign the answer sheet to protect the security of the exam and maintain the validity of the scores.
- Upon the discretion of the CISM Certification Committee, any candidate can be disqualified who is discovered engaging in any kind of misconduct, such as giving or receiving help; using notes, papers or other aids; attempting to take the exam for someone else; or removing test materials or notes from the testing room. The testing agency will provide the CISM Certification Committee with records regarding such irregularities. The committee will review reported incidents, and all committee decisions are final.
- Candidates may not take the exam question booklet after completion of the exam.

GRADING THE CISM EXAM AND RECEIVING RESULTS

The exam consists of 200 items. Candidate scores are reported as a scaled score. A scaled score is a conversion of a candidate's raw score on an exam to a common scale. ISACA uses and reports scores on a common scale from 200 to 800. A candidate must receive a score of 450 or higher to pass the exam. A score of 450 represents a minimum consistent standard of knowledge as established by ISACA's CISM Certification Committee. A candidate receiving a passing score may then apply for certification if all other requirements are met.

The CISM exam contains some questions that are included only for research and analysis purposes. These questions are not separately identified and are not used to calculate the candidate's final score.

Passing the exam does not grant the CISM designation. To become a CISM, each candidate must complete all requirements, including submitting an application and receiving approval for certification.

A candidate receiving a score less than 450 is not successful and can retake the exam by registering and paying the appropriate exam fee for any future exam administration. To assist with future study, the result letter each candidate receives includes a score analysis by content area. There are no limits to the number of times a candidate can take the exam.

Approximately five weeks after the exam date, the official exam results are mailed to candidates. Additionally, with the candidate's consent on the registration form, an e-mail message containing the candidate's pass/fail status and score will be sent to paid candidates.

This e-mail notification is only sent to the address listed in the candidate's profile at the time of the initial release of the results. To ensure the confidentiality of scores, exam results are not reported by telephone of fax. To prevent e-mail notification from being sent to a spam folder, the candidate should add *exam@isaca.org* to their address book, white list or safe senders list.

In order to become CISM-certified, candidates must pass the CISM exam and must complete and submit an application for certification (and must receive confirmation from ISACA that the application is approved). The application is available on the ISACA web site at *www.isaca.org/cismapp*. Once the application is approved, the applicant will be sent confirmation of the approval. The candidate is not CISM certified, and cannot use the CISM designation, until the candidate's application is approved. A processing fee of US $50 must accompany CISM applications for certification.

For those candidates not passing the examination, the score report contains a subscore for each job domain. The subscores can be useful in identifying those areas in which the candidate may need further study before retaking the exam. Unsuccessful candidates should note that taking either a simple or weighted average of the subscores does not derive the total scaled score. Candidates receiving a failing score on the exam may request a rescoring of their answer sheet. This procedure ensures that no stray marks, multiple responses or other conditions interfered with computer scoring. Candidates should understand, however, that all scores are subjected to several quality control checks before they are reported; therefore, rescores most likely will not result in a score change. Requests for hand scoring must be made in writing to the certification department within 90 days following the release of the exam results. Requests for a hand score after the deadline date will not be processed. All requests must include a candidate's name, exam identification number and mailing address. A fee of US $75 must accompany this request.

Page intentionally left blank

GLOSSARY

A

Acceptable interruption window
The maximum period of time that a system can be unavailable before compromising the achievement of the organization's business objectives

Acceptable use policy
A policy that establishes an agreement between users and the organization and defines for all parties the ranges of use that are approved before gaining access to a network or the Internet

Access controls
The processes, rules and deployment mechanisms that control access to information systems, resources and physical access to premises

Access path
The logical route that an end user takes to access computerized information. Typically it includes a route through the operating system, telecommunications software, selected application software and the access control system.

Access rights
The permission or privileges granted to users, programs or workstations to create, change, delete or view data and files within a system, as defined by rules established by data owners and the information security policy

Accountability
The ability to map a given activity or event back to the responsible party

Address Resolution Protocol (ARP)
Defines the exchanges between network interfaces connected to an Ethernet media segment in order to map an IP address to a link layer address on demand

Administrative control
The rules, procedures and practices dealing with operational effectiveness, efficiency and adherence to regulations and management policies

Advance encryption standard (AES)
The international encryption standard that replaced 3DES

Alert situation
The point in an emergency procedure when the elapsed time passes a threshold and the interruption is not resolved. The organization entering into an alert situation initiates a series of escalation steps.

Algorithm
A finite set of step-by-step instructions for a problem-solving or computation procedure, especially one that can be implemented by a computer

Alternate facilities
Locations and infrastructures from which emergency or backup processes are executed, when the main premises are unavailable or destroyed. This includes other buildings, offices or data processing centers.

Alternate process
Automatic or manual process designed and established to continue critical business processes from point-of-failure to return-to-normal

Annual loss expectancy (ALE)
The total expected loss divided by the number of years in the forecast period yielding the average annual loss

Anomaly detection
Detection on the basis of whether the system activity matches that defined as abnormal

Anonymous File Transfer Protocol (AFTP)
A method of downloading public files using the File Transfer Protocol (FTP). AFTP does not require users to identify themselves before accessing files from a particular server. In general, users enter the word "anonymous" when the host prompts for a username. Anything can be entered for the password, such as the user's e-mail address or simply the word "guest." In many cases, an AFTP site will not prompt a user for a name and password.

Antivirus software
An application software deployed at multiple points in an IT architecture. It is designed to detect and potentially eliminate virus code before damage is done, and repair or quarantine files that have already been infected

Application controls
The policies, procedures and activities designed to provide reasonable assurance that objectives relevant to a given automated solution (application) are achieved

Application layer
In the Open Systems Interconnection (OSI) communications model, the application layer provides services for an application program to ensure that effective communication with another application program in a network is possible. The application layer is not the application that is doing the communication; it is a service layer that provides these services.

Application programming interface (API)
A set of routines, protocols and tools referred to as "building blocks" used in business application software development. A good API makes it easier to develop a program by providing all the building blocks related to functional characteristics of an operating system that applications need to specify, for example, when interfacing with the operating system (e.g., provided by Microsoft Windows, different versions of UNIX). A programmer utilizes these APIs in developing applications that can operate effectively and efficiently on the platform chosen.

Application service provider (ASP)
Also known as managed service provider (MSP), it deploys, hosts and manages access to a packaged application to multiple parties from a centrally managed facility. The applications are delivered over networks on a subscription basis.

Architecture
Description of the fundamental underlying design of the components of the business system, or of one element of the business system (e.g., technology), the relationships among them, and the manner in which they support the organization's objectives

Asymmetric key
A cipher technique in which different cryptographic keys are used to encrypt and decrypt a message

Attack signature
A specific sequence of events indicative of an unauthorized access attempt. Typically a characteristic byte pattern used in malicious code or an indicator, or set of indicators, that allows the identification of malicious network activities.

Audit trail
A visible trail of evidence enabling one to trace information contained in statements or reports back to the original input source

Authentication
The act of verifying the identity (i.e., user, system)

Authorization
Access privileges granted to a user, program, or process or the act of granting those privileges

Availability
Information that is accessible when required by the business process now and in the future

B

Backup center
An alternate facility to continue IT/IS operations when the primary data processing (DP) center is unavailable

Baseline security
The minimum security controls required for safeguarding an IT system based on its identified needs for confidentiality, integrity, and/or availability protection

Benchmarking
A systematic approach to comparing an organization's performance against peers and competitors in an effort to learn the best ways of conducting business. Examples include benchmarking of quality, logistic efficiency and various other metrics.

Bit
The smallest unit of information storage; a contraction of the term "binary digit;" one of two symbols "0" (zero) and "1" (one) that are used to represent binary numbers

Bit copy
Provides an exact image of the original and is a requirement for legally justifiable forensics

Bit-stream image
Bit-stream backups, also referred to as mirror image backups, involve the backup of all areas of a computer hard disk drive or other type of storage media. Such backups exactly replicate all sectors on a given storage device including all files and ambient data storage areas.

Botnet
A large number of compromised computers that are used to create and send spam or viruses or flood a network with messages such as a denial-of-service attack

Brute force attack
Repeatedly trying all possible combinations of passwords or encryption keys until the correct one is found

Business case
Documentation of the rationale for making a business investment, used both to support a business decision on whether to proceed with the investment and as an operational tool to support management of the investment through its full economic life cycle

Business continuity plan (BCP)
A plan used by an organization to respond to disruption of critical business processes. Depends on the contingency plan for restoration of critical systems

Business dependency assessment
A process of identifying resources critical to the operation of a business process

Business impact
The net effect, positive or negative, on the achievement of business objectives

Business impact analysis/assessment (BIA)
Evaluating the criticality and sensitivity of information assets. An exercise that determines the impact of losing the support of any resource to an organization, establishes the escalation of that loss over time, identifies the minimum resources needed to recover, and prioritizes the recovery of processes and supporting system. This process also includes addressing: income loss, unexpected expense, legal issues (regulatory compliance or contractual), interdependent processes, and loss of public reputation or public confidence.

Business Model for Information Security (BMIS)
A holistic and business-oriented model that supports enterprise governance and management information security, and provides a common language for information security professionals and business management

C

Capability Maturity Model (CMM)
Contains the essential elements of effective processes for one or more disciplines. It also describes an evolutionary improvement path from ad hoc, immature processes, to disciplined, mature processes, with improved quality and effectiveness.

Certificate (certification) authority (CA)
A trusted third party that serves authentication infrastructures or enterprises and registers entities and issues them certificates

Certificate revocation list (CRL)
An instrument for checking the continued validity of the certificates for which the certification authority (CA) has responsibility. The CRL details digital certificates that are no longer valid. The time gap between two updates is very critical and is also a risk in digital certificates verification.

Certification practice statement
A detailed set of rules governing the certificate authority's operations. It provides an understanding of the value and trustworthiness of certificates issued by a given certificate authority (CA).

Stated in terms of the controls that an organization observes, the method it uses to validate the authenticity of certificate applicants and the CA's expectations of how its certificates may be used

Chain of custody
A legal principle regarding the validity and integrity of evidence. It requires accountability for anything that will be used as evidence in a legal proceeding to ensure that it can be accounted for from the time it was collected until the time it is presented in a court of law. This includes documentation as to who had access to the evidence and when, as well as the ability to identify evidence as being the exact item that was recovered or tested. Lack of control over evidence can lead to it being discredited. Chain of custody depends on the ability to verify that evidence could not have been tampered with. This is accomplished by sealing off the evidence, so it cannot be changed, and providing a documentary record of custody to prove that the evidence was, at all times, under strict control and not subject to tampering.

Chain of evidence
A process and record that shows who obtained the evidence, where and when the evidence was obtained, who secured the evidence and who had control or possession of the evidence. The "sequencing" of the chain of evidence follows this order: collection and identification, analysis, storage, preservation, presentation in court, return to owner.

Challenge/response token
A method of user authentication that is carried out through use of the Challenge Handshake Authentication Protocol (CHAP). When a user tries to log onto the server using CHAP, the server sends the user a "challenge," which is a random value. The user enters a password, which is used as an encryption key to encrypt the "challenge" and return it to the server. The server is aware of the password. It, therefore, encrypts the "challenge" value and compares it with the value received from the user. If the values match, the user is authenticated. The challenge/response activity continues throughout the session and this protects the session from password sniffing attacks. In addition, CHAP is not vulnerable to "man-in-the-middle" attacks because the challenge value is a random value that changes on each access attempt.

Change management
A holistic and proactive approach to managing the transition from a current to a desired organizational state

Checksum
A mathematical value that is assigned to a file and used to "test" the file at a later date to verify that the data contained in the file have not been maliciously changed.

A cryptographic checksum is created by performing a complicated series of mathematical operations (known as a cryptographic algorithm) that translates the data in the file into a fixed string of digits called a hash value, which is then used as the checksum. Without knowing which cryptographic algorithm was used to create the hash value, it is highly unlikely that an unauthorized person would be able to change data without inadvertently changing the corresponding checksum. Cryptographic checksums are used in data transmission and data storage. Cryptographic checksums are also known as message authentication codes, integrity check values, modification detection codes or message integrity codes.

Chief information officer (CIO)
The most senior official of the enterprise who is accountable for IT advocacy, aligning IT and business strategies, and planning, resourcing and managing the delivery of IT services, information and the deployment of associated human resources. In some cases, the CIO role has been expanded to become the chief knowledge officer (CKO) who deals in knowledge, not just information. Also see chief technology officer.

Chief information security officer (CISO)
Responsible for managing information risk, the information security program, and ensuring appropriate confidentiality, integrity and availability of information assets

Chief security officer (CSO)
Typically responsible for physical security in the organization although increasingly the CISO and CSO roles are merged

Chief technology officer (CTO)
The individual who focuses on technical issues in an organization

Cloud computing
An approach using external services for convenient on-demand IT operations using a shared pool of configurable computing capability. Typical capabilities include infrastructure as a service (IaaS), platform as a service (PaaS) and software as a service (SaaS), e.g., networks, servers, storage, applications and services, that can be rapidly provisioned and released with minimal management effort or service provider interaction. This cloud model is composed of five essential characteristics (on-demand self service, ubiquitous network access, location independent resource pooling, rapid elasticity, and measured service). It allows users to access technology-based services from the network cloud without knowledge of, expertise with, or control over, the technology infrastructure that supports them and provides four models for enterprise access (Private cloud, Community cloud, Public cloud, and Hybrid cloud).

COBIT 5
Formerly known as Control Objectives for Information and related Technology (COBIT); now used only as the acronym in its fifth iteration. A complete, internationally accepted framework for governing and managing enterprise information and technology (IT) that supports enterprise executives and management in their definition and achievement of business goals and related IT goals. COBIT describes five principles and seven enablers that support enterprises in the development, implementation, and continuous improvement and monitoring of goodIT-related governance and management practices.

Earlier versions of COBIT focused on control objectives related to IT processes, management and control of IT processes and IT governance aspects. Adoption and use of the COBIT framework are supported by guidance from a growing family of supporting products. (See *www.isaca.org/cobit* for more information.)

COBIT 4.1 and earlier
Formerly known as Control Objectives for Information and related Technology (COBIT). A complete, internationally accepted process framework for IT that supports business and IT executives and management in their definition and achievement of business goals and related IT goals by providing a comprehensive IT governance, management, control and assurance model. COBIT describes IT processes and associated control objectives, management guidelines (activities, accountabilities, responsibilities and performance metrics) and maturity models. COBIT supports enterprise management in the development, implementation, continuous improvement and monitoring of good IT-related practices.

Common vulnerabilities and exposures (CVE)
A system that provides a reference method for publicly known information-security vulnerabilities and exposures. MITRE Corporation maintains the system, with funding from the National Cyber Security Division of the United States Department of Homeland Security.

Compensating control
An internal control that reduces the risk of an existing or potential control weakness resulting in errors and omissions

Computer forensics
The application of the scientific method to digital media to establish factual information for judicial review. This process often involves investigating computer systems to determine whether they are or have been used for illegal or unauthorized activities. As a discipline, it combines elements of law and computer science to collect and analyze data from information systems (e.g., personal computers, networks, wireless communication and digital storage devices) in a way that is admissible as evidence in a court of law.

Confidentiality
The protection of sensitive or private information from unauthorized disclosure

Configuration management
The control of changes to a set of configuration items over a system life cycle

Content filtering
Controlling access to a network by analyzing the contents of the incoming and outgoing packets and either letting them pass or denying them based on a list of rules. Differs from packet filtering in that it is the data in the packet that are analyzed instead of the attributes of the packet itself (e.g., source/target IP address, transmission control protocol [TCP] flags)

Contingency plan
A plan used by an organization or business unit to respond to a specific systems failure or disruption

Continuous monitoring
The process implemented to maintain a current security status for one or more information systems or for the entire suite of information systems on which the operational mission of the enterprise depends. The process includes: 1) the development of a strategy to regularly evaluate selected IS controls/metrics, 2) recording and evaluating IS-relevant events and the effectiveness of the enterprise in dealing with those events, 3) recording changes to IS controls, or changes that affect IS risks, and 4) publishing the current security status to enable information-sharing decisions involving the enterprise.

Control
The means of managing risk, including policies, procedures, guidelines, practices or organizational structures which can be of an administrative, technical, management or legal nature

Control center
Hosts the recovery meetings where disaster recovery operations are managed

Controls policy
A policy defining control operational and failure modes, e.g., fail secure, fail open, allowed unless specifically denied, denied unless specifically permitted

Corporate governance
The system by which enterprises are directed and controlled. The board of directors is responsible for the governance of their enterprise. It consists of the leadership and organizational structures and processes that ensure the enterprise sustains and extends strategies and objectives.

COSO
Committee of Sponsoring Organizations of the Treadway Commission. Its 1992 report "Internal Control--Integrated Framework" is an internationally accepted standard for corporate governance. See *www.coso.org*.

Cost-benefit analysis
A systematic process for calculating and comparing benefits and costs of a project, control or decision

Countermeasures
Any process that directly reduces a threat or vulnerability

Criticality
A measure of the impact that the failure of a system to function as required will have on the organization.

Criticality analysis
An analysis to evaluate resources or business functions to identify their importance to the organization, and the impact if a function cannot be completed or a resource is not available

Cryptographic algorithm
A well-defined computational procedure that takes variable inputs, including a cryptographic key, and produces an output

Cryptographic strength
A measure of the expected number of operations required to defeat a cryptographic mechanism

Cryptography
The art of designing, analyzing and attacking cryptographic schemes

Cyclical redundancy check (CRC)
A method to ensure that data have not been altered after being sent through a communication channel

D

Damage evaluation
The determination of the extent of damage that is necessary to provide for an estimation of the recovery time frame and the potential loss to the organization

Data classification
The assignment of a level of sensitivity to data (or information) that results in the specification of controls for each level of classification. Levels of sensitivity of data are assigned according to predefined categories as data are created, amended, enhanced, stored or transmitted. The classification level is an indication of the value or importance of the data to the organization.

Data custodian
The individual(s) and/or department(s) responsible for the storage and safeguarding of computerized data

Data Encryption Standard (DES)
An algorithm for encoding binary data. It is a secret key cryptosystem published by the National Bureau of Standards (NBS), the predecessor of the US National Institute of Standards and Technology (NIST). DES and its variants have been replaced by the Advanced Encryption Standard (AES).

Data integrity
The property that data meet with a priority expectation of quality and that the data can be relied on

Data leakage
Siphoning out or leaking information by dumping computer files or stealing computer reports and tapes

Data leak protection (DLP)
A suite of technologies and associated processes that locate, monitor and protect sensitive information from unauthorized disclosure

Data mining
A technique used to analyze existing information, usually with the intention of pursuing new avenues to pursue business

Data normalization
A structured process for organizing data into tables in such a way that it preserves the relationships among the data

Data owner
The individual(s), normally a manager or director, who has responsibility for the integrity, accurate reporting and use of computerized data

Data warehouse
A generic term for a system that stores, retrieves and manages large volumes of data. Data warehouse software often includes sophisticated comparison and hashing techniques for fast searches, as well as advanced filtering.

Decentralization
The process of distributing computer processing to different locations within an organization

Decryption key
A digital piece of information used to recover plaintext from the corresponding ciphertext by decryption

Defense in depth
The practice of layering defenses to provide added protection. Defense in depth increases security by raising the effort needed in an attack. This strategy places multiple barriers between an attacker and an organization's computing and information resources.

Degauss
The application of variable levels of alternating current for the purpose of demagnetizing magnetic recording media. The process involves increasing the alternating current field gradually from zero to some maximum value and back to zero, leaving a very low residue of magnetic induction on the media. Degauss loosely means: to erase.

Demilitarized zone (DMZ)
A screened (firewalled) network segment that acts as a buffer zone between a trusted and untrusted network. A DMZ is typically used to house systems such as web servers that must be accessible from both internal networks and the Internet.

Denial-of-service (DoS) attack
An assault on a service from a single source that floods it with so many requests that it becomes overwhelmed and is either stopped completely or operates at a significantly reduced rate

Digital certificate
A process to authenticate (or certify) a party's digital signature; carried out by trusted third parties

Digital code signing
The process of digitally signing computer code to ensure its integrity

Disaster declaration
The communication to appropriate internal and external parties that the disaster recovery plan is being put into operation

Disaster notification fee

The fee the recovery site vendor charges when the customer notifies them that a disaster has occurred and the recovery site is required. The fee is implemented to discourage false disaster notifications.

Disaster recovery plan (DRP)
A set of human, physical, technical and procedural resources to recover, within a defined time and cost, an activity interrupted by an emergency or disaster

Disaster recovery plan desk checking
Typically a read-through of a disaster recovery plan without any real actions taking place. Generally involves a reading of the plan, discussion of the action items and definition of any gaps that might be identified

Disaster recovery plan walk-through
Generally a robust test of the recovery plan requiring that some recovery activities take place and are tested. A disaster scenario is often given and the recovery teams talk through the steps they would need to take to recover. As many aspects of the plan should be tested as possible.

Discretionary access control (DAC)
A means of restricting access to objects based on the identity of subjects and/or groups to which they belong. The controls are discretionary in the sense that a subject with a certain access permission is capable of passing that permission (perhaps indirectly) on to any other subject.

Disk mirroring
The practice of duplicating data in separate volumes on two hard disks to make storage more fault tolerant. Mirroring provides data protection in the case of disk failure because data are constantly updated to both disks.

Distributed denial-of-service (DDoS) attack
A denial-of-service (DoS) assault from multiple sources

Domain name system (DNS)
A hierarchical database that is distributed across the Internet that allows names to be resolved into IP addresses (and vice versa) to locate services such as web and e-mail servers

Dual control
A procedure that uses two or more entities (usually persons) operating in concert to protect a system resource so that no single entity acting alone can access that resource

Due care
The level of care expected from a reasonable person of similar competency under similar conditions

Due diligence
The performance of those actions that are generally regarded as prudent, responsible and necessary to conduct a thorough and objective investigation, review and/or analysis

Dynamic Host Configuration Protocol (DHCP)
A protocol used by networked computers (clients) to obtain IP addresses and other parameters such as the default gateway, subnet mask and IP addresses of domain name system (DNS) servers from a DHCP server. The DHCP server ensures that all IP addresses are unique (e.g., no IP address is assigned to a second client while the first client's assignment is valid [its lease has not expired]). Thus, IP address pool management is done by the server and not by a human network administrator.

E

Electronic data interchange (EDI)
The electronic transmission of transactions (information) between two enterprises. EDI promotes a more efficient paperless environment. EDI transmissions can replace the use of standard documents, including invoices or purchase orders.

Electronic funds transfer (EFT)
The exchange of money via telecommunications. EFT refers to any financial transaction that originates at a terminal and transfers a sum of money from one account to another.

Encryption
The process of taking an unencrypted message (plaintext), applying a mathematical function to it (encryption algorithm with a key) and producing an encrypted message (ciphertext)

Enterprise governance
A set of responsibilities and practices exercised by the board and executive management with the goal of providing strategic direction, ensuring that objectives are achieved, ascertaining that risks are managed appropriately and verifying that the enterprise's resources are used responsibly.

Exposure
The potential loss to an area due to the occurrence of an adverse event

External storage
The location that contains the backup copies to be used in case recovery or restoration is required in the event of a disaster

F

Fail-over
The transfer of service from an incapacitated primary component to its backup component

Fail safe
Describes the design properties of a computer system that allow it to resist active attempts to attack or bypass it

Fall-through logic
An optimized code based on a branch prediction that predicts which way a program will branch when an application is presented

Firewall
A system or combination of systems that enforces a boundary between two or more networks typically forming a barrier between a secure and an open environment such as the Internet

Flooding
An attack that attempts to cause a failure in a system by providing more input than the system can process properly

Forensic copy
An accurate bit-for-bit reproduction of the information contained on an electronic device or associated media, whose validity and integrity has been verified using an accepted algorithm

Forensic examination
The process of collecting, assessing, classifying and documenting digital evidence to assist in the identification of an offender and the method of compromise

G

Guideline
A description of a particular way of accomplishing something that is less prescriptive than a procedure

H

Harden
To configure a computer or other network device to resist attacks

Hash function
An algorithm that maps or translates one set of bits into another (generally smaller) so that a message yields the same result every time the algorithm is executed using the same message as input. It is computationally infeasible for a message to be derived or reconstituted from the result produced by the algorithm or to find two different messages that produce the same hash result using the same algorithm.

Help desk
A service offered via telephone/Internet by an organization to its clients or employees that provides information, assistance and troubleshooting advice regarding software, hardware or networks. A help desk is staffed by people who can either resolve the problem on their own or escalate the problem to specialized personnel. A help desk is often equipped with dedicated customer relationship management (CRM) software that logs the problems and tracks them until they are solved.

Honeypot
A specially configured server, also known as a decoy server, designed to attract and monitor intruders in a manner such that their actions do not affect production systems

Hot site
A fully operational offsite data processing facility equipped with hardware and system software to be used in the event of a disaster

Hypertext Transfer Protocol (HTTP)
A communication protocol used to connect to servers on the World Wide Web. Its primary function is to establish a connection with a web server and transmit hypertext markup language (HTML), extensible markup language (XML) or other pages to the client browsers.

I

Identification
The process of verifying the identity of a user, process or device, usually as a prerequisite for granting access to resources in an information system

Impact analysis
A study to prioritize the criticality of information resources for the organization based on costs (or consequences) of adverse events. In an impact analysis, threats to assets are identified and potential business losses determined for different time periods. This assessment is used to justify the extent of safeguards that are required and recovery time frames. This analysis is the basis for establishing the recovery strategy.

Incident
Any event that is not part of the standard operation of a service and that causes, or may cause, an interruption to, or a reduction in, the quality of that service

Incident handling
An action plan for dealing with intrusions, cybertheft, denial-of-service attack, fire, floods, and other security-related events. It is comprised of a six-step process: Preparation, Identification, Containment, Eradication, Recovery, and Lessons Learned.

Information security
Ensures that only authorized users (confidentiality) have access to accurate and complete information (integrity) when required (availability)

Information security governance
The set of responsibilities and practices exercised by the board and executive management with the goal of providing strategic direction, ensuring that objectives are achieved, ascertaining that risks are managed appropriately and verifying that the enterprise's resources are used responsibly

Information security program
The overall combination of technical, operational and procedural measures, and management structures implemented to provide for the confidentiality, integrity and availability of information based on business requirements and risk analysis

Integrity
The accuracy, completeness and validity of information

Internal controls
The policies, procedures, practices and organizational structures designed to provide reasonable assurance that business objectives will be achieved and undesired events will be prevented or detected and corrected

Internet service provider (ISP)
A third party that provides individuals and organizations access to the Internet and a variety of other Internet-related services

Interruption window
The time the company can wait from the point of failure to the restoration of the minimum and critical services or applications. After this time, the progressive losses caused by the interruption are excessive for the organization.

Intrusion detection
The process of monitoring the events occurring in a computer system or network to detect signs of unauthorized access or attack

Intrusion detection system (IDS)
Inspects network and host security activity to identify suspicious patterns that may indicate a network or system attack

Intrusion prevention system (IPS)
Inspects network and host security activity to identify suspicious patterns that may indicate a network or system attack and then blocks it at the firewall to prevent damage to information resources

IP Security (IPSec)
A set of protocols developed by the Internet Engineering Task Force (IETF) to support the secure exchange of packets

ISO/IEC 15504
ISO/IEC 15504 *Information technology—Process assessment.* ISO/IEC 15504 provides a framework for the assessment of processes. The framework can be used by organizations involved in planning, managing, monitoring, controlling and improving the acquisition, supply, development, operation, evolution and support of products and services.

ISO/IEC 17799
Originally released as part of the British Standard for *Information Security* in 1999 and then as the *Code of Practice for Information Security Management* in October 2000, it was elevated by the International Organization for Standardization (ISO) to an international code of practice for information security management. This standard defines information's confidentiality, integrity and availability controls in a comprehensive information security management system. The latest version is ISO/IEC 17799:2005.

ISO/IEC 27001
An international standard, released in 2005 and revised in 2013, that defines a set of requirements for an information security management system. Prior its adoption by the ISO, this standard was known as BS 17799 Part 2, which was originally published in 1999.

ISO/IEC 27002
A code of practice that contains a structured list of suggested information security controls for organizations implementing an information security management system. Prior to its adoption by ISO/IEC, this standard existed as BS 77799.

ISO/IEC 31000
ISO 31000:2009 *Risk management—Principles and guidelines.* Provides principles and generic guidelines on risk management. It is industry- and sector-agnostic and can be used by any public, private or community enterprise, association, group or individual.

IT governance
The responsibility of executives and the board of directors; consists of the leadership, organizational structures and processes that ensure that the enterprise's IT sustains and extends the organization's strategies and objectives

IT steering committee
An executive management-level committee that assists the executive in the delivery of the IT strategy, oversees day to day management of IT service delivery and IT projects and focuses on implementation aspects

IT strategic plan
A long-term plan(i.e., three- to five-year horizon) in which business and IT management cooperatively describe how IT resources will contribute to the enterprise's strategic objectives (goals)

IT strategy committee
A committee at the level of the board of directors to ensure that the board is involved in major IT matters and decisions. The committee is primarily accountable for managing the portfolios of IT-enabled investments, IT services and other IT resources. The committee is the owner of the portfolio.

K

Key goal indicator (KGI)
A measure that tells management, after the fact, whether an IT process has achieved its business requirements; usually expressed in terms of information criteria

Key performance indicator (KPI)
A measure that determines how well the process is performing in enabling the goal to be reached. A KPI is a lead indicator of whether a goal will likely be reached, and a good indicator of capability, practices and skills. It measures an activity goal, which is an action that the process owner must take to achieve effective process performance.

Key risk indicator (KRI)
A subset of risk indicators that are highly relevant and possess a high probability of predicting or indicating important risk

L

Least privilege
The principle of allowing users or applications the least amount of permissions necessary to perform their intended function

M

Mail relay server
An electronic mail (email) server that relays messages so that neither the sender nor the recipient is a local user

Malicious code
Software (e.g., Trojan horse) that appears to perform a useful or desirable function, but actually gains unauthorized access to system resources or tricks a user into executing other malicious logic

Malware
Software designed to infiltrate, damage or obtain information from a computer system without the owner's consent

Malware is commonly taken to include computer viruses, worms, Trojan horses, spyware and adware. Spyware is generally used for marketing purposes and, as such, is not malicious, although it is generally unwanted. Spyware can, however, be used to gather information for identity theft or other clearly illicit purposes.

Mandatory access control (MAC)
A means of restricting access to data based on varying degrees of security requirements for information contained in the objects and the corresponding security clearance of users or programs acting on their behalf.

Man-in-the-middle attack (MitM)
An attack strategy in which the attacker intercepts the communication stream between two parts of the victim system and then replaces the traffic between the two components with the intruder's own system, eventually assuming control of the communication.

Masqueraders
Attackers that penetrate systems by using the identity of legitimate users and their login credentials

Maximum tolerable outages (MTO)
Maximum time the organization can support processing in alternate mode

Media access control (MAC)
Applied to the hardware at the factory and cannot be modified, MAC is a unique, 48-bit, hard-coded address of a physical layer device, such as an Ethernet local area network (LAN) or a wireless network card.

Message authentication code
An American National Standards Institute (ANSI) standard checksum that is computed using the Data Encryption Standard (DES)

Message digest
A cryptographic checksum, typically generated for a file that can be used to detect changes to the file; Secure Hash Algorithm-1 (SHA-1) is an example of a message digest algorithm.

Mirrored site
An alternate site that contains the same information as the original. Mirror sites are set up for backup and disaster recovery as well as to balance the traffic load for numerous download requests. Such download mirrors are often placed in different locations throughout the Internet.

Mobile site
The use of a mobile/temporary facility to serve as a business resumption location. They can usually be delivered to any site and can house information technology and staff.

Monitoring policy
Rules outlining or delineating the way in which information about the use of computers, networks, applications and information is captured and interpreted.

Multipurpose Internet mail extension (MIME)
A specification for formatting non-ASCII messages so that they can be sent over the Internet. Many email clients now support MIME, which enables them to send and receive graphics, audio and video files via the Internet mail system. In addition, MIME supports messages in character sets other than ASCII.

N

Net present value (NPV)
Calculated by using an after-tax discount rate of an investment and a series of expected incremental cash outflows (the initial investment and operational costs) and cash inflows (cost savings or revenues) that occur at regular periods during the life cycle of the investment. To arrive at a fair NPV calculation, cash inflows accrued by the business up to about five years after project deployment also should be taken into account.

Network address translation (NAT)
Basic NATs are used when there is a requirement to interconnect two IP networks with incompatible addressing. However, it is common to hide an entire IP address space, usually consisting of private IP addresses, behind a single IP address (or in some cases a small group of IP addresses) in another (usually public) address space. To avoid ambiguity in the handling of returned packets, a one-to-many NAT must alter higher level information such as Transmission Control Protocol (TCP)/User Datagram Protocol (UDP) ports in outgoing communications and must maintain a translation table so that return packets can be correctly translated back.

Network-based intrusion detection (NID)
Provides broader coverage than host-based approaches but functions in the same manner detecting attacks using either an anomaly-based or signature-based approach or both

Nonintrusive monitoring
The use of transported probes or traces to assemble information, track traffic and identify vulnerabilities

Nonrepudiation
The assurance that a party cannot later deny originating data; that is, it is the provision of proof of the integrity and origin of the data and can be verified by a third party. A digital signature can provide nonrepudiation.

O

Offline files
Computer file storage media not physically connected to the computer; typically tapes or tape cartridges used for backup purposes

Open Shortest Path First (OSPF)
A routing protocol developed for IP networks. It is based on the shortest path first or link state algorithm.

Open Source Security Testing Methodology
An open and freely available methodology and manual for security testing

Outcome measure
Represents the consequences of actions previously taken; often referred to as a lag indicator. An outcome measure frequently focuses on results at the end of a time period and characterizes historical performance. It is also referred to as a key goal indicator (KGI) and is used to indicate whether goals have been met. Can be measured only after the fact and, therefore, is called a lag indicator.

P

Packet
Data unit that is routed from source to destination in a packet-switched network. A packet contains both routing information and data. Transmission Control Protocol/Internet Protocol (TCP/IP) is such a packet-switched network.

Packet filtering
Controlling access to a network by analyzing the attributes of the incoming and outgoing packets, and either letting them pass or denying them based on a list of rules

Packet sniffer
Software that observes and records network traffic

Packet switched network
Individual packets follow their own paths through the network from one endpoint to another and reassemble at the destination.

Partitions
Major divisions of the total physical hard disk space

Passive response
A response option in intrusion detection in which the system simply reports and records the problem detected, relying on the user to take subsequent action

Password cracker
A tool that tests the strength of user passwords searching for passwords that are easy to guess. It repeatedly tries words from specially crafted dictionaries and often also generates thousands (and in some cases, even millions) of permutations of characters, numbers and symbols.

Penetration testing
A live test of the effectiveness of security defenses through mimicking the actions of real-life attackers

Personally Identifiable Information (PII)
Information that can be used alone or with other sources to uniquely identify, contact or locate a single individual

Pharming
This is a more sophisticated form of a man-in-the-middle (MITM) attack. A user's session is redirected to a masquerading website. This can be achieved by corrupting a domain name system (DNS) server on the Internet and pointing a URL to the masquerading web site's IP address.

Phishing
This is a type of electronic mail (email) attack that attempts to convince a user that the originator is genuine, but with the intention of obtaining information for use in social engineering. Phishing attacks may take the form of masquerading as a lottery organization advising the recipient or the user's bank of a large win; in either case, the intent is to obtain account and personal identification number (PIN) details. Alternative attacks may seek to obtain apparently innocuous business information, which may be used in another form of active attack.

Policy
Overall intention and direction as formally expressed by management

Port
A hardware interface between a CPU and a peripheral device. Can also refer to a software (virtual) convention that allows remote services to connect to a host operating system in a structured manner

Privacy
Freedom from unauthorized intrusion or disclosure of information an individual

Private key
A mathematical key (kept secret by the holder) used to create digital signatures and, depending on the algorithm, to decrypt messages or files encrypted (for confidentiality) with the corresponding public key

Procedure
A document containing a detailed description of the steps necessary to perform specific operations in conformance with applicable standards. Procedures are defined as part of processes.

Proxy server
A server that acts on behalf of a user. Typically proxies accept a connection from a user, make a decision as to whether or not the user or client IP address is permitted to use the proxy, perhaps perform additional authentication, and then complete a connection to a remote destination on behalf of the user.

Public key
In an asymmetric cryptographic scheme, the key that may be widely published to enable the operation of the scheme

R

Reciprocal agreement
Emergency processing agreements among two or more organizations with similar equipment or applications. Typically, participants promise to provide processing time to each other when an emergency arises.

Recovery action
Execution of a response or task according to a written procedure

Recovery point objective (RPO)
Determined based on the acceptable data loss in case of a disruption of operations. It indicates the earliest point in time to which it is acceptable to recover data. It effectively quantifies the permissible amount of data loss in case of interruption.

Recovery time objective (RTO)
The amount of time allowed for the recovery of a business function or resource after a disaster occurs

Redundant Array of Inexpensive Disks (RAID)
Provides performance improvements and fault-tolerant capabilities, via hardware or software solutions, by writing to a series of multiple disks to improve performance and/or save large files simultaneously

Redundant site
A recovery strategy involving the duplication of key information technology components, including data or other key business processes, whereby fast recovery can take place

Request for proposal (RFP)
A document distributed to software vendors requesting them to submit a proposal to develop or provide a software product

Residual risk
The remaining risk after management has implemented risk response

Resilience
The ability of a system or network to resist failure or to recover quickly from any disruption, usually with minimal recognizable effect

Return on investment (ROI)
A measure of operating performance and efficiency, computed in its simplest form by dividing net income by the total investment over the period being considered

Return on security investment (ROSI)
An estimate of return on security investment based on how much will be saved by reduced losses divided by the investment

Risk
The combination of the probability of an event and its consequence. (ISO/IEC 73). Risk has traditionally been expressed as Threats x Vulnerabilities = Risk.

Risk analysis
The initial steps of risk management: analyzing the value of assets to the business, identifying threats to those assets and evaluating how vulnerable each asset is to those threats. It often involves an evaluation of the probable frequency of a particular event, as well as the probable impact of that event.

Risk assessment
A process used to identify and evaluate risk and potential effects. Risk assessment includes assessing the critical functions necessary for an organization to continue business operations, defining the controls in place to reduce organization exposure and evaluating the cost for such controls. Risk analysis often involves an evaluation of the probabilities of a particular event.

Risk avoidance
The process for systematically avoiding risk, constituting one approach to managing risk

Risk mitigation
The management and reduction of risk through the use of countermeasures and controls

Risk tolerance
The acceptable level of variation that management is willing to allow for any particular risk while pursuing its objectives

Risk transfer
The process of assigning risk to another organization, usually through the purchase of an insurance policy or outsourcing the service

Robustness
The ability of systems to withstand attack, operate reliably across a wide range of operational conditions and to fail gracefully outside of the operational range

Role-based access control
Assigns users to job functions or titles. Each job function or title defines a specific authorization level.

Root cause analysis
A process of diagnosis to establish origins of events, which can be used for learning from consequences, typically of errors and problems

Rootkit
A software suite designed to aid an intruder in gaining unauthorized administrative access to a computer system

S

Secret key
A cryptographic key that is used with a secret key (symmetric) cryptographic algorithm, that is uniquely associated with one or more entities and is not made public. The same key is used to both encrypt and decrypt data. The use of the term "secret" in this context does not imply a classification level, but rather implies the need to protect the key from disclosure.

Secure hash algorithm (SHA)
A hash algorithm with the property that is computationally infeasible 1) to find a message that corresponds to a given message digest, or 2) to find two different messages that produce the same message digest

Security information and event management (SIEM)
SIEM solutions are a combination of the formerly disparate product categories of SIM (security information management) and SEM (security event management). SIEM technology provides real-time analysis of security alerts generated by network hardware and applications. SIEM solutions come as software, appliances or managed services, and are also used to log security data and generate reports for compliance purposes. Capabilities include:
- **Data aggregation:** SIEM/LM (log management) solutions aggregate data from many sources, including network, security, servers, databases and applications, providing the ability to consolidate monitored data to help avoid missing crucial events.
- **Correlation:** Looks for common attributes, and links events together into meaningful bundles. This technology provides the ability to perform a variety of correlation techniques to integrate different sources, in order to turn data into useful information.
- **Alerting:** The automated analysis of correlated events and production of alerts, to notify recipients of immediate issues.
- **Dashboards:** SIEM/LM tools take event data and turn them into informational charts to assist in seeing patterns, or identifying activity that is not forming a standard pattern.

- **Compliance:** SIEM applications can be employed to automate the gathering of compliance data, producing reports that adapt to existing security, governance and auditing processes.
- **Retention:** SIEM/SIM solutions employ long-term storage of historical data to facilitate correlation of data over time, and to provide the retention necessary for compliance requirements.

Security metrics
A standard of measurement used in management of security-related activities

Segregation/separation of duties (SoD)
A basic internal control that prevents or detects errors and irregularities by assigning to separate individuals the responsibility for initiating and recording transactions and for the custody of assets. Segregation/separation of duties is commonly used in large IT organizations so that no single person is in a position to introduce fraudulent or malicious code without detection.

Sensitivity
A measure of the impact that improper disclosure of information may have on an organization

Service delivery objective (SDO)
Directly related to business needs, SDO is the level of services to be reached during the alternate process mode until the normal situation is restored

Service level agreement (SLA)
An agreement, preferably documented, between a service provider and the customer(s)/user(s) that defines minimum performance targets for a service and how they will be measured

Session key
A single-use symmetric key used for a defined period of communication between two computers, such as for the duration of a single communication session or transaction set

Shell programming
A script written for the shell, or command line interpreter, of an operating system; it is often considered a simple domain-specific programming language. Typical operations performed by shell scripts include file manipulation, program execution and printing text. Usually, shell script refers to scripts written for a UNIX shell, while COMMAND.COM (DOS) and cmd.exe (Windows) command line scripts are usually called batch files.Others, such as AppleScript, add scripting capability to computing environments lacking a command line interface. Other examples of programming languages primarily intended for shell scripting include digital command language (DCL) and job control language (JCL).

Sniffing
The process by which data traversing a network are captured or monitored

Social engineering
An attack based on deceiving users or administrators at the target site into revealing confidential or sensitive information

Split knowledge/split key
A security technique in which two or more entities separately hold data items that individually convey no knowledge of the information that results from combining the items; a condition under which two or more entities separately have key components that individually convey no knowledge of the plaintext key that will be produced when the key components are combined in the cryptographic module

Spoofing
Faking the sending address of a transmission in order to gain illegal entry into a secure system

Standard
A mandatory requirement, code of practice or specification approved by a recognized external standards organization, such as International Organization for Standardization (ISO)

Symmetric key encryption
System in which a different key (or set of keys) is used by each pair of trading partners to ensure that no one else can read their messages. The same key is used for encryption and decryption.

System owner
Person or organization having responsibility for the development, procurement, integration, modification, operation and maintenance, and/or final disposition of an information system

T

Threat
Anything (e.g., object, substance, human) that is capable of acting against an asset in a manner that can result in harm. A potential cause of an unwanted incident. (ISO/IEC 13335)

Threat agent
Methods and things used to exploit a vulnerability. Examples include determination, capability, motive and resources.

Threat analysis
An evaluation of the type, scope and nature of events or actions that can result in adverse consequences; identification of the threats that exist against information assets. The threat analysis usually also defines the level of threat and the likelihood of it materializing.

Threat assessment
The identification of types of threats to which an organization might be exposed

Threat event
Any event where a threat element/actor acts against an asset in a manner that has the potential to directly result in harm

Threat model
Used to describe a given threat and the harm it could to do a system if it has a vulnerability

Threat vector
The method a threat uses to exploit the target

Token
A device that is used to authenticate a user, typically in addition to a user name and password. A token is usually a device that displays a pseudo random number that changes every few minutes.

Total cost of ownership (TCO)
Includes the original cost of the computer plus the cost of: software, hardware and software upgrades, maintenance, technical support, training, and certain activities performed by users

Trusted system
A system that employs sufficient hardware and software assurance measures to allow its use for processing simultaneously a range of sensitive or classified information

Tunneling
Commonly used to bridge between incompatible hosts/routers or to provide encryption; a method by which one network protocol encapsulates another protocol within itself

Two-factor authentication
The use of two independent mechanisms for authentication, (e.g., requiring a smart card and a password); typically the combination of something you know, are or have

U

Uniform resource locator (URL)
The global address of documents and other resources on the World Wide Web. The first part of the address indicates what protocol to use; the second part specifies the IP address or the domain name where the resource is located (e.g., *http://www.isaca.org*).

V

Virtual private network (VPN)
A secure private network that uses the public telecommunications infrastructure to transmit data. In contrast to a much more expensive system of owned or leased lines that can only be used by one company, VPNs are used by enterprises for both extranets and wide areas of intranets. Using encryption and authentication, a VPN encrypts all data that pass between two Internet points, maintaining privacy and security.

Virus signature files
The file of virus patterns that are compared with existing files to determine if they are infected with a virus or worm

Voice-over IP (VoIP)
Also called IP Telephony, Internet Telephony and Broadband Phone, a technology that makes it possible to have a voice conversation over the Internet or over any dedicated Internet Protocol (IP) network instead of over dedicated voice transmission lines

Vulnerability
A weakness in the design, implementation, operation or internal controls in a process that could be exploited to violate system security

Vulnerability analysis
A process of identifying and classifying vulnerabilities

W

Warm site
Similar to a hot site, but not fully equipped with all of the necessary hardware needed for recovery

Web hosting
The business of providing the equipment and services required to host and maintain files for one or more web sites and provide fast Internet connections to those sites. Most hosting is "shared," which means that web sites of multiple companies are on the same server to share/reduce costs.

Web server
Using the client-server model and the World Wide Web's Hypertext Transfer Protocol (HTTP), Web server is a software program that serves web pages to users.

Wide area network (WAN)
A computer network connecting different remote locations that may range from short distances, such as a floor or building, to long transmissions that encompass a large region or several countries

Worm
A programmed network attack in which a self-replicating program does not attach itself to programs, but rather spreads independently of users' action

Wi-Fi protected access 2 (WPA2)
The replacement security method for WPA for wireless networks that provides stronger data protection and network access control. It provides enterprise and consumer Wi-Fi users with a high level of assurance that only authorized users can access their wireless networks. Based on the ratified IEEE 802.11i standard, WPA2 provides government-grade security by implementing the National Institute of Standards and Technology (NIST) FIPS 140-2 compliant advanced encryption standard (AES) encryption algorithm and 802.1X-based authentication.

ACRONYMS

The CISM candidate should be familiar with the following list of acronyms. These acronyms are the only standalone abbreviations used in examination questions.

CD	Compact Disk
CD-ROM	Compact Disk Read Only Memory
DMZ	Demilitarized zone
HTML	Hypertext Markup Language
ID	Identification
IP	Internet Protocol
IPS	Intrusion prevention system
IPSec	Internet Protocol Security
IS	Information systems
ISP	Internet service provider
IT	Information technology
OS	Operating system
URL	Uniform resource locator
XML	Extensible Markup Language

In addition to the aforementioned acronyms, candidates may also wish to become familiar with the following additional acronyms. Should any of these abbreviations be used in examination questions, their meanings would be included when the acronym appears.

AESRM	Alliance for Enterprise Security Risk Management
AIW	Acceptable interruption window
ALE	Annual loss expectancy
API	Application programming interface
AS/NZS	Australian Standard/New Zealand Standard
ASCII	American Standard Code for Information Interchange
ASIC	Application-specific integrated circuit
ASP	Application service provider
ATM	Asynchronous Transfer Mode
AV	Asset value
BCI	Business Continuity Institute
BCM	Business continuity management
BCP	Business continuity planning
BGP	Border Gateway Protocol
BI	Business intelligence
BIA	Business impact analysis
BIMS	Biometric information management and security
BIOS	Basic input/output system
BITS	Banking Information Technology Standards
BLP	Bell-LaPadula
BLP	Bypass label process
BS	British Standard
CA	Certificate authority
CASPR	Commonly accepted security practices and recommendations
CEO	Chief executive officer
CERT	Computer emergency response team
CFO	Chief financial officer
CIM	Computer-integrated manufacturing
CIO	Chief information officer
CIRT	Computer incident response team
CISO	Chief information security officer
CMM	Capability Maturity Model
COO	Chief operating officer
COOP	Continuity of operations plan
CORBA	Common Object Request Broker Architecture
COSO	Committee of Sponsoring Organizations of the Treadway Commission
CPO	Chief privacy officer
CPU	Central processing unit
CRM	Customer relationship management
CSA	Control self-assessment
CSF	Critical success factor
CSIRT	Computer security incident response team
CSO	Chief security officer
CSRC	Computer Security Resources Center (USA)
CTO	Chief technology officer
CVE	Common vulnerabilities and exposures
DAC	Discretionary access controls
DBMS	Database management system
DCE	Distributed control environment
DCE	Data communications equipment
DCE	Distributed computing environment
DCL	Digital command language
DDoS	Distributed denial of service
DES	Data Encryption Standard
DHCP	Dynamic Host Configuration Protocol
DNS	Domain name system
DNSSEC	Domain Name Service Secure
DoS	Denial of service
DOSD	Data-oriented system development
DR	Disaster recovery
DRII	Disaster Recovery Institute International
DRP	Disaster recovery planning
EDI	Electronic data interchange
EER	Equal error rate
EF	Exposure factor
EFT	Electronic funds transfer
EGRP	External Gateway Routing Protocol
EIGRP	Enhanced Interior Gateway Routing Protocol
EU	European Union
FAIR	Factor analysis of information risk
FAR	False-acceptance rate
FCPA	Foreign Corrupt Practices Act
FIPS	Federal Information Processing Standards (USA)
FISMA	Federal Information Security Management Act (USA)
FSA	Financial Security Authority (USA)
GAS	Generalized audit software
GLBA	Gramm-Leach-Bliley Act (USA)
GMI	Governance Metrics International
HD-DVD	High definition/high density-digital video disc
HIDS	Host-based intrusion detection system
HIPAA	Health Insurance Portability and Accountability Act (USA)
HIPO	Hierarchy Input-Process-Output
HR	Human resources
HTTP	Hypertext Transfer Protocol
I/O	Input/output
ICT	Information and communication technologies
IDEFIX	Integration Definition for Information Modeling
IDS	Intrusion detection system
IEC	International Electrotechnical Commission

IETF	Internet engineering task force
IFAC	International Federation of Accountants
IIA	Institute of Internal Auditors
IMT	Incident management team
IPF	Information processing facility
IPL	Initial program load
IPMA	International Project Management Association
IPRs	Intellectual property rights
IPS	Intrusion-prevention system
IRP	Incident response plan
IRT	Incident response team
ISF	Information Security Forum
ISO	International Organization for Standardization
ISSA	Information System Security Association
ISSEA	International System Security Engineering Association
ITGI	IT Governance Institute
ITIL	Information Technology Infrastructure Library
JCL	Job control language
KGI	Key goal indicator
KLOC	Kilo lines of code
KPI	Key performance indicator
KRI	Key risk indicator
L2TP	Layer 2 Tunneling Protocol
LAN	Local area network
LCP	Link Control Protocol
M&A	Mergers and Acquisition
MAC	Mandatory access control
MAO	Maximum allowable outage
MIME	Multipurpose Internet mail extension
MIS	Management information system
MitM	Man-in-the-middle
MTD	Maximum tolerable downtime
MTO	Maximum tolerable outage
NAT	Network address translation
NCP	Network Control Protocol
NDA	Nondisclosure agreement
NFPA	National Fire Protection Association
NIC	Network interface card
NIDS	Network intrusion detection system
NIST	National Institute of Standards and Technology (USA)
NPV	Net present value
OCSP	Online Certificate Status Protocol
OCTAVE	Operationally Critical Threat, Asset and Vulnerability Evaluation
OECD	Organization for Economic Co-operation and Development
OEP	Occupant emergency plan
OSI	Open systems interconnection
OSPF	Open Shortest Path First
PAN	Personal area network
PCI DSS	Payment Card Industry Data Security Standard
PDCA	Plan-do-check-act
PKI	Public key infrastructure
PMBOK	Project Management Body of Knowledge
POS	Point-of-sale
PPPoE	Point-to-point Protocol over Ethernet
PRA	Probabilistic risk assessment
PSTN	Public switched telephone network
PVC	Permanent virtual circuit
QA	Quality assurance
RAID	Redundant array of inexpensive disks
ROI	Return on investment
ROSI	Return on security investment
RPO	Recovery point objective
RRT	Risk Reward Theorem/Tradeoff
RSA	Rivest, Shamir and Adleman (RSA stands for the initials of the developers last names)
RTO	Recovery time objective
S/HTTP	Secure Hypertext Transfer Protocol
SABSA	Sherwood Applied Business Security Architecture
SCADA	Supervisory Control and Data Acquisition
SDLC	System development life cycle
SDO	Service delivery objective
SEC	Securities and Exchange Commission (USA)
SIEM	Security information and event management
SIM	Security information management
SLA	Service level agreement
SMART	Specific, measurable, achievable, relevant, time-bound
SMF	System management facility
SOP	Standard operating procedure
SPI	Security Parameter Index
SPICE	Software process improvement and capability determination
SPOC	Single point of contact
SPOOL	Simultaneous peripheral operations online
SQL	Structured Query Language
SSH	Secure Shell
SSL	Secure Sockets Layer
SSO	Single sign-on
TCO	Total cost of ownership
TCP	Transmission Control Protocol
TLS	Transport layer security
UDP	User Datagram Protocol
USB	Universal Serial Bus
VAR	Value at risk
VoIP	Voice-over IP
VPN	Virtual private network
XBRL	Extensible Business Reporting Language

Page intentionally left blank

INDEX

A

B

C

D

E

F

H

I

U

V